Handbook of Behavioral Economics - Foundations and Applications 2

Handbook of Behavioral Economics - Foundations and Applications 2

Edited by

B. Douglas Bernheim

Stefano DellaVigna

David Laibson

North-Holland

An imprint of Elsevier

North-Holland is an imprint of Elsevier
Radarweg 29, PO Box 211, 1000 AE Amsterdam, Netherlands
The Boulevard, Langford Lane, Kidlington, Oxford OX5 1GB, United Kingdom

Notices

Knowledge and best practice in this field are constantly changing. As new research and experience broaden our
understanding, changes in research methods, professional practices, or medical treatment may become necessary.

Practitioners and researchers must always rely on their own experience and knowledge in evaluating and using
any information, methods, compounds, or experiments described herein. In using such information or methods
they should be mindful of their own safety and the safety of others, including parties for whom they have a
professional responsibility.

To the fullest extent of the law, neither the Publisher nor the authors, contributors, or editors, assume any liability
for any injury and/or damage to persons or property as a matter of products liability, negligence or otherwise, or
from any use or operation of any methods, products, instructions, or ideas contained in the material herein.

Library of Congress Cataloging-in-Publication Data
A catalog record for this book is available from the Library of Congress

British Library Cataloguing-in-Publication Data
A catalogue record for this book is available from the British Library

ISBN: 978-0-444-63375-0

For information on all North-Holland publications
visit our website at https://www.elsevier.com/books-and-journals

Working together
to grow libraries in
developing countries

www.elsevier.com • www.bookaid.org

Publisher: Zoe Kruze
Acquisition Editor: Jason Mitchell
Editorial Project Manager: Shellie Bryant
Production Project Manager: Vignesh Tamil
Designer: Alan Studholme

Typeset by VTeX

Contents

Contributors

Daniel J. Benjamin

University of Southern California, Los Angeles, CA, United States of America

National Bureau of Economic Research, Cambridge, MA, United States of America

Amitabh Chandra

Harvard Kennedy School, Cambridge, MA, United States of America

Harvard Business School, Boston, MA, United States of America

National Bureau of Economic Research, Cambridge, MA, United States of America

Keith Marzilli Ericson

Questrom School of Business, Boston University, Boston, MA, United States of America

National Bureau of Economic Research, Cambridge, MA, United States of America

Erik Eyster

London School of Economics, London, United Kingdom of Great Britain and Northern Ireland

University of California, Santa Barbara, CA, United States of America

Xavier Gabaix

Harvard University, Cambridge, MA, United States of America

National Bureau of Economic Research, Cambridge, MA, United States of America

Benjamin Handel

UC Berkeley, Berkeley, CA, United States of America

Michael Kremer

Harvard University, Cambridge, MA, United States of America

National Bureau of Economic Research, Cambridge, MA, United States of America

David Laibson

Department of Economics, Harvard University, Littauer Center, Cambridge, MA, United States of America

National Bureau of Economic Research, Cambridge, MA, United States of America

Gautam Rao
Harvard University, Cambridge, MA, United States of America
National Bureau of Economic Research, Cambridge, MA, United States of America

Frank Schilbach
MIT, Cambridge, MA, United States of America
National Bureau of Economic Research, Cambridge, MA, United States of America

Joshua Schwartzstein
Harvard Business School, Boston, MA, United States of America

Introduction to the series

The aim of the Handbooks in Economics series is to produce Handbooks for various branches of economics, each of which is a definitive source, reference, and teaching supplement for use by professional researchers and advanced graduate students. Each Handbook provides self-contained surveys of the current state of a branch of economics in the form of chapters prepared by leading specialists on various aspects of this branch of economics. These surveys summarize not only received results but also newer developments, from recent journal articles and discussion papers. Some original material is also included, but the main goal is to provide comprehensive and accessible surveys. The Handbooks are intended to provide not only useful reference volumes for professional collections but also possible supplementary readings for advanced courses for graduate students in economics.

Kenneth J. Arrow[†]
Michael D. Intriligator[†]

[†] Deceased.

Preface

Behavioral economics has come a long way from the big bang of Kahneman and Tversky's seminal papers in the 1970s. Richard Thaler and a few fellow travelers including George Akerlof, Colin Camerer, Robert Frank, George Loewenstein, Tom Schelling, Robert Shiller, and Robert Sugden promulgated behavioral ideas in the early 1980s, but most economists initially rejected the behavioral approach, especially the concept of imperfect rationality. A lot has changed since then.

Today, most journals in economics routinely publish behavioral papers. In fact, all of the so-called "top-5" journals currently have at least one co-editor who has worked in behavioral economics. Many departments now offer doctoral classes or even fields in behavioral economics, including "early adopters" (e.g., Berkeley, Cal Tech, Carnegie Mellon, Cornell, Harvard, Stanford, and Zurich) as well as many other leading departments (e.g., Bonn, Brown, Chicago, Columbia, LSE, MIT, NYU, Princeton, Toulouse, Wharton, and Yale).

During the 2017–18 academic year, the chairs of the economics departments at Harvard, Stanford, and Chicago all counted behavioral economics as one of their primary interests (as did the previous chair at UC Berkeley), a fact that is not lost on the editors of this Handbook. And, of course, Richard Thaler received the 2017 Nobel Prize in Economics for laying out the foundations of the field. George Akerlof, Daniel Kahneman, Tom Schelling, Robert Shiller, and Jean Tirole have also received Nobel Prizes, in part, or wholly for their seminal contributions to behavioral economics.

It seems that behavioral economics has gained a measure of acceptance within the broader discipline. While there is still much we do not know, and certainly much more that we do not deeply understand, we now have a much better sense for key behavioral patterns concerning choice and beliefs within the realms of risk, time, and social preference. Furthermore, as this Handbook demonstrates, behavioral economics has permeated all fields of economics.

This is not to say that behavioral economics has avoided growing pains. In fact, the main challenge that has confronted aspiring behavioral economists coincides with a key motivation for this Handbook: there is no comprehensive graduate-level reference resource on behavioral economics. This state of affairs likely reflects the difficulties any individual author (or small team of coauthors) would face in attempting to provide comprehensive, cutting-edge summaries of research in a range of subfields, particularly given the frenetic pace at which research is progressing. Hence we arrived at the idea of this two-volume Handbook. For Volume 1 (published in late 2018) and the companion Volume 2 that you are currently reading (published in early 2019), we have called upon leaders in behavioral economics to contribute their expertise and synthesize their subfields. To maximize coordination and improve coverage, we held a conference in August 2016 at which the authors presented preliminary plans for their chapters.

We divided each Volume into two main areas, *Theory* and *Applications*. The chapters on *Theory* provide an overview of key behavioral models. Naturally, they also include discussions of evidence and applications, but they primarily focus on broad concepts and principles common to a wide range of economic problems. Volume 1 includes one *Theory* chapter, which examines reference-dependent preferences. Volume 2 includes four *Theory* chapters: intertemporal choice, errors in probabilistic reasoning, errors in strategic reasoning, and limited attention. (We hoped to also include a chapter on social preferences, but it could not be finished by our publication deadline.)

Chapters on *Applications* highlight how behavioral economics has informed research within traditional subfields of economics. Naturally, they also include discussions of pertinent theory, but each focuses on themes pertaining to a single subfield. Volume 1 includes three chapters that broadly concern finance; they cover the topics of asset pricing, household finance, and corporate finance. Two other chapters in Volume 1 cover applications in industrial organization and public economics. A final chapter in Volume 1 cuts across multiple applied subfields by focusing on structural methods in behavioral economics. Volume 2 includes two applied chapters: development economics and health-care economics. (Interested readers looking for material on labor economics, should consult the upcoming volume of the Handbook of Labor Economics planned for 2020.)

In our view, this lengthy list of theoretical topics and areas of application reflects the breadth and depth of behavioral contributions to the field of economics. While a detailed summary of the chapters would be out of place, we will briefly mention some of the notable features of the chapters in Volume 2. The preface to Volume 1 contains a similar overview of the chapters published there.

The first chapter is about "Intertemporal Choice." Starting with models of hyperbolic discounting and present bias, the literature on intertemporal choice has expanded into a rich panoply of different but related models, which are discussed in this chapter by coauthors Keith Ericson and David Laibson. The chapter characterizes the commonalities of these different theoretical threads by identifying a key shared property. "Present-focused preferences" describes the large class of models that prioritize present flows of experienced utility. Present-focused preferences may or may not coincide with a preference for commitment or preferences that are dynamically inconsistent. Present-*biased* preferences—which *are* dynamically inconsistent and which *do* induce a taste for commitment if agents are at least partially sophisticated—are one special case of present-focused preferences. Ericson and Laibson go on to identify 10 stylized facts in the intertemporal choice literature and 16 open questions.

The second chapter in Volume 2 is about "Errors in Probabilistic Reasoning and Judgment Biases." Daniel Benjamin reviews both theory and evidence, with the goal of creating a unified understanding of the interrelationships among different theories of biased beliefs. The chapter discusses biases in beliefs about random processes, biases in belief updating, the representativeness heuristic (which may provide a unifying theory of multiple biases), and interactions between biased belief updating and other features of the decision-making environment. The chapter carefully discusses evidence both for and against each hypothesized bias. The author also discusses practical applications in which these biases play an important role.

The third chapter in Volume 2 is about "Errors in Strategic Reasoning." The author of this chapter, Erik Eyster, has four goals. First, the chapter provides a user's guide for several of the most widely used behavioral solution concepts for strategic settings. The chapter begins with the taxonomy of strategic errors and describes how existing solution concepts address each of these errors. Empirical evidence is presented to substantiate each type of error and evaluate each solution concept. Second, the chapter draws out similarities and differences amongst the solution concepts. Third, the chapter explores how these solution concepts have succeeded and failed, and identifies fruitful directions for future research. The final goal of the chapter is to engage with mainstream economics and to describe how behavioral models of strategic decision-making should be incorporated into applied economics.

The fourth chapter in Volume 2 (which concludes our list of *Theory* chapters) is about "Behavioral Inattention." Xavier Gabaix argues that inattention is a theme that connects much of behavioral economics. This chapter discusses the most basic models of attention allocation and suggests a unified framework. Then the chapter discusses the methods used to measure attention. It then compares and contrasts the various theories of attention, both behavioral and Bayesian. It finally discusses applications and open questions in the attention literature.

The final two chapters in Volume 2 are Applications. The fifth chapter is "Behavioral Development Economics." Coauthors Michael Kremer, Gautam Rao, and Frank Schilbach review classical topics within development economics, such as high rates of return without high rates of growth, the slow spread of technological innovation, low investments in health, and difficulties faced by farmers and other entrepreneurs. Within each realm, they tie the results to behavioral phenomena. A key theme is that the behavioral features that matter in developing countries are largely the same ones that matter in developed countries, including reference dependence, present bias, and social preferences. At the same time, the different institutions in developing countries make some themes of more obvious importance. For example, high rates of self-employment mean a potentially greater role for behavioral factors to affect labor supply. Similarly, since market competition is limited and most firms are very small, there may be greater scope for "behavioral firms", which fail to maximize profits.

The sixth chapter in Volume 2 is "Behavioral Economics and Health-Care Markets." Coauthors Amitabh Chandra, Benjamin Handel, and Joshua Schwartzstein outline the fast-growing evidence of behavioral phenomena within health economics and focus on a few key topics. A first topic is the choice of insurance plans. Faced with an often long list of complex insurance options, consumers make choices that appear to be sub-optimal, in some cases even choosing dominated plans. Inertia and limited attention are two key behavioral features that have proven important to understand insurance plan choice. The authors also highlight the benefits of a framework that allows for "behavioral hazards" in health-treatment choices, instead of assuming maximizing choices, especially given the robust evidence of consumer mistakes in the area. Allowing for such behavioral frictions often can change the analysis of health care markets in the presence of adverse selection and moral hazard.

This final chapter closes the suite of thirteen chapters—six in this Volume 2 and seven in Volume 1—summarizing advances in behavioral economics. Given the remarkable progress in the field in even the last ten years, we delight in the thought of what a future Handbook volume may look like in 2030. Perhaps some areas of application which we did not cover, like macroeconomics, will have blossomed beyond what we can imagine now. New modeling areas will be calling for attention, though we would be surprised if some of the classics covered here—like reference dependence and time preferences – will not be a key focus. Time will tell. We would be foolish placing any additional predictions knowing what we know about overconfidence.

B. Douglas Bernheim
Stefano DellaVigna
David Laibson

Intertemporal choice*

1

Keith Marzilli Ericson[a,b,*], David Laibson[c,b]

[a]*Questrom School of Business, Boston University, Boston, MA, United States of America*
[b]*National Bureau of Economic Research, Cambridge, MA, United States of America*
[c]*Department of Economics, Harvard University, Littauer Center, Cambridge, MA, United States of America*
Corresponding author: e-mail address: kericson@bu.edu

Contents

* Acknowledgments: We are grateful to the volume editors Doug Bernheim and Stefano DellaVigna, who offered terrific insight and guidance on our chapter. We also received excellent advice from George Loewenstein and Matthew Rabin. We also thank all of the participants at the SITE 2016 Conference who shared feedback with us. Much of our thinking on this topic has emerged and evolved from our collaborations and conversations with Jonathan Cohen and John White. Lea Nagel provided outstanding research assistance. We gratefully acknowledge financial support from The Pershing Square Fund for Research on the Foundations of Human Behavior, the Boston University Angiola M. Noe Research Fund, and the National Institute of Aging R01 (R01AG021650).

ISSN 2352-2399, https://doi.org/10.1016/bs.hesbe.2018.12.001

1 Introduction

Most decisions have consequences that play out over time. How much should I spend today and how much should I save? How many hours should I work on a problem set tonight and what work should I postpone? Should I have a candid conversation with an under-performing co-worker or delay the awkward interaction? Is it worth getting out of bed to take my medicine, or is it OK to skip a night? Should I exercise this afternoon, or check all of my social media accounts today and exercise tomorrow?

Whether in the workplace, the marketplace, on vacation, or at home, almost all decisions have an intertemporal dimension. If one makes these decisions with any foresight at all, it is necessary to somehow weigh utility flows (i.e., costs and benefits) that occur at different points in time.

These questions also dominate many of our world's leading policy questions. How much to invest for the future is at the heart of myriad policy issues, including education, health, retirement, energy and the environment.

For much of the twentieth century, the working model of intertemporal choice was the (exponential) discounted utility model developed by Ramsey (1928) and Samuelson (1937), which features time-separable utility flows that are exponentially discounted: i.e., utility flows are discounted with the function δ^t, where δ is the discount factor and t is the horizon of the utility flow. This framework has many things to recommend it, including parsimony, generality/portability, and a single welfare criterion (which is implied by dynamically consistent preferences).[1] But the exponential discounting utility model is not descriptively accurate.

People seem to struggle when they make intertemporal tradeoffs, a phenomenon which has been extensively discussed by moral philosophers, political economists, psychologists, and policymakers. Writings about self-control and self-management are almost as old as written language itself.[2] As literature developed in the ancient

---

[1] For another early formal analysis of intertemporal choice, see Koopmans (1960).

[2] For example, the 'wisdom book', *The Maxims of Ptahhotep* includes numerous recommendations for self-restraint. This text was likely written during the Old Kingdom or the Middle Kingdom of Ancient Egypt (Fox, 1983, dates the book to the 21st century BCE).

world, the focus on self-control intensified. Greek philosophy contains many analyses about the challenges and virtues of self-management. Plato reports that Socrates described the soul as a charioteer (reason) with a pair of horses, one "noble" and the other one unruly and difficult to control.[3] Aristotle emphasized the virtue of temperance and the human propensity to engage in self-defeating behaviors. "For moral excellence is concerned with pleasures and pains; it is on account of the pleasure that we do bad things and it is on account of the pain that we abstain from noble ones." For Aristotle, an intemperate person has an appetite for pleasant things and chooses them at the cost of other, better things.[4] Issues of self-control were explored by David Hume ("reason is the slave to the passions") and Adam Smith (who distinguished between self-defeating "passions" and far-sighted "interests").[5] Much of the soft and hard paternalism reflected in the modern welfare state is an effort to influence intertemporal choices (e.g., see the discussion of Social Security in Feldstein, 1985).

While much of economics in the mid-twentieth century modeled individuals as having a clear objective function and no self-control problems, research exploring self-control and intertemporal choice has blossomed in recent decades. Important milestones include two volumes published by the Russell Sage Foundation on intertemporal choice, edited respectively by Loewenstein and Elster (1992) and Loewenstein et al. (2003). For a highly influential review of the development of the field see Frederick et al. (2002). Subsequent reviews include Chabris et al. (2010) and Sprenger (2015). Cohen et al. (2016) review the conceptual and methodological challenges associated with the measurement of intertemporal preferences. Cohen et al. also discuss relevant neuroimaging evidence, which we completely omit from this current review.[6]

In this handbook chapter, we review the latest research on intertemporal choice and identify important open questions for our understanding of human behavior. We begin (Section 2) by examining formal models of intertemporal choice, because models provide a lens with which to examine empirical evidence and help identify new questions to explore. Most models we review share the unifying feature of giving some special priority to the present. To formalize the idea that the present is qualitatively treated differently than other periods, we introduce a meta-category of models: *present-focused preferences* exist if agents are more likely in the present to choose an action that generates immediate experienced utility, than they would be if all the consequences of the actions in their choice set were delayed by the same amount of time. More informally, this amounts to people choosing more impatiently for the present than they do for the future.

We intentionally use the term present-*focus*, rather than the more common term present-*bias*, because bias implies a prejudgment that the behavior is a mistake.

---

[3] See *Phaedrus* sections 246a–254e. Also see discussion of in Chapter 7 of Nussbaum (2001).

[4] See *Nicomachean Ethics, Book II Chapter 3 and Book III Chapters 10–11* (W.D. Ross translation).

[5] On Hume, see Radcliffe (2018). On Smith, see Ashraf et al. (2005).

[6] See Camerer et al. (2015) for a related discussion of the literature on neuroeconomics.

Models that produce present-focused preferences include: hyperbolic and quasi-hyperbolic discounting (i.e., models with present bias); temptation that is experienced when choosing for now but not when choosing for the future; an interaction between myopic and planner selves; objective counter-party risks; and distortions in the perception of time or in forecasting the future. *Present-focused preferences* serve as a meta-category that identifies key commonalities among most of the models in the intertemporal choice literature. We also identify the key contrasts that differentiate the large number of present-focused models. Specifically, in Section 2.7 we provide a table that summarizes some of these differences.

In Section 3, we identify 10 key empirical regularities that have been well-documented in the literature: high required rates of return for money, higher required rates of return for consumption, preference reversals, procrastination, naiveté, large effect of transactions costs, a demand for commitment, the existence of paternalistic policies, and a preference for improving sequences. We accompany each of these 10 regularities with a closely related open question.

1. Why do individuals have such a high required rate of return for money if impatience is fundamentally about consumption flows rather than financial flows?
2. How substitutable is consumption (and effort) across time? How does the substitution of consumption affect measured discount rates?
3. What are the key mechanisms that cause preference reversals?
4. Why do people underestimate their own procrastination? What are the relative roles of naiveté about present-focus versus other explanations for underestimating procrastination, such as overconfidence about the effort required and limited memory?
5. Why don't people learn and anticipate their present-focused behavior? What can help people correctly anticipate their future present-focused behavior?
6. Is the large effect of small transactions costs on behavior primarily related to present focus, or is it some other channel?
7. Why do households have such low levels of liquid net wealth, relatively high levels of illiquid net wealth, and high marginal propensities to consume out of liquid wealth changes?
8. Why is pure commitment so rare in markets and why is willingness to pay for commitment usually so low (even in lab experiments designed to measure the taste for commitment)?
9. What welfare criterion should we use to evaluate intertemporal tradeoffs?
10. How do we integrate models of discounting with the other factors leading to a preference for improving sequences? When does a preference for an improving sequence become important relative to discounting?

In Section 4 we present six more open questions:

11. How soon is "now"? How fast does value decline over time?
12. What types of decisions involve temptation? How quantitatively important is temptation (as opposed to present-bias)?

13. How important are a variety of mechanisms for intertemporal choice, including probability weighting, trust, and heuristics, both in the lab and in the field? What role do alternative psychological conceptions play in intertemporal choice?
14. How stable are time preferences? How general are they across domains?
15. How malleable is time preference? How effective are self-management techniques?
16. Are households saving optimally for retirement?

Section 5 concludes.

2 Present-focused preferences: theoretical commonalities

All animals, including humans, tend to pursue instant gratification, even when such immediate rewards are obtained by foregoing a substantially larger amount of delayed gratification. In Section 3, we discuss both the qualitative and quantitative evidence (from the field and the lab) for this empirical regularity. In the current section, we describe several related theoretical frameworks that all generate a preference for immediate gratification. We focus on their similarities and accordingly group these conceptual frameworks together into a category that we call "present-focused preferences."

Present-focused preferences exist if agents are more likely in the present to choose an action that generates immediate experienced utility, than they would be if all the consequences of the actions in their choice set were delayed by the same amount of time.[7]

Our definition compares an agent's action in a situation in which they choose for the present to one in which they choose for the future (in a binding way)—for instance suppose eating ice cream delivered more immediate experienced utility than eating kale. Then, an agent displays present-focus if when choosing for today, they choose ice cream over kale, but when choosing for tomorrow, they choose kale over ice cream.

Circumstances that elicit such binding actions do not only arise in the laboratory or in artificial environments (though binding choices are easier to create in a controlled environment). Consider the person who tends to eat ice cream when it is immediately available, but tends to explicitly or implicitly choose not to eat ice cream in the future by not putting ice cream into his shopping cart at the supermarket.

Our definition of present-focused preferences refers to actions that generate immediate experienced utility—for instance, eating your favorite food, relaxing with friends, creating art or music, sexual activity, enjoyable hobbies, drinking alcohol, or recreational drug use.[8] Increased immediate experienced utility can be derived

---

[7] By "more likely", we mean weakly more likely and at least in some contexts strictly more likely.
[8] See Loewenstein (1996) for a related discussion of visceral drives.

not only from engaging in pleasurable or gratifying activities, but also by postponing activities that give immediate displeasure: consider a researcher who postpones working on a referee report whenever she can, but agrees to write the referee report in the first place (when the deadline is far away). In this example, the referee report generates instant displeasure (e.g., reading the paper is a slog), but generates long-term benefits (e.g., knowledge of the literature, or a reputation or self-image for being a good citizen).

Practical identification of activities that generate immediate experienced utility is conceptually challenging but can be approached in multiple ways. First, one could ask people which activities give them immediate pleasure, and even ask them to report that pleasure on a quantitative scale (see Wertenbroch, 1998, Field Study 1, and related conceptualizations in DellaVigna and Malmendier, 2004, 2006, and Oster and Morton, 2005).[9] Second, one could ask people which activities give *other* people immediate pleasure, both qualitatively and quantitatively. Third, one could measure willingness to pay for (marginal) experiences that only have immediate consequences: e.g., the willingness to pay for eating ice cream normally vs. having the same (unhealthy) ingredients safely ingested while one's taste buds are numbed. Fourth, one could measure neural activity during different activities and thereby identify activities that generate immediate neural activation in pleasure circuits (e.g., with neural probes in non-human animals—e.g., Schultz et al., 1997—or with fMRI in humans—e.g., Rangel et al., 2008; Hare et al., 2009).

The definition of present-focused preferences is intentionally unconstrained with respected to the nature/existence of self-control problems, issues that we will return to throughout this Section. Moreover, even though present-focused preferences generate dynamically inconsistent *choices*—that is, the choice between x and y made at date t for date t' is different from the choice between x and y at date t'—they may result from dynamically consistent *preferences* (which we define below). *Preferences* can be dynamically *consistent* even if *choices* are dynamically *inconsistent*.

A standard definition of dynamic consistency in preferences is as follows: *Dynamic consistency in preferences between dates t and $t' > t$ arises when a person's state contingent preferences for actions taken at date t', expressed at date t, are consistent with her state contingent preferences for actions taken at date t', expressed at date t'. Dynamic inconsistency in preferences arises if there is any pair of values t and $t' > t$, which is not characterized by dynamic consistency in preferences.*[10] In this definition "state contingency" incorporates all aspects of the choice. The state includes

---

[9]   See the large literature on subjective well-being, including experiments that triangulate choice data with self-reported data on tastes (e.g., Hare et al., 2009; Kahneman and Deaton, 2010; and Stevenson and Wolfers, 2013). These measures have also been used in practical domains. For example, most hospitals now have pain scales posted on the walls, so that patients can identify the level of discomfort that they are experiencing.

[10]   Some types of dynamic inconsistency arise in domains that are unrelated to time preferences (e.g., Andreoni et al., 2016a).

both internal phenomena like a twisted ankle (which would make exercise difficult and suboptimal) as well as external constraints, like the absence of a tempting good in a choice set. All of these contingencies are absorbed into the state contingency referred to in the definition of dynamic consistency of preferences.

The question of whether preferences are dynamically consistent can be applied to a model. One can ask what a particular model implies about the state-contingent preferences that are held at date t (for choices implemented at date t') and compare them to the state-contingent preferences that will be held at date t'. Likewise, the definition can be practically deployed as a series of hypothetical questions asked at date t: "What would you like to choose at date t' conditional on state X, knowing that you are not binding yourself to this answer?"

As we will emphasize below, some theories that generate present-focused preferences feature dynamically inconsistent preferences (e.g., present bias, which is discussed in Section 2.1). However, other theories that generate present-focused preferences feature dynamically consistent preferences (e.g., temptation models, which are discussed in Section 2.2).

We will also discuss the issue of commitment. Some theories that generate present-focused preferences feature a taste for commitment: *a strictly preferred restriction of one's own future choice set*. Here we are interested only in the intra-personal taste for commitment—e.g., a smoker who is trying to quit and chooses to flush her cigarettes down the toilet. We exclude any inter-personal strategic reasons for commitment—e.g., a general who burns a bridge *behind* her army, signaling to the opposing forces that her soldiers will fight to the death now that retreat is not an option. In this chapter, when we discuss the phenomenon of commitment we refer exclusively to the taste for (or choice of) commitment that arises from pure, intra-personal mechanisms.

We conclude the chapter by presenting a 2×2 table, which reviews all of the theories of present-focused preferences and organizes them along two dimensions: dynamic consistency of preferences and a taste for commitment. We will end up filling all four boxes with theories that fall under the broad rubric of present-focused preferences. We first discuss these theories in isolation, before drawing them together at the end of Section 2.

2.1 Present-biased preferences

The name present-*focused* preferences is a variation (and generalization) of the concept of present-*biased* preferences. Present-focused preferences include both present-biased preferences and many other related models. Present-biased preferences are the most commonly used intertemporal choice model in behavioral economics, so we describe it first.

Present bias (Laibson, 1997, O'Donoghue and Rabin, 1999a, 1999b) is also referred to as *quasi-hyperbolic discounting*, which highlights its intellectual debt to the earlier literature on hyperbolic discounting (e.g., Loewenstein and Prelec, 1992).[11] Present-biased preferences are expressed:

$$U_t = u_t + \beta\delta u_{t+1} + \beta\delta^2 u_{t+2} + \beta\delta^3 u_{t+3} + \cdots . \tag{1}$$

Here U_t is total utility, u_t is flow utility in period t, β is the present bias parameter, and δ is the long-run discount factor. Phelps and Pollak (1968) first used this framework to model *intergenerational* preferences, in contrast to the intra-personal preferences that we discuss now. For Phelps and Pollak, u_t is the utility of generation t and u_{t+1} is the utility of generation $t + 1$. In the behavioral economics literature, the discounting is intra-personal instead of being inter-generational. Accordingly, u_t is the utility flow that an agent experiences during period t and u_{t+1} is the utility flow that the same agent experiences during period $t + 1$.

In this framework (like most other intertemporal choice models in economics) the object being discounted is a stream of utility flows, which are distinct, in principle, from financial flows. In other words, the theory is about how agents discount pleasures and pains experienced at particular points in time, and not about how agents think about the timing of financial events (e.g., whether my fully anticipated paycheck is auto-deposited in my bank account on Friday or Monday—assuming that the interest rate is zero and my short-term liquidity is more than adequate to cover all of my expenses and other transactions over the weekend). The distinction between utility discounting and money discounting is reviewed in Sections 3.1 and 3.2, as well as in Cohen et al. (2016). To our knowledge this distinction was first clearly articulated by Ramsey (1928): "This rate of discounting future utilities must, of course, be distinguished from the rate of discounting future sums of money. If I can borrow or lend at a rate r I must necessarily be equally pleased with an extra £1 now and an extra £(1 + r) in a year's time, since I could always exchange the one for the other. My marginal rate of discount for money is, therefore, necessarily r, but my rate of discount for utility may be quite different, since the marginal utility of money to me may be varying by my increasing or decreasing my expenditure as time goes on."

To illustrate the importance of the timing of utility flows, consider the example of exercise (e.g., gym attendance). In most applications, exercise is assumed to have immediate logistical, and psychic costs and delayed health benefits (e.g., DellaVigna and Malmendier, 2004, 2006), which will engender a self-defeating pattern of low levels of exercise, even among those who pay for gym memberships. However, the opposite self-regulation problem might apply to people who greatly enjoy the physical sensation of exercising. These presumably rare types will tend to exercise too much, for the same reasons (in the model) that the rest of us watch too much television and eat too many donuts. Modelers need to be careful in the assumptions that

---

[11] For earlier examples from the psychology literature, see Herrnstein (1961) and Ainslie (1975). For a different, but conceptually related functional form, see Benhabib et al. (2010). For a closely related formulation based on salience, see Akerlof (1991).

they make about the timing of utility flows (for example, see the related analysis in Augenblick et al., 2015) and the valence of utility flows.

In this model it is natural to place bounds on the discounting parameters: $0 < \beta \leq 1$ and $0 < \delta \leq 1$. In the literature, the notation distinguishes the term 'discount factor', which refers to a specific weighting parameter β or δ, and 'discount function', which refers to the function of horizon-dependent utility weights, which, for present-biased preferences, is given by

$$D(t) = \begin{cases} 1 & \text{if } t = 0, \\ \beta \delta^t & \text{if } t \geq 1. \end{cases} \quad (2)$$

In Eqs. (1) and (2), β is not exponentiated (whereas δ is). Because of this difference, it is helpful to rewrite these preferences as

$$U_t = u_t + \beta \left[\delta u_{t+1} + \delta^2 u_{t+2} + \delta^3 u_{t+3} + \cdots \right]. \quad (3)$$

Written this way, it is clear that present biased preferences embed a continuation payoff stream that is weighted by β and then exponentially discounted thereafter. When $\beta = 1$ these preferences revert to exponential discounting. (As a general point, it is useful when behavioral models nest the classical model as a special case.) In typical calibration/estimation of these discounting factors, $\beta \ll 1$ and $\delta \cong 1$.

Present-biased preferences are *present-focused*. Under present-biased preferences, $\beta < 1$ engenders a preference to experience pleasurable activities in the present instead of the future. For example, assume that exercise has an immediate cost of c and a delayed (health) benefit of b. Assume that all of these utility flows are differences relative to an alternative activity which we will call napping. To further simplify this example, assume that $\delta = 1$. If $b > c > \beta b$, then the present-biased agent prefers to nap today and to commit to exercise tomorrow:

$$-c + \beta b < 0,$$
$$\beta(-c + b) > 0.$$

Present-biased preferences are dynamically inconsistent: e.g., in this example, the agent at time t prefers to exercise at time $t' > t$ and the agent at time t' prefers to nap at time t'.

Present-biased preferences engender a (potential) preference for commitment if the agent has sophisticated or partially sophisticated beliefs (see Strotz, 1955; Phelps and Pollak, 1968; Laibson, 1997, and O'Donoghue and Rabin, 1999a, 1999b; however, see Laibson, 2015 for reasons that commitment might still not arise in practice even for partially or fully sophisticated agents). Sophisticated beliefs imply that the agent has a correct theory of her own future time preferences.

Partially sophisticated beliefs (i.e., partially naïve beliefs) imply that she recognizes that she is present-biased, but she believes that her future selves ($t' > t$) will each have a higher value of β then those future selves will actually have $\beta(t') < E_t[\beta(t')] < 1$ (O'Donoghue and Rabin, 1999a, 1999b). In the literature, $\hat{\beta}$ is used as a short-hand for $E_t[\beta(t')]$. Fully naïve beliefs imply that the agent believes that her future selves will not be present biased at all: $\hat{\beta} = 1$. Accordingly, fully naïve beliefs imply that a present-biased agent won't have a preference for commitment. She believes that all future selves will act according to her current preferences for their future actions.

Present-biased preferences are a special case within a large class of discounting models that are distinguished by high discount rates in the short-run and low discount-rates in the long-run—i.e., a monotonically falling discount rate (see Strotz, 1955). The discount rate is the local rate of decline in the discount function, $D(t)$. In discrete time models, the local rate of decline of the discount function (per unit of time) is

$$-\frac{D(t+1) - D(t)}{D(t)}. \tag{4}$$

In continuous time models (with differentiable discount functions), the local rate of decline of the discount function is

$$-\frac{D'(t)}{D(t)}. \tag{5}$$

Under exponential discounting, the discrete-time discount rate is $1 - \delta$ and the continuous-time discount rate is $-\ln \delta \approx 1 - \delta$.[12] These discount rates are constant, and therefore not horizon dependent.

Contrast this with the case of present bias. Under present-biased discounting in discrete time, the short-run discount rate is $1 - \beta\delta$ and the long-run discount rate is $1 - \delta < 1 - \beta\delta$.

There are also generalizations of present-bias in continuous time, which we omit in this short survey (see Harris and Laibson, 2012). Continuous-time implementations generate desirable modeling properties, such as smooth policy functions, equilibrium uniqueness, and—like the exponential discounting model—a single value function that the individual uses to judge their own welfare.

2.2 Unitary-self models with temptation

Present-biased preferences induce dynamically inconsistent preferences. As such preferences began to gain influence in the 1990s, some economists pointed out that many of the phenomena that were being explained by models with dynamically inconsistent preferences, could also be explained by models with rational beliefs and dynamically consistent preferences (e.g., Dekel et al., 2001; Gul and Pesendorfer, 2001; Laibson, 2001; Bernheim and Rangel, 2004; Dekel et al., 2009; Gul and Pesendorfer, 2004; Noor, 2007, 2011; Lipman and Pesendorfer, 2013). Some of these unitary-self models are called *temptation models*. (A related psychology literature also studies temptation effects: e.g., Baumeister et al., 1998; Muraven et al., 1998;

---

[12] This approximation represents a first-order Taylor expansion.

Muraven and Baumeister, 2000.) Present-biased models also feature temptation properties, though the nature of the temptation is different, as we will explain below.

Unitary-self models of self-control problems come in many different particular forms. They are related by the principle that choice *sets* affect utility, including the *options that are not chosen* (see Kreps, 1979). Consider an example in which a decision-maker at time t can, in principle, engage in two mutually exclusive activities during a future period $t' > t$: exercise or nap. Assume that exercise has immediate consequences that are hedonically aversive, and therefore exercise is not tempting. By contrast, assume that nap has immediate consequences that are pleasurable, and therefore nap is tempting. Suppose that the decision-maker must choose her choice set for period t' during t. At period t, the decision-maker has preferences over three possible choice sets for period t': {exercise, nap}, {exercise}, {nap}. A singleton choice set implies that the decision-maker must choose that action (there is no opt-out).

Two scenarios illustrate some of the key ideas in this literature: "commitment with strong temptation" and "commitment with weak temptation." For all of the analysis in this subsection, we will assume that there is no risk/uncertainty, thereby *removing* the classical option-value reason for preferring flexibility (however, see Kreps, 1979, for an alternative framework in which agents have a preference for flexibility for its own sake).

Commitment with strong temptation: The period t preferences over choice sets available at time t', could take the following form:

$$\{\underline{\text{exercise}}\} \succ \{\text{exercise}, \underline{\text{nap}}\} \sim \{\underline{\text{nap}}\}. \tag{6}$$

To simplify exposition, we underline the outcome that occurs at period t' conditional on each choice set that could be chosen in period t. In this scenario, during period t the decision-maker prefers that at period t' she will exercise without the temptation to nap. Therefore, she chooses to tie her own hands by compelling herself to exercise at time t'. If the choice set {exercise, nap} were available at period t', then nap would be chosen (because nap is the tempting option and, in the current scenario, this temptation is *strong*). Consequently, at time period 0, the agent is indifferent between the (future) choice sets {exercise, nap}, which will induce the tempting action of napping, and the restrictive choice set {nap}. In either case, she'll nap. (This is the same type of temptation that emerges in the model of present bias.)

Commitment with weak temptation: The period t preferences over choice sets available at time t', could take the following form:

$$\{\underline{\text{exercise}}\} \succ \{\underline{\text{exercise}}, \text{nap}\} \succ \{\underline{\text{nap}}\}. \tag{7}$$

At date t, the decision-maker prefers that at time t' she will exercise without the temptation to nap (as before). Therefore, she chooses to tie her own hands by compelling herself to exercise at time t'. If the choice set {exercise, nap} were available at time period t', then exercise would still be chosen. Even though nap is the tempting option, this temptation is weak, so exercise would still be chosen at period t'. But the agent does pay some utility cost when she rejects a tempting option *that is in her immediate choice set*, so at date t, Eq. (7) features two strict inequalities, reflecting the costs of temptation.

In these analyses, temptation plays two roles. First, it can affect the final choice, as it does in the first example (strong temptation). The availability of the option to nap causes nap to be chosen in period t' (even though it is preferred to remove that option during period t so it isn't in the consideration set at period t').

Second, temptation can affect welfare, even when it does not affect the final choice. In the second example (weak temptation), exercise is chosen whenever it is available. However, the decision-maker still strictly prefers to remove nap from her choice set. In this scenario, nap is a temptation that makes the decision-maker worse off, even though she never chooses it when exercise is available. Intuitively, it is psychologically costly to resist a temptation.[13]

Let's now generalize this example. Consider an agent at time t who has two *immediate* choices to make from *unrestricted* choice sets: do I choose to exercise or nap at time t and do I choose (now at time t) to exercise or nap at time t'. The choices made at time t for time t' will be implemented by choosing singleton choice sets for time t', thereby committing actions at time t'.

Under strong temptation, the agent will choose to nap at time t and will commit to exercise at time t', implying that these preferences are present-focused.

Under weak temptation, the agent will choose to exercise at time t and will also commit to exercise at time t'. Moreover, at time t, the agent will *strictly* prefer (i.e., she is willing to pay) to restrict her choice set at time t', even though this commitment does not affect her choice at time t'. This phenomenon—willingness to pay for commitments that do not actually affect one's choices—is not predicted by present-biased preferences (see 4.2 for evidence of such commitments). Present-biased agents may be willing to pay for commitment, but only if that commitment changes their choices.

Summing up, the unitary-self model with temptation features dynamically consistent preferences (all selves have aligned state-contingent preferences, where the contingency includes the relevant choice set). The unitary-self model also features commitment, unless the agent is naïve about her preferences (e.g., see Ahn et al., 2017).

2.3 Multiple-self models with simultaneous selves

A different branch of present-focused models is based on the idea that competing sets of interests simultaneously pull the decision-maker in different directions (e.g.,

---

[13] Though rarely discussed, temptation effects could, in principle, have effects opposite in sign to those discussed in this subsection. If a decision-maker takes pride/pleasure in successfully resisting temptations, then a third case could arise. *Self-satisfaction when resisting temptation:* The period 0 preferences over choice sets available at time 1, could take the following form: {exercise, nap} ≻ {exercise} ≻ {nap}. At date 0, the decision-maker prefers that at time 1 she will exercise and she foresees that she will take extra pleasure in exercising if she does so by using her own willpower, instead of relying on an extrinsic commitment mechanism. See Kreps (1979).

Thaler and Shefrin, 1981; Shefrin and Thaler, 1988; Hoch and Loewenstein, 1991; Loewenstein, 1996; Bernheim and Rangel, 2004; Loewenstein and O'Donoghue, 2004; McClure et al., 2004, 2007; Fudenberg and Levine, 2006, 2011, 2012; Brocas and Carrillo, 2008a, 2008b, 2012; Jackson and Yariv, 2014, 2015).

This conceptualization of simultaneously competing internal interests can be traced back to Greek philosophers and probably has even earlier precedents. In the field of economics, the idea originates with Smith (1759),[14] who adopted a framework that echoed classical sources with which he would have been familiar (e.g., Plato's discussion of Socrates, referenced in the introduction). Smith contrasted two sets of motivational systems: passions, which tend to be myopic, and a far-sighted internal spectator who attempts to rein in the free expression of our passions. "The spectator does not feel the solicitations of our present appetites. To him the pleasure which we are to enjoy a week hence, or a year hence, is just as interesting as that which we are to enjoy this moment." Related models reappeared in the economics literature with the contributions of Thaler and Shefrin (1981) and Shefrin and Thaler (1988). They hypothesized competition between a myopic "doer" and a far-sighted (and dynamically consistent) "planner."

Subsequent contributions (e.g., Fudenberg and Levine, 2006, 2011, 2012) have used formal frameworks that populate a middle-ground between the planner-doer model of Thaler and Shefrin and the unitary-self models described in the previous subsection.[15]

Fudenberg and Levine begin their 2006 paper with a quote from McIntosh (1969): "The idea of self-control is paradoxical unless it is assumed that the psyche contains more than one energy system, and that these energy systems have some degree of independence from each other." Fudenberg and Levine model two types of selves that play a repeated stage game: a patient (dynamically consistent) long-run self and a sequence of myopic short-run selves. These two types of selves share the same preferences over the immediate outcomes of each current stage-game. However, only the long-run self cares about payoffs in future stage games. Fudenberg and Levine assume that each stage game is played in two phases. In the first sub-period of the phase game, the long-run self chooses to exert a level of (costly) self-control that influences the preferences of the current short-run self. In the second sub-period of the stage game, the short-run self takes the final decision.

Models with simultaneously competing selves also fit into the general class of present-focused models. Here too, (unconstrained) agents are relatively more likely to choose hedonically pleasurable activities for the present, than they are to commit to choose the same hedonically pleasurable activities for the future. For example, in the

---

[14] See Ashraf et al. (2005) for a fascinating review of the rich veins of behavioral economics that can be found in the work of Adam Smith, especially *The Theory of Moral Sentiments* (1759).

[15] "While we find the language of multiple 'selves' to be suggestive, the model can equally well be interpreted as describing the behavior of a single 'self' whose overall behavior is determined by the interaction of two subsystems" (Fudenberg and Levine, 2006, p. 1450).

model of Fudenberg and Levine, the current short-run self wants to experience immediate pleasures, making it difficult (i.e., costly) for the long-run self to dictate the outcome. In equilibrium, unconstrained choices for the present will be biased toward immediate gratification because the long-run self won't be willing to exert enough costly self-control to force the hand of the myopic short-run self. However, when the same person makes binding commitments for the future, the current short-run self doesn't care about what will happen, so it can be easily manipulated by the long-run self. Accordingly, choices made for the future will be less prone to favor short-run pleasures.

Multiple-self models with simultaneous selves feature a preference for commitment. The long-run self typically wants to restrict future choice sets to make it easier to resist the drives of future short-run selves.

It is unclear how to categorize multiple-self models with simultaneous selves with respect to the property of dynamic consistency of preferences. The long-run selves in these models are (usually) dynamically consistent in their preferences. The long-run selves may *appear* to be dynamically inconsistent because of their fraught interactions with their myopic selves. The myopic short-run selves create drives that the long-run selves need to resist or, if that is very costly, accept. Once one properly accounts for these myopic psychological drives, and the psychic costs that must be paid to overcome them, the long-run selves have dynamically consistent preferences (just like the unitary self in the temptation models).

Nevertheless, it would be odd to say that the *full* set of preferences is dynamically consistent in multiple-self models with simultaneous selves. These models feature competing preferences (e.g., the preferences of long-run and short-run selves), which are not aligned.

2.4 Objective risks that reduce future value

Objective risks can create another source of present-focused preferences. Assume that future rewards may be 'lost' before they are received—e.g., the counter-party making the promise of the future payment could go bankrupt or skip town. If the hazard rate of such losses is horizon dependent, $\rho(\tau)$, then a perfectly patient decision-maker should discount rewards at rate $\rho(\tau)$ at horizon τ. If this hazard is constant, discounting will appear exponential, but a changing hazard can generate discount functions with a hyperbolic shape (see Sozou, 1998; Azfar, 1999; Weitzman, 2001; Halevy, 2005; Dasgupta and Maskin, 2005; Fernández-Villaverde and Mukherji, 2006; Halevy, 2014, 2015).

Hyperbolic discounting can be generated by uncertainty about what the hazard rate is (even if it is a constant rate). For instance, Sozou (1998), Azfar (1999), and Weitzman (2001) assume that $\rho(\tau)$ is not horizon-dependent, so $\rho(\tau)$ is a constant, and ρ is not known because it has been drawn from a distribution. Consequently, at every point in time the true (realized) value of ρ has a posterior distribution that is changing. The more time that passes without a loss, the more likely that one of the low values for ρ was originally drawn. This generates intertemporal choices that are equivalent to those that would be generated by a discount rate that declines as the horizon increases (e.g., hyperbolic discounting).[16]

This is another example of present-focused preferences arising from an agent whose preferences are dynamically consistent. In this scenario, the agent will look as if she has hyperbolic time preferences (in the sense that her discount rate is declining with the horizon), but she won't have a self-control problem, she won't have dynamically inconsistent preferences, and she won't view commitment as something valuable. She will always prefer more choice to less (all else equal).

This is an illustration of a more general point: exponential discounting is sufficient, but not necessary for dynamically consistent preferences. If all selves agree on the same (non-stationary) non-exponential discount function, then they will have dynamically consistent preferences.

2.5 **Models with psychometric distortions**

Models with psychometric distortions posit that time and risk are perceived with psychological distortions that tend to generate present-focused preferences. For example, suppose time is perceived with a concave (subjective) transformation (as argued by Read, 2001; Takahashi, 2005; Ebert and Prelec, 2007, and Zauberman et al., 2009). To fix ideas, suppose that agents discount with an exponential discount function, $D(\tau(t)) = \delta^{\tau}$, but that they perceive objective time, t, with a concave transformation $\tau(t)$. Then the discount rate inferred by the social scientist (with respect to objective time), will be given by

$$-\frac{D'(\tau(t))}{D(\tau(t))}\tau'(t) = (-\ln \delta)\tau'(t).$$

Note that when $\tau'(t) = 1$, so that subjective and objective slopes align, the researcher will simply impute a constant discount rate, $-\ln \delta$. However, if τ is a concave function, the imputed discount rate is declining as the objective horizon, t, increases. To see this, take the derivative of the imputed discount rate with respect to the discounting horizon:

$$\frac{d[(-\ln \delta)\tau'(t)]}{dt} = (-\ln \delta)\tau''(t) < 0.$$

Hence, the agent's psychometric distortion in the perception of time produces behavior that mimics the behavior that one observes when the discount function has a declining discount rate in the (objective) horizon of the discounted reward. Relatively high short-run (effective) discount rates and relatively low long-run (effective) discount rates generate present-focused preferences for the same reasons that we see them in Section 2.1.

---

[16] Dasgupta and Maskin (2005) show that while Souzou's model cannot explain preference reversals, uncertainty about when payoffs will be realized can.

This mechanism is one microfoundation for hyperbolic discounting. However, this version of hyperbolic discounting is different from the one implied by present bias. For example, this psychometric distortion does not seem to imply a motive for commitment. Rather a psychometrically distorted view of the future is like an optical illusion. When you become aware of the optical illusion, you try to correct your misperception (i.e., make some effort at debiasing), rather than restricting your future choice sets. On the other hand, psychometric distortions do tend to generate dynamic inconsistency in preferences: an agent with distorted time perception has preferences for future tradeoffs which are inconsistent with the preferences that she will actually have in the future.

In the model above, agents perceive objective time with a distortion, leading to present-focus. Agents might instead perceive *delays* between two options with distortions, such that the delay between t' and t is perceived as $\tau(t' - t)$ rather than $\tau(t') - \tau(t)$. This psychometric distortion of delays can be one source of *subadditivity* (Read, 2001; Scholten and Read, 2006; see also Glimcher et al., 2007; and Kable and Glimcher, 2010).[17] Specifically, subadditivity arises when discounting over a time interval is greater when the interval is divided into subintervals, which is a robust empirical regularity. Subadditivity produces choices that mimic a key property of hyperbolic discounting: diminishing discount rates as the length of the discounting period is increased. Despite this similarity with hyperbolic discounting, discounters who exhibit subadditivity will not choose commitment and their preferences will be dynamically consistent.[18] Neither perceiving delays with distortions nor subadditivity generate present-focused preferences, since an additional delay is perceived the same regardless of whether it begins now or in the future. As a result, a sub-additive agent will make the same choice today (e.g., 1 util now vs. x utils tomorrow) as she will for the future (1 util in t days vs. x utils in $t+1$ days).[19]

Other psychometric distortions produce present-focused preferences. For example, subjective probability distortions, such as the probability weighting function of Kahneman and Tversky (1979), will produce behavior that mimics hyperbolic discounting. Specifically, if the present is perceived to be risk free (in the sense that promised rewards will be delivered with certainty), but the near future is perceived to introduce a tiny amount of risk, then the existence of a certainty effect (whereby a very small amount of risk is subjectively treated like a large reduction in likelihood), will generate behavior like present bias. For related arguments see the non-expected utility frameworks in Prelec and Loewenstein (1991), Quiggin and Horowitz (1995),

---

[17] Subadditivity may be rational if there is implicit information (e.g., about riskiness) in the way that information is elicited from subjects. For example, it may be that any delay in payment is associated with an implied risk, and the magnitude of the risk is not (highly) dependent on the length of the delay. Under this interpretation, subadditivity could be included in Section 2.5.

[18] Specifically, their views about tradeoffs between utils at t and utils at $t' > t$ does not depend on when (on or before date t) they are asked to express this preference.

[19] Cohen et al. (2016) discuss the evidence for two distinct features of hyperbolic discounting: discount rates fall as a front-end delay is added and as the length of the discounting period is increased. Subadditivity can account for the latter regularity.

Keren and Roelofsma (1995), Weber and Chapman (2005), Halevy (2008), Epper et al. (2011), Baucells and Heukamp (2012), Andreoni and Sprenger (2012a), Epper and Fehr-Duda (2015a, 2015b), Chakraborty (2017). These models do not generate a demand for commitment, but they do generate dynamically inconsistent preferences.

Heuristic reasoning can also generate present-focused preferences. Proportional reasoning can lead to behavior that has many of the properties generated by a hyperbolic discount function. For example, if a delay from 0 days to 1 day seems like a large delay (because the average delay is 1/2) but a delay from 100 days to 101 days seems like a small delay because the average is 100 1/2, then agents may respond more aversively to rewards that are delayed in the former than in the latter case (Rubinstein, 2003; Read et al., 2013; Ericson et al., 2015). Agents that are using heuristic reasoning will not choose commitment, but they will express dynamically inconsistent preferences.

The focusing model of Kőszegi and Szeidl (2013) also generates present focused preferences in some circumstances. In this model, consumers choose among multidimensional consumption vectors, where each dimension represents an attribute. The consumer maximizes focus-weighted utility, which disproportionately weights attributes in which her options generate a greater range of consumption utility. Their model produces no present-focus when simply trading off utility at two different dates. However, agents may display present-focus when they frame a choice (like exercising today) as an isolated current decision with a salient up-front cost (going to the gym) and a stream of tiny non-salient benefits (being slightly healthier, each day over the next few years because you exercised once). When instead framing the decision as a continuous stream of exercise (in the future) and a stream of *large* health benefits (that arise from a consistent routine of exercising), the agent makes a more patient choice. The all-in or all-out decision leads to patient choices, because now the streams of costs and benefits are both large and the focusing bias does not make the cost of exercise disproportionately salient. Agents with focusing bias will not choose commitment if the bias is a perceptual error, but they will express dynamically inconsistent preferences.

2.6 Models of myopia

The concept of myopic decision-making has been discussed for millennia. Though it is not possible to locate the intellectual origin of this idea there are many historical milestones.[20] For example, von Böhm-Bawerk (1890) wrote that "we possess inadequate power to imagine and to abstract, or that we are not willing to put forth the necessary effort, but in any event we limn a more or less incomplete picture of our future wants and especially of the remotely distant ones. And then, there are all of those wants that never come to mind at all."

---

[20] See Loewenstein (1992) for a review of the 19th and 20th century intellectual history of theories of intertemporal choice.

Pigou (1920) similarly observed "that our telescopic faculty is defective, and that we, therefore, see future pleasures, as it were, on a diminished scale. That this is the right explanation is proved by the fact that exactly the same diminution is experienced when, apart from our tendency to forget ungratifying incidents, we contemplate the past."

Even if we stipulate that people are "myopic," it is not at all clear what that formally means. Loosely speaking, myopia is a failure to clearly see the future when it is forecastable in principle (e.g., if one "took their head out of the sand" or "stopped living completely in the moment").[21]

Gabaix and Laibson (2017) model myopia as the consequence of *cognitive* noise that reduces the accuracy of signals about future events (see also related work by Commons et al., 1982, 1991). Because agents know that their signals are noisy, they shade those signals toward their prior, causing their forecasts to be relatively unresponsive to true variation in future rewards. Consequently, future utility flows are given less weight than they would have if perceptions were not noisy. This implies that the agent will exhibit present-focused preferences: the agent's choices will reflect greater sensitivity to the attributes—positive and negative—that are experienced in the present.

The model of Gabaix and Laibson produces behavior that mimics much of the behavior that arises under hyperbolic discounting. However, the model generates no taste for commitment because the agents are not encumbered by a self-control problem; their only problem is that they are unable to see clearly into the future. The model assumes that agents have *underlying* dynamically consistent preferences. However, the agent may not be able to act on these preferences because her noisy perceptions of future payoffs undermine the expression of these preferences, leading her to *exhibit* preferences that appear to be dynamically inconsistent to an outside observer who doesn't appreciate her perceptual limitations.

Other forms of myopia also produce behavior that appears to be characteristic of dynamically inconsistent preferences. For example, one could interpret the focusing model of Kőszegi and Szeidl (2013) as a model of selective myopia (i.e., overlooking the attributes that are not focal). This model implies no commitment and generates (expressed) preferences that will appear to be dynamically consistent to an outside observer. See Frederick (2005) for another mechanism that can produce myopia: a low propensity to engage in cognitive reflection. See also Steele and Josephs (1990) for alcohol-induced myopia.

2.7 Overview of models of present-focused preferences

We have reviewed a large family of models that feature present-focused preferences. These models share the property that agents choose more impatiently for the present than when they choose for the future. Commonalities of models in the intertemporal

---

[21] Early formulations of myopia were developed by Brown and Lewis (1981) and Jéhiel (1995).

Table 1 Present-focused models categorized by two properties: commitment (rows) and dynamic consistency of preferences (columns).

	Dynamically consistent preferences	Dynamically inconsistent preferences
Commitment	• Unitary-self temptation models: 2.2 • Long-term self in multiple-self models: 2.3	• Present-bias with partial sophistication: 2.1 • Other forms of hyperbolic discounting: 2.1
No Commitment	• Exponential discounting: 2.1 • Objective risks (non-exponential discounting): 2.4 • Myopia: 2.6	• Present-bias with perfect naiveté: 2.1 • Psychometric distortions: 2.5 • Myopia: 2.6

Note: Each model is discussed in the associated subsection.

choice literature have been noted by many authors (e.g., Barro, 1999; Krusell et al., 2010; Gustman and Steinmeier, 2012; Gabaix and Laibson, 2017).

Despite this core similarity, the models in this literature have many contrasting properties, some of which are summarized in Table 1. The taste for commitment (which is captured in the rows of the table) is a particularly important differentiator, because this is directly observable in choices. In other words, we can (in principle) observe this smoking gun if we can find settings in which commitment is purely choice-set restricting and not confounded by other benefits (like tax advantages in illiquid retirement savings plans). However, see Laibson (2015, 2018) for reasons that we may not expect to see commitment in practice. For example, exogenous uncertainty may make commitment undesirable even for fully sophisticated present-biased agents who would commit themselves in an idealized world with no uncertainty.

Dynamic consistency of preferences is captured in the columns of Table 1. Dynamic consistency in preferences is not measurable by observing (binding) choices. Rather it is a property of a model. As an empirical object, it is measured by asking people about their current state-contingent preferences (in future states).

2.8 Models that do not generate present-focused preferences

Finally, we conclude Section 2 by emphasizing that there are other influential models of intertemporal choice that do not fall into the category of present-focused preferences. Present-focused preferences undergird a large part of the intertemporal choice literature, but not all of it.

Habits and related reference-point effects lead agents to experience larger utility flows when they can favorably compare current consumption to their own past consumption, to consumption of their peers, or to consumption that they had expected (e.g., Ryder and Heal, 1973; Becker and Murphy, 1988; Loewenstein, 1988; Abel, 1990; Hoch and Loewenstein, 1991; Loewenstein and Sicherman, 1991; Loewenstein and Prelec, 1992, 1993; Prelec and Loewenstein, 1998; Campbell and Cochrane, 1999; Laibson, 2001; Kőszegi and Rabin, 2009). Some of these models generate present-focused preferences, as in the preferred calibration of Kőszegi and Rabin (2009). But most of these theoretical mechanisms have the effect of leading agents to choose consumption profiles with a relatively higher slope (i.e., less consumption now and more consumption in the future), so the comparisons to past consumption will be more favorable over the lifecycle.

Anticipation effects also encourage consumers to move rewarding events into the future so they can be savored in advance (Loewenstein, 1987; Caplin and Leahy, 2001; Kreps, 1998). This idea has a long history. Loewenstein (1987) quotes Alfred Marshall on the topic: "When calculating the rate at which a future benefit is discounted, we must be careful to make allowance for the pleasures of expectation" (Marshall, 1891, p. 178).

Finally, there is a class of models that have implications for the timing of the resolution of uncertainty (e.g., Kreps and Porteus, 1978; Epstein and Zin, 1989; Weil, 1990). Depending on the calibration of these models, they can either rationalize a preference for early or late resolution of uncertainty.

3 Empirical regularities and open puzzles

We turn now to a series of well-established empirical regularities, each of which is also associated with some important open questions. Additionally, we identify a number of additional open questions for future research.

3.1 Preferences over monetary receipt timing

Empirical regularity 1. *Individuals require a high rate of return (RRR) for money earlier versus later tradeoffs.*

One of the primary ways time preference has been measured has been with Money Earlier or Later (MEL) experiments, in which subjects choose between X dollars at an early date or Y dollars at a later date.[22] While the models we discuss above are—almost always—fundamentally about the discounting of *utility*, it is hard to directly give an individual a unit of utility. Money is easily measured, is socially important, and is a placeholder for reward (albeit one that can be easily intertemporally shifted). Accordingly, a large literature examines how individuals choose between money earlier and later.

To describe the indifference points generated by individuals making choices over financial flows, we follow Cohen et al. (2016) and study the required rate of return (RRR). If an individual is indifferent between $\$x_1$ at time t_1 and $\$x_2$ at a later time t_2, we define the RRR between time t_1 and t_2 to be $\ln \frac{x_2}{x_1}$. (This is approximately the percentage difference between the rewards received in the respective periods.) Likewise,

---

[22]   This section and Section 2 draw in part on Cohen et al. (2016).

we define the annualized RRR as[23]

$$\frac{1}{(t_2 - t_1)} \ln \frac{x_2}{x_1},$$

where time units are measured in years. For comparability, it will often be convenient to annualize the RRR, though this hides some important information about the type of choices from which the RRR was estimated.

Note that the RRR is not a preference parameter. The discount rate for *utility* requires additional assumptions on when and how financial flows translate into utility: does the receipt of money correspond to receipt of utility at that time? Does utility increase approximately linearly in the amount of money received, or is there substantial curvature even over small amounts of money? Cohen et al. highlight the difficulty of interpreting what MEL experiments imply for discounting of utility, and present different models that are used to translate MEL choices into (estimated) discount functions.

The first published MEL paper is Thaler (1981), who showed a number of anomalies using hypothetical MEL questions, including the key finding that the annualized RRR declines as the time horizon gets longer (holding the earlier payment date fixed).[24] Kirby (1997) used incentive compatible (sealed second bid) auctions to measure the RRR at different time horizons, and found similar results, finding that a hyperbolic function fit the data better than the exponential discount function. The MEL design was used by several other economists after Thaler (e.g. Loewenstein and Thaler, 1989; Prelec and Loewenstein, 1991); it was popularized in the psychology literature by Kirby and Herrnstein (1995). MEL experiments now account for a large share of intertemporal choice research (Cohen et al., 2016).

There are many anomalies that characterize measured RRR's. An influential review (Frederick et al., 2002) documented numerous regularities uncovered in MEL experiments. For instance, as discussed above, the annualized RRR falls as the horizon, d, between t_1 and $t_2 = t_1 + d$ increases. There is also a robust magnitude effect (RRR's decrease as the magnitude of both $\$x_1$ and $\$x_2$ are proportionately scaled up). Moreover, as discussed in Section 2.5, there is *subadditivity* in MEL choices: individuals are more impatient over a delay if that delay is subdivided into smaller intervals (Read, 2001; Read and Roelofsma, 2003). Consider three delays: $t_1 < t_2 < t_3$, and two indifferences: $\{\$x_1, t_1\} \sim \{\$x_2, t_2\}$ and $\{\$x_2, t_2\} \sim \{\$x_3, t_3\}$. Transitivity implies that $\{\$x_1, t_1\} \sim \{\$x_3, t_3\}$, but subadditivity implies that the individual will strictly prefer $\{\$x_3, t_3\}$ to $\{\$x_1, t_1\}$. This complicates any easy aggregation of choices into a simple RRR.

---

[23] These definitions are derived from the following implicit definition of an instantaneous annual rate of return, r: $\exp(r[t_2 - t_1]) = \frac{x_2}{x_1}$.

[24] We believe that the first implementation in humans was an unpublished working paper by Maital and Maital (1977). A related stream of work studied discounting in animal behavior (e.g. Chung and Herrnstein, 1967; Ainslie, 1975).

Finally, the method used to elicit choices can affect measured preferences.[25] The literature has used a variety of methods, most commonly multiple price lists, matching/fill-in-the blank, or convex time budget tasks.

There is no single RRR that summarizes an individual's preference over money. However, we can summarize some of the quantitative stylized facts that have emerged from this literature. For payments now versus later, Thaler (1981) found median annualized RRRs of 20–30% for delays of 3–5 years, and annualized RRRs of 40–345 percent for delays of 1 month, depending on the magnitude of the rewards in his choice set. In the earliest paper to examine discounting in a representative sample (with incentivized choice), Harrison et al. (2002) conduct a field experiment in Denmark, and find an average annual RRR of 28% (with substantial individual heterogeneity), based on choices between an earlier payment in 1 month and later payments at delays of 6 to 36 months. Dohmen et al. (2010) study a representative sample of Germans who (repeatedly) chose between a payment now or a payment in 12 months, and report a median annualized RRR of about 30%.

An annual RRR of 30% is high (for instance, higher than almost all credit card APRs). However, note that these RRRs are estimated from choices with delays of months to years. Choices measured from delays of only days yield even higher annualized RRRs, as summarized by Frederick et al. (2002).

A second wave of experiments aims at measuring the discount function for a time-separable utility model. This typically requires accounting for potential curvature in the utility function.[26] The literature also typically assumes a "consume-on-receipt model" in which individuals consume the money on the date they receive it. The consume-on-receipt assumption is different from an optimization model in which individuals smooth consumption across periods. (See a detailed discussion below and in Cohen et al., 2016.)

Discount rates are typically lower once utility is adjusted for curvature. Andersen et al. (2008) measure utility curvature from choices over gambles (a "double multiple price list," one for time and one for risk). They estimate an average discount rate of about 10% per year for a representative sample of experimental participants in Denmark. Andreoni and Sprenger (2012a) introduce a convex time budget method to

---

[25] Freeman et al. (2016) compare two "matching methods" (that of Becker et al., 1964, henceforth BDM, and a sealed second price auction) with multiple price lists and find a significant difference between RRRs measured with the BDM mechanism and multiple price lists. Hardisty et al. (2013) compare matching with multiple price lists and find that matching has fewer demand characteristics. (Multiple price lists can anchor subjects or suggest a reasonable range of choices.)

[26] Abdellaoui et al. (2010), Olea and Strzalecki (2014), and Ericson and Noor (2015) provide alternative methods for measuring characteristics of discounting without measuring utility curvature. Noor (2009) highlights the importance of accounting for curvature and background consumption in reaching conclusions about the shape of the discount function.

account for utility curvature, and estimate an average annual discount rate of 25 to 35% for college students.[27]

It is worth noting that utility curvature for small payments requires two assumptions: that payments are consumed on the day (or period, however defined) the payments are received (without crowd out), and that individuals have small scale risk aversion. The first assumption requires a strong degree of narrow bracketing, and is at odds with field evidence measuring marginal propensities to consume. The second assumption is empirically plausible, though it is at odds with the theoretical prediction of the expected utility model that utility should be approximately linear with respect to small gains or losses (Rabin, 2000). Another line of work argues that attitudes over risk do not describe consumption utility curvature (see Andreoni and Sprenger, 2012b; Abdellaoui et al., 2013, and Cheung, 2016).

Another literature examines RRR for money outside the lab. This literature has some advantages over lab-based questions, but also raises methodological questions. One of the most influential papers was written by Hausman (1979), who examined the tradeoff between upfront prices when buying appliances v. the long-run operating costs (energy efficiency), and found implied annualized RRR's of about 20%. However, the tradeoffs may not have been salient to individuals (see a discussion in Allcott and Greenstone, 2012).

There is also an ongoing debate about the RRR implied by individuals' willingness to pay for fuel efficiency: Dreyfus and Viscusi (1995) estimate an RRR of 11–17%; Allcott and Wozny (2014) estimate an RRR of about 15%. Busse et al. (2013) estimate RRR's that range from −6.2% to +20.9%, depending on their assumptions, and argue that the RRR is similar to the range of interest rates paid by borrowers.

In another classic paper, Warner and Pleeter (2001) examine the choice between an annuity and a lump sum payment. They show that most enrollees selected the lump-sum, implying a RRR that exceeds 17%. This paper has been widely interpreted as evidence for under-annuitization. However, this estimate had important confounds: choosing the annuity came with additional requirements to be in the reserves; lump-sum recipients also received a variety of additional benefits not given to annuity recipients (see Simon et al., 2014).

Similarly, Coile et al. (2002) find that individuals claim Social Security payments too early; under reasonable discount rates, most would be better off delaying claiming and effectively purchasing a larger annuity. This can be interpreted as evidence for a high RRR or may instead be linked to lack of knowledge about the rules and tradeoffs that exist in the Social Security system (Brown et al., 2017). There is also a more general puzzle about low levels of annuitization (Benartzi et al., 2011; Beshears et al., 2014).

---

[27] Andreoni et al. (2015) compare the performance of the convex time budget to the double multiple price list method (utility curvature measured from risky choices) and find that the convex time budget predicts better.

Open question 1. *Why do individuals have such a high RRR for money if impatience is fundamentally about consumption flows rather than financial flows?*

The money-earlier-or-later (MEL) literature raises fundamental methodological questions. A body of theoretical research argues against inferring discount rates from MEL studies because financial flows are fungible. Money flows are about financing, and distinct from the actual timing of consumption. Coller and Williams (1999) develop a model in which MEL choices reveal an individual's discount rate only if the revealed annualized RRR is strictly between her borrowing and lending rates.[28] In their framework, an individual's annualized RRR reflects either her financing costs/return or her discount rate. However, Cubitt and Read (2007) show that the censored data techniques of Coller and Williams are not applicable when agents have concave utility functions and pick interior points of their choice sets: even when an observed RRR (imputed from binary choices) is between an individual's borrowing and lending rate, it will not reveal their discount rate but rather joint information about both the curvature of their utility function and their discount rate.[29]

To utilize the MEL paradigm, the literature has often explicitly or implicitly assumed a consume-on-receipt model, in which individuals consume payments when they get them (e.g. Thaler, 1981; Kirby and Herrnstein, 1995; Loewenstein and Prelec, 1992; Andersen et al., 2008; Benhabib et al., 2010; Halevy, 2014, 2015). Yet the estimated marginal propensity to consume out of financial receipts is much lower than one: people don't instantly consume everything they receive on the day of receipt. For instance, Johnson et al. (2006) examined spending responses to receipt of a tax rebate ($300–$600) that households knew would be coming and found that in the 3-month period after receiving the payment, households spend 20–40% of the payment on non-durables; Parker et al. (2013) found similar effects.

Evidence specific to MEL studies also provides evidence against the consume-on-receipt model. Reuben et al. (2015) looked at the check cashing behavior for participants paid in MEL studies, and found that only about half of participants cashed their check within two weeks of receipt, even though they had chosen a smaller immediate payment than a 2-week delayed payment. However, note that consumption could occur without cashing the check.

One might rescue the consume-on-receipt assumption if experimental participants made choices *as if* they would consume on receipt, even if they do not. However, research we discuss in the next section suggests that individuals discount money differently than real consumption rewards (Augenblick et al., 2015). Moreover, both Carvalho et al. (2016) and Dean and Sautmann (2018) show that MEL decisions were affected by income shocks, providing evidence against this narrow bracketing assumption (see also Cassidy, 2017). Similarly, Krupka and Stephens (2013) show that changes in the inflation rate and in income are correlated with MEL decisions.

---

[28] See also Chabris et al. (2008) for another analysis of the confounds posed by intertemporal substitution, as well as other problems associated with the MEL paradigm.

[29] See Andreoni et al. (2018) for evidence against arbitrage as an explanation for behavior on intertemporal choice tasks.

As a result, it remains an open question how to interpret behavior in MEL studies, and the extent to which it informs us about discount rates versus other factors such as heuristics, trust, risk, or probability weighting. (We discuss some of these alternative factors in Section 4.3.)

3.2 Preferences over consumption timing

Empirical regularity 2. *Individuals require a high rate of return (RRR) for real rewards. Choices over real rewards display robust present-focused preferences. When estimated with structural models, short-run discount rates are high.*

If discounting is over utility flows, a promising experimental design is to give individuals choices over time-yoked consumption, such as food or leisure—what we will term "real rewards." The literature on real rewards and intertemporal choice was inaugurated by Mischel and Ebbesen (1970) and Mischel et al. (1989) with the famous "marshmallow test" conducted with children. There were many different design variants, aimed at testing strategies that enabled self-control, but the different paradigms shared a common structure: participants were brought to a lab, and were told they could have one candy/cookie now or wait until the experimenter returned and have two. Marshmallows weren't always used, but they have become the canonical example of how the experiment was run. Some subjects took the "marshmallow" immediately, others waited for some time before taking the sooner marshmallow, while still others waited for experimenter to return (typically 15 minutes) to receive both marshmallows. The marshmallow test is commonly assumed to measure individual differences in impatience, and some evidence shows that behavior in the test is predictive of later life outcomes.[30] However, Michel's original intent was to investigate the effect of different strategies for implementing self-control (rather than persistent individual differences). Moreover, McGuire and Kable (2012, 2013) argue that participants who waited some time, then took a single marshmallow, might be better interpreted as learning about their environment (i.e. learning how long it would take for the experimenter to return) rather than failing to implement self-control.

Many studies show that RRR for real rewards are typically higher than for money: see e.g. Odum and Rainaud (2003), Odum et al. (2006), Estle et al. (2007), Lawyer et al. (2010), Tsukayama and Duckworth (2010), Reuben et al. (2010), and Ubfal (2016). Some papers find extremely high RRR.[31] McClure et al. (2007) employed time-dated juice rewards in a neuroimaging experiment in which participants were asked to choose one of two time-yoked water/juice squirts (subjects were thirsty,

---

[30] A literature using small subgroup analyses found that performance in the marshmallow task predicted SAT scores years later (Shoda et al., 1990). A recent conceptual replication (Watts et al., 2018) found a correlation about half the size as the original correlation, and which was reduced by 2/3 when controls for childhood background were included. Benjamin et al. (2018) report that the (childhood) marshmallow task does not predict mid-life measures of capital formation.

[31] For more detail, see the discussion in Cohen et al. (2016).

because they were denied fluid for three hours before the experiment and then fed salty snacks at the start of the experiment). They assume linear utility and estimate a quasi-hyperbolic discounting model that treats immediate juice as "now" but delays as small and 1 min in the future. They estimate $\beta = 0.52$ and δ close to 1.

Converting those RRR's into discount rates requires the researcher to account for curvature in the utility function, where curvature is now not over money, but over the real reward itself. Augenblick et al. (2015) show that participants in their study discount monetary rewards differently from real effort tasks. Estimating a quasi-hyperbolic discounting model separately for both money and effort, they find very little present-bias for money ($\beta = 0.97$) but more present-bias for effort: $\beta = 0.89$.

Testing for the existence of present-bias (or more generally present-focused preferences) does not require accounting for the curvature of utility (however, quantifying present-bias does). Present-bias (or present-focused preferences) can be demonstrated when the *type* of real rewards chosen systematically differs when individuals choose for immediate consumption versus for future consumption. In this paradigm, participants make choices between "long-term gratification" and "short-term gratification" goods. For instance, Read and van Leeuwen (1998) examined the choice between healthy and unhealthy snacks. Across conditions, unhealthy snacks were chosen 51% of the time when offered for consumption one week in the future, while the same unhealthy snacks were chosen 83% of the time when offered for immediate consumption. Similar results were shown by Read et al. (1999) in a paradigm in which participants choose between "high-brow" and "low-brow" movies. Studies like this make a conceptual distinction between goods that generate immediate utility costs and future utility benefits—what DellaVigna and Malmendier (2004, 2006) call "investment goods"—and goods with the opposite time profile—or "leisure goods" (see the related discussion in Section 2, where we discuss the measurement of experienced utility, and Banerjee and Mullainathan, 2010 on "temptation goods").

Finally, in contrast to the experimental literature, studies using field choices have inferred discount rates explicitly for consumption. Laibson et al. (2017) use the method of simulated moments (MSM) to estimate a lifecycle consumption model with present bias, estimating $\beta = 0.5$ and $\delta = 0.987$ (see also Angeletos et al., 2001). Other papers have used job search behavior to calibrate discounting models. DellaVigna and Paserman (2005) find β often near 0.9 (depending on assumptions). Paserman (2008) estimates β separately by income and finds that $\beta = 0.4$–0.5 for low and moderate wage workers, but less present bias for high wage workers ($\beta = 0.9$).

Food consumption provides another way to calibrate discounting models, and results are not consistent with exponential discounting. Using caloric intake data on food stamp recipients, Shapiro (2005) estimates high short-run discounting; imposing the exponential model, he estimates an unreasonable annual discount *factor* of 0.23—implying a discount rate of $-\ln(0.23)$—but when estimating a quasi-hyperbolic model and assuming log-utility, he roughly calibrates $\beta = 0.96$. Mastrobuoni and Weinberg (2009) examine food consumption of liquidity constrained social security recipients and find $\beta = 0.91$–0.94.

Open question 2. *How substitutable is consumption (and effort) across time? How does the substitution of consumption affect measured discount rates?*

Real rewards appear promising because they deliver incremental utility flows at a given time; moreover discounting of real rewards appears different than discounting of money receipt. Yet, in theory, consumption studies can introduce similar confounds: individuals can change consumption in other areas of life to offset experimentally induced consumption. For instance, consider an individual choosing how much to work (as opposed to relax) in a lab session today v. next week. If the individual works more in the lab right now, they could offset that by relaxing more after they leave the lab. Moreover, present choices may appear different from future choices: if an individual's plans for today are largely fixed but future plans are flexible, effort in the lab today will be incremental effort for the day, while planned effort for next week can be offset by reducing effort outside the lab. If, for instance, utility is aggregated at the day level and can easily be adjusted outside the lab, the utility experience in a given hour in the lab need not impact utility that day.

As intertemporal choice research increasingly moves toward using real consumption rewards, estimates of how substitutable utility is across time and structural models that account for offsetting behavior are needed.

3.3 Preference reversals

Empirical regularity 3. *Individuals exhibit (present-focused) preference reversals.*

One of the key anomalies of the intertemporal choice literature is the concept of preference reversals. Indeed, in our view, the unifying theme of the (behavioral) intertemporal choice literature is the concept of preference-focused preferences (introduced in Section 2), which boils down to a preference reversal. Recall our earlier definition: ***Present-focused preferences*** *exist if agents are relatively more likely to currently choose actions that generate instant gratification, than they are to currently choose the same (binding) actions for future periods.* We hasten to remind the reader that preference reversals are not the same as dynamic inconsistency in preferences, a point we will return to below.

Read and van Leeuwen (1998) present a canonical example of a preference reversal. In their study experimental participants are asked to choose among six snacks (two healthy and four unhealthy)[32] to be delivered after seven days. We'll refer to the asking date as day 0 and the delivery date as day 7. On day 0, the participants are not told that they will have an opportunity to revisit this choice on day 7, an important design decision, that we will discuss momentarily. Read and van Leeuwen create a 2×2 design, where they vary the degree of satiation at day 0 ("after lunch time,"

---

[32] The six snacks, rank-ordered from most to least healthy are apples (1.33), bananas (1.67), crisps (3.91), borrelnoten (4.08), Mars bars (4.67), and Snickers bars (5.33). The numbers in parentheses are the average rank-ordering.

when they are presumably satiated, or "in the late afternoon, around 4:30 or 5:00," when they are presumably not satiated) and the degree of satiation at day 7. Experimental participants are told on day 0 when the snack will be delivered on day 7. In other words, they know at day 0 whether they will receive the day-7 snack after lunch time or in the late afternoon.

In the always satiated condition (asked when satiated and delivered when satiated), 26% of participants choose an unhealthy snack at date 0 (to be delivered on day 7), and 70% of participants choose an unhealthy snack on day 7. In the always non-satiated condition (asked when non-satiated and delivered when non-satiated), 78% of participants choose an unhealthy snack at date 0 (to be delivered on day 7), and 92% of participants choose an unhealthy snack on day 7. (There is a ceiling effect in the always non-satiated condition.)

In both the always satiated condition and the always non-satiated condition there is a switch on day 7 towards snacks that offer greater instant gratification (e.g., a Snickers bar vs. an apple). This is the essence of present-focused preferences. When people choose the snack to be eaten "now" they are relatively more likely to choose snacks that offer instant gratification than when they choose (what they think will be a binding) choice 7 days in advance. Many of the models discussed in Section 2 would predict this type of "preference reversal," although they offer different explanations for the reversal.

Many related studies have documented preference reversals, including Read et al. (1999), DellaVigna and Malmendier (2004, 2006), Badger et al. (2007), Milkman et al. (2009), Augenblick et al. (2015), Sadoff et al. (2015), Kuchler and Pagel (2018), and Fedyk (2018).[33] It is also important to note that preference reversals come in three broad methodological categories. First, strong form preference reversals occur when the same decision is made by the same person at an early date and then again at a later date (as in Read and van Leeuwen, 1998). Semi-strong form preference reversals occur when the same person makes a decision now and also makes a decision for the future. Weak form preference reversals occur when different people make the now decision and the later decision.

Open question 3. *What are the key mechanisms that cause preference reversals?*

Preference reversals are consistent with *both* dynamically *in*consistent preferences *and* dynamically consistent preferences. For example, present-bias generates preference reversals of the type that we have just discussed due to dynamically *in*consistent preferences (see Section 2.1). Present-biased agents heavily weight immediate rewards (which are not β-discounted) relative to delayed rewards (which are β-discounted), leading present-biased agents to more frequently choose candy (and other unhealthy snacks) when they are available immediately, compared to when they

---

[33] Preference reversals also emerge in other domains. For example, Andreoni et al. (2016a) document preference reversals in social preferences.

are available at a delay. Read and van Leeuwen (1998) interpret their results as evidence for present-biased preferences, but this is not the only way to understand their findings.

Unitary-self models (which feature dynamically consistent preferences), also predict preference reversals. Here the mechanism is the temptation effects that are assumed to arise when decisions are being made in the moment (i.e., for eating candy now) but do not arise when decisions are being made for the future. In other words, candy now is tempting, but candy next week is not tempting. Accordingly, an agent will more readily choose candy now than candy later. All of this can be explained with a model in which agents are dynamically consistent. Specifically, the agent says that she would like to choose fruit later *if* she can commit herself. However, she does not prefer to choose fruit later if she can't commit herself, because she anticipates that the temptation effects (that will arise later if she hasn't pre-committed) will make choosing fruit later suboptimal. In this sense, she is dynamically consistent. On day 0, she only prefers fruit later if she can pre-commit herself to choose fruit later (i.e., if she can restrict her choice set). On day 0, she prefers candy later if she can't restrict her day-7 choice set.[34]

Of course, (dynamically inconsistent) present-bias and (dynamically consistent) temptation effects are mutually compatible. In other words, they are likely both present in human motivation. One open challenge is to identify and measure their quantitative contributions. A related open challenge is to understand the role that naiveté plays in all of these intertemporal choice models. For example, a naïve agent with temptation preferences may not appreciate how temptation will affect her later choices, leading the agent to look nearly indistinguishable from a naïve present-biased agent. Accordingly, it is important to understand not only the underlying mix of preferences that agents have, but also to understand their meta-awareness of these preferences.

3.4 Procrastination

Empirical regularity 4. *We procrastinate and deadlines can help.*

While many people agree that procrastination is widespread, we do not have a precise, commonly shared definition of procrastination. In our discussion here, we will define someone as procrastinating if, when completing a costly task, there is delay that appears suboptimal from their *own* perspective. Procrastination, is by our definition, a problem, and can result from different models.[35]

---

[34] See Sadoff et al. (2015) for related evidence from a field experiment.

[35] Alternatively, one can view procrastination through the lens of a model and define it more precisely. For instance, through the lens of present-bias, procrastination can be defined as additional delay in completing a costly task relative to the benchmark of a time-consistent model with correct beliefs (e.g. as in Ericson, 2017).

Anecdotal examples of procrastination abound, perhaps most famously in Akerlof's (1991) discussion of how he continually put off returning a box to a friend—and showed how small mistakes could lead to large welfare losses: each day, the loss from delaying one more day was small, but the overall cost of delaying versus sending at the start was quite large.

The theoretical analysis of procrastination through the lens of present-bias was developed in a series of papers by O'Donoghue and Rabin (1999a, 1999b, 2001). For naïve individuals completing a single task, present-bias quite intuitively leads to excess (and unpredicted) delay; but behavior of present-biased individuals can become quite complex for sophisticates, or when there are multiple tasks from which to choose. For instance, there are special circumstances in which sophisticates may sometimes complete a task *earlier* than a time-consistent individual because they recognize if they delay today they will delay even more in the future; as a result, present-bias needn't always lead to procrastination. However, in most settings, agents with present bias (i.e., $\beta < 1$, holding all else equal), will procrastinate more than agents without present bias, whether the present-biased agents are naïve or sophisticated.

Nor does every behavior that looks like problematic delay qualify as procrastination. For instance, it is widely observed that people—especially students—wait until right before a deadline to act, and this is often interpreted as procrastination. Yet this behavior can emerge quite naturally if there is little value to completing the task in advance of the deadline (see Fischer, 2001's theoretical analysis). If individuals did not describe waiting until the deadline to be inefficient, this wouldn't qualify as procrastination in our definition.

Much of the systematic evidence on the extent of procrastination comes from the laboratory (Augenblick et al., 2015) or from field experiments with students (e.g., Fedyk, 2018). There is also an older literature in education, not well-known by economists, examining procrastination in students. For instance, Solomon and Rothblum (1984) found many students self-report "procrastinating" in preparing for exams and that they also report wanting to reduce procrastination, though it is unclear how subjects defined procrastination.

Procrastination is often closely connected to naiveté (but naiveté is not necessary for procrastination—see Carroll et al., 2009). DellaVigna and Malmendier (2004, 2006) have a pair of papers that examine procrastination behavior in the context of gym attendance; we discuss the role of naiveté in these papers in the next section. DellaVigna and Malmendier (2006) show that individuals take "too long" to cancel their gym contract after their last attendance (an average of about 2 months). Calibrations suggest that a sophisticated person would cancel in a few days, while naiveté can explain the much longer observed delay. DellaVigna and Malmendier (2004) show that firms will design contracts to take advantage of this procrastination on cancellation behavior, creating contracts with automatic renewal and switching and cancellation costs.

Other research identifies behavior that is likely procrastination and shows it is connected to other behaviors that result from present-focus. For instance, Brown and

Previtero (2016) show the people who wait until the last day of health plan open enrollment to enroll ("procrastinators") take longer to sign up for 401(k) plans, contribute less to those plans, and are more likely to take the default fund allocation in the 401(k). Similarly, Reuben et al. (2015) measure how quickly individuals complete various tasks (e.g. application to university and mandatory surveys); procrastinators on those measures take longer to cash their payment check.

Deadlines are a type of commitment device that may reduce procrastination. Ariely and Wertenbroch (2002) provide influential evidence on deadlines that is often interpreted as evidence about procrastination. They assigned one section of students to fixed, evenly spaced deadlines for class assignments, while students in the other section got to choose their own deadlines at the beginning of the semester. One key fact is that when given the choice, about two-thirds of their study participants do self-impose binding deadlines (with financial penalties), suggesting some sophistication about a self-control problem. However, these self-imposed deadlines were less binding, on average than the evenly spaced deadlines. Second, performance on assignments was lower in the self-chosen deadline condition than in the evenly spaced deadlines. They show similar results in a lab-based proofreading task. The paper suggests the interpretation that students do not set self-imposed deadlines "optimally," from the perspective of maximizing class performance. However, it is possible that students in the self-chosen deadline condition could be trading off preferences for flexibility in other areas of life against performance in this class; in this view, self-chosen deadlines could lead to lower class performance but higher individual welfare.

However, it is not always the case that interim deadlines increase performance; there is a tradeoff between overcoming procrastination and maintaining flexibility. Burger et al. (2011) conduct deadline experiments for subjects completing online tasks. They found that interim deadlines lowered performance (as measured by completion rates), in contrast to Ariely and Wertenbroch's (2002) results. Similarly, Bisin and Hyndman (2018) examine an experiment in which participants have to complete tasks online. While they find robust demand for self-imposed deadlines, they also find that deadlines did not increase completion rates. Bisin and Hyndman estimate a structural model of present-bias and conclude that present-bias is widespread.

Evidence on procrastination and deadlines outside of students and lab experiments is more limited (however, see, Kaur et al., 2010, 2015; Duflo et al., 2011). Frakes and Wasserman (2017) provide intriguing evidence on procrastination in patent examiners. They find that work is "end loaded" right before deadlines and argue that non-procrastinating examiners would spread work evenly over time, while a procrastinator who wants to make their target would cluster work at the end of each quota period. They provide evidence that end loaded work is of lower quality. Moreover, it is likely that telecommuting (as opposed to working in the office) could exacerbate procrastination; indeed, they find that end-loading increases when a telecommuting program is introduced.

3.4.1 Explanations for procrastination

Procrastination is often explained by time inconsistent preferences. However, limited attention or memory can also explain excess delay, and can interact with present-bias in counter-intuitive ways (see Ericson, 2017). For example, Choi et al. (2002) examine procrastination behavior in the context of retirement savings for white-collar workers. Out of every 100 workers, 68 say that their savings rate is too low. When asked about future intentions, 24 of those 68 say they plan to increase their savings rate in the next two months. Yet data on contribution rates reveal that only 3 of those 24 actually do so (over the next four months). Similarly, at a financial education seminar, virtually all non-participating employees said they planned to join the retirement savings plan, but only 14% followed through. A combination of delay due to present-bias and then forgetting may explain this, as employees typically either make changes almost immediately after their financial education seminar or not at all.

Another explanation for procrastination is the planning fallacy. Kahneman and Tversky (1979) identified the concept of the *planning fallacy:* people typically underestimate how long it will take to complete a task. The planning fallacy could be in part due to mispredicting future present focus; the phenomenon is typically closely linked to incorrect beliefs about how much work will be required. However, evidence on the planning fallacy suggests that misprediction has an important component apart from any issues of present-focus (e.g., a military contractor mispredicting the time to delivery on a major weapons project).

Open question 4. *Why do people underestimate their own procrastination? What are the relative roles of naiveté about present-focus versus other explanations for underestimating procrastination, such as overconfidence about the effort required and limited memory?*

Evidence on forecasts of task completion (e.g. Augenblick and Rabin, 2018; Fedyk, 2018) show that people underestimate how long it will take to complete a task; estimated models of present-bias also often show substantial naiveté (see following section).

One open question is why people are naïve about their present-focus, which we discuss more extensively in the next section. However, there are at least two other explanations for underestimating procrastination that do not rely on present-focus: overestimating memory (attention) and underestimating how much work a task will be.

Individuals might not complete a task because they forget to do it for some period of time. The issue of limited memory is taken up in a pair of papers by Ericson (2011, 2017). Ericson (2011) finds experimental evidence that individuals are overconfident about the probability they will remember to complete a task in the future. Ericson (2017) models the interaction between limited memory and present-bias and shows that structural models can produce biased estimates of present-bias if they incorrectly assume complete memory.

Empirically, lengthening deadlines can lower eventual task completion rates (Shu and Gneezy, 2010; Taubinsky, 2014). Having more time to complete a task should not lower completion rates in a model of present-bias but can lower completion rates with limited memory (see Taubinsky, 2014; Ericson, 2017). This suggests that limited memory or inattention is important for explaining procrastination, yet we do not have calibrated estimates of this mechanism.

3.5 Naiveté

Empirical regularity 5. *People partially but do not fully anticipate their extent of future present-focus.*

Do individuals correctly anticipate the extent of their future present-focus? That is are they sophisticated, or naïve? A body of evidence indicates that people are at least *partially* naïve about their present-focus: they may recognize they will in the future act in a present-focused manner, but do not recognize the extent of this present-focus. Some evidence suggests that individuals are fully naïve (they think they will act like a time-consistent exponential discounter in the future).

We focus on naiveté about present-focus, which is a subset of incorrect beliefs. As a concept it is distinct from overconfidence about ability, over-optimism about future challenges, or projection bias. Nonetheless, it can be difficult in practice to distinguish among competing types of incorrect beliefs. For instance, not saving much for the future today could result from expectations that you will save more tomorrow, or that you will have a much higher income tomorrow. Similarly, persistent failure to complete a task could arise from present bias and naiveté (O'Donoghue and Rabin, 1999a, 1999b) or from continually and incorrectly believing that the cost of completing the task will be lower tomorrow than it is today. Moreover, Ericson (2017) shows that overconfidence about memory/inattention can lead to a failure to act and may be mistaken for present-bias.

Early evidence on naiveté comes from DellaVigna and Malmendier (2006), who show a pattern of naiveté in the choice of gym contracts. First, individuals too often choose a contract with a flat fee (at an effective rate of $17 per expected visit), even though the pay per visit is cheaper ($10 per visit fee). Moreover, users in the monthly contract are more likely to stay enrolled beyond one year than users committing for a year. This is surprising because monthly members pay higher fees for the option to cancel each month, and suggests they over-estimated the probability they would actually follow through on canceling.

While DellaVigna and Malmendier (2006) rely on contract choice to identify misprediction of future gym attendance, Acland and Levy (2015) directly elicit beliefs about future attendance and find that individuals over-predict their future gym attendance by 1–2 visits per week. (Moreover, participants in their study also failed to anticipate the extent to which incentives would increase their future behavior, which Acland and Levy attribute to projection bias.)

Ariely and Wertenbroch (2002)'s finding that equally spaced deadlines lead to better performance than self-chosen deadlines may be evidence of partial naiveté. However, as we suggested in Section 3.4, participants in their study may have valued the flexibility of the later, self-chosen deadlines.

Stronger evidence on incorrect beliefs in the classroom setting comes from Wong (2008), who asks students when it would be ideal to start preparing for the final and when they predict they will start preparing for the final. On average, students predicted they would start about 2.5 days later than ideal, which Wong interprets as awareness of a self-control problem. However, subsequent data on when students actually start preparing for the exam indicate that they started preparing an average of about 2 days later than predicted; Wong classifies more than half the sample as either fully or partially naïve and only a quarter as sophisticated (predictions within ± 1 day of actual). Wong's results could indicate naiveté about present-bias but could also be consistent with overconfidence about future free time or about remembering to prepare.

Augenblick and Rabin (2018) examine present-bias and sophistication/naiveté about present-bias in a real effort task. They estimate a β of about 0.8 but estimate a $\hat{\beta}$ near 1 (individual's implied perception of the β that will determine their choices in the future, see Section 2.1). They cannot reject the null hypothesis of no perceived present bias and can reject the hypothesis that individuals have an accurate perception of present bias.

Whether individuals are sophisticated or naïve about their present-focus matters for the contracts that individuals will choose in equilibrium as well as for welfare. For instance, firms will design contracts with backloaded fees if individuals are naïve about the probability they will procrastinate on taking costly action to cancel a contract (e.g. gym membership) in the future (DellaVigna and Malmendier, 2004). Heidhues and Kőszegi (2010) show that even a small amount of naiveté in credit contract choices will lead individuals to have discontinuously lower welfare than a sophisticated individual: firms design credit contracts with large penalties for deferring repayment and naïve individuals choose these contracts because they underestimate the probability they will pay these penalties.

Evidence suggests that people hold more accurate beliefs about others' procrastination than their own. For instance, Fedyk (2018) estimates a structural model of present-bias on participants completing a real-effort task. While individuals' forecast of their own behavior implies a substantial degree of naiveté, their forecasts for others were much more accurate.

Using field data on consumption, Kuchler and Pagel (2018) provide a method to classify people as sophisticated or naïve based on how an individual's level of financial resources affects the sensitivity of their consumption to paycheck receipt. Their model shows that sophisticates, but not naïfs, will act more patiently when there are more resources available. They examine credit card payments and compare self-set debt paydown plans to actual behavior. While many users fail to follow through, individuals their method identifies as sophisticates are in fact more likely to stick to their plan.

Open question 5. *Why don't people learn and anticipate their present-focused behavior? What can help people correctly anticipate their future present-focused behavior?*

There are a number of open questions about naiveté. Given that individuals repeatedly make consumption decisions, it is perhaps surprising that they do not learn (more quickly) about their miscalibrated beliefs. One hypothesis is that individuals do learn, but learn in narrow, domain-specific contexts. Therefore, they do not learn generally about the fact they make present-focused decisions. Under this hypothesis, individuals might learn that they will procrastinate on preparing for exams, but when they encounter a new decision (e.g. job search), they don't realize they will procrastinate. Yet we see naiveté even in contexts where individuals have experience (e.g. students in the study of Wong, 2008), so they may not even learn in specific domains. It is likely that wishful thinking plays some role here. People would like to believe in a rosy future, and naïve beliefs help to make that possible. This would explain why people are asymmetrically naïve about their own future behavior, and not about the behavior of others (see Fedyk, 2018).

3.6 The effect of transactions costs

Empirical regularity 6. *Small changes in transactions costs often have large effects on behavior.*

The behavioral economics literature has emphasized that small changes in transactions costs or choice architecture sometimes have anomalously large changes on behavior (for reviews see Thaler and Sunstein, 2008 or Beshears et al., 2018b, which is Chapter 3 of Volume 1 of this Handbook). Default settings (Madrian and Shea, 2001; Johnson and Goldstein, 2003; Beshears et al., 2008; Choi et al., 2009) are posed as the canonical example of such effects. For example, setting a default of non-enrollment in a 401(k) plan leads to a participation rate of approximately 40% after one year of tenure as an employee. By contrast, setting a default of enrollment (and letting employees opt out if they prefer), leads to a participation rate of approximately 90% after one year of tenure. Results like this have been reproduced in dozens of studies (for a meta-analysis see Jachimowicz et al., 2018).[36]

Other examples of highly impactful transaction cost manipulations abound. For example, offering parents of a high school senior immediate assistance and a streamlined process to complete the Free Application for Federal Student Aid, raised the likelihood that their child completed (at least) two years of college from 28% to 36% (Bettinger et al., 2012). Enabling individuals to almost effortlessly opt into a retirement savings plan at a pre-selected contribution rate and asset allocation, increased enrollment rates by 10 to 20 percentage points (Beshears et al., 2013). Enabling students to send an extra free ACT report to a college (rather than charging $6 for that marginal report), led ACT-takers to send more reports and applications relative to SAT-takers, widening the range of colleges

---

[36] Note however that defaults have complex distal effects that often dilute their impact (Abadie and Gay, 2006; Beshears et al., 2018b; Choukhmane, 2018).

they sent scores to and improving admissions to selective colleges (Pallais, 2015). Related effects have been observed in take-up of social benefits (Currie, 2004; Aizer, 2007; Bhargava and Manoli, 2015) and medical adherence (Thornton, 2008; Banerjee et al., 2010; Milkman et al., 2011, 2013).

Open question 6. *Is the large effect of small transactions costs on behavior primarily related to present focus, or is it some other channel?*

The outsized impact of small incentives, including disincentives like transactions costs, is likely due to many different mechanisms. Present bias (and other closely related present-focused mechanisms) have been used to explain why agents are particularly responsive to immediate transactions costs and immediate rewards for task completion (e.g., Carroll et al., 2009). These immediate transaction costs can be particularly impactful because they lead agents who are partially or fully naïve to postpone doing the task because they falsely believe that they are going to complete the task in the near future (e.g., Akerlof, 1991; O'Donoghue and Rabin, 1999a, 1999b). This catalyzes a long (even infinite) cycle of self-defeating procrastination. Related empirical evidence points to present bias as a key mechanism that explains why transactions costs (and defaults specifically) are so effective in influencing behavior (e.g., Brown and Previtero, 2016; Goda et al., 2018; Blumenstock et al., 2018).

However, there are other mechanisms that are also probably important. For example, status quo bias (Samuelson and Zeckhauser, 1988) is likely driven by many complementary channels (not just present-focused preferences), including confusion, anchoring effects (e.g., Bernheim et al., 2015a), endorsement effects (e.g., Benartzi, 2001; Brown et al., 2007; Beshears et al., 2008), and inattention/memory (e.g., Gabaix, 2014; Ericson, 2017).

As nudges become increasingly popular in the policy context, it will be useful to identify the rich set of mechanisms that cause these nudges to be effective. Unpacking the many complementary mechanisms and identifying their quantitative contribution will be important as we push this research program forward.

3.7 Lack of liquidity on household balance sheets

Empirical regularity 7. *Households tend to hold very low levels of liquid assets.*

Households around the world tend to hold very low levels of *liquid* assets, despite the fact that they tend to hold relatively large stocks of *illiquid* assets. These facts are compiled in Chapter 3 of Volume 1 of this Handbook (Beshears et al., 2018b, Table 1 and Appendix A), and we quickly touch on them here as well. These results are derived from the 2016 (U.S.) Survey of Consumer Finances.

The median value of net liquid assets starts at $1000 for households in the 21–30 age category and rises to $6719 for households in the 61–70 age category. (Other percentiles are presented in Chapter 3 of Volume 1.) Accordingly, even households on the brink of retirement have little liquid net worth.

On the other hand, total net worth (which includes illiquid assets, nets out corresponding collateralized liabilities, and *excludes* Social Security claims, which are involuntarily accumulated) shows robust growth over the life course. The median value of total net worth starts at \$7611 for households in the 21–30 age category and rises to \$209,227 in the 61–70 age category.

These results jointly imply that the typical U.S. household is living without a large buffer of liquid assets and doing almost all of its voluntary wealth accumulation in illiquid assets.

The financial health of U.S. households appears more strained when debt is broken out of the balance sheet. In any given month, half of households are borrowing on at least one of their credit cards (i.e., not making their full payment when they pay their card—see Zinman, 2015 and Laibson et al., 2017). Finally, in any given year 12 million U.S. households (5% of the adult population) take out a payday loan (Pew Charitable Trusts, 2012). About one million households file for personal bankruptcy each year and one in ten households has filed for bankruptcy at some point in their lives (Stavins, 2000).

As a corollary to these low levels of liquid wealth (and high levels of borrowing), households also tend to have anomalously high propensities to consume out of changes in liquid wealth, whether that change in liquidity is anticipated or unanticipated (e.g., Shea, 1995; Gross and Souleles, 2002; Stephens, 2003; Shapiro and Slemrod, 2003; Shapiro, 2005; Mastrobuoni and Weinberg, 2009; Parker et al., 2013; Broda and Parker, 2014; Ganong and Noel, 2017; Gross et al., 2016).

Aguiar and Hurst (2005) offer a countervailing view, emphasizing that the simultaneous fall in income and consumption expenditure at retirement does not coincide with a fall in caloric consumption. They argue that the systemic drop in consumption *expenditure* is *not* anomalous because households maintain a smooth consumption of calories between the pre- and post-retirement periods (by shopping more frugally and doing more home production of meals). However, Stephens and Toohey (2018) are unable to replicate this caloric-smoothing result using new data and instead find that caloric intake falls as households enter retirement (mirroring the fall in consumption expenditure).

Open question 7. *Why do households have such low levels of liquid net wealth, relatively high levels of illiquid net wealth, and high marginal propensities to consume out of liquid wealth changes?*

These stylized facts are particularly hard to explain because these empirical regularities tend to occur in the same households. For example, households that borrow on their credit cards tend to also accumulate large stocks of illiquid wealth (see Laibson et al., 2017). Accordingly, household heterogeneity can offer only a partial explanation of these regularities.

In the behavioral economics literature, the principle explanation for these balance sheet and consumption facts has been present bias (Laibson, 1997; Angeletos et al., 2001; Skiba and Tobacman, 2008; Laibson et al., 2017). Households with present bias have a hard time holding on to liquid assets, which tend to get quickly spent on consumption expenditures. Indeed, households with present bias (e.g., $\beta < 0.8$) will tend to borrow on credit cards. However, present biased households will be willing to invest in illiquid assets (including durables) with modest rates of return, because the household's *long-run* discount rate is only $\ln \delta \cong 1 - \delta$, which is typically estimated to be below the long-run real (after-tax, risk adjusted) return that households can obtain on assets like housing or (matched) 401(k) contributions. Laibson et al. (2017) use the method of simulated moments to estimate preference parameters in a lifecycle consumption model. Using data on voluntary wealth formation and credit card borrowing to identify preference parameters, they estimate $\beta = 0.51$, $\delta = 0.99$, and a coefficient of relative risk aversion of 1.3.

Models outside the behavioral literature have taken a different approach to explaining low levels of liquidity, high levels of borrowing, high levels of illiquid wealth formation and the high marginal propensity to consume out of changes in liquidity. For example, Kaplan and Violante (2014) assume that the real, after-tax return on liquid wealth is -1.48%, the real, after-tax interest rate on credit card borrowing is 6%, and the real, after-tax and risk-adjusted return on illiquid assets is 6.29%, generating a high level of credit card borrowing, little liquid wealth buffering, and aggressive investment in illiquid assets (see also Kaplan et al., 2014).

Future work will continue to explore the mechanisms that explain the balance sheet behavior and consumption dynamics of households.

3.8 Commitment

Empirical regularity 8. *People sometimes demand commitment devices.*

Many of the theories that generate present-focused preferences predict that, under the right circumstances, agents will choose commitment 'for its own sake' (see Table 1 in Section 2.7). By this we mean that agents will prefer to restrict their choice set holding all else equal, which we refer to as a pure commitment. For present-biased agents, such a restriction prevents them from making a suboptimal choice in the future (e.g., a pre-paid or shame-inducing gym trainer forces one to exercise; likewise an irreversible temporary web-or phone-blocker like Freedom keeps one on task). For agents with temptation (see Section 2.2), commitment removes temptation costs, which can be beneficial *even* if the tempting good is not chosen when it is available.

Agents sometimes do choose *pure* commitments that are not confounded by tied inducements, like financial incentives,[37] but such pure commitments are rarely observed in markets (Laibson, 2015). When trying to identify pure commitments in the field, only a handful come to mind, such as web blockers, which do not seem to be used widely, even in developed economies.[38] We suspect that personal trainers are

---

[37] For example, a 401(k) savings plan is an *impure* commitment, because it is tied to financial incentives like matching dollars and favorable tax treatment, so it is not clear whether people invest money in 401(k)'s for their commitment properties or despite them.

[38] Other exotic examples include a series of alarm clocks that jump off the night table and run around the bedroom until the groggy sleeper chases them down. Such alarm clocks do exist, but they appear to have a limited market. Likewise, the commitment website stickK has not gone viral.

also hired mostly for their commitment effects, though this is not an example of a pure commitment.

Most practical "commitments" seem to be corrupted by impurities. For example, standard amortization mortgages (with fixed payments that end when the principal is repaid) are sometimes advocated in the financial advice literature as a forcing mechanism that helps people with self-control problems systematically shed their housing debt. But mortgages are also a tax-advantaged financing vehicle for home buying. So it's not clear why people take them up: to solve a self-control problem or, simply, to get tax advantaged financing. Perhaps the lack of popularity of interest-only mortgages provides a hint that amortization mortgages deliver some special benefits, but such an inference is somewhat speculative.

Some other *apparent* commitments may simply arise from naiveté. For example, Wertenbroch (1998) documents that consumers prefer to buy vice goods in small packages and virtue goods in large (volume discount) packages, which is reflected in firms' pricing decisions. These patterns could arise because of commitment *or* because consumers *naively* anticipate that they won't want to eat more than a small serving of ice cream and accordingly buy ice cream in packages that forego volume discounts. If you think you are only going to eat ice cream today (because you believe you will prefer to eat healthfully tomorrow), then you should buy only a small container of ice cream. Hence, small packaging could be a sign of commitment or it could be a sign of naiveté.

The commitment evidence from experiments is less muddy. In lab studies and field experiments researchers have been able to systematically observe pure commitment behavior (e.g., see Ariely and Wertenbroch, 2002; Ashraf et al., 2006; Bryan et al., 2010; Houser et al., 2018; Giné et al., 2010; Kaur et al., 2010, 2015; Royer et al., 2015; Bisin and Hyndman, 2018; Augenblick et al., 2015; Alsan et al., 2017; Casaburi and Macchiavello, 2018; Schilbach, 2017; Beshears et al., 2018c). For example, Schilbach (2017), implements a field study in which the experimental participants are rickshaw drivers in India, a population with a high level of alcohol consumption. Schilbach finds economically (and statistically) significant demand for a pure commitment device. About a third of study subjects choose to forgo about 10% of their daily incomes for a week to receive monetary payments conditional on a zero blood alcohol test that would otherwise be received unconditionally.

Open question 8. *Why is pure commitment so rare in markets and why is willingness to pay for commitment usually so low (even in lab experiments designed to measure the taste for commitment)?*

As noted above, pure commitment is rarely observed in organic ('real-world') markets that have not been designed by behavioral economists (e.g., Bernheim et al., 2016). While pure commitment is routinely observed in lab and field experiments (see the list above), willingness to pay for such commitment is typically zero (e.g., Augenblick et al., 2015). In other words, the typical experimental participant is not willing to *pay* for the privilege of tying their hands (by committing to a particular outcome that is strictly dominated by what they could have achieved without commitment). Only a handful of studies reveal a substantial willingness to pay for commitment: e.g., Casaburi and Macchiavello (2018), and Beshears et al. (2018c), report that an overwhelming majority of participants are willing to pay for commitment, and Schilbach (2017) finds that a third of subjects are willing to pay 10% of their daily income for commitment.

There are several hypotheses for the overall pattern of weak demand for commitment (see Laibson, 2015, 2018). First, agents may be fully or partially naïve. Second, commitment may be costly to generate (e.g., personal trainers). Third, extrinsic uncertainty may make commitment suboptimal (if the commitment technology can't condition on all states of nature). Fourth, many types of commitment may already be embedded in other institutions that serve multiple purposes. For example, the 401(k) system provides both a commitment technology—penalties for early withdrawal—and a saving subsidy, crowding out incipient demand for a pure commitment technology (e.g., a savings account that is illiquid and offers no saving subsidy). Many social institutions may have this hybrid property of providing commitment and other services. For example, many large employers provide multiple forcing mechanisms that counteract workers' self-control problems (e.g., deadlines, progress reports, retirement savings programs, etc.—see Laibson, 2018). Finally, self control may be achieved through internal punishments instead of external commitment technologies (see Bernheim et al., 2015b).

3.9 Paternalistic policy and welfare

Empirical regularity 9. *Many public policies seem paternalistic and aimed at addressing present-focused behavior.*

Many government policies seem rooted in a paternalistic desire to at least partially offset present-focused behavior. The most explicit is provision for retirement: in the U.S., social security benefits offer protection to myopic or present-focused individuals who do not save for retirement. Indeed, as far back as in Feldstein (1985), setting the optimal level of social security benefits was discussed as a tradeoff of benefits for myopic individuals against costs from distorting private saving and other economic behavior. Illiquid defined contribution retirement savings accounts also help provide a commitment device for savers. Laibson et al. (1998) show that this commitment can be appealing for present-biased individuals. (Note that U.S. accounts are more liquid than in some other developed countries; see Beshears et al. (2015) for a discussion.) Several recent papers have acquired that illiquid accounts and compulsory savings are an optimal response if agents have present-biased preferences (e.g., Amador et al., 2006; Moser and Olea de Souza e Silva, 2017; Beshears et al., 2018a).

Compulsory education laws are also naturally—and often explicitly—explained as a counter to present-focused decisions of children (see Lavecchia et al., 2014). Restrictions on payday borrowing as well as caps on interest rates (usury laws) can be motivated in part by an intent to counter present-focused behavior (see e.g. Skiba,

2012 on what restrictions on payday lending can be rationalized by present-focused behavior and what cannot).

Paternalism can interact with present-focused behavior to lead to somewhat surprising predictions: for instance, Lockwood (2016) shows that present-bias can lead to optimal tax policy to have negative marginal tax rates at low incomes, similar to the design of the Earned Income Tax Credit in the U.S.

The existence of paternalistic policy plus naiveté about present-focus may at first seem a puzzle, but recall that individuals are better at predicting the present-focus of others than themselves, and these laws can be interpreted as paternalistic control of others, rather than a preference for commitment (Fedyk, 2018; also see Albrecht et al., 2011). Moreover, Laibson (2018) shows that naïve individuals can use model-free forecasts to choose contexts (e.g. firms/employers) that have a reputation for generating satisfaction. In this case, individuals don't want paternalism, but do want institutions that produce benefits for the stakeholders (whether or not the paternalism is made explicit).

Open question 9. *What welfare criterion should we use to evaluate intertemporal tradeoffs?*

A welfare criterion is needed in order to evaluate policy. While economists often rely on revealed preference, dynamically inconsistent preferences pose new challenges and how to evaluate welfare is disputed. Suppose an individual plans to contribute to a retirement savings plan next month (a patient choice), but when next month arrives changes her plans and spends the money (an impatient choice). Which choice makes the individual better off? Revealed preference has no obvious answer.

Normative analysis for intertemporal choice has been discussed through the lens of present bias (Laibson, 1997). A common choice is to simply evaluate welfare from the long-run perspective (setting $\beta = 1$), on the grounds that these are the preferences that are persistent; an alternative is the multi-self Pareto-criterion, which treats each self as a different person (e.g., Laibson et al., 1998).

There is a fundamental philosophical debate about the extent to which observed choices should be linked to normative preferences. Bernheim and Rangel (2009) and Bernheim (2016) argue that normative evaluation must be linked to choice and propose a welfare criterion that never overrules a choice; as a result, it is sometimes undiscerning (i.e., cannot rank two outcomes). In contrast, Beshears et al. (2008) argue that *normative preferences* (that represent an individual's actual interests and that should be used for analysis) can diverge from revealed preferences (that rationalize an action), and propose a variety of ways of identifying normative preferences. (See also Sugden, 2004.) See the Handbook chapter in Volume 1 on Behavioral Public Economics (Bernheim and Taubinsky, 2018) for more discussion of these issues.

The existence of paternalistic policies may reflect some important information about the appropriate welfare criteria: voters seem to demand and policy-makers seem to create paternalistic policies. It is an open question how informative the existence of paternalistic policies should be for informing welfare judgments. Policy can be mistaken, or policy may be insightful, or, most likely a bit of both. We might also be able to make inferences (in part) from the retirement savings systems and other human resource norms that have been developed by non-profit institutions that are concerned about the well-being of their employees (beyond the universal issues of recruitment and retention).

There has been a long tradition of not using revealed preference estimates of discount rates for normative analysis. Sen (1957) argues that the social discount rate should differ from the individual discount rate—"for, among other things, while the individuals die the nation does not." Schelling (1995) notes the importance of conceptually distinguishing pure time preference for one's own consumption from preferences for redistribution across generations, while Gollier (2013) highlights that the discount rate that should be used for an investment project depends on whether the project is financed by reducing current consumption or reallocating productive capital. Relatedly, Goulder and Williams (2012) similarly distinguish between a social-welfare discount rate and finance discount rate based on the marginal product of capital.

This normative discount rate has been particularly important for evaluating climate change and potential policy responses. Stern (2007, 2008) highlights how the social and private discount rates are distinct concepts; market interest rates reflect the private decisions of individuals but are not necessarily informative of the social discount rate, which also reflects ethical considerations.[39]

3.10 Preference for improving sequences

Empirical regularity 10. *Individuals typically display both impatience and preferences for improvement over time.*

Typically, individuals have (weakly) positive time preference: all else equal, they would rather have something earlier rather than later. However, there is one important exception: individuals seem to prefer sequences of outcomes that improve over time. For instance, Barsky et al. (1997) show that participants prefer their real consumption path either to be flat or to rise over time (the modal subject prefers to it be flat, but the mean is a rising profile); when the real interest rate is zero, impatience and standard assumptions of separable discounted utility would predict a declining consumption profile. Similarly, Loewenstein and Sicherman (1991) show that participants prefer an increasing wage profile,[40] and Chapman (2000) shows that subjects typically prefer improving sequences of health outcomes (e.g. headaches that get better over time rather than worse).

---

[39] However, even if the social discount rate is lower than the market interest rate, a policy maker might still wish to use the market interest rate as a return hurdle. Why invest in a public project with social return r when there exists a private project that can be used to generate a social return $r' > r$ that the government could pursue instead (Cropper and Laibson, 1998)?

[40] Read and Powell (2002) elicit verbal reasons for subjects' choices over sequences over money, and find that subjects typically match income to desired consumption.

Open question 10. *How do we integrate models of discounting with the other factors leading to a preference for improving sequences? When does a preference for an improving sequence become important relative to discounting?*

Loewenstein and Prelec (1993) identified three related motivations for preferring an improving sequence: anticipatory utility, reference points, and a recency effect in evaluating experiences. Anticipatory utility can lead to preferences for improving sequences, if individuals prefer delaying pleasurable experiences so that they can savor them (Loewenstein, 1987; see also Caplin and Leahy, 2001); for instance, people prefer to delay receiving a kiss from a movie star by a few days, while also preferring to get through a painful shock immediately. Loss aversion with respect to reference points based on past consumption—adaptive reference points[41]—can also lead to a preference for increasing consumption, as can habit-based models (Ryder and Heal, 1973; Abel, 1990). Finally, because experiences may be evaluated with a "peak-end" rule (Kahneman et al., 1993), individuals may prefer a better ending over a better beginning. It would be useful to quantitatively incorporate these motivations into a model of intertemporal choice that also involves discounting.

Moreover, Frederick and Loewenstein (2008) show that elicitation method matters for preferences over sequences: when choosing among sequences that differ in trend, people prefer increasing sequences; with other elicitation methods (allocation or pricing tasks), the preference for improving sequences disappears. If different motivations become salient with different tasks, which tasks best reflect economically relevant decisions?

4 Puzzles without associated empirical regularities
4.1 How soon is now?

Open question 11. *How soon is "now"? How fast does value decline over time?*

What is the duration of the "present" for present-focused models? Using a present-biased (i.e., quasi-hyperbolic) discounting model requires distinguishing between "now" and later. Of course, this discretization of time into the present versus the future is a simplification, but even a generalized hyperbolic discounting model requires a calibration of how fast value declines as you move forward.

Evidence on preferences over consumption suggests an extremely quick drop off in value over time, on the order of minutes. McClure et al. (2007) examined choices over juice and water consumption for thirsty subjects and found strong preference for drinking "now" versus more in 5 minutes, but substantially more patient choices between 20 and 25 minutes in the future.

Augenblick et al. (2015) examine choices over when to exert effort and find present-bias for effort "now" (to be started in a few minutes) versus weeks later.

---

[41] See DellaVigna et al. (2017) and Thakral and Tô (2017) on adaptive reference points.

Recently, Augenblick (2018) traces out discounting over effort tasks at short horizons (hours and days) and finds a discount factor of 0.94 for a delay of a few hours, 0.91 for one day, and 0.87 for one week. However, the interpretation of these results depends on the extent to which individuals can substitute effort across time; while today's plans may be fixed, individuals may respond to increased requirements for effort in experiments in the future by reducing effort in other areas of their life.

A different picture emerges for discounting of monetary payments, which could be a result of a distinction between preferences over consumption versus financial flows. Balakrishnan et al. (2017) measure MEL choices using the convex time budget, comparing immediate payments, end of day payments, and future payments (using electronic payments for Kenyan subjects). They find little present-bias for end of day payments (about 4 hours delay) but do find present bias for immediate payments (β around 0.9).[42] In contrast, structural models with annual periods (e.g. Angeletos et al., 2001) implicitly treat consumption anytime "this year" as immediate. The connection between the assumptions of these structural models and the experimental literature remains to be explored.

If there is limited present-bias beyond horizons of a few hours, the impact of present-bias on many decisions seems limited. For instance, purchasing goods online, even with next-day delivery, wouldn't provide an immediate reward. Many expensive, durable goods (cars, computers) are only received at hours or days delay, and even clothing is not usually worn immediately after being purchased. However, there may be some transactional utility that makes the purchase of certain goods pleasurable in itself—i.e., buying a sports car or a special piece of clothing.

4.2 The role of temptation

Open question 12. *What types of decisions involve temptation? How quantitatively important is temptation (as opposed to present-bias)?*

Intuition suggests that there is a cost to resisting temptation that is not captured in discounted utility models (whether they be time-consistent or present-biased), since in these discounted utility models the *outcome* (and not the cognitive process that gets the household to that end-point) solely determines an individual's welfare. Suppose you choose fruit as an afternoon snack; in a discounted utility model, your welfare is the same regardless of whether fruit was the only option, or you chose fruit over an unhealthy (but delicious) alternative. An alternative class of models allows for the possibility that resisting an unchosen alternative is costly (e.g. Gul and Pesendorfer, 2001; Fudenberg and Levine, 2006).

Toussaert (2018) provides evidence on the existence of costly temptation. Participants in her experiment chose between either reading a story (the potentially

---

[42] Similarly, Andreoni and Sprenger (2012a) find no present-bias for payments made via check at the end of the day. However, Augenblick et al. (2015) made immediate monetary payments in cash and found β near 1 for money.

"tempting" alternative) or completing a task for pay. About a third of her subjects preferred to limit their options for future work so that they could not read the story. This could be explained by either a desire to remove a tempting alternative that is costly to resist, or as a commitment device to change their future behavior. However, Toussaert shows that the desire to limit their options wasn't driven by a desire to change their future behavior, since most participants predicted that they would do the task even if they had a choice. Moreover, consistent with a cost of resisting temptation, task performance was lower when participants were assigned to have the option to stop the task and read the story (even though they kept doing the task).

Other research also provides suggestive evidence that individuals want to limit their option set not merely to change their outcome but to reduce their costs of exercising self-control. Sadoff et al. (2015) examine the desire for commitment to healthy v. unhealthy foods in a food delivery service, and find that individuals who demand commitment are more likely to be dynamically consistent in their prior behavior. Similarly, examining gym attendance, Royer et al. (2015) write, "we observe demand for commitment by those who appear on the surface not to need it." This is hard to explain through the lens of present-biased discounted utility models but is naturally explained by models of costly temptation.

It is an open question how important temptation costs are for policy. Toussaert (2018) provides evidence of the existence of temptation, but the design had to be carefully constructed to rule out the alternative story in which participants demand commitment because they fear they might give in and choose the tempting alternative. Thus, her context has a tempting task where, perhaps unusually, people almost always resist temptation. Toussaert's design also likely estimates a lower bound on the role of temptation, since it is a joint test for both temptation preference *and* sophistication about those preferences: subjects have to predict that they will face costs of self-control. However, the literature examining time discounting and present-bias has typically found substantial naiveté (see Section 3.5).

It is difficult to distinguish costly temptation from other models such as present-bias (and note, the existence of costly temptation doesn't rule out an important role for present-bias). Indeed, under certain conditions, Krusell et al. (2010) show for strong enough costs of temptation (such that you always give in), behavior will be equivalent to that of present bias.[43] A smoking gun indicator for costly temptation is a willingness-to-pay to remove tempting things from your choice set that you wouldn't choose anyway. But it is difficult to distinguish that motivation from willingness-to-pay for commitment if there is a small likelihood that you succumb to temptation. Future work may explore biometric data and subjective wellbeing measures to help measure pure temptation effects.

Large temptation costs could impact the evaluation of many policies, since in these models even options that are rarely if ever chosen could have substantial welfare impacts. Hence, smoking bans might increase the welfare of former smokers who

---

[43] Krusell et al. (2010) show this equivalence for consumption choice under constant-relative-risk aversion preferences. It is unclear how general this result can be made.

have quit, but who no longer have to resist the temptation of smoking. The availability of social media on smart phones might reduce welfare, even when people aren't using their cell phones. Finally, deadlines might be valuable because they lower the self-control costs of working on a project, even if they don't ultimately change when the project is completed.

4.3 Other mechanisms and complementary psychological conceptions

Open question 13. *How important are a variety of mechanisms for intertemporal choice, including probability weighting, trust, and heuristics, both in the lab and in the field? What role do alternative psychological conceptions play in intertemporal choice?*

Discounted utility (as well as other models of present-focus) is fundamentally a theory of time preference. Yet intertemporal choices also reflect other factors, such as risk, heuristics, or even framing that are distinct from pure time preference. We do not yet have a clear picture of how quantitatively important these other factors are.

4.3.1 Risk

An alternative motivation for discounting the receipt of future rewards is that the reward may disappear—e.g. the payment may not be made, or the individual may die, etc.[44] A common concern in interpreting MEL tasks is whether subjects trust that payments will be delivered, and experimenters attempt to maintain high reliability in when payments are received. Risk that a future reward might disappear can lead to discounting apart from pure time preference, as discussed in Section 2.4.

Other work moves beyond expected utility models. Halevy (2008) argues that the present is different from the future in that the future is uncertain; in non-expected utility models, this can lead to diminishing impatience (see also Saito, 2011). Along these lines, Epper et al. (2011) show experimental evidence that individuals who are prone to more probability distortions also discount money more hyperbolically, and show that, since future events are uncertain, probability distortions can lead to hyperbolic discounting.

Other work shows interactions between risk and time that are not predicted by expected utility. For instance, Anderson and Stafford (2009) find that the presence of risk makes individuals less patient (adjusting for the level of risk); see also Ahlbrecht and Weber (1997). Andreoni and Sprenger (2012b) show that participants seem to display a preference for certainty, though Cheung (2015) shows that those results are at least partially driven by a motive for diversifying across dates and thereby hedging payment risk (because the risks are independent); see also Miao and Zhong (2015) and a reply by Andreoni and Sprenger (2015).

---

[44] McGuire and Kable (2013) argue that behavior in the original marshmallow task is driven by trust and changing beliefs about how long it would be necessary to wait for the larger reward.

4.3.2 Heuristics

It may be cognitively difficult to discount. For instance, evidence on exponential growth bias (Stango and Zinman, 2009) indicates that people get exponentiation wrong and tend to linearize exponential functions; this poses a challenge for discounted utility models. Given cognitive difficulties, individuals may rely on heuristics. Various models of intertemporal choice heuristics have been proposed in which choice is a function of proportional and absolute differences on time and reward dimension, as well as other factors (Read et al., 2013; Ericson et al., 2015). Ericson et al. (2015) conduct a cross-validated intertemporal choice model comparison showing that heuristic models predict better out of sample than discounted utility models, though Wulff and van den Bos (2017) show that some of their results depend on the model of noise and individual heterogeneity.

Heuristic models of intertemporal choice seem promising but are currently limited in their applicability. It remains an open question whether heuristic models generalize beyond lab-based MEL choices. Can economists use them to explain any other behaviors? Moreover, it may be fruitful to develop a model that nests both heuristics and discounted utility, allowing researchers to estimate a parameter capturing the extent of deviation from expected utility.

4.3.3 Other theories

Alongside the economics literature is a psychological literature examining intertemporal choice, and it may be fruitful to examine the relationship between the psychological and economic models.[45] For instance, personality psychology characterizes individuals not via their discount factor, but via concepts such as conscientiousness and grit.[46] Conscientiousness is one of the "big five" personality measures, and may include some aspects of self-control (Roberts et al., 2005). Grit, defined as perseverance and passion for long-term goals, has been argued to be distinct from self-control (Duckworth and Gross, 2014) and associated with measures of life success (Duckworth et al., 2007). How does grit translate into an economic model? Can grit be captured by a utility function that places less weight on the cost of effort? Or is grit an increased ability to forecast and make salient future benefits of present costly actions?

Other work examines factors that affect the construction of intertemporal choice. Query theory (Weber et al., 2007; Appelt et al., 2011) can be used to understand the process of making an intertemporal choice. Weber et al. (2007) show that manipulating the order in which individuals think of different reasons for their choice can lead to more or less impulsivity. Another line of work examines the role of emotion in intertemporal choice, showing that sadness increases impatience (Lerner et al., 2013) and that gratitude decreases impatience (DeSteno et al., 2014).

---

[45] For a review of related psychological research on behavior change, see Duckworth et al. (2018).

[46] See also discussion of the connection between economics and personality psychology in Borghans et al. (2008), and Becker et al. (2012).

4.4 Stability and domain generality

Open question 14. *How stable are time preferences? How general are they across domains?*

In discounted utility models, time preference applies to utility, and so the same discount factor applies to all domains of choice. Yet it is an open question whether different types of consumption are discounted in similar ways.

Cohen et al. (2016) review how predictive money-earlier-or-later (MEL) studies are for other domains. Many studies show that impatience in MEL tasks is weakly correlated with other behaviors. For instance, Meier and Sprenger (2011) find that MEL discounting is correlated with individuals' credit scores, and a series of papers shows that children's MEL choices predict future behavior (Bettinger and Slonim, 2007; Castillo et al., 2011; Sutter et al., 2013; Golsteyn et al., 2013).[47] Aggregating field behaviors into single indices increases the correlation with MEL behavior (Chabris et al., 2008). However, as discussed previously, preferences over the timing of money receipt can (and should in an optimizing model) diverge from preferences over other rewards, since receipt of money is not the same as consumption.

There is limited work comparing consumption-based measures of time preference to field behavior. A classic non-monetary task is the marshmallow test (Mischel and Ebbesen, 1970; Mischel et al., 1989), which is correlated with personality scales that measure self-regulatory capacity; it has some predictive power for early-life outcomes (Shoda et al., 1990; Watts et al., 2018) and no predictive power for mid-life outcomes (Benjamin et al., 2018). Burks et al. (2012) develop an analogue of the marshmallow task, in which individuals trade off waiting longer for monetary compensation. They conclude that while this measure is correlated with smoking, it "does not predict outcomes very well", and that a quasi-hyperbolic model measured from MEL choices does a better job.

It would be interesting to examine how time preferences over different domains of consumption are correlated, but evidence is limited here. A number of studies examine money and another domain (e.g. health and money in Chapman, 1996 or effort and money in Augenblick et al., 2015). Other studies examine field behaviors that could be a function of time preferences but also other factors (e.g. smoking, obesity; see Chabris et al., 2008, Falk et al., 2015, 2016). The best evidence on discounting of different types of goods comes from developing countries. Ubfal (2016) estimates good specific discount rates (e.g. for sugar, rice, meat) and rejects the hypothesis that discount rates are the same across goods.

Correlations between measured time preference (whatever the method) and field behaviors have multiple interpretations, as behaviors in both the lab and field are functions not only of time preference, but also cognitive ability, knowledge, beliefs,

---

[47] Another type of correlation is between measures of restlessness, aggression, or impulsivity in children and their future outcomes (Cadena and Keys, 2012; Moffitt et al., 2011); it is unclear how to interpret these measures in a model of discounting utility.

and preferences. For instance, more patient MEL behavior is correlated with measures of cognitive ability (Burks et al., 2009; Dohmen et al., 2010, and Benjamin et al., 2013). Thus, unconditional correlations between MEL behavior and other behaviors include some effect of cognitive ability. Why cognitive ability and MEL behavior are correlated is another puzzle. One explanation is that more patience leads to more investment in human capital. An alternative explanation is that higher cognitive ability makes it more likely that individuals treat MEL decisions "rationally" as a financing decision rather than a consumption decision; their choices thus reveal their market interest rate rather than a discount rate for utils.

Finally, the role of noise in eliciting or constructing preference may be important. Test-retest correlations of discount rates measured from MEL behavior are similar to other personality measures: 0.6 to 0.8 in Kirby (2009), and 0.5 in Meier and Sprenger (2015). Yet it is also rare that a discounting model strongly predicts an individual's choices; the form of noise used to estimate discounting parameters can be quite important. For instance, it may matter whether noise is additive (so that as rewards are scaled up, an individual is less likely to make a "mistake") or multiplicative (so that mistakes are equally likely for high stakes choices), or some hybrid case.

4.5 Malleability and self-management

Open question 15. *How malleable is time preference? How effective are self-management techniques?*

Commitment is one self-management strategy. Yet there are other ways individuals might alter their intertemporal choices.

Early childhood interventions have been shown to have large impacts on later life outcomes; much of this effect comes from non-cognitive skills, potentially including self-regulation and/or time preference (Heckman et al., 2006). However, we are unaware of direct evidence showing the effect of early childhood interventions on conventional measures of time preference (MEL or real consumption choices). Heckman et al. (2013) show that an early childhood intervention improved academic motivation (e.g. "showing initiative") and externalizing behaviors (e.g. disruption of class, aggressive behaviors) that seem plausibly related to time preference or self-control.

One hypothesis is that cognitive load can affect impatience, a prediction that can be produced by cost-of-self-control models. The evidence here is mixed. Deck and Jahedi (2015) provide experimental evidence that increasing cognitive load leads to more impatience over money, but not over consumption goods (see also Shiv and Fedorikhin, 1999; Hinson et al., 2003).[48] Closely connected is the hypothesis that scarcity leads to myopic or impatient behavior, supported by experimental studies

---

[48] Exogenously increasing time for deliberation has been shown to lead to more patient decisions (Dai and Fishbach, 2013; Imas et al., 2017).

(Shah et al., 2012; see also Haushofer and Fehr, 2014). Carvalho et al. (2016) examine choices of low-income individuals before versus after payday (generating a short-lived change in financial pressure). They show that before payday, choices are more impatient over money, but are *not* more impatient over real effort tasks; this is naturally explained via liquidity constraints, rather than changing time preferences.

Other work has shown that a "growth mindset" (a belief that intelligence is malleable rather than fixed) predicts greater academic performance (Dweck, 1986; Blackwell et al., 2007). Meta-analyses have found small effects of mindset interventions (Sisk et al., 2018) with larger effects for low-socio-economic status students. A large-scale replication of a growth-mindset intervention found significant, though small effects (Yeager et al., 2018). While the growth mindset is likely best captured as a change in beliefs about self-efficacy and the connection between effort and reward, it might also impact decisions about self-control. (See also our discussion of "grit" in Section 4.3.3.)

4.6 Retirement saving adequacy

Open question 16. *Are households saving optimally for retirement?*

Since the work of Hamermesh (1984) and Mariger (1987) there has been an active literature studying consumption dynamics around retirement and the closely related question of the adequacy of household retirement savings.[49] There are strong advocates of two positions: that households save too little and that households save optimally. There is also a small set of papers that argue that many households are tightwads and accordingly save too much (e.g., Rick et al., 2007).

Many studies have shown that, on average, consumption expenditure falls around retirement (e.g., Bernheim et al., 2001; Angeletos et al., 2001; Haider and Stephens, 2007; Olafsson and Pagel, 2018). Many rational mechanisms might explain this drop, including a decline in work-related expenditures, a shift toward home production (i.e., leisure-consumption substitution), and a greater propensity to shop for low-cost consumption goods (e.g., more time for coupon clipping or traveling a greater distance to purchase goods on sale).

Bernheim et al. (2001) show that the decline in consumption expenditure at retirement is not associated with the decline in work-related expenditures. Relatedly, Ganong and Noel (2017) show that work-related expenditures do not account for a substantial change in expenditure when a member of a household separates from an employer.

A hypothesized shift toward home production at retirement, which would smooth *total* market and non-market consumption even as market-based consumption *expenditure* fell, was first supported by the finding that *caloric* consumption did not drop at retirement (Aguiar and Hurst, 2005). However, subsequent work has challenged

---

[49] For a review of the literature on consumption and savings, see Attanasio and Weber (2010).

that finding with new data (Stephens and Toohey, 2018). It now appears that caloric consumption does fall on average at retirement, though it is still not clear how to interpret that finding. It is possible that retirees expend less energy than employed people (holding age fixed). It would be useful to longitudinally follow the caloric intake of a person who is not in the labor force and passes from a period in which their spouse is employed to a period in which their spouse is retired. Of course, even this empirical strategy presents confounds if the retirement of one's spouse changes one's own level of physical activity.

There is evidence for the hypothesized mechanism that retirees purchase less expensive goods in retirement (holding quality fixed): e.g., Aguiar and Hurst (2007), Hurd and Rohwedder (2013) and Agarwal et al. (2015). But it is not clear whether this behavior reflects a rational plan for lifecycle behavior (i.e., another example of rational substitution between leisure and consumption expenditure) or the consequence of financial pressure/distress that leads retirees to search for bargains.

There is also a literature that studies wealth accumulation. For example, Scholz et al. (2006) use a structural model to analyze the optimality of lifecycle wealth formation and report that the vast majority of households are saving optimally. Here too there are challenges of interpretation. Key parameters make a large difference in these models (Skinner, 2007). For example, if households experience large incremental costs when they have children, then it is optimal for expenditure to fall sharply when children leave the home, and by extension for balance sheet wealth for households on the brink of retirement (who are largely empty nesters) to be low. For evidence that consumption expenditure changes relatively little when children start to live independently, see Dushi et al. (2015).

In surveys, households overwhelmingly report that they are saving less than they think they should (e.g., Bernheim, 1991, 1995; Farkas and Johnson, 1997; Choi et al., 2002), though it is hard to interpret this attitudinal measure. Such perceived undersaving is consistent with models of present-bias, which have been used to explain wealth accumulation, credit card borrowing, and consumption-income comovement, including the drop in consumption expenditure at retirement (Angeletos et al., 2001; Laibson et al., 2003, 2017).

The extreme sensitivity between savings behavior and institutional nudges (e.g., auto-enrollment) suggests that savings behavior is not consistent with a rational actor model (e.g., Madrian and Shea, 2001). But this does not necessarily imply that households are undersaving on average. It is possible that paternalistic policies (like Social Security and other pensions) are structured so that on average households accumulate wealth optimally, even though each individual household is not necessarily at its own private optimum (Fadlon and Laibson, 2017).

5 Conclusion

A set of key stylized facts have been documented in the literature on intertemporal choice. These facts are largely at odds with the once-dominant exponential discounted utility model. A variety of models with the feature of present-focus have been developed to describe how humans make intertemporal choices. While in many cases these models make similar predictions, they have important distinctions that can affect the advice we give individuals, the policies we develop, and the welfare judgments we make.

As a result, despite a robust literature, there is a need for new empirical evidence to address the important open questions that we identify and to distinguish among various present-focused models. There is thus room for much new work in the field of intertemporal choice, which may be furthered by new experimental paradigms. Much of the laboratory research we review relies on monetary tradeoffs, but the connection between these money choices and experienced utility is itself unclear and a subject of ongoing research. Real effort laboratory tasks are a promising methodology that poses considerable advantages over experiments based on time-linked monetary payoffs (e.g. Augenblick et al., 2015; Augenblick and Rabin, 2018; Fedyk, 2018), but these methods are also imperfect. Other sources of data, such as household balance sheet data (Laibson et al., 2017), spending transactions (e.g. Ganong and Noel, 2017; Kuchler and Pagel, 2018) or caloric intake (Aguiar and Hurst, 2005; Stephens and Toohey, 2018) will complement the methods that have been deployed in the historical literature. Ultimately, there probably isn't a right answer to our methodological quest. Progress will likely come from many different methods that jointly paint a more complete and compelling picture of our intertemporal preferences.

References

Abadie, A., Gay, S., 2006. The impact of presumed consent legislation on cadaveric organ donation: a cross-country study. Journal of Health Economics 25 (4), 599–620.

Abdellaoui, M., Attema, A.E., Bleichrodt, H., 2010. Intertemporal tradeoffs for gains and losses: an experimental measurement of discounted utility. The Economic Journal 120 (545), 845–866.

Abdellaoui, M., Bleichrodt, H., l'Haridon, O., Paraschiv, C., 2013. Is there one unifying concept of utility? An experimental comparison of utility under risk and utility over time. Management Science 59 (9), 2153–2169.

Abel, A.B., 1990. Asset prices under habit formation and catching up with the Joneses. The American Economic Review 80 (2), 38–42.

Acland, D., Levy, M.R., 2015. Naiveté, projection bias, and habit formation in gym attendance. Management Science 61 (1), 146–160.

Agarwal, S., Pan, J., Qian, W., 2015. The composition effect of consumption around retirement: evidence from Singapore. The American Economic Review 105 (5), 426–431.

Aguiar, M., Hurst, E., 2005. Consumption versus expenditure. Journal of Political Economy 113 (5), 919–948.

Aguiar, M., Hurst, E., 2007. Life-cycle prices and production. The American Economic Review 97 (5), 1533–1559.

Ahlbrecht, M., Weber, M., 1997. An empirical study on intertemporal decision making under risk. Management Science 43 (6), 813–826.

Ahn, D.S., Iijima, R., Sarver, T., 2017. Naiveté About Temptation and Self-Control: Foundations for Naive Quasi-Hyperbolic Discounting. Cowles Foundation Discussion Papers 2099.

Ainslie, G., 1975. Specious reward: a behavioral theory of impulsiveness and impulse control. Psychological Bulletin 82 (4), 463–496.

Aizer, A., 2007. Public health insurance, program take-up, and child health. Review of Economics and Statistics 89 (3), 400–415.

Akerlof, G.A., 1991. Procrastination and obedience. The American Economic Review 81 (2), 1–19.

Albrecht, K., Volz, K.G., Sutter, M., Laibson, D.I., von Cramon, D.Y., 2011. What is for me is not for you: brain correlates of intertemporal choice for self and other. Social Cognitive and Affective Neuroscience 6 (2), 218–225.

Allcott, H., Greenstone, M., 2012. Is there an energy efficiency gap? The Journal of Economic Perspectives 26 (1), 3–28.

Allcott, H., Wozny, N., 2014. Gasoline prices, fuel economy, and the energy paradox. Review of Economics and Statistics 96 (5), 779–795.

Alsan, M., Beshears, J., Armstrong, W., Choi, J.J., Madrian, B.C., Nguyen, M.L.T., et al., 2017. A commitment contract to achieve virologic suppression in poorly adherent patients with HIV/AIDS. AIDS 31 (12), 1765–1769.

Amador, M., Werning, I., Angeletos, G.M., 2006. Commitment vs. flexibility. Econometrica 74 (2), 365–396.

Andersen, S., Harrison, G.W., Lau, M.I., Rutström, E.E., 2008. Eliciting risk and time preferences. Econometrica 76 (3), 583–618.

Anderson, L.R., Stafford, S.L., 2009. Individual decision-making experiments with risk and intertemporal choice. Journal of Risk and Uncertainty 38 (1), 51–72.

Andreoni, J., Aydin, D., Barton, B., Bernheim, B.D., Naecker, J., 2016a. When Fair Isn't Fair: Understanding Choice Reversals Involving Social Preferences. National Bureau of Economic Research Working Paper No. 25257.

Andreoni, J., Gravert, C., Kuhn, M.A., Saccardo, S., Yang, Y., 2018. Arbitrage or Narrow Bracketing? On Using Money to Measure Intertemporal Preferences. National Bureau of Economic Research Working Paper No. 25232.

Andreoni, J., Kuhn, M.A., Sprenger, C., 2015. Measuring time preferences: a comparison of experimental methods. Journal of Economic Behavior & Organization 116, 451–464.

Andreoni, J., Sprenger, C., 2012a. Estimating time preferences from convex budgets. The American Economic Review 102 (7), 3333–3356.

Andreoni, J., Sprenger, C., 2012b. Risk preferences are not time preferences. The American Economic Review 102 (7), 3357–3376.

Andreoni, J., Sprenger, C., 2015. Risk preferences are not time preferences: reply. The American Economic Review 105 (7), 2287–2293.

Angeletos, G., Laibson, D., Repetto, A., Tobacman, J., Weinberg, S., 2001. The hyperbolic consumption model: calibration, simulation, and empirical evaluation. The Journal of Economic Perspectives 15 (3), 47–68.

Appelt, K.C., Hardisty, D.J., Weber, E.U., 2011. Asymmetric discounting of gains and losses: a query theory account. Journal of Risk and Uncertainty 43 (2), 107–126.

Ariely, D., Wertenbroch, K., 2002. Procrastination, deadlines, and performance: self-control by precommitment. Psychological Science 13 (3), 219–224.

Aristotle, 2000. Nicomachean Ethics, 2nd ed. Hackett Publishing, Indianapolis/Cambridge. Translated, with introduction, by Terence Irwin.

Ashraf, N., Camerer, C.F., Loewenstein, G., 2005. Adam Smith, behavioral economist. The Journal of Economic Perspectives 19 (3), 131–145.

Ashraf, N., Karlan, D., Yin, W., 2006. Tying Odysseus to the mast: evidence from a commitment savings product in the Philippines. The Quarterly Journal of Economics 121 (2), 635–672.

Attanasio, O.P., Weber, G., 2010. Consumption and saving: models of intertemporal allocation and their implications for public policy. Journal of Economic Literature 48, 693–751.

Augenblick, N., 2018. Short-Term Time Discounting of Unpleasant Tasks. Working Paper.

Augenblick, N., Niederle, M., Sprenger, C., 2015. Working over time: dynamic inconsistency in real effort tasks. The Quarterly Journal of Economics 30 (3), 1067–1115.

Augenblick, N., Rabin, M., 2018. An experiment on time preference and misprediction in unpleasant tasks. The Review of Economic Studies. https://doi.org/10.1093/restud/rdy019. Forthcoming.

Azfar, O., 1999. Rationalizing hyperbolic discounting. Journal of Economic Behavior & Organization 38 (2), 245–252.

Badger, G.J., Bickel, W.K., Giordano, L.A., Jacobs, E.A., Loewenstein, G., Marsch, L., 2007. Altered states: the impact of immediate craving on the valuation of current and future opioids. Journal of Health Economics 26 (5), 865–876.

Balakrishnan, U., Haushofer, J., Jakiela, P., 2017. How Soon is Now? Evidence of Present Bias from Convex Time Budget Experiments. National Bureau of Economic Research Working Paper No. 23558.

Banerjee, A.V., Duflo, E., Glennerster, R., 2010. Improving immunisation coverage in rural India: clustered randomised controlled evaluation of immunisation campaigns with and without incentives. BMJ 340.

Banerjee, A., Mullainathan, S., 2010. The Shape of Temptation: Implications for the Economic Lives of the Poor. National Bureau of Economic Research Working Paper No. 15973.

Barro, R.J., 1999. Ramsey meets Laibson in the neoclassical growth model. The Quarterly Journal of Economics 114 (4), 1125–1152.

Barsky, R.B., Juster, F.T., Kimball, M.S., Shapiro, M.D., 1997. Preference parameters and behavioral heterogeneity: an experimental approach in the health and retirement study. The Quarterly Journal of Economics 112 (2), 537–579.

Baucells, M., Heukamp, F.H., 2012. Probability and time trade-off. Management Science 58 (4), 831–842.

Baumeister, R.F., Bratslavsky, E., Muraven, M., Tice, D.M., 1998. Ego depletion: is the active self a limited resource? Journal of Personality and Social Psychology 74 (5), 1252–1265.

Becker, A., Deckers, T., Dohmen, T., Falk, A., Kosse, F., 2012. The relationship between economic preferences and psychological personality measures. Annual Review of Economics 4, 453–478. https://doi.org/10.1146/annurev-economics-080511-110922.

Becker, G.M., Degroot, M.H., Marschak, J., 1964. Measuring utility by a single-response sequential method. Behavioral Science 9 (3), 226–232. https://doi.org/10.1002/bs.3830090304.

Becker, G.S., Murphy, K.M., 1988. A theory of rational addiction. Journal of Political Economy 96 (4), 675–700.

Benartzi, S., 2001. Excessive extrapolation and the allocation of 401(k) accounts to company stock. Journal of Finance 56 (5), 1747–1764.

Benartzi, S., Previtero, A., Thaler, R.H., 2011. Annuitization puzzles. The Journal of Economic Perspectives 25 (4), 143–164.

Benhabib, J., Bisin, A., Schotter, A., 2010. Present-bias, quasi-hyperbolic discounting, and fixed costs. Games and Economic Behavior 69 (2), 205–223.

Benjamin, D.J., Brown, S.A., Shapiro, J.M., 2013. Who is 'behavioral'? Cognitive ability and anomalous preferences. Journal of the European Economics Association 11 (6), 1231–1255. https://doi.org/10.1111/jeea.12055.

Benjamin, D.J., Laibson, D., Mischel, W., Peake, P.K., Shoda, Y., Steiny, A., Wilson, N.L., 2018. Predicting Mid-Life Capital Formation with Life-Course Measures of Self-Regulation. Working Paper.

Bernheim, B.D., 1991. The Vanishing Nest Egg: Reflections on Saving in America. Priority Press Publications, New York.

Bernheim, B.D., 1995. Do household appreciate their financial vulnerabilities? An analysis of actions, perceptions, and public policy. In: Tax Policy and Economic Growth. American Council for Capital Formation, Washington, DC.

Bernheim, B.D., 2016. The good, the bad, and the ugly: a unified approach to behavioral welfare economics. Journal of Benefit–Cost Analysis 7 (1), 12–68. https://doi.org/10.1017/bca.2016.5.

Bernheim, B.D., Fradkin, A., Popov, I., 2015a. The welfare economics of default options in 401(k) plans. The American Economic Review 105 (9), 2798–2837.

Bernheim, B.D., Meer, J., Novarro, N.K., 2016. Do consumers exploit commitment opportunities? Evidence from natural experiments involving liquor consumption. American Economic Journal: Economic Policy 8 (4), 41–69.

Bernheim, B.D., Rangel, A., 2004. Addiction and cue-triggered decision processes. The American Economic Review 94 (5), 1558–1590.

Bernheim, B.D., Rangel, A., 2009. Beyond revealed preference: choice-theoretic foundations for behavioral welfare economics. The Quarterly Journal of Economics 124 (1), 51–104. https://doi.org/10.1162/qjec.2009.124.1.51.

Bernheim, B.D., Ray, D., Yeltekin, S., 2015b. Poverty and self-control. Econometrica 83 (5), 1877–1911. https://doi.org/10.3982/ECTA11374.

Bernheim, B.D., Skinner, J., Weinberg, S., 2001. What accounts for the variation in retirement wealth among U.S. households? The American Economic Review 91 (4), 832–857. https://doi.org/10.1257/aer.91.4.832.

Bernheim, B.D., Taubinsky, D., 2018. Behavioral public economics. In: Bernheim, B.D., Laibson, D., DellaVigna, S. (Eds.), Handbook of Behavioral Economics, vol. 1. North-Holland, Amsterdam.

Beshears, J., Choi, J.J., Harris, C., Laibson, D., Madrian, B.C., 2018a. Optimal illiquidity. Mimeo.

Beshears, J., Choi, J.J., Hurwitz, J., Laibson, D., Madrian, B.C., 2015. Liquidity in retirement savings systems: an international comparison. The American Economic Review 105 (5), 420–425.

Beshears, J., Choi, J.J., Laibson, D., Madrian, B.C., 2008. The importance of default options for retirement saving outcomes: evidence from the United States. In: Kay, S.J., Sinha, T. (Eds.), Lessons from Pension Reform in the Americas. Oxford University Press, Oxford.

Beshears, J., Choi, J.J., Laibson, D., Madrian, B.C., 2013. Simplification and saving. Journal of Economic Behavior & Organization 95, 130–145.

Beshears, J., Choi, J.J., Laibson, D., Madrian, B.C., 2018b. Behavioral household finance. In: Bernheim, B.D., Laibson, D., DellaVigna, S. (Eds.), Handbook of Behavioral Economics, vol. 1. North-Holland, Amsterdam.

Beshears, J., Choi, J.J., Laibson, D., Madrian, B.C., Sakong, J., 2018c. Self Control and Liquidity: How to Design a Commitment Contract. Working Paper.

Beshears, J., Choi, J.J., Laibson, D., Madrian, B.C., Zeldes, S.P., 2014. What makes annuitization more appealing? Journal of Public Economics 116, 2–16.

Bettinger, E.P., Long, B.T., Oreopoulos, O., Sanbonmatsu, L., 2012. The role of application assistance and information in college decisions: results from the H&R block FAFSA experiment. The Quarterly Journal of Economics 127 (3), 1205–1242.

Bettinger, E., Slonim, R., 2007. Patience among children. Journal of Public Economics 91 (1–2), 343–363. https://doi.org/10.1016/j.jpubeco.2006.05.010.

Bhargava, S., Manoli, D., 2015. Psychological frictions and the incomplete take-up of social benefits: evidence from an IRS field experiment. The American Economic Review 105 (11), 3489–3529.

Bisin, A., Hyndman, K., 2018. Present-Bias, Procrastination and Deadlines in a Field Experiment. National Bureau of Economic Research Working Paper No. 19874.

Blackwell, L., Trzesniewski, K., Dweck, C.S., 2007. Implicit theories of intelligence predict achievement across an adolescent transition: a longitudinal study and an intervention. Child Development 78, 246–263.

Blumenstock, J., Callen, M., Ghani, T., 2018. Why do defaults affect behavior? Experimental evidence from Afghanistan. The American Economic Review 108 (10), 2868–2901.

von Böhm-Bawerk, Eugen, 1890. Capital and Interest: A Critical History of Economical Theory. Macmillan, London.

Borghans, L., Duckworth, A.L., Heckman, J.J., ter Weel, B., 2008. The economics and psychology of personality traits. The Journal of Human Resources 43, 972–1059.

Brocas, I., Carrillo, J.D., 2008a. Theories of the mind. The American Economic Review 98 (2), 175–180.

Brocas, I., Carrillo, J.D., 2008b. The brain as a hierarchical organization. The American Economic Review 98 (4), 1312–1346. https://doi.org/10.1257/aer.98.4.1312.

Brocas, I., Carrillo, J.D., 2012. From perception to action: an economic model of brain processes. Games and Economic Behavior 75 (1), 81–103. https://doi.org/10.1016/j.geb.2011.10.001.

Broda, C., Parker, J.A., 2014. The Economic Stimulus Payments of 2008 and the Aggregate Demand for Consumption. National Bureau of Economic Research Working Paper No. 20122.

Brown, D.J., Lewis, L.M., 1981. Myopic economic agents. Econometrica 49 (2), 359–368.

Brown, J.R., Kapteyn, A., Luttmer, E.F., Mitchell, O.S., 2017. Cognitive constraints on valuing annuities. Journal of the European Economic Association 15 (2), 429–462.

Brown, J.R., Liang, N., Weisbenner, S., 2007. Individual account investment options and portfolio choice: behavioral lessons from 401(k) plans. Journal of Public Economics 91 (10), 1992–2013.

Brown, J.R., Previtero, A., 2016. Saving for Retirement, Annuities and Procrastination. Working Paper.

Bryan, G., Karlan, D., Nelson, S., 2010. Commitment devices. Annual Review of Economics 2 (1), 671–698. https://doi.org/10.1146/annurev.economics.102308.124324.

Burger, N., Charness, G., Lynham, J., 2011. Field and online experiments on self-control. Journal of Economic Behavior & Organization 77 (3), 393–404. https://doi.org/10.1016/j.jebo.2010.11.010.

Burks, S.V., Carpenter, J.P., Goette, L., Rustichini, A., 2009. Cognitive skills affect economic preferences, strategic behavior, and job attachment. Proceedings of the National Academy of Sciences 106 (19), 7745–7750.

Burks, S., Carpenter, J., Götte, L., Rustichini, A., 2012. Which measures of time preference best predict outcomes: evidence from a large-scale field experiment. Journal of Economic Behavior & Organization 84 (1), 308–320. https://doi.org/10.1016/j.jebo.2012.03.012.

Busse, M.R., Knittel, C.R., Zettelmeyer, F., 2013. Are consumers myopic? Evidence from new and used car purchases. The American Economic Review 103 (1), 220–256. https://doi.org/10.1257/aer.103.1.220.

Cadena, B.C., Keys, B.J., 2012. Human Capital and the Lifetime Costs of Impatience. SSRN Scholarly Paper ID 1674068. Social Science Research Network.

Camerer, C.F., Cohen, J.D., Fehr, E., Glimcher, P.W., Laibson, D., 2015. Neuroeconomics. In: Kagel, J.H., Roth, A.E. (Eds.), Handbook of Experimental Economics, vol. 2. Princeton University Press, Princeton and Oxford.

Campbell, J.Y., Cochrane, J.H., 1999. By force of habit: a consumption-based explanation of aggregate stock market behavior. Journal of Political Economy 107 (2), 205–251.

Caplin, A., Leahy, J., 2001. Psychological expected utility theory and anticipatory feelings. The Quarterly Journal of Economics 116 (1), 55–79.

Carroll, G.D., Choi, J.J., Laibson, D., Madrian, B.C., Metrick, A., 2009. Optimal defaults and active decisions. The Quarterly Journal of Economics 124 (4), 1639–1674.

Carvalho, L., Meier, S., Wang, S., 2016. Poverty and economic decision-making: evidence from changes in financial resources at payday. The American Economic Review 106 (2), 260–284.

Casaburi, L., Macchiavello, R., 2018. Demand and supply of infrequent payments as a commitment device: evidence from Kenya. The American Economic Review. Forthcoming.

Cassidy, R., 2017. Are the Poor Really so Present-Biased? Evidence from a Field Experiment in Rural Pakistan. IFS Working Paper WP18/24.

Castillo, M., Ferraro, P., Jordan, J.L., Petrie, R., 2011. The today and tomorrow of kids: time preferences and educational outcomes of children. Journal of Public Economics 95 (11), 1377–1385.

Chabris, C.F., Laibson, D., Morris, C.L., Schuldt, J.P., Taubinsky, D., 2008. Individual laboratory-measured discount rates predict field behavior. Journal of Risk and Uncertainty 37 (2–3), 237–269.

Chabris, C.F., Laibson, D.I., Schuldt, J.P., 2010. Intertemporal choice. In: Durlauf, S.N., Blume, L.E. (Eds.), Behavioural and Experimental Economics. Palgrave Macmillan, London.

Chakraborty, A., 2017. Present Bias. Working Paper.

Chapman, G.B., 1996. Temporal discounting and utility for health and money. Journal of Experimental Psychology: Learning, Memory, and Cognition 22 (3), 771–791.

Chapman, G.B., 2000. Preferences for improving and declining sequences of health outcomes. Journal of Behavioral Decision Making 13 (2), 203–218.

Cheung, S., 2015. Risk preferences are not time preferences: on the elicitation of time preference under conditions of risk: comment. The American Economic Review 105 (7), 2242–2260.

Cheung, S.L., 2016. Recent developments in the experimental elicitation of time preference. Journal of Behavioral and Experimental Finance 11, 1–8.

Choi, J.J., Laibson, D., Madrian, B.C., 2009. Mental accounting in portfolio choice: evidence from a flypaper effect. The American Economic Review 99 (5), 2085–2095.

Choi, J.J., Laibson, D., Madrian, B.C., Metrick, A., 2002. Defined contribution pensions: plan rules, participant choices, and the path of least resistance. In: Poterba, J.M. (Ed.), Tax Policy and the Economy, vol. 16. National Bureau of Economic Research, MIT Press, Cambridge.

Choukhmane, T., 2018. Default Options and Retirement Savings Dynamics. Working Paper.

Chung, S., Herrnstein, R.J., 1967. Choice and delay of reinforcement. Journal of the Experimental Analysis of Behavior 10 (1), 67–74. https://doi.org/10.1901/jeab.1967.10-67.

Cohen, J.D., Ericson, K.M., Laibson, D., White, J.M., 2016. Measuring Time Preferences. National Bureau of Economic Research Working Paper No. 22455.

Coile, C., Diamond, P., Gruber, J., Jousten, A., 2002. Delays in claiming social security benefits. Journal of Public Economics 84 (3), 357–385. https://doi.org/10.1016/S0047-2727(01)00129-3.

Coller, M., Williams, M.B., 1999. Eliciting individual discount rates. Experimental Economics 2 (2), 107–127. https://doi.org/10.1023/A:1009986005690.

Commons, M.L., Woodford, M., Ducheny, J.R., 1982. How reinforcers are aggregated in reinforcement-density discrimination and preference experiments. In: Commons, M.L., Herrnstein, R.J., Rachlin, H. (Eds.), Quantitative Analyses of Behavior. Vol. 2, Matching and Maximizing Accounts. Ballinger, Cambridge, pp. 25–78.

Commons, M.L., Woodford, M., Trudeau, E.J., 1991. How each reinforcer contributes to value: 'noise' must reduce reinforcer value hyperbolically. In: Commons, M.L., Nevin, J.A., Davison, M.C. (Eds.), Signal Detection: Mechanisms, Models, and Applications. Lawrence Erlbaum Associates, Hillsdale, pp. 139–168.

Cropper, M.L., Laibson, D.I., 1998. The Implications of Hyperbolic Discounting for Project Evaluation. World Bank Publications.

Cubitt, R.P., Read, D., 2007. Can intertemporal choice experiments elicit time preferences for consumption? Experimental Economics 10 (4), 369–389. https://doi.org/10.1007/s10683-006-9140-2.

Currie, J., 2004. The Take Up of Social Benefits. National Bureau of Economic Research Working Paper No. 10488.

Dai, X., Fishbach, A., 2013. When waiting to choose increases patience. Organizational Behavior and Human Decision Processes 121 (2), 256–266.

Dasgupta, P., Maskin, E., 2005. Uncertainty and hyperbolic discounting. The American Economic Review 95 (4), 1290–1299.

Dean, M., Sautmann, A., 2018. Credit Constraints and the Measurement of Time Preferences. Working Paper.

Deck, C., Jahedi, S., 2015. The effect of cognitive load on economic decision making: a survey and new experiments. European Economic Review 78, 97–119. https://doi.org/10.1016/j.euroecorev.2015.05.004.

Dekel, E., Lipman, B.L., Rustichini, A., 2001. Representing preferences with a unique subjective state space. Econometrica 69 (4), 891–934.

Dekel, E., Lipman, B.L., Rustichini, A., 2009. Temptation-driven preferences. The Review of Economic Studies 76 (3), 937–971. https://doi.org/10.1111/j.1467-937X.2009.00560.x.

DellaVigna, S., Lindner, A., Reizer, B., Schmieder, J., 2017. Reference-dependent job search: evidence from Hungary. The Quarterly Journal of Economics 132 (4), 1969–2018.

DellaVigna, S., Malmendier, U., 2004. Contract design and self-control: theory and evidence. The Quarterly Journal of Economics 119 (2), 353–402.

DellaVigna, S., Malmendier, U., 2006. Paying not to go to the gym. The American Economic Review 96 (3), 694–719.

DellaVigna, S., Paserman, M.D., 2005. Job search and impatience. Journal of Labor Economics 23 (3), 527–588.

DeSteno, D., Li, Y., Dickens, L., Lerner, J.S., 2014. Gratitude: a tool for reducing economic impatience. Psychological Science 25 (6), 1262–1267.

Dohmen, T., Falk, A., Huffman, D., Sunde, U., 2010. Are risk aversion and impatience related to cognitive ability? The American Economic Review 100 (3), 1238–1260.

Dreyfus, M.K., Viscusi, W.K., 1995. Rates of time preference and consumer valuations of automobile safety and fuel efficiency. The Journal of Law & Economics 38 (1), 79–105.

Duckworth, A., Gross, J.J., 2014. Self-control and grit: related but separable determinants of success. Current Directions in Psychological Science 23 (5), 319–325.

Duckworth, A., Peterson, C., Matthews, M.D., Kelly, D.R., 2007. Grit: perseverance and passion for long-term goals. Journal of Personality and Social Psychology 92, 1087–1101.

Duckworth, A.L., Laibson, D., Milkman, K.L., 2018. Beyond willpower: strategies for reducing failures of self-control. Psychological Science in the Public Interest. Forthcoming.

Duflo, E., Kremer, M., Robinson, J., 2011. Nudging farmers to use fertilizer: theory and experimental evidence from Kenya. The American Economic Review 101 (6), 2350–2390.

Dushi, I., Munell, A.H., Sanzenbacher, G.T., Webb, A., 2015. Do Households Increase Their Savings When the Kids Leave Home? Center for Retirement Research at Boston College Working Paper No. 2015-26.

Dweck, C.S., 1986. Motivational processes affecting learning. The American Psychologist 41, 1040–1048.

Ebert, J.E.J., Prelec, D., 2007. The fragility of time: time-insensitivity and valuation of the near and far future. Management Science 53 (9), 1423–1438. https://doi.org/10.1287/mnsc.1060.0671.

Epper, T., Fehr-Duda, H., 2015a. The Missing Link: Unifying Risk Taking and Time Discounting. Working Paper No. 096. University of Zurich.

Epper, T., Fehr-Duda, H., 2015b. Comment on 'Risk preferences are not time preferences': balancing on a budget line. The American Economic Review 105 (7), 2261–2271.

Epper, T., Fehr-Duda, H., Bruhin, A., 2011. Viewing the future through a warped lens: why uncertainty generates hyperbolic discounting. Journal of Risk and Uncertainty 43 (3), 169–203. https://doi.org/10.1007/s11166-011-9129-x.

Epstein, L.G., Zin, S.E., 1989. Substitution, risk aversion, and the temporal behavior of consumption and asset returns: a theoretical framework. Econometrica 57 (4), 937–969.

Ericson, K.M., 2011. Forgetting we forget: overconfidence and memory. Journal of the European Economic Association 9 (1), 43–60.

Ericson, K.M., 2017. On the interaction of memory and procrastination: implications for reminders, deadlines, and empirical estimation. Journal of the European Economic Association 15 (3), 692–719.

Ericson, K.M., Noor, J., 2015. Delay Functions as the Foundation of Time Preference: Testing for Separable Discounted Utility. National Bureau of Economic Research Working Paper No. 21095.

Ericson, K.M., White, J.M., Laibson, D., Cohen, J.D., 2015. Money earlier or later? Simple heuristics explain intertemporal choices better than delay discounting does. Psychological Science 26 (6), 826–833. https://doi.org/10.1177/0956797615572232.

Estle, S.J., Green, L., Myerson, J., Holt, D.D., 2007. Discounting of monetary and directly consumable rewards. Psychological Science 18 (1), 58–63. https://doi.org/10.1111/j.1467-9280.2007.01849.x.

Fadlon, I., Laibson, D., 2017. Paternalism and Pseudo-Rationality. National Bureau of Economic Research Working Paper No. 23620.

Falk, A., Becker, A., Dohmen, T., Enke, B., Huffman, D., Sunde, U., 2015. The Nature and Predictive Power of Preferences: Global Evidence. IZA Discussion Papers No. 9504.

Falk, A., Becker, A., Dohmen, T., Enke, B., Huffman, D., Sunde, U., 2016. The Preference Survey Module: A Validated Instrument for Measuring Risk, Time, and Social Preferences. IZA Discussion Papers No. 9674.

Farkas, S., Johnson, J., 1997. Miles to Go: A Status Report on Americans' Plans for Retirement. Public Agenda, New York.

Fedyk, A., 2018. Asymmetric Naivete: Beliefs about Self-Control. SSRN Scholarly Paper ID 2727499. Social Science Research Network.

Feldstein, M., 1985. The optimal level of social security benefits. The Quarterly Journal of Economics 100 (2), 303–320.

Fernández-Villaverde, J., Mukherji, A., 2006. Can We Really Observe Hyperbolic Discounting? Working Paper.

Fischer, C., 2001. Read this paper later: procrastination with time-consistent preferences. Journal of Economic Behavior & Organization 46 (3), 249–269.

Fox, M.V., 1983. Ancient Egyptian rhetoric. Rhetorica: A Journal of the History of Rhetoric 1 (1), 9–22.

Frakes, M.D., Wasserman, M.F., 2017. Procrastination in the Workplace: Evidence from the U.S. Patent Office. National Bureau of Economic Research Working Paper No. 22987.

Frederick, S., 2005. Cognitive reflection and decision making. The Journal of Economic Perspectives 19 (4), 25–42.

Frederick, S., Loewenstein, G., 2008. Conflicting motives in evaluations of sequences. Journal of Risk and Uncertainty 37 (2–3), 221–235.

Frederick, S., Loewenstein, G., O'Donoghue, T., 2002. Time discounting and time preference: a critical review. Journal of Economic Literature 40 (2), 351–401.

Freeman, D., Manzini, P., Mariotti, M., Mittone, L., 2016. Procedures for eliciting time preferences. Journal of Economic Behavior & Organization 126, 235–242. https://doi.org/10.1016/j.jebo.2016.03.017.

Fudenberg, D., Levine, D.K., 2006. A dual-self model of impulse control. The American Economic Review 96 (5), 1449–1476.

Fudenberg, D., Levine, D.K., 2011. Risk, delay, and convex self-control costs. American Economic Journal: Microeconomics 3 (3), 34–68. https://doi.org/10.1257/mic.3.3.34.

Fudenberg, D., Levine, D.K., 2012. Timing and self-control. Econometrica 80 (1), 1–42.

Gabaix, X., 2014. A sparsity-based model of bounded rationality. The Quarterly Journal of Economics 129 (4), 1661–1710.

Gabaix, X., Laibson, D., 2017. Myopia and Discounting. Working Paper.

Ganong, P., Noel, P., 2017. Consumer Spending During Unemployment: Positive and Normative Implications. Working Paper.

Giné, X., Karlan, D., Zinman, J., 2010. Put your money where your butt is: a commitment contract for smoking cessation. American Economic Journal: Applied Economics 2 (4), 213–235.

Glimcher, P.W., Kable, J., Louie, K., 2007. Neuroeconomic studies of impulsivity: now or just as soon as possible? The American Economic Review 97 (2), 142–147.

Goda, G.S., Levy, M.R., Manchester, C.F., Sojourner, A., Tasoff, J., 2018. Mechanisms Behind Retirement Saving Behavior: Evidence from Administrative and Survey Data. TIAA Institute Research Dialogue 140.

Gollier, C., 2013. The debate on discounting: reconciling positivists and ethicists. Chicago Journal of International Law 13 (2), 549–564.

Golsteyn, B.H.H., Grönqvist, H., Lindahl, L., 2013. Time Preferences and Lifetime Outcomes. IZA Discussion Paper No. 7165.

Goulder, L.H., Williams, R.C., 2012. The choice of discount rate for climate change policy evaluation. Climate Change Economics 03 (04).

Gross, D.B., Souleles, N.S., 2002. Do liquidity constraints and interest rates matter for consumer behavior? Evidence from credit card data. The Quarterly Journal of Economics 117 (1), 149–185.

Gross, T., Notowidigdo, M.J., Wang, J., 2016. The Marginal Propensity to Consume Over the Business Cycle. National Bureau of Economic Research Working Paper No. 22518.

Gul, F., Pesendorfer, W., 2001. Temptation and self-control. Econometrica 69 (6), 1403–1435. https://doi.org/10.1111/1468-0262.00252.

Gul, F., Pesendorfer, W., 2004. Self-control and the theory of consumption. Econometrica 72 (1), 119–158.

Gustman, A.L., Steinmeier, T.L., 2012. Policy effects in hyperbolic vs. exponential models of consumption and retirement. Journal of Public Economics 96 (5–6), 465–473. https://doi.org/10.1016/j.jpubeco.2012.02.001.

Haider, S.J., Stephens Jr., M., 2007. Is there a retirement-consumption puzzle? Evidence using subjective retirement expectations. Review of Economics and Statistics 89 (2), 247–264.

Halevy, Y., 2005. Diminishing Impatience: Disentangling Time Preference from Uncertain Lifetime. Working Paper. University of British Columbia.

Halevy, Y., 2008. Strotz meets Allais: diminishing impatience and the certainty effect. The American Economic Review 98 (3), 1145–1162.

Halevy, Y., 2014. Some Comments on the Use of Monetary and Primary Rewards in the Measurement of Time Preferences. Technical Report. University of British Columbia.

Halevy, Y., 2015. Time consistency: stationarity and time invariance. Econometrica 83 (1), 335–352.

Hamermesh, D.S., 1984. Consumption during retirement: the missing link in the life cycle. Review of Economics and Statistics 66 (1), 1–7.

Hardisty, D.J., Thompson, K.F., Krantz, D.H., Weber, E.U., 2013. How to measure time preferences: an experimental comparison of three methods. Judgment and Decision Making 8 (3), 236–249.

Hare, T.A., Camerer, C.F., Rangel, A., 2009. Self-control in decision-making involves modulation of the vmPFC valuation system. Science 324 (5927), 646–648.

Harris, C., Laibson, D., 2012. Instantaneous gratification. The Quarterly Journal of Economics 128 (1), 205–248.

Harrison, G.W., Lau, M.I., Williams, M.B., 2002. Estimating individual discount rates in Denmark: a field experiment. The American Economic Review 92 (5), 1606–1617.

Haushofer, J., Fehr, E., 2014. On the psychology of poverty. Science 344 (6186), 862–867.

Hausman, J.A., 1979. Individual discount rates and the purchase and utilization of energy-using durables. Bell Journal of Economics 10 (1), 33–54.

Heckman, J., Pinto, R., Savelyev, P., 2013. Understanding the mechanism through which an influential early childhood program boosted adult outcomes. The American Economic Review 103 (6), 2052–2086.

Heckman, J.J., Stixrud, J., Urzua, S., 2006. The effects of cognitive and noncognitive abilities on labor market outcomes and social behavior. Journal of Labor Economics 24 (3), 411–482.

Heidhues, P., Kőszegi, B., 2010. Exploiting naïvete about self-control in the credit market. The American Economic Review 100 (5), 2279–2303.

Herrnstein, R.J., 1961. Relative and absolute strength of response as a function of frequency of reinforcement. Journal of the Experimental Analysis of Behavior 4 (3), 267–272. https://doi.org/10.1901/jeab.1961.4-267.

Hinson, J.M., Jameson, T.L., Whitney, P., 2003. Impulsive decision making and working memory. Journal of Experimental Psychology: Learning, Memory, and Cognition 29 (2), 298–306.

Hoch, S.J., Loewenstein, G.F., 1991. Time-inconsistent preferences and consumer self-control. Journal of Consumer Research 17 (4), 492–507.

Houser, D., Schunk, D., Winter, J., Xiao, E., 2018. Temptation and commitment in the laboratory. Games and Economic Behavior 107, 329–344.

Hurd, M.D., Rohwedder, S., 2013. Heterogeneity in spending change at retirement. The Journal of the Economics of Ageing 1–2, 60–71.

Imas, A., Kuhn, M.A., Mironova, V., 2017. Waiting to Choose. Working Paper. Carnegie Mellon University.

Jachimowicz, J., Duncan, S., Weber, E.U., Johnson, E.J., 2018. When and Why Defaults Influence Decisions: A Meta-Analysis of Default Effects. SSRN Working Paper ID 2727301.

Jackson, M., Yariv, L., 2014. Present bias and collective dynamic choice in the lab. The American Economic Review 104 (12), 4184–4204.

Jackson, M., Yariv, L., 2015. Collective dynamic choice: the necessity of time inconsistency. American Economic Journal: Microeconomics 7 (4), 150–178.

Jéhiel, P., 1995. Limited horizon forecast in repeated alternate games. Journal of Economic Theory 67 (2), 497–519.

Johnson, D.S., Parker, J.A., Souleles, N.S., 2006. Household expenditure and the income tax rebates of 2001. The American Economic Review 96 (5), 1589–1610.

Johnson, E.J., Goldstein, D., 2003. Do defaults save lives? Science 302 (5649), 1338–1339.

Kable, J.W., Glimcher, P.W., 2010. An "as soon as possible" effect in human intertemporal decision making: behavioral evidence and neural mechanisms. Journal of Neurophysiology 103 (5), 2513–2531.

Kahneman, D., Deaton, A., 2010. High income improves evaluation of life but not emotional well-being. Proceedings of the National Academy of Sciences 107 (38), 16489–16493.

Kahneman, D., Fredrickson, B.L., Schreiber, C.A., Redelmeier, D.A., 1993. When more pain is preferred to less: adding a better end. Psychological Science 4 (6), 401–405.

Kahneman, D., Tversky, A., 1979. Prospect theory: an analysis of decision under risk. Econometrica 47 (2), 263–291.

Kaplan, G., Violante, G.L., 2014. A model of the consumption response to fiscal stimulus payments. Econometrica 82 (4), 1199–1239.

Kaplan, G., Violante, G.L., Weidner, J., 2014. The Wealthy Hand-to-Mouth. National Bureau of Economic Research Working Paper No. 20073.

Kaur, S., Kremer, M., Mullainathan, S., 2010. Self-control and the development of work arrangements. The American Economic Review 100 (2), 624–628.

Kaur, S., Kremer, M., Mullainathan, S., 2015. Self-control at work. Journal of Political Economy 123 (6), 1227–1277.

Keren, G., Roelofsma, P., 1995. Immediacy and certainty in intertemporal choice. Organizational Behavior and Human Decision Processes 63 (3), 287–297.

Kirby, K.N., 1997. Bidding on the future: evidence against normative discounting of delayed rewards. Journal of Experimental Psychology: General 126 (1), 54–70. https://doi.org/10.1037/0096-3445.126.1.54.

Kirby, K.N., 2009. One-year temporal stability of delay-discount rates. Psychonomic Bulletin & Review 16 (3), 457–462. https://doi.org/10.3758/PBR.16.3.457.

Kirby, K.N., Herrnstein, R.J., 1995. Preference reversals due to myopic discounting of delayed reward. Psychological Science 6 (2), 83–89. https://doi.org/10.1111/j.1467-9280.1995.tb00311.x.

Koopmans, T., 1960. Stationary ordinal utility and impatience. Econometrica 28, 287–309.

Kőszegi, B., Rabin, M., 2009. Reference-dependent consumption plans. The American Economic Review 99 (3), 909–936.

Kőszegi, B., Szeidl, A., 2013. A model of focusing in economic choice. The Quarterly Journal of Economics 128 (1), 53–104.

Kreps, D.M., 1979. A representation theorem for "preference for flexibility". Econometrica 47 (3), 565–577.

Kreps, D.M., 1998. Anticipated utility and dynamic choice. In: Jacobs, D., Kalai, E., Kamien, M. (Eds.), Frontiers of Research in Economic Theory: The Nancy L. Schwartz Memorial Lectures, 1983–1997. In: Econometric Society Monographs. Cambridge University Press, Cambridge.

Kreps, D.M., Porteus, E.L., 1978. Temporal resolution of uncertainty and dynamic choice theory. Econometrica, 185–200.

Krupka, E.L., Stephens Jr., M., 2013. The stability of measured time preferences. Journal of Economic Behavior & Organization 85, 11–19. https://doi.org/10.1016/j.jebo.2012.10.010.

Krusell, P., Kuruşçu, B., Smith Jr., A.A., 2010. Temptation and taxation. Econometrica 78 (6), 2063–2084. https://doi.org/10.3982/ECTA8611.

Kuchler, T., Pagel, M., 2018. Sticking to Your Plan: The Role of Present Bias for Credit Card Paydown. National Bureau of Economic Research Working Paper No. 24881.

Laibson, D., 1997. Golden eggs and hyperbolic discounting. The Quarterly Journal of Economics 112 (2), 443–477. https://doi.org/10.1162/003355397555253.

Laibson, D., 2001. A cue-theory of consumption. The Quarterly Journal of Economics 116 (1), 81–119.

Laibson, D., 2015. Why don't present-biased agents make commitments? The American Economic Review 105 (5), 267–272.

Laibson, D., 2018. Private paternalism, the commitment puzzle, and model-free equilibrium. AEA Papers and Proceedings 108, 1–21.

Laibson, D., Maxted, P., Repetto, A., Tobacman, J., 2017. Estimating Discount Functions with Consumption Choices over the Lifecycle. Working Paper.

Laibson, D., Repetto, A., Tobacman, J., 2003. A debt puzzle. In: Aghion, P., Frydman, R., Stiglitz, J., Woodford, M. (Eds.), Knowledge, Information and Expectations in Modern Macroeconomics: In Honor of Edmund S. Phelps. Princeton University Press, Princeton.

Laibson, D., Repetto, A., Tobacman, J., 1998. Self-control and saving for retirement. Brookings Papers on Economic Activity 1998 (1), 91–196.

Lavecchia, A., Liu, H., Oreopoulos, P., 2014. Behavioral Economics of Education: Progress and Possibilities. National Bureau of Economic Research Working Paper No. 20609.

Lawyer, S.R., Williams, S.A., Prihodova, T., Rollins, J.D., Lester, A.C., 2010. Probability and delay discounting of hypothetical sexual outcomes. Behavioural Processes 84 (3), 687–692. https://doi.org/10.1016/j.beproc.2010.04.002.

Lerner, J.S., Li, Y., Weber, E.U., 2013. The financial cost of sadness. Psychological Science 24 (1), 72–79.

Lipman, B.L., Pesendorfer, W., 2013. Temptation. In: Acemoglu, D., Arellano, M., Dekel, E. (Eds.), Advances in Economics and Econometrics: Tenth World Congress, vol. 1. Cambridge University Press, New York.

Lockwood, B., 2016. Optimal Income Taxation with Present Bias. Working Paper.

Loewenstein, G., 1987. Anticipation and the valuation of delayed consumption. The Economic Journal 97 (387), 666–684. https://doi.org/10.2307/2232929.

Loewenstein, G., 1988. Frames of mind in intertemporal choice. Management Science 34 (2), 200–214. https://doi.org/10.1287/mnsc.34.2.200.

Loewenstein, G., 1992. The fall and rise of psychological explanations in the economics of intertemporal choice. In: Loewenstein, G., Elster, J. (Eds.), Choice Over Time. Russell Sage Foundation, New York.

Loewenstein, G., 1996. Out of control: visceral influences on behavior. Organizational Behavior and Human Decision Processes 65 (3), 272–292. https://doi.org/10.1006/obhd.1996.0028.

Loewenstein, G., Elster, J. (Eds.), 1992. Choice over Time. Russell Sage Foundation, New York.

Loewenstein, G., O'Donoghue, T., 2004. Animal Spirits: Affective and Deliberative Processes in Economic Behavior. SSRN Scholarly Paper ID 539843. Social Science Research Network.

Loewenstein, G., Prelec, D., 1992. Anomalies in intertemporal choice: evidence and an interpretation. The Quarterly Journal of Economics 107 (2), 573–597.

Loewenstein, G.F., Prelec, D., 1993. Preferences for sequences of outcomes. Psychological Review 100 (1), 91–108.

Loewenstein, G., Read, D., Baumeister, R.F. (Eds.), 2003. Time and Decision. Russell Sage Foundation, New York.

Loewenstein, G., Sicherman, N., 1991. Do workers prefer increasing wage profiles? Journal of Labor Economics 9 (1), 67–84.

Loewenstein, G., Thaler, R.H., 1989. Anomalies: intertemporal choice. Journal of Economic Perspectives 3 (4), 181–193. https://doi.org/10.1257/jep.3.4.

Madrian, B.C., Shea, D.F., 2001. The power of suggestion: inertia in 401 (k) participation and savings behavior. The Quarterly Journal of Economics 116 (4), 1149–1187.

Maital, S., Maital, S., 1977. Time preference, delay of gratification and the intergenerational transmission of economic inequality: a behavioral theory of income distribution. In: Ashenfelter, O.C., Oates, W.E. (Eds.), Essays in Labor Market Analysis: In Memory of Yochanan Peter Comay. John Wiley and Sons, New York.

Mariger, R.P., 1987. A life-cycle consumption model with liquidity constraints: theory and empirical results. Econometrics 55 (3), 533–557.

Marshall, A., 1891. Principles of Economics, 2nd ed. Macmillan, London.

Mastrobuoni, G., Weinberg, M., 2009. Heterogeneity in intra-monthly consumption patterns, self-control, and savings at retirement. American Economic Journal: Economic Policy 1 (2), 163–189. https://doi.org/10.1257/pol.1.2.163.

McClure, S.M., Ericson, K.M., Laibson, D.I., Loewenstein, G., Cohen, J.D., 2007. Time discounting for primary rewards. The Journal of Neuroscience 27 (21), 5796–5804. https://doi.org/10.1523/JNEUROSCI.4246-06.2007.

McClure, S.M., Laibson, D.I., Loewenstein, G., Cohen, J.D., 2004. Separate neural systems value immediate and delayed monetary rewards. Science 306 (5695), 503–507. https://doi.org/10.1126/science.1100907.

McGuire, J.T., Kable, J.W., 2012. Decision makers calibrate behavioral persistence on the basis of time-interval experience. Cognition 124 (2), 216–226.

McGuire, J.T., Kable, J.W., 2013. Rational temporal predictions can underlie apparent failures to delay gratification. Psychological Review 120 (2), 395–410.

McIntosh, D., 1969. The Foundations of Human Society. University of Chicago Press, Chicago.

Meier, S., Sprenger, C., 2011. Time discounting predicts creditworthiness. Psychological Science 23 (1), 56–58. https://doi.org/10.1177/0956797611425931.

Meier, S., Sprenger, C., 2015. Temporal stability of time preferences. Review of Economics and Statistics 97 (2), 273–286.

Miao, B., Zhong, S., 2015. Comment on 'Risk preferences are not time preferences': separating risk and time preference. The American Economic Review 105 (7), 2272–2286.

Milkman, K.L., Beshears, J., Choi, J.J., Laibson, D., Madrian, B.C., 2011. Using implementation intentions prompts to enhance influenza vaccination rates. Proceedings of the National Academy of Sciences 108 (26), 10415–10420.

Milkman, K.L., Beshears, J., Choi, J.J., Laibson, D., Madrian, B.C., 2013. Planning prompts as a means of increasing preventive screening rates. Preventive Medicine 56 (1), 92–93.

Milkman, K.L., Rogers, T., Bazerman, M.H., 2009. Highbrow films gather dust: time-inconsistent preferences and online DVD rentals. Management Science 55 (6), 1047–1059.

Mischel, W., Ebbesen, E.B., 1970. Attention in delay of gratification. Journal of Personality and Social Psychology 16 (2), 329–337. https://doi.org/10.1037/h0029815.

Mischel, W., Shoda, Y., Rodriguez, M.I., 1989. Delay of gratification in children. Science 244 (4907), 933–938. https://doi.org/10.1126/science.2658056.

Moffitt, T.E., Arseneault, L., Belsky, D., Dickson, N., Hancox, R.J., Harrington, H., et al., 2011. A gradient of childhood self-control predicts health, wealth, and public safety. Proceedings of the National Academy of Sciences 108 (7), 2693–2698.

Moser, C., Olea de Souza e Silva, P., 2017. Optimal paternalistic savings policies.

Muraven, M., Baumeister, R.F., 2000. Self-regulation and depletion of limited resources: does self-control resemble a muscle? Psychological Bulletin 126 (2), 247–259.

Muraven, M., Tice, D.M., Baumeister, R.F., 1998. Self-control as a limited resource: regulatory depletion patterns. Journal of Personality and Social Psychology 74 (3), 774–789. https://doi.org/10.1037/0022-3514.74.3.774.

Noor, J., 2007. Commitment and self-control. Journal of Economic Theory 135 (1), 1–34.

Noor, J., 2009. Hyperbolic discounting and the standard model: eliciting discount functions. Journal of Economic Theory 144 (5), 2077–2083.

Noor, J., 2011. Temptation and revealed preference. Econometrica 79 (2), 601–644.

Nussbaum, M.C., 2001. 'This story isn't true': madness, reason and recantation in the Phaedrus. In: The Fragility of Goodness: Luck and Ethics in Greek Tragedy and Philosophy. Cambridge University Press, Cambridge, pp. 200–234.

O'Donoghue, T., Rabin, M., 1999a. Doing it now or later. The American Economic Review 89 (1), 103–124.

O'Donoghue, T., Rabin, M., 1999b. Incentives for procrastinators. The Quarterly Journal of Economics 114 (3), 769–816.

O'Donoghue, T., Rabin, M., 2001. Choice and procrastination. The Quarterly Journal of Economics 116 (1), 121–160.

Odum, A.L., Baumann, A.A.L., Rimington, D.D., 2006. Discounting of delayed hypothetical money and food: effects of amount. Behavioural Processes 73 (3), 278–284. https://doi.org/10.1016/j.beproc.2006.06.008.

Odum, A.L., Rainaud, C.P., 2003. Discounting of delayed hypothetical money, alcohol, and food. Behavioural Processes 64 (3), 305–313. https://doi.org/10.1016/S0376-6357(03)00145-1.

Olafsson, A., Pagel, M., 2018. The Retirement-Consumption Puzzle: New Evidence from Personal Finances. National Bureau of Economic Research Working Paper No. 24405.

Olea, J.L.M., Strzalecki, T., 2014. Axiomatization and measurement of quasi-hyperbolic discounting. The Quarterly Journal of Economics 129 (3), 1449–1499.

Oster, S.M., Morton, F.M.S., 2005. Behavioral biases meet the market: the case of magazine subscription prices. The BE Journal of Economic Analysis & Policy 5 (1).

Pallais, A., 2015. Small differences that matter: mistakes in applying to college. Journal of Labor Economics 33 (2), 493–520.

Parker, J.A., Souleles, N.S., Johnson, D.S., McClelland, R., 2013. Consumer spending and the economic stimulus payments of 2008. The American Economic Review 103 (6), 2530–2553.

Paserman, M.D., 2008. Job search and hyperbolic discounting: structural estimation and policy evaluation. The Economic Journal 118 (531), 1418–1452. https://doi.org/10.1111/j.1468-0297.2008.02175.x.

Pew Charitable Trusts, 2012. Who Borrows, Where They Borrow, and Why – Pew Center on the States. Payday Lending in America Report Series. Pew Charitable Trusts, Philadelphia.

Phelps, E.S., Pollak, R.A., 1968. On second-best national saving and game-equilibrium growth. The Review of Economic Studies 35 (2), 185–199. https://doi.org/10.2307/2296547.

Pigou, A.C., 1920. The Economics of Welfare. Macmillan, London.

Plato, 1925. Plato in Twelve Volumes. Translated by Harold N. Fowler, vol. 9. Harvard University Press, Cambridge, MA. London, William Heinemann Ltd.

Prelec, D., Loewenstein, G., 1991. Decision making over time and under uncertainty: a common approach. Management Science 37 (7), 770–786.

Prelec, D., Loewenstein, G., 1998. The red and the black: mental accounting of savings and debt. Marketing Science 17 (1), 4–28.

Quiggin, J., Horowitz, J., 1995. Time and risk. Journal of Risk and Uncertainty 10 (1), 37–55.

Rabin, M., 2000. Risk aversion and expected-utility theory: a calibration theorem. Econometrica 68 (5), 1281–1292.

Radcliffe, E.S., 2018. Hume, Passion, and Action. Oxford University Press, Oxford.

Ramsey, F.P., 1928. A mathematical theory of saving. Economic Journal 38, 543–559.

Rangel, A., Camerer, C., Montague, P.R., 2008. A framework for studying the neurobiology of value-based decision making. Nature Reviews Neuroscience 9 (7), 545–556.

Read, D., 2001. Is time-discounting hyperbolic or subadditive? Journal of Risk and Uncertainty 23 (1), 5–32. https://doi.org/10.1023/A:1011198414683.

Read, D., Frederick, S., Scholten, M., 2013. DRIFT: an analysis of outcome framing in intertemporal choice. Journal of Experimental Psychology: Learning, Memory, and Cognition 39 (2), 573–588.

Read, D., Loewenstein, G., Kalyanaraman, S., 1999. Mixing virtue and vice: combining the immediacy effect and the diversification heuristic. Journal of Behavioral Decision Making 12 (4), 257–273.

Read, D., Powell, M., 2002. Reasons for sequence preferences. Journal of Behavioral Decision Making 15 (5), 433–460.

Read, D., Roelofsma, P.H.M.P., 2003. Subadditive versus hyperbolic discounting: a comparison of choice and matching. Organizational Behavior and Human Decision Processes 91 (2), 140–153.

Read, D., van Leeuwen, B., 1998. Predicting hunger: the effects of appetite and delay on choice. Organizational Behavior and Human Decision Processes 76 (2), 189–205.

Reuben, E., Sapienza, P., Zingales, L., 2010. Time discounting for primary and monetary rewards. Economics Letters 106 (2), 125–127.

Reuben, E., Sapienza, P., Zingales, L., 2015. Procrastination and impatience. Journal of Behavioral and Experimental Economics 58, 63–76.

Rick, S.I., Cryder, C.E., Loewenstein, G., 2007. Tightwads and spendthrifts. Journal of Consumer Research 34 (6), 767–782.

Roberts, B.W., Chernyshenko, O.S., Stark, S., Goldberg, L.R., 2005. The structure of conscientiousness: an empirical investigation based on seven major personality questionnaires. Personnel Psychology 58 (1), 103–139.

Royer, H., Stehr, M., Sydnor, J., 2015. Incentives, commitments, and habit formation in exercise: evidence from a field experiment with workers at a Fortune-500 company. American Economic Journal: Applied Microeconomics 7 (3), 51–84.

Rubinstein, A., 2003. 'Economics and psychology?' The case of hyperbolic discounting. International Economic Review 44 (4), 1207–1216.

Ryder, H.E., Heal, G., 1973. Optimal growth with intertemporally dependent preferences. The Review of Economic Studies 40 (1), 1–31.

Sadoff, S., Samek, A., Sprenger, C., 2015. Dynamic Inconsistency in Food Choice: Experimental Evidence from a Food Desert. Becker Friedman Institute for Research in Economics Working Paper No. 2572821, CESR-Schaeffer Working Paper No. 2015-027.

Saito, K., 2011. Strotz meets Allais: diminishing impatience and the certainty effect: comment. The American Economic Review 101 (5), 2271–2275.

Samuelson, P., 1937. A note on measurement of utility. The Review of Economic Studies 4 (2), 155–161. https://doi.org/10.2307/2967612.

Samuelson, W., Zeckhauser, R., 1988. Status quo bias in decision making. Journal of Risk and Uncertainty 1, 7–59.

Schelling, T.C., 1995. Intergenerational discounting. Energy Policy 23 (4–5), 395–401.

Schilbach, F., 2017. Alcohol and Self-Control: A Field Experiment in India. Working Paper.

Scholten, M., Read, D., 2006. Discounting by intervals: a generalized model of intertemporal choice. Management Science 52 (9), 1424–1436.

Scholz, J.K., Seshadri, A., Khitatrakun, S., 2006. Are americans saving "optimally" for retirement? Journal of Political Economy 114 (4), 607–643.

Schultz, W., Dayan, P., Montague, R.R., 1997. A neural substrate of prediction and reward. Science 275, 1593–1599.

Sen, A.K., 1957. A note on Tinbergen on the optimum rate of saving. The Economic Journal 67 (268), 745–748.

Shah, A.K., Mullainathan, S., Shafir, E., 2012. Some consequences of having too little. Science 338 (6107), 682–685.

Shapiro, J.M., 2005. Is there a daily discount rate? Evidence from the food stamp nutrition cycle. Journal of Public Economics 89, 303–325.

Shapiro, M.D., Slemrod, J., 2003. Did the 2001 tax rebate stimulate spending? Evidence from taxpayer surveys. Tax Policy and the Economy 17, 83–109.

Shea, J., 1995. Union contracts and the life-cycle/permanent-income hypothesis. The American Economic Review 85 (1), 186–200.

Shefrin, H.M., Thaler, R.H., 1988. The behavioral life-cycle hypothesis. Economic Inquiry 26 (4), 609–643.

Shiv, B., Fedorikhin, A., 1999. Heart and mind in conflict: the interplay of affect and cognition in consumer decision making. Journal of Consumer Research 26 (3), 278–292.

Shoda, Y., Mischel, W., Peake, P.K., 1990. Predicting adolescent cognitive and self-regulatory competencies from preschool delay of gratification: identifying diagnostic conditions. Developmental Psychology 26 (6), 978–986.

Shu, S., Gneezy, A., 2010. Procrastination of enjoyable experiences. Journal of Marketing Research 47, 933–944.

Simon, C.J., Warner, J.T., Pleeter, S., 2014. Discounting, cognition, and financial awareness: new evidence from a change in the military retirement system. Economic Inquiry 53 (1), 318–334.

Sisk, V.F., Burgoyne, A.P., Sun, J., Butler, J.L., Macnamara, B.N., 2018. To what extent and under which circumstances are growth mind-sets important to academic achievement? Two meta-analyses. Psychological Science 29 (4), 549–571.

Skiba, P.M., 2012. Regulation of payday loans: misguided? Washington and Lee Law Review 69 (2), 1023–1049.

Skiba, P.M., Tobacman, J., 2008. Payday Loans, Uncertainty and Discounting: Explaining Patterns of Borrowing, Repayment, and Default. Vanderbilt Law and Economics Research Paper No. 08-33. Available at https://doi.org/10.2139/ssrn.1319751.

Skinner, J., 2007. Are you sure you're saving enough for retirement? The Journal of Economic Perspectives 21 (3), 59–80.

Smith, A., 1759. The Theory of Moral Sentiments. A. Miller, A. Kincaid, and J. Bell, Strand and Edinburgh.

Solomon, L.J., Rothblum, E.D., 1984. Academic procrastination: frequency and cognitive-behavioral correlates. Journal of Counseling Psychology 31 (4), 503–509.

Sozou, P.D., 1998. On hyperbolic discounting and uncertain hazard rates. Proceedings of the Royal Society B: Biological Sciences 265 (1409), 2015–2020.

Sprenger, C., 2015. Judging experimental evidence on dynamic inconsistency. American Economic Review 105 (5), 280–285.

Stango, V., Zinman, J., 2009. Exponential growth bias and household finance. The Journal of Finance 64 (6), 2807–2849.

Stavins, J., 2000. Credit card borrowing, delinquency, and personal bankruptcy. New England Economic Review 2000 (July/August), 15–30.

Steele, C.M., Josephs, R.A., 1990. Alcohol myopia: its prized and dangerous effects. The American Psychologist 45 (8), 921–933.

Stephens, M., 2003. '3rd of tha month': do social security recipients smooth consumption between checks? The American Economic Review 93 (1), 406–422.

Stephens Jr., M., Toohey, D., 2018. Changes in Nutrient Intake at Retirement. National Bureau of Economic Research Working Paper No. 24621.

Stern, N., 2007. The Economics of Climate Change: The Stern Review. Cambridge University Press, Cambridge.

Stern, N., 2008. The economics of climate change. The American Economic Review 98 (2), 1–37.

Stevenson, B., Wolfers, J., 2013. Subjective well-being and income: is there any evidence of satiation? The American Economic Review 103 (3), 598–604.

Strotz, R.H., 1955. Myopia and inconsistency in dynamic utility maximization. The Review of Economic Studies 23 (3), 165–180.

Sugden, R., 2004. The opportunity criterion: consumer sovereignty without the assumption of coherent preferences. The American Economic Review 94, 1014–1033.

Sutter, M., Kocher, M.G., Glätzle-Rüetzler, D., Trautmann, S.T., 2013. Impatience and uncertainty: experimental decisions predict adolescents' field behavior. The American Economic Review 103 (1), 510–531.

Takahashi, T., 2005. Loss of self-control in intertemporal choice may be attributable to logarithmic time-perception. Medical Hypotheses 65 (4), 691–693.

Taubinsky, D., 2014. From Intentions to Actions: A Model and Experimental Evidence of Inattentive Choice. Working Paper.

Thakral, N., Tô, L., 2017. Daily Labor Supply and Adaptive Reference Points. Working Paper.

Thaler, R., 1981. Some empirical evidence on dynamic inconsistency. Economics Letters 8 (3), 201–207.

Thaler, R.H., Shefrin, H.M., 1981. An economic theory of self-control. Journal of Political Economy 89 (2), 392–406.

Thaler, R.H., Sunstein, C.R., 2008. Nudge: Improving Decisions about Health, Wealth, and Happiness. Yale University Press.

Thornton, R.L., 2008. The demand for, and impact of, learning HIV status. The American Economic Review 98 (5), 1829–1863.

Toussaert, S., 2018. Eliciting temptation and self-control through menu choices: a lab experiment. Econometrica 86 (5), 859–889.

Tsukayama, E., Duckworth, A.L., 2010. Domain-specific temporal discounting and temptation. Judgment and Decision Making 5 (2), 72–82.

Ubfal, D., 2016. How general are time preferences? Eliciting good-specific discount rates. Journal of Development Economics 118, 150–170.

Warner, J.T., Pleeter, S., 2001. The personal discount rate: evidence from military downsizing programs. The American Economic Review 91 (1), 33–53.

Watts, T.W., Duncan, G.J., Quan, H., 2018. Revisiting the marshmallow test: a conceptual replication investigating links between early delay of gratification and later outcomes. Psychological Science 29 (7), 1159–1177.

Weber, B.J., Chapman, G.B., 2005. The combined effects of risk and time on choice: does uncertainty eliminate the immediacy effect? Does delay eliminate the certainty effect? Organizational Behavior and Human Decision Processes 96 (2), 104–118.

Weber, E.U., Johnson, E.J., Milch, K.F., Changwong, H., Brodscholl, J.C., Goldstein, D.G., 2007. Asymmetric discounting in intertemporal choice: a query-theory account. Psychological Science 18 (6), 516–523.

Weil, P., 1990. Nonexpected utility in macroeconomics. The Quarterly Journal of Economics 105 (1), 29–42.

Weitzman, M., 2001. Gamma discounting. The American Economic Review 91 (1), 260–271.

Wertenbroch, K., 1998. Consumption self-control by rationing purchase quantities of virtue and vice. Marketing Science 17 (4), 317–337.

Wong, W., 2008. How much time-inconsistency is there and does it matter? Evidence of self-awareness, size, and effects. Journal of Economic Behavior & Organization 68 (3–4), 645–656.

Wulff, D.U., van den Bos, W., 2017. Modelling choices in delay discounting. Psychological Science 29 (11), 1890–1894.

Yeager, D.S., Hanselman, P., Paunesku, D., Hulleman, C., Dweck, C., Muller, C., et al., 2018. Where and for Whom Can a Brief, Scalable Mindset Intervention Improve Adolescents' Educational Trajectories? PsyArXiv Working Paper. https://doi.org/10.31234/osf.io/md2qa.

Zauberman, G., Kim, B.K., Malkoc, S.A., Bettman, J.R., 2009. Discounting time and time discounting: subjective time perception and intertemporal preferences. Journal of Marketing Research 46 (4), 543–556. https://doi.org/10.1509/jmkr.46.4.543.

Zinman, J., 2015. Household debt: facts, puzzles, theories, and policies. Annual Review of Economics 7, 251–276.

Errors in probabilistic reasoning and judgment biases

Daniel J. Benjamin[a,b,c]

[a]*University of Southern California, Los Angeles, CA, United States of America*
[b]*National Bureau of Economic Research, Cambridge, MA, United States of America*
e-mail address: daniel.benjamin@gmail.com

Contents

[c] For helpful comments, I am grateful to Andreas Aristidou, Nick Barberis, Maya Bar-Hillel, Pedro Bordalo, Colin Camerer, Christopher Chabris, Gary Charness, Samantha Cherney, James Choi, Bob Clemen, Alexander Coutts, Chetan Dave, Angus Deaton, Juan Dubra, Craig Fox, Nicola Gennaioli, Tom Gilovich, David Grether, Zack Grossman, Ori Heffetz, Jon Kleinberg, Lawrence Jin, Annie Liang, Chuck Manski, Josh Miller, Don Moore, Ted O'Donoghue, Jeff Naecker, Collin Raymond, Alex Rees-Jones, Rebecca Royer, Adam Sanjurjo, Josh Schwartzstein, Tali Sharot, Andrei Shleifer, Josh Tasoff, Richard Thaler, Joël van der Weele, George Wu, Basit Zafar, Chen Zhao, Daniel Zizzo, conference participants at the 2016 Stanford Institute for Theoretical Economics, and the editors of this Handbook, Doug Bernheim, Stefano DellaVigna, and David Laibson. I am grateful to Matthew Rabin for extremely valuable conversations about the topics in this chapter over many years. I thank Peter Bowers, Ruoxi Li, Rebecca Royer, and especially Tushar Kundu for outstanding research assistance.

1 Introduction

Probabilistic beliefs are central to decision-making under risk. Therefore, systematic errors in probabilistic reasoning can matter for the many economic decisions that involve risk, including investing for retirement, purchasing insurance, starting a business, and searching for goods, jobs, or workers. This chapter reviews what psychologists and economists have learned about such systematic errors. At the cost of some precision, throughout this chapter I will use the term *belief biases* as shorthand for "errors in probabilistic reasoning." By *bias*, in this chapter I will mean any deviation from correct reasoning about probabilities or Bayesian updating.[1]

This chapter's area of research—which is often called "judgment under uncertainty" or "heuristics and biases" in psychology—was introduced by the psychologist

---

[1] My use of the same term "bias" for all of these deviations is not meant to obscure the distinctions between them in terms of their psychological origins. For example, the gambler's fallacy (the belief that heads is likely to be followed by tails; Section 2.1) is a mistaken mental model of independent random processes, while Non-Belief in the Law of Large Numbers (the belief that the distribution of a sample mean is independent of sample size; Section 3.2) is a failure to understand or apply a deep statistical principle. These differences can matter, for example, for who makes the errors, under what circumstances, and the likelihood that interventions could reduce the bias.

Ward Edwards and his students and colleagues in the 1960s (e.g., Phillips and Edwards, 1966). This topic was the starting point of the collaboration between Daniel Kahneman and Amos Tversky. Their seminal early papers (e.g., Tversky and Kahneman, 1971, 1974) jump-started an enormous literature in psychology and influenced thinking in many other disciplines, including economics.

Despite so much work by psychologists and despite being one of the original topics of modern behavioral economics, to date belief biases have received less attention from behavioral economists than time, risk, and social preferences. Belief biases have also made few inroads in applied economic research, with the important exception of behavioral finance (see Chapters "Psychology-Based Models of Asset Prices and Trading Volume" (by Barberis) and "Behavioral Corporate Finance" (by Malmendier) of this Handbook). I suspect that is because in many available datasets, beliefs have been unobserved. But today, datasets are becoming much more plentiful, and it is easier than ever to collect one's own data. Therefore in my view, the relative lack of attention paid to belief biases makes them an especially exciting area of research, rife with opportunities for innovative work. For some topics in this chapter, particularly beliefs about random sequences (Section 2) and prior-biased updating (Section 8), the body of evidence and theory is relatively mature. For these topics, the biases could be fairly straightforwardly incorporated into applied economic models or explored in new empirical settings. For other topics, such as many aspects of beliefs about sample distributions (Section 3) and features of biased inference (Section 5), there are basic questions about what the facts are and how to model them that remain poorly addressed. For those topics, careful experimental work and modeling could fundamentally reshape how these biases are understood.

This chapter has three specific goals. First, I have tried to organize the topics in a natural way for economists. For example, I review biased beliefs about random samples before discussing biased inferences because, according to the standard model in economics, beliefs about random samples are a building block for inference. I hope that this organization will facilitate more systematic study of the biases and integration into economics.

Second and relatedly, I have tried to highlight when and how different biases may be related to each other. For example, some of the biases about random samples may underlie some of the biases about inferences. Sometimes, belief biases are presented in a way that makes them seem like an unmanageable laundry list of unrelated items. By emphasizing possible connections, I hope to point researchers in the direction of a smaller number of unifying principles. At the same time, I have tried to highlight when different biases may push in opposite directions or even jointly imply logically inconsistent beliefs, cases which raise interesting challenges for modeling and applications.

Third, I have tried to convey how much evidence there is for (and against) each putative bias. Often, papers focused on a particular bias review existing evidence somewhat selectively. While it is impossible to be comprehensive, and while I have surely missed papers inadvertently, for each topic I attempted to find as many papers as I could that provide relevant evidence from both economics and psychology. In some cases, I was surprised by what I learned. For example, as discussed in Section 4, the evidence overwhelmingly indicates that people tend to infer too little from signals rather than too much, even from small samples of signals. Another example is discussed in Section 9: while discussions of the literature often take for granted that people update their beliefs more in response to good news than bad news, and while the psychology research is nearly unanimously supportive, the evidence from experimental economics taken as a whole is actually rather muddy, and it leaves me puzzled as to whether and under what circumstances there is an asymmetry.

For each bias, in addition to discussing the most compelling evidence for and against it, which is usually from laboratory experiments, I also try to highlight the most persuasive field evidence and existing models of the bias. While I mention modeling challenges as they arise, I return in Section 10 to briefly discuss some of the challenges common to many of the belief biases.

Due to space constraints, I cannot cover all belief biases, or even most of them.[2] The biases I focus on all relate to beliefs about random samples and belief updating. I chose these topics because they are core issues for most applications of decision making under risk, they allow the chapter to tell a fairly coherent narrative, and some of them have not been well covered in other recent reviews. In addition, admittedly, this chapter is tilted toward topics I am more familiar with.

An especially major omission from this chapter is *overconfidence*, which is probably the most widely studied belief distortion in economics to date and is discussed at some length in Chapters "Psychology-Based Models of Asset Prices and Trading Volume" (by Barberis) and "Behavioral Corporate Finance" (by Malmendier) of this Handbook. The term "overconfidence" is unfortunately used to refer to several distinct biases—and for the sake of clarity, I advocate adopting terminology that distinguishes between distinct meanings. One meaning is *overprecision*, a bias toward beliefs that are too certain (for reviews, see Lichtenstein et al., 1982, and Moore et al., 2015). Relatedly, the biased belief that one's own signal is more precise than others' signals has been argued to be important for understanding trading in financial markets (e.g., Daniel et al., 1998), as well as for social learning and voting; this bias is discussed in Chapter "Errors in Strategic Reasoning" (by Eyster) of this Handbook, which addresses biases in beliefs about other people.[3] Another meaning is *overop-*

---

[2] Moreover, because this chapter is organized around specific biases, it omits discussion of related work that is less tightly connected to the psychological evidence. For example, Barberis et al. (1998) is among the seminal papers that incorporated belief biases into an economic model. Yet it is only barely mentioned in this chapter because its core assumption—that stocks switch between a mean-reverting state and a positively autocorrelated state—does not fit neatly with the evidence on people's general beliefs about i.i.d. processes (described in Section 2).

[3] While the key feature of this bias is the *relative* precision of one's own versus others' signals, models of the bias typically assume that agents believe that their own signal is more precise than it is, and therefore agents overinfer from their own signal. Relevantly for such models, the evidence reviewed in Section 4 of this chapter indicates that people generally *underinfer* rather than overinfer (see also Section 10.1). Therefore, it would be more realistic to assume that agents underinfer from their own signal, even if they believe that others observe less precise signals (and thus infer even less than they do).

timism, a bias toward beliefs that are too favorable to oneself (a classic early paper is Weinstein, 1980; for a review, see Windschitl and O'Rourke, 2015). Although I do not discuss overoptimism in this chapter, biases in belief updating, in particular those reviewed in Sections 5.1, 6, and 8, are relevant to how overoptimistic beliefs are maintained in the face of evidence. A closely related omission is *motivated beliefs*, an important class of biases related to having preferences over beliefs (a classic review is Kunda, 1990; for a recent review, see Bénabou and Tirole, 2016). While I do not discuss the broad literature on motivated beliefs, preference-biased updating (reviewed in Section 9) is considered to be one potential mechanism that helps people end up with the beliefs they want.

Other omissions from this chapter include: *vividness bias*, according to which hearing an experience described more vividly, or experiencing it oneself, may cause it to have a greater impact on one's beliefs (e.g., Nisbett and Ross, 1980; an early review is Taylor and Thompson, 1982, which concludes that the evidence is not strong; for a recent meta-analysis, see Blondé and Girandola, 2016); and *hindsight bias*, according to which, ex post, people overestimate how much they and others knew ex ante (Fischhoff, 1975; for a recent review, see Roese and Vohs, 2012, and for an economic model, see Madarász, 2012). I do not review the evidence on how people draw inferences from samples about population means, proportions, variances, and correlations (for reviews, see Peterson and Beach, 1967; Juslin et al., 2007).[4] I also do not cover the *availability heuristic*, according to which judgments about the likelihood of an event is influenced by how easily examples or instances come to mind (Tversky and Kahneman, 1974; for a review, see Schwarz and Vaughn, 2002), but Gennaioli and Shleifer's (2010) model of representativeness, discussed in Section 7.3 of this chapter, is related to it.

Although some of the biases in this chapter might be understood as people not paying attention to relevant aspects of a judgment problem, I do not review the literature on inattention since that is the focus of Chapter "Behavioral Inattention" (by Gabaix) of this Handbook. I also do not at all address biases in probabilistic beliefs about other people or their behavior. Many of those biases are covered in Chapter "Errors in Strategic Reasoning" (by Eyster) of this Handbook. However, in Section 10 of this chapter, I briefly mention some of the modeling challenges that arise when applying the biases discussed here in environments with strategic interaction.

I will also not separately discuss the sprawling literature on *debiasing*—which refers to interventions designed to reduce biases—although some of this work will come up in the context of specific biases. Debiasing strategies come in three forms (Roy and Lerch, 1996): (i) modifying the presentation of a problem to elicit the appropriate mental procedure; (ii) training people to think correctly about a problem;

---

[4] Recent work in this vein has concluded that people tend to overlook selection biases and treat sample statistics as unbiased estimators of population statistics (Juslin et al., 2007). Much of the economics research on errors in strategic reasoning has focused on such failure to account for selection bias (see Chapter "Errors in Strategic Reasoning" (by Eyster) of this Handbook). In the experimental economics literature, Enke (2017) recently explored this error in a non-strategic setting.

and (iii) doing the calculations for people, so that they merely need to provide the inputs to the calculations. The classic review is Fischhoff (1982), and a more recent review is Ludolph and Schulz (2017). Some recent work has suggested that instructional games may be more effective than traditional training methods at persistent debiasing that generalizes across decision making contexts (Morewedge et al., 2015).

While I mention throughout the chapter when belief elicitation was incentivized, I do not discuss the literature on how to elicit beliefs in an incentive-compatible way. For a recent review, see Schotter and Trevino (2014).

There are a number of literature reviews that partially overlap the material covered in this chapter. Some of these are oriented around belief updating and are therefore similar to this chapter in terms of topics covered (Peterson and Beach, 1967; Edwards, 1968; DuCharme, 1969; Slovic and Lichtenstein, 1971; Grether, 1978; Fischhoff and Beyth-Marom, 1983). Others are reviews of the behavioral decision research literature more broadly that have substantial sections devoted to biases in probabilistic beliefs (Rapoport and Wallsten, 1972; Camerer, 1995; Rabin, 1998; DellaVigna, 2009). Relative to this chapter, Dhami (2017, Part VII, Chapter 1) is a textbook-style treatment that covers a much broader range of judgment biases but in less depth. This chapter builds on and updates these earlier reviews. For the biases it addresses, this chapter aims to broadly cover the available evidence from both psychology and economics with an eye toward formal modeling and incorporation into economic analyses.

The chapter has five parts and is organized as follows. The first part examines biased beliefs about random processes: Section 2 is about sequences (e.g., a sequence of coin flips), and Section 3 is about sampling distributions (e.g., the number of heads out of ten flips). An overarching theme is that, while some biases about sampling-distribution beliefs seem to result from biases in beliefs about sequences, there are additional biases that are specific to sampling-distribution beliefs. The second part of the chapter examines biases in belief updating. On the basis of a review and meta-analysis of the experimental evidence, Section 4 lays out a set of stylized facts. The central lesson is that people underweight *both* the information from signals *and* their priors—errors that I refer to as underinference and base-rate neglect, respectively. Section 5 discusses the three main theories of underinference, and Section 6 discusses base-rate neglect. The third part of the chapter is Section 7, which focuses on the representativeness heuristic, generally considered to be a unifying theory for many of the biases discussed earlier in the chapter. I highlight that the representativeness heuristic has several distinct components and that efforts to formalize it have focused on one component at a time. At the end of the section, I reflect on the merits of modeling the representativeness heuristic as opposed to specific biases. The fourth part of the chapter examines interactions between biased updating and other features of the updating situation. Section 8 focuses on a type of confirmation bias I call "prior-biased updating," according to which people update less when the signal points toward the opposite hypothesis as their prior. Section 9 reviews the evidence on what I call "preference-biased updating," which posits that people update less when the signal favors their less-preferred hypothesis. The final part of the chapter is Section 10, which draws general lessons from the chapter as a whole, reflects on challenges in this area of research, advocates for connecting better to field evidence and other areas of economics, and highlights some possible directions for future work.

2 Biased beliefs about random sequences
2.1 The gambler's fallacy and the Law of Small Numbers

The *gambler's fallacy* (GF) refers to the mistaken belief that, in a sequence of signals known to be i.i.d., observing one signal reduces the likelihood of next observing that same signal. For example, people think that when a coin flip comes up heads, the next flip is more likely to come up tails.

The GF has long been observed among gamblers and is one of the oldest documented biases. Laplace (1814), who anticipated much of the literature on errors in probabilistic reasoning (Miller and Gelman, 2018), described people's belief that the fraction of boys and girls born each month must be roughly balanced, so that if more of one sex has been born, the other sex becomes more likely. The first systematic study of the GF was Alberoni (1962a, 1962b), who reported many experiments showing that, with i.i.d. binomial signals, people think a streak of a signals is less likely than a sequence with a mix of a and b signals.[5]

Rabin (2002) and Oskarsson et al. (2009) provided reviews of the extensive literature documenting the GF in surveys and experiments. While most of this evidence comes from undergraduate samples, Dohmen et al. (2009) surveyed a representative sample of the German population, asking about the probability of a head following the sequence TTTHTHHH. While 60% of the sample gave the correct answer of 50%, the GF was the dominant direction of bias, with 21% of the sample giving answers less than 50% and 9% of the sample giving answers greater than 50%.

Rabin (2002) pointed out ways in which some of the laboratory evidence is not fully compelling. For example, in experiments involving coin flips (or other 50–50 binomial signals) that ask participants to guess the next flip in a sequence, either guess has an equal chance of being correct. Moreover, many of the experiments are unincentivized. However, there have been experiments that address these concerns. For example, Benjamin et al. (2018b) conducted two incentivized experiments in which they elicited participants' beliefs about the probability of a head following streaks of

---

[5] Laplace (1814) and Alberoni (1962a, 1962b) both provided explanations of the GF that anticipated Tversky and Kahneman's (1971) theory, the Law of Small Numbers, which is discussed below. Specifically, Laplace conjectured that the GF results from misapplying the logic of sampling without replacement, which is exactly the intuition captured by Rabin's (2002) model of the Law of Small Numbers, also discussed below. Alberoni's "Principle of the Best Sample" is essentially a restatement of Tversky and Kahneman's description of the Law of Small Numbers: "[People believe that the most likely] sample is that which, without presenting a cyclic structure, reflects the composition of the system of expectations in the whole and in each of its parts" (Alberoni, 1962a, p. 253).

heads of each possible length up to 9. Like Dohmen et al., they found that the majority of reported beliefs were the correct answer of 50%, but the incorrect answers predominantly exhibited the GF. On average, their participants (undergraduates and a convenience sample of adults) assessed a 44% to 50% chance that a first flip would be a head but only a 32% to 37% chance that a flip following 9 heads would be a head.[6]

Most field evidence of behavior consistent with the GF is from gambling settings, such as dog- and horse-race betting (Metzger, 1985; Terrell and Farmer, 1996), roulette playing in casinos (Croson and Sundali, 2005), and lottery-ticket purchasing (e.g., Clotfelter and Cook, 1993; Terrell, 1994). For example, using individual-level administrative data from the Danish national lottery, Suetens et al. (2016) found that players placed roughly 2% fewer bets on numbers that won in the previous week.

Chen et al. (2016) examined three other field settings: judges' decisions in refugee asylum court, reviews of loan applications, and umpires' calls on baseball pitches. In all three settings, they found that decision making is negatively autocorrelated, controlling for case quality. For example, even though the quality of referee asylum cases appears to be serially uncorrelated conditional on observables, Chen et al. estimated that a judge is up to 3.3% more likely to deny asylum in the current case if she approved it in the previous case. To explain their findings, Chen et al. theorized that judges think of underlying case quality as an i.i.d. process and thus, due to the GF, when the previous case was (say) positive, the decision maker's prior belief about underlying case quality is negative for the next case. This prior belief then influences the decision in the next case. While Chen et al. persuasively ruled out a number of alternative explanations, they acknowledged that they cannot rule out "sequential contrast effects" (e.g., Pepitone and DiNubile, 1976; Simonsohn, 2006; Bhargava and Fisman, 2014), in which the decision maker's perception of (rather than belief about) case quality is influenced by the previous case.

A related literature in economics examines whether people randomize when playing a game that has a unique Nash equilibrium in mixed strategies. Equilibrium play requires that the sequence of actions be unpredictable and hence serially independent, but in laboratory games, experimental participants often alternate actions more often than they should (for a review, see Rapoport and Budescu, 1997). In the largest field study to date, Gauriot et al. (2016) analyzed data on half a million serves made by professional tennis players and find that players switch their direction too often (see

---

[6] Miller and Sanjurjo (2018) pointed out conditions under which GF-like beliefs are actually *correct* rather than being a bias. Specifically, fixing an i.i.d. sequence, say, a sequence of coin flips, and any streak length, they show that the (true) frequency of a head following a streak of heads *within that sequence* is less than 50%. Moreover, this frequency is decreasing in the streak length. Roughly speaking, the reason is that the expected frequency of heads in the entire sequence is 50%, so knowing that some of the flips are heads makes it more likely that the others are tails. Miller and Sanjurjo's result, however, is not relevant for much of the evidence on the GF. For example, Dohmen et al. and Benjamin, Moore, and Rabin asked about the probability of a head following a specific sequence of flips, questions for which the correct answer is always 50%. Miller and Sanjurjo's result *is* relevant for evidence of the hot-hand bias, however, as discussed in Section 2.2.

also Walker and Wooders, 2001; Hsu et al., 2007). This excessive switching could reflect the mistaken GF intuition for what random sequences look like.

As an explanation of the GF, Tversky and Kahneman (1971) proposed that "people view a sample randomly drawn from a population as highly representative, that is, similar to the population in all essential characteristics" (p. 105). They called this mistaken intuition a belief in the *Law of Small Numbers* (LSN), a tongue-in-cheek name which conveys the idea that people believe that the Law of *Large* Numbers applies also to small samples.[7] Tversky and Kahneman highlighted two implications of the LSN. First, it generates the GF: after (say) a streak of heads, a tail is needed to ensure that the overall sequence reflects the unbiasedness of the coin. Second, belief in the LSN should cause people to infer too much from small samples.

There is very little evidence in support of the latter prediction. The evidence Tversky and Kahneman presented was from surveys of academic psychologists showing that they underestimate sampling variation and expect statistically significant results obtained in small samples to replicate at unrealistically high rates. For example, they described to their survey respondents an experiment with 15 participants that obtained a statistically significant result ($p < 0.05$) with $t = 2.46$. If a subsequent experiment with 15 more participants obtained a statistically insignificant result in the same direction with $t = 1.70$, most of Tversky and Kahneman's respondents said they would view that result as a "failure to replicate"—even though the second result is more plausibly viewed as supportive. However, as Oakes (1986) discussed, the interpretation of this evidence in terms of the LSN is confounded by other errors in understanding statistics, including a heuristic of treating results that cross the statistical significance threshold as much more likely to reflect "true" effects than they do. In additional surveys of academic psychologists, Oakes found that his respondents exhibited similar overinference from statistically significant results obtained in larger samples, indicating that the misinterpretations are not specific to small samples. Moreover, as discussed in Section 4 of this chapter, the experimental evidence on inference taken as a whole suggests that even in small samples, people generally *underinfer* rather than overinfer.

Rabin (2002) proposed a formal model of the LSN (see also Rapoport and Budescu, 1997, for a model of the belief that i.i.d. processes tend to alternate). Signals are known to be drawn i.i.d., with a signals having rate θ and b signals having rate $1 - \theta$. Because the agent is a believer in the LSN, she forms beliefs as if the signals are drawn *without replacement* from an urn of finite size M containing θM a signals (where θM is assumed to be an integer). The model directly generates the GF: after (say) an a signal is drawn, there is one fewer a signal in the urn, so the probability that the next signal is a is $\dfrac{\theta M - 1}{M - 1}$, which is smaller than θ.

---

[7] To help flesh out the LSN, Bar-Hillel (1982) directly asked experimental participants to judge the "representativeness" of different samples. She found that their judgments were influenced by a variety of factors. For example, a sample was judged to be more representative if its mean matched the population mean and if none of the sample observations were repeats.

When the true rate is unknown and must be inferred by the agent, the model implies that the agent will err in the direction of overinference, ending up with a posterior belief that is too extreme. For example, suppose there are two states of the world: in state A, the rate of a signals is high (θ_A), whereas in state B, it is low ($\theta_B < \theta_A$). The agent thinks the probability of aa is $\pi(aa|A) = \theta_A \cdot \left(\frac{\theta_A M - 1}{M - 1} \right)$ if the state is A and $\pi(aa|B) = \theta_B \cdot \left(\frac{\theta_B M - 1}{M - 1} \right)$ if the state is B. While the agent thinks the streak aa is less likely than it is regardless of the state, the agent thinks it is especially unlikely in state B since $\frac{\pi(aa|B)}{\pi(aa|A)} < \left(\frac{\theta_B}{\theta_A} \right)^2$. Consequently, the agent interprets aa as stronger evidence in favor of state A than it truly is. In Rabin's example, if the agent thinks an average fund manager has a 50% chance of success in each year, then he thinks a manager with two consecutive successful years is less likely to be average than she is.[8]

This overinference in turn implies that, when the agent observes a small number of signals from many sources, she exaggerates the amount of variation in rates across sources. For example, suppose all fund managers are average, and the agent observes the last two years of performance for many managers. Because the agent underestimates how often average managers will have consecutive good or bad years, she will think the number of fund managers with such consecutive years is inconsistent with all managers being average and will instead conclude that there must be a mix of good and bad managers.

This model is useful for straightforwardly elucidating this and other basic implications of belief in the LSN. However, Rabin highlights that the model has artificial features that limit its suitability for many applications; for example, since the urn only contains M signals, the urn must be "renewed" at some point in order for the model to make predictions about sequences longer than length M. To address these limitations, Rabin and Vayanos (2010) introduced a more generally applicable model of belief in the LSN (see also Teguia, 2017, for a related model in a portfolio-choice setting).

While both the Rabin (2002) and Rabin and Vayanos (2010) models describe the GF, they do not fully capture the psychology of the LSN that *any* sample should be representative of the population. Benjamin et al. (2018b) illustrated this point in an experiment regarding beliefs about coin flips. They generated a million sequences of a million coin flips and had participants make incentivized guesses about how often different outcomes occurred. In some questions, they randomly chose a location in the sequence (e.g., the 239,672nd flip out of the 1 million) and asked participants to guess how often, when there had been a streak of 1, 2, or 5 consecutive heads at that

---

[8] Although Rabin's (2002) model generates both the GF and overinference, given the lack of evidence for the latter, it is worth noting that overinference does not necessarily follow from the belief in the GF. The GF for a signals entails that $\pi(a|a, A) < \pi(a|A)$ and $\pi(a|a, B) < \pi(a|B)$. Overinference after two a signals entails that $\frac{\pi(a|a, A)}{\pi(a|a, B)} < \frac{\pi(a|A)}{\pi(a|B)}$, but this is not implied by the GF inequalities.

location, the next flip was a head. Participants' mean probabilities were 44%, 41%, and 39%, consistent with the GF. In other questions, Benjamin, Moore, and Rabin randomly chose 1, 2, or 5 *non-consecutive* flip locations in the sequence at random and asked participants to guess how often, when all of these flips had been heads, another randomly chosen flip would be a head. Participants' mean probabilities—45%, 42%, and 41%—were nearly the same as those for consecutive flips. Since these flips are non-consecutive, the Rabin (2002) and Rabin and Vayanos (2010) models do not predict any GF. In fact, Benjamin et al. proved that whenever a sequence of flip *locations* is chosen i.i.d., the resulting sequence of flips must be i.i.d. regardless of whether the flips themselves are serially dependent. Therefore, *no* model of the LSN in which an agent's beliefs are internally consistent could explain why people expect negative autocorrelation in flips from random locations. Section 10.2 of this chapter contains a brief general discussion of some of the conceptual and modeling challenges raised by belief biases that generate internally inconsistent beliefs.

2.2 The hot-hand bias

The term *hot hand* comes from basketball. A basketball player is said to have a hot hand when she is temporarily better than usual at making her shots. The term has come to be used more generally to describe a random process in which outcomes sometimes enter a "hot" state and have temporarily higher probability than normal. Much of the literature is framed as testing whether people suffer from the *hot-hand fallacy*, a belief in the hot hand when the random process is actually i.i.d. In light of evidence (discussed below) that there truly is a hot hand in settings such as basketball, Miller and Sanjurjo (2015) introduced the more general term *hot-hand bias* to refer to a mistaken belief about the degree to which there is a hot hand. I will use the term "hot-hand bias" to mean that people believe a random process has more of a hot hand than it does, regardless of whether the process actually has a hot hand. An agent with the bias will have an exaggerated expectation that a streak of an outcome will continue because a streak is indicative that the outcome is hot.

The cleanest evidence for hot-hand bias comes from settings where people believe in a hot hand even though the outcomes are known to be i.i.d.—the case referred to above as the "hot-hand fallacy." For example, as pointed out originally by Laplace (1814), lottery players place more bets on numbers that have won repeatedly in the recent past, implying that they mistakenly believe in a hot hand (e.g., Suetens et al., 2016; see Croson and Sundali, 2005, for evidence from roulette, and Camerer, 1989, and Brown and Sauer, 1993, for evidence from sports betting markets). This bias appears prima facie to be the opposite of the GF because the GF says that numbers that won recently are believed to be *less* likely to win again. Empirically, Suetens et al. (2016) found evidence for both: after a lottery number won once, players bet less on it, but when a streak of two or more wins occurred, players bet more the longer the streak. Theoretically, Gilovich et al. (1985) and others have argued not only that the two biases co-exist but that the hot-hand bias is a consequence of the GF: to someone who suffers from the GF, an i.i.d. process looks like it has too many streaks, so a belief in the hot hand arises to explain the apparent excess of streaks.

Rabin and Vayanos (2010) formally developed this argument that hand-hand bias can arise from belief in the GF. Rabin and Vayanos assumed that an agent dogmatically believes that one component of the process is negatively correlated, as per the GF, but puts positive probability (even if very small) on the possibility that the process has a hot hand. After observing an i.i.d. process for a sufficiently long time and updating Bayesianly about the probability of a hot state, the agent will come to believe with certainty that there is a hot state. With the resulting combined GF/hot-hand beliefs, the agent will expect high-frequency negative autocorrelation, but will expect positive autocorrelation once a long enough streak has occurred. Applying their model to investors' beliefs about i.i.d. stock returns, Rabin and Vayanos argued that it explains several puzzles in finance, such as why investors believe that stock returns are partially predictable and hence active mutual fund managers can outperform the stock market.

This theory of hot-hand bias arising from and coexisting with the GF is consistent with several observations. First, Suetens et al.'s (2016) evidence mentioned above—that lottery players bet less on a number after it comes up once but more after a streak—fits the theory nicely. Moreover, Suetens et al. (2016) found that the lottery players exhibiting the hot-hand bias also tend to be those exhibiting the GF. However, Dillon and Lybbert (2018) interpret the evidence from different lottery data, as well as the evidence in Suetens et al., as indicating that most lottery players exhibit *only* the GF, with the observation of hot-hand bias driven by a small minority who bet on the most recently drawn number. Second, Asparouhova et al. (2009) found that when experimental participants are asked to predict the next outcome of a process and are not informed that the process is i.i.d., they predict reversals of single outcomes and continuation of streaks, again the pattern implied by the theory. Finally, for random processes whose i.i.d. nature is arguably well understood by people (such as coin flips and roulette spins), the GF is by far the dominant belief. For example, as mentioned in Section 2.1, Benjamin et al. (2018b) asked participants the probability of a head following streaks of different lengths up to 9 heads and found that the perceived likelihood of a head is declining monotonically in the length of the streak. The theory of hot-hand bias arising from the GF implies that for a random process where people put near-zero prior probability on the existence of the hot hand, the hot-hand bias should *not* arise—unless people observe the process for a very long time. Consistent with this, over 1000 draws of binary i.i.d. processes, Edwards (1961a) found that experimental participants predicted reversals of streaks for the first 200 draws (see also Lindman and Edwards, 1961) but continuation of streaks for the last 600 draws.

On the other hand, Guryan and Kearney's (2008) finding of a "lucky store effect" may be a challenging observation for the theory. In data on weekly lottery drawings from Texas, they found that stores that sold a winning ticket sold substantially more tickets in subsequent weeks, with the effect persisting for up to 40 weeks. This seems to be a case of hot-hand bias without the GF. As a possible reconciliation with the theory, Guryan and Kearney speculated that in this context, lottery players might have a strong prior on a hot hand, for example, because of a belief in the store clerk's karma.

In the psychology literature, a variety of factors have been proposed to explain when the GF versus hot-hand bias occurs (Oskarsson et al., 2009). For example, Ayton and Fischer (2004) found that experimental participants anticipated negative autocorrelation in roulette spins but positive autocorrelation for successes in human prediction of the outcomes of roulette spins. They proposed that the GF dominates for natural processes, whereas the hot-hand bias dominates when human performance is involved (see also Caruso et al., 2010). While this theory cannot explain evidence of the GF after a single outcome and the hot-hand bias after a streak as in Suetens et al. (2016), it is complementary with Rabin and Vayanos's model insofar as it provides a theory to explain people's prior probability of a hot hand, which is taken as exogenous in Rabin and Vayanos's model.

Much of the field evidence on the hot hand comes from professional sports. Identifying a hot-hand bias in such settings is tricky because sports performance is typically *not* i.i.d. Since confidence, anxiety, focus, and fatigue vary over time, a true hot hand is plausible, as is its opposite, a cold hand. Yet accurately estimating the magnitude of a true hot hand in performance is itself challenging for several reasons, including that performance affects outcomes only probabilistically (Stone, 2012) and that endogenous responses by the other team may counteract positive autocorrelation in a player's performance (e.g., Rao, 2009). Bar-Eli et al. (2006) reviewed the sizeable literature testing for a true hot hand in a variety of sports.

Gilovich et al.'s (1985) seminal paper introducing the hot-hand fallacy focused on the context of basketball. The paper attracted a lot of attention because it made a surprising empirical claim: contrary to strongly held beliefs of fans, players, and coaches, there is *not* a hot hand in basketball. Gilovich et al. made this claim on the basis of evidence from three studies. First, they analyzed the shot records of 9 players from a National Basketball Association (NBA) team over a season and found no evidence of positive autocorrelation for any of the players. Second, they analyzed the free-throw records of 9 players from another NBA team and, again, found no evidence of autocorrelation. Finally, they ran a shooting experiment with 26 collegiate basketball players and found evidence of positive autocorrelation for only one player. They also found, in incentivized bets, that both shooters and observers expected positive autocorrelation, but in fact neither shooters nor observers could predict the shooters' performance better than chance. From the contrast between the widespread belief in the hot hand and the absence of it in the data, Gilovich et al. inferred that beliefs are biased. Subsequent work replicated and extended Gilovich et al.'s findings (e.g., Koehler and Conley, 2003; Avugos et al., 2013).

Miller and Sanjurjo (2014, 2017) recently identified a subtle statistical bias in earlier analyses that overturns the conclusion of no hot hand in basketball. Put simply, Gilovich et al. and others had inferred that there is no true hot hand because the empirical frequency of making a second shot in a row, $\hat{p}$(hit|hit), is roughly equal to the unconditional frequency of making a shot, $\hat{p}$(hit). While the details vary with the statistical method, roughly speaking, $\hat{p}$(hit|hit) is estimated as the ratio of two empirical frequencies: $\hat{p}$(hit then hit)$/\hat{p}$(hit). But when making shots is i.i.d., $\hat{p}$(hit then hit) and $\hat{p}$(hit) are positively correlated in a finite sample. Consequently, $\hat{p}$(hit|hit) is biased downward relative to the true conditional probability, p(hit|hit) (as explained by Rinott and Bar-Hillel, 2015, in a comment on an earlier version of Miller and Sanjurjo, 2018). Thus, the evidence that $\hat{p}$(hit|hit) is roughly equal to $\hat{p}$(hit) implies that the *true* probability p(hit|hit) is actually greater than p(hit). In re-analyses of earlier data, Miller and Sanjurjo (2014, 2017) found that this bias is substantial. Correcting for the bias, they concluded that there is evidence for a hot hand in basketball. In a new shooting experiment with many more shots per participant, Miller and Sanjurjo (2014) again concluded that many players have a hot hand. Miller and Sanjurjo (2017) re-analyzed Gilovich et al.'s betting data, pooling across bettors to increase power, and concluded that overall, the bettors *did* predict shooters' performance better than chance. By showing that there is a hot hand, these new analyses and evidence re-opens—but does not answer—what is, in my view, the key question: whether there is a hot-hand *bias* in basketball, i.e., a belief in a stronger hot hand than there really is.

In two other sports, recent papers found both a true hot hand and evidence for a bias. Among Major League Baseball players, Green and Zwiebel (2017) found that recent performance predicts subsequent performance for both batters and pitchers, and the magnitudes are substantial (although the analysis did not control for player-ballpark interaction effects, which can be important in baseball). However, pitchers overreact to recent good performance by batters, indicating that they believe that the hot hand is stronger than it is. For example, they walk batters who have recently been hitting home runs more than can be justified based on the batters' hot hand. Among players in the World Darts Championship, Jin (2018) found a substantial hot hand but also found that players' willingness to take a high-risk/high-reward shot increases by more than it should in light of their hot hand.

Intriguingly, Stone and Arkes (2018) found that the committee of experts that seeds collegiate basketball teams into the "March Madness" tournament *underreacts* to momentum heading into the tournament—which is the opposite of the hot-hand bias. Stone and Arkes argue that their evidence is most consistent with the committee not appreciating the predictive value of recent performance. It is not clear how to reconcile this finding with evidence from other contexts of hot-hand bias or of base-rate neglect (as discussed in Section 6).

2.3 Additional biases in beliefs about random sequences

Almost all research on beliefs about random sequences have focused on the LSN and the hot-hand bias, and as discussed in Section 2.2 above, for purely mechanical random processes such as coin flips, the LSN is the relevant bias. Kleinberg et al. (2017) have found, however, that (current models of) the LSN provides far from a complete theory of people's perceptions about random sequences. Kleinberg et al. asked 471 online experimental participants to generate 25 random sequences of 8 coin flips. Using the empirical frequencies calculated from this large number ($471 \times 25 = 11,775$) of 8-flip sequences, Kleinberg et al. generated the (approximately) optimal prediction of the probability that participants will generate a head on the next flip after any given sequence of fewer than 8 flips. They also used the experimental data to estimate the parameters of the Rabin (2002) and Rabin and Vayanos (2010) models of the LSN, and then they generated predictions from the estimated models. In an independent validation sample, they compared the predictive success of the models with that of the optimal prediction. They found that the models achieved no more than 15% of the reduction in mean squared error (relative to random guessing) attained by the optimal prediction. This finding implies that there are additional systematic biases in people's beliefs about coin flips beyond what is captured in current models of the LSN.[9]

This intriguing result raises two further questions that remain largely unresolved. First, is the remainder of the potentially attainable predictive power (the other 85%) comprised of biases that are as predictive or more predictive of people's beliefs as the LSN, or is it comprised of many "minor" biases, each of which individually has very little predictive power? If the latter, then the benefit from identifying and modeling any given additional bias may not be worth the opportunity cost of investing research resources elsewhere.

Second, are these other biases generalizable across domains—as the LSN is—or are they specific to this setting (e.g., to coin flips)? If the latter, then again, the benefit from identifying the biases may be small. Kleinberg et al. provide some evidence on the generalizability question, showing that the optimal predictions from the 8-flip data continue to perform well when applied to 7-flip data and to i.i.d. sequences using a different alphabet than H and T.

Despite the open questions, Kleinberg et al.'s results nonetheless should make us humble about our current state of knowledge and raise the possibility that the payoffs to discovering the nature of the additional biases could be substantial.

3 Biased beliefs about sampling distributions

Throughout this chapter, I will use the term *sampling distribution* to refer the distribution of the *number* of a and b signals. For example, for a sample of size 2, the sampling distribution specifies the probabilities of three events: 0 a's and 2 b's, 1 a and 1 b, and 2 a's and 0 b's.

---

[9] Is 15% of the way toward the optimal prediction large or small? The performance of other economic models provide a natural benchmark. While Kleinberg et al.'s analysis has not yet been carried out for other models, related exercises have been conducted. Using laboratory data on choices under risk and ambiguity, Peysakhovich and Naecker (2017) compared the mean squared error of predictions made by existing economic models with that of predictions made by machine learning algorithms (trained on the same laboratory data used to estimate the models). They found that the probability-weighting model achieved *all* of the predictive gains of the machine learning algorithms, whereas models of ambiguity aversion fell far short of the predictive power of the algorithms. Fudenberg and Liang (2018) used a related approach to study initial play in strategic-form games and found that models of level-k thinking (see Chapter "Errors in Strategic Reasoning" (by Eyster) of this Handbook) achieved ∼50–80% of the attainable predictive power, depending on specification.

Whereas the previous section reviewed research on people's beliefs about the likelihood of particular random sequences, this section focuses on people's sampling-distribution beliefs. At the end of the section, I discuss the extent to which people's beliefs about sampling distributions may or may not be consistent with their beliefs about the sequences that must logically underlie the distributions.

3.1 Partition dependence

Bayesian beliefs satisfy a normative principle called extensionality: if two events correspond to the same set of states, then the probabilities of the two events must be equal. In this section, I discuss a bias in which people's beliefs violate this principle: people assign greater total probability to an event when it is described as the union of subevents rather than as a single event. Following Fox and Rottenstreich (2003), I refer to this bias as *partition dependence* because beliefs depend on how the state space is partitioned into events. Partition dependence is not only an important bias in itself, but it is also a potential confound for evidence on other belief biases, and for that reason, it comes up throughout this section and later in this chapter.

Partition dependence was first systematically studied by Tversky and Koehler (1994). Drawing on extensive existing evidence (e.g., Teigen, 1974a; Olson, 1976; Fischhoff et al., 1978) and new experiments, Tversky and Koehler found that people assign greater total probability to an event when it is "unpacked" into subevents. For example, when Tversky and Koehler asked undergraduates to estimate the frequency of death by natural causes, the mean estimate was 56%. When they instead asked about three mutually exclusive subcategories—heart disease, cancer, and other natural causes—the mean estimates were 18%, 20%, and 29%, which add up to 67%. Even for decision-theory experts, unpacking an event has been found to increase the probability assigned to it, although typically less dramatically than for non-experts (e.g., Fox and Clemen, 2005). Similarly for subject-matter experts; for example, in several surveys of physicians, Redelmeier et al. (1995) described a patient exam and asked the physicians to assign probabilities to various possible diagnoses or prognoses. As in the results with other samples, unpacked events were assigned higher total probabilities.

Sonnemann et al. (2013) found evidence that partition dependence is reflected in behavior in a range of experimental markets and naturally occurring betting markets. For example, in an experimental market, students traded contingent claims on professional basketball and soccer outcomes. For some participants, an interval of outcomes comprised a single contingent claim (e.g., an NBA team will win from 4 to 11 games during the playoffs), while for other participants, that same interval was unpacked into two contingent claims (e.g., 4–7 and 8–11). To combat the worry that participants might infer that the market designer chose the intervals to be equally probable, each group of participants was informed about the contingent claims that other groups traded. Sonnemann et al. found higher sum-total prices for unpacked contingent claims than for their corresponding packed contingent claims, and the differences persisted over the 8 weeks of the experiment.

Tversky and Koehler (1994) proposed a formal model of partition dependence called *support theory* (see also Rottenstreich and Tversky, 1997). To establish notation, Ω is the set of all possible states of the world. A subset of Ω is called an *event* and is denoted $E \subseteq \Omega$. A *partition* of Ω is a set of mutually exclusive events that jointly cover the state space Ω. In the above example from Tversky and Koehler, heart disease, cancer, and other natural causes are three events that form a partition. In support theory, there exists a function $s(\cdot)$, defined independent of the partition, that maps any event into a strictly positive number. The function $s(\cdot)$, which is called the *support function*, captures the strength of belief in each possible event. In particular, if the agent's beliefs are elicited using partition ε, then the agent's belief about any event $E \subseteq \Omega$ is:

$$\pi(E|\varepsilon) = \frac{s(E)}{\sum_{F \in \varepsilon} s(F)}. \tag{3.1}$$

The key property of the support function is: For any mutually exclusive events E' and E'',

$$s(E') + s(E'') \geq s(E' \cup E''). \tag{3.2}$$

If Eq. (3.2) always holds with equality, then $s(\cdot)$ represents a standard subjective probability (and equals a subjective probability if rescaled so that $\sum_{F \in \varepsilon} s(F) = 1$). Whenever Eq. (3.2) holds with strict inequality, the support function is said to be *subadditive*. Subadditivity is the central feature of support theory because it captures the evidence that unpacking an event generates a higher total probability than asking about it as a single event. Tversky and Koehler provided properties on the observed subjective probabilities that imply Eqs. (3.1)–(3.2), and Ahn and Ergin (2010) provided a decision-theoretic axiomatization.

The vast majority of evidence on partition dependence is consistent with subadditivity, and the few studies that found the opposite identified mechanisms generating those results that may not be relevant more generally (Macchi et al., 1999; Sloman et al., 2004). For example, Sloman et al. (2004) argued that when an event is unpacked into subevents that are atypical, attention is directed away from the typical members, which may reduce the event's perceived likelihood. For instance, they found that death by "pneumonia, diabetes, cirrhosis, or any other disease" was judged as less likely than death by "any disease" (40% versus 55%).

As Tversky and Koehler and others pointed out, depending on the setting, subadditivity could result from a variety of psychological mechanisms, including imperfect memory for unmentioned events, salience of mentioned events, ambiguity in the way packed events are described, and an implicit suggestion that mentioned events are more likely than unmentioned ones. Fox and Rottenstreich (2003) provided evidence that subadditivity can also result from a bias toward assigning equal probability to each category, i.e., the reported probabilities are compressed toward a uniform distribution ("ignorance prior") across categories.[10] In a series of studies, Fox and Clemen (2005) found that subadditivity persists in settings where other mechanisms are unlikely to be at play. For example, in one study, MBA students were asked to rate the probabilities that particular business schools would be ranked #1 in the next *Business Week* rankings. Some participants assigned probabilities to six categories: (i) Chicago, (ii) Harvard, (iii) Kellogg, (iv) Stanford, (v) Wharton, and (vi) None of the above. Other participants assigned probabilities to two categories: (i) Chicago, Harvard, Kellogg, Stanford, or another school other than Wharton, and (ii) Wharton. This design rules out many possible mechanisms for subadditivity because the same set of schools was mentioned to both groups of participants, and yet subadditivity was observed: the median probability assigned to Wharton was 30% in the first group but 60% in the second group. Fox and Clemen concluded that compression accounts for the robust evidence of subadditivity across settings.

Of particular relevance for discussion later in this section, Teigen (1974a), Olson (1976), and Benjamin et al. (2018b) reported evidence of partition dependence in sampling-distribution beliefs for binomial signals that is consistent with Fox and Clemen's compression mechanism. For example, Benjamin, Moore, and Rabin elicited from each participant the probability distribution of outcomes of ten flips of a fair coin. This distribution was elicited with four different ways of partitioning the outcomes:

(A) 0, 1, 2, 3, 4, 5, 6, 7, 8, 9, 10 heads (11-bin partition)
(B) 0–3, 4, 5, 6, 7–10 heads (5-bin partition)
(C) 0–4, 5, 6–10 heads (3-bin partition)
(D) Each possible number of heads (0–10) elicited separately (eleven 2-bin partitions)

In partitions A–C, the outcome categories were presented together on the same screen, and participants' probabilities were restricted to sum to 100%. For D, each possible number of heads was asked about on a separate screen, and there was no requirement that the total sum to 100%. Questions in D, such as "What percentage of ten-flip sets include exactly 4 HEADS and 6 TAILS?", are believed to induce 2-bin partitions because they effectively ask about the probability of a given outcome as opposed to any other outcome (e.g., Fox and Rottenstreich, 2003). Each participant provided sampling-distribution beliefs in response to each of A–D, which were presented in a random order and interspersed with other questions.

Table 1 shows participants' mean beliefs for each of these partitions, in each of two experiments. Two patterns are clear. First, there is subadditivity. For example, across partitions A–C, the total probability assigned to 0–4 heads is smallest when it

---

[10] Fox and Rottenstreich suggested that this psychological mechanism may also underlie the *1/n heuristic* (Benartzi and Thaler, 2001), in which people allocate their money equally across the investment options offered to them. The same mechanisms that generate subadditivity in probability judgments might also underlie what has been called the *part-whole bias* in the contingent valuation literature (e.g., Bateman et al., 1997), in which the sum of people's valuations of the components of a good add up to more than people's valuation of the whole.

Table 1 Experimental participants' mean beliefs for each bin (from Benjamin et al., 2018b).

Experiment 1 (convenience sample of 104 adults)

Partition	Number of heads out of 10 flips											Sum
	0	1	2	3	4	5	6	7	8	9	10	
(A)	6.1%	6.4%	8.0%	9.0%	12.3%	20.0%	12.7%	8.9%	7.3%	6.5%	2.7%	100%
(B)		18.3%			21.5%	28.1%	18.3%			13.8%		100%
(C)			33.9%			36.2%			29.9%			100%
(D)	18.0%	36.0%	35.9%	36.7%	38.2%	39.4%	37.7%	34.2%	29.7%	27.9%	11.1%	345%

Experiment 2 (308 undergraduates)

Partition	Number of heads out of 10 flips											Sum
	0	1	2	3	4	5	6	7	8	9	10	
(A)	2.2%	3.8%	5.5%	9.3%	15.1%	28.3%	14.9%	9.2%	5.5%	3.9%	2.4%	100%
(B)		15.9%			18.3%	32.1%	18.1%			15.6%		100%
(C)			34.0%			32.9%			33.2%			100%
(D)	4.3%	6.7%	11.8%	16.6%	26.4%	34.3%	24.7%	17.4%	11.9%	6.6%	3.9%	164.7%

is described as a single event, higher when unpacked to the two events 0–3 heads and 4 heads, and highest when further unpacked to five events: 0, 1, 2, 3, and 4 heads. Second, relative to the correct probability distribution, participants' mean beliefs are compressed toward a uniform distribution in all partitions. One consequence is that the probabilities sum to more than 100% in D (where they were not constrained to sum to 100%), consistent with similar evidence from previous work (e.g., Teigen, 1974a, 1974b; Redelmeier et al., 1995).

Partition dependence raises fundamental issues about interpreting and measuring beliefs. For example, if reported beliefs depend on the partition, then does it make sense to talk about a person's "true" beliefs? Within the subjective expected utility tradition, a natural approach would be to define a person's true beliefs as those implied by the person's behavior, but the evidence from Sonnemann et al. (2013) mentioned above indicates that doing so would not uniquely pin down beliefs because behavior is also partition dependent. Indeed, in Ahn and Ergin's (2010) decision-theoretic framework, the beliefs implied by behavior depend on the partition relevant to the decision problem. A related question is whether there are better and worse partitions to use when eliciting beliefs, when the purpose is to aid someone in decision making. The answer to this question presumably depends on the psychological mechanism that generates partition dependence. For example, if a particular description of events causes people to forget about some of the states of the world, then beliefs induced by that description are suspect. On the other hand, if subadditivity is due to people compressing beliefs toward a uniform distribution, then beliefs are biased regardless of which partition is used to elicit them. These normative issues have been largely unaddressed in the context of belief elicitation, but they are analogous to issues that have been raised for framing effects in general; for discussion, see Chapter "Behavioral Public Economics" (by Bernheim and Taubinsky) of this Handbook.

Related to the issue of "true" beliefs, partition dependence raises a thorny conceptual problem that needs to be addressed before proceeding with the rest of this section: since reported beliefs depend on the partition, which partition should be used for the purpose of defining other sampling-distribution biases? For example, when a coin is flipped 10 times, do people overestimate the probability of 4 heads as in partition D of Table 1, or underestimate it as in partition A?

One way to define and study other belief biases separately from partition dependence is to write down a model of how beliefs are affected by partition dependence, use the model to undo its effects, and then examine the resulting beliefs. Such an approach posits the existence of latent *root beliefs*, which are what the beliefs would be if they were purged of partition dependence. The root beliefs are never directly observed but may be inferred using the model, and then other belief biases can be defined in terms of how the root beliefs deviate from the correct probabilities. This approach has been taken by Clemen and Ulu (2008) and Prava et al. (2016). For example, Clemen and Ulu proposed a model that extends support theory by assuming that observed beliefs are a mixture of the root beliefs with a uniform distribution over the events in a partition. Using their model, Clemen and Ulu proposed a method of inferring root beliefs from observed beliefs, demonstrated their method in an experiment, and found that the inferred root beliefs exhibited little or no partition dependence.

In later parts of this section, when attempting to disentangle other biases in sampling-distribution beliefs from partition dependence, I will refer back to a similar approach taken by Benjamin et al. (2018b). Benjamin, Moore, and Rabin proposed a quite general framework that does not make functional form assumptions, and they proved some results regarding inferences that can be drawn about the root beliefs in this framework. Specifically, denoting the root belief about event E as $r(E)$, they assumed that the support of an event is a continuous, positive-valued function of the agent's root belief:

$$s(E) = g\big(r(E)\big) \tag{3.3}$$

for all $E \subseteq \Omega$. The function g has two key properties. First, it is strictly increasing. This assumption means that one event has greater support than another if and only if the root beliefs assign it greater probability. The assumption implies that there is a special situation in which root beliefs can be inferred: when the reported beliefs are equal to each other. That is, if there is some partition in which the agent reports that each event has equal probability, then the agent's root beliefs also assign equal probability to each event.

Second, g is weakly concave. Given the other assumptions, this assumption is essentially equivalent to inequality (3.2). It ensures that the reported beliefs are a compressed version of the root beliefs. It implies that there is another special situation in which inferences can be drawn about the root beliefs: when the *correct* probabilities of each event in a partition are equal to each other. In that case, we know that, relative to the root beliefs, the reported beliefs are biased toward the correct probabilities. Therefore, in whatever direction the reported beliefs are biased relative to the correct probabilities, the root beliefs are biased in the same direction (and are even further away from correct). Partition dependence is problematic for the growing literatures in many areas of economics that rely on survey elicitations of people's beliefs (for a review, see Manski, 2018). An early example is Viscusi (1990), who asked a representative sample "Among 100 cigarette smokers, how many of them do you think will get lung cancer because they smoke?" The mean response was 42.6—surely a dramatic overestimate of the true probability. This finding is often interpreted as suggesting that, if people were better informed about the health risks of smoking, they would smoke *more*. However, the partition of the state space of the consequences of smoking as {get lung cancer, not get lung cancer} would be expected, per compression, to lead people to assign an especially high probability to the event of getting lung cancer. Thus, unless the state space is partitioned this way when people are deciding whether to smoke, it is not clear how to relate the reported belief to the prevalence of smoking behavior.

More generally, partition dependence implies that in order to elicit the beliefs that are relevant for decision making, the beliefs must be elicited using the same partition that people use when making the decision. This in turn means that economists will need to study what partitions people use. This is an important direction for research that, as far as I am aware, has not been explored.

3.2 Sample-size neglect and Non-Belief in the Law of Large Numbers

A striking regularity regarding sampling-distribution beliefs is *sample-size neglect*. It was first documented by Kahneman and Tversky (1972a). In an initial demonstration, they told one group of participants that 1000 babies are born a day in a certain region, and they asked,

> On what percentage of days will the number of boys among 1000 babies be as follows:
>
> Up to 50 boys
> 50 to 150 boys
> 150 to 250 boys
> . . .
> 850 to 950 boys
> More than 950 boys
> Note that the categories include all possibilities, so your answers should add up to about 100%.

They asked another group of participants the analogous question about 100 babies, and they asked a third group about 10 babies (with the outcomes 0, 1, 2, . . . , 9, and 10 boys). As per the Law of Large Numbers, the correct sampling distribution puts more mass on the mean as the sample size gets larger. However, as shown in Fig. 1A, all three groups reported the same distribution over sample proportions. Kahneman and Tversky called this distribution the "universal distribution" for a binomial with rate 50%. With the same three sample sizes, Kahneman and Tversky similarly elicited beliefs about two other distributions: a binomial with rate 80% (Fig. 1B) and a normal distribution (not shown). For both, participants' subjective sampling distributions for the sample mean were again invariant to sample size. Kahneman and Tversky did not investigate sample sizes smaller than 10 but noted that they did not expect sample-size neglect to hold ". . . when the sample is small enough to permit enumeration of possibilities" (p. 441); as mentioned in Section 3.5 below, it seems likely that people hold correct beliefs about sample sizes of 1 (although I am not aware of any evidence).[11]

Despite pre-dating Tversky and Koehler (1994) by two decades, Kahneman and Tversky (1972a) anticipated the potentially confounding effect of partition depen-

---

[11] The idea that people may find it easier to reason correctly about small samples than large samples may be consistent with research in numerical cognition, which has found that people (as well as infants and non-human animals) have different cognitive systems for perceiving and thinking intuitively about small versus large numbers (for reviews, see, e.g., Feigenson et al., 2004; Anobile et al., 2016). In the so-called "subitizing" range of numbers (up to about four), people precisely keep track of the individual objects, whereas for larger numbers, people rely on an approximate representation of magnitude. Research on these different systems has focused on performance on perception and arithmetic tasks, not probabilistic reasoning. One might conjecture that intuitions for probabilistic reasoning are built in to the small-number system but not the large-number system.

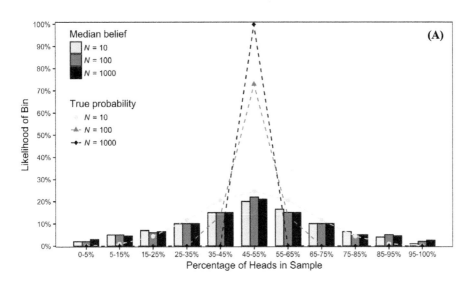

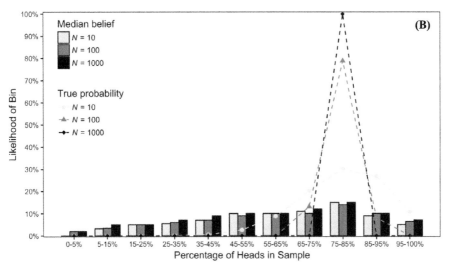

FIGURE 1

(A) Sample-size neglect for binomial with rate $\theta = 0.5$ (from Kahneman and Tversky, 1972a), (B) sample-size neglect for binomial with rate $\theta = 0.8$ (from Kahneman and Tversky, 1972a).

dence. They emphasized that "in contrast [to previous studies], subjects evaluate[d] the *same* number of categories for all sample sizes" (p. 441). Indeed, according to the model of partition dependence in Eqs. (3.1) and (3.3), if the bins are held constant and if the function g is assumed to be the same across sample sizes, then the insensitivity of the reported-belief distributions to sample size implies that the root-belief distributions are also the same across sample sizes.

There have been several replications and extensions of Kahneman and Tversky's elicitation of full sampling-distributions beliefs. Recently, Benjamin et al. (2018b) elicited subjective sampling distributions about flips of a fair coin. They asked about samples of size 10, 1000, and 1 million, each with the same 11-bin partition used by Kahneman and Tversky. Despite incentivizing participants' responses and eliciting all three distributions from each participant, they found identical subjective sampling distributions across the three sample sizes. In an early replication, Olson (1976) reinforced Kahneman and Tversky's concern about the potentially confounding influence of partition dependence. Olson asked different groups of undergraduates to provide the sampling distribution for the percentage of boys born in regions with 100 and 1000 babies born per day. When he used the same 11-bin partition as Kahneman and Tversky, he found identical distributions like they did. However, Olson also elicited the distributions using other partitions. For example, he asked another group of participants about the 100-baby distribution, but this time using an 11-bin partition with the outcomes $<46, 46, 47, \ldots, 53, 54$, and >54 boys. He found that the probabilities that participants assigned to these 11 bins were similar to those they assigned when the 11 bins corresponded to Kahneman and Tversky's partition. For instance, the median participant assigned only a slightly higher probability to the lowest category in the new partition—3% for <46 boys—than to the lowest category in Kahneman and Tversky's partition—1% for 0–5 boys—even though the true probability is much higher in the first case (18% versus roughly 0%).

Kahneman and Tversky interpreted sample-size neglect as showing that "The notion that sampling variance decreases in proportion to sample size is apparently not part of man's repertoire of intuitions" (p. 444). Sedlmeier and Gigerenzer (1997) proposed a more specific hypothesis: when asked about the distribution of means across samples, people instead give an answer about the distribution of outcomes within a sample. Among several pieces of evidence, the most telling comes from Sedlmeier (1994, Study 2, as described by Sedlmeier and Gigerenzer), who replicated and extended Kahneman and Tversky's elicitation of sampling-distribution beliefs about a normal distribution. Similar to prior work, Sedlmeier's experimental participants constructed distributions for the mean height of Israeli soldiers for sample sizes of 20 and 200—and, as in prior findings, the two distributions were identical. Another group of participants constructed distributions for height (as opposed to mean height) for these two sample sizes, i.e., distributions of heights for 20 soldiers and for 200 soldiers. These two distributions looked extremely similar, as they should, but they were also extremely similar to the distributions of mean height produced by the other participants, suggesting that the participants had no intuition that the two tasks were different.

Kahneman and Tversky reported further evidence of sample-size neglect from other questions that did not require participants to construct a distribution and are arguably less subject to confounding from partition dependence. For example, they asked whether a hospital with 45 births per day or one with 15 births per day would record more days with at least 60% of births being boys, or whether the two hospitals would have "About the same" number of days. Although the correct answer is the smaller hospital, more than half the participants chose "About the same," and roughly equal numbers chose the larger and smaller hospitals. This finding again points to people not understanding that the variance of the sampling distribution shrinks with sample size. It has been replicated in several dozen studies involving many variants of the judgment problem (for a review, see Lem et al., 2011).

Notwithstanding the evidence described above, people do seem to have two intuitions about the role of sample size, both originally identified by Bar-Hillel (1979). First, when asked directly, people expect the mean from a larger sample to be closer to the population mean. In a particularly clean demonstration, Well et al. (1990, Experiment 2) asked about the average height of the men registering at two conscription registration centers, one in which 25 men register per day and one in which 100 register per day, and told participants that the national average height in the population of men is 5 feet 9 inches. Similar to the hospital problem, one group of undergraduates was asked which center has more days when the average height exceeds 6 feet, and only 8% gave the correct answer of the smaller center. However, another group was asked which center will measure an average height closer to the national average on a particular day, and a third group was asked which will have more days when the average height is between 5 feet 6 inches and 6 feet (a 6-inch interval around the national average). In these latter two conditions, respectively 59% and 56% gave the correct answer. Well, Pollatsek, and Boyce concluded that although people have some basic understanding of the Law of Large Numbers, they do not understand its implications for the variance of the sampling distribution. I further discuss people's intuition that large samples are more likely to have means close to the population mean in Section 3.4.

Relatedly, Evans and Dusoir (1977, Experiment 2) hypothesized that when the question itself makes the logic clear to people, they can understand that extreme outcomes are less likely in large samples. Several studies have found evidence that has been interpreted as supporting this hypothesis (e.g., Bar-Hillel, 1979; Pelham and Neter, 1995, Study 1). For example, Bar-Hillel (1979) posed a version of the hospital problem with 15 and 5 births per day and asked which hospital recorded more days on which *all* the babies born were boys. In this problem, over half the participants correctly chose the smaller hospital and only a quarter chose "About the same." Bar-Hillel (1982) reported further evidence from versions of the problem that asked different groups of participants which hospital had more days in which the percentage of births being boys was over 60%, over 70%, over 80%, and 100%. She found that as the percentage became more extreme, more participants gave the correct answer. This seems to contradict the evidence from eliciting the full sampling distribution, discussed above, that people construct the same "universal distribution" regardless of sample size, even in the tails of the distribution, but constructing the distribution is arguably a more difficult task that does not give clues as to the correct intuition.

Second, people have an *incorrect* intuition that what matters for getting a sample mean close to the population mean is the *ratio* of the sample size to the population size, rather than the absolute sample size. Mathematically, as long as a sample is drawn with replacement, only the absolute sample size matters (and even if a sample is drawn without replacement, the ratio matters very little as long as the ratio is small). In one of Bar-Hillel's (1979, Experiment 4) studies, she described two urns, one containing 10 beads and one containing 100 beads, each with the same unknown proportions of red and green beads. She asked participants whether they would be more likely to correctly guess the majority color if they took 9 draws with replacement from the small urn or 15 draws with replacement from the large urn. 72 out of 110 participants erroneously chose the smaller number of draws from the small urn, presumably because it has a higher ratio of draws to urn size. Evans and Bradshaw (1986) also found evidence that experimental participants incorrectly believe they can draw stronger inferences when the ratio of sample size to population size is larger. I am not aware of any work that has explored the psychology underlying this intuition or its broader implications.

Benjamin et al. (2016) proposed a model to capture sample-size neglect. They called the bias that generates sample-size neglect *Non-Belief in the Law of Large Numbers (NBLLN)*. In the model, signals are drawn i.i.d. from a binomial distribution whose rate of a signals is θ. The agent, however, forms beliefs as if any particular sample is generated by a two-step process: (i) a "subjective rate" β is drawn from some distribution that has mean θ and full support on [0, 1], called the "subjective-rate distribution"; and then (ii) the signals for the sample are drawn i.i.d. from a binomial distribution whose rate is β. This model directly generates sample-size neglect in large samples: if β were the actual rate, the proportion of a signals in a large sample would be β (by the Law of Large Numbers). Therefore, in a large sample, the probability density that the agent assigns to any proportion of signals (say, 60% of babies are boys) is equal to the probability density that the subjective-rate distribution assigns to β equaling that value. In other words, as the sample size gets large, the agent's subjective sampling distribution for the mean converges to the subjective-rate distribution. Thus, in the model, the subjective-rate distribution is the "universal distribution" that the agent believes characterizes any large enough sample—and Kahneman and Tversky's evidence indicates that a sample size of 10 is already "large enough." For a sample size of one, the model implies that the agent has correct sampling-distribution beliefs. For any sample size larger than one, the agent's subjective sampling distribution is flatter than the correct distribution (due to the randomness of β), and the agent believes that tail events are more likely than they are.

Benjamin, Rabin, and Raymond used the model as a tool to explore the implications of sample-size neglect in a number of settings, including risky decision making. A number of implications follow from the agent's belief that the tails of the sampling distribution—such as all a's or all b's—are more likely than they are. To give some examples, if winning a lottery requires matching all numbers, and matching each number has probability θ, then the agent will overestimate his chance of winning and be too willing to play. If success at a job fair requires getting at least one job offer, and getting any job offer has probability θ, then the agent will overestimate his chance of getting no offers and will undervalue attending. If each of many stocks has positive expected value and earns money with independent probability θ, then the agent overestimates the variance of payoffs in a diversified portfolio and hence will undervalue diversification.

Similarly, the model predicts that people will undervalue a repeated, positive-expected-value gamble. Benartzi and Thaler (1999) reported evidence from several studies on attitudes toward repeated gambles and long-term investing that they interpreted as consistent with sample-size neglect (related evidence is reported in Keren and Wagenaar, 1987; Keren, 1991, and Redelmeier and Tversky, 1992). For example, when undergraduate experimental participants were asked the probability of a net loss after 150 repetitions of a 90%/10% bet to gain $0.10/lose $0.50, participants' mean estimate was 24%—a dramatic overestimate relative to the correct probability of 0.3%. When actually offered this repeated gamble, only 49% accepted it. Yet 90% said they would accept a single-play bet that had the true distribution of money outcomes implied by the repeated bet, suggesting that they would have accepted the repeated bet if they had correctly understood the distribution of outcomes.

NBLLN also has implications for how people draw inferences. I will defer discussion of these implications until Section 5.1.

3.3 Sampling-distribution-tails diminishing sensitivity

As discussed above, NBLLN implies sample-size neglect: for large enough sample sizes, people's subjective sampling distribution is determined by a "universal distribution" that is invariant to sample size. This in turn implies that for large sample sizes, the tails of the subjective sampling distribution are fat relative to the true tails. There is also some evidence that the tails of the "universal distribution" are *flat* relative to the true tails. NBLLN implies some flatness, but the amount of flatness is greater than can be explained by Benjamin et al.'s (2016) model of NBLLN. Benjamin et al. (2016, Appendix C) conjectured that this excess flatness is due to another bias, which they called sampling-distribution-tails diminishing sensitivity (SDTDS): people think of unlikely outcomes as similar to each other.

Apparent flatness of the tails is evident in Fig. 1B, which shows Kahneman and Tversky's survey data for the binomial with rate 0.8. In the true distribution for a sample size of 100, as one goes from 45–55% to 35–45% to 25–35% heads, the probability declines at an exponential rate, from 0.73 to 0.14 to 0.001. In contrast, the median participant's estimate declines much more slowly, from 0.22 to 0.15 to 0.10. Much of the other evidence from experimental participants' constructed sampling distributions also features flat tails (e.g., Wheeler and Beach, 1968; Peterson et al., 1968, Study 2; Teigen, 1974b). All of this evidence, however, is confounded by partition dependence, which would compress participants' estimates relative to their root beliefs.

In experiments designed to identify sampling-distribution beliefs separately from compression, Benjamin et al. (2018b) found evidence of flat tails for sample sizes of 1000 and 1 million. For example, experimental participants' sampling distribution for 1000 coin flips was elicited using the 5-bin partition: 0–487, 488–496, 497–503, 504–512, and 513–1000 heads. This partition was chosen because each bin has roughly equal true probability. Consequently, as discussed in Section 3.1, the deviation of beliefs away from equality indicates the direction of bias in root beliefs net of partition dependence. Mean beliefs had a "W" shape, overweighting the middle bin and extreme-tail bins but underweighting the intermediate-tail bins: mean beliefs were 26%, 13%, 21%, 14%, and 27%, compared with the true probabilities of 21.5%, 19.8%, 16.5%, 19.8%, and 21.5%, respectively. The combination of overweighting extreme tails but underweighting intermediate tails implies that the tail beliefs are too flat.

3.4 Overweighting the mean and the fallacy of large numbers

As discussed in Section 3.2, when people construct sampling distributions for samples of different sizes, they do not assign higher probability to the population mean in the larger sample size. Yet, as also discussed there, there is much evidence that when people are asked directly, they do have an intuition that when the sample is larger, the sample mean is likely to be closer to the population mean. Moreover, from experiments that control for confounding from partition dependence, there is some evidence that when people construct sampling distributions, they assign *too much* weight to the population mean. For example (as mentioned in Section 3.3), in five-bin elicitations of beliefs about samples of 1000 and 1 million coin flips, Benjamin et al. (2018b) found that relative to the true probabilities, experimental participants overweighted both the extreme-tail bins and the middle bin. Olson (1976) also found evidence that points to overweighting the mean, net of partition dependence. For instance (as also discussed in Section 3.3), some of his experimental participants constructed sampling distributions for how often a 100-baby sample would have different percentages of boys. Among participants where the middle bin in an 11-bin partition was 45–55 boys, participants' median estimate was 40% (the true probability is 68%). Among a different group of participants where the middle bin in an 11-bin partition was exactly 50 boys, participants' median estimate was actually slightly *higher*: 45% (the true probability is 8%).

Further evidence comes from Klos et al. (2005), who asked their experimental participants a set of questions about four repeated gambles. For example, one gamble was a 50–50 chance to win 200 euros or lose 100 euros. When participants were asked about the standard deviation of payoffs or about probability of a loss, it was clear that participants assigned too much probability mass to the tails, replicating Benartzi and Thaler's (1999) evidence of NBLLN. But participants were also asked the probability that the outcome would fall within ±100 euros of the expected value in 5 or 50 repetitions of the gamble. While the true probability is 21% for 5 repetitions and 7% for 50 repetitions, participants' mean estimates were dramatically too high: 47% and 58%.

This evidence is consistent with people having some correct Law of Large Numbers intuition. Yet the *overestimation* of the probability that the sample mean will match the population mean is more suggestive of the Law of Small Numbers (LSN) bias discussed in Section 2.1. The (incorrect) LSN intuition is that extreme sample realizations tend to be counteracted by additional signals (as opposed to the correct Law of Large Numbers intuition, which is that the effect of extreme sample realizations on the sample mean is diluted by additional signals). However, the LSN bias by itself does not explain why, in Klos, Weber, and Weber's experiment, participants' estimates—contrary to the true probabilities—are *higher* for 50 repetitions than for 5 repetitions. Klos, Weber, and Weber's comparison between 50 and 5 repetitions was motivated as a test of Paul Samuelson's (1963) hypothesis that people suffer from a "fallacy of large numbers." Samuelson had hypothesized that people have a specific misunderstanding of the Law of Large Numbers: while the correct idea is that for fixed $\epsilon > 0$, $p\left(\frac{1}{N}\sum_{i=1}^{N} s_i - \theta < \epsilon\right) \to 1$ as $N \to \infty$, he argued people incorrectly think that $p\left(\sum_{i=1}^{N} s_i - N\theta < \epsilon\right) \to 1$. In words, the Law of Large Numbers states that the *mean* of the signals in the sample becomes arbitrarily close to the population rate. The fallacy states incorrectly that the *sum total* of the signals becomes arbitrarily close to its expected value.[12]

Psychologically, the fallacy of large numbers is closely related to the LSN: it is the belief that the GF is stronger in larger samples. More precisely, the GF is the belief that below-average realizations and above-average realizations tend to cancel out in any sample, whereas the fallacy of large numbers states that below-average and above-average realizations will *perfectly* cancel out in an arbitrarily large sample.

The fallacy-of-large-numbers hypothesis is plausible but logically contradicts sample-size neglect/NBLLN: if people's sampling-distribution beliefs are pinned down by a "universal distribution" over proportions regardless of sample size, then they would believe that the probability of the outcome $\sum_{i=1}^{N} s_i$ ending up in any fixed interval converges to zero as $N \to \infty$. Because of this contradiction, Benartzi and Thaler (1999) interpreted their evidence of NBLLN (see Section 3.2) as casting doubt on the fallacy-of-large-numbers hypothesis. But this internal inconsistency between biases could be a case where which bias occurs depends on which question a person is asked; for related discussion, see Sections 3.2, 3.4, and 10.2. Another possibility is that the fallacy-of-large-numbers hypothesis is not the correct explanation of Klos, Weber, and Weber's evidence. I am not aware of other tests of the hypothesis.

---

[12] For readers unfamiliar with the "fallacy of large numbers" hypothesis, some orientation regarding its history may be helpful. Samuelson noted that an MIT colleague said he would turn down a single gamble like the one studied by Klos, Weber, and Weber (a 50–50 chance to win 200 euros or lose 100 euros) but accept many repetitions of the gamble. Samuelson argued that his colleague's willingness to accept many repetitions was a mistake, and he proposed the fallacy of large numbers to explain the supposed mistake. Benartzi and Thaler (1999) documented behavior like that of Samuelson's colleague in surveys and experiments (see Section 3.2), but they argued that people's error is turning down the single gamble (due to loss aversion; see Chapter "Reference-Dependent Preferences" (by O'Donoghue and Sprenger) in this Handbook), rather than accepting the repeated gamble. Moreover, as noted below, Benartzi and Thaler interpreted their evidence of NBLLN as evidence *against* the fallacy-of-large-numbers hypothesis.

Overall, my reading of the data is that NBLLN coexists with a sampling-distribution bias of overweighting the mean, which may be due to the LSN. At this point, there is not enough evidence for a confident judgment about whether there is also a fallacy-of-large-numbers bias.

3.5 Sampling-distribution beliefs for small samples

All of the evidence discussed so far has been from sample sizes of at least 10. There are two papers that elicited subjective sampling distributions for smaller sample sizes. Wheeler and Beach (1968) elicited two binomial sampling distributions, with rates $\theta = 0.6$ and 0.8 and both with a sample size of $N = 8$. They found that their participants' distributions were too flat.[13] Peterson et al. (1968, Study 2) elicited nine binomial sampling distributions, with the three rates $\theta = 0.6$, 0.7, and 0.8 and the three sample sizes $N = 3$, 5, and 8. They found that participants' sampling distributions were roughly correct for $N = 3$ but were flatter than the correct distributions for $N = 5$ and especially for $N = 8$. In all cases, beliefs were elicited using a partition that binned each possible outcome separately (e.g., 0, 1, 2, and 3). Thus, the evidence from both papers confounds the root-belief distributions with compression due to partition dependence, which would also flatten reported-belief distributions. Taking compression into account, Peterson et al.'s results may suggest that people's root-belief distributions are *too peaked* for sample sizes of 3, rather than too flat.

Using an elicitation designed to control for compression, Benjamin et al. (2018b) studied beliefs about samples of 10 coin flips and found no evidence that participants' root-belief distribution was too flat. Specifically, they elicited beliefs using the 5-bin partition 0–3, 4, 5, 6, and 7–10 heads, which is the partition that comes closest to equal true probabilities in each bin (17%, 21%, 25%, 21%, and 17%). According to the model of compression effects in Section 3.1, with such a partition, the direction of bias of reported beliefs also indicates the direction of bias of root beliefs. In both their convenience sample of adults and their sample of undergraduates, Benjamin et al. found that mean beliefs were approximately correct (18%, 22%, 28%, 18%, and 14% for the adults and 16%, 18%, 32%, 18%, and 16% for the students), except with some overweighting of the middle bin. These results suggest that, for sample sizes of 10, people's root-belief distribution is roughly correct or too peaked.

Putting the scant evidence together, it suggests that for sample sizes between one and 10, people's root-belief sampling distributions may be too peaked. I am not aware of any evidence regarding beliefs about samples of size one, probably because such an elicitation would be weird for experimental participants. It seems likely that such

---

[13] Wheeler and Beach's study had a sequence of stages, and the sampling distributions were elicited three times over the course of the study. In between, the participants observed realized samples, made bets about which distribution each sample was drawn from, and then received feedback about whether they were correct (see Section 4.1 for further discussion). While participants' sampling distributions were too flat at the beginning of the experiment (prior to any feedback), by the end of the experiment the distributions were too peaked.

beliefs are correct: people would believe that the probability of an a signal in a single draw when the rate is known to be θ is equal to θ.

3.6 Summary and comparison of sequence beliefs with sampling-distribution beliefs

Psychologists have identified two main biases in people's beliefs about sequences of random events: the GF and the hot-hand bias, both of which may be due to the LSN (Sections 2.1 and 2.2). The LSN also appears to influence people's beliefs about sampling distributions, causing them to assign too much probability to the possibility that the sample mean will be close to the population rate (Section 3.4).

People's sampling-distribution beliefs, however, are also influenced by other biases: partition dependence (Section 3.1), NBLLN (Section 3.2), and perhaps SDTDS (Section 3.3). Summarizing all of the evidence from Section 3 and focusing on what can be inferred about root beliefs: for "small" sample sizes (say, smaller than 10), people think the sampling distribution is too peaked, while for non-small sample sizes, people think the sampling distribution has tails that are too fat and too flat but also that put too much weight at the mean. Most of this evidence can be rationalized by LSN dominating at the small sample sizes and by LSN, NBLLN, and SDTDS jointly influencing beliefs at the larger sample sizes.

People's sampling-distribution beliefs are internally inconsistent due to partition dependence. Even if we put this aside by focusing on root beliefs, people's sampling-distribution beliefs are inconsistent with their sequence beliefs because several biases (such as NBLLN and SDTDS) influence sampling-distribution but not sequence beliefs.

In some direct tests in which sampling-distribution beliefs and sequence beliefs were elicited from the same experimental participants, Benjamin et al. (2018b) reported evidence of such inconsistency (suggestive evidence of such inconsistency was also reported by Teigen, 1974a). For example, experimental participants' root beliefs about the distribution of the number of heads out of 10 coin flips are roughly correct, as mentioned in Section 3.5. This would imply that people think 9 heads out of 10 flips is 10 times more likely than 10 heads out of 10 flips. But, as per the GF, they believe that heads is roughly half as likely as tails following a streak of 9 heads. And since, given the GF, participants surely think that the nine other ways to get 9 heads out of 10 are at least as likely as HHHHHHHHHT, their sequence beliefs imply that 9 out of 10 heads should be at least 20 times more likely than 10 out of 10 heads.

This internal inconsistency means that people's beliefs about a random sample will depend on whether they are thinking about the sequence of signals or the distribution generated by that sequence. Economic models have generally not drawn this distinction, and I am not aware of work that studies when people think about sequences versus distributions, but these will be important issues to work out. I briefly discuss some of the related modeling challenges in Section 10.2.

4 Evidence on belief updating

Belief updating is the revision of beliefs upon receipt of new information. The core component of the neoclassical theory of probabilistic beliefs is the assumption that people update beliefs according to Bayes' Theorem. This section is about the evidence on deviations from Bayesian updating. The review in this section aims to be comprehensive, except that I focus on settings where people are motivated only to be accurate; I defer discussion of settings where people also have preferences over which state of the world is true until Section 9.

For simplicity, I will describe Bayesian updating (and deviations from it) in the case where there are two states of the world, A and B. Denote the agent's *prior* beliefs, before observing new signals, by $p(A)$ and $p(B)$. Bayes' Theorem prescribes how to update the prior beliefs to *posterior* beliefs after observing some set of signals, S:

$$p(A|S) = \frac{p(S|A)p(A)}{p(S|A)p(A) + p(S|B)p(B)} \tag{4.1}$$

$$p(B|S) = \frac{p(S|B)p(B)}{p(S|A)p(A) + p(S|B)p(B)} \tag{4.2}$$

where $p(S|A)$ is the likelihood of observing S in state A, and $p(S|B)$ is the likelihood of observing S in state B.[14] It is often useful to write Bayes' Theorem in its posterior-odds form, obtained by dividing Eq. (4.1) by Eq. (4.2):

$$\frac{p(A|S)}{p(B|S)} = \frac{p(S|A)p(A)}{p(S|B)p(B)} \tag{4.3}$$

This equation states that the posterior odds of state A to state B, $\dfrac{p(A|S)}{p(B|S)}$, is equal to the likelihood ratio, $\dfrac{p(S|A)}{p(S|B)}$, times the prior odds, $\dfrac{p(A)}{p(B)}$.

Much of the evidence on how people update their beliefs comes from what I will refer to as *updating problems*. In an updating problem, experimental participants are given priors and a set of signals from which the likelihoods could be calculated, and then their posterior beliefs are elicited. To illustrate this type of problem, Edwards (1968, pp. 20–21) gave a hypothetical example:

> Imagine two urns filled with millions of poker chips. In the first urn, 70 percent of the chips are red and 30 percent are blue. In the second urn, 70 percent are blue

---

[14] Bayes' Theorem is an immediate consequence of the definition of conditional probability, $p(X|Y) = \dfrac{p(X \cap Y)}{p(Y)}$. Using this definition for the first and last equalities: $p(A|S) = \dfrac{p(A \cap S)}{p(S)} = \dfrac{p(S \cap A)}{p(S \cap A) + p(S \cap B)} = \dfrac{p(S|A)p(A)}{p(S|A)p(A) + p(S|B)p(B)}$, and $p(B|S)$ is derived analogously.

and 30 percent are red. Suppose one of the urns is chosen randomly and a dozen chips are drawn from it: eight red chips and four blue chips. What are the chances that the chips came from the urn with mostly red chips? (Give your answer as a percentage.)

Here, the two states are $A = \{$mostly red urn$\}$ and $B = \{$mostly blue urn$\}$, the prior probabilities are $p(A) = p(B) = 0.5$, and assuming that the chips are drawn with replacement (as in most of the experiments), the likelihoods can be calculated using the binomial distribution.

Biased updating can be identified by comparing people's posteriors with the correct posteriors. For example, Edwards reports that in his example, the intuitive answer for most people is roughly 70% or 80%. The correct answer is calculated by plugging the likelihoods, $p(S|A) = \binom{12}{8}(0.7)^8(0.3)^4 = 0.231$ and $p(S|B) = \binom{12}{8}(0.3)^8(0.7)^4 = 0.008$, and the priors into Eq. (4.1). Doing so yields a correct answer of 97%—much larger than most people anticipate! In this example, people underinfer, meaning that they infer less from the evidence than they should.

This section reviews the evidence on such deviations of people's posterior beliefs from normatively correct posterior beliefs in updating problems. Although Edwards's example is hypothetical, there are many dozens of experiments that have been conducted in which poker chips are actually drawn out of bookbags in front of the participants (or balls are drawn out of urns, etc.). These are often called *bookbag-and-poker-chip experiments*. Most of the evidence reviewed in this section comes from bookbag-and-poker-chip experiments.

Most of these experiments were published in the psychology literature during 1964–1973 and are unfamiliar to economists.[15] Some historical context helps to understand why. The pioneers in studying deviations from Bayesian updating were Ward Edwards, a psychologist, and his student, Larry Phillips (Edwards and Phillips, 1964; Phillips and Edwards, 1966). Edwards had written two important early reviews of behavioral decision research (1954, 1961b) and a seminal paper introducing psychologists to Bayesian statistics that remains a classic among statisticians (Edwards et al., 1963). It was thus natural for him and other psychologists at the time to ask how people's actual updating compares to Bayes' Theorem. The bookbag-and-poker-chip paradigm was the workhorse in this active literature.

As discussed in Section 7 of this Chapter, Daniel Kahneman and Amos Tversky's persuasive "heuristics and biases" research program, beginning with Tversky and Kahneman (1971) and Kahneman and Tversky (1972a), redirected psychologists' attention toward understanding the psychological processes underlying belief judgments. In the meantime, Edwards's interests shifted toward designing computer programs to aid people in applying Bayes' Theorem to their priors and likelihood judgments (Edwards, 1968). After 1973, the psychology literature on biased belief

---

[15] This literature also included a number of experiments on deviations from the Bayesian model of demand for information (e.g., Green et al., 1964; Edwards and Slovic, 1965). For economists, this work is also unfamiliar but relevant. I do not review it here.

updating became dominated by the sort of hypothetical updating scenarios that Kahneman and Tversky employed (which more closely resembled real-world situations than Edwards's abstract environments did).

Economists were influenced by Kahneman and Tversky's work. When David Grether (1980) conducted the first economics experiments on belief updating, he framed it as testing whether Kahneman and Tversky's representativeness heuristic describes people's beliefs when people are financially motivated and experienced, and he did not mention the earlier psychology literature at all.[16] Yet instead of posing hypothetical judgment scenarios via surveys as Kahneman and Tversky had done, Grether adopted the bookbag-and-poker-chip paradigm as his experimental methodology in order to make the random process transparent to participants and to better control the information that participants might use to fill in unspecified scenario details. Subsequent economics experiments have continued to use the bookbag-and-poker-chip paradigm but have built on the findings of the precursor economics experiments rather than on the much earlier psychology experiments.

This section draws on both the earlier psychology literature and the more recent experiments in economics and psychology. To help organize this large body of evidence, I will supplement the literature review with a meta-analysis. To organize the findings, throughout the section I summarize a sequence of "stylized facts" that I will refer back to in subsequent sections of this chapter.

4.1 Conceptual framework

To organize the evidence on belief-updating biases, I will use the following reduced-form model introduced by Grether (1980)[17]:

$$\pi(A|S) = \frac{p(S|A)^c p(A)^d}{p(S|A)^c p(A)^d + p(S|B)^c p(B)^d} \tag{4.4}$$

$$\pi(B|S) = \frac{p(S|B)^c p(B)^d}{p(S|A)^c p(A)^d + p(S|B)^c p(B)^d}, \tag{4.5}$$

where $p(\cdot)$ refers to a true probability, $\pi(\cdot)$ refers to a person's (possibly biased) belief, and $c, d \geq 0$. The parameter c measures biased use of the likelihoods, and d measures biased use of the priors. Bayes' Theorem is the special case $c = d = 1$.

---

[16] In personal correspondence, David Grether told me that early drafts of his paper had referenced the bookbag-and-poker-chip literature in psychology (as he had done in his review paper, Grether, 1978), but his recollection is that a referee asked him to remove those references.

[17] To be more precise, Eqs. (4.4)–(4.6) are the implicit model underlying Grether's specification. Grether introduced the empirical regression specification in Eq. (4.15) below (both with and without the indicator term), which can be derived by taking the logarithm of Eq. (4.6) below and adding a constant term and an error term. Many subsequent economics papers have followed Grether (1980) in estimating this equation or its sequential-sample analog, Eq. (4.21) below, introduced by Grether (1992). For an alternative organizing framework, see Epstein et al. (2008).

I will not treat c and d as (fixed) structural parameters that *explain* people's updating. Instead, I use them merely to *describe* deviations from Bayesian updating. Much of this section focuses on establishing stylized facts about how c and d vary with features of the updating problem. In subsequent sections, I take these stylized facts as given and discuss theories of biased updating.

To interpret the magnitudes of c and d, it is helpful to write the model in the posterior-odds form that is analogous to Eq. (4.3). Dividing Eq. (4.4) by Eq. (4.5):

$$\frac{\pi(A|S)}{\pi(B|S)} = \left[\frac{p(S|A)}{p(S|B)}\right]^c \left[\frac{p(A)}{p(B)}\right]^d. \tag{4.6}$$

From this equation, it is clear that $c < 1$ corresponds to updating as if the signals provided less information about the state than they actually do (*underinference*).[18] Symmetrically, $c > 1$ means updating as if the signals are more informative than they are (*overinference*). Similarly, $d < 1$ corresponds to treating the priors as less informative than they are and $d > 1$ to the opposite. Following the literature (which I review in Section 6), I call the former *base-rate neglect*. (There is no accepted term for the latter because it is rare empirically, as we will see, but it could be called "base-rate over-use.")

This conceptual model has three important properties. First, when the priors are equal, $p(A) = p(B)$, the value of d does not matter for updating; the bias in posterior beliefs is entirely driven by c. Therefore, biases in inference can be isolated by studying settings with equal priors. For instance, in Edwards's (1968) example above, since the prior probabilities of the two urns are equal, we can describe people's biased posteriors as resulting from underinference. In this section I exploit this property to study biased inferences.

Second and symmetrically, when the likelihoods are equal, $p(S|A) = p(S|B)$, the bias in updating is entirely determined by d, and therefore, deviations from optimal use of prior information can be isolated by studying settings with equal likelihoods. Such settings are discussed in Section 6.

Third, and related to the first two properties, while researchers sometimes speak as if what matters for biased updating is whether likelihoods are underweighted or overweighted *relative* to priors, in fact the *absolute* values of c and d both matter. For example, suppose that $c = d < 1$, so that the relative weighting of likelihoods and priors is correct, but both are underweighted (as we will see is usually the case). Then in general, the agent's posterior odds will be biased—with c fully driving the bias if the priors are equal and with d fully driving the bias if the likelihoods are equal, as already noted. Therefore, contrary to what is sometimes said, the evidence for base-rate neglect (discussed in this section) is not in tension with the evidence (also discussed in this section) that people generally underinfer.

---

[18] In the literature, what I refer to as underinference is often called "conservatism." To keep the distinction between theory and evidence clear, I reserve the term conservatism to refer to a particular theory of underinference discussed in Section 5.2.

The c and d parameters can be estimated from updating from simultaneous samples, in which people update in response to a one-shot sample of signals, or from updating from sequential samples, in which people update dynamically as additional signals are observed. Because the latter is more complex, I begin with evidence from simultaneous samples in Section 4.2 and then turn to evidence from sequential samples in Section 4.3.[19]

4.2 Evidence from simultaneous samples

Here I will review a set of stylized facts regarding biased inferences and biased use of priors that have emerged from simultaneous-sample experiments. I will both describe the results from specific experiments as well as report a meta-analysis intended to summarize the evidence from the literature as a whole. The meta-analysis extends the earlier meta-analysis reported by Benjamin et al. (2016, Appendix D) with additional data[20] and new analyses.

The vast majority of bookbag-and-poker-chip experiments focus on a particular class of updating problems: there are two states of the world, A and B; there are two signals, a and b; and the signals are drawn i.i.d., with probability θ_A of an a signal in state A and θ_B in state B. Participants are given the prior probabilities, and then they either observe a sequence of signals, such as $aabab$, or they are just told the total number of realized a and b signals, N_a and N_b. In simultaneous-sample experiments, participants' posterior beliefs are elicited only once, after the complete sample has been realized.

Most simultaneous-sample experiments further restrict attention to symmetric updating problems, in which (like in Edwards's example above) the probability of an a signal in state A is equal to the probability of a b signal in state B: $\theta \equiv \theta_A = 1 - \theta_B$. In the literature the parameter θ, which quantifies how diagnostic of the state any given signal is, is called the *diagnosticity* parameter. Without loss of generality, it is conventional to label the states as A or B such that $\theta > \frac{1}{2}$.

While the narrative literature review in this section is broader (for example, it includes non-binomial updating problems), the meta-analysis is restricted to two-state, binomial, symmetric updating problems. It uses the results from the 16 papers I could identify that (i) face experimental participants with updating problems from this class and (ii) report all the variables needed to calculate the correct answer—$p(A)$, $p(B)$, θ, N_a, and N_b—as well as the participants' mean or median posterior beliefs for at

---

[19] Recently, Augenblick and Rabin (2018) showed how a researcher can infer the directions of deviation of c and d from one based on observing how a person's probabilistic beliefs change in response to signals, even when the signals are not observed by the researcher. I am not aware of any empirical work yet that has estimated the biases using this approach.

[20] Specifically, here I add data from 6 new papers to the meta-analysis sample, bringing the total number of papers to 16. In addition, I conduct a new meta-analysis of 5 sequential-sample papers by combining sequential observations from 3 of the papers included in the earlier analysis with sequential-sample data from 2 new papers. The sequential-sample meta-analysis is discussed in Section 4.3 below.

least one such problem. I have posted on an Online Appendix on my website all of the data and code underlying these analyses.[21]

I first ask: how commonly do people underinfer versus overinfer? To address this question, I focus on updating problems in which the prior probabilities of the two states are equal because, as noted above in Section 4.1, in these problems any error in people's posterior beliefs can be attributed to biased inference. I measure experimental participants' posterior beliefs using log posterior odds, $\ln\left(\dfrac{\pi(A|S)}{\pi(B|S)}\right)$. This quantity is positive if participants believe that state A is more likely and negative if they believe that state B is more likely.

For each of the inference problems included in the meta-analysis, Fig. 2 Panel A plots participants' log posterior odds on the y-axis against the correct log posterior odds, $\ln\left(\dfrac{p(A|S)}{p(B|S)}\right)$, on the x-axis. The identity line (the dashed line in the figure) corresponds to Bayesian inference. To interpret the regression slope (the solid line), note that taking the logarithm of Eq. (4.6), participants' log posterior odds can be written

$$\ln\left(\frac{\pi(A|S)}{\pi(B|S)}\right) = c\ln\left(\frac{p(S|A)}{p(S|B)}\right) + d\ln\left(\frac{p(A)}{p(B)}\right),$$ (4.7)

and taking the logarithm of Eq. (4.3), the correct log posterior odds are

$$\ln\left(\frac{p(A|S)}{p(B|S)}\right) = \ln\left(\frac{p(S|A)}{p(S|B)}\right) + \ln\left(\frac{p(A)}{p(B)}\right).$$ (4.8)

In both equations, the prior-odds term vanishes because the updating problems are restricted to those with equal priors:

$$\ln\left(\frac{\pi(A|S)}{\pi(B|S)}\right) = c\ln\left(\frac{p(S|A)}{p(S|B)}\right),$$ (4.9)

$$\ln\left(\frac{p(A|S)}{p(B|S)}\right) = \ln\left(\frac{p(S|A)}{p(S|B)}\right).$$ (4.10)

Substituting Eq. (4.10) into Eq. (4.9) yields

$$\ln\left(\frac{\pi(A|S)}{\pi(B|S)}\right) = c\ln\left(\frac{p(A|S)}{p(B|S)}\right).$$ (4.11)

---

[21] Although Grether (1992) does not report all the needed variables, David Grether provided this data to me and gave me permission to share it, so it is included in the meta-analysis and made available on an Online Appendix on my website. I have also posted data from asymmetric updating problems (where $\theta_A \neq 1 - \theta_B$) on the Online Appendix on my website, even though these data are not included in the meta-analysis.

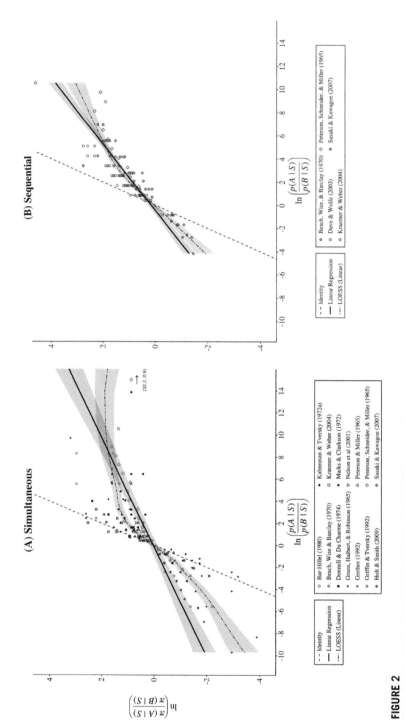

FIGURE 2

Participants' log-posterior-odds versus Bayesian log-posterior-odds. Panel (A): restricted to updating problems with equal priors. Panel (B): restricted to updating problems with equal initial priors, and log-posterior-odds are calculated from final posteriors. LOESS is implemented in R with a span of 0.75. Shaded regions are 95% confidence intervals.

Table 2 Regression of participants' log-posterior-odds on Bayesian log-posterior-odds.

	(A) Simultaneous		(B) Sequential	
	(1) **All data**	**(2)** **Only incentivized**	**(1)** **All data**	**(2)** **Only incentivized**
$\ln(p(S|A)/p(S|B))$	0.201	0.383	0.349	0.528
	(0.063)	(0.028)	(0.025)	(0.018)
Constant	0.029	−0.064	0.153	0.062
	(0.087)	(0.089)	(0.055)	(0.037)
R^2	0.462	0.764	0.808	0.965
#obs	147	76	111	43
#papers	14	6	5	2

Notes: Panel A: restricted to updating problems with equal priors. Panel B: restricted to updating problems with equal initial priors, and log-posterior-odds are calculated from final posteriors. Heteroskedasticity-robust standard errors in parentheses.

Therefore, the regression slope in the figure is a measure of c that is averaged across the updating problems included in the analysis. At each point in the figure, the ratio $\ln\left(\frac{\pi(A|S)}{\pi(B|S)}\right) / \ln\left(\frac{p(A|S)}{p(B|S)}\right)$ is a measure of the biased-inference parameter c for that inference problem.[22] Points below the identity line in the first quadrant and above the identity line in fourth quadrant correspond to underinference ($c < 1$).

From Fig. 2 Panel A, it can be seen that in these experiments, participants underinfer more often than they overinfer. The slope of the regression line is $\hat{c} = 0.20$, with a standard error of 0.063—far smaller than one. The figure also shows a locally linear regression curve, which suggests that the underinference tends to be more extreme when the correct inference is stronger.

The first column of Table 2 Panel A shows the linear regression results displayed in Fig. 2 Panel A. In the second column, the analysis is restricted to updating problems from incentivized experiments. In those experiments, the estimate is $\hat{c} = 0.38$, with a standard error of 0.028, indicating somewhat less but still substantial underinference on average and less noisy behavior.

---

[22] In the psychology literature on bookbag-and-poker-chip experiments, this quantity was referred to as the "accuracy ratio" (Peterson and Miller, 1965), and it was typically the main measure of biased updating relative to Bayes' Theorem. Sometimes, these experiments studied updating problems in which the priors are not equal, in which case the prior-odds terms in Eqs. (4.7) and (4.8) do not vanish, so the accuracy ratio reflects a mixture of c and d: $\dfrac{\ln\left(\frac{\pi(A|S)}{\pi(B|S)}\right)}{\ln\left(\frac{p(A|S)}{p(B|S)}\right)} = \dfrac{c\ln\left(\frac{p(S|A)}{p(S|B)}\right) + d\ln\left(\frac{p(A)}{p(B)}\right)}{\ln\left(\frac{p(S|A)}{p(S|B)}\right) + \ln\left(\frac{p(A)}{p(B)}\right)}$. In order to identify biased inference separately from evidence on biased use of prior information, I focus throughout this section on estimators that distinguish between c and d.

In experiments with binomial signals that did not meet all the criteria for inclusion in the meta-analysis, underinference has also been the general finding.[23] In addition, underinference has been the usual finding in experiments where, instead of the signals being binomial, the signals are multinomial.[24] When a signal is drawn from a normal distribution, underinference has occurred when the signal realization is far from its expected value in either state, and otherwise, nearly Bayesian inference or overinference has occurred.[25]

To summarize:

Stylized Fact 1. Underinference is by far the dominant direction of bias.

This conclusion may be surprising since, in our personal experiences, many of us observe people jumping to conclusions. After discussing the rest of the evidence and various theories, Section 10.1 returns to this apparent tension and discusses potential reconciliations. Section 5 discusses the leading theories for explaining underinference.

I next ask: how is underinference related to sample size, $N = N_a + N_b$? As a measure of the bias in inference, I will use the updating-problem-specific estimate $\hat{c}$ discussed above, $\ln\left(\frac{\pi(A|S)}{\pi(B|S)}\right) / \ln\left(\frac{p(A|S)}{p(B|S)}\right)$.

A number of papers have manipulated sample size while holding constant other features of the inference problem and reported the results in such a way that the relationship between N and $\hat{c}$ can be seen. Every such paper has found that larger N is associated with more underinference as measured by smaller $\hat{c}$.[26]

Turning to the meta-analysis sample, which includes studies that do not manipulate N, Fig. 3 Panel A plots the inference measure against N. The value of $\hat{c}$ is mostly smaller than one, as expected given that underinference is the predominant direction of bias. The slope of the regression line is negative, indicating that $\hat{c}$ is smaller at larger sample sizes. A locally linear regression suggests that the relationship between underinference and sample size is steeper at smaller sample sizes.

Stylized Fact 2. Underinference (as measured by $\hat{c}$) is more severe the larger the sample size.

Are inferences biased at a sample size of 1? While the regression line in Fig. 3 Panel A suggests that there is underinference when $N = 1$, the value of the regression

---

[23] For example, Chinnis and Peterson (1968), Peterson and Swensson (1968), Sanders (1968), De Swart (1972a, 1972b), and Antoniou et al. (2015).

[24] For example, Beach (1968), Phillips et al. (1966, Study 1), Dale (1968), Martin (1969), Martin and Gettys (1969), Shanteau (1972), and Chapman (1973).

[25] Nearly Bayesian inference was found by DuCharme and Peterson (1968, Studies 1 and 2) and DuCharme (1970, Studies 1 and 2), while overinference was found by Gustafson et al. (1973).

[26] I have found nine such papers: Green et al. (1965), Pitz (1967), Peterson et al. (1968, Study 2), Peterson and Swensson (1968), Sanders (1968), Kahneman and Tversky (1972a), Griffin and Tversky (1992, Study 1), Nelson et al. (2001, Study 1), and Kraemer and Weber (2004).

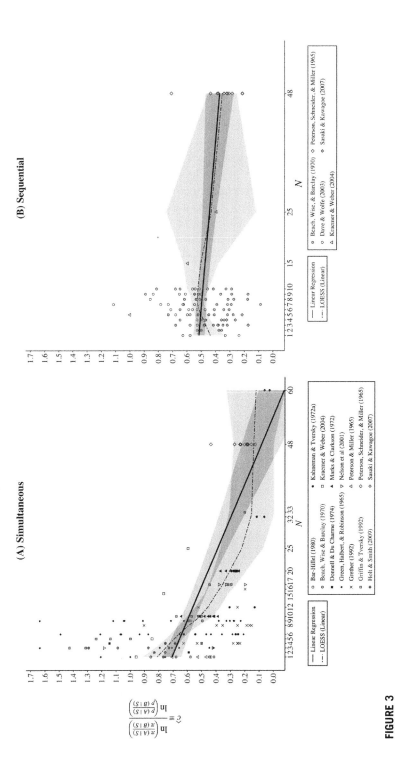

FIGURE 3

Inference measure $\hat{c}$ versus sample size N. Panel (A): restricted to updating problems with equal initial priors, N refers to final sample size, and log-posterior-odds are calculated from final posteriors. Panel (B): restricted to updating problems with equal priors. LOESS is implemented in R with a span of 0.75. Shaded regions are 95% confidence intervals.

line here relies largely on extrapolation from larger sample sizes. Focusing only on the 16 updating problems with $N = 1$, the mean $\hat{c}$ is 0.70 with a standard error of 0.057; restricted to the 7 updating problems from incentivized experiments, the mean is 0.86 with a standard error of 0.078. Thus, the data from the meta-analysis sample points to underinference from a sample size of 1.[27]

Among experiments with binomial updating problems and a sample size of 1 that did not meet all the criteria for inclusion in the meta-analysis, nearly all found substantial underinference or slight underinference,[28] with one exception (Robalo and Sayag, 2014).[29] One experiment observed overinference in an experimental condition with asymmetric rates that are close to each other (Peterson and Miller, 1965, $\theta_A = 0.6$, $\theta_B = 0.4$). In an experiment with a sample size of 1 in which the signal was drawn from a multinomial distribution, Phillips et al. (1966) found nearly Bayesian inference. As noted above, when a single signal is drawn from a normal distribution, underinference has occurred when the signal realization is far from its expected value in either state but not otherwise.[30]

Thus, while there are exceptions (which may or may not be systematic), the evidence from $N = 1$ samples can be summarized as generally finding underinference:

Stylized Fact 3. On average, people underinfer after observing only a single signal.

I next ask which features of the sample matter most for people's inferences. It turns out that for Bayesian inferences in (symmetric) inference problems, a sufficient statistic is the *difference* between the number of a and b signals: $N_a - N_b$. This fact can be seen by specializing Eq. (4.3) to the case of symmetric, binomial signals:

$$
\frac{p(A|S)}{p(B|S)} = \left[\frac{\binom{N}{N_a} \theta^{N_a}(1-\theta)^{N_b}}{\binom{N}{N_a}(1-\theta)^{N_a}\theta^{N_b}} \right] \left[\frac{p(A)}{p(B)} \right]
$$

$$
= \left(\frac{\theta}{1-\theta} \right)^{(N_a - N_b)} \left[\frac{p(A)}{p(B)} \right]. \tag{4.12}
$$

---

[27] For sample sizes of 2, 3, 4, 5, and 6, the corresponding mean $\hat{c}$ is 0.73 (SE $= 0.07$), 0.98 (SE $= 0.10$), 0.52 (SE $= 0.08$), 1.06 (SE $= 0.09$), and 0.67 (SE $= 0.10$), respectively. Thus, the broad impression is underinference across these small sample sizes, but we cannot reject overinference for sample sizes of 3 and 5.

[28] Substantial underinference was found by Dave and Wolfe (2003) and Gettys and Manley (1968, Studies 1 and 2), whereas slight underinference was found by Chinnis and Peterson (1968), Peterson and Swensson (1968, Study 1), Kraemer and Weber (2004), Sasaki and Kawagoe (2007), and Ambuehl and Li (2018).

[29] Robalo and Sayag (2014) studied a symmetric binomial updating problem with 60–40 priors. Their experimental participants did not have posteriors that are systematically less extreme than Bayesian posteriors. Depending on the degree of base-rate neglect, their evidence could be consistent with either Bayesian inference or overinference.

[30] DuCharme and Peterson (1968, Studies 1 and 2), DuCharme (1970, Studies 1 and 2), and Gustafson et al. (1973).

Kahneman and Tversky (1972a) pointed out that this feature of normatively correct inferences is counterintuitive. For example, to most of us, 2 a's out of 2 feels like much stronger evidence in favor of state A than 51 a's out of 100, but in fact they are equally strong evidence because $N_a - N_b = 2$ in both cases. Rather than relying on the sample *difference*, $N_a - N_b$, Kahneman and Tversky hypothesized that people intuitively draw inferences on the basis of the sample *proportion*, N_a/N.

Kahneman and Tversky tested this hypothesis in a set of ten hypothetical updating problems[31] was (p. 447):

> Consider two very large decks of cards, denoted A and B. In deck A, 2/3 of the cards are marked a, and 1/3 are marked b. In deck B, 1/3 of the cards are marked a, and 2/3 are marked b. One of the decks has been selected by chance, and 12 cards have been drawn at random from it, of which 8 are marked a and 4 are marked b. What do you think the probability is that the 12 cards were drawn from deck A, that is, from the deck in which most of the cards are marked a?

In this problem, which is similar to Edwards's problem quoted above, the proportion of a signals is 2/3, and the difference between the number of a and b signals is 4. Similarly, as in Edwards's problem, the median subject reported a belief of 70%, much weaker than the correct posterior of 94%. Two other problems, each asked to a different group of subjects, were the same except that the numbers of a and b signals were changed from 8 and 4 (in the quoted problem above) to 4 and 2 in one problem and to 40 and 20 in the other. These problems hold constant the proportion of a signals but, by manipulating the sample size, change the true probabilities to 80% and 99.9999%, respectively. Yet, consistent with Kahneman and Tversky's hypothesis, the median subject's reported belief was virtually unaffected: 68% and 70%, respectively.

In other problems, Kahneman and Tversky varied the proportion but held constant the difference and found that people reported a higher belief in state A when the proportion of a signals was higher. Kahneman and Tversky's finding that beliefs depend *only* on the sample proportion is an extreme result[32]; other experiments in the literature (discussed next) also find support for the hypothesis that people's inferences

---

[31] In the original statement of the problem, the cards were marked "X" and "O." I've changed them to "a" and "b" for consistency of notation with the rest of this chapter. Moreover, while Kahneman and Tversky quote directly from their problem with $\theta = 5/6$, I instead describe their other set of problems, with $\theta = 2/3$, for greater comparability with Edwards' illustrative problem above.

[32] Kahneman and Tversky's results are also extreme in another way: they find that the median subject's posterior belief is completely insensitive to the diagnosticity parameter θ. For example, in three updating problems identical to the those mentioned above but with $\theta = 5/6$ instead of 2/3, the median subject's posterior belief was 70% in all three cases. As discussed below, such complete insensitivity to θ has not been observed in updating problems more generally. Why were Kahneman and Tversky's results so extreme? A possible explanation is that the median subject was following a simple heuristic of setting their posterior belief $\pi(A|N_a, N_b)$ roughly *equal* to the sample proportion N_a/N. As Kahneman and Tversky pointed out, for all three sample proportions they investigated, the median subject's posterior belief was very nearly equal to the sample proportion and was insensitive to both N and θ. Earlier, Beach et al. (1970) proposed that people follow this heuristic (and cite Kriz, 1967 as having proposed it even earlier). Beach,

are influenced by the sample proportion, but they generally find that the difference between the number of a and b signals also matters.

Evans and Dusoir (1977) also found that many people rely on sample proportion over sample size (in a more complex experiment, Evans and Pollard (1982) reach the same conclusion). They asked undergraduates to make pairwise judgments such as whether a sample of coin flips with 8 heads and 2 tails provides stronger or weaker evidence of a heads-biased coin than a sample of 70 heads and 30 tails. When sample proportion and sample size considerations conflicted, as in this example, more than two-thirds of participants endorsed the sample with the larger proportion as providing more evidence.

Griffin and Tversky (1992) quantified the relative roles of sample size and sample proportions in driving people's inferences. They posed twelve updating problems to each of their undergraduate participants, with equal priors for the two states and the diagnosticity parameter θ fixed at $\frac{3}{5}$. Across the twelve problems, the number of signals varied from 3 to 33, and the sample proportion varied from 0.53 (9 a's out of 17) to 1 (3 a's out of 3 and 5 out of 5). To assess how participants' use of sample size and sample proportion deviated from Bayesian inference, Griffin and Tversky estimated a regression equation that nests Bayesian inference as a special case. I will derive this regression in four steps.

The starting point is the formula for Bayesian inference in symmetric binomial problems, Eq. (4.12), when the priors are equal:

$$\frac{p(A|S)}{p(B|S)} = \left(\frac{\theta}{1-\theta} \right)^{(N_a - N_b)}.$$

The first step is to obtain a linear equation by taking the double logarithm[33]:

$$\ln \left(\ln \left(\frac{p(A|S)}{p(B|S)} \right) \right) = \ln(N_a - N_b) + \ln \left(\ln \left(\frac{\theta}{1-\theta} \right) \right).$$

Wise, and Barclay found evidence consistent with this heuristic in simultaneous-sample updating problems but not sequential-sample updating problems. Marks and Clarkson (1972) found that roughly 2/5 of their experimental participants seemed to follow this heuristic. As discussed below, Griffin and Tversky (1992) found that their median participant's posterior was somewhat sensitive to N and θ, which is inconsistent with the median participant reporting beliefs according to this heuristic.

[33] Griffin and Tversky ensured that all of the terms in this equation are well defined by setting $\theta = \frac{3}{5} > \frac{1}{2}$ and posing updating problems in which $N_a > N_b$. In the meta-analysis data I analyze below, I guarantee $\theta > \frac{1}{2}$ by labeling the states such that state A has the higher rate of a signals. However, $N_a > N_b$ does not hold for all of the observations. To include in the analysis the observations where $N_a < N_b$, I exploit the symmetry of the updating problem, switching N_a and N_b and replacing participants' posterior odds $\frac{\pi(A|S)}{\pi(B|S)}$ in Eq. (4.14) by $\frac{\pi(B|S)}{\pi(A|S)}$. For example, if participant's posterior odds were $\frac{1}{3}$ after observing a 4 b's and 1 a, I enter it into the analysis as if the odds were 3 after having observed 4 a's and 1 b. I drop the 25 observations for which $N_a = N_b$ in the simultaneous-sample experiments and 16 such observations in the sequential-sample experiments.

Second, to separate out the role of the sample proportion, the sample-difference term is decomposed into the sum of a sample-proportion term and a sample-size term:

$$\ln\left(\ln\left(\frac{p(A|S)}{p(B|S)}\right)\right) = \ln\left(\frac{N_a - N_b}{N}\right) + \ln(N) + \ln\left(\ln\left(\frac{\theta}{1-\theta}\right)\right).$$

Third, this rule for Bayesian inference is generalized by allowing the coefficients to differ from one, and a response-error term is added:

$$\ln\left(\ln\left(\frac{\pi(A|S)}{\pi(B|S)}\right)\right) = \alpha_0 + \alpha_1 \ln\left(\frac{N_a - N_b}{N}\right) + \alpha_2 \ln(N)$$
$$+ \alpha_3 \ln\left(\ln\left(\frac{\theta}{1-\theta}\right)\right) + \epsilon. \tag{4.13}$$

Finally, because θ did not vary across their updating problems, Griffin and Tversky absorbed the θ term into the constant:

$$\ln\left(\ln\left(\frac{\pi(A|S)}{\pi(B|S)}\right)\right) = \tilde{\alpha}_0 + \alpha_1 \ln\left(\frac{N_a - N_b}{N}\right) + \alpha_2 \ln(N) + \epsilon. \tag{4.14}$$

The null hypothesis of Bayesian inference is $\alpha_1 = \alpha_2 = 1$. By estimating regression Eq. (4.14), Griffin and Tversky tested whether the sample proportion and sample size are weighted as much as they should be according to Bayesian inference as well as how they are weighted relative to each other.

Griffin and Tversky reported estimates of $\hat{\alpha}_1 = 0.81$ and $\hat{\alpha}_2 = 0.31$, respectively.[34] To interpret these results, note first that the hypothesis $\alpha_1 = \alpha_2$ is rejected; thus, experimental participants are not drawing inferences based on the difference between the number of a signals and the number of b signals. Next, the results indicate that both α_1 and α_2 are smaller than one, consistent with underinference on average (Stylized Fact 1), and $\alpha_2 < 1$ points to greater underinference from larger samples (Stylized Fact 2). Since the hypothesis $\alpha_1 = 1$ and $\alpha_2 = 0$ is rejected, Griffin and Tversky's results are less extreme than Kahneman and Tversky's (1972a): participants' inferences are not *entirely* driven by the sample proportion; they do take sample size into account to some extent. Finally, the results indicate that $\alpha_1 > \alpha_2$, meaning that relative to (the correct) equal weighting of sample proportion and sample size, sample proportion influences inferences by more.

Griffin and Tversky's regression can be replicated in the meta-analysis data. Because this data has variation in θ, I estimate Eq. (4.13) rather than Eq. (4.14). The first

---

[34] Specifically, Griffin and Tversky (p. 416) wrote: "For the median data, the observed regression weight for strength (.81) was almost 3 times larger than that for weight (.31)." However, when I estimate Eq. (4.14) using the median data reported in Griffin and Tversky, I find $\tilde{\alpha}_0 = 0.44$ (SE $= 0.115$), $\hat{\alpha}_1 = 1.02$ (SE $= 0.094$), and $\hat{\alpha}_2 = 0.17$ (SE $= 0.064$). In personal communication with Dale Griffin, we were unable to recover how the regression in the paper differed from my regression. Regardless of which estimates are used, the main conclusions are the same.

Table 3   Regression of participants' log-log-posterior-odds on features of the observed sample.

	(A) Simultaneous			(B) Sequential		
	(1) All data	**(2)** All data	**(3)** Only incentivized	**(1)** All data	**(2)** All data	**(3)** Only incentivized
$\ln N$	0.411	0.412	0.562	0.773	0.771	1.024
	(0.049)	(0.050)	(0.082)	(0.056)	(0.055)	(0.071)
$\ln\left(\frac{2N_a - N}{N}\right)$	0.848	0.850	0.870	0.805	0.804	0.829
	(0.071)	(0.075)	(0.117)	(0.073)	(0.073)	(0.070)
$\ln\ln\left(\frac{\theta}{1-\theta}\right)$	0.394	0.395	0.515	0.640	0.643	1.275
	(0.082)	(0.082)	(0.097)	(0.151)	(0.149)	(0.480)
$I\left\{\frac{N_a}{N} = \theta\right\}$		0.022			0.269	
		(0.086)			(0.149)	
Constant	−0.052	−0.053	−0.120	−0.610	−0.620	−0.726
	(0.080)	(0.082)	(0.104)	(0.096)	(0.095)	(0.151)
R^2	0.631	0.631	0.648	0.713	0.720	0.895
#obs	147	147	76	111	111	43
#papers	14	14	6	5	5	2

Notes: Panel A: restricted to updating problems with equal priors. Panel B: restricted to updating problems with equal initial priors, and log-log-posterior-odds are calculated from final posteriors. States A and B are labeled so as to maximize the number of observations included in the regression; see footnote 33. Heteroskedasticity-robust standard errors in parentheses.

column of Table 3 Panel A shows the results. The estimates are consistent with Griffin and Tversky's reported estimates, not only qualitatively but even quantitatively: the estimated coefficient on sample proportion, $\hat{\alpha}_1$, is 0.85 with a standard error of 0.071, and the estimated coefficient on sample size, $\hat{\alpha}_2$, is 0.41 with a standard error of 0.049. (I discuss the coefficient on the θ term below.) The third column of the table repeats the analysis but restricted to incentivized experiments, and the results are similar. Thus, while sample size matters to some extent, the sample proportion has a much greater impact on participants' inferences on average.

Stylized Fact 4. Rather than depending on the sample difference, $N_a - N_b$, people's inferences are largely driven by the sample proportion, $\dfrac{N_a - N_b}{N}$.

Beginning with Grether (1980), several papers have investigated the hypothesis that the sample proportion has an especially large impact on inference when it equals the rate of a signals in one of the states. Grether's idea was that if the sample proportion equals (say) θ_A, then participants can rely on the representativeness heuristic (discussed in Section 7) in drawing an inference in favor of state A. Elaborating on this idea, Camerer (1987) referred to the hypothesis that people draw stronger inferences when the sample proportion exactly matches one of the rates as *exact representativeness*.

In Grether's experiment, the prior probability of state A varied across conditions, equaling $1/3$, $1/2$, or $2/3$. The probability of an a signal was $\theta_A = 2/3$ in state A and $\theta_B = 1/2$ in state B. Experimental participants observed a set of $N = 6$ signals and guessed whether the state was A or B. In some conditions, participants were paid a bonus for guessing accurately. To analyze his data, Grether ran a regression corresponding to Eq. (4.7) but with indicator variables for the observed sample proportion matching the states' rates:

$$
\ln\left(\frac{\pi(A|S)}{\pi(B|S)}\right) = \beta_0 + \beta_1 \ln\left(\frac{p(S|A)}{p(S|B)}\right) + \beta_2 \ln\left(\frac{p(A)}{p(B)}\right) + \beta_3 I\left\{\frac{N_a}{N} = \theta_A\right\}
$$
$$
+ \beta_4 I\left\{\frac{N_a}{N} = \theta_B\right\} + \eta. \tag{4.15}
$$

Because participants reported a guess about the state rather than a posterior probability, Grether estimated a logistic regression version of this equation, and thus the absolute magnitudes of the coefficients are not straightforward to interpret. Across various specifications and subsamples, his results generally indicated $\hat{\beta}_3 > 0$ and $\hat{\beta}_4 < 0$, consistent with exact representativeness. However, in two similar experiments conducted subsequently, Grether (1992) found much more equivocal evidence.

Camerer (1987, 1990) aimed to test whether biased updating would survive in markets. He conducted an experimental asset market, in which participants traded a state-contingent asset. In each round of the experiment, participants observed a set of $N = 3$ signals before trading. The probability of an a signal was $2/3$ in state A and $1/3$ in state B. Consistent with exact representativeness, he found that when the observed sample contained 2 a's and 1 b, the price of a state-contingent asset that pays off in state A was too high, and when the observed sample contained 1 a and 2 b's, the price of a state-contingent asset that pays off in state B was too high.

To assess the evidence regarding "exact representativeness" more broadly in bookbag-and-poker-chip experiments, I analyze the meta-analysis sample. Because this sample has variation in N and θ and is restricted to updating problems with equal priors, I estimate a version of Eq. (4.13) rather than Eq. (4.15). Specifically, Column 2 of Table 3 Panel A shows the results when I have included an indicator for the sample proportion being equal to θ. (There is no indicator for the sample proportion being equal to $1 - \theta$ because, as per footnote 33, all observations are coded such that $\theta > \frac{1}{2}$ and $N_a > N_b$.)

The coefficient on this indicator is 0.02, with a standard error of 0.086. The sign is in accordance with what exact representativeness would predict, but the standard error is much larger than the point estimate. Thus, I find little evidence for exact representativeness in the meta-analysis sample, but the estimate is too noisy to draw strong conclusions.

Stylized Fact 5. While some experiments have found evidence of overinference, or less underinference, when the observed sample proportion equals the rate in one of the states, it has not been robustly seen across experiments.

As a final question about inference: how is underinference related to the diagnosticity parameter, θ? Almost every study[35] that varies θ while holding constant other features of the updating problem has found greater underinference (as measured by $\hat{c}$) for θ further from $\frac{1}{2}$, with the exceptions of Gettys and Manley (1968), who found no relationship, and Shanteau (1972), who found the opposite in a multinomial-signal experiment.

Turning to the meta-analysis data, Fig. 4 Panel A plots $\hat{c}$ against diagnosticity θ. The slope of the regression line is -0.97 with a standard error of 0.27. The negative slope indicates that as θ increases, there is more underinference on average, consistent with what the individual studies have found.

To control for other factors that affect inferences and to examine whether participants adequately account for θ (compared to Bayesian inference), I return to Table 3 Panel A and examine the coefficient on the diagnosticity term. As noted above, Bayesian inference implies that the coefficient on $\ln\left(\ln\left(\frac{\theta}{1-\theta}\right)\right)$ should equal one. Instead, as seen in Column 1, the coefficient estimate is 0.39 (standard error $= 0.082$). The estimate remains similar, 0.52 (standard error $= 0.097$), when the sample is restricted to incentivized studies (Column 3). The fact that this coefficient is in between zero and one indicates that subjects' inferences take the different rates of a signals across states into account but less strongly than they should.

In asymmetric updating problems (which are excluded from the meta-analysis), there is some evidence that people overinfer when the rate of a signals in state A is similar to the rate in state B. As mentioned above, Peterson and Miller (1965) found overinference in inference problems with a single signal when the rates were $(\theta_A, \theta_B) = (0.6, 0.43)$, but they found underinference when the rates were further apart: $(\theta_A, \theta_B) = (0.83, 0.17)$, $(\theta_A, \theta_B) = (0.71, 0.2)$, and $(\theta_A, \theta_B) = (0.67, 0.33)$. Griffin and Tversky (1992, Study 3) posed a set of updating problems in which the number of a signals is 7, 8, 9, or 10. When the rates were far apart, $(\theta_A, \theta_B) = (0.6, 0.25)$, their experimental participants underinferred: the median posterior beliefs that the state is A were 0.60, 0.70, 0.80, and 0.90, respectively, whereas a Bayesian's posteriors would be 0.95, 0.98, 0.998, and 0.999. In contrast, when the rates were close together, $(\theta_A, \theta_B) = (0.6, 0.5)$, the participants overinferred, with median posterior beliefs 0.55, 0.66, 0.75, and 0.85, respectively, compared to a Bayesian's posteriors of 0.54, 0.64, 0.72, and 0.80.[36] Grether (1992, Study 2) also

---

[35] Green et al. (1965), Peterson and Miller (1965), Sanders (1968), Peterson and Swensson (1968, Studies 1 and 2), Peterson et al. (1968, Study 2), Beach et al. (1970), Kahneman and Tversky (1972a), Donnell and DuCharme (1975). Vlek (1965) and Vlek and Van der Heijden (1967) are cited in Slovic and Lichtenstein (1971) as also finding this result, but I have not been able to track down those papers.

[36] Griffin and Tversky's (1992, Study 3) evidence may also be related to a hypothesis, proposed by Vlek (1965), that people underinfer by more when an event occurs that is unlikely in both states. In a test of

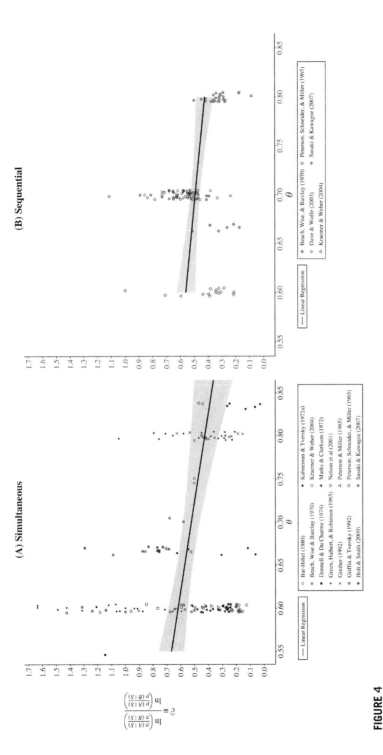

FIGURE 4

Inference measure $\hat{c}$ versus diagnosticity θ. Panel (A): restricted to updating problems with equal priors. Panel (B): restricted to updating problems with equal initial priors, and log-posterior-odds are calculated from final posteriors. Shaded regions are 95% confidence intervals.

found overinference in asymmetric updating problems with $(\theta_A, \theta_B) = (0.67, 0.5)$. Recently, in simultaneous-sample updating problems with a single signal, Ambuehl and Li (2018) also found underinference when θ_A and θ_B are far apart and overinference when they are close together.

Stylized Fact 6. Underinference (as measured by $\hat{c}$) is more severe the larger is the diagnosticity parameter θ. In asymmetric inference problems, people may overinfer when the rates θ_A and θ_B are close together.

To conclude the summary of evidence from simultaneous-updating experiments, I turn to biased use of priors. Five bookbag-and-poker-chip experiments that manipulated the priors found that people under-use prior information relative to what is prescribed by Bayes' Theorem, and two found that people over-use prior information.[37]

To examine the evidence across studies, I now add into the meta-analysis sample the updating problems with unequal priors. Whereas we had focused on problems with equal priors in order to isolate biased inference, we cannot follow the analogous strategy here of focusing on problems with equal likelihoods because there is little evidence from such problems, and the results require more nuanced discussion; I defer discussion of that evidence to Section 6. Therefore, in order to identify biased use of priors, I will need to control for biased inferences.

To do so, I exploit the fact that we previously estimated biased inferences in regression Eq. (4.13). The fitted values from that regression tell us what people's posterior odds would be in an updating problem with equal priors. Here, I will treat the fitted values as telling us what people's (biased) subjective likelihood ratio would be, before it is combined with the prior odds. That is, we replace Eq. (4.6) by[38]

$$\frac{\pi(A|S)}{\pi(B|S)} = \frac{\pi(S|A)}{\pi(S|B)} \left[\frac{p(A)}{p(B)} \right]^d, \tag{4.16}$$

---

this hypothesis, Beach (1968) ran a bookbag-and-poker-chip experiment with multinomial signals: the letters A–F written on the back of a card. Cards were drawn from one of two decks, a red deck and a green deck, which had different proportions of the letters. Different groups of participants faced decks with the same likelihood ratios for the letters but different probabilities. For example, for one group, the probability of an F card was 0.03 for the red deck and 0.06 for the green deck, and for another group, 0.16 and 0.32. Holding the likelihood ratio fixed, Beach found greater underinference when the probabilities were smaller, consistent with Vlek's hypothesis. Slovic and Lichtenstein (1971) reported that Vlek (1965) and Vlek and Van der Heijden (1967) found similar results, but I have been unable to obtain those papers.

[37] Those that found under-use are Green et al. (1965), Bar-Hillel (1980), Griffin and Tversky (1992, Study 2), Grether (1992, Study 3), and Holt and Smith (2009), while those that found over-use are Peterson and Miller (1965) and Grether (1992, Study 2).

[38] Alternatively, we could consider directly estimating Eq. (4.6), but I do not do so because it is misspecified if treated as a "structural" model: as discussed above, the results from estimating Eq. (4.13) tell us that the exponent c depends on sample size, sample proportion, and diagnosticity in the updating problem.

where $\dfrac{\pi(S|A)}{\pi(S|B)}$ is a person's subjective likelihood ratio, and for any given updating problem, we use Eq. (4.13) to obtain an estimate of the logarithm of this subjective likelihood ratio, $\ln\left(\widehat{\dfrac{\pi(S|A)}{\pi(S|B)}}\right)$.[39] Next, we take the logarithm of Eq. (4.16) and isolate the prior ratio on the right side:

$$\ln\left(\frac{\pi(A|S)}{\pi(B|S)}\right) - \ln\left(\widehat{\frac{\pi(S|A)}{\pi(S|B)}}\right) = d\ln\left(\frac{p(A)}{p(B)}\right). \tag{4.17}$$

Fig. 5 plots the left-hand side of Eq. (4.17) against the right-hand side. If experimental participants correctly use prior odds, then $d = 1$, so the points should fall along the identity line (the dashed line). Instead, the slope of the regression line (the solid line) is less than one, indicating under-use of prior odds.

For more formal evidence, I estimate the regression equation:

$$\ln\left(\frac{\pi(A|S)}{\pi(B|S)}\right) - \ln\left(\widehat{\frac{\pi(S|A)}{\pi(S|B)}}\right) = \gamma_0 + \gamma_1\ln\left(\frac{p(A)}{p(B)}\right) + \zeta. \tag{4.18}$$

The results are shown in Table 4. The first column represents the regression illustrated in Fig. 5, while the second column restricts the data to experiments with unequal priors, which is the subset of the data that identifies γ_1. As expected, the estimate of d, $\widehat{\gamma}_1$, is essentially the same in both columns: 0.60 with a standard error of 0.066. This estimate of d is substantially smaller than one, indicating that on average people under-use prior information.

The third column of Table 4 re-runs the analysis from column 1, this time restricted to incentivized experiments. In this case, the estimate of d is 0.43 with a standard error of 0.086, indicating even more extreme under-use of priors. Thus, both the evidence from individual papers and the evidence from the meta-analysis point rather strongly to under-use of prior information.

Stylized Fact 7. People exhibit base-rate neglect.

---

[39] There is a nuance: the predicted value from Eq. (4.13) is an estimator for $\ln\left(\ln\left(\frac{\pi(A|S)}{\pi(B|S)}\right)\right)$, but for Eq. (4.17), what is needed is an estimate of $\ln\left(\frac{\pi(A|S)}{\pi(B|S)}\right)$. Simply exponentiating the estimate $\ln\left(\ln\left(\widehat{\frac{\pi(A|S)}{\pi(B|S)}}\right)\right)$ is not a consistent estimator for $\ln\left(\frac{\pi(A|S)}{\pi(B|S)}\right)$ due to Jensen's inequality. I therefore generate an estimate of $\ln\left(\frac{\pi(A|S)}{\pi(B|S)}\right)$ by calculating $e^{\widehat{\mu}+\frac{1}{2}\widehat{\sigma}^2}$, where $\widehat{\mu} = \ln\left(\ln\left(\widehat{\frac{\pi(A|S)}{\pi(B|S)}}\right)\right)$ and $\widehat{\sigma}^2$ is the estimated variance of the residual from Eq. (4.13). This estimator is consistent under the assumption that $\ln\left(\frac{\pi(A|S)}{\pi(B|S)}\right)$ is normally distributed.

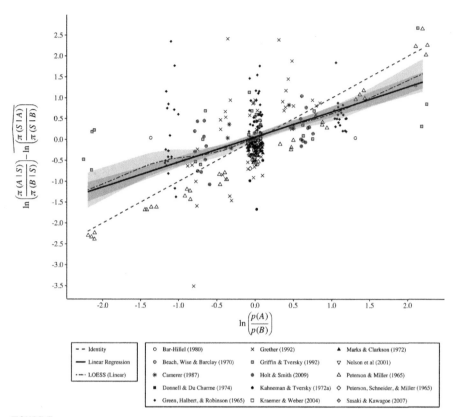

- - Identity	○ Bar-Hillel (1980)	✕ Grether (1992)	▲ Marks & Clarkson (1972)
— Linear Regression	◔ Beach, Wise & Barclay (1970)	▣ Griffin & Tversky (1992)	▽ Nelson et al (2001)
- · LOESS (Linear)	✳ Camerer (1987)	⊕ Holt & Smith (2009)	△ Peterson & Miller (1965)
	■ Donnell & Du Charme (1974)	◆ Kahneman & Tversky (1972a)	◇ Peterson, Schneider, & Miller (1965)
	◆ Green, Halbert, & Robinson (1965)	▢ Kraemer & Weber (2004)	◈ Sasaki & Kawagoe (2007)

FIGURE 5

Participants' log-posterior-odds adjusted for inference biases versus log-prior-odds.
Simultaneous-sample updating problems only. LOESS is implemented in R with a span of 0.75. Shaded regions are 95% confidence intervals.

Table 4 Regression of participants' log-posterior-odds adjusted for inference biases on log-prior-odds.

	(1) All data	(2) Only unequal priors	(3) Only incentivized
$\ln(p(A)/p(B))$	0.601	0.601	0.434
	(0.066)	(0.066)	(0.086)
Constant	0.064	0.120	0.149
	(0.039)	(0.066)	(0.053)
R^2	0.321	0.398	0.145
#obs	296	149	167
#papers	15	7	6

Notes: *Simultaneous-sample updating problems only. Heteroskedasticity-robust standard errors in parentheses.*

While the experiments discussed in Section 6 have been the focus of the literature on base-rate neglect, Stylized Fact 7 shows that the evidence for base-rate neglect extends to bookbag-and-poker-chip experiments.[40]

4.3 Evidence from sequential samples

Up until now, I have focused on bookbag-and-poker-chip experiments in which the sample was presented simultaneously. A number of bookbag-and-poker-chip experiments, however, have been sequential-sample experiments: participants observe a sample sequentially and report updated beliefs after each new signal (or set of signals) is observed. I now turn to the evidence from these experiments.

An initial conceptual question—which matters for how the data should be analyzed—is how people "group" signals. In the terminology of Benjamin et al. (2016, Appendix A), who provide formal definitions, one hypothesis is that people are *acceptive*: they group together signals that are presented to them together, and they treat sets of signals presented separately as distinct samples. For example, suppose two independent signals are observed sequentially. If people are acceptive, then they would update their beliefs after each signal, with their updated beliefs after the first signal becoming their priors when updating in response to the next signal. Another leading hypothesis is that people are *pooling*: at any point in time, people pool all the signals they have received up until that point and update from their initial priors using the pooled sample.

For a Bayesian updater, the grouping of the signals is irrelevant. Continuing with the example of two independent signals, suppose that a Bayesian is acceptive and hence updates after each signal. Using Eq. (4.3), her posterior odds after the first signal are

$$\frac{p(A|s_1)}{p(B|s_1)} = \frac{p(s_1|A)}{p(s_1|B)} \frac{p(A)}{p(B)},$$

and her posterior odds after the second signal are

---

[40] Few papers have addressed the question of whether giving people feedback leads to more accurate updating, but what evidence there is suggests only limited impact. Specifically, two papers have studied the effect of telling experimental participants the correct posterior probabilities after each updating problem. Martin and Gettys (1969) compared the effect of doing so with the effect of merely telling them the true state. The group that received posterior-probability feedback underinferred by less than the group that received true-state feedback, but over 200 trials, there was no detectable learning in either group, except possibly very early on. Donnell and DuCharme (1975) found that telling experimental participants the correct posterior probabilities after each of 60 updating problems eliminated their underinference, with almost all of the learning occurring in the first 10 trials. However, when participants were then faced with a new updating problem for which naïve participants tend to infer correctly, they overinferred. Donnell and DuCharme concluded that the feedback had caused participants to report more extreme beliefs but not to become better at drawing inferences.

$$\frac{p(A|s_1, s_2)}{p(B|s_1, s_2)} = \frac{p(s_2|A)}{p(s_2|B)} \frac{p(A|s_1)}{p(B|s_1)} = \frac{p(s_2|A)}{p(s_2|B)} \left(\frac{p(s_1|A)}{p(s_1|B)} \frac{p(A)}{p(B)} \right)$$
$$= \frac{p(s_1, s_2|A)}{p(s_1, s_2|B)} \frac{p(A)}{p(B)}.$$

If instead, she updates after the second signal by pooling both signals and updating from her original priors, then her posterior odds after the second signal are

$$\frac{p(A|s_1, s_2)}{p(B|s_1, s_2)} = \frac{p(s_1, s_2|A)}{p(s_1, s_2|B)} \frac{p(A)}{p(B)},$$

which are the same as the posterior odds from updating sequentially.

For a biased updater, however, grouping matters (see Cripps, 2018, for related discussion). Using Eq. (4.6), if the agent is acceptive, then her posterior odds after the first signal are

$$\frac{\pi(A|s_1)}{\pi(B|s_1)} = \left[\frac{p(s_1|A)}{p(s_1|B)} \right]^{c(1)} \left[\frac{p(A)}{p(B)} \right]^{d},$$

where $c(N)$ denotes the bias in inference from a sample of size N (recall from Stylized Fact 2 that underinference is increasing in sample size). Her posterior odds after the second signal are

$$\frac{\pi(A|s_1, s_2)}{\pi(B|s_1, s_2)} = \left[\frac{p(s_2|A)}{p(s_2|B)} \right]^{c(1)} \left[\frac{p(A|s_1)}{p(B|s_1)} \right]^{d}$$
$$= \left[\frac{p(s_2|A)}{p(s_2|B)} \right]^{c(1)} \left[\left[\frac{p(s_1|A)}{p(s_1|B)} \right]^{c(1)} \left[\frac{p(A)}{p(B)} \right]^{d} \right]^{d}$$
$$= \left[\frac{p(s_2|A)}{p(s_2|B)} \right]^{c(1)} \left[\frac{p(s_1|A)}{p(s_1|B)} \right]^{c(1)d} \left[\frac{p(A)}{p(B)} \right]^{d^2}. \qquad (4.19)$$

In contrast, if she pools the signals and then updates, then her posterior odds are

$$\frac{\pi(A|s_1, s_2)}{\pi(B|s_1, s_2)} = \left[\frac{p(s_1, s_2|A)}{p(s_1, s_2|B)} \right]^{c(2)} \left[\frac{p(A)}{p(B)} \right]^{d}$$
$$= \left[\left(\frac{p(s_2|A)}{p(s_2|B)} \right) \left(\frac{p(s_1|A)}{p(s_1|B)} \right) \right]^{c(2)} \left[\frac{p(A)}{p(B)} \right]^{d}$$
$$= \left[\frac{p(s_2|A)}{p(s_2|B)} \right]^{c(2)} \left[\frac{p(s_1|A)}{p(s_1|B)} \right]^{c(2)} \left[\frac{p(A)}{p(B)} \right]^{d}. \qquad (4.20)$$

Eq. (4.20) differs from Eq. (4.19) for two reasons: if the agent updates separately after each signal, then (i) the bias in inference is the bias corresponding to a sample size of 1 rather than 2, and (ii) the information from the first signal is incorporated into the agent's prior when the second signal is processed, and so her biased use of priors affects how the first signal enters into her final posterior. These differences can matter not only for the analysis of experimental data, but also for the implications of biased updating in real-world environments. For further discussion of the implications of (i) and (ii), see Sections 5.1 and 6, respectively.

Only two papers have explicitly tested experimentally between different grouping hypotheses, and both find evidence against pooling. Pooling predicts that people's posterior beliefs should not depend on how signals are presented. In incentivized updating problems, Kraemer and Weber (2004) found that mean beliefs of experimental participants presented with a sample of 3 a signals and 2 b signals differed marginally from those of experimental participants who were instead shown the same signals as two separate samples, one with 3 a's and 0 b's and one with 0 a's and 2 b's. Kraemer and Weber similarly found a difference in posteriors when participants were presented with a single sample of 13 a's and 12 b's, as opposed to a sequence of two samples, 13 a's and 0 b's and then 0 a's and 12 b's. Shu and Wu (2003, Study 3) found that participants who observed 10 signals one at a time reported a different posterior belief than participants who observed the same 10 signals two at a time or five at a time.

Although less clean, comparisons between participants' posteriors in simultaneous-sample versus sequential-sample experiments also bear on the pooling hypothesis. Holding constant other features of the updating problems, pooling predicts no differences in participants' posteriors. Sanders (1968) found less extreme posterior odds in sequential-sample updating problems, while Beach et al. (1970) found more extreme posterior odds.

To obtain a more systematic comparison, I extended the meta-analysis sample to incorporate updating problems in which participants were asked to report posteriors after each signal in a sequence. As before, I restrict the sample to problems with equal (initial) priors. Figs. 2–4 and Tables 2–3 each have a Panel B, which repeats exactly the analysis from Panel A but applied to these sequential-sample updating problems.

The figures and tables suggest that the same qualitative conclusions from the simultaneous-sample experiments carry over to the sequential-sample experiments: on average, participants' final posteriors are less extreme when updating from larger final sample sizes and more diagnostic rates. These qualitative conclusions also hold in every individual sequential-sample experiment that manipulated sample size N or diagnosticity θ.[41]

The pooling hypothesis, however, predicts that the results should be the same *quantitatively*, but differences between the sequential-sample and simultaneous-sample results are apparent in all the figures and tables. Table 3 Panel B provides another piece of evidence against the pooling hypothesis: the estimated constant term

---

[41] For sample size, the experiments are Phillips et al. (1966), Peterson and Swensson (1968), Sanders (1968), and Kraemer and Weber (2004); for diagnosticity, Phillips and Edwards (1966, Study 1 and 3), Pitz et al. (1967), Peterson and Swensson (1968), Sanders (1968), Chinnis and Peterson (1968), and Beach et al. (1970).

is statistically distinguishable from zero, which suggests that regression Eq. (4.13) is misspecified for the sequential-sample updating problems. Across sequential-sample and simultaneous-sample experiments with multinomial signals that held constant the final samples observed by participants, Labella and Koehler (2004) found that participants had final posteriors that differed in several ways, which is again inconsistent with the pooling hypothesis. While the evidence is not overwhelming, taken all together it casts substantial doubt on pooling.

Stylized Fact 8. In sequential-sample updating problems, people do not "pool" the signals (i.e., update as if they had observed a single, simultaneous sample).

Therefore, I tentatively conclude that people are acceptive, updating after each set of signals they observe—with the caveat that this conclusion has not been interrogated empirically.

Given that people underinfer (Stylized Fact 1) and under-use priors (Stylized Fact 7), one would expect to see that the final posterior odds in sequential-sample experiments are less extreme than Bayesian posterior odds. Indeed, essentially all sequential-sample experiments that I am aware of have found final posterior odds that are less extreme than Bayesian.[42] This is also true on average for the meta-analysis sample, as shown in Fig. 2 Panel B and Table 2 Panel B.

The quantitative differences between Panels A and B of the figures and tables are difficult to interpret directly. If people are not pooling (Stylized Fact 8), then even if the *initial* prior odds put equal weight on the two states, people's subsequent prior odds in general will not. Consequently, their posterior odds at the end of a sequential sample reflect the effects of both biased inference and biased use of the priors.

To disentangle the two, following Grether (1992), economists typically estimate a panel-data version of Eq. (4.15) (without the indicators for exact representativeness):

$$
\ln\left(\frac{\pi(A|s_1, s_2, \ldots, s_t)}{\pi(B|s_1, s_2, \ldots, s_t)}\right)
$$
$$
= \beta_0 + \beta_1 \ln\left(\frac{p(s_t|A)}{p(s_t|B)}\right) + \beta_2 \ln\left(\frac{\pi(A|s_1, s_2, \ldots, s_{t-1})}{\pi(B|s_1, s_2, \ldots, s_{t-1})}\right) + \eta_t, \qquad (4.21)
$$

---

[42] The papers for which this is true are Peterson et al. (1965b), Peterson et al. (1965a), Phillips and Edwards (1966), Phillips et al. (1966), Beach (1968), Chinnis and Peterson (1968), Dale (1968), Peterson and Swensson (1968), Sanders (1968), Beach et al. (1970), Edenborough (1975), Dave and Wolfe (2003), Kraemer and Weber (2004), and Sasaki and Kawagoe (2007). The one, partial exception is Strub (1969), who finds that while it is true for naïve experimental participants, participants with extensive training update Bayesianly.

where the initial priors are assumed to be correct $\left(\dfrac{\pi(A)}{\pi(B)} = \dfrac{p(A)}{p(B)} \right)$. This specification implicitly assumes that people are acceptive in grouping signals. As in Eq. (4.15), $\hat{\beta}_1$ is an estimate of c and $\hat{\beta}_2$ is an estimate of d.[43]

From the eight papers[44] that have estimated Eq. (4.21), the range of $\hat{\beta}_1$ is 0.25–1.23, with an inverse-variance-weighted mean of 0.53 (SE = 0.012). Taking this mean as an overall estimate of c, it indicates that participants underweight the likelihood ratio. From these same papers, the range of $\hat{\beta}_2$ is 0.51–1.88, with an inverse-variance-weighted mean of 0.88 (SE = 0.009). This estimate of d is consistent with base-rate neglect. Two other sequential-sample experiments also found evidence of base-rate neglect but did not estimate d (Phillips and Edwards, 1966, Experiment 1; Phillips et al., 1966).

Stylized Fact 9. In sequential updating problems, people both underinfer and exhibit base-rate neglect.

Several papers have examined updating at the individual-level and have found that, upon receiving a signal, one-third to one-half of participants do not update at all (e.g., Möbius et al., 2014; Coutts, 2017; Henckel et al., 2017). While Coutts concluded that the underweighting of the likelihood ratio is driven by these observations, the other papers found that participants update by less than a Bayesian even when these observations are omitted.

From sequential-sample updating experiments, two other regularities are worth noting. First, several experiments have found a *primacy effect*, meaning that signals observed early in the sequence have a greater impact on final beliefs than signals observed in the middle of the sequence (Peterson and DuCharme, 1967; Roby, 1967; Dale, 1968; De Swart and Tonkens, 1977), although DuCharme (1970) did not find a primacy effect.

---

[43] Möbius et al. (2014) pointed out that OLS is not a consistent estimator for Eq. (4.21) for two reasons: (a) $\ln\left(\dfrac{\pi(A|s_1, s_2, \ldots, s_{t-1})}{\pi(B|s_1, s_2, \ldots, s_{t-1})} \right)$ is correlated with c and d (if there is heterogeneity in c and d across participants) and (b) $\ln\left(\dfrac{\pi(A|s_1, s_2, \ldots, s_{t-1})}{\pi(B|s_1, s_2, \ldots, s_{t-1})} \right)$ has measurement error. In Möbius et al.'s experiment (discussed in more detail in Section 9), participants updated beliefs about their performance on an IQ quiz, and different participants faced different versions of the quiz. Möbius et al. estimated Eq. (4.21) using IV, using the quiz difficulty as an instrument for $\ln\left(\dfrac{\pi(A|s_1, s_2, \ldots, s_{t-1})}{\pi(B|s_1, s_2, \ldots, s_{t-1})} \right)$. Barron (2016) is the only other paper I am aware of that has addressed (a) and (b) and also did so using an IV estimation method. Both Möbius et al. and Barron found that their IV results are similar to their OLS results, but the estimates for Eq. (4.21) from other papers should interpreted with the caveat that they do not address (a) and (b).

[44] These papers are Grether (1992), Möbius et al. (2014), Holt and Smith (2009), Barron (2016), Charness and Dave (2017), Coutts (2017), Gotthard-Real (2017), and Buser et al. (2018). The analysis yielding the numbers reported in this paragraph are described in an Online Appendix on my website. Note that while Charness and Dave is included in the range of coefficients, it isn't included in the calculation of the inverse-variance-weighted mean since standard errors are not reported.

Stylized Fact 10. In sequential updating problems, signals observed early in the sequence have a greater impact on final beliefs than signals observed in the middle of the sequence.

The primacy effect is predicted by prior-biased updating, as discussed further in Section 8.

Second, several studies have found a *recency effect*, meaning that the most recently observed signals have a greater impact on final beliefs than signals observed in the middle of the sequence (e.g., Pitz and Reinhold, 1968; Shanteau, 1970, Study 2; Marks and Clarkson, 1972; Edenborough, 1975; Grether, 1992, Experiment 3).[45]

Stylized Fact 11. In sequential updating problems, the most recently observed signals have a greater impact on final beliefs than signals observed in the middle of the sequence.

The recency effect is predicted by base-rate neglect, as discussed further in Section 6. Both primary and recency effects provide further evidence against the *pooling* hypothesis, and hence constitute additional evidence for Stylized Fact 8.[46]

5 Theories of biased inference

Most of the stylized facts outlined in the previous section had already been identified fifty years ago in the psychology literature on bookbag-and-poker-chip experiments. Much of the work in that literature focused on testing three main theories to explain those regularities. These three theories remain the leading candidate explanations.

---

[45] Unfortunately, it seems that there have been no experiments that aimed to identify both primacy and recency effects. Indeed, the typical experiment on "order effects" in this literature compares participants' posteriors after two sequences, one whose first half is mostly *a* signals and whose second half is mostly *b* signals, and another which is the reverse. Such a design can only identify which of the two effects dominates, and indeed, much of the literature has been framed in terms of whether there is a primacy *or* a recency effect.

[46] What is the effect of feedback and training on updating in sequential-sample experiments? Unfortunately, there is only a small amount of evidence, which I judge to be inconclusive. Phillips and Edwards (1966, Study 2) had their experimental participants report posteriors after each signal and told their experimental participants the true state after each of four 20-signal sequences. Posteriors were closer to Bayesian at the end of the fourth sequence than at the end of the first sequence but remained not extreme enough. Strub (1969) ran a sequential-sample updating experiment among a group of naïve participants and a group of trained participants, undergraduates who had received 114 hours of lecture sessions, demonstrations, problem-solving sessions, and other training in dealing with probabilities, including prior participation in bookbag-and-poker-chip experiments. Relative to the naïve participants, the trained participants had final posteriors that were much closer to Bayesian on average across updating problems, but the results are not reported in enough detail to evaluate whether the trained participants had biased beliefs in the updating problems considered separately.

This section reviews each of these in turn, in light of the current state of evidence and more recent and specific conceptualizations of the theories.[47]

5.1 Biased sampling-distribution beliefs

Since people's sampling-distribution beliefs presumably influence their inferences, it is natural to look to sampling-distribution biases to provide an explanation of people's biased inferences. And indeed, biased sampling-distribution beliefs was a leading theory in the psychology literature on bookbag-and-poker-chip experiments (e.g., Peterson and Beach, 1967; Edwards, 1968; Slovic and Lichtenstein, 1971). Yet the theory was not explored much, and it received little attention in the subsequent literature (e.g., it is not mentioned at all by Fischhoff and Beyth-Marom, 1983).

To discuss the theory formally, suppose an agent updates according to Bayes' Theorem but using her biased sampling-distribution beliefs, $\pi(S|A)$ and $\pi(S|B)$, in place of the true likelihoods, $p(S|A)$ and $p(S|B)$.[48] If the agent has no additional biases, then her posterior beliefs will be:

$$\pi(A|S) = \frac{\pi(S|A)p(A)}{\pi(S|A)p(A) + \pi(S|B)p(B)} \tag{5.1}$$

$$\pi(B|S) = \frac{\pi(S|B)p(B)}{\pi(S|A)p(A) + \pi(S|B)p(B)}. \tag{5.2}$$

To see this theory's implications about inferences, it is helpful to rewrite the agent's posterior beliefs in odds form:

$$\frac{\pi(A|S)}{\pi(B|S)} = \frac{\pi(S|A)}{\pi(S|B)} \frac{p(A)}{p(B)}. \tag{5.3}$$

Eq. (5.3) predicts underinference whenever $\frac{\pi(S|A)}{\pi(S|B)}$ is less extreme than the correct likelihood ratio $\frac{p(S|A)}{p(S|B)}$.

For this theory to be qualitatively consistent with the evidence that people underinfer in general (Stylized Fact 1) and especially so for updating problems with larger sample sizes (Stylized Fact 2), people's sampling-distribution beliefs would have to be too flat relative to the true distributions and especially flat at larger sample sizes.

---

[47] Reflecting these more specific conceptualizations, I will refer to the three theories by different names than were used in the older literature. That literature referred to the "misperception hypothesis," "misaggregation hypothesis," and "response-bias hypothesis." Instead, I call them biased sampling-distribution beliefs, conservatism bias, and extreme-belief aversion, respectively.

[48] As far as I am aware, none of the work on belief updating has taken partition-dependence into account (see Section 3.1). An implicit assumption in what follows is that the agent's posterior beliefs and sampling-distribution beliefs are elicited using the same partition of the state space. Otherwise, partition-dependence would distort these beliefs relative to each other.

As discussed in Sections 3.5 and 3.2, people's sampling-distribution beliefs appear to have these features.

Two experiments have directly tested Eq. (5.3) in the case of equal priors, when it simplifies to $\dfrac{\pi(A|S)}{\pi(B|S)} = \dfrac{\pi(S|A)}{\pi(S|B)}$. The first is Peterson et al. (1968, Study 2). In stage one of their study, they elicited participants' posteriors beliefs in each of the 57 possible updating problems defined by the binomial parameter values $\theta = 0.6, 0.7, 0.8$ and the three sample sizes $N = 3, 5, 8$. Stage one replicated the usual findings of underinference on average and greater underinference with larger N and larger θ. In stage two, Peterson et al. elicited nine binomial sampling distributions, with each of the binomial parameter values $\theta = 0.6, 0.7, 0.8$ and each of the three sample sizes $N = 3, 5, 8$. As previously mentioned in Section 3.5, Peterson et al. found that participants' sampling distributions were nearly correct for $N = 3$ but were flatter than the correct distributions for $N = 5$ and especially for $N = 8$. Peterson et al. tested Eq. (5.3) by comparing the distributions produced in stage two to the inferences elicited in stage one.[49] When they plotted experimental participants' median log-posterior-odds calculated from stage two, $\ln\left(\dfrac{\pi(A|S)}{\pi(B|S)}\right)$, against participants' log-likelihood-odds calculated from stage one, $\ln\left(\dfrac{\pi(S|A)}{\pi(S|B)}\right)$, they found that "most points cluster extremely close to the identity line" (p. 242).[50]

The other paper is Wheeler and Beach (1968). Their study also had a sequence of stages. In the first stage, participants reported their beliefs about two binomial sampling distributions, with parameter values $\theta = 0.6$ and 0.8, both with a sample size of $N = 8$. As previously mentioned in Section 3.5, these sampling distributions were too flat. In the second stage, participants bet on whether particular samples of size 8 (e.g., 6 a's out of 8) came from an urn where the rate of a signals was 0.6 or an urn where the rate was 0.8. The prior probabilities of the two urns were equal. After each of 100 bets, which were incentivized, participants were told which urn was correct. To test Eq. (5.3), Wheeler and Beach compared the first 20 bets with

---

[49] Peterson et al.'s study had two further stages. Stage three was designed to de-bias participants' sampling-distribution beliefs. Stage four repeated stage one, with no sampling distributions visible to the participants. The purpose of stage four was to test whether the de-biasing of participants' sampling-distribution beliefs from stage three also de-biased their inferences. Peterson et al. found that underinference was reduced in stage four relative to stage one, but they do not report participants' sampling-distribution beliefs in stage three. Thus it is not possible to assess the consistency between these beliefs and participants' posteriors in stage four.

[50] There were a few exceptions, which occurred in updating problems where the observed sample was in the far tail of the sampling distribution: 0, 1, 7, or 8 a's out of 8, and 0 or 5 a's out of 5. In these cases, participants inferred more strongly than would be expected given their sampling distributions. Peterson et al. suggested that these exceptions may be driven by participants assigning probabilities many times too high to these very unlikely samples, which have true probabilities smaller than 1%. While participants were allowed to estimate likelihoods smaller than 1%, Peterson et al. noted that doing so was inconvenient in their design. Peterson et al. also noted that the discrepancies could also be due to the fact that estimation errors in very small likelihoods can have a large effect on the likelihood odds.

participants' initial sampling distributions.[51] Their results were similar to Peterson et al.'s: there was a tight correspondence between inferences and sampling-distribution beliefs.

Both of these studies support the theory that people's inferences are consistent with Bayes' Theorem applied to their beliefs about sampling distributions. Both also suggest that the flatness of these distributions may account for the general finding of underinference. However, both had small numbers of participants: only 24 undergraduates in Peterson, DuCharme, and Edwards and 17 in Wheeler and Beach.

There is other, less direct evidence bearing on the biased-sampling-distribution theory of biased inferences. In particular, if the theory were true, then features of people's sampling-distribution beliefs (reviewed in Section 3) would be reflected in their inferences (reviewed in Section 4). I outline three of these possible links in turn, with the caveat that the evidence is thin regarding the latter two features of people's sampling-distribution beliefs.

First, in non-small samples—e.g., a sample size of at least 10—people's subjective sampling distributions are based on the *proportion* of *a* signals rather than the number of *a* signals (see Section 3.2). As Kahneman and Tversky (1972a) pointed out, if people's inferences are based on these distributions, then, for non-small sample sizes, people's inferences will depend on the sample proportion, as they indeed seem to (Stylized Fact 4).

Second, there is some evidence that people's sampling-distribution beliefs overweight the mean (see Section 3.4). If so, people put too much weight on sample proportions matching the population rate. This feature of sampling-distribution beliefs may explain "exact representativeness," the (not entirely robust) evidence that overinference occurs when the sample proportion matches the rate of one of the states (Stylized Fact 5).

Third, there is a bit of evidence that people's sampling-distribution beliefs have flat tails (see Section 3.3). This may be why people underinfer by more when the rates in the two states are further apart (Stylized Fact 6). If (say) the state is A, then the most likely samples will have sample proportions close to θ_A. The agent will overestimate the likelihood of these samples in state B because the agent's state-B sampling distribution has fat tails and will therefore underinfer on average—and this overestimation and consequent underinference will be more severe the further apart are θ_A and θ_B.

---

[51] Like Peterson et al., Wheeler and Beach found that in inference problems with sample realizations in the tails, participants inferred more strongly than would be expected given their sampling distributions. Wheeler and Beach's study had further stages after the initial set of 100 bets: participants' sampling distributions were re-elicited, then they faced another 100 bets, their sampling distributions were elicited one last time, and then they faced a final 20 bets. The purpose of this procedure was to give participants feedback and experience about the sampling distributions. Participants' sampling distributions elicited at the beginning of the study were somewhat too peaked rather than too flat. In addition to testing Eq. (5.3) with data from the initial bets, Wheeler and Beach also tested it with data from the end of the study, comparing participants' 20 bets with their final sampling distributions, and they again found a tight correspondence.

Thus, the biased-sampling-distribution theory may be consistent with nearly all of the stylized facts regarding biased inference reviewed in Section 4, with one important exception: the theory almost certainly *cannot* explain why underinference occurs on average in samples of size one (Stylized Facts 3 and 9). In order for the theory to do so, people would have to believe that the probability of an *a* signal in a single draw when the rate is known to be θ is not equal to θ. As noted in Section 3.5, I am not aware of any direct evidence, but such a result seems implausible.

Several of the biases in people's sampling-distribution beliefs discussed above have not been captured in formal models. However, two features of people's subjective sampling distributions—generally being too flat and being based on the proportion of *a* signals in large samples—are reflected in Benjamin et al.'s (2016) model of Non-Belief in the Law of Large Numbers (NBLLN). In addition to drawing out the implications of NBLLN for sampling-distribution beliefs, Benjamin et al. explored implications of NBLLN for biased inferences in economic settings, under the assumption of Eqs. (5.1)–(5.2).[52]

In their model, signals are drawn i.i.d. from a binomial distribution whose rate of *a* signals is θ. The agent correctly understands that the probability of a single signal being *a* is θ, but her subjective sampling distribution is biased for sample sizes N larger than one. The Law of Large Numbers implies that, as $N \to \infty$, the true sampling distribution over the proportion of *a* signals, N_a/N, converges to a point

---

[52] Edwards (1968, pp. 34–35) sketched a different model of biased sampling distribution beliefs: $\pi(N_a = n_a|A) = \dfrac{p(N_a = n_a|A)^\varphi}{\sum_{n=1}^{N} p(N_a = n|A)^\varphi}$, where $\varphi \in [0, 1]$, and similarly for beliefs about state B. The agent has correct sampling-distribution beliefs if $\varphi = 1$ and uniform-distribution beliefs if $\varphi = 0$, while if $0 < \varphi < 1$, the agent's subjective sampling distribution is flatter than the true distribution, so the agent underinfers on average. Edwards also pointed out that in symmetric updating problems ($\theta_A = 1 - \theta_B$), the denominators in states A and B are equal, so $\dfrac{\pi(N_a = n_a|A)}{\pi(N_a = n_a|B)} = \left(\dfrac{p(N_a = n_a|A)}{p(N_a = n_a|B)}\right)^\varphi$. Therefore, in symmetric updating problems, the parameter φ is equal to the measure of biased inference c in Eq. (4.6). While Edwards's analysis stopped here, the model could be extended to capture sample-size neglect by replacing the constant φ with a decreasing function of sample size, $\varphi(N)$ with $\varphi(1) = 1$ and $\varphi(N) \to \dfrac{\breve{\varphi}}{N} > 0$ for N large, where $\breve{\varphi}$ is a constant. Because $\varphi(1) = 1$, the agent's sampling-distribution beliefs are correct when $N = 1$. In this model, for a large sample of binomial signals, it can be shown that the agent's subjective sampling distribution over sample proportions, $\pi\left(\dfrac{N_a}{N} = x|A\right)$, converges to a doubly-truncated normal distribution, $\dfrac{\phi(x)}{\Phi(1) - \Phi(0)}$, where ϕ is the pdf of a normal distribution with mean θ_A and variance $\dfrac{\theta_A(1 - \theta_A)}{\breve{\varphi}}$, Φ is its cdf, and the distribution is truncated at 0 and 1. In this formula for the "universal distribution," the parameter $\breve{\varphi}$ enters the variance the way a sample size would, so it can be interpreted as the universal distribution's "effective sample size." Relative to Benjamin, Rabin, and Raymond's model of NBLLN, this model has several disadvantages: it is less tractable for some purposes because the mean of the large-sample distribution of proportions is not equal to θ_A (it is biased toward 0.5), and it is more difficult to combine with models of biased beliefs about random sequences.

mass at θ. As explained in Section 3.2, the agent instead believes that the sampling distribution of N_a/N converges to a "universal distribution" that has mean θ but full support on $(0, 1)$. Thus, the agent's subjective sampling distribution for large samples is very flat relative to the true sampling distribution.

When combined with Eqs. (5.1)–(5.2), the model's basic implications for inference are straightforward. Let the agent's universal distributions for binomials with rates θ_A and θ_B be denoted $\pi_\infty\left(\dfrac{N_a}{N}|A\right)$ and $\pi_\infty\left(\dfrac{N_a}{N}|B\right)$, respectively. From Eq. (5.3), the agent's posterior odds after observing a large sample containing N_a a-signals will be

$$\frac{\pi(A|N_a \text{ out of } N)}{\pi(B|N_a \text{ out of } N)} = \frac{\pi_\infty\left(\frac{N_a}{N}|A\right)}{\pi_\infty\left(\frac{N_a}{N}|B\right)} \frac{p(A)}{p(B)} \tag{5.4}$$

Eq. (5.4) formalizes two of the links between sampling-distribution beliefs and biased inferences that have already been noted above. First, since the universal distributions are based on sample proportions, so are the agent's inferences in a large sample. Second, in large samples, because the agent's subjective sampling distribution is too flat, the agent underinfers. Furthermore, while the Bayesian will learn the true state with certainty in an infinite sample, the agent will remain uncertain even after observing an infinite sample. For example, if the true state is A, then (due to the Law of Large Numbers) the sample proportion will converge to the state-A rate θ_A with probability one. The agent's likelihood ratio in Eq. (5.4) will therefore converge to $\dfrac{\pi_\infty\left(\frac{N_a}{N} = \theta_A|A\right)}{\pi_\infty\left(\frac{N_a}{N} = \theta_A|B\right)}$, which is the ratio of the pdfs of the universal distributions, evaluated at θ_A. Since this likelihood ratio is a finite number, the agent's inference is limited.

Because the likelihood ratio is finite, it is clear from Eq. (5.4) that the agent's priors will continue to matter no matter how large a sample the agent observes. For this reason, Benjamin, Rabin, and Raymond argue that NBLLN can serve as an "enabling bias" for misbeliefs people have about themselves. In particular, if people have overoptimistic priors about their own abilities or preferences (for reasons unrelated to NBLLN), NBLLN may explain why they remain overoptimistic despite a lifetime of experience.

Benjamin, Rabin, and Raymond also explored the implications of NBLLN for people's demand for information. What is crucial for demand for information is what the agent *expects* to infer. While a Bayesian's expectations about his own inferences are correct, an agent with NBLLN has incorrect expectations because she has mistaken beliefs about the distribution of samples she will observe. Surprisingly, these mistaken beliefs can cause the agent to have *greater* willingness to pay for an intermediate-sized sample than a Bayesian would have. In particular, because the agent's subjective sampling distribution is too flat, she thinks an extreme proportion of a signals that would be very informative about the state is more likely than it is. The agent may be willing to pay for the sample in the hope of such an extreme sample realization, even though a Bayesian would recognize that such an outcome is too unlikely to be worth paying for.

For a large sample, however, the agent anticipates drawing a weaker inference than a Bayesian would draw for any possible realization of the sample proportion (because a Bayesian will learn the truth in a large enough sample, while the agent's inference will be limited). Therefore, an agent with NBLLN always has lower willingness to pay for a large sample than a Bayesian would have. Benjamin, Rabin, and Raymond argue that this lack of demand for large samples is a central implication of NBLLN, which may contribute to explaining why statistical data is rarely provided by the market, as well as why people often rely on anecdotes rather than seeking larger samples.

For drawing out the implications of biased inferences when samples are observed sequentially, a crucial issue is how people group signals, as discussed in Section 4.3. For an agent with NBLLN, it makes all the difference whether 100 signals are grouped as a single sample, in which case she dramatically underinfers, or as 100 samples of size one, in which case she updates correctly after each signal and ends up with the same posteriors as a Bayesian!

As per Stylized Fact 8, there is evidence against the hypothesis that people "pool" all signals they have observed into a single large sample. It may therefore be reasonable to hypothesize that people are "acceptive" of the way signals are presented to them, processing signals as a sample when the signals are presented together. This evidence, however, relates only to how signals are grouped *retrospectively*, after they are observed. The implications of NBLLN in many dynamic environments also depends on how the agent expects to group signals she hasn't yet observed. There is no necessary reason why people would *prospectively* group signals the same way they retrospectively group signals. Differences between retrospective and prospective grouping can generate dynamically inconsistent behavior. An important lesson that emerges from formally modeling NBLLN is the need for evidence on how people group signals both retrospectively and prospectively.

5.2 Conservatism bias

The theory of biased inference that received by far the most attention in the literature on bookbag-and-poker-chip experiments is *conservatism bias*: when updating to posterior beliefs, people underweight their likelihood beliefs. Phillips and Edwards (1966) introduced conservatism bias and modeled it as

$$\frac{\pi(A|S)}{\pi(B|S)} = \left[\frac{p(S|A)}{p(S|B)}\right]^c \frac{p(A)}{p(B)}. \tag{5.5}$$

Formally, this equation is the special case of Eq. (4.6) in which biased use of prior information is abstracted away ($d = 1$). Conceptually, however, there is a key difference: whereas Eq. (4.6) is intended as a reduced-form description used to summarize evidence from updating problems, conservatism bias is a structural model of the actual process of forming beliefs. Psychologically, conservatism bias is hypothesized to result from the difficulty of aggregating different sources of information (e.g., Slovic and Lichtenstein, 1971).

In a comparison with other theories of biased inference, Edwards (1968) cites three pieces of evidence in favor of conservatism bias. First, in several sequential-sample updating experiments conducted with symmetric binomial signals, estimates of the conservatism parameter c were found to be roughly independent of the numbers of a and b signals that occurred in a sample (Phillips and Edwards, 1966, Experiments 1 and 3; Peterson et al., 1965a, as reported by Edwards, 1968; also in a multinomial-signal experiment: Shanteau, 1972).[53] This stability of estimates of c supported its interpretation as a structural parameter, and it is a challenging fact for alternative theories to explain.[54] It should be noted, however, that estimates of c were known to be smaller when the diagnosticity parameter θ was larger (Phillips and Edwards, 1966) and, in sequential-sample experiments, when the sample size N was larger (Peterson et al., 1965a), as per Stylized Facts 6 and 2. While there was no clear explanation for the dependence on θ, greater conservatism for larger sample sizes had a ready interpretation: aggregating more information is more difficult.

Second, in settings where participants themselves provide the likelihood estimates, participants nonetheless update too little relative to Bayes' Theorem (e.g., Hammond et al., 1967; Grinnell et al., 1971). For example, in some experiments, participants were asked to estimate the likelihood of different signals (e.g., reconnaissance reports) in different states of the world (e.g., impending war), and then they observed certain signals and were asked to update their beliefs (e.g., Edwards et al., 1968). In such an experiment, participants' biased posteriors cannot be attributed to biased sampling-distribution beliefs because the perceived likelihoods are elicited directly. This evidence, however, is not sufficient to conclude that participants update too little relative to Bayes' Theorem. One concern is that, while participants provide point estimates of the likelihoods, participants may in fact be uncertain about the likelihoods or report their point estimates with error. In either case, Bayes' Theorem applied to participants' point estimates is the wrong benchmark for comparing with participants' posteriors. Another concern is that Bayes' Theorem was calculated assuming that the signals are independent conditional on the states, but participants' beliefs about the likelihoods were typically not elicited in sufficient detail to test that assumption.

Third, people underinfer for sample sizes of one (Stylized Facts 3 and 9). This observation can be explained by conservatism bias, while as discussed above, it is a

---

[53] At first blush, this observation seems inconsistent with "exact representativeness"—stronger inferences when the observed sample proportion equals the rate in one of the states—as per Stylized Fact 5. However, the estimates of the conservatism parameter c presented in these papers were averaged across sample sizes, so it is not possible to assess whether or not there was evidence of exact representativeness.

[54] The model of sampling-distribution beliefs sketched in footnote 52 *does* imply that, in symmetric binomial updating problems, the measure of biased inference c is independent of the numbers of a and b signals in the sample. For Edwards (1968), explaining that observation was an important desideratum for evaluating a theory of underinference.

challenging observation to explain by biased sampling-distribution beliefs. Extreme-belief aversion, discussed next, is a competing explanation for this observation.

5.3 Extreme-belief aversion

Extreme-belief aversion is the term used by Benjamin et al. (2016, Appendix C) to refer to an aversion to holding or expressing beliefs close to certainty.[55] As a simple example, suppose there are two possible states, A and B, and the true probability of A is p. An agent with extreme-belief aversion would report that the probability of A is $\pi = f(p)$, where $f(p) > p$ for p sufficiently close to 0 and $f(p) < p$ for p sufficiently close to 1. Note that extreme-belief aversion is not specifically a theory of biased inference but rather a theory about bias in *any beliefs*.[56]

DuCharme (1970) argued that extreme-belief aversion is a major confound in belief-updating experiments that explains much of the evidence that had been interpreted as underinference. In support of this view, DuCharme reported two experiments. Both were sequential-sample bookbag-and-poker-chip experiments with two states and normally distributed signals. Using the results of each experiment, DuCharme produced a plot like Fig. 2, graphing participants' log posterior odds ($\ln\left(\dfrac{\pi}{1-\pi}\right)$) against the Bayesian log posterior odds ($\ln\left(\dfrac{p}{1-p}\right)$). Both experiments resulted in similar plots: for Bayesian odds between -1 and $+1$, participants' odds virtually coincided with the Bayesian odds, but for Bayesian odds more extreme than -1 or $+1$, participants' odds were less extreme than the Bayesian odds. The plot was similar whether or not the data was restricted to the posteriors reported by participants after just a single signal had been observed. In an earlier paper that also reported two experiments with normally distributed signals, DuCharme and Peterson (1968) had found similar results. The results of these experiments are difficult to reconcile with conservatism bias but consistent with extreme-belief aversion.

Extreme-belief aversion is a distortion toward less extreme posteriors that does not depend on whether the correct posteriors are extreme due to an extreme likelihood or an extreme prior. Thus, extreme-belief aversion is a confound not only for findings that have been interpreted as underinference (Stylized Fact 1) but also

---

[55] The more general term *extremeness aversion* is sometimes used to refer to a desire to avoid both extreme judgments and extreme choices (e.g., Lewis et al., forthcoming).

[56] Extreme-belief aversion resembles probability weighting but is conceptually distinct. Probability weighting is a bias in how beliefs are *used* in decision making (rather than a bias in how they are formed or reported); it is discussed in Chapter "Reference-Dependent Preferences" (by O'Donoghue and Sprenger) of this Handbook. Extreme-belief aversion is also distinct from an aversion to reporting a response at the extremes of the response scale, a bias that is sometimes called floor and ceiling effects. Such floor and ceiling effects have been documented in bookbag-and-poker-chip experiments. For example, experimental participants report less extreme beliefs when reporting their beliefs as probabilities, which are bounded between zero and one, than when reporting their beliefs as odds or log-odds, which have a response scale that is unbounded on at least one end (Phillips and Edwards, 1966, Experiment III). However, floor and ceiling effects seem unlikely to account for DuCharme and Peterson's (1968) evidence mentioned below because they elicited respondents' posterior odds, so the response scale did not have a floor or ceiling.

those that have been interpreted as base-rate neglect (Stylized Fact 7). Moreover, the extreme-belief aversion explanation of these findings applies equally to sequential-sample and simultaneous-sample experiments (Stylized Fact 9) and to samples of any size. In particular, extreme-belief aversion provides an explanation for the apparent evidence of underinference after just a single signal (Stylized Fact 3), a fact that biased sampling-distribution beliefs cannot explain.

Based on the particular shape of extreme-belief aversion observed in his plots of the results mentioned above, DuCharme (1970) argued that the bias can also explain the evidence that has been interpreted as underinference being more severe on average when sample sizes are larger (Stylized Fact 2) and when the population rates θ_A and θ_B are further apart (Stylized Fact 6).[57] These stylized facts are based on measuring the amount of underinference by c, which is equal to $\ln\left(\frac{\pi}{1-\pi}\right) / \ln\left(\frac{p}{1-p}\right)$ in updating problems with equal priors (see Section 4.1 and the discussion of Fig. 2 in Section 4.2). DuCharme's plots imply that $c \approx 1$ when the Bayesian log posterior odds are within the interval $[-1, +1]$, but $c < 1$ when the Bayesian odds are more extreme. Both larger sample sizes and population rates that are further apart make the expected Bayesian odds more extreme, leading in expectation to more severe underinference as measured by c.

The theory of extreme-belief aversion has not been developed in much detail. It is worth exploring whether extreme-belief aversion is actually the same phenomenon as compression of probabilities toward a uniform distribution, discussed in Section 3.1 in the context of partition dependence. Such compression would indeed lead people to avoid reporting beliefs close to certainty. Whether or not the two biases are the same, they raise similar conceptual challenges.

Extreme-belief aversion probably contributes to biased updating, and it is a certainly a confound that should be taken into account when interpreting the evidence from updating experiments. However, Benjamin et al. (2016, Appendix C) argued that the stylized facts discussed in Section 4 cannot be entirely attributed to extreme-belief aversion. If extreme-belief aversion were the only bias at play, then experimental participants' reported posteriors (π) would be a fixed transformation of the correct posteriors ($\pi = f(p)$). That implies that in any two problems where the correct posteriors are the same, experimental participants' reported posteriors would also be the same. There are several clean test cases that contradict this prediction. For example, consider four of the updating problems in Griffin and Tversky's (1992, Study 1) belief-updating experiment (described in Section 4.2): 3 out of 3 a signals, 4 out

---

[57] These stylized facts are not implied by the general definition of extreme-belief aversion given above. For example, an extreme-belief averse agent could have posterior beliefs such that $\ln\left(\frac{\pi}{1-\pi}\right) = \chi \ln\left(\frac{p}{1-p}\right)$ for some constant $\chi \in (0, 1)$. In that case, the measure of underinference c would be equal to χ regardless of how extreme the Bayesian posterior odds $\ln\left(\frac{p}{1-p}\right)$ are. If extreme-belief aversion took this form, then DuCharme's plot would have been a line through zero with slope χ.

of 5 a signals, 6 out of 9 a signals, and 10 out of 17 a signals. Because the difference between the number of a and b signals is always 3, the correct posterior is the same in all four problems. Experimental participants' median posteriors, however, were less extreme in the problems with larger sample sizes. Other, similar examples from Griffin and Tversky (1992)'s Study 1 and Kraemer and Weber (2004) also provide evidence of Stylized Fact 2 that is unconfounded by extreme-belief aversion.

Analogously, there are examples from Griffin and Tversky's (1992) Study 2 where the correct posteriors are the same across updating problems with different prior probabilities. Consistent with base-rate neglect (Stylized Fact 7), participants' posteriors were less extreme in the problems with more extreme priors. Similarly, Griffin and Tversky's (1992) Study 3 and Kahneman and Tversky (1972a) provide evidence, unconfounded by extreme-belief aversion, that participants underinfer when the rates θ_A and θ_B are further apart (Stylized Fact 6) and draw inferences based on sample proportions (Stylized Fact 4).

5.4 Summary

There is evidence for all three of the theories reviewed in this section: biased sampling-distribution beliefs, conservatism bias, and extreme-belief aversion. Biases in sampling-distribution beliefs are a natural starting point and may explain many of the stylized facts about biased inference from Section 4. To date, however, formal models of people's sampling-distribution beliefs capture only some of the relevant biases. In my judgment, this theory is particularly ripe for theoretical development and application in field settings. Evidence on how people group signals is needed in order to understand how the biases play out in dynamic settings.

Biased sampling-distribution beliefs seem unlikely to explain why people underinfer from single signals, whereas extreme-belief aversion and conservatism bias could explain that evidence. In my view, experiments designed to disentangle the theories from each other and assess their relative magnitudes should be a priority.

6 Base-rate neglect

The evidence reviewed in Section 4 indicates that in updating problems, with or without incentives for accuracy, people on average under-use prior information (Stylized Facts 7 and 9). This phenomenon was apparent from the psychology literature on bookbag-and-poker-chips—indeed, it was documented by Phillips and Edwards (1966, Experiment 1) in one of the first such experiments—but it was largely ignored in that literature. Kahneman and Tversky (1973) made this bias a focus of attention in the literature on errors in probabilistic reasoning and labeled it *base-rate neglect*.

Among various other surveys and experiments, Kahneman and Tversky (1973) presented an elegant demonstration of base-rate neglect and its properties. They asked experimental participants to assign a probability to the event that Jack is an engineer rather than a lawyer based on the following description:

> Jack is a 45 year old man. He is married and has four children. He is generally conservative, careful, and ambitious. He shows no interest in political and social issues and spends most of his free time on his many hobbies which include home carpentry, sailing, and mathematical puzzles.

There were two groups of participants. Both were provided the same description, but one group was told that it was randomly drawn from a set of 100 descriptions consisting of 30 engineers and 70 lawyers, while the other was told that the set included 70 engineers and 30 lawyers. Although we do not know participants' assessment of the likelihood ratio based on the description, $\dfrac{\pi(S|A)}{\pi(S|B)}$, Bayes' Theorem (Eq. (4.3)) implies that the first group of subjects should have posterior odds $\dfrac{\pi(S|A)}{\pi(S|B)}\dfrac{0.70}{0.30}$, and the second group should have posterior odds $\dfrac{\pi(S|A)}{\pi(S|B)}\dfrac{0.30}{0.70}$. Bayes' Theorem therefore allows us to make an unambiguous prediction about the *ratio* of the posterior odds across the two groups: it should be $\dfrac{0.70/0.30}{0.30/0.70} \approx 5.4$. Contrary to this, the first group's mean probability that Jack is an engineer (averaged across this description and four similar others) was 55%, and the second group's was 50%, yielding a ratio of only $\dfrac{0.55/0.45}{0.50/0.50} \approx 1.2$. Thus, manipulation of the base rates had less of an effect on the posterior probabilities than would be prescribed by Bayes' Theorem. Such base-rate neglect in response to the description of Jack has been replicated many times, but whereas Kahneman and Tversky found complete neglect of base rates, in some other experiments, participants' posteriors reflected the base rates to some extent but less than they should according to Bayes' Rule (Koehler, 1996, Table 1).

To provide some insight when base-rate neglect occurs, Kahneman and Tversky then conducted two more versions of the same experiment. In one version, participants were given "no information whatsoever about a person chosen at random from the sample." In that case, participants reported probabilities that were equal to the base rates. Thus, in the absence of updating, participants understood the base rates correctly, and no base-rate neglect occurred.

In the other version of the experiment, participants were given the following description, which was intended to be completely uninformative regarding whether the person is a lawyer or engineer:

> Dick is a 30 year old man. He is married with no children. A man of high ability and high motivation, he promises to be quite successful in his field. He is well liked by his colleagues.

In this case, in both the 70%–30% and the 30%–70% groups, the median probability assigned to Dick being an engineer was 50%—implying complete base-rate neglect in this case. Participants relied on the description to make their judgment, even though the description was uninformative. Some subsequent experiments have also found base-rate neglect in response to uninformative descriptions (Wells and Harvey, 1978; Ginosar and Trope, 1987), but others instead found that participants' posteriors were equal to their priors (Swieringa et al., 1976; Ginosar and Trope, 1980; Fischhoff and Bar-Hillel, 1984; Hamilton, 1984). Manipulating the instructions, participant pool, and implementation of the experiment, Zukier and Pepitone (1984) and Gigerenzer et al. (1988) found that base-rate neglect sometimes occurs in response to uninformative descriptions and sometimes does not. Overall, the evidence for base-rate neglect in response to an uninformative description is much less robust than that for an informative description, but when there is an effect, it goes in the direction of base-rate neglect.

Taken together, the results of the no-description and the uninformative-description versions of the experiment have an important implication: base-rate neglect is triggered by *updating* the prior with information from a new signal. For a base-rate neglecter, there is a distinction between receiving no signal, in which case no updating occurs, and receiving an uninformative signal, which may cause updating and hence base-rate neglect to occur. For a Bayesian agent, in contrast, there would be no difference across these two cases.

To explain their results, Kahneman and Tversky (1973) argued that people judge probabilities based on the "representativeness" of the personality sketch to a lawyer or engineer, whereas the base rates are not relevant to judgments of representativeness (see Section 7.1 for further discussion). Nisbett et al. (1976) suggested another psychological mechanism: the likelihood information is weighted more heavily because it is "vivid, salient, and concrete," whereas the base rates are "remote, pallid, and abstract." Bar-Hillel (1980) argued that base-rate neglect is more general than either of these explanations would predict. She documented base-rate neglect in a sequence of updating problems that specified both the base rates and the likelihoods as (abstract) statistics. For example, one of the most famous problems is the Cab Problem (originally due to Kahneman and Tversky, 1972b):

> Two cab companies operate in a given city, the Blue and the Green (according to the color of cab they run). Eighty-five percent of the cabs in the city are Blue, and the remaining 15% are Green.
>
> A cab was involved in a hit-and-run accident at night.
>
> A witness later identified the cab as a Green cab.
>
> The court tested the witness' ability to distinguish between Blue and Green cabs under nighttime visibility conditions. It found that the witness was able to identify each color correctly about 80% of the time, but confused it with the other color about 20% of the time.
>
> What do you think are the chances that the errant cab was indeed Green, as the witness claimed?

In this problem, the correct answer is $\dfrac{(0.8)(0.15)}{(0.8)(0.15) + (0.2)(0.85)} \approx 41\%$. Bar-Hillel (1980) found that only about 10% of her high school graduate respondents gave a response to this question close to the correct answer. The modal answer, which was given by 36% of respondents, was 80%. This answer reflects complete base-rate neglect. The same basic result has been replicated many times, including with much more extreme base rates (e.g., 99% Blue and 1% Green; Murray et al., 1987).

Bar-Hillel argued that the key variable underlying base-rate neglect is relevance: when the base rate is the only relevant information available, people use it; when other information is also relevant, people prioritize the information in order of relevance. Thus, people use the base rates more when they seem more relevant to the particular instance in the updating problem. Base-rate neglect in the Cab Problem could be explained by the observation that many participants believed the color distribution of cabs was irrelevant, as documented by informal interviews with respondents and experimental evidence from Lyon and Slovic (1976). Relevance, in turn, is influenced by specificity: when people have information about some population (e.g., 15% of cabs are Green) but also have information about a subset of that population (e.g., a witness identified that particular cab as Green), the latter seems more relevant for making a judgment about a member of the subset (e.g., the chances that the errant cab was Green). Specificity can also be achieved via a causal relationship. For example, in a variant of the Cab Problem, Tversky and Kahneman (1980) described the base rates by telling respondents "85% of the cab accidents in the city involve [blue] cabs," implying that blue cabs cause more accidents than green cabs. In this causal framing, they found far lower rates of base-rate neglect. In a sequence of updating problems, Bar-Hillel manipulated the relevance of the base rates in different ways and showed that the degree of base-rate neglect varied accordingly. For example, base-rate neglect was largely eliminated in a variant of the Cab Problem where the specificity of the likelihood information was reduced to be comparable to that of the base rate (the witness did not see the cab but remembers hearing an intercom, which are installed in 80% of the Green cabs and 20% of the Blue cabs).

Much subsequent research on base-rate neglect has used updating problems like the Cab Problem, which specify both the prior probabilities and the likelihoods and are contextualized in hypothetical, realistic scenarios. Two examples from the economics literature are Dohmen et al. (2009), who documented widespread base-rate neglect in a representative sample of 988 Germans, and Ganguly et al. (2000), who found base-rate neglect in market experiments with financial incentives. While Bar-Hillel's (1980) and some other results show a high frequency of complete base-rate neglect, most of the evidence is less extreme and instead indicates that people's inferences usually do incorporate base rates to some extent, albeit less fully than prescribed by Bayes' Rule (Koehler, 1996). The evidence from bookbag-and-poker-chip experiments reviewed in Section 4 similarly points to underweighting of priors, rather than complete neglect (at least on average).

Troutman and Shanteau (1977) conducted two sequential-sample bookbag-and-poker-chip experiments whose results further suggest that it is the act of updating that triggers base-rate neglect. Beads were drawn with replacement from one of two boxes with equal prior probabilities. In one of the experiments, Box *A* contained 70/30/50 red/white/blue beads, and box *B* contained 30/70/50. To give a flavor of the results, after an initial sample of two white beads, experimental participants' mean probability assigned to box A was 69.9%. The experimenter then drew a "null sample," consisting of no beads at all, and asked participants to update their beliefs. Participants' mean probability declined to 66.9% (SE of the change $= 1.0\%$). To show that participants understood the lack of information contained in the null sample, Troutman and Shanteau presented another sequence in which the null sample occurred first. In that case, participants' mean probability was 50%.[58]

Much of the literature has focused on factors that increase or reduce the extent of base-rate neglect (for reviews, see Koehler, 1996, and Barbey and Sloman, 2007). For example, based on a literature review and two experiments, Goodie and Fantino (1999) concluded that base-rate neglect can be reduced but nonetheless persists even after extensive training with explicit feedback. Many papers have focused on the effect of framing the updating problem in terms of frequencies versus probabilities. After reviewing this literature, Barbey and Sloman (2007) conclude that frequency formats weaken base-rate neglect but do not eliminate it.

Researchers have discussed the pervasiveness of base-rate neglect in a variety of field settings, including psychologists' interpretations of diagnostic tests (Meehl and Rosen, 1955), courts' judgments in trials (Tribe, 1971), and doctors' diagnoses of patients (Eddy, 1982). In two experiments, Eide (2011) found that law students exhibit a similar degree of base-rate neglect in the Cab Problem as the usual undergraduate samples. In experiments with realistic hypothetical scenarios, school psychologists were found to be more confident but less accurate in assessing learning disability when base-rate information was supplemented with individuating information (Kennedy et al., 1997).

Benjamin et al. (2018a) analyzed the implications of a formal model of base-rate neglect:

$$\frac{\pi(A|S)}{\pi(B|S)} = \frac{p(S|A)}{p(S|B)} \left[\frac{p(A)}{p(B)} \right]^d \tag{6.1}$$

---

[58] Troutman and Shanteau also found in both experiments that when participants observed an "irrelevant sample" of all blue beads or a "mixed" sample of one red and one white bead—both are which are uninformative regarding A versus B—participants' posterior probability of Box A was similarly moderated toward 50%, and these effects were larger than that of the null sample. Shanteau (1975) had similarly found that experimental participants' beliefs were moderated toward 50% after observing a mixed sample. Across several sequential-sample experiments modeled on Troutman and Shanteau's, Labella and Koehler (2004) did not replicate these results, finding instead that participants' posteriors were unaffected by an irrelevant sample and became *more extreme* after a mixed sample. (Labella and Koehler did not study the effect of a "null sample.") However, in a simultaneous-sample version of their experiment, Labella and Koehler did find that participants' posteriors were weaker when an additional, mixed set of signals was included in the sample. The "null sample" result is a cleaner test of whether base-rate neglect is triggered by updating because observing an irrelevant or mixed sample could affect beliefs for two additional reasons discussed in this chapter. First, it may moderate beliefs if inferences are drawn based on the sample proportion (Stylized Fact 4), including in sequential samples if inferences are based on the pooled sample. Second, it could make beliefs more extreme due to prior-biased updating (Section 8) (which is indeed how Labella and Koehler interpreted their finding of more extreme beliefs after a mixed sample).

with $0 < d < 1$. Eq. (6.1) is the special case of Eq. (4.6) in which biased inferences are abstracted away ($c = 1$). However, unlike Eq. (4.6), Eq. (6.1) is treated as a structural model of the belief-updating process. In this model, neglect of base rates (i.e., population frequencies), as in the evidence discussed above, is treated as a special case of underweighting priors in general. As per the evidence from Kahneman and Tversky (1973) discussed above, it is assumed that the agent updates whenever a signal is observed, even if the signal is uninformative.

A number of implications follow directly from Eq. (6.1). First, whereas a Bayesian treats all signals symmetrically, a base-rate neglecter is affected more by recent than less recent signals. To see this, note that the base-rate neglecter's posterior odds after one signal are

$$\frac{\pi(A|s_1)}{\pi(B|s_1)} = \frac{p(s_1|A)}{p(s_1|B)} \left[\frac{p(A)}{p(B)}\right]^d;$$

and after two signals,

$$\frac{\pi(A|s_1, s_2)}{\pi(B|s_1, s_2)} = \frac{p(s_2|A)}{p(s_2|B)} \left[\frac{p(s_1|A)}{p(s_1|B)}\right]^d \left[\frac{p(A)}{p(B)}\right]^{d^2}. \tag{6.2}$$

Because the older signal becomes part of the prior when the new signal arrives, the older signal is down-weighted twice, whereas the new signal is down-weighted only once. Thus, base-rate neglect provides an explanation of the "recency effects" observed in the bookbag-and-poker-chip experiments (Stylized Fact 11). As discussed below, in economic settings, these recency effects can generate adaptive expectations and extrapolative beliefs.

Second, the base-rate neglecter's long-run beliefs fluctuate in accordance with an ergodic (stationary long-run) distribution. Iterating the derivation of Eq. (6.2) and taking the logarithm, the agent's log posterior odds after observing t signals are $\sum_{\tau=0}^{t} d^{t-\tau} l_\tau$, where $l_\tau \equiv \frac{p(s_\tau|A)}{p(s_\tau|B)}$ denotes the log likelihood of the τth signal for $\tau > 0$ and $l_0 \equiv \frac{\pi(A)}{\pi(B)}$ denotes the log prior odds. Since this sum is an AR(1) process, it converges in the limit $t \to \infty$ to an ergodic distribution, as long as the l_τ's are bounded. Thus, while a Bayesian will eventually identify the true state with certainty, a base-rate neglecter will never become fully confident, and her beliefs will forever fluctuate even if the environment is fundamentally stationary.

This in turn implies that in settings where the agent observes many signals, base-rate neglect will cause her to ultimately become underconfident about the state. Such underconfidence contrasts with the impression one might get from examples like the Cab Problem, where base-rate neglect causes people to be overly swayed by a signal indicative of an event that is unlikely given the base rates. While base-rate neglect can cause people to "jump to conclusions" after a single signal that goes in the opposite direction of the base rates—as in almost all of the updating problems used to study base-rate neglect—in the long run it is a force for persistent uncertainty (see Section 10.1 for related discussion).

Third and finally, Eq. (6.1) has a counterintuitive implication that Benjamin, Bodoh-Creed, and Rabin call the *moderation effect*: when the agent's prior in favor of a state is sufficiently strong, a supportive signal can *dampen* the agent's belief about the state! The moderation effect occurs because the new signal has less of an impact on the agent's posterior than down-weighting the prior. Although surprising, there is evidence of the moderation effect in existing data. For example, consider the updating problems in Griffin and Tversky's (1992) Study 2, where the rate of *a* signals was 0.6 in state A and 0.4 in state B, participants were informed about a sample of size 10, and the prior probability of state A was 90%. When the sample contained 5 *a*'s, participants reported a median posterior of 60%; when 6 *a*'s, 70%; and when 7 *a*'s, 85%. In all of these cases, the participants' posterior belief was *lower* than the prior of 90%, consistent with a moderation effect. (Their posterior belief exceeded 90% only when the sample had at least 8 *a*'s.)

Benjamin, Bodoh-Creed, and Rabin drew out the implications of base-rate neglect in settings of persuasion, reputation-building, and expectations formation. The results are particularly straightforward in a simple expectations formation setting. Suppose the agent is forming expectations about some parameter θ, say, the expected return of some asset. The agent's current prior is normally distributed, $N\left(\theta_0, \frac{1}{v_0}\right)$, with some mean θ_0 and precision v_0. The agent then updates her beliefs after observing a noisy signal of θ drawn from a normal distribution, $x \sim N\left(\theta, \frac{1}{v_x}\right)$, with precision v_x. As is well known, a Bayesian's posterior would be normally distributed and centered around a precision-weighted mean of the prior mean θ_0 and the signal x:

$$E[\theta|x] = \frac{v_0}{v_0 + v_x}\theta_0 + \frac{v_x}{v_0 + v_x}x = \theta_0 + \left(\frac{v_x}{v_0 + v_x}\right)(x - \theta_0).$$

The base-rate neglecter's posterior also turns out to be normally distributed, but centered around a different mean:

$$E_{BRN}[\theta|x] = \frac{v_0/d^2}{v_0/d^2 + v_x}\theta_0 + \frac{v_x}{v_0/d^2 + v_x}x$$

$$= \theta_0 + \left(\frac{v_x}{v_0/d^2 + v_x}\right)(x - \theta_0). \tag{6.3}$$

Because base-rate neglect causes the agent to treat the prior as less informative than it is, the base-rate neglecter updates as if the precision of the prior distribution is shrunken by a factor of d^2. Consequently, as shown in Eq. (6.3), the agent's expectations are overly influenced by the recently observed signal. Such expectations can generate extrapolative beliefs, in which the agent over-extrapolates from recent returns when predicting future returns. As discussed in Chapter "Psychology-Based Models of Asset Prices and Trading Volume" (by Barberis) of this Handbook, extrapolative beliefs are an important ingredient in explaining a variety of puzzles in finance.

When studying the implications of base-rate neglect in field settings, a crucial issue is how people group signals (as previously discussed in Sections 4.3 and 5.1). Benjamin, Bodoh-Creed, and Rabin make the plausible assumption that beliefs are updated after each new signal is observed, but there are other possibilities. For example, all previously observed signals could be pooled together into a single sample. If the agent then updates using her original priors and the pooled sample, then earlier signals would *not* be down-weighted more than recent signals. While Stylized Fact 8 summarizes evidence against such pooling, the evidence is relatively thin. In settings where the agent's future beliefs are relevant, it also matters whether or not the agent believes she will exhibit base-rate neglect and how she anticipates grouping signals she may receive in the future. There is no evidence on these issues.

7 The representativeness heuristic

In his Nobel lecture, Daniel Kahneman (2002) recollected how his collaboration with Amos Tversky began when he invited Tversky to give a guest lecture in his graduate psychology course at Hebrew University in 1968–1969. Tversky, whom as a Ph.D. student had been mentored by Ward Edwards, lectured about conservatism bias. Kahneman was deeply skeptical for a number of reasons, including the everyday experience that—contrary to conservatism bias—people commonly jump to conclusions on the basis of little data. Kahenman's reaction shook Tversky's faith in thinking about people as merely a biased version of Bayesian, and they met for lunch to discuss their experiences and hunches about how people *really* judge probabilities.

Their collaboration blossomed into the enormously influential "heuristics and biases" research program (see, e.g., Gilovich et al., 2002). To explain this research program, Tversky and Kahneman (1974) drew an analogy with visual perception. People perceive objects as physically closer when they can be seen more sharply. This perceptual heuristic has some validity but leads to systematic errors when visibility is unusually good or poor. Similarly, Tversky and Kahneman argued, a small number of simple heuristics are useful for a wide range of complex probabilistic judgments but also generate systematic biases.

7.1 Representativeness

The first heuristic Kahneman and Tversky (1972a) proposed—and the central one for probabilistic reasoning—is the *representativeness heuristic*. They defined it as "evaluat[ing] the probability of an uncertain event, or a sample, by the degree to which it is: (i) similar in essential properties to its parent population; and (ii) reflects the salient features of the process by which it is generated" (p. 431).[59] Across several papers (Kahneman and Tversky, 1972a, 1973; Tversky and Kahneman, 1983), Kahneman and Tversky argued that the representativeness heuristic is the psychological process that generates the LSN (Section 2.1), sample-size neglect (Section 3.2), and base-rate neglect (Section 6), as well as several other biases such as the conjunction fallacy (described below).[60] For each of these biases, Kahneman and Tversky reported evidence from many different surveys and experiments.

Kahneman and Tversky (1972a) focused on people's beliefs about random samples. They argued that in order for a sample to be representative of the population from which it is drawn, it must satisfy both parts of the definition of representativeness: (i) the sample proportions must match the population rate, and (ii) systematic patterns must be absent. They called part (i) the LSN, and some of the evidence is described in Section 2.1. As an example of part (ii), they pointed to prior findings that people judged fair-coin-flip sequences with a pattern, such as HTHTHTHT, to be less likely than sequences that have the same number of heads and tails but no obvious pattern (e.g., Tune, 1964).

Kahneman and Tversky (1973) argued that sample-size neglect and base-rate neglect are consequences of the representativeness heuristic because sample sizes and base rates do not enter into judgments of representativeness. Similarly, the representativeness heuristic explains why regression to the mean is not intuitive to people, since it is also unrelated to representativeness.

Tversky and Kahneman (1983) introduced a new bias, the conjunction fallacy, which they argued could be caused by each of several mechanisms, including the representativeness heuristic. The conjunction fallacy is when people believe that the conjunction of two events, A *and* B, has higher probability than one of its constituents, say, A. Such a belief violates a basic law of probability. In one of several examples, Tversky and Kahneman reported results from a series of variants of the now-famous "Linda problem." In this problem, respondents were first given a brief description of Linda:

> Linda is 31 years old, single, outspoken and very bright. She majored in philosophy. As a student, she was deeply concerned with issues of discrimination and social justice, and also participated in anti-nuclear demonstrations.

---

[59] Kahneman and Frederick (2002) further developed the theory of the representativeness heuristic. In their formulation, when people are asked to make judgments about probability, they instead give the answer to the much simpler question about representativeness. They argue that such "attribute substitution" is a general characteristic of intuitive judgment: when asked a question that would be difficult and effortful to answer (requiring "System 2" thinking), people answer a much simpler question (that has an effortless and quick "System 1" answer) whenever they can.

[60] Later, Kahneman and Tversky (1982) drew a distinction between judgments *of* representativeness, relating to judgments about whether a random sample is representative (including the biases discussed in Sections 2 and 3), and judgments *by* representativeness, relating to use of the representativeness heuristic to make predictions and judge probabilities (including biased inference and base-rate neglect). Kahneman and Tversky argued that the evidence supported both hypotheses.

In one of the variants, 142 undergraduates were asked which of two statements (presented in a random order) is more probable:

Linda is a bank teller.
Linda is a bank teller and is active in the feminist movement.

Tversky and Kahneman predicted that people would commit the conjunction fallacy because the description of Linda was constructed to be representative of a feminist and not representative of a bank teller. Consistent with the conjunction fallacy, 85% of respondents indicated that the second statement was more likely. A natural alternative explanation is that interpret "Linda is a bank teller" as implying that she is not active in the feminist movement, but a majority of respondents still committed the conjunction fallacy when the first statement was replaced by "Linda is a bank teller whether or not she is active in the feminist movement."

Tentori et al. (2004) reviewed evidence that the conjunction fallacy is robust to many potential confounds and persists when participants make incentivized bets and when the problem is framed in terms of frequencies. While Zizzo et al. (2000) found that making the error more obvious to participants reduced the frequency of the fallacy, Zizzo et al. and Stolarz-Fantino et al. (2003, Experiment 5) found that for participants given feedback or monetary rewards, the effect occurred at rates similar to those for control participants. On the other hand, Charness et al. (2010) found that it is much less common when experimental participants are incentivized or work in teams. For an overview of non-representativeness-based explanations of the conjunction fallacy, see Fisk (2016).

While a wide array of biases can be accounted for by the representativeness heuristic, critics allege that representativeness is too vague and flexible a concept to be useful (e.g., Evans and Pollard, 1982, p. 101; Gigerenzer, 1996).[61] The theory po-

---

[61] Gerd Gigerenzer's (1996) critiques were aimed broadly at the heuristics-and-biases research program and were empirical as well as theoretical. The central empirical claim was that many of the biases are weaker when problems are framed in terms of frequencies rather than probabilities. Kahneman and Tversky (1996) agreed with this claim (and indeed, Tversky and Kahneman (1983) anticipated it) but emphasized that the biases nonetheless largely persist in a frequency framing. Theoretically, Gigerenzer disputed the normative status of the Bayesian model and, more relevantly for economics, he argued that the proposed heuristics were too vague. For example, Gigerenzer (1996, p. 592) wrote: "Explanatory notions such as representativeness remain vague, undefined, and unspecified with respect both to the antecedent conditions that elicit (or suppress) them and also to the cognitive processes that underlie them... The problem with these heuristics is that they at once explain too little and too much. Too little, because we do not know when these heuristics work and how; too much, because, post hoc, one of them can be fitted to almost any experimental result." Gigerenzer's own research program differed in both research strategy and emphasis. The research strategy pursued by him and his colleagues focused on specifying precise algorithms to fit experimental data on people's judgments (e.g., Gigerenzer et al., 2011). Their emphasis was on the high quality of the resulting judgments, rather than on deviations from Bayesian reasoning. This work is less relevant for economics than Kahneman and Tversky's both because the kinds of judgments studied are less central and because the Bayesian model already provides a good "as if" model of unbiased judgments. A recent, related line of work in cognitive science aims to explain biases as resulting from optimal cognitive strategies given limited cognitive resources (e.g., Lieder et al., 2018). Such work holds

tentially has many degrees of freedom if "similar in essential properties" and "salient features of the process" can be defined differently in different settings. A related critique is that it merely creates the appearance of parsimony by giving a single name to distinct phenomena. The most pointed version of the critique is that representativeness is merely a label for, or redescription of, intuitive judgments of probability (Gigerenzer, 1996, p. 594), rather than an explanation of them.

In their original presentation of representativeness, Kahneman and Tversky (1972a, p. 431) anticipated this concern but argued that the agreement in people's judgments adequately pinned down its meaning:

> Representativeness, like perceptual similarity, is easier to assess than to characterize. In both cases, no general definition is available, yet there are many situations where people agree which of two stimuli is more similar to a standard, or which of two events is more representative of a given process. In this paper... we consider cases where the ordering of events according to representativeness appears obvious, and show that people consistently judge the more representative event to be the more likely, whether it is or not.

In subsequent work, Tversky and Kahneman (1983) identified some regularities in judgments of representativeness. First, it is directional: it is natural to describe an outcome (e.g., a sample) as representative of a causally prior entity (e.g., a population), but usually not vice-versa. Second, when both can be described in the same terms, such as the mean or other salient statistics, then representativeness partly reduces to similarity of these statistics. However, as noted above, sharing features of the random process is also relevant. Third, common instances are usually more representative than rare events. However, there are notable exceptions; for example, a narrow interval around the mode of a distribution is often more representative than a wider interval near the tail that has greater probability mass (an observation related to the evidence discussed in Section 3.4 that people's sampling-distribution beliefs overweight the mean). Fourth, an attribute is more representative of a class if it is more diagnostic, i.e., if its relative frequency in that class is higher than in a reference class. For example, 65% of undergraduates surveyed by Tversky and Kahneman stated that it is more representative of Hollywood actresses "to be divorced more than 4 times" than "to be Democratic," even though 83% of a different sample of undergraduates stated that, among Hollywood actresses, more are Democratic than divorced more than 4 times. The reason, Tversky and Kahneman argued, is that the odds of Hollywood actresses *relative to other women* being four-times divorced is much greater than the odds of Hollywood actresses *relative to other women* being Democratic. Fifth, an unrepresentative instance of a category can nonetheless be representative of a superordinate category (e.g., a chicken is not a representative bird, but it is a fairly representative animal).

---

promise of answering Gigerenzer's directives to be specific about cognitive processes and to make precise predictions, while keeping the focus on biases that result from relying on heuristics.

Formal modeling of representativeness provides the most persuasive response to the vagueness critique. Tenenbaum and Griffiths (2001) formalized the notion of representativeness as diagnosticity (the fourth regularity in the list above). To do so, they need to specify the relevant reference classes. For example, suppose the reference class for a fair coin is a usually alternating coin. Then the sequence HHTHTTTH is more representative of a fair coin than HTHTHTHT because the likelihood ratio $\frac{p(\text{HHTHTTTH}|\text{fair})}{p(\text{HTHTHTHT}|\text{fair})}$, which equals 1, is greater than the likelihood ratio $\frac{p(\text{HHTHTTTH}|\text{alternating})}{p(\text{HTHTHTHT}|\text{alternating})}$, which is less than 1. Tenenbaum and Griffiths did not propose an ex ante theory of the reference class, so its specification remains a degree of freedom in operationalizing this notion of representativeness.

7.2 The strength-versus-weight theory of biased updating

In an influential paper, Griffin and Tversky (1992) proposed a theory that aims to unify many updating biases within a common framework. According to their theory, the psychological process of belief updating has two stages: people form an initial impression based on the "strength" of the evidence, and then they adjust this impression based on the "weight" of the evidence. The strength, or extremeness, of the evidence is determined by its representativeness. The weight, or credence, of the evidence reflects other factors that matter for normatively correct updating. The adjustment for weight is insufficient, causing people's updating to be excessively influenced by the representativeness-related features of the evidence. The predictions of the theory then come from specifying what is strength and what is weight. Griffin and Tversky applied their theory to seven belief biases, three of which are relevant for this chapter and discussed here.

First, following Kahneman and Tversky (1972a), they identified the proportion of a signals in a sample with the representativeness of the sample (see Section 3.2). Thus, they theorized that in drawing inferences from a sample of binary signals, the sample proportion $\left(\frac{N_a - N_b}{N}\right)$ is strength and the sample size (N) is weight. The theory then explains why inferences are too sensitive to sample proportion (Stylized Fact 4) and insufficiently sensitive to sample size (Stylized Fact 2). In their Study 1, Griffin and Tversky posed twelve simultaneous-sample bookbag-and-poker-chip updating problems that vary in sample proportion and sample size; this study is discussed in Section 4.2, and its results are included in Section 4's meta-analysis. Consistent with the theory, when estimating Eq. (4.14), Griffin and Tversky found that the coefficient on sample proportion is greater than the coefficient on sample size.

Griffin and Tversky also found (consistent with the relatively small coefficient on sample size) that their experimental participants overinferred from sample sizes of 3 and 5 and underinferred from sample sizes of 9, 17, and 33. Based on this finding, they suggested that their theory might reconcile the general finding that experimental participants in bookbag-and-poker-chip experiments underinfer (Stylized Fact 1) with the evidence from Tversky and Kahneman (1971) that scientific researchers conclude too much from evidence obtained in small samples. However, this suggestion is not compelling. The sample sizes for the research studies examined by Tversky and Kahneman (1971) were 15, 20, 40, and 100, which are in the range of sample sizes where Griffin and Tversky find *under*inference. Moreover, as shown in Fig. 3A and discussed in Section 4, Griffin and Tversky's finding of overinference is unusual; overinference is *not* the predominant pattern across bookbag-and-poker-chip experiments for sample sizes of 3 and 5. With more complete financial incentives than Griffin and Tversky, Antoniou et al. (2015) replicated their Study 1 results but found underinference for all sample sizes when they controlled for risk preferences over the incentives (see Fig. 3 from their 2013 working paper).

Second, Griffin and Tversky argued that their theory could explain base-rate neglect (Stylized Fact 7) if the likelihood information is the strength of the evidence and the prior probabilities of the states are the weight. This supposition follows from the argument that prior probabilities do not enter into judgments of representativeness, as discussed above. In their Study 2, Griffin and Tversky posed twenty-five updating problems that vary the prior probabilities of the two states and the number of a's in a sample of 10 signals; this study is included in Section 4's meta-analysis on the use of prior probabilities in updating. Their results provide particularly clean evidence that experimental participants' posteriors are not sensitive enough to the prior probabilities.

Third, as discussed in Section 8.2 in the context of Fischhoff and Beyth-Marom's (1983) explanation of prior-biased updating, Griffin and Tversky argued that people focus on how well the evidence fits a "given" hypothesis but not how well it fits an "alternative" hypothesis. To apply this idea to a bookbag-and-poker-chip updating problem, suppose the likelihood of a sample under state A, $p(S|A)$, is higher than the likelihood under state B, $p(S|B)$. The higher likelihood is identified with the strength of the evidence and the lower likelihood with the weight. For example (as also described in Section 3.2), in Griffin and Tversky's Study 3, they posed updating problems in which the number of a signals is 7, 8, 9, or 10. When the rates were close together, $(\theta_A, \theta_B) = (0.6, 0.5)$, the experimental participants overinferred, reporting posteriors too favorable to state A. However, when the rates were further apart, $(\theta_A, \theta_B) = (0.6, 0.25)$, the participants' posteriors were only slightly less favorable to state A, and thus they dramatically underinferred. Griffin and Tversky argued that this is because when evaluating the likelihood ratio, $\dfrac{p(S|A)}{p(S|B)}$, participants' overweighted the numerator and underweighted the denominator. They argued that this application of their theory explains why people underinfer by more in bookbag-and-poker-chip experiments when the rates are further apart (Stylized Fact 6).

Griffin and Tversky's strength-versus-weight theory is appealing because it explains so many biases, but it is not clear how useful the theory is for economists. It amounts to saying that people primarily judge posterior probabilities according to representativeness but also incorporate Bayesian reasoning to some extent. Economic models of biased updating generally nest pure bias and Bayesian updating as polar cases and assume that people are in between (for discussion, see Section 10.2). For economists, the challenge in capturing the strength-versus-weight theory, then, is the same as the challenge in capturing other representativeness-based theories: formalizing what representativeness means.

7.3 Economic models of representativeness

All of the models discussed in previous sections of this chapter are designed to capture biases that have been attributed to the representativeness heuristic. Most directly, Rabin's (2002) and Rabin and Vayanos's (2010) models of the Law of Small Numbers are aimed directly at formalizing judgments of how representative a sample is of the population from which it is drawn.

Zhao (2018) proposed a model that formalizes the sense of representativeness based on similarity. He assumed that people judge the likelihood of A given S by assessing the similarity of A to S, and he proposed an axiomatic characterization of an ordinal similarity index. Under some assumptions, the judged similarity of A to S is the geometric mean of the two conditional probabilities: $p(A|S)^\varsigma p(S|A)^{1-\varsigma}$, where $0 < \varsigma < 1$. Zhao showed that his model can accommodate the conjunction fallacy. For example, consider the Linda problem. According to the model, an agent's belief that Linda is a bank teller (BT) *and* a feminist (F), conditional on the description of Linda as a social-justice activist (the signal S), depends on the similarity of BT $\cap$ F to S, which equals $p(\mathrm{BT} \cap \mathrm{F}|S)^\varsigma p(S|\mathrm{BT} \cap \mathrm{F})^{1-\varsigma}$. By comparison, the agent's conditional belief that Linda is a bank teller depends on the similarity of BT to S, which equals $\pi(\mathrm{BT}|S) = p(\mathrm{BT}|S)^\varsigma p(S|\mathrm{BT})^{1-\varsigma}$. The former can be larger than the latter if $p(S|\mathrm{BT} \cap \mathrm{F})$ is sufficiently larger than $p(S|\mathrm{BT})$. Zhao also showed that his model generates base-rate neglect: dividing the similarity of state A to signal S by the similarity of state B to signal S gives

$$\left(\frac{p(A|S)^\varsigma p(S|A)^{1-\varsigma}}{p(B|S)^\varsigma p(S|B)^{1-\varsigma}} \right) = \frac{p(S|A)}{p(S|B)} \left(\frac{p(A|S)p(S)}{p(S|A)} \frac{p(S|B)}{p(B|S)p(S)} \right)^\varsigma$$

$$= \frac{p(S|A)}{p(S|B)} \left(\frac{p(A)}{p(B)} \right)^\varsigma .$$

This is the same as the formula for base-rate neglect in Eq. (6.1), with the base-rate neglect parameter d equal to the similarity parameter ς. For economic applications, it is a limitation of Zhao's framework that the similarity judgment is an ordinal measure, i.e., defined up to a monotonic transformation. Because of that, the resulting similarity judgments cannot directly be treated as probabilistic beliefs for the purposes of decision making.

Gennaioli and Shleifer (2010) proposed a model that, like Tenenbaum and Griffiths (2001), formalizes the sense of representativeness based on diagnosticity. The key idea underlying Gennaioli and Shleifer's model is that, when people are judging the probability of some event, the states of the world that are most representative of the event are most likely to come to an agent's mind, i.e., to be remembered or attended to. People then overestimate the probabilities of these states. Gennaioli and

Shleifer refer to the bias in what comes to mind as *local thinking*. Implementations of this idea in different environments have been developed not only in Gennaioli and Shleifer (2010) but also in Bordalo et al. (2016) and Bordalo et al. (2018), each of which is described below.

Gennaioli and Shleifer (2010) applied their model to explain several biases, including the conjunction fallacy. To illustrate, consider the Linda problem. There are two dimensions of the state space: bank teller (BT) versus social worker (SW) and feminist (F) versus non-feminist (NF). Suppose that the true probabilities of each of four states are:

	Feminist	Non-Feminist
Bank Teller	20%	10%
Social Worker	60%	10%

When assessing the probability of an event that fully pins down the state, the agent's belief is correct because there is no scope for biased attention or recall to play a role; e.g., the agent's belief about the probability that Linda is a bank teller and a feminist, $\pi(BT \cap F)$, is the true probability, $p(BT \cap F) = 20\%$. However, when assessing the probability of an event that leaves uncertainty about the state, then the agent differentially attends to (or remembers) the states that are more representative of the event. This assessment can be broken down into two steps. First, given the focal event, the representativeness of each possible "scenario" (some event along a different dimension) is judged according to its diagnosticity. For the focal event {Linda is a bank teller}, the representativeness of the scenario that she is a feminist is $\dfrac{p(F|BT)}{p(F|SW)} = \dfrac{20\%/(20\% + 10\%)}{60\%/(60\% + 10\%)} = 0.78$, and the representativeness of the scenario that she is a non-feminist is $\dfrac{p(NF|BT)}{p(NF|SW)} = \dfrac{10\%/(20\% + 10\%)}{10\%/(60\% + 10\%)} = 2.33$. Second, the agent judges the probability of the focal event by aggregating across all scenarios, weighted by their representativeness. In the starkest and simplest case, the agent puts full weight on the most representative scenario. In that case, when judging the probability of the event {Linda is a bank teller}, the agent thinks only about the scenario in which Linda is a non-feminist, and thus $\pi(BT) = p(BT \cap NF) = 10\%$. Since $\pi(BT)$ is smaller than $\pi(BT \cup F)$, the agent has committed the conjunction fallacy.

The model also generates a form of base-rate neglect. In the Linda-problem example, when told that Linda is a bank teller, the agent becomes certain that Linda is a non-feminist despite the fact that, unconditional on bank teller versus social worker, former activists like Linda are much more likely to be feminists (80% probability) than non-feminists (20% probability). This base-rate neglect occurs because the agent's judgments of the representativeness of Linda depend only on the conditional probabilities $p(F|BT)$, $p(F|SW)$, $p(NF|BT)$, and $p(NF|SW)$ and not on the base rates $p(F)$ and $p(NF)$.

Gennaioli and Shleifer also developed an extension of their model to capture some of the evidence of partition dependence reviewed in Section 3.1. Consider an example similar to theirs (based on Fischhoff, Slovic, and Lichtenstein, 1978). There are three possible causes of car failure: the state space is {battery problems, fuel problems, and ignition problems}. People are asked the probability that a car's failure to start is *not* due to battery problems. The model aims to explain why, when asked to assign probabilities to three bins {battery, fuel, ignition}, people report a higher total probability for non-battery causes than when asked to assign probabilities to the two bins {battery, non-battery}. Suppose the true probabilities are p(battery) = 60%, p(fuel) = 30%, and p(ignition) = 10%. When asked to assign probabilities to all three states, the agent is not biased and judges the probability of non-battery as π(non-battery | {battery, fuel, ignition}) = p(fuel) + p(ignition) = 40%. However, when asked to assign probabilities to {battery, non-battery}, the agent's assessment of the probability of the event {non-battery} is distorted by overweighting the likelihood of its constituent states according to their representativeness. Analogous to the Linda-problem example, this distortion can be broken down into two steps. In the first step, the representativeness of each constituent state is judged. The representativeness of {fuel} is $\dfrac{p(\text{fuel}|\text{non-battery})}{p(\text{fuel}|\text{battery})}$, while the representativeness of {ignition} is $\dfrac{p(\text{ignition}|\text{non-battery})}{p(\text{ignition}|\text{battery})}$. Unfortunately, in this environment, these measures of representativeness are not well-defined because the denominators are zero. Gennaioli and Shleifer therefore extended their model by proposing that when these likelihood ratios are not well-defined, people instead measure representativeness by just the numerators. Thus, the representativeness of {fuel} is p(fuel|non-battery) $= \dfrac{30\%}{30\% + 10\%} = 0.75$, and the representativeness of {ignition} is p(ignition|non-battery) $= \dfrac{10\%}{30\% + 10\%} = 0.25$. In the second step, the agent judges the probability of the event {non-battery} by aggregating across its constituent states, weighted by their representativeness. In the stark case where the most representative state is given full weight, the agent judges the probability of {non-battery} to be equal to the probability of {fuel}: π(non-battery | {battery, non-battery}) = p(fuel) = 30%. This perceived probability is smaller than π(non-battery | {battery, fuel, ignition}) = 40%. The psychology of the model is that when the agent assesses the probability of the event {non-battery}, the possibility of ignition problems (the less representative state) does not come to mind.

Bordalo et al. (2016) applied the representativeness-as-diagnosticity idea to stereotyping. This model develops the logic underlying Tversky and Kahneman's (1983) example, mentioned above, of why "being divorced more than 4 times" is a stereotype of Hollywood actresses. Adapting an example from Bordalo et al., consider the stereotype of Florida residents being elderly. There are two groups, Florida residents and U.S. residents overall. According to the 2010 Census, the percentage of residents 65 and over is 17% in Florida and 13% in the US overall. The model assumes that the agent knows these percentages but does not remember them. When assessing the age distribution of Florida residents, the more representative scenarios (i.e., age intervals) are differentially recalled or attended to. The

65+ age group is more representative of Florida residents than the <65 age group because $\dfrac{p(\text{age } 65+ |\text{FL})}{p(\text{age } 65+ |\text{US})} > \dfrac{p(\text{age} < 65|\text{FL})}{p(\text{age} < 65|\text{US})}$. Consequently, the agent's assessment $\pi(\text{age } 65+ |\text{FL})$ is an overestimate relative to $p(\text{age } 65+ |\text{FL})$, while $\pi(\text{age} < 65|\text{FL})$ is an underestimate. This example illustrates the two central implications of the model: stereotypes have a "kernel of truth," but they can nonetheless be extremely inaccurate. In addition to providing a number of other illustrative examples (such as Asians are good at math, Republicans are rich, Tel Aviv is dangerous), Bordalo et al. reports laboratory experiments with abstract groups and exogenous frequencies, as well as an empirical application to survey data on actual and perceived ethical views of liberals and conservatives across many political issues. The results overall are consistent with the model. Arnold et al. (2018) and Alesina et al. (2018) find that the kernel-of-truth hypothesis provides a good explanation of judges' bias against blacks in bail decisions and residents' beliefs about immigrants, respectively. A parameter of the model governing how strongly representativeness influences beliefs is also estimated to have similar values across papers that estimate it (Bordalo et al., 2016; Arnold et al., 2018).

Bordalo et al. (2018) explored how representativeness-influenced beliefs may generate extrapolative expectations in asset markets (discussed in detail in Chapter "Psychology-Based Models of Asset Prices and Trading Volume" (by Barberis) of this Handbook). The state of the economy at time t is denoted ω_t. The rational expectation of ω_t at time $t - 1$ is $E[\omega_t|\omega_{t-1}] \equiv f(\omega_{t-1})$. The key assumption in this setting is that at time t, when forecasting next period's state ω_{t+1}, the agent assigns higher probability to states that are more representative of ω_t relative to $f(\omega_{t-1})$, i.e., states with larger $\dfrac{p(\omega_{t+1}|\omega_t)}{p(\omega_{t+1}|f(\omega_{t-1}))}$. Intuitively, the most representative state is the one that has experienced the largest increase in its likelihood based on recent news. Thus, the agent's forecast of next period's state is given by the probability density function:

$$\pi(\omega_{t+1}|\omega_t) = p(\omega_{t+1}|\omega_t)\left(\frac{p(\omega_{t+1}|\omega_t)}{p(\omega_{t+1}|f(\omega_{t-1}))}\right)^{\rho}\frac{1}{Z}, \qquad (7.1)$$

where $\rho > 0$ is the parameter governing how strongly representativeness influences beliefs and $Z \equiv \displaystyle\int_{+\infty}^{x=-\infty} p(\omega_{t+1} = x|\omega_t)\left(\frac{p(\omega_{t+1} = x|\omega_t)}{p(\omega_{t+1} = x|f(\omega_{t-1}))}\right)^{\rho} dx$ is a normalizing constant. Bordalo, Gennaioli, and Shleifer refer to the mean of the beliefs in Eq. (7.1) as "diagnostic expectations" because the beliefs overweight states that are most diagnostic of ω_t relative to $f(\omega_{t-1})$.

These beliefs turn out to have a particularly convenient form when ω_t follows an AR(1) process whose shocks are distributed normally with mean zero and variance σ^2. In that case, $\pi(\omega_{t+1}|\omega_t)$ is a normal distribution with variance σ^2 and mean

$$E_t[\omega_{t+1}] + \rho(E_t[\omega_{t+1}] - E_{t-1}[\omega_{t+1}]). \qquad (7.2)$$

It is clear from Eq. (7.2) that diagnostic expectations for period $t + 1$ overreact to the new information received at time t. It is this property of diagnostic expectations that generates extrapolative expectations. Bordalo, Gennaioli, and Shleifer embed diagnostic expectations in a dynamic macroeconomic model and show that it can explain several facts about credit cycles that are difficult to reconcile with a rational-expectations model.

The local-thinking model of representativeness reviewed in this subsection has two main limitations. First, additional assumptions may be needed to apply it in new settings. For example, a key ingredient for diagnostic expectations is the assumption that representativeness for ω_{t+1} is assessed by its diagnosticity for ω_t relative to $f(\omega_{t-1})$. Although it may be plausible, this assumption does not follow from the local-thinking model. As discussed above, applying the model to explain partition dependence requires an assumption about how representativeness is judged when the likelihood ratio is not well-defined. More generally, it is not clear how to apply the model in settings that do not fit the basic setup of existing applications. For example, does the model make predictions about people's beliefs about the distribution of 100 flips of a fair coin, and if so, how should the model be specified? An important challenge going forward is to specify a set of assumptions or guidelines that eliminate the degrees of freedom in applying the model.

Second, the model does not explain the representativeness-related biases that motivate it across the range of settings in which those biases are observed. For example, the model's explanation of partition dependence is that people do not fully remember or attend to all of an event's constituent states; in the example above, when the event is described as "non-battery problems," the agent thinks only of fuel but not ignition problems. Yet partition dependence is observed even when an event is described as the union of its constituent states—e.g., "either fuel or ignition problems" instead of "non-battery problems" (as in many of Tversky and Koehler's (1994) examples)—a case when there is little scope for differential memory or attention to play a role in generating the bias. The evidence discussed in Section 3.2 on people's sampling-distribution beliefs about coin flips pertains to partition dependence in which an event is described explicitly as the union of its constituent states (e.g., "0, 1, 2, or 3 heads").[62] Similarly, the model has no mechanism for explaining base-rate neglect in simple updating problems where attention and memory are unlikely to play large roles, as in much of the evidence reviewed in Sections 4 and 6.

Advocates of the local-thinking model would argue that it represents a different approach to behavioral-economic theory than the models discussed in earlier sections. While those models aim to capture the psychology and experimental evidence regarding a particular bias, the local-thinking model aims to capture a central intuition about representativeness that cuts across biases. The model is also motivated as much by empirical examples as by the psychology evidence. Moreover, the attention

---

[62] In the partition-dependence literature, the cases where the event is described explicitly as unions of its constituent states are called *explicit disjunctions*, and other cases are called *implicit disjunctions*. Using that terminology, the local-thinking model provides an explanation for the latter but not the former.

and memory mechanisms underlying the local-thinking model are consistent with its orientation toward empirical applications, since field settings often do have scope for such mechanisms to play a role. Because of this orientation, advocates would argue, the model may hold promise of organizing a wider array of evidence from field settings.

7.4 Modeling representativeness versus specific biases

Kahneman and Tversky's work on representativeness had a far more profound influence on economics than Edwards's earlier work on conservatism bias. Indeed, the early research in economics on errors in probabilistic reasoning—despite relying on bookbag-and-poker-chip experiments like Edwards's—was framed as testing whether the representativeness heuristic would persist in shaping beliefs under more stringent conditions, such as when people face incentives and have experience (e.g., Grether, 1980, 1992; Harrison, 1994) or face market discipline (e.g., Duh and Sunder, 1986; Camerer, 1989).

Much of the subsequent economic modeling, however, has focused on biases (the LSN, NBLLN, etc.), rather than on the representativeness heuristic per se. An advocate of modeling biases could argue that when heuristics generate nearly optimal probabilistic reasoning, the Bayesian model is an adequate "as if" representation. It is precisely the biases—the deviations from the Bayesian model—that are needed to improve the accuracy of economic analysis. Analogously, models of *deviations* from exponential discounting and expected utility have proven useful for economics, even in the absence of more detailed models of the psychological processes underlying intertemporal and risky decision making.

Yet modeling the representativeness heuristic is appealing. Doing so holds the promise of capturing many biases at once and of explaining why particular biases may be more or less powerful under certain circumstances. On the other hand, because judgments of representativeness are so psychologically rich, it may be that no simple economic model can capture more than a narrow slice of the wide range of phenomena that representativeness encompasses.

In my opinion, both approaches have merit. Any model, whether of a bias or a heuristic, should be evaluated by the usual criteria of good economic models: broad applicability, predictive sharpness, and empirical accuracy. I further discuss these and other modeling issues in Section 10.2.

8 Prior-biased inference

In this section and the next, I return to the topic of inference. In this section, I review evidence and theory related to drawing inferences in a manner that is biased in favor of current beliefs. Informal observations of such a bias date back at least to Francis Bacon (1620). In the psychology literature, the term *confirmation bias* is commonly used to refer to a variety of different psychological processes related to seeking out, interpreting, and preferentially recalling information or generating arguments supportive of one's current beliefs (e.g., Nickerson, 1998). The work I review falls under the umbrella of confirmation bias but is narrowly focused on updating from signals that have been observed. To reflect my relatively narrow focus, I adopt the new term *prior-biased inference*.

8.1 Conceptual framework

To be more precise about what I mean by prior-biased inference, I build on the reduced-form empirical model from Section 4.1, Eq. (4.6), rewritten here for convenience:

$$\frac{\pi(A|S)}{\pi(B|S)} = \left[\frac{p(S|A)}{p(S|B)}\right]^c \left[\frac{p(A)}{p(B)}\right]^d.$$

Recall from Section 4 that in general it has been found that $c < 1$ (Stylized Facts 1 and 9), and in symmetric binomial updating problems, $c = c(N, \theta)$ is decreasing in the sample size N (Stylized Fact 2) and in the diagnosticity parameter θ (Stylized Fact 6). Prior-biased inference is the possibility that c may depend on whether a newly observed signal reinforces or weakens current priors.

Specifically, as in Charness and Dave (2017),[63] I describe the bias as a discrete difference in the amount by which beliefs are updated depending on whether the signal is confirming or disconfirming[64]:

$$\frac{\pi(A|S)}{\pi(B|S)} = \left[\frac{p(S|A)}{p(S|B)}\right]^{c_0 + I\{S \text{ is confirming}\} \cdot c_{\text{conf}} + I\{S \text{ is disconfirming}\} \cdot c_{\text{disconf}}} \left[\frac{p(A)}{p(B)}\right]^d,$$

$$(8.1)$$

where $I\{S$ is confirming$\}$ equals 1 if $\dfrac{p(A)}{p(B)}$ and $\dfrac{p(S|A)}{p(S|B)}$ are both greater than 1 or both less than 1, and $I\{S$ is disconfirming$\}$ equals 1 if one of them is greater than 1

---

[63] To be more precise, Eq. (8.1) is the implicit model underlying Charness and Dave's (2017) empirical specification, which is Eq. (8.2) below.

[64] There are other reasonable specifications that have not been explored. For example, a continuous and symmetric version of prior-biased inference would be:

$$\ln\left(\frac{\pi(A|S)}{\pi(B|S)}\right) = c_0 \ln\left(\frac{p(S|A)}{p(S|B)}\right) + d \ln\left(\frac{p(A)}{p(B)}\right) + c_{00}\left[\ln\left(\frac{p(S|A)}{p(S|B)}\right) \cdot \ln\left(\frac{p(A)}{p(B)}\right)\right].$$

In this specification, prior-biased inference amounts to adding an interaction term to Eq. (4.7). The measure of biased inference is then a continuous function of the priors, $c_0 + c_{00} \ln\left(\frac{p(A)}{p(B)}\right)$, and consistent with this specification, Pitz et al. (1967, Figs. 2–4) found that the difference between confirming and disconfirming signals in the amount of inference is increasing in the difference between the priors. Interestingly, in this specification, the bias could alternatively be described as having the constant c_0 as the measure of biased inference but having the measure of base-rate neglect be a continuous function of the likelihoods: $d + c_{00} \ln\left(\frac{p(S|A)}{p(S|B)}\right)$.

and the other is less than 1. As before, d is a measure of base-rate neglect. Now, however, there are three reduced-form parameters describing biased inference: c_0 when the priors are equal, $c_0 + c_{conf}$ when the signal is confirming of current beliefs, and $c_0 + c_{disconf}$ when the signal is disconfirming of current beliefs. The prior-biased-inference hypothesis is $c_{conf} \geq 0 \geq c_{disconf}$, with at least one inequality strict.

In the literature, the term "confirmation bias" is sometimes used to mean the opposite of base-rate neglect: $d > 1$. However, the evidence reviewed in Sections 4 and 6 indicate that base-rate neglect ($d < 1$) is the general direction of bias (Stylized Fact 7). With prior-biased inference defined as in Eq. (8.1), it is separately identifiable from base-rate neglect, and the two biases can coexist. What I call prior-biased inference is identified by the *asymmetric* response to signals that confirm versus disconfirm current priors.

Although conceptually distinct in my formulation, prior-biased inference and base-rate neglect will often push in opposite directions in a particular updating problem because prior-biased inference tends to reinforce an agent's current beliefs, while base-rate neglect will often move an agent's beliefs away from certainty (for further discussion, see Section 10.1). Moreover, despite the general tendency for people to underinfer (Stylized Fact 1), if $c_0 + c_{conf} > 1$, then prior-biased inference would cause people to overinfer when they receive confirming signals.

8.2 Evidence and models

The evidence usually adduced for confirmation bias comes from *belief polarization* experiments, in which the beliefs of people with different priors who observe the same mixed signals are typically found to move *further apart*. In a classic experiment, Lord et al. (1979) recruited 24 proponents and 24 opponents of capital punishment to be experimental participants (selected based on how they had filled out an in-class political questionnaire). The participants read a brief summary of a study that either found evidence in favor of capital punishment as a deterrent or found opposite evidence. The participants were then asked to report the change in their attitudes. Next, the participants read a detailed account of the study. The change in their attitudes was again elicited, and they were also asked to judge the quality and convincingness of the study. After reading the brief summary, which did little more than provide an unambiguous statement of the study's conclusion, proponents and opponents both reported that their attitudes moved in the direction of the study's conclusion. In contrast, after participants read the detailed account, which included information about the study's procedures, criticisms of the study, and rebuttals to the criticisms, participants whose prior beliefs disagreed with the conclusion reverted to their prior beliefs. Moreover, participants whose prior attitudes agreed with the study's conclusion judged the study to be valid and convincing, while those whose prior beliefs disagreed with the conclusion highlighted flaws and alternative explanations. Finally, after participants read the detailed accounts of both the pro- and anti-capital punishment studies, belief polarization occurred, with both proponents and opponents reporting that their attitudes had become more extreme but in opposite directions.

This belief-polarization effect has been replicated across a range of contexts, including political beliefs such as the causes of climate change (Fryer et al., 2017), interpersonal beliefs such as a person's level of academic skills (Darley and Gross, 1983), and consumer beliefs about brand quality (Russo et al., 1998). Reviews of the literature that are critical (e.g., Miller et al., 1993; Gerber and Green, 1999) have highlighted that the effect is not always found, and when it is, it shows up when participants' *changes* in beliefs are elicited but not when the before and after *levels* of their beliefs are elicited and compared.

Belief polarization is often interpreted as evidence of a bias relative to Bayesian updating. In particular, as Lord et al. (1979) argued informally, while it is *not* an error for people to infer that a study that aligns with their priors is higher quality, it *is* an error when people go on to use their prior-influenced assessment of the study to update their prior in opposite directions.[65] Baliga et al. (2013) formally proved that agents cannot update in opposite directions in a simple Bayesian model, but they showed that polarization can occur if agents are ambiguity averse. Moreover, a number of researchers have shown that belief polarization can be consistent with Bayesian reasoning in richer models (e.g., Dixit and Weibull, 2007; Andreoni and Mylovanov, 2012; Jern et al., 2014; Benoît and Dubra, 2018). For instance, Benoît and Dubra (2018) showed how belief polarization can occur when people have private information about an "ancillary matter" that does not have direct bearing on the issue of interest but matters for the interpretation of evidence. To give a concrete example, in the Lord, Ross, and Lepper experiment, this ancillary matter might be the proposition that studies reaching right-wing conclusions tend to be politically motivated and less intellectually honest. People who believe that proposition are more likely to have discounted evidence in favor of capital punishment as a deterrent *in the past* and are therefore more likely to enter the experiment as an opponent of capital punishment. They are also more likely to discount the evidence in favor of capital punishment as a deterrent *during the experiment*. If both proponents and opponents of capital punishment update their priors when reading the study that confirms their views but discount the evidence from the other study, then their beliefs will polarize.[66]

At the cost of being more abstract than the belief-polarization experiments, sequential bookbag-and-poker-chip experiments provide cleaner evidence for prior-biased inference. These experiments rule out many alternative explanations by studying fully specified updating problems; for example, they leave little room for unobserved "ancillary matters." However, confirmation bias is generally thought to be stronger when people observe ambiguous data that could be interpreted as either consistent or inconsistent with the currently favored hypothesis (Nickerson, 1998).

---

[65] Fryer et al. (2017) formalize this error of "two-step updating" described by Lord, Ross, and Lepper.

[66] Some of the subsequent experiments are cleaner than the Lord, Ross, and Lepper experiment because the prior is randomly assigned. For example, in Darley and Gross's (1983) experiment, before watching a video of a nine-year-old girl and rating her academic skills, participants were either told that her family was of high or low socioeconomic status. As Rabin and Schrag (1999) noted, such a design rules out non-common priors as a possible explanation for belief polarization.

To the extent that the data in bookbag-and-poker-chip experiments is unambiguous, such experiments may understate the magnitude of prior-biased inference that may occur when the information content of signals is more subject to interpretation.

In the earliest bookbag-and-poker-chip experiment that directly investigated prior-biased inference, Pitz et al. (1967) posed updating problems like those described in Section 4.3. The prior probabilities of the two states, A and B, were equal. The probability of a signal matching the state, θ, was known to participants and equal to 0.6, 0.7, or 0.8. Ten participants saw chunks of $N = 5$ signals at a time, ten saw chunks of $N = 10$ signals, and ten saw chunks of $N = 20$ signals. Consistent with the evidence reviewed in Section 4.2, underinference was greater when the sample size of signals was larger (larger N) and when the signals were more discriminable (larger θ). Moreover—consistent with prior-biased inference—Pitz, Downing, and Reinhold found less underinference when the signals confirmed the currently favored hypothesis. When they examined individual-level updating, Pitz, Downing, and Reinhold found that, following a single disconfirming signal, many participants revised their beliefs as if they had observed a confirming signal or did not revise their beliefs at all. In sequential-updating experiments in which participants updated after a single signal at a time, Geller and Pitz (1968) and Pitz (1969) replicated these findings, but in two experiments with normally distributed signals, DuCharme and Peterson (1968) found the opposite (i.e., stronger inference in response to a disconfirming signal).

In sequential updating experiments that begin with equal priors on the two states, prior-biased inference predicts that signals observed early on will have a greater impact on final beliefs than signals observed later: the early signals will move the priors to assign higher probability to one of the states, and then subsequent updating will be biased in favor of that state. As mentioned in Section 4.3, such "primacy effects" have indeed been found in most sequential-sample experiments that tested for them (Stylized Fact 10).

Three sequential updating experiments in the economics literature have reported tests for prior-biased inference. One of these experiments found evidence of it (Charness and Dave, 2017) and two did not (Eil and Rao, 2011; Möbius et al., 2014), but none found the opposite.[67]

In Charness and Dave's (2017) experiment, the prior probabilities of the two states were equal, and the probability of a signal matching the state was $\theta = 0.7$. Each participant observed six signals sequentially and, after each signal, recorded his subjective probability of the states. Participants were incentivized for accuracy. Charness

---

[67] Across the experiments in this literature, there are several regularities that may be related to prior-biased updating but which I do not discuss because I do not know how to interpret these regularities. For example, Pitz et al. (1967), Shanteau (1972), and Buser et al. (2018) found that, fixing the diagnosticity of the signal θ, the absolute change in beliefs (in units of probability) when updating does not depend on the priors. As another example, Coutts (2017) found a kind of primacy effect in which signals observed more frequently in the past were weighted more heavily when observed subsequently.

and Dave's regression equation is based on the logarithm of Eq. (8.1)[68]:

$$\ln\left(\frac{\pi(A|s_1, s_2, \ldots, s_t)}{\pi(B|s_1, s_2, \ldots, s_t)}\right)$$

$$= \beta_0 + \beta_1 \ln\left(\frac{p(s_t|A)}{p(s_t|B)}\right) + \beta_2 \ln\left(\frac{\pi(A|s_1, s_2, \ldots, s_{t-1})}{\pi(B|s_1, s_2, \ldots, s_{t-1})}\right)$$

$$+ \beta_3 I\{s_t \text{ is confirming}\} + \beta_4 I\{s_t \text{ is disconfirming}\} + \eta_t, \qquad (8.2)$$

where $I\{s_t$ is confirming$\}$ equals 1 if $\dfrac{\pi(A|s_1, s_2, \ldots, s_{t-1})}{\pi(B|s_1, s_2, \ldots, s_{t-1})}$ and $\dfrac{p(s_t|A)}{p(s_t|B)}$ are both greater than 1 or both less than 1, and $I\{s_t$ is disconfirming$\}$ equals 1 if one of them is greater than 1 and the other is less than 1.

Charness and Dave estimated both $\hat{\beta}_1$ and $\hat{\beta}_2$ to be less than one, consistent with underinference and base-rate neglect in updating problems that start from equal priors (as per Stylized Fact 9). Moreover, they estimated $\hat{\beta}_3 > 0$ and $\hat{\beta}_4 < 0$, consistent with prior-biased inference. Charness and Dave also found that $\hat{\beta}_1 + \hat{\beta}_3 > 1$, meaning that their experimental participants overinferred when a confirming signal was observed. Although Pitz et al. (1967) did not report estimates from regression Eq. (8.2), their experimental participants often overinferred after a confirming signal in updating problems with low diagnosticity ($\theta = 0.6$) and extreme priors, but underinferred after a confirming signal in updating problems with high diagnosticity ($\theta = 0.7$ or 0.8) or nearly equal priors.

What explains the prior-biased inference that has been observed in bookbag-and-poker-chip experiments? Fischhoff and Beyth-Marom (1983, pp. 247–248) proposed that, rather than correctly using the likelihood ratio to draw inferences, people assess how consistent the signal is with the hypothesis they are testing—which is generally the currently favored hypothesis—and do not take into account its consistency with other hypotheses. That proposal dovetails nicely with Pitz et al.'s (1967, p. 391) suggestion that participants may "not perceive isolated disconfirming events as being, in fact, contradictory to their favored hypothesis. For example, if they are fairly certain that the 80 per cent red bag is being used, a single occurrence of a blue chip will not be unexpected, and consequently may not lead to a decrement in subjective certainty." Fischhoff and Beyth-Marom argued that this bias of ignoring alternative hypotheses helps explain a variety of other observations. For example, when psychics offer universally valid personality descriptions, people are often impressed by how well it fits them without regard to the fact that it would fit others equally well. As discussed in Section 7.2, Griffin and Tversky (1992) subsequently argued that this same bias ex-

---

[68] Charness and Dave parameterized the regression slightly differently, replacing $\ln\left(\dfrac{p(s_t|A)}{p(s_t|B)}\right)$ with a dummy taking the value 1 if the tth signal is a and -1 if the tth signal is b. This specification is equivalent to Eq. (8.2), but the coefficients β_1, β_3, and β_4 in Eq. (8.2) need to be multiplied by 0.847 in order to equal the corresponding coefficients in Charness and Dave's specification.

plains why people underinfer by more in bookbag-and-poker-chip experiments when the signal rates are further apart (Stylized Fact 6).

Second, Pitz, Downing, and Reinhold (p. 391) speculated that prior-biased inference may arise because participants are unwilling to report a decrease in confidence once they have "committed" to supporting one state as more likely. As a test of this hypothesis, Pitz (1969) conducted a sequential bookbag-and-poker-chip experiment in which he manipulated the salience of the participants' posterior after the last signal when reporting their next posterior. He found prior-biased updating when participants reported posteriors after each signal and their posterior after the previous signal was visually displayed, but prior-biased updating was almost completely eliminated when the previous posterior was not displayed or when participants reported posteriors only at the end of a sequence of signals. However, a contrary result was found in another bookbag-and-poker-chip experiment (Beach and Wise, 1969): participants who reported beliefs after each signal ended up with virtually the same posteriors as participants who reported beliefs only after a sequence of signals. In a formal model related to the commitment hypothesis, Yariv (2005) assumed that an agent has a preference for consistency and can choose her beliefs. She showed that when the observed signal confirms the agent's prior, the agent may choose posteriors that are overconfident.

Eil and Rao (2011) proposed another hypothesis to explain prior-biased updating: people want their guesses to be correct, so they view confirming evidence as "good news" and update more strongly in response to good news than bad news. However, this hypothesis presupposes that *preference*-biased inference occurs, but as discussed in the next section, the evidence on preference-biased inference taken as a whole is not straightforward to interpret.

Rabin and Schrag (1999) proposed a formal model of what they call "confirmatory bias" in order to study the implications of prior-biased updating. The central assumption is that the agent sometimes misperceives disconfirming signals as confirming. This assumption is meant to capture many of the psychological mechanisms that may underlie confirmation bias. While misperception seems implausible as a literal description of the psychology underlying prior-biased inference in bookbag-and-poker-chips experiments, it actually fits nicely with the evidence that experimental participants sometimes update in the wrong direction in response to disconfirming signals, although it cannot explain the evidence of overinference from confirming signals mentioned above.

Formally, the agent begins with equal priors on the two states A and B and observes a sequence of i.i.d. signals, $s_t \in \{a, b\}$, where the signal matches the state with probability $\theta > \frac{1}{2}$ and does not match with probability $1 - \theta$. If the agent's priors are equal, or if she observes a signal that matches the state that she currently thinks is more likely, then her *perceived signal* is equal to the true signal s_t. However, if she observes a signal that does not match the state favored by her current priors, then with probability $q > 0$ she misperceives the disconfirming signal to be a confirming signal. The agent is unaware that she misperceives signals. She updates using Bayes' Rule but using the perceived signals instead of the true signals.

Rabin and Schrag drew out several main implications of the model. First, relative to a Bayesian who observed the same number of *a* and *b* signals, the agent on average will have overconfident beliefs. That is because the agent is likely to have misperceived some disconfirming signals as confirming her current beliefs, causing her to believe more strongly than she should in her currently favored hypothesis.

Second and surprisingly, if a Bayesian observer sees that a sufficiently biased agent believes that one state, say *A*, is more likely despite having perceived a sufficiently mixed set of signals, then the Bayesian observer may conclude that the *other* state is in fact more likely. The reason is that some of the signals that the agent perceived as *a* signals were likely to have been *b* signals, which in turn means that *b* signals were likely the majority. This implication, while striking, inherently applies to a scenario that is very unlikely because it requires that the signals are highly informative (θ close to 1), in which case the sample perceived by the agent is unlikely to be sufficiently mixed.

Third, if the bias is sufficiently severe or the signals are sufficiently uninformative (θ close to $\frac{1}{2}$), then when observing an infinite sequence of signals, there is positive probability that the agent will converge to certainty on belief in the wrong state. That is because once the agent starts believing in the wrong state, confirmatory bias is likely to cause her to perceive subsequent signals as continually building support for that hypothesis.

Pouget et al. (2017) examined the implications of Rabin and Schrag's model in financial markets, assuming that some fraction of traders are rational and some fraction have confirmatory bias. They showed that the model can explain three well-known observations. First, excess volume arises simply because rational and biased traders disagree and are therefore willing to trade. Second, excess volatility occurs because the biased traders are too optimistic following an initial positive signal and too pessimistic following an initial negative signal. Third, momentum arises and bubbles occur because once biased traders are optimistic, they underreact to negative signals, so future prices are expected to be higher than current prices. Pouget, Sauvagnat, and Villeneuve also derived some novel predictions of the model: differences of opinion among traders are larger following a sequence of mixed signals; traders are less likely to update their beliefs in the same direction as the current signal when previous signals have pointed in the opposite direction; and traders are less likely to update their beliefs in the same direction as the current signal when previous belief changes have been in the opposite direction. They found evidence consistent with these predictions using quarterly earnings surprises as a proxy for signals, dispersion in analysts' earnings forecasts as a proxy for differences of opinion, and analysts' revisions of annual earnings as a measure of beliefs updating.

9 Preference-biased inference

This section discusses another potential inference bias, which I call *preference-biased inference*: when people receive "good news" (i.e., information that increases expected utility), they update more than when they receive "bad news." In the literature, this bias has been referred to as *asymmetric updating* (Möbius et al., 2014) or the *good news-bad news effect* (Eil and Rao, 2011). Almost all of the research on this bias has been relatively recent. Preference-biased inference is a possible mechanism underlying a bias toward optimistic beliefs.

My focus on biased inference from signals that have been observed is (again) narrow relative to a broader literature in psychology and behavioral economics related to a range of psychological processes that can cause beliefs to become optimistic, such as strategic ignorance (avoiding information sources that may reveal bad news; see Golman et al., 2017, for a review) and self-signaling (taking actions that one later interprets as impartially revealing good news; e.g., Quattrone and Tversky, 1984; Bodner and Prelec, 2003; Bénabou and Tirole, 2011). There is evidence for several such processes. For example, strongly pointing to strategic ignorance, many people at risk for Huntington's disease refuse to be tested even though the test is inexpensive and accurate (Oster et al., 2013), and similarly for HSV (Ganguly and Tasoff, 2016).

9.1 Conceptual framework

To be precise about preference-biased inference, I once again elaborate on the reduced-form empirical model from Section 4.1, Eq. (4.6):

$$
\frac{\pi(A|S)}{\pi(B|S)} = \left[\frac{p(S|A)}{p(S|B)} \right]^{c} \left[\frac{p(A)}{p(B)} \right]^{d}.
$$

In preference-biased inference, people draw stronger inferences—i.e., c is larger—in response to a signal that favors the state that they prefer. Without loss of generality, suppose expected utility in state A, denoted U_A, is at least as large as expected utility in state B, denoted U_B. Following Möbius et al. (2014), I describe the bias as a discrete difference in the amount by which beliefs are updated depending on whether the signal is good news or bad news:

$$
\frac{\pi(A|S)}{\pi(B|S)} = \left[\frac{p(S|A)}{p(S|B)} \right]^{c_0 + I\{S \text{ is good news}\} \cdot c_{\text{good}} + I\{S \text{ is bad news}\} \cdot c_{\text{bad}}} \left[\frac{p(A)}{p(B)} \right]^{d}, \quad (9.1)
$$

where $I\{S$ is good news$\}$ equals 1 if $S = a$ and $U_A > U_B$, $I\{S$ is bad news$\}$ equals 1 if $S = b$ and $U_A > U_B$, and both indicators equal 0 if $U_A = U_B$. As always, d is a measure of base-rate neglect, but now there are three reduced-form parameters describing biased inference: c is the same biased-inference measure discussed in Section 4, which alone governs the bias if the agent has no preference between states; $c + c_{\text{good}}$ is the measure of biased inference in response to good news; and $c + c_{\text{bad}}$ is the measure of biased inference in response to bad news. The preference-biased-inference hypothesis is $c_{\text{good}} > c_{\text{bad}}$.

Note that this specification of the preference-biased-inference hypothesis does not require that $c_{\text{good}} \geq 0$ or $c_{\text{bad}} \leq 0$; it is conceivable that having "valenced" signals (i.e., that are good or bad news) could affect the overall amount of underinference or overinference relative to having unvalenced signals.

9.2 Evidence and models

In one of the pioneering papers on preference-biased inference,[69] Möbius et al. (2014) argued that it may arise as an "optimal bias" for agents who get utility directly from holding optimistic beliefs. In Möbius et al.'s model, which builds on the theoretical framework from Brunnermeier and Parker (2005), agents can choose ex ante (i.e., before observing any signals) the weight they put on the likelihood ratio—the value of c in Eq. (4.6)—for each possible signal they might observe. The benefit of deviating from Bayesian updating is that beliefs can end up being more optimistic, but the cost is that biased beliefs can lead to suboptimal behavior. In the model, the agent optimally chooses to weight bad news less than good news. Moreover, to offset the increased risk of suboptimal behavior, the agent optimally chooses to underweight the likelihood ratio for all signals. Thus, the agent has conservatism bias (as in Section 5.2) but is more conservative in response to bad news than good news. Bénabou (2013) proposed a model in which an agent can choose whether or not to process a signal that has been observed (i.e., to not pay attention to it, explain it away, or not think about it); if the agent gets anticipatory utility from putting high probability on the good state, then the agent may selectively ignore bad news.

In the economics literature, the evidence regarding preference-biased inference comes from sequential-updating experiments, in which participants are updating about a preference-relevant event. Möbius at al. conducted one of the earliest such experiments. Each participant took an IQ test. The two states of the world are $A = \{$scored in top half of the IQ test$\}$ and $B = \{$scored in bottom half$\}$. Participants' beliefs were measured both before and after the IQ test and then again after each of four, independent binary signals. Each signal matched the true state with probability $\theta = 0.75$. The belief elicitation was incentive compatible.

Möbius et al. estimated a regression equation corresponding to the logarithm of Eq. (9.1) above:

$$\ln\left(\frac{\pi(A|s_1, s_2, \ldots, s_t)}{\pi(B|s_1, s_2, \ldots, s_t)}\right)$$
$$= \delta_1 I\{s_t = a\} \ln\left(\frac{p(s_t|A)}{p(s_t|B)}\right) + \delta_2 I\{s_t = b\} \ln\left(\frac{p(s_t|A)}{p(s_t|B)}\right)$$
$$+ \delta_3 \ln\left(\frac{\pi(A|s_1, s_2, \ldots, s_{t-1})}{\pi(B|s_1, s_2, \ldots, s_{t-1})}\right) + \zeta_t. \tag{9.2}$$

In terms of Eq. (9.1), δ_1 gives an estimate of $c + c_{\text{good}}$, δ_2 gives an estimate of $c + c_{\text{bad}}$, and δ_3 gives an estimate of the base-rate neglect parameter d. Möbius et al. found $\hat{\delta}_1 = 0.27$ (SE $= 0.01$) and $\hat{\delta}_2 = 0.17$ (SE $= 0.03$).[70] Both are less than one, indicating

---

[69] All results from Möbius et al. are from the most recent, 2014 working paper, but the original working paper is from 2007.

[70] For the coefficient on the prior ratio, Möbius et al. estimate $\hat{\delta}_3 = 0.98$ (SE $= 0.06$). Since this coefficient is essentially one, it indicates that there is no base-rate neglect in Möbius et al.'s data. As discussed in Section 4.3, most sequential-sample experiments find stronger evidence of base-rate neglect.

underinference in response to both good and bad news. Moreover, the estimates imply $c_{good} > c_{bad}$, consistent with preference-biased inference.

Experiments on preference-biased inference typically include a control condition in which participants are updating about an event that is *not* preference-relevant. In Möbius et al.'s control condition, participants repeated the updating task, except with reference to the performance of a robot rather than their own performance. The robot's initial probability of being a high type was set equal to the multiple of 0.05 closest to the participant's post-IQ-test belief about herself. That way, the state of the world about which the participant was updating had essentially the same prior probability and differed only in not being preference-relevant. In this control condition, Möbius et al. found less underinference overall and no asymmetry.[71]

While Möbius et al. found that bad news was underweighted by more than good news, the evidence from similar experiments taken as a whole is mixed. Three papers have found stronger inference from good news: Möbius et al. (2014), Eil and Rao (2011), and Charness and Dave (2017). The opposite result—stronger inference from *bad* news—was found in three papers: Ertac (2011) and Coutts (2017), as well as by Kuhnen (2015) for outcomes that take place in the loss domain (but not those that take place in the gain domain). Five papers have tested and found no evidence for asymmetry: Grossman and Owens (2012), Buser et al. (2018), Schwardmann and Van der Weele (2016), Barron (2016), and Gotthard-Real (2017). Note also that while Eil and Rao (2011) found stronger inference from good news for participants' beliefs about their own beauty, they found no evidence for asymmetry for participants' beliefs about their own IQ.

There does not appear to be a neat explanation for the puzzling differences in results across experiments. Coutts (2017) suggested that since the experiments differ in the prior probability of state A, what appears to be preference-biased inference might actually be driven by prior-biased inference. However, Möbius et al. (2014) and Eil and Rao (2011) found evidence for preference-biased inference despite not finding prior-biased inference. Moreover, three papers tested for preference-biased inference with controls for priors or for prior-biased inference (Schwardmann and Van der Weele, 2016; Charness and Dave, 2017; Coutts, 2017) and reached different conclusions about the presence and direction of preference-biased inference.[72]

---

[71] This is the result with their preferred sample restrictions, including only participants who updated at least once in the correct direction and never in the wrong direction (their Table 4 Column I). In the full sample, the amount of underinference is stronger overall and asymmetric, with greater updating in response to a signals (their Table 4 Column III).

[72] As noted at the end of Section 8.2, Eil and Rao (2011) hypothesized the opposite: that what appears to be evidence for prior-biased inference may actually be due to preference-biased inference, if people consider prior-supporting signals to be good news. Consistent with this hypothesis, Eil and Rao found little evidence of prior-biased inference when separately examining updating in response to signals that are good versus bad news, but the data are quite noisy. Their intriguing hypothesis does not appear to have been tested in other papers. However, the mixed overall evidence regarding preference-biased inference, combined with the relatively stronger evidence overall regarding prior-biased inference, leans against this hypothesis.

Another hypothesis is that different results across experiments may arise from differences in signal structure, which varies a great deal across the experiments. For example, different from Möbius et al. (2014), Ertac (2011) elicited participants' probabilities of scoring in the top, middle, or bottom tercile on a math quiz, and then provided a perfectly informative signal that performance is top/not-top or bottom/not-bottom. However, there are opposite results even across experiments with similar signal structures. For instance, Coutts's (2017) design is similar to Möbius et al.'s (2014), except with $\theta = 0.67$ instead of 0.75.

In parallel with the economics literature on preference-biased inference, there is a literature in psychology and neuroscience based on a different experimental design. In the pioneering experiment, Sharot et al. (2011) presented participants with 80 randomly ordered short descriptions of negative life events, such as having one's car stolen or having Parkinson's disease. Participants were asked the likelihood of the event happening to them (without incentives for accuracy). Participants were then shown the population base rate of the event, and their belief was re-elicited. "Good news" is defined as learning that the base rate is lower than the participant's initial probability. Almost all of the experiments in this literature find that the absolute change in participants' probabilities is larger in response to good news than bad news.[73]

Wiswall and Zafar (2015) reported a related study as part of a broader field experiment on the effects of providing information about earnings on students' beliefs and choices of undergraduate major. They provided 240 students with mean earnings of age-30 individuals and 255 students with the same information broken down by college major. Pooling across the two groups, they found that the information caused students who learned that they had overestimated population earnings to revise their own expected earnings downward by $159 per $1000, while those who had underestimated earnings revised upward by $347 per $1000. As Wiswall and Zafar highlight, however, the difference is far from statistically distinguishable, with a p-value of 0.327.

These experiments, however, have a design limitation: because receipt of good news versus bad news is not randomly assigned—whether the news is good or bad depends on one's prior belief—those who receive good news about a particular event may differ on unobservables from those who receive bad news. For example, those who are more optimistic about an event may also be more confident about it and therefore update less in response to news. (The bookbag-and-poker-chip experiments discussed above eliminate such confounds by randomly assigning good and bad news.) Wiswall and Zafar partially addressed such a potential confound by test-

---

[73] The experiments finding such asymmetric updating include Sharot et al. (2012a), Sharot et al. (2012b), Moutsiana et al. (2013), Chowdhury et al. (2014), Garrett and Sharot (2017), Garrett et al. (2014), Korn et al. (2014), Kuzmanovic et al. (2015, 2016), and Krieger et al. (2016). An exception is Shah et al. (2016), who argued that the findings of asymmetry are due to a variety of methodological limitations with this kind of study design. Garrett and Sharot (2017), however, argued that the original findings are robust to addressing these limitations.

ing whether any asymmetric response to good news versus bad news is associated with demographics they measured, and they found no evidence for such correlation.

Beginning with Kuzmanovic et al. (2015), some recent work in psychology and neuroscience overcomes this limitation by randomly assigning bogus base-rate information (e.g., Marks and Baines, 2017).[74] For example, Kuzmanovic et al. followed the same basic design as Sharot et al.—eliciting the participant's belief about likelihood of an event, providing the population base rate, and then re-eliciting the participant's belief—but told the participant that the population base rate is equal to the participant's belief plus or minus a random number. These experiments confirm the finding from the earlier studies that participants update more in response to good news than bad news.[75]

Taken all together, the evidence on preference-biased inference is confusing. In the economics literature, there are many bookbag-and-poker-chip experiments that reach opposite conclusions, and there the obvious candidate explanations for the differences in findings do not seem to be right. In the psychology and neuroscience literature, the experiments are based on a different design, and the results are nearly unanimous in finding evidence in favor of preference-biased inference. Sorting out the reasons why different experiments reach different conclusions should be a priority.

10 Discussion

This chapter has reviewed a range of belief biases. In this final section, I comment on some interrelated, overarching issues that relate to many of the biases and to the literature as a whole.

---

[74] Within experimental economics, providing bogus information is viewed as deceptive, and deceiving experimental participants is generally considered unacceptable (or at least unethical), especially if non-deceptive methods could be used instead. A non-deceptive method of randomizing the numbers provided to participants would be to show them actual numbers obtained from different sources (as was done in a different context by Cavallo et al., 2016).

[75] A related strand of work in psychology and neuroscience conducts two-armed bandit experiments. In each round, participants can receive a payoff from either of two bandits, which give rewards at different, unknown rates. The rate of reinforcement learning is estimated separately in response to better-than-expected outcomes and worse-than-expected outcomes (i.e., positive and negative reward prediction errors). Lefebvre et al. (2017) found that experimental participants learn at a higher rate from better-than-expected outcomes. Palminteri et al. (2017) replicated this finding but also found that when the counterfactual payoffs from the unchosen bandit is also revealed in each round, then for these counterfactual payoffs, participants learn at a higher rate from *worse*-than-expected outcomes. Palminteri et al. interpreted their result as consistent with prior-biased inference: people update more in response to information that confirms their current choice.

10.1 **When do people update too much or too little?**

Do people update too much or too little, relative to Bayesian updating? The predominant view in the literature has shifted over time. The early literature focused exclusively on conservatism bias and characterized people as generally underinferring. As mentioned in Section 7, upon first learning about this literature from Amos Tversky in 1968, Daniel Kahneman (2002) recalled thinking "The idea that people were conservative Bayesian did not seem to fit with the everyday observation of people commonly jumping to conclusions." Much of Kahneman and Tversky's work, especially on the LSN (Tversky and Kahneman, 1971) and base-rate neglect (Kahneman and Tversky, 1982), focused on examples of people updating too much. Enamored with the new methods and findings from research on representativeness, psychologists lost interest in the conservatism literature and started doubting its methods and conclusions. As Fischhoff and Beyth-Marom (1983) summarized the general view at the time:

> In the end, this line of research [on bookbag-and-poker-chip experiments] was quietly abandoned... This cessation of activity seems to be partly due to the discovery of the base-rate fallacy, which represents the antithesis of conservatism and other phenomena that led researchers to conclusions such as the following: "It may not be unreasonable to assume that... the probability estimation task is too unfamiliar and complex to be meaningful" (Pitz et al., 1967, p. 392). "Evidence to date seems to indicate that subjects are processing information in ways fundamentally different from Bayesian... models" (Slovic and Lichtenstein, 1971, p. 728). "In his evaluation of evidence, man is apparently not a conservative Bayesian; he is not Bayesian at all" (Kahneman and Tversky, 1972a, p. 450).

My view—hopefully communicated throughout this chapter—is that *whether* people update too much or too little is the wrong question. A better question is *when* we may expect one versus the other.

Here is a broad-brush summary, focusing on several of the main biases reviewed in this chapter and on the usual case of updating about state *A* versus *B* from independent binomial signals, with *a* signals having probability $\theta_A > \frac{1}{2}$ in state *A* and probability $\theta_B < \frac{1}{2}$ in state *B*. By and large, people update too little, with three exceptions. First, when θ_A and θ_B are close together, people overinfer from signals and hence update too much (Section 4.1). Second, people may overinfer and thus update too much due to prior-biased updating, when the signal goes in the *same* direction of the priors (Section 8). Third, people may update too much due to base-rate neglect, when the priors are extreme and the signal goes in the *opposite* direction of the priors (Section 6). As noted in Section 8.1, these latter two biases—prior-biased updating and base-rate neglect—push in opposite directions. A plausible conjecture is that prior-biased updating dominates when the priors are close to 50–50 whereas base-rate neglect dominates when the priors are extreme, but I am not aware of any work that has directly examined how these two biases interact.

10.2 Modeling challenges

Following Barberis et al. (1998), many models of belief biases have been what Rabin (2013) calls *quasi-Bayesian*, meaning that the agent has the wrong model of the world but is fully Bayesian with respect to that wrong model. Of those discussed in this chapter, only the models of the LSN (Rabin, 2002; Rabin and Vayanos, 2010) are quasi-Bayesian. The model of prior-biased updating (Rabin and Schrag, 1999) is closely related; the agent is Bayesian but misreads some of the signals she observes. Quasi-Bayesian and *misread-signal models* are attractive analytically because the standard machinery for studying Bayesian models can be brought to bear. They are also attractive theoretically because the agent's beliefs are logically consistent (despite being incorrect); as discussed below, logical inconsistencies raise thorny issues that have barely begun to be studied.

The quasi-Bayesian and misread-signal models that have been proposed to date are also examples of what Rabin (2013) calls *portable extensions of existing models* (PEEMs). PEEMs are defined by two properties: (i) they embed the Bayesian model as a special case for particular values of one or more bias parameters, and (ii) they are portable across environments in the sense that the independent variables are the same as for existing models. PEEMs are attractive for a number of reasons. Most relevantly for the discussion here, once the parameters of a PEEM are pinned down by empirical estimates, the model has no degrees of freedom beyond those that are already available in the Bayesian model.

The models of NBLLN (Benjamin et al., 2016), partition dependence (Benjamin et al., 2018b), base-rate neglect (Benjamin et al., 2018a), and local thinking (Gennaioli and Shleifer, 2010) are neither quasi-Bayesian models nor PEEMs. The models are not PEEMs because they fail criterion (ii): there is an independent variable that is irrelevant for a Bayesian agent but relevant in the model. In particular, as discussed in Sections 4.3, 5.1, and 6, for the models of NBLLN and base-rate neglect, the grouping of signals needs to be specified in order to pin down the model's predictions (more generally, He and Xiao (2017) show that grouping will matter for *any* non-Bayesian updating rule). For partition dependence, it is the set of bins that is a crucial new independent variable. For the model of local thinking, as discussed in Section 7.3, additional assumptions may be needed to apply it outside the context where it has been formulated.

Because the models have new independent variables that must be specified in applications, the models have degrees of freedom that the Bayesian model does not have. In some cases, these degrees of freedom may not be a problem for studying the model in an experiment because, by framing the judgment problem in a particular way, the experimenter can plausibly control the new independent variables. In applied settings, however, a researcher will often not have such control and may not observe, say, how an agent groups the signals she observes or how she partitions the state space into bins when formulating her beliefs.

When the degrees of freedom are left unspecified, the models are less powerful than the Bayesian model because they rule out fewer possible observations (i.e., assumptions can be made ex post to rationalize what was observed). To turn a non-

PEEM into a PEEM, additional modeling is needed to pin down the values of the free parameters as a function of observable characteristics of the judgment problem.[76] In the cases of NBLLN, partition dependence, base-rate neglect, and local thinking, there is currently little evidence available to guide such modeling. New experiments will be needed to provide that evidence.

Because these models are not quasi-Bayesian, the agent's beliefs are not internally consistent across different framings of the same judgment problem. This is not necessarily a problem in individual decision-making environments as long as the agent always views the problem in the same frame, but it raises the question of what an agent would believe if she views the same problem with different frames over time. Would the agent always use the current frame, despite knowing that she herself had previously thought about the problem differently?

Additional complications arise in environments with strategic interaction between agents. Such environments often require assumptions about higher-order beliefs about agents' biases and framing of the judgment problem, not only what Agent 1 believes about Agent 2 but also what Agent 1 believes Agent 2 believes about Agent 1, etc. A natural assumption is naïveté: Agent 1 believes that other agents make the same predictions and draw the same inferences as she does. But what if Agent 1 knows that other agents frame the information differently (say, Agent 1 observes 20 samples of individual signals but knows that Agent 2 observes the entire sample of 20 signals at once), or if the other agent's behavior is inconsistent with holding the same beliefs as Agent 1? Addressing these and other questions requires an equilibrium concept that can accommodate belief biases. Chapter "Errors in Strategic Reasoning" (by Eyster) of this Handbook addresses these and related issues in the context of several errors in reasoning, but it does not study the same biases that are the focus of this chapter. There is much fertile ground for new evidence and theory to begin to understand how errors in probabilistic reasoning play out dynamically and in environments with strategic interaction.

10.3 Generalizability from the lab to the field

Much of the evidence reviewed in this chapter has been from bookbag-and-poker-chip experiments or similarly abstract laboratory studies. Such studies typically provide the cleanest evidence on errors in probabilistic reasoning because the properties of the random processes and the information provided to participants can be tightly controlled. This control enables researchers to rule out alternative interpretations of apparent belief biases. Yet laboratory evidence is often prone to concerns about generalizability: laboratory behavior may give a misleading impression of how people behave in the field settings that are of primary interest to economists. I will

---

[76] The same issue arises with other models in behavioral economics, for example, with the reference point in models of reference-dependent preferences. As discussed in Chapter "Reference-Dependent Preferences" (by O'Donoghue and Sprenger), recent work on loss aversion has devoted substantial attention to understanding how the reference point for gains and losses is endogenously determined.

briefly highlight six potentially relevant differences between the typical laboratory environment and the typical field setting that could limit generalizability: incentives, experience, markets, populations, problem structure, and framing.

Grether's (1980) seminal economic experiments on errors in probabilistic reasoning were motivated by questions of whether the biases found in psychology experiments would also be found in settings where participants were incentivized and experienced and where the random processes were made transparent and credible. To achieve transparency and credibility, Grether (1980) adopted the bookbag-and-poker-chip experimental design and drew balls from urns in front of participants. In addition to testing for deviations from Bayesian updating, he also studied the robustness of these deviations to incentives for correct answers and experience with the same updating problem. In earlier work from psychology, there was also some attention to the effect of incentives (e.g., Phillips and Edwards, 1966) and experience (e.g., Martin and Gettys, 1969; Strub, 1969). Aggregating over findings from many papers, the meta-analysis results from Section 4 suggest that, overall, the presence of incentives in bookbag-and-poker-chip experiments does not eliminate deviations from Bayesian updating. Among papers that examine the effect of experience, a typical finding is that it reduces but does not eliminate bias (e.g., Camerer, 1987). I am not aware of any systematic overview of the effects of experience.

Other groundbreaking, early economics papers in this literature addressed whether deviations from Bayesian updating would persist in experimental asset markets and influence market outcomes (Duh and Sunder, 1986; Camerer, 1987; Anderson and Sunder, 1995; Camerer, 1990). In general, these papers found that base-rate neglect and exact representativeness do influence market prices, although the effects are weak and reduced when experimental participants gain experience (for a brief review, see Camerer, 1995, pp. 605–608). The work has addressed only a few of the many relevant questions that might be asked about markets. For example, one might conjecture that in life insurance markets, where supply-side competition may drive prices to marginal cost (as determined by actuarial tables), in equilibrium belief biases influence quantities (i.e., who buys insurance) rather than prices.

While much of the laboratory evidence on belief biases to date is from student samples, a number of papers have examined generalizability to other populations. For example, Dohmen et al. (2009) found that the GF is widespread in a representative sample from the German population. There is relatively little evidence, however, on how the *magnitude* of biases compares across populations. Since students are often found to be less biased than other, less educated, demographic groups, it seems likely that evidence from student samples understates the prevalence and magnitude of biases. Relevant to the question of how much bias can be expected in particular field settings, some research has studied how individual characteristics are correlated with biases (e.g., Stanovich and West, 1998; Stanovich, 1999). Relatedly, for making predictions about how biases interact, it may be valuable to know how biases are correlated with each other in the population (for some work along these lines, see, e.g., Stango et al., 2017; Falk et al., 2018; Chapman et al., 2018).

A longstanding generalizability concern is related to differences in problem structure between the lab and the field. Specifically, people's beliefs may result from heuristics or mental models that are well adapted to real-world problems—i.e., they do not lead to systematic biases in naturalistic environments—but that cause biased responses in the problems posed in the lab. For example, Winkler and Murphy (1973) argued that real-world random processes are typically different from the i.i.d. processes in bookbag-and-poker-chip experiments, e.g., featuring positive autocorrelation and non-stationarity. They argued that in these real-world settings, people update correctly, but when faced with the unfamiliar, artificial i.i.d. settings created in the lab, people behave as they would when facing real-world random processes. This behavior generates underinference in i.i.d. settings, but researchers would be mistaken to generalize that people underinfer in the field. The force of the problem-structure critique is weakened by a lack of evidence or clear intuition on what the relevant real-world random processes actually looks like (indeed, while Winkler and Murphy posited positive autocorrelation of real-world random processes in order to explain underinference, the GF is sometimes rationalized by arguing that real-world random processes are *negatively* correlated). Moreover, while experimental participants surely do bring some expectations from their everyday experiences into the lab, the problem-structure critique does not provide a plausible explanation for all of the lab evidence. For example, everyone has enough experience with coin flips to understand what the random process is when told that a fair coin is being flipped, and much of the evidence for the GF and other biases can be (and has been) generated using coin flips. Furthermore, if a particular version of the critique predicts that people form beliefs as if outcomes were generated by a specific, non-i.i.d. (but internally consistent) random process, then it cannot explain why people's beliefs are internally inconsistent, with beliefs depending on the question they are asked (see Section 3.6).

Another generalizability concern is that whether and how people are biased depends on how problems are framed. Most famously, some biases are smaller in magnitude when problems are posed in terms of frequencies rather than probabilities, and frequencies have been argued to be more common in field settings (e.g., Tversky and Kahneman, 1983; Gigerenzer and Hoffrage, 1995).

More generally, the cognitive processes underlying belief formation and revision, such as perception, attention, and memory, plausibly operate differently in natural environments than they do in abstract settings. For example, people may pay more attention or process information more effectively when they are more familiar with or more interested in the context. Some versions of this concern can be and have been studied in the lab. For example, in a bookbag-and-poker-chip experiment with accounting students as participants, Eger and Dickhaut (1982) found less underinference when the experiment was framed in terms of an accounting problem rather than as an abstract problem. Yet it is not necessarily the case that biases are smaller in more naturalistic settings; for example, Ganguly et al. (2000) found that base-rate neglect was *stronger* in an experimental market when it was framed in terms of buying and selling stocks than in terms of abstract balls and urns.

All of the above evidence notwithstanding, the most compelling response to concerns about generalizability to the field is field studies. Of the topics discussed in this chapter, the GF, the hot-hand bias, and base-rate neglect are relatively well documented in field settings. Most of the other biases in this chapter are in need of more field evidence. For example, could it be that preference-biased updating powerfully influences our political and social beliefs, even if it is difficult to reliably observe in bookbag-and-poker experiments? For biases lacking much field evidence, I urge caution in generalizing from abstract laboratory settings, and as discussed further in 10.5 below, I advocate field studies as a high priority.

10.4 Connecting with other areas of economics

In behavioral finance, research on forecasting errors has drawn on the biases reviewed in this chapter. In particular, the LSN, base-rate neglect, and local thinking have been argued to be leading contributors to extrapolative expectations; see Chapter "Psychology-Based Models of Asset Prices and Trading Volume" (by Barberis) of this Handbook.

The relevance of errors in probabilistic reasoning to economics, however, should be far broader. Indeed, as noted at the very beginning of this chapter, belief biases could matter for any context of decision making under risk, including portfolio choice, insurance purchasing, and search and experimentation. Belief biases should also be crucial for research on stereotyping and statistical discrimination, since these can be based on erroneous beliefs (e.g., Bordalo et al., 2016; Bohren et al., 2018). Belief biases should similarly be central to the study of persuasion, since persuaders will aim to exploit the biases of persuadees. Yet these and other areas of economics remain virtually untouched by insights from the literature on belief biases and are thus fertile ground for enterprising researchers.

There are at least two other literatures within economics which, to date, have proceeded almost completely independently from the work reviewed in this chapter despite being closely related. The first is the line of work on sticky expectations (e.g., Gabaix and Laibson, 2002; Mankiw and Reis, 2002) and learning in macroeconomics (see, e.g., Evans and Honkapohja, 2001). Research in macroeconomics may benefit from the accumulated evidence and theorizing about belief biases, and behavioral economists should take on the challenge of explaining key features of macroeconomic beliefs.

The second is the literature on survey measurement of expectations (e.g., Viscusi, 1990; Manski, 2018; Coibion et al., 2018). Sampling-distribution biases would be especially relevant to that literature, and in particular, the survey literature should be aware of and correct for partition dependence (Section 3.1) and extreme-belief aversion (Section 5.3). Conversely, experimental research that elicits sampling distributions would benefit from methodological advances in the survey literature, such as modeling and adjusting for measurement error and for rounding of numerical answers (e.g., Giustinelli et al., 2018).

10.5 Some possible directions for future research

To end this chapter, I highlight three directions for future research that seem to me to be especially important. First, although the tradition in behavioral economics has been to focus on one bias at a time, studying several biases at once will often be essential in research on belief biases. Doing so may be necessary to separately identify the biases. For example, partition dependence can be a confound for assessing other sampling-distribution biases, biased inference is often confounded with biased use of prior information, and prior-biased updating and preference-biased updating are often confounded with each other. Studying biases jointly will also be important to assess the robustness of the predictions that arise from one bias to the presence of another bias. For example, as discussed above in Section 10.1, prior-biased updating and base-rate neglect make opposite predictions about whether people will update too much or too little; studying the interaction between the biases will be necessary to understand when one or the other dominates.

Second, the efforts to model belief biases have taught us that some additional evidence is needed as an input to further modeling, and new experiments should collect that evidence. For example, as discussed in Sections 4.3, 5.1, and 6, when modeling how people update after observing a sequence of signals, predictions may hinge on an assumption about how people group the signals. Few experiments to date have addressed that question (with the exceptions of Shu and Wu, 2003, and Kraemer and Weber, 2004). In many dynamic settings, another important modeling assumption is what people expect about how their own beliefs will evolve if they observe additional signals. Similarly, in strategic interactions, a key assumption is what people believe about how others' beliefs will evolve. Evidence is needed to inform those assumptions, as well.

Finally, the vast majority of evidence on belief biases comes from laboratory studies; more field evidence is needed to probe generalizability (as discussed in Section 10.3) and to assess the economic importance of the biases. Most existing field evidence is from gambling (e.g., Metzger, 1985), lotteries (e.g., Clotfelter and Cook, 1993), and sports (e.g., Gilovich et al., 1985), environments where the true probabilities are known or can be reliably estimated and where data have long been publicly available. However, recent work has begun to examine other settings. For example, Chen et al. (2016) studied reviews of loan applications and judges' decisions in refugee asylum court (in addition to umpires' calls on baseball pitches), and Augenblick and Rabin (2018) studied how beliefs evolve over time in prediction markets. As has occurred with other areas of behavioral economics, once it becomes clear that errors in probabilistic reasoning matter in a range of economically relevant field settings, this area of research will become part of mainstream economics.

References

Ahn, D.S., Ergin, H., 2010. Framing contingencies. Econometrica 78 (2), 655–695.
Alberoni, F., 1962a. Contribution to the study of subjective probability. I. The Journal of General Psychology 66 (2), 241–264.

Alberoni, F., 1962b. Contribution to the study of subjective probability: prediction. II. The Journal of General Psychology 66 (2), 265–285.

Alesina, A., Miano, A., Stantcheva, S., 2018. Immigration and Redistribution. Working Paper.

Ambuehl, S., Li, S., 2018. Belief updating and the demand for information. Games and Economic Behavior 109, 21–39.

Anderson, M.J., Sunder, S., 1995. Professional traders as intuitive Bayesians. Organizational Behavior and Human Decision Processes 64 (2), 185–202.

Andreoni, J., Mylovanov, T., 2012. Diverging opinions. American Economic Journal: Microeconomics 4 (1), 209–232.

Anobile, G., Cicchini, G.M., Burr, D.C., 2016. Number as a primary perceptual attribute: a review. Perception 45 (1–2), 5–31.

Antoniou, C., Harrison, G.W., Lau, M.I., Read, D., 2013. Revealed Preference and the Strength/Weight Hypothesis. Warwick Business School, Finance Group.

Antoniou, C., Harrison, G.W., Lau, M.I., Read, D., 2015. Subjective Bayesian beliefs. Journal of Risk and Uncertainty 50 (1), 35–54.

Arnold, D., Dobbie, W., Yang, C.S., 2018. Racial bias in bail decisions. The Quarterly Journal of Economics 133 (4), 1885–1932.

Asparouhova, E., Hertzel, M., Lemmon, M., 2009. Inference from streaks in random outcomes: experimental evidence on beliefs in regime shifting and the Law of Small Numbers. American Management Science 55 (11), 1766–1782.

Augenblick, N., Rabin, M., 2018. Belief Movement, Uncertainty Reduction, & Rational Updating. Working Paper.

Avugos, S., Bar-Eli, M., Ritov, I., Sher, E., 2013. The elusive reality of efficacy performance cycles in basketball shooting: analysis of players' performance under invariant conditions. International Journal of Sport and Exercise Psychology 11 (2), 184–202.

Ayton, P., Fischer, I., 2004. The hot hand fallacy and the gambler's fallacy: two faces of subjective randomness? Memory & Cognition 32 (8), 1369–1378.

Bacon, F., 1620. The New Organon and Related Writings. Liberal Arts Press, New York.

Baliga, S., Hanany, E., Klibanoff, P., 2013. Polarization and ambiguity. American Economic Review 103 (7), 3071–3083.

Bar-Eli, M., Avugos, S., Raab, M., 2006. Twenty years of "hot hand" research: review and critique. Psychology of Sport and Exercise 7 (6), 525–553.

Bar-Hillel, M., 1979. The role of sample size in sample evaluation. Organizational Behavior and Human Performance 24 (2), 245–257.

Bar-Hillel, M., 1980. The base-rate fallacy in probability judgments. Acta Psychologica 44 (3), 211–233.

Bar-Hillel, M., 1982. Studies of representativeness. In: Kahneman, D., Slovic, P., Tversky, A. (Eds.), Judgment Under Uncertainty: Heuristics and Biases. Cambridge University Press, New York, pp. 69–83.

Barberis, N., Shleifer, A., Vishny, R., 1998. A model of investor sentiment. Journal of Financial Economics 49 (3), 307–343.

Barbey, A.K., Sloman, S.A., 2007. Base-rate respect: from ecological rationality to dual processes. Memory & Cognition 30 (3), 241–254.

Barron, K., 2016. Belief Updating: Does the 'Good-News, Bad-News' Asymmetry Extend to Purely Financial Domains? WZB Discussion Paper, SP II 2016-309.

Bateman, I., Munro, A., Rhodes, B., Starmer, C., Sugden, R., 1997. Does part-whole bias exist? An experimental investigation. The Economic Journal 107 (441), 322–332.

Beach, L.R., 1968. Probability magnitudes and conservative revision of subjective probabilities. Journal of Experimental Psychology 77 (1), 57–63.

Beach, L.R., Wise, J.A., 1969. Subjective probability revision and subsequent decisions. Journal of Experimental Psychology 81 (3), 561–565.

Beach, L.R., Wise, J.A., Barclay, S., 1970. Sample proportions and subjective probability revisions. Organizational Behavior and Human Performance 5 (2), 183–190.

Bénabou, R., 2013. Groupthink: collective delusions in organizations and markets. Review of Economic Studies 80 (2), 429–462.

Bénabou, R., Tirole, J., 2011. Identity, morals, and taboos: beliefs as assets. The Quarterly Journal of Economics 126 (2), 805–855.

Bénabou, R., Tirole, J., 2016. Mindful economics: the production, consumption, and value of beliefs. Journal of Economic Perspectives 30 (3), 141–164.

Benartzi, S., Thaler, R.H., 1999. Risk aversion or myopia? Choices in repeated gambles and retirement investments. Management Science 45 (3), 346–381.

Benartzi, S., Thaler, R.H., 2001. Naïve diversification strategies in defined contribution savings plans. American Economic Review 91 (1), 79–98.

Benjamin, D., Bodoh-Creed, A.L., Rabin, M., 2018a. Base-Rate Neglect: Foundations and Implications. Working Paper.

Benjamin, D., Moore, D., Rabin, M., 2018b. Biased Beliefs About Random Samples: Evidence from Two Integrated Experiments. Working Paper.

Benjamin, D., Rabin, M., Raymond, C., 2016. A model of non-belief in the Law of Large Numbers. Journal of the European Economic Association 14 (2), 515–544.

Benoît, J-P., Dubra, J., 2018. When do Populations Polarize? An Explanation. Working Paper.

Bhargava, S., Fisman, R., 2014. Contrast effects in sequential decisions: evidence from speed dating. Review of Economics and Statistics 96 (3), 444–457.

Blondé, J., Girandola, F., 2016. Revealing the elusive effects of vividness: a meta-analysis of empirical evidences assessing the effect of vividness on persuasion. Social Influence 11 (2), 111–129.

Bodner, R., Prelec, D., 2003. Self-signaling and diagnostic utility in everyday decision making. In: Brocas, I., Carrillo, J.D. (Eds.), The Psychology of Economics Decisions. Vol. 1. Rationality and Well-being. Oxford University Press, New York, pp. 105–126.

Bohren, A., Imas, A., Rosenberg, M., 2018. The Dynamics of Discrimination: Theory and Evidence. Working Paper.

Bordalo, P., Coffman, K., Gennaioli, N., Shleifer, A., 2016. Stereotypes. The Quarterly Journal of Economics 131 (4), 1753–1794.

Bordalo, P., Gennaioli, N., Shleifer, A., 2018. Diagnostic expectations and credit cycles. Journal of Finance 73 (1), 199–227.

Brown, W.O., Sauer, R.D., 1993. Does the basketball market believe in the "hot hand"? Comment American Economic Review 83 (5), 1377–1386.

Brunnermeier, M., Parker, J., 2005. Optimal expectations. American Economic Review 95 (4), 1092–1118.

Buser, T., Gerhards, L., Van der Weele, J., 2018. Measuring responsiveness to feedback as a personal trait. Journal of Risk and Uncertainty 56 (2), 165–192.

Camerer, C.F., 1987. Do biases in probability judgment matter in markets? Experimental evidence. American Economic Review 77 (5), 981–997.

Camerer, C.F., 1989. Does the basketball market believe in the 'hot hand'? American Economic Review 79 (5), 1257–1261.

Camerer, C.F., 1990. Do markets correct biases in probability judgment? Evidence from market experiments. In: Kagel, J.H., Green, L. (Eds.), Advances in Behavioral Economics, Vol. 2. Ablex Publishing Company, Norwood, NJ, pp. 125–172.

Camerer, C.F., 1995. Individual decision making. In: Kagel, J.H., Roth, A.E. (Eds.), Handbook of Experimental Economics. Princeton University Press, Princeton, NJ, pp. 587–703.

Caruso, E., Waytz, A., Epley, N., 2010. The intentional mind and the hot hand: perceiving intentions makes streaks seem likely to continue. Cognition 116 (1), 149–153.

Cavallo, A., Cruces, G., Perez-Truglia, R., 2016. Learning from potentially biased statistics. Brookings Papers on Economic Activity 2016 (1), 59–108.

Chapman, C., 1973. Prior probability bias in information seeking and opinion revision. American Journal of Psychology 86 (2), 269–282.

Chapman, J., Dean, M., Ortoleva, P., Snowberg, E., Camerer, C., 2018. Econographics. Working Paper.

Charness, G., Dave, C., 2017. Confirmation bias with motivated beliefs. Games and Economic Behavior 104, 1–23.

Charness, G., Karni, E., Levin, D., 2010. On the conjunction fallacy in probability judgment: new experimental evidence regarding Linda. Games and Economic Behavior 68 (2), 551–556.

Chen, D., Moskowitz, T., Shue, K., 2016. Decision making under the gambler's fallacy: evidence from asylum judges, loan officers, and baseball umpires. The Quarterly Journal of Economics 131 (3), 1181–1242.

Chinnis, J.O., Peterson, C.R., 1968. Inference about a nonstationary process. Journal of Experimental Psychology 77 (4), 620–625.

Chowdhury, R., Sharot, T., Wolfe, T., Düzel, E., Dolan, R.J., 2014. Optimistic update bias increases in older age. Psychological Medicine 44 (9), 2003–2012.

Clemen, R.T., Ulu, C., 2008. Interior additivity and subjective probability assessment of continuous variables. Management Science 54 (4), 835–851.

Clotfelter, C.T., Cook, P.J., 1993. The "gambler's fallacy" in lottery play. Management Science 39 (12), 1521–1525.

Coibion, O., Gorodnichenko, Y., Kamdar, R., 2018. The formation of expectations, inflation, and the Phillips curve. Journal of Economic Literature 56 (4), 1447–1491.

Coutts, A., 2017. Good news and bad news are still news: experimental evidence on belief updating. Experimental Economics, 1–27.

Cripps, M.W., 2018. Divisible Updating. Working Paper.

Croson, R., Sundali, J., 2005. The gambler's fallacy and the hot hand: empirical data from casinos. The Journal of Risk and Uncertainty 30 (3), 195–209.

Dale, H.C.A., 1968. Weighing evidence: an attempt to assess the efficiency of the human operator. Ergonomics 11 (3), 215–230.

Daniel, K., Hirshleifer, D., Subrahmanyam, A., 1998. Investor psychology and security market under- and overreactions. Journal of Finance 53 (6), 1839–1885.

Darley, J., Gross, P., 1983. A hypothesis-confirming bias in labeling effects. Journal of Personality and Social Psychology 44 (1), 20–33.

Dave, C., Wolfe, K., 2003. On Confirmation Bias and Deviations From Bayesian Updating. Working Paper.

DellaVigna, S., 2009. Psychology and economics: evidence from the field. Journal of Economic Literature 47 (2), 315–372.

De Swart, J.H., 1972a. Effects of diagnosticity and prior odds on conservatism in a bookbag-and-pokerchip situation. Acta Psychologica 36 (1), 16–31.

De Swart, J.H., 1972b. Conservatism as a function of bag composition. Acta Psychologica 36 (3), 197–206.

De Swart, J.H., Tonkens, R.I.G., 1977. The influence of order of presentation and characteristics of the datagenerator on opinion revision. Acta Psychologica 41 (2), 101–117.

Dhami, S., 2017. The Foundations of Behavioral Economic Analysis. Oxford University Press, Oxford, UK.

Dillon, B., Lybbert, T.J., 2018. Biased Bets in the Haitian Lottery. Working Paper.

Dixit, A., Weibull, J., 2007. Political polarization. Proceedings of the National Academy of Sciences 104 (18), 7351–7356.

Dohmen, T., Falk, A., Huffman, D., Marklein, F., Sunde, U., 2009. Biased probability judgment: evidence of incidence and relationship to economic outcomes from a representative sample. Journal of Economic Behavior and Organization 72 (3), 903–915.

Donnell, M.L., DuCharme, W.M., 1975. The effect of Bayesian feedback on learning in an odds estimation task. Organizational Behavior and Human Performance 14 (3), 305–313.

DuCharme, W., 1969. A Review and Analysis of the Phenomenon of Conservatism in Human Inference. Systems Report No. 46-5. Rice University.

DuCharme, W., 1970. Response bias explanation of conservative human inference. Journal of Experimental Psychology 85 (1), 66–74.

DuCharme, W., Peterson, C., 1968. Intuitive inference about normally distributed populations. Journal of Experimental Psychology 78 (2), 269–275.

Duh, R.R., Sunder, S., 1986. Incentives, learning and processing of information in a market environment: an examination of the base-rate fallacy. In: Moriarity, S. (Ed.), Laboratory Market Research. University of Oklahoma Press, Norman, Oklahoma, pp. 50–79.

Eddy, D.M., 1982. Probabilistic reasoning in clinical medicine: problems and opportunities. In: Kahneman, D., Slovic, P., Tversky, A. (Eds.), Judgment Under Uncertainty: Heuristics and Biases. Cambridge University Press, New York, pp. 249–267.

Edenborough, R., 1975. Order effects and display persistence in probabilistic opinion revision. Bulletin of the Psychonomic Society 5 (1), 39–40.

Edwards, W., 1954. The theory of decision making. Psychological Bulletin 51 (4), 380–417.

Edwards, W., 1961a. Probability learning in 1000 trials. Journal of Experimental Psychology 62 (4), 385–394.

Edwards, W., 1961b. Behavioral decision theory. Annual Review of Psychology 12, 473–498.

Edwards, W., 1968. Conservatism in human information processing. In: Kleinmuntz, B. (Ed.), Formal Representation of Human Judgment. Wiley, New York, pp. 17–52.

Edwards, W., Lindman, H., Savage, L., 1963. Bayesian statistical inference for psychological research. Psychological Review 70 (3), 193–242.

Edwards, W., Phillips, L.D., 1964. Man as transducer for probabilities in Bayesian command and control systems. In: Shelly, M.W., Bryan, G.L. (Eds.), Human Judgments and Optimality. Wiley, New York, pp. 360–401.

Edwards, W., Phillips, L.D., Hays, W.L., Goodman, B.C., 1968. Probabilistic information processing systems: design and evaluation. IEEE Transactions on Systems Science and Cybernetics 4 (3), 248–265.

Edwards, W., Slovic, P., 1965. Seeking information to reduce the risk of decisions. American Journal of Psychology 78, 188–197.

Eger, C., Dickhaut, J., 1982. An examination of the conservative information-processing bias in an accounting framework. Journal of Accounting Research 20 (2), 711–723.

Eide, E., 2011. Two Tests of the Base Rate Neglect Among Law Students. Working Paper.

Eil, D., Rao, J., 2011. The good news-bad news effect: asymmetric processing of objective information about yourself. American Economic Journal: Microeconomics 3 (2), 114–138.

Enke, B., 2017. What You See Is All There Is. Working Paper.

Epstein, L.G., Noor, J., Sandroni, A., 2008. Non-Bayesian updating: a theoretical framework. Theoretical Economics 3 (2), 193–229.

Ertac, S., 2011. Does self-relevance affect information processing? Experimental evidence on the response to performance and non-performance feedback. Journal of Economic Behavior and Organization 80 (3), 532–545.

Evans, G.W., Honkapohja, S., 2001. Learning and Expectations in Macroeconomics. Princeton University Press.

Evans, J.St.B.T., Bradshaw, H., 1986. Estimating sample-size requirements in research design: a study of intuitive statistical judgment. Current Psychological Research & Reviews 5 (1), 10–19.

Evans, J.St.B.T., Dusoir, A.E., 1977. Proportionality and sample size as factors in intuitive statistical judgement. Acta Psychologica 41 (2), 129–137.

Evans, J.St.B.T., Pollard, P., 1982. Statistical judgement: a further test of the representativeness construct. Acta Psychologica 51 (2), 91–103.

Falk, A., Becker, A., Dohmen, T., Enke, B., Huffman, D., Sunde, U., 2018. Global Evidence on Economic Preferences. University of Bonn and University of Mannheim. Mimeo.

Feigenson, L., Dehaene, S., Spelke, E., 2004. Core systems of number. Trends in Cognitive Sciences 8 (7), 307–314.

Fischhoff, B., 1975. Hindsight is no equal to foresight: the effect of outcome knowledge on judgment under uncertainty. Journal of Experimental Psychology: Human Perception and Performance 1 (3), 288–299.

Fischhoff, B., 1982. Debiasing. In: Kahneman, D., Slovic, P., Tversky, A. (Eds.), Judgment Under Uncertainty: Heuristics and Biases. Cambridge University Press, New York, pp. 331–339.

Fischhoff, B., Bar-Hillel, M., 1984. Diagnosticity and the base-rate effect. Memory & Cognition 12 (4), 402–410.

Fischhoff, B., Beyth-Marom, R., 1983. Hypothesis evaluation from a Bayesian perspective. Psychological Review 90 (3), 239–260.

Fischhoff, B., Slovic, P., Lichtenstein, S., 1978. Fault trees: sensitivity of estimated failure probabilities to problem representation. Journal of Experimental Psychology 4 (2), 330–344.

Fisk, J.E., 2016. Conjunction fallacy. In: Pohl, R.F. (Ed.), Cognitive Illusions: Intriguing Phenomena in Judgement, Thinking and Memory. Psychology Press, London, pp. 25–43.

Fox, C.R., Clemen, R., 2005. Subjective probability assessment in decision analysis: partition dependence and bias toward the ignorance prior. Management Science 51 (9), 1417–1432.

Fox, C.R., Rottenstreich, Y., 2003. Partition priming in judgment under uncertainty. Psychological Science 14 (3), 195–200.

Fryer, R., Harms, P., Jackson, M., 2017. Updating Beliefs when Evidence is Open to Interpretation: Implications for Bias and Polarization. Working Paper.

Fudenberg, D., Liang, A., 2018. Predicting and Understanding Initial Play. Working Paper.

Gabaix, X., Laibson, D., 2002. The 6D bias and the equity-premium puzzle. NBER Macroeconomics Annual 16, 257–312.

Ganguly, A., Kagel, J., Moser, D., 2000. Do asset market prices reflect traders' judgment biases? Journal of Risk and Uncertainty 20 (3), 219–245.

Ganguly, A., Tasoff, J., 2016. Fantasy and dread: the demand for information and the consumption utility of the future. Management Science 63 (12), 4037–4060.

Garrett, N., Sharot, T., 2017. Optimistic update bias holds firm: three tests of robustness following Shah et al. Consciousness and Cognition 50, 12–22.

Garrett, N., Sharot, T., Faulkner, P., Korn, C.W., Roiser, J.P., Dolan, R.J., 2014. Losing the rose tinted glasses: neural substrates of unbiased belief updating in depression. Frontiers in Human Neuroscience 8, 639.

Gauriot, R., Page, L., Wooders, J., 2016. Nash at Wimbledon: Evidence from Half a Million Serves. Working Paper.

Geller, E.S., Pitz, G.F., 1968. Confidence and decision speed in the revision of opinion. Organizational Behavior and Human Performance 3 (2), 190–201.

Gennaioli, N., Shleifer, A., 2010. What comes to mind. The Quarterly Journal of Economics 125 (4), 1399–1433.

Gerber, A., Green, D., 1999. Misperceptions about perceptual bias. Annual Review of Political Science 2, 189–210.

Gettys, C.F., Manley, C.W., 1968. The probability of an event and estimates of posterior probability based upon its occurrence. Psychonomic Science 11 (2), 47–48.

Gigerenzer, G., 1996. On narrow norms and vague heuristics: a reply to Kahneman and Tversky (1996). Psychological Review 103 (3), 592–596.

Gigerenzer, G., Hell, W., Blank, H., 1988. Presentation and content: the use of base rates as a continuous variable. Journal of Experimental Psychology: Human Perception and Performance 14 (3), 513–525.

Gigerenzer, G., Hoffrage, U., 1995. How to improve Bayesian reasoning without instruction: frequency formats. Psychological Review 102 (4), 684–704.

Gigerenzer, G., Hertwig, R., Pachur, T. (Eds.), 2011. Heuristics: The Foundations of Adaptive Behavior. Oxford University Press, New York.

Gilovich, T., Griffin, D., Kahneman, D. (Eds.), 2002. Heuristics: The Foundations of Adaptive Behavior. Cambridge University Press, New York, NY.

Gilovich, T., Vallone, R., Tversky, A., 1985. The hot hand in basketball: on the misperception of random sequences. Cognitive Psychology 17 (3), 295–314.

Ginosar, Z., Trope, Y., 1980. The effects of base rates and individuating information on judgments about another person. Journal of Experimental Social Psychology 16, 228–242.

Ginosar, Z., Trope, Y., 1987. Problem solving in judgment under uncertainty. Journal of Personality and Social Psychology 52 (3), 464–474.

Giustinelli, P., Manski, C.F., Molinari, F., 2018. Tail and Center Rounding of Probabilistic Expectations in the Health and Retirement Study. Working Paper.

Golman, R., Hagmann, D., Loewenstein, G., 2017. Information avoidance. Journal of Economic Literature 55 (1), 96–135.

Goodie, A.S., Fantino, E., 1999. What does and does not alleviate base-rate neglect under direct experience. Journal of Behavioral Decision Making 12 (4), 307–335.

Gotthard-Real, A., 2017. Desirability and information processing: an experimental study. Economics Letters 152, 96–99.

Green, P.E., Halbert, M.H., Minas, J.S., 1964. An experiment in information buying. Journal of Advertising Research 4, 17–23.

Green, P.E., Halbert, M.H., Robinson, P.J., 1965. An experiment in probability estimation. Journal of Marketing Research 2 (3), 266–273.

Green, B., Zwiebel, J., 2017. The hot-hand fallacy: cognitive mistakes or equilibrium adjustments? Evidence from major league baseball. Management Science, Articles in Advance, 1–34.

Grether, D.M., 1978. Recent psychological studies of behavior under uncertainty. In: Papers and Proceedings of the Ninetieth Annual Meeting of the American Economic Association. American Economic Review 68 (2), 70–74.

Grether, D.M., 1980. Bayes rule as a descriptive model: the representativeness heuristic. The Quarterly Journal of Economics 95 (3), 537–557.

Grether, D.M., 1992. Testing Bayes rule and the representativeness heuristic: some experimental evidence. Journal of Economic Behavior and Organization 17 (1), 31–57.

Griffin, D., Tversky, A., 1992. The weighing of evidence and the determinants of confidence. Cognitive Psychology 24 (3), 411–435.

Grinnell, M., Keeley, S.M., Doherty, M.E., 1971. Bayesian predictions of faculty judgments of graduate school success. Organizational Behavior and Human Performance 6 (3), 379–387.

Grossman, Z., Owens, D., 2012. An unlucky feeling: overconfidence and noisy feedback. Journal of Economic Behavior and Organization 84 (2), 510–524.

Guryan, J., Kearney, M.S., 2008. Gambling at lucky stores: empirical evidence from state lottery sales. American Economic Review 98 (1), 458–473.

Gustafson, D.H., Shukla, R.K., Delbecq, A., Walster, G.W., 1973. A comparative study of differences in subjective likelihood estimates made by individuals, interacting groups, Delphi groups, and nominal groups. Organizational Behavior and Human Performance 9 (2), 280–291.

Hamilton, M.M., 1984. An Examination of Processing Factors Affecting the Availability of Consumer Testimonial Information in Memory. Unpublished dissertation. Johns Hopkins University, Baltimore, MD.

Hammond, K.R., Kelly, K.J., Schneider, R.J., Vancini, M., 1967. Clinical inference in nursing: revising judgments. Nursing Research 16 (1), 38–45.

Harrison, G.W., 1994. Expected utility theory and the experimentalists. In: Hey, J.D. (Ed.), Experimental Economics. Physica, Heidelberg, pp. 43–73.

He, X.D., Xiao, D., 2017. Processing consistency in non-Bayesian inference. Journal of Mathematical Economics 70, 90–104.

Henckel, T., Menzies, G., Moffatt, P., Zizzo, D., 2017. Belief Adjustment: A Double Hurdle Model and Experimental Evidence. Working Paper.

Holt, C.A., Smith, A.M., 2009. An update on Bayesian updating. Journal of Economic Behavior and Organization 69 (2), 125–134.

Hsu, S-H., Huang, C-Y., Tang, C-T., 2007. Minimax play at Wimbledon: comment. American Economic Review 97 (1), 517–523.

Jern, A., Chang, K.K., Kemp, C., 2014. Belief polarization is not always irrational. Psychological Review 121 (2), 206–224.

Jin, L., 2018. Evidence of Hot-Hand Behavior in Sports and Medicine. Working Paper.

Juslin, P., Winman, A., Hansson, P., 2007. The *Naïve* intuitive statistician: a naïve sampling model of intuitive confidence intervals. Psychological Review 114 (3), 678–703.

Kahneman, D., 2002. The Sveriges Riksbank prize in economic sciences in memory of Alfred Nobel. In: Frängsmyr, T. (Ed.), Les Prix Nobel, The Nobel Prizes 2002. Stockholm, 2003.

Kahneman, D., Frederick, S., 2002. Representativeness revisited: attribute substitution in intuitive judgment. In: Gilovich, T., Griffin, D., Kahneman, D. (Eds.), Heuristics of Intuitive Judgment: Extensions and Applications. Cambridge University Press, New York, pp. 49–81.

Kahneman, D., Tversky, A., 1972a. Subjective probability: a judgment of representativeness. Cognitive Psychology 3 (3), 430–454.

Kahneman, D., Tversky, A., 1972b. On prediction and judgment. Oregon Research Institute Bulletin 12 (4).

Kahneman, D., Tversky, A., 1973. On the psychology of prediction. Psychological Review 80 (4), 237–251.

Kahneman, D., Tversky, A., 1982. Judgments of and by representativeness. In: Kahneman, D., Slovic, P., Tversky, A. (Eds.), Judgment Under Uncertainty: Heuristics and Biases. Cambridge University Press, New York, pp. 84–98.

Kahneman, D., Tversky, A., 1996. On the reality of cognitive illusions: a reply to Gigerenzer's critique. Psychological Review 103 (3), 582–591.

Kennedy, M.L., Willis, W.G., Faust, D., 1997. The base-rate fallacy in school psychology. Journal of Psychoeducational Assessment 15 (4), 292–307.

Keren, G., 1991. Additional tests of utility theory under unique and repeated conditions. Journal of Behavioral Decision Making 4 (4), 297–304.

Keren, G., Wagenaar, W.A., 1987. Violation of utility theory in unique and repeated gambles. Journal of Experimental Psychology: Learning, Memory, and Cognition 13 (3), 387–391.

Kleinberg, J., Liang, A., Mullainathan, S., 2017. The Theory is Predictive, but is it Complete? An Application to Human Perception of Randomness. Working Paper.

Klos, A., Weber, E.U., Weber, M., 2005. Investment decisions and time horizon: risk perception and risk behavior in repeated gambles. Management Science 51 (12), 1777–1790.

Koehler, J.J., 1996. The base rate fallacy reconsidered: descriptive, normative and methodological challenges. Behavioral and Brain Sciences 19 (1), 1–53.

Koehler, J.J., Conley, C., 2003. The "hot hand" myth in professional basketball. Journal of Sport and Exercise Psychology 25 (2), 253–259.

Korn, C.W., Sharot, T., Walter, H., Heekeren, H.R., Dolan, R.J., 2014. Depression is related to an absence of optimistically biased belief updating about future life events. Psychological Medicine 44 (3), 579–592.

Kraemer, C., Weber, M., 2004. How do people take into account weight, strength, and quality of segregated vs. aggregated data? Experimental evidence. The Journal of Risk and Uncertainty 29 (2), 113–142.

Krieger, J.L., Murray, F., Roberts, J.S., Green, R.C., 2016. The impact of personal genomics on risk perceptions and medical decision-making. Nature Biotechnology 34 (9), 912–918.

Kriz, J., 1967. Der Likelihood Quotient zur erfassung des subjektiven signifikanzniveaus. Forschungsbericht No. 9. Institute for Advanced Studies, Vienna.

Kuhnen, C.M., 2015. Asymmetric learning from financial information. Journal of Finance 70 (5), 2029–2062.

Kunda, Z., 1990. The case for motivated reasoning. Psychological Bulletin 108 (3), 480–498.

Kuzmanovic, B., Jefferson, A., Vogeley, K., 2015. Self-specific optimism bias in belief updating is associated with high trait optimism. Journal of Behavioral Decision Making 28 (3), 281–293.

Kuzmanovic, B., Jefferson, A., Vogeley, K., 2016. The role of the neural reward circuitry in self-referential optimistic belief updates. Neuroimage 133, 151–162.

Labella, C., Koehler, D., 2004. Dilution and confirmation of probability judgments based on nondiagnostic evidence. Memory & Cognition 32 (7), 1076–1089.

Laplace, P.S., 1814. Essai Philosophique sur les Probabilités. Courcier, Paris.

Lefebvre, G., Lebreton, M., Meyniel, F., Bourgeois-Gironde, S., Palminteri, S., 2017. Behavioural and neural characterization of optimistic reinforcement learning. Nature Human Behavior 1, 1–9, 0067.

Lem, S., Dooren, W.V., Gillard, E., Verschaffel, L., 2011. Sample size neglect problems: a critical analysis. Studia Psychologica: Journal for Basic Research in Psychological Sciences 53 (2), 123–135.

Lewis, J., Gaertig, C., Simmons, J.P., forthcoming. Extremeness aversion is a cause of anchoring. Psychological Science. Available from: https://doi.org/10.1177/0956797618799305. (Accessed 19 December 2018).

Lichtenstein, S., Fischhoff, B., Phillips, L.D., 1982. Calibration of probabilities: the state of the art to 1980. In: Kahneman, D., Slovic, P., Tversky, A. (Eds.), Judgment Under Uncertainty: Heuristics and Biases. Cambridge University Press, New York, pp. 306–334.

Lieder, F., Griffiths, T.L., Hsu, M., 2018. Overrepresentation of extreme events in decision making reflects rational use of cognitive resources. Psychological Review 125 (1), 1–32.

Lindman, H., Edwards, W., 1961. Supplementary report: unlearning the gambler's fallacy. Journal of Experimental Psychology 62 (6), 630.

Lord, C.G., Ross, L., Lepper, M.R., 1979. Biased assimilation and attitude polarization: the effects of prior theories on subsequently considered evidence. Journal of Personality and Social Psychology 37 (11), 2098–2109.

Ludolph, R., Schulz, P.J., 2017. Debiasing health-related judgments and decision making: a systematic review. Medical Decision Making 38 (1), 3–13.

Lyon, D., Slovic, P., 1976. Dominance of accuracy information and neglect of base rates in probability estimation. Acta Psychologica 40 (4), 287–298.

Macchi, L., Osherson, D., Krantz, D.H., 1999. A note on superadditive probability judgment. Psychological Review 106 (1), 210–214.

Madarász, K., 2012. Information projection: model and applications. The Review of Economic Studies 79 (3), 961–985.

Mankiw, N.G., Reis, R., 2002. Sticky information versus sticky prices: a proposal to replace the new Keynesian Phillips curve. The Quarterly Journal of Economics 117 (4), 1295–1328.

Manski, C.F., 2018. Survey measurement of probabilistic macroeconomic expectations: progress and promise. NBER Macroeconomics Annual 32 (1), 411–471.

Marks, J., Baines, S., 2017. Optimistic belief updating despite inclusion of positive events. Learning and Motivation 58, 88–101.

Marks, D.F., Clarkson, J.K., 1972. An explanation of conservatism in the bookbag-and-pokerchips situation. Acta Psychologica 36 (2), 145–160.

Martin, D.W., 1969. Data conflict in a multinomial decision task. Journal of Experimental Psychology 82 (1), 4–8.

Martin, D.W., Gettys, C.F., 1969. Feedback and response mode in performing a Bayesian decision task. Journal of Applied Psychology 53 (5), 413–418.

Meehl, P.E., Rosen, A., 1955. Antecedent probability and the efficiency of psychometric signs, patterns, or cutting scores. Psychological Bulletin 52 (3), 194–216.

Metzger, M.A., 1985. Biases in betting: an application of laboratory findings. Psychological Reports 56 (3), 883–888.

Miller, J.B., Gelman, A., 2018. Laplace's Theories of Cognitive Illusions, Heuristics, and Biases. Working Paper.

Miller, J.B., Sanjurjo, A., 2014. A Cold Shower for the Hot Hand Fallacy. IGIER Working Paper 518. Bocconi University, Milan.

Miller, J.B., Sanjurjo, A., 2015. Is It a Fallacy to Believe in the Hot Hand in the NBA Three-Point Contest? Working Paper.

Miller, J.B., Sanjurjo, A., 2017. A Visible (Hot) Hand? Expert Players Bet on the Hot Hand and Win. Working Paper.

Miller, J.B., Sanjurjo, A., 2018. Surprised by the hot hand fallacy? A truth in the Law of Small Numbers. Econometrica 86 (6), 2019–2047.

Miller, A.G., McHoskey, J.W., Bane, C.M., Dowd, T.G., 1993. The attitude polarization phenomenon: role of response measure, attitude extremity, and behavioral consequences of reported attitude change. Journal of Personality and Social Psychology 64 (4), 561–574.

Möbius, M.M., Niederle, M., Niehaus, P., Rosenblat, T.S., 2014. Managing Self-Confidence. Working Paper.

Moore, D.A., Tenney, E.R., Haran, U., 2015. Overprecision in judgment. In: Keren, G., Wu, G. (Eds.), Blackwell Handbook of Judgment and Decision Making. Wiley, New York, pp. 182–212.

Morewedge, C.K., Yoon, H., Scopelliti, I., Symborski, C.W., Korris, J.H., Kassam, K.S., 2015. Debiasing decisions: improved decision making with a single training intervention. Policy Insights from the Behavioral and Brain Sciences 2 (1), 129–140.

Moutsiana, C., Garrett, N., Clarke, R.C., Lotto, R.B., Blakemore, S-J., Sharot, T., 2013. Human development of the ability to learn from bad news. Proceedings of the National Academy of Sciences of the United States of America 110 (41), 16396–16401.

Murray, J., Iding, M., Farris, H., Revlin, R., 1987. Sample-size salience and statistical inference. Bulletin of the Psychonomic Society 25 (5), 367–369.

Nelson, M.W., Bloomfield, R., Hales, J.W., Libby, R., 2001. The effect of information strength and weight on behavior in financial markets. Organizational Behavior and Human Decision Processes 86 (2), 168–196.

Nickerson, R.S., 1998. Confirmation bias: a ubiquitous phenomenon in many guises. Review of General Psychology 2 (2), 175–220.

Nisbett, R.E., Borgida, E., Crandall, R., Reed, H., 1976. Popular induction: information is not necessarily informative. In: Carroll, J.S., Payne, J.W. (Eds.), Cognition and Social Behavior. Erlbaum, Hillsdale, N.J., pp. 113–133.

Nisbett, R.E., Ross, L., 1980. Human Inference: Strategies and Shortcomings of Social Judgment. Prentice-Hall, Englewood Cliffs, N.J.

Oakes, M., 1986. Statistical Inference: A Commentary for the Social and Behavioral Sciences. Wiley, New York.

Olson, C.L., 1976. Some apparent violations of the representativeness heuristic in human judgment. Journal of Experimental Psychology: Human Perception and Performance 2 (4), 599–608.

Oskarsson, T., Van Boven, L., McClelland, G.H., Hastie, R., 2009. What's next? Judging sequences of binary events. Psychological Bulletin 135 (2), 262–285.

Oster, E., Shoulson, I., Dorsey, E.R., 2013. Optimal expectations and limited medical testing: evidence from Huntington disease. American Economic Review 103 (2), 804–830.

Palminteri, S., Lefebvre, G., Kilford, E.J., Blakemore, S-J., 2017. Confirmation bias in human reinforcement learning: evidence from counterfactual feedback processing. PLoS Computational Biology 13 (8), e1005684.

Pelham, B.W., Neter, E., 1995. The effect of motivation of judgment depends on the difficulty of the judgment. Journal of Personality and Social Psychology 68 (4), 581–594.

Pepitone, A., DiNubile, M., 1976. Contrast effects in judgments of crime severity and the punishment of criminal violators. Journal of Personality and Social Psychology 33 (4), 448–459.

Peterson, C.R., Beach, L.R., 1967. Man as an intuitive statistician. Psychological Bulletin 68 (1), 29–46.

Peterson, C.R., DuCharme, W.M., 1967. A primacy effect in subjective probability revision. Journal of Experimental Psychology 73 (1), 61–65.

Peterson, C.R., DuCharme, W.M., Edwards, W., 1968. Sampling distributions and probability revisions. Journal of Experimental Psychology 76 (2), 236–243.

Peterson, C.R., Miller, A.J., 1965. Sensitivity of subjective probability revision. Journal of Experimental Psychology 70 (1), 117–121.

Peterson, C.R., Schneider, R.J., Miller, A.J., 1965a. Sample size and the revision of subjective probabilities. Journal of Experimental Psychology 69 (5), 522–527.

Peterson, C.R., Swensson, R.G., 1968. Intuitive statistical inferences about diffuse hypotheses. Organizational Behavior and Human Performance 3 (1), 1–11.

Peterson, C.R., Ulehla, Z.J., Miller, A.J., Bourne, L.E., Stilson, D.W., 1965b. Internal consistency of subjective probabilities. Journal of Experimental Psychology 70 (5), 526–533.

Peysakhovich, A., Naecker, J., 2017. Using methods from machine learning to evaluate behavioral models of choice under risk and ambiguity. Journal of Economic Behavior and Organization 133, 373–384.

Phillips, L.D., Edwards, W., 1966. Conservatism in a simple probability inference task. Journal of Experimental Psychology 72 (3), 346–354.

Phillips, L.D., Hays, W.L., Edwards, W., 1966. Conservatism in complex probabilistic inference. IEEE Transactions on Human Factors in Electronics HFE-7 (1), 7–18.

Pitz, G.F., 1967. Sample size, likelihood, and confidence in a decision. Psychonomic Science 8 (6), 257–258.

Pitz, G.F., 1969. The influence of prior probabilities on information seeking and decision-making. Organizational Behavior and Human Performance 4 (3), 213–226.

Pitz, G.F., Downing, L., Reinhold, H., 1967. Sequential effects in the revision of subjective probabilities. Canadian Journal of Psychology 21 (5), 381–393.

Pitz, G.F., Reinhold, H., 1968. Payoff effects in sequential decision-making. Journal of Experimental Psychology 77 (2), 249–257.

Pouget, S., Sauvagnat, J., Villeneuve, S., 2017. A mind is a terrible thing to change: confirmatory bias in financial markets. The Review of Financial Studies 30 (6), 2066–2109.

Prava, V.R., Clemen, R.T., Hobbs, B.F., Kenney, M.A., 2016. Partition dependence and carryover biases in subjective probability assessment surveys for continuous variables: model-based estimation and correction. Decision Analysis 13 (1), 51–67.

Quattrone, G.A., Tversky, A., 1984. Causal versus diagnostic contingencies: on self-deception and on the Voter's illusion. Journal of Personality and Social Psychology 46 (2), 237–248.

Rabin, M., 1998. Psychology and economics. Journal of Economic Literature 36 (1), 11–46.

Rabin, M., 2002. Inference by believers in the Law of Small Numbers. The Quarterly Journal of Economics 117 (3), 775–816.

Rabin, M., 2013. Incorporating limited rationality into economics. Journal of Economic Literature 51 (2), 528–543.

Rabin, M., Schrag, J.L., 1999. First impressions matter: a model of confirmatory bias. The Quarterly Journal of Economics 114 (1), 37–82.

Rabin, M., Vayanos, D., 2010. The gambler's and hot-hand fallacies: theory and applications. The Review of Economic Studies 77 (2), 730–778.

Rao, J.M., 2009. Experts' Perceptions of Autocorrelation: The Hot Hand Fallacy Among Professional Basketball Players. Working Paper.

Rapoport, A., Budescu, D.V., 1997. Randomization in individual choice behavior. Psychological Review 104 (3), 603–617.

Rapoport, A., Wallsten, T.S., 1972. Individual decision behavior. Annual Review of Psychology 23, 131–176.

Redelmeier, D.A., Koehler, D.J., Liberman, V., Tversky, A., 1995. Probability judgement in medicine: discounting unspecified possibilities. Medical Decision Making 15 (3), 227–230.

Redelmeier, D.A., Tversky, A., 1992. On the framing of multiple prospects. Psychological Science 3 (3), 191–193.

Rinott, Y., Bar-Hillel, M., 2015. Comments on a "Hot Hand" Paper by Miller and Sanjurjo (2015). Discussion Paper Series from The Federmann Center for the Study of Rationality. The Hebrew University, Jerusalem.

Robalo, P., Sayag, R., 2014. Paying is Believing: The Effect of Costly Information on Bayesian Updating. Working Paper.

Roby, T.B., 1967. Belief states and sequential evidence. Journal of Experimental Psychology 75 (2), 236–245.

Roese, N.J., Vohs, K.D., 2012. Hindsight bias. Perspectives on Psychological Science 7 (5), 411–426.

Rottenstreich, Y., Tversky, A., 1997. Unpacking, repacking, and anchoring: advances in support theory. Psychological Review 104 (2), 406–415.

Roy, M.C., Lerch, F.J., 1996. Overcoming ineffective mental representations in base-rate problems. Information Systems Research 7 (2), 233–247.

Russo, J.E., Meloy, M.G., Medvec, V.H., 1998. Predecisional distortion of product information. Journal of Marketing Research 35 (4), 438–452.

Samuelson, P.A., 1963. Risk and uncertainty: a fallacy of large numbers. Scientia 98, 108–113.

Sanders, A.F., 1968. Choice among bets and revision of opinion. Acta Psychologica 28, 76–83.

Sasaki, S., Kawagoe, T., 2007. Belief Updating in Individual and Social Learning: A Field Experiment on the Internet. Discussion Paper 690. The Institute of Social and Economic Research, Osaka University.

Schotter, A., Trevino, I., 2014. Belief elicitation in the lab. Annual Review of Economics 6, 103–128.

Schwardmann, P., Van der Weele, J., 2016. Deception and Self-Deception. Working Paper.

Schwarz, N., Vaughn, L.A., 2002. The availability heuristic revisited: ease of recall and content of recall as distinct sources of information. In: Gilovich, T., Griffin, D., Kahneman, D. (Eds.), Heuristics and Biases: The Psychology of Intuitive Judgment. Cambridge University Press, New York, NY, pp. 103–119.

Sedlmeier, P., 1994. People's appreciation of sample size in frequency distributions and sampling distributions. University of Chicago. Unpublished manuscript.

Sedlmeier, P., Gigerenzer, G., 1997. Intuitions about sample size: the empirical Law of Large Numbers. Journal of Behavioral Decision Making 10 (1), 33–51.

Shah, P., Harris, A.J.L., Bird, G., Catmur, C., Hahn, U., 2016. A pessimistic view of optimistic belief updating. Cognitive Psychology 90, 71–127.

Shanteau, J.C., 1970. An additive model for sequential decision making. Journal of Experimental Psychology 85 (2), 181–191.

Shanteau, J.C., 1972. Descriptive versus normative models of sequential inference judgment. Journal of Experimental Psychology 93 (1), 63–68.

Shanteau, J.C., 1975. Averaging versus multiplying combination rules of inference judgment. Acta Psychologica 39, 83–89.

Sharot, T., Guitart-Masip, M., Korn, C.W., Chowdhury, R., Dolan, R.J., 2012a. How dopamine enhances an optimism bias in humans. Current Biology 22 (16), 1477–1481.

Sharot, T., Kanai, R., Marston, D., Korn, C.W., Rees, G., Dolan, R.J., 2012b. Selectively altering belief formation in the human brain. Proceedings of the National Academy of Sciences of the United States of America 109 (42), 17058–17062.

Sharot, T., Korn, C.W., Dolan, R.J., 2011. How unrealistic optimism is maintained in the face of reality. Nature Neuroscience 14 (11), 1475–1479.

Shu, S., Wu, G., 2003. Belief Bracketing: Can Partitioning Information Change Consumer Judgments? Working Paper.

Simonsohn, U., 2006. New Yorkers commute more everywhere: contrast effects in the field. The Review of Economics and Statistics 88 (1), 1–9.

Sloman, S.A., Rottenstreich, Y., Wisniewski, E., Hadjichristidis, C., Fox, C.R., 2004. Typical versus atypical unpacking and superadditive probability judgment. Journal of Experimental Psychology: Learning, Memory, and Cognition 30 (3), 573–582.

Slovic, P., Lichtenstein, S., 1971. Comparison of Bayesian and regression approaches to the study of information processing in judgment. Organizational Behavior and Human Performance 6 (6), 649–744.

Sonnemann, U., Camerer, C.F., Fox, C.R., Langer, T., 2013. How psychological framing affects economic market prices in the lab and field. Proceedings of the National Academy of Sciences of the United States of America 110 (29), 11779–11784.

Stango, V., Yoong, J., Zinman, J., 2017. The Quest for Parsimony in Behavioral Economics: New Methods and Evidence on Three Fronts. Working Paper.

Stanovich, K.E., 1999. Who is Rational? Studies of Individual Differences in Reasoning. Lawrence Earlbaum Associates, Mahwah, NJ.

Stanovich, K.E., West, R.F., 1998. Individual differences in rational thought. Journal of Experimental Psychology: General 127 (2), 161–188.

Stolarz-Fantino, S., Fantino, E., Zizzo, D.J., Wen, J., 2003. The conjunction effect: new evidence for robustness. American Journal of Psychology 116 (1), 15–34.

Stone, D.F., 2012. Measurement error and the hot hand. The American Statistician 66 (1), 61–66.

Stone, D.F., Arkes, J., 2018. March Madness? Underreaction to hot and cold holds in NCAA basketball. Economic Inquiry 56 (3), 1724–1747.

Strub, M.H., 1969. Experience and prior probability in a complex decision task. Journal of Applied Psychology 53 (2), 112–117.

Suetens, S., Galbo-Jørgensen, C.B., Tyran, J-R., 2016. Predicting lotto numbers: a natural experiment on the gambler's fallacy and the hot-hand fallacy. Journal of the European Economic Association 14 (3), 584–607.

Swieringa, R., Gibbins, M., Larsson, L., Sweeney, J.L., 1976. Experiments in the heuristics of human information processing. Journal of Accounting Research 14, 159–187.

Taylor, S.E., Thompson, S.C., 1982. Stalking the elusive "vividness" effect. Psychological Review 89 (2), 155–181.

Teguia, A., 2017. Law of Small Numbers and Hysteresis in Asset Prices and Portfolio Choices. Working Paper.

Teigen, K.H., 1974a. Overestimation of subjective probabilities. Scandinavian Journal of Psychology 15 (1), 56–62.

Teigen, K.H., 1974b. Subjective sampling distributions and the additivity of estimates. Scandinavian Journal of Psychology 15 (1), 50–55.

Tenenbaum, J.B., Griffiths, T.L., 2001. The rational basis of representativeness. In: Moore, J.D., Stenning, K. (Eds.), Proceedings of the 23rd Annual Conference of the Cognitive Science Society. Erlbaum, Hillsdale, N.J., pp. 1036–1041.

Tentori, K., Bonini, N., Osherson, D., 2004. The conjunction fallacy: a misunderstanding about conjunction? Cognitive Science 28 (3), 467–477.

Terrell, D., 1994. A test of the gambler's fallacy: evidence from pari-mutuel games. Journal of Risk and Uncertainty 8 (3), 309–317.

Terrell, D., Farmer, A., 1996. Optimal betting and efficiency in parimutuel betting markets with information costs. The Economic Journal 106 (437), 846–868.

Tribe, L.H., 1971. Trial by mathematics: precision and ritual in the legal process. Harvard Law Review 84 (6), 1329–1393.

Troutman, C.M., Shanteau, J., 1977. Inferences based on nondiagnostic information. Organizational Behavior and Human Performance 19 (1), 43–55.

Tune, G.S., 1964. Response preferences: a review of some relevant literature. Psychological Bulletin 61 (4), 286–302.

Tversky, A., Kahneman, D., 1971. Belief in the Law of Small Numbers. Psychological Bulletin 76 (2), 105–110.

Tversky, A., Kahneman, D., 1974. Judgment under uncertainty: heuristics and biases. Science 185 (4157), 1124–1131.

Tversky, A., Kahneman, D., 1980. Causal schemas in judgments under uncertainty. In: Fishbein, M. (Ed.), Progress in Social Psychology, Vol. 1. Erlbaum, Hillsdale, NJ, pp. 49–72.

Tversky, A., Kahneman, D., 1983. Extensional versus intuitive reasoning: the conjunction fallacy in probability judgment. Psychological Review 90 (4), 293–315.

Tversky, A., Koehler, D.J., 1994. Support theory: a nonextensional representation of subjective probability. Psychological Review 101 (4), 547–567.

Viscusi, W.K., 1990. Do smokers underestimate risks? Journal of Political Economy 98 (6), 1253–1269.

Vlek, C.A.J., 1965. The Use of Probabilistic Information in Decision Making. Psychological Institute Report No. 009-65. University of Leiden, Netherlands.

Vlek, C.A.J., Van der Heijden, L.H.C., 1967. Subjective Likelihood Functions and Variations in the Accuracy of Probabilistic Information Processing. Psychological Institute Report No. E 107-67. University of Leiden, Netherlands.

Walker, M., Wooders, J., 2001. Minimax play at Wimbledon. American Economic Review 91 (5), 1521–1538.

Weinstein, N.D., 1980. Unrealistic optimism about future events. Journal of Personality and Social Psychology 39 (5), 806–820.

Well, A.D., Pollatsek, A., Boyce, S.J., 1990. Understanding the effects of sample size on the variability of the mean. Organizational Behavior and Human Decision Processes 47 (2), 289–312.

Wells, G.L., Harvey, J.H., 1978. Naïve attributors' attributions and predictions: what is informative and when is an effect an effect? Journal of Personality and Social Psychology 36 (5), 483–490.

Wheeler, G., Beach, L.R., 1968. Subjective sampling distributions and conservatism. Organizational Behavior and Human Performance 3 (1), 36–46.

Windschitl, P.D., O'Rourke, J.L., 2015. Optimism biases: types and causes. In: Keren, G., Wu, G. (Eds.), Blackwell Handbook of Judgment and Decision Making. Wiley, New York, pp. 431–455.

Winkler, R.L., Murphy, A.H., 1973. Experiments in the laboratory and the real world. Organizational Behavior and Human Performance 10 (2), 252–270.

Wiswall, M., Zafar, B., 2015. How do college students respond to public information about earnings? Journal of Human Capital 9 (2), 117–169.

Yariv, L., 2005. I'll See It When I Believe It – A Simple Model of Cognitive Consistency. Working Paper.

Zhao, C., 2018. Representativeness and Similarity. Working Paper.

Zizzo, D.J., Stolarz-Fantino, S., Wen, J., Fantino, E., 2000. A violation of the monotonicity axiom: experimental evidence on the conjunction fallacy. Journal of Economic Behavior and Organization 41 (3), 263–276.

Zukier, H., Pepitone, A., 1984. Social roles and strategies in prediction: some determinants of the use of base-rate information. Journal of Personality and Social Psychology 47 (2), 349–360.

Errors in strategic reasoning

3

Erik Eyster[a,b,c]

[a]*London School of Economics, London, United Kingdom of Great Britain and Northern Ireland*
[b]*University of California, Santa Barbara, CA, United States of America*
e-mail address: E.Eyster@lse.ac.uk

Contents

[c] I thank the editors, Vince Crawford, Ignacio Esponda, Tristan Gagnon-Bartsch, Ryan Oprea, Matthew Rabin, Rani Spiegler, and Georg Weizsäcker for helpful comments or discussions, as well as Maria Kogelnik and Krittanai Laohakunakorn for invaluable research assistance.

Handbook of Behavioral Economics, Volume 2
ISSN 2352-2399, https://doi.org/10.1016/bs.hesbe.2018.11.003

1 Introduction

In the 1970s and 1980s, economists began to move beyond neoclassical models of price-taking and perfect competition towards a new generation of models that explicitly incorporate strategic interaction. Nearly all applied economic theory today—be it information economics, political economy, industrial organization, etc.—revolves around explicit accounts of strategic interaction. Depending upon the environment of interest, economists invoke a myriad of different assumptions about people's information, preferences, and choice sets.

The most popular non-cooperative, game-theoretic equilibrium concepts have the feature that each player plays in such a way as to maximize her payoffs given the equilibrium behavior of the other players. This can be interpreted as players correctly predicting how other people behave, learning rationally from other people's behavior, and making optimal choices given their beliefs. The development of these now-standard game-theoretic solution concepts kick-started tremendous conceptual advances in virtually all fields of economics, as well as in related disciplines. To give but one example, models of strategic competition amongst firms and models of competitive bidding in auctions have utterly transformed the field of industrial organization.[1] Not only did game theory improve social scientists' understanding of much of human behavior, but it provided a tool for policy-makers to devise better policy. For instance, governments have used the predictions of auction theory—itself predicated upon standard game-theoretic solution concepts—to raise more revenue when auctioning off government debt or assets.

Despite the enormous success of the "Game-Theory Revolution", experimental and empirical economists have challenged the empirical validity of its core assumptions. Copious laboratory and some field evidence suggests that people err in predicting others' behavior, learning from others, and choosing optimally. Some of these errors appear to be systematic. In recent years, economists have proposed a new generation of solution concepts that relax the stringent rationality assumptions that underlie standard game-theoretic solution concepts. This chapter reviews the evidence on errors in strategic reasoning as well as developments in modeling how people strategically interact when they commit errors. In order to describe those errors and the new generation of models, I begin by briefly reviewing "standard" game theory.

---

[1] Tirole (1988) gives a lucid textbook treatment of many such models.

1.1 Game-theory background

The most popular non-cooperative, game-theoretic solution concept was developed by John Nash (1950, 1951).[2] In a "Nash equilibrium" (NE) of a game, each "player" of the game chooses an action, or distribution over actions, that maximizes her expected utility given the distribution over actions chosen in equilibrium by the game's other players. For example, firms engaging in Cournot competition independently and simultaneously choose quantities of production before learning the market price, which depends negatively upon their collective production. In a Nash equilibrium of the Cournot game, each firm chooses the quantity that maximizes its profits given the quantity choices of its rivals. We can think of each firm as best responding to correct beliefs about other firms' actions, given an understanding of its own payoff function.

In many settings, Nash equilibrium offers a panoply of predictions, some of which seem unreasonable. The duopoly model of Stackelberg differs from Cournot competition with two firms in that a "leader" firm chooses its quantity first, after which a "follower" firm, with the benefit of observing the leader, chooses its quantity. Whereas the leader simply chooses a quantity q_1, the follower's plan of action specifies a quantity for every possible choice of the leader, $q_2(q_1)$. This game possesses an infinity of Nash equilibria. Most of these equilibria have the property that for some choices $\hat{q}_1$ of the leader, the follower chooses $q_2(\hat{q}_1)$ that does not maximize its profits. So long as the leader chooses something other than $\hat{q}_1$ in a Nash equilibrium, the follower may indeed be maximizing its expected profits. Nevertheless, this behavior seems unreasonable: why would a rational follower not maximize its profits given the leader's choice? Surely the Stackelberg leader should recognize that the follower will best respond to any quantity choice. Selten (1965) proposed a refinement of the set of Nash equilibria of a game that excludes equilibria built upon these so-called incredible threats.

Selten's solution was to extend Nash equilibrium in the original game to Nash equilibrium in all "subgames", portions of the entire game that constitute games in their own right. Formally, Selten defined a subgame-perfect Nash equilibrium (SPNE) to be a Nash equilibrium in which players also play Nash equilibria of every subgame of the original game. In the Stackelberg game, for example, every feasible choice of quantity by the leader defines a subgame that begins (and ends) with the follower's choice. Subgame perfection strengthens Nash equilibrium in the Stackelberg game by requiring that the follower make an optimal choice in every such subgame; equivalently, the follower must choose a best response to the every possible action of the leader, even those that the leader does not choose. This restriction reduces the infinite set of Nash equilibria of the Stackelberg game to a unique SPNE prediction. In finite games like the Stackelberg game in which players move sequentially one at a time such that the mover at any given point in time observes all previous moves,

---

[2] Because this chapter deals exclusively with non-cooperative game theory, the adjective "non-cooperative" will be dropped henceforth for brevity.

SPNE coincides with the notion of backwards induction, where one starts by figuring out what the last player will do in all contingencies, then what the penultimate player will do in all contingencies given the last player's plan of action, etc.

In many strategic situations of interest to economists, people do not know other people's preferences or information, or others' beliefs about their own preferences or information. Harsanyi (1967a) and Harsanyi (1967b) proposed a parsimonious approach to deal with such uncertainty by describing it through an underlying "state of nature" that governs the payoffs of the game. According to the Harsanyi approach, each player begins with a common prior probability distribution over the set of possible states of nature. Asymmetric information can then be modeled though private information about the state of nature. A pure strategy in such a "Bayesian game" maps a player's private information (or type) into her actions. In a "Bayesian Nash equilibrium" (BNE), each player's strategy maximizes her expected payoff given her opponents' strategies.

In the past fifty years, many game theorists have added profound insights to the now canonical work of Nash, Selten, and Harsanyi (who shared the 1994 Nobel Prize in Economics). This chapter could not possibly adequately convey the depth and ingenuity of the great number of such contributions. Instead, its goal is to describe how economists, psychologists and other researchers over the past fifty years have deepened our understanding of strategic decision-making by identifying systematic departures from standard game-theoretic predictions as well as by incorporating insights from psychology and related disciplines into new concepts of strategic decision-making.

1.2 Behavioral-game-theory background

From Nash equilibrium to SPNE to Bayesian Nash equilibrium, traditional game theory has exacted more and more stringent demands on its actors' cognition. In a Nash equilibrium, people optimally respond to correct beliefs about others' equilibrium behavior.[3] In a SPNE, people not only correctly predict how others behave, but they also correctly predict how others would behave in contingencies that do not arise. A Stackelberg leader who chooses the quantity $q_1 = 1$, for example, must not only predict how the follower will respond to $q_1 = 1$, but also must foresee how the follower would react to any other choice $q_1' \neq 1$. Bayesian Nash equilibrium requires not only that people correctly predict what actions others choose, but also that they correctly assess how others' actions correlate with those other people's private information. Moreover, people are assumed to hold correct beliefs about the distribution of other people's private information. As Richard Thaler has often remarked in public lectures, every time a smart game theorist discovers some novel and subtle implica-

---

[3] People could also play a Nash equilibrium simply because each person has learned through trial and error which of her actions produces the highest average payoff. See Fudenberg and Levine (1998) for such learning stories. Even in cases where people come to play Nash equilibrium through some learning process, to the extent that they think about others' behavior, they should hold correct beliefs.

tion of rationality, our profession reacts by immediately assuming that all agents in our models have already figured it out!

Copious lab and some field evidence suggests that people do not interact in strategic situations as predicted by standard game-theoretic equilibrium concepts. People fail to best respond to others' behavior: they do not play Nash equilibria. They do not always backwards induct: they do not play SPNE. They under-appreciate the correlation between other people's private information and their actions: they do not play BNE. Much early experimental game theory was devoted to documenting such anomalies. Colin Camerer's pathbreaking textbook *Behavioural Game Theory* as well as Sanjit Dhami's 160-page-long chapter "The Evidence on Strategic Human Choice" in his encyclopedic tome *The Foundations of Behavioural Economic Analysis* provide superlative overviews of that literature.

In recent years, researchers have sought to build upon the empirical evidence about imperfections in human reasoning by building formal game-theoretic solution concepts that explicitly subsume some of the documented failings of human reasoning. This chapter reviews that literature by organizing it around different categories of error that people may commit in strategic situations. For each category, I provide evidence of the error, review models that embed the error, and illustrate applications.

1.3 **Chapter aims**

This chapter has three primary goals. Firstly, it aims to categorize errors that people make in strategic settings and provide lab or field evidence to substantiate each type of error.

Secondly, the chapter attempts to provide a user's guide for several of the most widely used "behavioral" solution concepts. Rather than describe each of these models in sequence, before comparing and contrasting them, the chapter puts the taxonomy of errors front and center and describes how popular existing solution concepts address each of these errors. Some solution concepts encompass only a single category of error, whereas others cut across different categories. Many recent experimental papers identify behavior in a laboratory game incongruent with Nash-equilibrium predictions, enumerate several alternative solution concepts alongside their predictions, and run horseraces between different concepts.[4] Horseraces between solution concepts appeal to insiders in the literature. Yet by focusing exclusively on statistical goodness of fit, this literature sometimes obscures *intuitiveness of fit*. How do the different solution concepts explain the data? Throughout the chapter, I try to keep focus on the mechanisms through which different solution concepts explain datasets.

Behavioral game theory should not merely aspire to explain data in laboratory experiments. Rather, it should aim to use laboratory and field evidence—enriched by intuition and thought experiments—to develop theoretical models that can be used to predict human behavior in domains of interest to economists. A third goal of the

---

[4] Solution concepts that preclude certain outcomes must be "noised up" by adding error terms of one form or another.

chapter is to describe how various solution concepts have been adopted into applied economics and how these solution concepts might influence the field even more.

This chapter complements rather than substitutes for the surveys by Camerer (2003) and Dhami (2016). Those excellent works provide a far more comprehensive view of the work on experimental game theory than possible within the confines of this chapter. Crawford et al. (2013) give a rich account of the laboratory evidence that focuses on the Level-k model, which features prominently in this chapter. Goeree et al.'s (2016) monograph on Quantal-Response Equilibrium lays out both the theory and empirics behind that solution concept, which also looms large in this chapter. Relative to those works, this chapter places greater emphasis on categories of error, similarities between solution concepts, and application to Economics.

1.4 Exclusions

Several forms of "behavioral" phenomena are excluded from the chapter. A large strand of the behavioral literature has studied other-regarding preferences. In a landmark experiment, Güth et al. (2000) asked a "proposer" to propose a split of x DM between herself and a responder. The responder could either accept the offer, in which case it was implemented, or reject the offer, in which case both parties received zero. Since a purely self-interested responder prefers any $x > 0$ to the nothing gained by rejecting the proposer's offer, and is indifferent between $x = 0$ and rejecting the proposer's offer, the unique SPNE has the proposer offer nothing and be accepted. Yet the average amount offered to the responder in the lab greatly exceeds the SPNE prediction of zero, and non-zero offers are frequently rejected. This "Ultimatum Game" experiment, replicated thousands of times, inspired a wave of theorizing about social preferences. Most prominently, Fehr and Schmidt (1999) proposed a model of preferences in which people dislike inequity across players' payoffs.

Rabin (1993) takes a different approach to explain why people choose "fair" actions in games. Unlike older models of unconditional altruism in which players are assumed to weight others' utilities positively (Andreoni, 1990), Rabin's model allows players to care positively or negatively about one another's payoffs. He does this by drawing upon the game-theoretic concept of Psychological Nash Equilibrium developed a few years earlier by Geanakoplos et al. (1989). In a Psychological Nash equilibrium, players' preferences depend upon their beliefs about others' actions, and others' beliefs about their actions. Rabin models each player's concern for another player's payoff as depending upon her perception of the other's kindness, which depends upon her beliefs about that other player's actions.[5]

Because the models of Fehr and Schmidt (1999) and Rabin (1993) do not incorporate errors in strategic reasoning, they do not belong in this chapter. However, some

---

[5] By dint of being a static model, Rabin's does not satisfactorily account for behavior in the ultimatum game. Dufwenberg and Kirchsteiger (2004) and Falk and Fischbacher (2006) extend Rabin's concept to extensive-form games.

of the evidence that they seek to explain might also include errors in strategic reasoning. For example, a proposer in the ultimatum game might make an offer that gets rejected because she mispredicts how the responder will behave. Due to the difficulty inherent in disentangling social preferences from strategic errors, this chapter focuses on experimental evidence from environments that do not seem to trigger strong distributional or reciprocity concerns, and argues in various places that lab evidence inconsistent with standard theory owes its explanation to errors in strategic reasoning rather than social preferences.

Another major theme of behavioral economics is time-inconsistency. The most popular way to model this is with the β–δ model popularized by Laibson (1997), in which the intertemporal preferences of someone in period t over instantaneous utilities received in periods $t, t+1, t+2, \ldots$ is

$$U^t(u_t, u_{t+1}, \ldots) = u_t + \beta \sum_{\tau=t+1}^{\infty} \delta^{\tau-t} u_\tau,$$

for $\beta, \delta \in [0, 1]$. In period t, the decision-maker weights u_{t+2} δ times as much as u_{t+1}, whereas in period $t+1$, the decision-maker weights u_{t+2} only $\beta\delta$ times as much as u_{t+1}. Intuitively, the person is present-biased.

Following the pioneering work of Strotz (1955), the standard way to analyze the behavior of a single decision-maker with such preferences over time has become through the formulation of a "multi-self game". We can think of Person 1 as moving $t = 1$ to maximize U^1, Person 2 as moving $t = 2$ to maximize U^2, etc. Most economists analyzing such games assume that the decision-maker is sophisticated: in each period t, she correctly predicts U^τ, for $\tau \geq t$, namely she correctly predicts her future preferences and, hence, behavior. However, O'Donoghue and Rabin (1999) (foreshadowed by Akerlof, 1991) introduce the alternative assumption that people naively underappreciate their own future taste for immediate gratification. The simplest, and most extreme, form of naivety is for the person in period t to think that her period $\tau > t$ preferences over utility flows $(u_\tau, u_{\tau+1}, \ldots)$ will agree with her period-t preferences over such flows. This coincides with the person in period t believing that future selves have $\beta = 1$.

Such mispredictions about future preferences create misprediction about future behavior. Nevertheless, the β–δ model and its variants are also excluded from this chapter for two reasons. First, mispredicting your own tastes differs fundamentally from mispredicting others behavior. Second, the naive β–δ model is extensively analyzed in the chapter by Beshears, Choi, Laibson, and Madrian in this handbook.

Indeed, any heuristic or bias that people may employ will have some implication for strategic reasoning. Each of the errors described in Daniel Benjamin's chapter in this volume has implications in strategic settings. For example, drawing upon evidence from Kahneman and Tversky, Rabin (2002) and Rabin and Vayanos (2010) develop models of the "Law of Small Numbers" under which people expect small samples to conform to the underlying population distribution more than they do. Rabin (2002) shows that a consequence is that people inferring about a parameter that characterizes the parent population infer more from small samples than prescribed by Bayes' Rule. Clearly this has implications for strategic reasoning in that a Player 1 who recognizes that Player 2 suffers from the Law of Small Numbers might behave differently. To take an example from the paper, mutual fund managers may understand that their clients read more into past performance about future performance than warranted, and tailor their behavior accordingly.

Xavier Gabaix's chapter in this volume surveys the literature on bounded rationality. Broadly speaking, this chapter includes models in which the bounds take the form of limits on people's strategic sophistication, such as the Level-k model, but excludes those in which the bounds constrain people's computational abilities or restrict the complexity of their strategies. For example, several game-theory papers model people as finite automata, namely machines with a limited number of states and rules that govern the transition from one state to another. Rubinstein (1986), for instance, looks at repeated games amongst finite automata that have the minimal number of states necessary to implement equilibrium.

I exclude bounded rationality for two reasons. Human cognition, of course, has its limits. But this does not mean that the most fruitful way to analyze strategic errors comes through those constraints. Indeed, in some settings, people work very hard to make enticing errors, when getting the right answer would be much simpler.[6] A second reason for excluding models of bounded rationality is that they are inherently models of rationality. To give an analogy, there is an old tradition in economics of including asymmetric information amongst other forms of bounded rationality. Today, however, most economists would not find anything irrational about not having access to certain information. If people can only keep track of two categories—due to a prohibitive cost of entertaining a third—then there is nothing irrational about optimizing in the face of these constraints. Similarly, when attention is costly, there is nothing irrational about being optimally inattentive.

Many researchers have explored how people learn to play equilibrium, or something other than equilibrium, when playing the same game repeatedly. (Fudenberg and Levine (1998) provides an excellent textbook treatment of the literature.) Consider a two-player game in which each player has two actions. The popular model of "reinforcement learning" (Roth and Erev, 1995) has each player mix over actions in proportion to "propensities" that are updated every period. When Player 1 chooses action a and earns a payoff of x, the propensity for a rises by x minus x_{min}, Player 1's minimum payoff in the game; the propensity for b does not change. As a consequence, a gets reinforced and becomes more likely to be repeated whenever it earns a high payoff, given Player 2's action. Fudenberg and Levine (1998) propose an alternative learning rule that differs from reinforcement learning by also using information on counterfactual payoffs. If Player 1 observes Player 2's action and knows her own payoff function, then she could compute what her payoff from b would have

---

[6] Eyster et al. (2018) provide some experimental evidence along these lines.

been if chosen.[7] "Fictitious play" differs from reinforcement learning by updating the propensities for both actions in every period. These and other learning models assume far less sophistication or knowledge of the environment than the solution concepts described in this chapter. In most economic settings of interest to economists, people know with whom they interact and have theories—albeit possibly incomplete or wrong theories—about how those other people behave. For this reason, the chapter mostly omits the literature on learning, except insofar as theorizing about learning has inspired various solution concepts.

Finally, the chapter also omits the literature on cheap talk. In games with multiple Nash equilibria, having the ability to communicate before playing the game might help players to coordinate on efficient equilibria. A number of experimental papers explore the extent to which various communication protocols enhance efficiency in games. Even though various experiments reveal interesting shortcomings in strategic reasoning, because this literature does not revolve around that issue, it is not covered.

1.5 Modeling approaches

In recent years, economists have developed several alternatives to traditional game-theoretic solution concepts of Nash equilibrium, subgame-perfect Nash equilibrium, sequential equilibrium, Bayesian Nash equilibrium, and perfect Bayesian equilibrium. Some of the new concepts embed directed psychological errors of the sort discussed in elsewhere in the Handbook. Others revolve around computational limitations.

The goal of these models ought to be to deepen our understanding of human decision-making. In part, this comes from fitting data, whether it come from the lab or the field. In part, it also comes from fitting our intuition. Good models also ought to make good out-of-sample predictions. We want models that are portable across settings in order to be able to apply them to new environments. We also want for these models to offer predictions in settings that interest economists such as markets, bargaining, auctions, etc.

Broadly speaking, the models follow three approaches. The psychology-and-economics approach tries to incorporate into game-theoretic equilibrium concepts various errors that people have been documented to commit in psychology experiments, economics experiments, or in the field. An example is Madarasz's (2015) projection equilibrium. We are all familiar with "Monday-Morning Quarterbacking", whereby sports fans project after-the-fact knowledge onto coaches and players during the contest. A coach who called an unsuccessful play is regarded as dumb rather than unlucky. Numerous psychology experiments suggest that people project information onto others. Based on this evidence, Madarasz develops a game-theoretic model in which players project their private information onto other parties. A prospective tenant haggling for a good deal on rent, for example, might mistakenly believe that the

---

[7] Camerer and Ho (1998) define a learning rule that incorporates both reinforcement learning and fictitious play.

landlord knows more about his preferences that she actually does. Typically, solution concepts which follow this approach are equilibrium-like in that players do everything right except to commit the one error of interest.

Another school of thought follows a procedural-rationality approach. In Stahl and Wilson (1994) and Nagel's (1995) Level-k and related models, players are thought to have limited scope for strategic reasoning, or to think that their opponents have limited scope. In some cases, these procedural models bear a tight resemblance to theories of mind. Children playing Hide-and-Seek, for instance, try to outsmart one another: "since she thinks I'll hide there, I'll instead hide here". But in more complex environments, the relationship between the procedural model and the players' thought process becomes more nebulous, as we shall see in Section 3.

Another approach draws its inspiration from notions of learning. By interacting repeatedly in the same type of strategic setting, people come to learn many features of their environment and others' behavior, but do not necessarily learn everything of interest. Eventually, people come to best respond to those things that they do learn, but not necessarily to things that they don't learn. The leading example of this type of model is self-confirming equilibrium of Fudenberg and Kreps (1998) and Fudenberg and Levine (1993).[8] This extensive-form solution concept has players correctly predict what happens along the equilibrium path but possibly mispredict what would happen at unreached decision nodes off the equilibrium path. The idea is that someone who learns to play a game through repeated interactions will learn how other people behave in contingencies that do arise, but will not necessarily learn for contingencies that do not arise.

A very different view is espoused by Ariel Rubinstein, who compares economic models to fairytales (Rubinstein, 2006). Rather than convey any larger lesson transferable across settings, the economist-fabulist uses formal models to convey insight without imbuing those models with any external validity. For example, one could tell a story in which Hansel and Gretel, after stealing three gingerbreads from a witch's house, bargain over how to divide their spoils. Having woken up too late to eat breakfast before the day's outing, Hansel is famished and desperate to eat as soon as possible. When Gretel opens negotiations by offering Hansel one gingerbread—and keeping the other two for herself—Hansel accepts immediately. The children's negotiation might illustrate how greater impatience can lower one's equilibrium payoff but need not suggest that greater impatience would be negatively correlated with payoff outside of the Black Forest. The model depicts a slice of reality, and Rubinstein argues that this particular slice should not be presumed to make better predictions than any other slice.

In my opinion, he is too pessimistic about our profession's ability to produce genuine, non-trivial and transferable insights about human behavior. For example, few people unschooled in microeconomic theory understand tax incidence. While it is intuitive that the payer of the tax should bear the burden of the tax, economists understand that this need not be the case; indeed, what matters is not who formally pays

---

[8] See also Battigalli (1987).

the tax but rather the elasticities of demand and supply. Even the simplest supply-and-demand analysis can provide transferable insight just beyond the reach of someone unschooled in economic theory.

In the domain of strategic behavior, researchers have identified several regularities that cut across a variety of different settings. People do not appear to think through other people's incentives as thoroughly as they should. In games in which others have dominant actions, people do not always best respond to those dominant actions: they seemingly underestimate other people's rationality. In dynamic settings, people underappreciate the extent to which other people's behavior in the future depends upon what happens in the present. In settings with asymmetric information, this leads people to underestimate the correlation between other people's actions and their hidden information.

Solution concepts that embed these errors, and are written in such a way so as to apply across different settings, will allow economists to see the implications of these errors in a range of environments. These models will allow economists to estimate parameters of traditional interest (e.g., preferences and information) and improve the accuracy of our predictions.[9]

2 Setup and taxonomy of errors

One aim of this chapter is to present different solutions in common notation to facilitate comparisons. I begin by defining games with a degree of generality sufficient for the introduction of all of the different solution concepts in the chapter, using the Bayesian games approach of Harsanyi (1967b). In a Bayesian Game, all of players' uncertainty about payoffs, information, etc. can be summarized through some underlying state of nature about which the players have private information. Let Ω be the set of states of nature, taken to be finite for ease of exposition. Each player k has some private information about the state of nature, which is represented by the partition of Ω denoted by $\mathcal{T}_k$ with typical element t_k.[10] When the state is $\omega \in \Omega$, Player k learns that $\omega \in t_k \in \mathcal{T}_k$. For any given state ω, let $t_k(\omega)$ denote the element $t_k \in \mathcal{T}_k$ with the property that $\omega \in t_k$.

Following Harsanyi, assume that the players share a common prior belief, or have "common priors" over Ω: before learning their types, players share the prior belief that the probability distribution p describes the likelihood of states in Ω.

Consider again the example of Cournot competition from the Introduction, in which firms now have constant marginal costs known only to themselves. Firm 1's marginal cost belongs to $\{c_1, c_1'\}$ and Firm 2's to $\{c_2, c_2'\}$. The state comprises a pair of

---

[9] Rabin (2013) articulates the case for "portable extensions of existing models" that allow economists to add behavioral elements to any textbook economic model.

[10] The assumption that $\mathcal{T}_k$ partitions Ω means that every pair of distinct $t_k, t_k' \in \mathcal{T}_k$ has empty intersection, and $\cup_{t_k \in \mathcal{T}_k} t_k = \Omega$.

marginal costs, and $\Omega = \{(c_1, c_2), (c_1', c_2), (c_1, c_2'), (c_1', c_2')\}$. When Firm 1 knows its own marginal cost but not Firm 2's, then $\mathcal{T}_1 = \{\{(c_1, c_2), (c_1, c_2')\}, \{(c_1', c_2), (c_1', c_2')\}\}$. This means that when Firm 1 learns its marginal cost is c_1, it learns that the state $\omega \in \{(c_1, c_2), (c_1, c_2')\}$; since both possible values of Firm 2's marginal cost belong to that set, Firm 1 does not learn Firm 2's marginal cost.

Let $\{1, 2, \ldots, N\}$ be the set of players of the game.[11] Each Player k in the game has a finite set of available actions, A_k. For simplicity, we assume that A_k does not depend upon t_k: for instance, firms' ability to produce does not depend upon their marginal costs.[12] In a dynamic game such as the Stackelberg game described in the Introduction, the follower, Player 2, has a large set of available "action plans", which specify for every quantity of the leader, a quantity of his own. Most authors refer to these "action plans" as strategies. In this chapter, the term strategy is reserved for a use described below, and the terms "action" and "action plan" are used synonymously. Hence, in a dynamic game, the set A_k consists of all action plans for Player k. Henceforth, let $A = A_1 \times A_2 \times \ldots A_N$.

The players' payoffs depend upon all players' actions, as well as the (possibly unknown) state of nature, $u_k : A \times \Omega \to \mathbb{R}$. A finite Bayesian game is some ordered tuple

$$G = (\Omega, A_1, \ldots, A_N; \mathcal{T}_1, \ldots, \mathcal{T}_N; p; u_1, \ldots, u_N),$$

where the set of players is implicit.

In a Bayesian game, a pure strategy s_k for Player k describes an action to be played in each state, namely $s_k : \Omega \to A_k$, which is measurable with respect to Player k's information partition; formally, for each $t_k \in \mathcal{T}_k$, and each $\omega, \omega' \in t_k$, $s_k(\omega) = s_k(\omega')$. This restricts Player k's chosen action to depend only upon things known to her. Letting $\triangle A_k$ be the set of probability distributions over A_k, a mixed strategy for Player k consists of $\sigma_k : \Omega \to \triangle A_k$, where once again for each $t_k \in \mathcal{T}_k$, and each $\omega, \omega' \in \mathcal{T}_k$, $\sigma_k(\omega) = \sigma_k(\omega')$. Let $\sigma_k(a_k|\omega)$ denote the probability that type Player k plays action a_k given the strategy σ_k in state ω. Let σ_{-k} be the strategies of all players apart from Player k, and $\sigma_{-k}(a_{-k}|\omega)$ be the probability that the players other than k take the action profile $a_{-k} \in A_{-k}$ in state ω.

Let $p(\omega|t_k)$ denote type t_k of Player k's belief that the state is ω conditional on type t_k; in particular, $p(\omega|t_k) := \frac{p(\omega)}{\sum_{\omega' \in t_k} p(\omega')}$. Players in Bayesian games face two sources of uncertainty: they do not know the state ω, nor do they know one another's chosen actions. To maximize her expected payoffs, type t_k of Player k would like to know the joint distribution of a_{-k} and ω. Because many models to be discussed

---

[11] This chapter adopts the convention of referring to odd-indexed players as "she" and even-indexed players as "he".

[12] Certain solution concepts impose this restriction to prevent players from holding beliefs inconsistent with the structure of the game. For example, consider a Hollywood studio that chooses whether to screen its film before auctioning the distribution rights (Forsythe et al., 1989), or wait until after the auction to show the film. When the studio screens *Moonlight*, distributors cannot plausibly believe that they are bidding for *La La Land*.

revolve around people neglecting the correlation between a_{-k} and ω, it is useful to write payoffs in a way that highlights this relationship.

Define $\overline{\sigma}_{-k}(t_k(\omega)) := \sum_{\omega' \in \Omega} p(\omega'|t_k(\omega))\sigma_{-k}(\omega')$, and $\overline{\sigma}_{-k}(a_{-k}|t_k(\omega))$ to be the probability that $\overline{\sigma}_{-k}(t_k(\omega))$ assigns to a_{-k}. From the perspective of type $t_k(\omega)$ of Player k, $\overline{\sigma}_{-k}(a_{-k}|t_k(\omega))$ describes the probability that players other than k use the action profile a_{-k} given that they follow the strategies σ_{-k}. In a Bayesian Nash equilibrium of the game G, in each state ω, Player k plays a_k with positive probability only when it solves

$$\max_{a_k \in A_k} \sum_{\omega' \in \Omega} \sum_{a_{-k} \in A_{-k}} p(\omega'|t_k(\omega))\sigma_{-k}(a_{-k}|\omega')u_k(a_k, a_{-k}; \omega').$$

The expected payoff to type $t_k(\omega)$ of Player k from playing action a_k when the other players use strategies σ_{-k} can be written as

$$\sum_{a_{-k} \in A_{-k}} \underbrace{\overline{\sigma}_{-k}(a_{-k}|t_k(\omega))}_{\text{opponents' predicted actions}} \sum_{\omega' \in \Omega} \underbrace{\Pr[\omega'|a_{-k}, t_k(\omega)]}_{\text{inference given actions}} \times \underbrace{u_k(a_k, a_{-k}; \omega')}_{\text{payoff}},$$

where $\Pr[\omega|a_{-k}, t_k]$ is the probability of state ω when the other players play actions a_{-k}, and Player k has type t_k. Note that $\Pr[\omega|a_{-k}, t_k]$ depends both upon the prior p and the other players' strategies σ_{-k}.

Assuming that the players know the game's payoffs as well as have correct probabilistic beliefs about the state of nature, they can err in three conceptually distinct ways. Firstly, someone may misjudge the probabilities with which her opponents choose different action profiles. In the formal language above, type t_k of Player k may misappraise $\overline{\sigma}_{-k}(a_{-k}|t_k)$. For example, in a static bargaining problem in which a proposer makes a take-it-or-leave-it offer to a responder, the proposer may misjudge the responder's likelihood of accepting different offers.[13] In our dynamic Stackelberg game, the leader may hold wrong beliefs about how the follower would react to different quantity choices q_1. In particular, the proposer may fail to do backwards induction. This falls under the category of failure to predict actions because actions in dynamic games refer to action plans.

Secondly, a player may fail to properly infer the other players' private information from their actions. In the language above, Player k could hold wrong beliefs about $\Pr[\omega'|a_{-k}, t_k(\omega)]$. Consider a wealth adviser who may or may not receive direct compensation for selling Fund A to a client. The adviser recommends either Fund A or bonds to the client. In a Bayesian Nash equilibrium, the client correctly perceives the relationship between the advisor's recommendation and her financial interest. An imperfectly rational investor instead might overlook this relationship, namely underinfer. The client could even get the relationship backward, namely misinfer.

---

[13] Likewise, the responder might mispredict the likelihood that the proposer makes different offers. But because the responder observes the proposer's offer, this would not matter.

Players may misjudge $\Pr[\omega|a_{-k}, t_k]$ for an entirely different reason. Rather than commit any error of inference, they may simply hold the wrong priors, or update their beliefs incorrectly based upon their private information. In the simple case in which a_{-k} does not vary with ω, then $\Pr[\omega|a_{-k}, t_k] = p(\omega|t_k)$. In this case, a player whose only error is to muddle the relationship between ω and a_{-k} would not commit an error, for there is no relationship to muddle. This player could, however, confuse $p(\omega|t_k)$ for any number of reasons—many of which are covered in Daniel Benjamin's chapter in this volume—including overconfidence, confirmatory bias, anchoring, etc. Whereas such errors do not make up the focus of this chapter, some are discussed as alternative hypotheses to errors in inference.

Finally, Player k might fail to best respond to her beliefs. Students and researchers who perfectly understand the consequences of their errors commit errors all the same, all the time. One interesting reason for which people may fail to best respond to their beliefs is that they may not hold consistent, unitary beliefs. When asked to predict whether a wealth adviser would be more apt to recommend Fund A when paid for doing so, few clients would hesitate to say yes. At some level, people understand that money incentivizes other people. Yet this does not mean that clients appreciate how a wealth advisor's recommendation of a fund signals her own stake in the matter. In a sense, people may hold two separate kinds of beliefs: those they use when explicitly thinking through the logic of others' actions, and those that they implicitly use when choosing their own actions.

Based on evidence that people err systematically in all three domains, economists have introduced solution concepts that embed such errors. The next three sections of this chapter explore each of these errors in sequence.

3 Mispredicting actions

Anyone trying to work out what to do in a strategic environment should reason about how others will act. In a Nash equilibrium, each player correctly predicts others' actions for all contingencies that arise; that is, they predict what others will do along the equilibrium path of play. People may err at such predictions in simple static games: a child, for instance, might mispredict the frequency of another child's actions when playing Hide-and-Seek. People also may err in dynamic games: a Stackelberg leader might mispredict how the follower will react to its quantity choice.

Researchers have modeled errors in predicting actions in two fundamentally different ways. A first approach builds off standard equilibrium concepts like Nash equilibrium and SPNE, and either relaxes some equilibrium condition or embeds some particular form of error. Models in this vein sometimes appeal to learning foundations: the solution concept is regarded as a rest point of some learning process. A second approach eschews equilibrium reasoning in favor of positing that people in novel environments introspect to develop theories of others' behavior, and then best respond to these theories. Different forms of introspection generate different predictions. The comparative advantage of the first approach lies in environments with

Table 1 Battle of the classes.

	B	S
B	2, −1	0, 0
S	0, −2	1, 2

which people have some basic familiarity or structural understanding, but where they misunderstand or neglect some important feature. The comparative advantage of the second approach comes in novel settings in which people fare badly at predicting others' behavior.

To better understand how people might introspect about others' reasoning, and reach the wrong conclusion, it is worthwhile to review reasons why people should correctly predict the actions of other people. In certain repeated settings, people might learn how others behave through repeated observation. After playing some number of points, Björn Borg might learn how frequently John McEnroe serves to his left versus to his right. In other cases, people might arrive at correct beliefs about others' behavior through introspection. In still other settings, might people combine an understanding of the preferences and information that characterize the game at hand with things they have learned in related, but distinct, settings. The buyer of a used car might understand from first principles that the seller likes money, and consequently would accept a higher offer with higher likelihood. From an internet search, she may have learned typical trading prices for the make and model of car. The buyer's predictions of the seller's behavior therefore combine learning with theory.

How might introspection lead players to correctly predict one another's actions? A rational person never chooses the action a over a second action b if b always delivers a higher payoff, regardless of how everyone else behaves. In the language of game theory, the action $a \in A_k$ is strictly dominated for Player k if some (possibly mixed) action $b \in A_k$ gives Player k a higher expected payoff, regardless of others' behavior. Rational people never play strictly dominated strategies.

Do players who know that their opponents are rational correctly predict their opponents' behavior? Let us begin with a complete-information game $G = (A_1, \ldots, A_N; u_1, \ldots, u_N)$ that lacks any uncertainty over players' payoffs or information. For each player k, eliminate those actions from A_k that are strictly dominated to form the new game $\tilde{G} = (\tilde{A}_1, \ldots, \tilde{A}_N; u_1, \ldots, u_N)$. Whenever A_k is nonempty, the set $\tilde{A}_k$ of undominated actions also must be nonempty, for it is impossible that for any $a, a' \in A_k$, a always gives higher payoffs than a', and vice versa. Thus $\tilde{G}$ itself describes a new game. If each player k not only is rational but also believes that every other player is rational, then she will play an action in $\tilde{A}_k$ that itself is undominated given that all other players play actions in the sets $\tilde{A}_j$.

In the game displayed in Table 1, Players 1 and 2 simultaneously choose classes at the gym, either Boxing (B) or Spinning (S), without the aid of any communication technology. Player 1 (who chooses rows) most wants to meet Player 2 for boxing class. But Player 2 (who chooses columns) abhors boxing, and most wants to coordinate on spinning. Because B is dominated for Player 2, he will, if rational, attend

Table 2 Costa Gomes et al.'s (2001) Game 6A.

	L	M	R
U	21, 26	52, 73	75, 44
D	88, 55	25, 30	59, 81

Table 3 Shelling's coordination game.

	Grand Central	Times Square
Grand Central	2, 2	0, 0
Times Square	0, 0	1, 1

spinning class. A rational Player 1 who appreciates that Player 2 is rational also then attends spinning. This game is said to be "dominance solvable" because the process of "iterated elimination of dominated actions" leads to a unique action for each player.

In games that have more available actions, higher levels of reasoning about rationality can eliminate more actions. Table 2 presents a game from Costa Gomes et al. (2001). In it, L is dominated for the column player. Given that a rational Column will never play L, a rational Row who believes that Column is rational will never play D. Finally, a rational Column who (i) believes that Row is rational and (ii) believes that Row believes that Column is rational, will choose M.

In games with finite sets of available actions, this procedure must terminate after a finite number of rounds. Rational players do not play actions eliminated in the first round, as described above. Rational players who believe that all other players are rational do not play actions eliminated in the second round, as in the example above. Rational players who believe that others are rational and that others believe that all are rational do not play actions eliminated in the third round, and so forth. The players are said to have common knowledge of rationality whenever each is rational, each knows that all are rational, each knows that all know that all are rational, etc. Whenever it is common knowledge that the players are rational, no player will play an action eliminated by iterated elimination of strictly dominated actions. For each player, the set of actions that survive iterated elimination of strictly dominated actions is the largest set consistent with common knowledge of rationality.

Whilst some games are dominance solvable, many games are not, and the set of actions for each player surviving iterated elimination of dominated actions will be quite large relative to the players' action spaces. Consider the following example, drawn from Schelling's (1984) famous work on focal points and described in Table 3. Two tourists in New York City without mobile phones wish to coordinate on a meeting spot for lunch. Their choices are to meet in the lobby of Grand Central Station or at Times Square. Each prefers the grandeur of Grand Central to the hurly-burly of Times Square but wants above all to meet: she receives a payoff of 2 for meeting at Grand Central, 1 for meeting at Times Square, and 0 for not meeting. There are two pure-strategy Nash equilibria of this game, in addition to a mixed-strategy equilibrium in which the two parties connect with probability five-ninths.

Because neither action in this game is strictly dominated, iterated elimination of strictly dominated actions does nothing to the game. Common knowledge of rationality does not have any implications in this setting. It is rational for Player 1 to go to Grand Central Station if she expects Player 2 to also go there. Such beliefs are consistent with Player 2 being rational whenever Player 2 expects Player 1 to go to Grand Central. The beliefs of Player 2 about Player 1's action are consistent with Player 1 being rational if Player 1 expects Player 2 to go to Grand Central Station, etc. In this way, Player 1 choosing to go to Grand Central Station is consistent with common knowledge of rationality. However, for an exactly analogous reason, Player 2 choosing to go to Times Square is consistent with common knowledge of rationality. Thus, common knowledge of rationality does not preclude that the couple meet with probability zero.

Bernheim (1984) and Pearce (1984) approach the question of how players should reason about other players' actions in a different way. A rational player should hold beliefs about what other players will do, possibly probabilistic, and best respond to those beliefs. Therefore, an action that is never a weak best response to others' behavior—that is, not a weak best response to any beliefs about others' play—will not be played by a rational actor. Consider the two-player game $G = (A_1, A_2; u_1, u_2)$. Define $\tilde{A}_k^0 = A_k$, and for $n \in \mathbb{N}$,

$$\tilde{A}_k^n = \{a_k \in \tilde{A}_k^{n-1} : \exists \alpha_j \in \Delta\left(\tilde{A}_j^{n-1}\right) \ s.t. \ \forall a_k' \in \tilde{A}_k^{n-1}, u_k(\alpha_j, a_k) \geq u_k(\alpha_j, a_k')\}, \tag{1}$$

those actions for Player k in $\tilde{A}_k^{n-1}$ that weakly best respond to some beliefs about how Player j might choose from $\tilde{A}_j^{n-1}$.

The action a_i for Player i is *k-rationalizable* if $a_i \in \cap_{n=0}^k \tilde{A}_i^n$. When $k = 1$, this means that Player i's action best responds to some beliefs about Player j. When $k = 2$, this means that Player i's action best responds to some beliefs about Player j consistent with j playing a best response to some beliefs about i's action. The action a_i is k-rationalizable if it is a best response to some (mixed) action of Player 2, which itself is a best response to some (mixed) action of Player 1, which itself is a best response to some (mixed) action of Player 2, and so forth up to k times. The action a_i for Player i is rationalizable if $a_i \in \cap_{n=0}^\infty \tilde{A}_i^n$. An action for Player 1 in a two-player game is "rationalizable" if it is a best response to some (mixed) action of Player 2, which itself is a best response to some (mixed) action of Player 1, which itself is a best response to some (mixed) action of Player 2, etc. In two-player games, Bernheim (1984) and Pearce's (1984) concept of "rationalizabilty" is equivalent to iterated elimination of dominated strategies. Hence, for the game in Table 3, both actions are rationalizable for both players. Thus, rationality—or even common knowledge of rationality—does not imply Nash equilibrium.[14]

---

[14] Nash equilibrium requires not only some form of rationality but also some coordination in players' beliefs. Aumann and Brandenburger (1995) provide a set of epistemic conditions for Nash equilibrium. The

Table 4 Kneeland's (2015) games.

Game 1	c	d		Game 2	c	d
a	15, 5	0, 10		a	15, 10	0, 5
b	5, 0	10, 5		b	5, 5	10, 0

3.1 Lab evidence

3.1.1 Reasoning about others' rationality

Rational players avoid dominated actions. People who perceive that others are rational recognize that others do not play dominated actions. In other words, in a complete-information game, a Player k who recognizes that others are rational should assign zero probability to $\overline{\sigma}_k(a_{-k})$ whenever for some $j \neq k$, a_j is dominated for Player j and is j's action in a_{-k}.

Do people recognize that others avoid dominated actions? In the game presented in Table 2 and an isomorphic game, Costa Gomes et al. (2001) find that only 62% of subjects play according to equilibrium. Kneeland (2015) pinpoints where players err through a very clever set of experiments. In Game 1 of Table 4 (taken from Kneeland, 2015), the row player does not have a dominant action. However, for the column player, c is dominated. If Row appreciates that Column is rational, then she should understand that Column will play d; if Row is rational as well, then she should play b. Now consider Game 2 in the table. Row's payoffs have not changed. But Column's dominant action has changed to c. If Row is rational and appreciates that Column is rational as well, then Row should play a. A Row who switches from b to a across games and therefore not only acts rationally but also recognizes Column's rationality. By contrast, Kneeland posits that a Row who is merely rational should hold beliefs about Column that do not vary across the two games. Intuitively, a Row who is merely rational would have no reason to believe, for example, Column plays d with probability $\frac{2}{3}$ in Game 1 but only with probability $\frac{1}{3}$ in Game 2, beliefs that would lead Row to choose b in Game 1 and a in Game 2.

Kneeland finds that whereas 93% of subjects are rational, only 74% of subjects perceive others as rational. That is, 26% of subjects fail to appreciate that (nearly all) others avoid playing dominated actions. This suggests that one-quarter of people doubt that others are rational or simply do not think through the implications of other people's rationality. In summary, one reason why people mispredict other people's actions seems to be that they do not think through how those other people should behave if rational.

Without access to data on past choices, people need information about other people's preferences to accurately predict these other people's behavior. Johnson et al.

---

simplest case is a that of a pure-strategy Nash equilibrium in a two-player game. Whenever both players know that they play (a_1, a_2), and both players are rational, then (a_1, a_2) must be a Nash equilibrium.

(2002) provide evidence that people do not always bother to learn their opponents' payoffs, even in rather simple games. They conduct experiments on a three-period, alternating-offer bargaining game, in which the pie available for division shrinks in every period, which is suggestive of the type of discounting due to impatience that economists use in many dynamic models. Subjects are told the size of the pie in the first period, but must click on boxes in the computer interface "Mouse Track" to uncover the size of the pie in later periods. Camerer et al. find that 19% do not look at the period-2 pie size, and 10% do not look at the period-3 pie size. Clearly, these subjects who do not look up others' payoffs cannot be reasoning via backwards induction; indeed, these subjects deviate most from SPNE.

Nagel (1995) introduces the p-beauty pageant, inspired by Keynes' famous comparison of financial markets to a fictitious newspaper "beauty contest" in which people are asked to choose the prettiest face yet rewarded for guessing the most popular reply.

> *"It is not a case of choosing those [faces] that, to the best of one's judgment, are really the prettiest, nor even those that average opinion genuinely thinks the prettiest. We have reached the third degree where we devote our intelligences to anticipating what average opinion expects the average opinion to be. And there are some, I believe, who practice the fourth, fifth and higher degrees."*
> **Keynes, *The General Theory of Employment, Interest and Money*, 1936**

In Nagel's game, each player chooses an integer between 0 and 100. The person who guesses closest to p times the average integer wins a prize. (In the event of a tie, the prize gets split evenly amongst those closest to p times the average.) Everyone else earns zero. Because its payoffs have a fixed sum, the p-beauty pageant falls into the category of zero-sum games.[15] Social preferences are unlikely to affect behavior in games such as the p-beauty pageant where people play for a fixed prize. Consequently, when people fail to play according to Nash equilibrium, they commit some form of error.

The p-beauty pageant has a unique rationalizable action for each player. Take the case where $p = \frac{1}{2}$. Since the average cannot exceed 100, choosing 50 does at least as well as choosing any number above 50. But then a rational player who knows that others are rational will conclude that the average will not exceed 50, in which case choosing 25 does at least as well as choosing any number above 25. Iterating this argument six times yields the conclusion that each player should play 0.[16]

Nagel (1995) provided the first of many experiments with this game. In her experiments, subjects' initial responses had spikes at $50p^k$, for $k = 0, 1, 2, \ldots$, with a

---

[15] The equivalence between fixed- and zero-sum games follows from the observation that adding a constant to all payoffs does not change equilibrium behavior.

[16] The game is also dominance solvable. Solving for Nash equilibrium requires few steps. Let $\bar{a}_{-k}$ be the average guess of players other than k. When $p = \frac{1}{2}$ Player k best responds by playing $a_k^* = \frac{1}{2}\bar{a}_{-k}$. With many players, $\bar{a}_{-k} \approx \bar{a}$, the average of all players' actions, which gives the approximation $a_k^* = \frac{1}{2}\bar{a}$. Since all players are symmetric, $a^* = \frac{1}{2}a^*$, namely all players choose 0 in the unique Nash equilibrium.

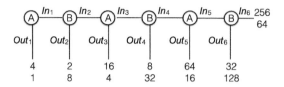

FIGURE 1

Centipede game.

median of 17 and mean of 27. Because someone who correctly predicts the mean should choose 13.5, the data reveal that a substantial majority of subjects either have trouble dividing by two or incorrectly predict others' actions.

Capra et al. (1999) run experiments using a game called the "Traveler's Dilemma", developed by Basu (1994). Basu tells the story of two tourists who bought identical souvenirs and packed them into their luggage, which the airline then lost. Knowing that the two bags have identical value, the airline offers to pay both parties their minimum claim. To deter over-claiming, the airline pays the lower claimant (if unique) R, which is deducted from the higher claimant's payout. In the experiments, claims take the forms of integers in $\{80, 81, \ldots, 200\}$, with $R > 1$ varying by treatment. The unique rationalizable outcome of the game is 80, irrespective of the value of $R > 1$. The reason is that if Person 1 claims a higher amount, say 81, then she must believe that Person 2 claims 82 with positive probability, which in turn requires that he believe that Person 1 claims 83 with positive probability, and so forth all the way up to 200, which is never a weak best response. Capra et al. (1999) find that for $R = 5, 10$, subjects play quite close to the top of the range, 200. By contrast, for larger values of $R = 50, 80$, they play very close to 80.

Fig. 1 shows a particular form of a perfect-information extensive-form game that is known as the Centipede Game, which was introduced by Rosenthal (1981) and first experimentally analyzed by McKelvey and Palfrey (1992). At nodes labeled A, Player A chooses between playing *Out* and ending the game of *In* and continuing, and likewise for Player B. The total payoffs double at each stage of the game, but the identity of the player receiving the larger share changes from one stage to the next. When Player B is rational, he will play Out_6 anytime the game gets that far. A Player A who correctly predicts Player B's choice at the game's final node–whether because Player A believes that Player B is rational or for some other reason—will play Out_5. This process of "backwards induction" leads to the unique outcome Out_1 with payoffs 4, 1.[17]

Many authors have analyzed play in the Centipede game. McKelvey and Palfrey (1992) find that only about 5% of games end with Out_1, as predicted by backwards induction and SPNE. Levitt et al. (2011) recruited pairs of chess masters at a chess tournament to play the Centipede Game and another related game against each others.

---

[17] The unique SPNE in this game has each player play out at each node.

Table 5 The Prisoners' Dilemma and Harmony Games.

Prisoners' Dilemma (PD)			Harmony Game (HG)		
	C	D		C	D
C	9, 9	3, 11	C	8, 8	2, 7
D	11, 3	5, 5	D	7, 2	1, 1

Successful strategizing in chess requires the use of backwards induction, so master chess players ought to perform well in this experiment. However, Levitt et al. (2011) find that only about 4% of chess masters finish the game in Out_1, with over half of games ending in Out_4 or Out_5.

Levitt et al. (2011) suggest that players in the Centipede game cooperate due to social preferences. Over one-third of Player B's eligible to move at the game's final node choose In_6, which entails voluntarily giving up 64 in order that her co-player gain 224. Note, however, that this generosity appears to surprise the last mover's co-player, for a Player A who anticipated B's choice frequency at the last node would rationally play In_5 (as $64 < \frac{1}{3}256 + \frac{2}{3}32 = 106\frac{2}{3}$); anticipating this, Player B would himself play In_4; etc. To the extent that social preferences do in fact influence choices in this game, players appear to underestimate their influence, and to mispredict one another's action plans.

Dal Bó et al. (2018) provide evidence that people fail to appreciate how other people's actions adapt to changes in environment by exploring voting over two games in Table 5. The Harmony Game can be derived from the Prisoner's Dilemma by taxing C by 1 and D by 4. Cell by cell, the Harmony Game gives lower payoffs than the Prisoner's Dilemma. Whereas D is a dominant action in the PD, C is dominant in the HG.

Consider a player who has played the PD a few times and settled into a D,D outcome. The player is now called upon to decide whether to change "policy" and switch to playing the HG. In any SPNE of the game where the "decider" first selects one of the two games, before both players play the chosen game, the decider must choose the Harmony Game: payoffs in the dominant-strategy equilibrium of the HG are 8, whereas they are only 5 in the PD. Indeed, so long as the decider is rational, and appreciates that the other player is rational, she must opt for the HG.

More generally, a decider who believes that the other player's probability of playing D in the HG will be at least 50 percentage points less than in the HG will prefer to play HG. Conversely, someone who has been playing C,C in the HG and has the opportunity to switch to the PD should accept so long as she expects the other player's probability of playing D to rise by no more than 50 percentage points. Dal Bó et al. (2018) find that a majority of subjects prefer to play PD, irrespective of whether they began by playing PD or HG.[18] Moreover, by eliciting subjects' beliefs about how

---

[18] These findings do not depend upon the voting rule used to select the games. Here this is presented as dictatorship, whilst the paper considers random dictatorship and majoritarian elections.

their co-players will play each of the two games, they establish that those subjects who believe that behavior will be most similar across the two games are most apt to vote for the Prisoner's Dilemma.

3.2 Field evidence

Many researchers have replicated Nagel's (1995) qualitative findings in the p-beauty pageant. These replications have taken a number of forms, most notably field experiments reported by Bosch-Domènech Montalvo et al. (2002). Subjects in these experiments were recruited through advertisements in three newspapers, the *Financial Times*, *Spektrum der Wissenchaft*, and *Expansión*, with each newspaper version being its own treatment. The three treatments had 1476, 2728, and 3696 participants, respectively, who mailed in their guesses in the hopes of winning substantial prizes. Like in Nagel's original experiment, subjects played very far from Nash equilibrium, and a large number of people played $50p$ and $50p^2$.

In games that are not dominance solvable, players may learn how others act by repeated observation of past actions. One realm where this occurs is professional sports. In tennis, players mix between serving into the two sides of the service box in order to keep their opponents at bay. Walker and Wooders (2001) explore whether tennis players play Nash equilibria by testing whether the server wins the same fraction of points when placing the first serve to the left as to the right. Because in each match, two players serve in two different directions (ad versus deuce courts, where lefty servers usually have an advantage serving into the ad court and righty servers into the deuce court), they split their data from ten Wimbledon Gentlemen's Singles finals into forty bins. In only one of those forty do Walker and Wooders reject the hypothesis of equal win percentages from serving left or right.[19]

A server who predictably mixes between left and right hands his opponent an advantage. Walker and Wooders test whether the location of servers is independent across time. If it is not, then either the receiver has wrong beliefs by failing to appreciate the time-dependence, or the server fails to best respond to the receiver's strategy. They reject the hypothesis of independence at the 5% level on their sample: servers alternate too much to be independent. Regrettably, Walkers and Wooders do not explore whether returners appreciate the correlation in serves. This could be done by looking at whether serving right pays off the same as serving left, conditional on past serves. For instance, someone who served right in the first point should be as often to win the second point serving left or right. A finding of a lower likelihood of winning with (R, L) than (R, R) would suggest that the receiver has indeed detected the correlation. In any event, Walker and Wooders' work shows that even with some of the highest stakes imaginable, the most experienced professionals still err systematically.[20]

---

[19] The players only send 6% of their serves up the center; including these would not affect the results.

[20] Gauriot et al. (2016) perform a similar analysis with a much larger dataset and find that professional women's players, but not men's players, alternate their serves too much. Palacios-Huerta (2003) analyzes

Simonsohn (2010) examines when buyers and sellers participate in eBay auctions for DVDs. He finds that 25% of bids take place from 5 to 9 p.m., whilst 37% of sellers time their auctions to end during these hours (often paying additional transaction costs to do so). He interprets this as evidence that sellers target times when demand is high—buyers like to shop online after work—but neglect that their competitors reason the same way. Consequently, sellers are 5 to 13 percentage points less likely to sell during those hours, at prices that are 4–6% lower. The fact that sellers of high-value bundled DVDs are as apt to during this period as low-value sellers suggests that the cost of seller's time does not explain the finding.[21]

3.3 Models

3.3.1 The Level-k model

The Level-k model describes non-equilibrium reasoning. Unlike Nash equilibrium, it does not rely on the assumption that people correctly anticipate others' actions. Indeed, Level-k practitioners aspire to capture people's initial responses to novel strategic situations. They argue that when players have not had the opportunity to learn from past behavior how others will choose their actions, they can only reach Nash equilibrium by means of difficult fixed-point reasoning, which seems implausible.

The Level-k model takes as its premise that people do at most k levels of reasoning. Specifically, the model put forward by Stahl and Wilson (1994) and Nagel (1995) goes as follows. A Level-0 type of Player i mixes over all actions in A_i according to some fixed distribution, which is typically taken to be the uniform distribution.[22] For $k \geq 1$, a Level-k player best responds to beliefs that all other players have level $k - 1$. Like k-rationalizability, the Level-k model is defined recursively and parameterized by an integer that represents players' depth of reasoning. Unlike k-rationalizability, the Level-k model typically offers unique predictions for any given k; it offers a se-

---

penalty-kicking in soccer. He finds that kickers score with equal frequency on average regardless of which side they target, and that kicks are serially independent.

[21] However, the paper does not test the hypothesis of seller error directly by auctioning off DVDs in the two markets and comparing prices. Consider the following simple example. Bidders have values $v \sim U[0, 1]$. During the day, there are 3 bidders and 1 seller. The auction takes the form of an ascending auction. With 3 bidders and 1 seller, the pivotal bidder has the median value, and the average revenue is $\frac{1}{2}$. Suppose that nighttime brings 5 bidders and 2 sellers. Like in Simonsohn's data, the proportion of sellers, 67% (2 of 3), who operate by night exceeds that of buyers, 62.5% (5 of 8). With 5 bidders and 2 sellers, the pivotal bidder again holds the median value, and the average revenue is again $\frac{1}{2}$. Now consider an entrant seller. Where should she sell? Simple intuition suggests indifference: both markets have the same average price. But a more careful reasoning suggests the larger market, since the entrant will lower the price by less in a thicker market. This intuition turns out to be correct. If the entrant enters the first market, the average revenue falls to $\frac{1}{4}$; if she enters the second market, it only falls to $\frac{1}{3}$. (On average, the third highest of three random variables distributed on $[0, 1]$ takes the expected value of $\frac{1}{4}$, while the fourth highest of five random variables distributed on $[0, 1]$ takes the expected value of $\frac{1}{3}$.)

[22] Practitioners do, however, often tailor the Level-0 distribution to the application.

lection from the set of k-rationalizable actions. It also has the advantage of being extremely tractable.

In some games, the Level-k model yields Nash equilibrium for small values of k. In the Prisoner's Dilemma, for example, Defect is a dominant strategy and thus chosen for all $k \geq 1$. Hence, players who are at least Level 1's in the Prisoner's Dilemma play Nash equilibrium. In other games, however, the Level-k model makes predictions very different than those of Nash equilibrium.

Consider again Nagel's (1995) p-beauty pageant. Players who uniformly mixed over all actions would on average play 50. Players who choose 25 play best a best response to the average being 50; they appear to be Level 1's. Players who play 12.5 play a best response to the average being 25; they appear to be Level 2's.[23] Alternatively, a player might play 12.5 because she believes that other players are rational and hence do not choose more than 50, and then that other players randomize uniformly over the remaining interval [0, 50]. In general, the Level-k predictions coincide with those of "$k - 1$ dominance", whereby players do $k - 1$ rounds of iterated deletion of strictly dominated actions and best respond to a uniform distribution over the remaining actions. Costa Gomes and Crawford (2006) explore behavior in asymmetric guessing games that allow them to cleanly separate these two hypotheses and find far more subjects adhering to Level-k than to dominance or indeed other models (Nash players, or people who best respond to the empirical distribution of play). Amongst those players identified as Level-k players, 20 of 35 (57%) are Level 1, 12 of 35 (34%) are Level 2, and 3 of 35 (9%) are Level 3.

The higher is k, the more behavior resembles Nash. Indeed, whenever the predictions of the Level-k model converge, they converge to a Nash equilibrium. That is, let a^1 be the (generically unique) Level-1 action profile, a^2 be the (generically unique) Level-2 action profile, etc. Whenever the sequence $a^k \to \hat{a}$, $\hat{a}$ is a Nash equilibrium. Notice thought that behavior in the Level-k model need not converge, as in asymmetric matching pennies.

In the p-beauty pageant, Nash equilibrium can be found by identifying the a such that $\frac{1}{2}a = a$. Alternatively, given that guesses are restricted to the integers, the Nash equilibrium can be computed by iterating a best-response operator some large but finite number of times, which seems almost equally implausible.

In the Level-k model, someone of type k believes that all of her opponents are of type $k - 1$. What if they are not so sure about their opponents' rationality? A Level-k type might believe that some opponents are Level $k - 1$, others are Level $k - 2$, etc. Camerer et al. (2004) propose such a model, which they call the "Cognitive-Hierarchy Model". The Cognitive-Hierarchy Model posits a distribution over cognitive types k, with probability mass function $f(k)$, and cdf $F(k)$. Each type k believes that the other players have Levels $0, 1, \ldots, k - 1$ with probabilities $\frac{f(0)}{F(k-1)}, \frac{f(1)}{F(k-1)}, \ldots, \frac{f(k-1)}{F(k-1)}$, respectively. In this way, a Level 2 might believe that she faces some mixture of Level 0

---

[23] As defined above, Level-0 players should mix uniformly over all actions and not primarily play 50, as needed to explain the disproportionate number of such choices in Nagel's data.

and Level 1's. Camerer et al. (2004) propose that the distribution of types follow a Poisson distribution, in which case the model has just one parameter to estimate.

The Level-k model is most convincing in complete-information games in which it might reasonably describe a theory of mind. People in certain strategic situations, particularly zero-sum ones like the p-beauty pageant, really sometimes do try to predict their opponents' actions by putting themselves in the other party's shoes and then attempt to stay one step ahead. (It is much harder to imagine that people actively reason according to the Cognitive-Hierarchy Model due to the difficulty in best responding to mixed distributions over others' actions.)

In other settings, however, where people want to be predictable, the Level-k model can rest on too much irrationality in the form of Level 0. Consider two firms competing in a procurement auction to supply some account. The client has no inherent preference over the two bidders and wishes to choose the lowest bidder. However, a Level-1 bidder believes that the client would choose randomly between the two bids, regardless of their amounts. To make things concrete, suppose that bids must come in the form of dollars and cents between 1.00 and 100.00, and that the service costs suppliers nothing to provide. Regarding all bids as equally likely to be accepted, a Level-1 bidder would bid 100.00. Then a Level 2 would bid 99.99, and a Level 3 99.98, etc. For the values of k typically estimated in the literature $k = 1, 2, 3$, bids would cluster near their maximum feasible value. This seems unlikely, and far less plausible than the Nash prediction of 1.00.[24]

Of course, the predictions of the Level-k model change with the specification of Level 0. Incorporating greater rationality into the specification of Level 0 for the buyer would lead to more conventional predictions about bidding in the simple procurement auction. Indeed, researchers frequently tailor their choice of Level-0 to the environment, which is both a feature and a bug of the model. On the one hand, the extra degree of freedom allows researchers to sensibly apply the Level-k model to a greater number of domains. On the other hand, it adds an element of artistry to application of the model. Certainly, the Level-k model would benefit from a theory of Level 0 that would apply across domains.

3.3.2 Self-confirming equilibrium

Fudenberg and Kreps (1998) and Fudenberg and Levine (1993) introduce the concept of a "Self-Confirming equilibrium (SCE)" to allow for players of extensive form games to mispredict one another's actions off the equilibrium path. SCE is motivated by an incomplete-learning story: players who repeatedly play the same game ought to learn how other players will behave along equilibrium path, whereas they need not learn correct beliefs off the equilibrium path.[25]

---

[24] Crawford and Iriberri (2007) make the case that the Level-k model captures a variety of anomalous behaviors in private- and common-values auctions. In these auctions, the seller's role is automated: the fact that the highest bidder wins is simply folded into the payoff function.

[25] Spiegler (2005) proposes an interesting solution concept for infinitely repeated games in which players hold correct off-equilibrium-path beliefs because they have previously tested one another's threats.

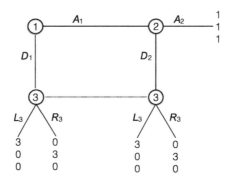

FIGURE 2

Selten's horse.

Fudenberg and Kreps (1998) illustrate SCE in the game of Fig. 2. Player 1 first decides whether to play A_1 or D_1. If she chooses A_1, then Player 2 chooses between A_2 or D_2. When Player 3 gets the opportunity to move, she does not know whether she is at the left or right decision node. In every Nash equilibrium, Player 1 or Player 2 must choose D. The reason is that they must hold correct and hence common beliefs about Player 3's action. Whenever Player 3 plays L_3 with probability greater than one-third, Player 1 wants to play D_1; whenever Player 3 plays L_3 with probability less than two-thirds, Player 2 wants to play D_2. Since at least one of these cases must hold true, at least one player must choose D.

Fudenberg and Kreps (1998) argue that (A_1, A_2) may be a reasonable outcome of a learning process. Why should Players 1 and 2 agree on Player 3's action plan if their own equilibrium behavior bars Player 3 from acting? In a self-confirming equilibrium, players must hold correct beliefs about others' actions along the equilibrium path, but can hold any form of incorrect beliefs about how other players might behave off the equilibrium path. In this way, self-confirming equilibrium allows players to mispredict others' action plans.[26]

Self-confirming equilibrium differs from other solution concepts in this section for two reasons. First, it does not guide researchers as to how people might mispredict one another's actions off the equilibrium path. Second, and more importantly, people only mispredict what would happen in contingencies that never arise in equilibrium.

---

[26] In two-player games, the set of self-confirming equilibria induces the same set of outcomes as the set of Nash equilibrium. The rationale is simple. Let σ^1, Player 1's strategy in some SCE, prescribe something different than Player 2's beliefs, σ^1_2, about Player 1's strategies in that SCE. In a SCE, σ^1 agrees with σ^1_2 on the equilibrium path. This means that σ^1_2 best responds to σ^2, Player 2's SCE strategy, since σ^1 does as well. Making the same argument the other way around, we see that (σ^1_2, σ^1_1) is a Nash equilibrium of the game.

3.3.3 Analogy-based-expectations equilibrium

Jehiel (2005) defines "analogy-based expectations equilibrium" in complete information games to embody the idea that people under-appreciate the extent to which other players' future actions depend upon the history of the game. Defining the concept requires introducing some extra terminology for extensive-form games. For simplicity, we consider two-player, complete-information, finitely-repeated games: in each period, both players choose actions simultaneously, having observed all past choices.

Define $G^T = (A_1, A_2; g_1, g_2)$ to be the T-fold repetition of the complete-information stage game G, in which Player k has the finite action space A_k and payoff function $g_k : A_1 \times A_2 \to \mathbb{R}$. In each period of the game, each player chooses some distribution over actions in the stage game; this choice can depend upon the history of the game in any way. Let $H^0 = Null$, $H^t = H^{t-1} \times (A_1 \times A_2)$ and $H = \cup_{t < T} H^t$, the set of all non-terminal histories of the repeated game.

A (behavioral) action plan for Player k specifies a mixture over A_k following any history: $\sigma_k : H \to \triangle A_k$. Let $\sigma_k^h(a_k)$ be the probability that σ_k assigns to a_k after history h. Let $\pi^\sigma(h)$ be the probability of reaching h when players use the profile of action plans σ.

Jehiel describes players' analogy classes through two partitions of histories. Let $\mathcal{P}_1$ and $\mathcal{P}_2$ be two partitions of histories, where $\mathcal{P}_k$ characterizes Player k's beliefs about j's action plan. Denote by P_k a typical element of $\mathcal{P}_k$, and $P_k(h)$ the set of all histories belonging to the same element of the partition $\mathcal{P}_k$ as h.

Player k's analogy-based perception of Player j's action plan, $\hat{\sigma}_j$, is consistent with $\sigma = (\sigma_j, \sigma_k)$ if for each $h \in H$ such that $\pi^\sigma(h) > 0$, and each $a_j \in A_i$,

$$\hat{\sigma}_j^h(a_j) = \frac{\sum_{h' \in P_k(h)} \pi^\sigma(h') \sigma_j^{h'}(a_j)}{\sum_{h' \in P_k(h)} \pi^\sigma(h')}.$$

Player k using analogy classes $\mathcal{P}_k$ judges the likelihood of Player j playing a_j following the history h to be a weighted average of the true probabilities with which Player j would play a_j after all histories in $P_k(h)$, with weights that agree with the probabilities of reaching the different histories in $P_k(h)$ according to σ. Since Player k's analogy classes filter his world view, they also should constrain his beliefs about how Player j would behave following histories precluded by σ. Jehiel defines $\hat{\sigma}_j$ to be strongly consistent with σ if it is consistent with σ and if there exists a sequence of completely mixed behavioral action plans for both players, $\tilde{\sigma}^n = (\tilde{\sigma}_j^n, \tilde{\sigma}_k^n) \to \sigma$, and a sequence of beliefs for Player k about Player j's strategy, $(\hat{\sigma}_j^n)$, such that for each $n \in \mathbb{N}$, $(\hat{\sigma}_j^n)$ is consistent with $\tilde{\sigma}^n$, and $(\hat{\sigma}_j^n) \to \hat{\sigma}_j$.

Let $u_k^h(\sigma_1|h, \sigma_2|h)$ be the expected total payoff to Player k in the repeated game conditional upon reaching the history h and given that the players use action plans

$\sigma_1|h$ and $\sigma_2|h$ from h forward. The strategy profile σ is an *analogy-based expectations equilibrium (ABEE)* if for each player k, each history $h \in H$, and each action plan from h onwards $\sigma'_k|h$, $u_k^h(\sigma_k|h, \hat\sigma_j|h) \geq u_k^h(\sigma'_k|h, \hat\sigma_j|h)$, where $\hat\sigma_j$ is strongly consistent with σ.

Consider the once-repeated Prisoner's Dilemma:

Prisoner's Dilemma

	C	D
C	12, 12	−2, 16
D	16, −2	0, 0

with analogy classes formed by dividing histories into those where no one has played D and those where someone has played D. Formally, for each $i = 1, 2$, let

$$\mathcal{P}_i = \{\{(Null), (Null; C, C)\}, \{(Null; C, D), (Null; D, C), (Null; D, D)\}\}$$

Let us ask whether it can be an ABEE for both players to play C in the first period and D in the second: for each i, $\sigma_i(Null) = C$, and for each $h \neq Null$, $\sigma_i(h) = D$. These strategies give $\pi^\sigma(Null) = \pi^\sigma(Null; C, C) = 1$ and for all other h, $\pi^\sigma(h) = 0$.

Clearly players find it optimal to play the dominant action D in the second period; each player also understands her own plan to play D in period 2. Let's check whether misperceptions of the other's action plan can allow for players to play C in the first period.

Since $\pi^\sigma(Null) = \pi^\sigma(Null; C, C) = 1$ and both belong to the same analogy class, given the strategies Player 1 believes that in the first period, as well as in the second period following mutual cooperation in the first period, Player 2 will play C half the time. Given her analogy partitions, she understands that Player 2 will play differently following a defection in period 1 than following no defection. Strong consistency forces Player 1 to correctly predict that Player 2 will defect in period 2 following a defection in period 1. Player 1's perceived payoff from playing C in the first period is then

$$\underbrace{\frac{1}{2}(12 + (-2)) + \frac{1}{2}(0)}_{\text{period-1 payoff}} + \underbrace{\frac{1}{2}\frac{1}{2}(16 + 0)}_{\text{period-2 payoff}} = 9$$

and from D

$$\underbrace{\frac{1}{2}(16 + 0)}_{\text{period-1 payoff}} + \underbrace{0}_{\text{period-2 payoff}} = 8.$$

Both players do indeed then prefer to cooperate in the first period. Their error lies in perceiving a benefit to period-1 cooperation that does not in reality exist: whereas players understand that defection in period 1 will trigger defection in period 2, they wrongly believe that by cooperating in period 1 they can induce probabilistic cooperation in period 2. This error therefore incentivizes cooperation in period 1. By contrast, any player who knows that the other is rational would understand that the other player will defect in period 2 no matter what, which undermines any incentive to cooperation in the first period.

Note that whereas SPNE makes a unique prediction in this game (always defect), ABEE offers a multiplicity of equilibria, even when holding the analogy classes fixed. Always defect is, for example, also an ABEE for the analogy classes above. It is the unique ABEE when players use the coarsest possible analogy classes, namely $\mathcal{P}_1 = \mathcal{P}_2 = \{H\}$, for any player who believes that her current choice of action has no bearing on her opponent's future actions optimally chooses to defect.

Although typically regarded as disjoint from behavioral economics, network economics often invokes behavioral assumptions for tractability purposes. In many dynamic models of learning from networks of friends, agents are assumed to be myopic and maximize expected utility for the current period alone (Bala and Goyal, 1998; Golub and Jackson, 2010) on the grounds that thinking through the future is implausibly complex. In certain settings, myopia coincides with an ABEE. (Myopic play can also be justified by appealing to Markov Perfect equilibrium, Maskin and Tirole, 2001, which precludes continuation strategies from depending upon play in elapsed periods.)

Now consider the finitely-repeated prisoner's dilemma in which each player groups histories by time period: h^t and $h^{t'}$ belong to the same analogy class if and only if $t = t'$. This means that each player believes that the other's action in any given period depends only upon the period. Since each player believes that her opponent's play in future periods does not depend upon her current action, she must play her part of a stage-game Nash equilibrium in every period. Note that myopic players would also play a stage-game Nash equilibrium in every period.

ABEE can generate cooperation in the finitely repeated Prisoner's Dilemma. But since the logic of the last example applies equally well to infinitely-repeated games (with discounted total payoffs), ABEE, equipped with the right analogy classes, can also rule out cooperation in the infinitely repeated Prisoner's Dilemma (where of course SPNE famously allows for cooperation).

3.3.4 Comparing Level k to ABEE in a dynamic game

Consider again the Stackelberg game in which the Leader chooses q_1 before the Follower observes q_1 and chooses q_2. Inverse demand in the market is given by $p = 1 - q_1 - q_2$, and firms have zero marginal costs.

In SPNE, the Follower chooses q_2 to maximize $q_2(1 - q_2 - q_1)$, which is done at $q_2 = \frac{1-q_1}{2}$. Understanding that, the Leader chooses q_1 to maximize $q_1 \frac{1-q_1}{2}$, which is done at $q_1^* = \frac{1}{2}$, and so $q_2^* = \frac{1}{4}$.

For the Level-k model, it is natural to take action spaces for the two players to be $[0, 1]$, as the inverse-demand formula becomes non-sensical for total quantity exceeding one. When the Follower has level 1 or higher, he best responds to q_1, as in the SPNE. However, when the Leader has level 1, she believes that the Follower randomizes uniformly over $[0, 1]$ and chooses q_1 to maximize

$$E[q_1(1 - q_1 - Q_2)] = q_1(1 - q_1 - E[Q_2]) = q_1\left(1 - q_1 - \frac{1}{2}\right).$$

Note that this was the same maximization problem solved by the *Follower* along the equilibrium path in the SPNE, and so we have $q_1^* = \frac{1}{4}$ for a level-1 Leader and then $q_2^* = \frac{1}{2}$ for a level-1 Follower. When the Leader has level 2 or above, she knows that the Follower plays as per SPNE and therefore does too.

Next consider ABEE. Despite having been defined above only for finitely repeated games, it is straightforward to extend the concept to encompass this game. Since the Follower observes the Leader's action, any analogy classes that he might use would not influence his decision-making. Suppose that the Leader uses the coarsest possible analogy partition, which entails believing that the Follower chooses the same distribution over quantities following every q_1. The Leader then chooses q_1 to best respond to $E[Q_2]$. Denoting that quantity q_1^*, the Follower will best respond to q_1^*. This yields the unique $q_2^*(q_1^*)$. Hence we have that $q_2^*(q_1^*)$ is a best response to q_1^*, and q_1^* is a best response to $q_2^*(q_1^*) = E[Q_2^*]$. This implies that the ABEE quantity choices correspond to those in Cournot competition: $(q_1^*, q_2^*(q_1^*)) = \left(\frac{1}{3}, \frac{1}{3}\right)$.

In the Stackelberg game, the Level-1 model turns the SPNE result on its head: the Leader (Follower) in Level-1 chooses the quantity of the Follower (Leader) in SPNE. This isometry is an artifact of parameters of the example. In general, whether the Leader acts less aggressively than in SPNE depends entirely on the mean quantity chosen by a level-0 Follower.

4 Underinference and misinference

One frequently identified error of inference is underinference: a person who underappreciates the relationship between other people's actions and those other people's private information learns too little from observing, or conditioning on, those other people's actions. Misinference refers to someone inferring the wrong information content from other people's actions. Although the two errors may at first appear to be opposites, they are in fact orthogonal. Underinference refers to how much people infer; misinference refers to what people infer when they do infer.

4.1 Folk wisdom on underinference

There is a tradition in economic theory of entertaining the possibility that people may fail to infer information from other people's actions. Perhaps the most prominent example comes from the finance literature. In a rational-expectations equilibrium (REE), market prices provide a signal of traders' private information. Lintner (1969) describes equilibrium in a financial model in which, contrary to REE, traders fail to infer anything from the market price. In their pioneering experiments on financial markets, Plott and Sunder (1988) explicitly test REE against Lintner's "Walrasian equilibrium". Although they find prices close to REE prices, subsequent researchers working with nearly experimental settings found substantial departures from REE pricing (Biais et al., 2005; Corgnet et al., 2017).

In a seminal paper, Milgrom and Stokey (1982) demonstrate that when it is common knowledge that traders are rational, asymmetry of information does not generate speculative trade. The reason is that rational traders learn from their counterparties' willingness to trade, which negates the effect of initial asymmetries. Consider the simplest example in which there are two possible states of nature $\Omega = \{\omega_1, \omega_2\}$, and the two traders share the common prior belief p over Ω. Trader 2 knows the state, but Trader 1 lacks private information. Formally, $\mathcal{T}_2 = \{\{\omega_1\}, \{\omega_2\}\}$ and $\mathcal{T}_1 = \{\Omega\}$. For instance, Trader 2 might have inside information about whether a corporate takeover will occur. A state-contingent trade t maps states of the world into payments from Trader 2 to Trader 1, namely $t : \Omega \to \mathbb{R}$. Such trades are zero-sum; traders bet against each other about the state of the world. Assume that the trade t occurs if and only if both traders simultaneously agree to it, as well as that both parties are risk neutral.

Consider a trade t with the property that $\sum_{\omega \in \Omega} p(\omega) t(\omega) > 0$; on average, it benefits Trader 1. If neither trader possessed private information, then Trader 2 would reject t, for its zero-sum nature implies that it harms Trader 2. How do traders behave with the private information? Trader 2 will of course accept the trade only in the state in which it benefits him. (Since $p \cdot t > 0$, it cannot benefit Trader 2 in both states.) What should Trader 1 do? Knowing that Trader 2 only accepts when the trade benefits Trader 2—and therefore harms Trader 1—a rational Trader 1 rationally rejects the trade.

Rational traders formulate their trading strategies based upon contingent reasoning, thinking through how their counterparts would act in each state of nature. When presenting their celebrated no-speculation result, Milgrom and Stokey (1982) explicitly discuss the possibility that traders may engage in what they call "naive behavior". In our example, such naive behavior entails Trader 1 accepting the trade because it has a positive expected value conditional upon Trader 1's information.

In a different context, Milgrom and Roberts (1986) propose this same notion of naivety, giving it greater prominence. Often people choose whether or not to disclose information, with the restriction that any information disclosed must be truthful. For example, French smoked-salmon purveyors supply their fish to supermarkets either by freezing it between catch and supermarket shelf, or without freezing it. Purveyors who do not freeze naturally advertise that fact on their labels. Legally, firms may not dissemble: those who do freeze may not legally advertise never-frozen fish. Freezers therefore face a choice of whether to explicitly mention that their product has been frozen or simply avoid any mention of freezing on their labels. A consumer who observes a label lacking a "never-frozen" claim should rationally infer that the salmon has in fact been frozen.[27] In their seminal work on such disclosure games, Milgrom

---

[27] This example comes from a talk at SITE 2016 by Peter Schwardmann on Ispano and Schwardmann (2016).

and Roberts discuss the possibility that real consumers may not draw that sort of sophisticated inference and explore how competition can protect such consumers.[28]

Despite the openness of some prominent members of the economic-theory vanguard to the possibility that people infer less than fully rationally, this tradition died out once the rational-expectations revolution took hold and economic theorists gravitated towards solution concepts with ever more stringent rationality assumptions.[29] To the extent that economists considered imperfections in human reasoning, they embraced models in which these imperfections were themselves optimal in the face of factors familiar to the profession: costs and constraints.

4.2 Lab evidence

A large and growing body of work in experimental economics has uncovered instances of underinference. Below, I try to give a sense of the literature through a few key findings. Many fine works are only mentioned in passing, or omitted.

4.2.1 Bilateral trade

Samuelson and Bazerman (1985) devised an elegant experiment to test whether people appreciate the adverse selection inherent in bilateral-trade settings with private information. In their "Acquire-a-Company Game", a firm puts itself for sale to a raider. The firm knows its own value, but the raider does not and believes that the value follows a uniform distribution on $[0, 1]$. The raider values the firm at a premium upon the firm's value. In particular, a firm worth v to itself is worth $\gamma v \geq v$ to the raider. The raider makes the firm a take-it-or-leave-it offer, which the firm accepts or rejects.[30]

A rational raider should recognize that if it offers b, the only types of firm that accept have $v < b$. Since v follows a uniform distribution on $[0, 1]$, this means that the average value of a firm that accepts b is only $\frac{b}{2}$. As a consequence, whenever $\gamma < 2$, having an offer of b accepted carries a surplus of $\frac{b}{2} - b < 0$; as a consequence, the BNE calls for the raider to offer 0. Samuelson and Bazerman (1985) find that for $\gamma = \frac{3}{2}$, subjects offer far more than zero; indeed, a majority offers more than 0.5. Subsequent studies have uncovered similar patterns of overbidding, which appears robust to learning. (See, inter alia, Ball et al., 1991, Carrillo and Palfrey, 2009, Fudenberg and Peysakhovich, 2014, Magnani and Oprea, 2014.)

One might imagine that bidders pay too much merely because they savour acquisition for its own sake rather than commit any error. Holt and Sherman (1994) investigate this possibility by tweaking the Acquire-a-Company Game such that the firm's value is drawn from a uniform distribution on $[v_0, v_0 + r]$. Here again, the firm

---

[28] Regulation in the form of mandatory disclosure policies may also help such consumers.

[29] Empirical economists have sometimes been more open to less-than-full rationality. See Dranove and Jin (2010) for various explanations, including some boundedly rational ones, for nondisclosure in the disclosure game.

[30] This game owes its inspiration to the pathbreaking work of Akerlof (1970).

with value v has a weakly dominant strategy of accepting if and only if the raider offers at least v. A rational raider therefore understands that an offer of $b \in [v_0, v_0 + r]$ gets accepted with probability $\frac{b - v_0}{r}$, and the firm's expected value conditional upon accepting is $\frac{b + v_0}{2}$. Hence, the raider solves

$$\max_b \frac{b - v_0}{r} \left(\gamma \frac{b + v_0}{2} - b \right),$$

which is achieved at $b^* = \frac{v_0}{2 - \gamma}$ for $\gamma < 2$. For Holt and Sherman's parameter choice of $\gamma = 1.5$, the rational bidder bids $b^* = 2v_0$.

A bidder who infers nothing about the firm's value based on its willingness to accept an offer believes that the average value of an acquired firm will be $\frac{v_0 + (v_0 + r)}{2}$. To predict the bid of such a raider, we must make some assumption about its perception of the relationship between its bid and the probability that the firm accepts the bid. Even a raider who fails to extract information from the firm's behavior is likely to recognize that the higher its offer, the more likely the firm accepts. By assuming that the raider holds correct beliefs about the relationship between its bid and the acceptance probability, we can isolate the effects of underinference from those of mispredicting others' actions.

Assuming that this bidder holds correct beliefs about the relationship between its bid and the probability of acceptance, it maximizes

$$\max_b \frac{b - v_0}{r} \left(\gamma \frac{v_0 + (v_0 + r)}{2} - b \right),$$

which is done at $b^* = \frac{\gamma + 1}{2} v_0 + \frac{\gamma}{4} r$. For Holt and Sherman's parameter choice $\gamma = 1.5$, this yields $b^* = \frac{5}{4} v_0 + \frac{3}{8} r$.

When r is high relative to v_0, a bidder who fails to infer bids more than a rational bidder. Holt and Sherman call this the "winner's-curse" treatment. This was the case in Samuelson and Bazerman's experiment, where $v_0 = 0$ and $r = 1$. On the other hand, when v_0 is high relative to r, then the bidder who fails to infer bids less than a rational bidder. Holt and Sherman call this the "loser's-curse" treatment. When $r = 2v_0$, then the two bidding rules coincide; Holt and Sherman call this the "no-curse" treatment.

Table 6 presents their data. The last column records the average bid $\bar{b}$ in each treatment. The third-to-last gives the BNE prediction. The second-to-last gives the prediction when the raider infers nothing conditional upon winning and correctly predicts the probability that each bid is accepted. In the winner's-curse treatment, subjects do indeed bid more than rational, with a mean of 3.78 compared to the rational prediction of 3. In the loser's-curse treatment, they bid less than rational, bidding 0.74 rather than the rational bid of 1.

4.2.2 Auctions

Many experimental papers examine bidding in auctions where bidders share a common but unknown value for the good being auctioned. Bidders do not know the

Table 6 Adverse selection (from Holt and Sherman, 1994).

Curse	r	v_0	γ	BNE	No inference	$\bar{b}$
No curse	2	1	1.5	2	2	2.03
Winner's	4.5	1.5	1.5	3	3.56	3.78
Loser's	0.5	0.5	1.5	1	0.81	0.74

object's value but instead each receive an unbiased signal about it. They commonly find evidence of the "winner's curse"—the tendency for the average winning bid to exceed the average value of the good being auctioned. One explanation for the winner's curse is that bidders do not correctly infer the information inherent in placing the highest bid. In a symmetric equilibrium of an n-bidder common-values auction, whenever people's bids increase in their signals, the highest bidder holds the highest signal. Despite each signal being unbiased, the maximum of the n bidders' signals is (on average) too high. Understanding this, rational bidders shade their bids below the level warranted by their private signals alone. Bidders who are less than fully rational may fail to adjust their assessments appropriately.

In a classic experiment, Bazerman and Samuelson (1983) auctioned off the contents of a transparent jar filled with pennies. Bidders could see the jar and its contents to form some estimate of the number of pennies, but did not know the number of pennies held by the jar. The jars of pennies were sold in sealed-bid, first-price auctions: every bidder submitted a sealed bid; the highest bidder won and paid her bid. In reality, each jar in each auction contained 800 pennies. In no Bayesian Nash equilibrium of the auction can the seller's expected revenue surpass $8. The reason is that if the revenue did exceed $8 on average, then at least one bidder must lose money on average, and any such bidder could do better by not bidding.

Nevertheless, Bazerman and Samuelson found that the average winning bid exceeded $10 in their experiments: subjects fall prey to the winner's curse and lost an average of slightly more than $2 per auction. One systematic error that could explain this pattern is that subjects might have systematically overestimated the number of pennies in the jar. Formally speaking, they may have held erroneous "prior beliefs"; for instance, someone who underestimates the volume of a penny would overestimate the penny capacity of the jar. This turns out not to have been the case. Bazerman and Samuelson elicited subjects' point beliefs about the number of pennies in the jar and found the opposite pattern: on average, people estimated that the jars contained only 513 pennies.

Kagel and Levin (1986) first put forward the idea that bidders in common-values auctions might fail to condition their estimates of the object's value on the event that they submit the winning bid. A bidder who fails to perform such conditioning would appraise the value of the good conditional upon her own private signal and the event that she wins as identical to its expected value conditional upon her private signal alone. In the context of the pennies, let e_i be bidder i's estimate of the value of the penny jar based upon her visual impression of the jar. Let v be the value of the pennies. Let V and E_i denote the random variables representing value and a

Bidder i's signal. A rational bidder i with estimate e_i should recognize that the expected value of the pennies conditional upon winning (in a symmetric equilibrium) is $E[V|E_i = e_i, e_i \geq E_j \forall j] < E[V|E_i = e_i]$. That is, each bidder must take into account that when she wins, her own estimate e_i exceeds everyone else's estimate; consequently, the event that she wins the auction conveys negative information about the value of the object. A naive bidder overlooks this subtlety.

A great many papers demonstrate that bidders in experimental common-values auctions suffer the "winner's curse". Kagel and Levin (2002) provide a comprehensive review of the literature. These experiments differ in a number of details, including auction format (first-price, second-price, Dutch auction, English auction, presence or absence of reserve price, etc.), number of bidders, and value and signal structures. Avery and Kagel (1997) employ a particularly elegant design in which Bidders 1 and 2 receive two iid signals s_1 and s_2, respectively, and compete in a second-price auction for an object worth $v = s_1 + s_2$. This setting has been dubbed the "Wallet Auction" for its resemblance to a situation in which the money contents of two bidders' wallets are auctioned, where each bidder knows exactly how much money her wallet contains.

The unique symmetric Bayesian Nash equilibrium of this second-price auction is for each bidder to bid $b(s_i) = 2s_i$.[31] Bayesian Nash equilibrium in this environment does not depend upon the details of the distribution of the bidders' private signals. So long as Bidder 1 believes that Bidder 2 follows his equilibrium bidding rule of bidding twice his signal, Bidder 1's bid does not depend upon her beliefs about the distribution of Bidder 2's signals. Thus, non-common priors about each other's types cannot by itself explain anomalous bidding in this auction. In Bazerman and Samuelson (1983) experiment, holding incorrect beliefs about $p(\omega|t_k)$, e.g., underestimating the size of a penny, might explain the result in theory, although bidders reported beliefs suggest that it did not in practice. In Avery and Kagel's setting, by contrast, excluding the utterly improbable case in which bidders do not understand their own signals, no wrong beliefs about $p(\omega|t_k)$ can generate anomalous bidding.[32]

Avery and Kagel (1997) divide their subjects into two groups: inexperienced subjects have played only seven (unreported) practice auctions, and their reported data cover 18 auctions; experienced subjects have graduated from being inexperienced subjects after participating in 25 auctions. For each group, Avery and Kagel estimate a linear bidding rule $b_i = \alpha + \beta s_i$. The Bayesian-Nash predictions of $\alpha = 0, \beta = 2$ are reported in the second column of Table 7; Avery and Kagel's estimates are reported in the last column of that table. (I will return to the middle columns.)

---

[31] Suppose that Bidder 1 bids $b_1 > 2s_1$. This only affects her expected payoff when $b_1 > b_2 = 2s_2 > 2s_1$, in which case Bidder 1 pays $2s_2$ for an object worth only $s_1 + s_2 < 2s_2$, which is not a profitable deviation. Likewise, suppose that Bidder 1 bids $b_1 < 2s_1$. This only affects Bidder 1's expected payoff when $b_1 < 2s_2 < s_1$, in which case she gives up winning an object worth $s_1 + s_2$ for $2s_2 < s_1 + s_2$, which is not a profitable deviation. Asymmetric equilibria also exist in this auction. For details, as well as to see why this equilibrium is unique, see Avery and Kagel (1997).

[32] Risk aversion also cannot explain bidding something other than twice one's signal.

Table 7 Second-Price Auctions (from Avery and Kagel, 1997).

Subjects	BNE		$\chi = 0.75$		$\chi = 1$		Actual	
	α	β	α	β	α	β	$\bar{\alpha}$	$\bar{\beta}$
Inexperienced	0	2	1.875	1.25	2.5	1	2.64	1.13
($n = 299$)							(0.68)	(0.08)
Experienced	0	2	1.875	1.25	2.5	1	1.99	1.34
($n = 308$)							(0.35)	(0.05)

Avery and Kagel estimate that inexperienced subjects bid $b_i(s_i) = 2.64 + 1.13s_i$. In their experiment, $s_i \sim U[1, 4]$, so $E[S_i] = 2.5$. A bidder's expectation of the value of the object conditional upon her private signal alone is therefore $E[V|s_i] = 2.5 + s_i$. Bidders in Avery and Kagel's experiment bid very close to their expected value of the object conditional upon their private information alone. Experienced subjects bid $b_i(s_i) = 1.99 + 1.34s_i$, which also comes closer to their estimate based upon private signal alone than to the BNE bidding rule.

Ivanov et al. (2010) report experimental evidence on a two-bidder auction in which each bidder $i = 1, 2$ receives an independent signal x_i drawn from a uniform distribution on $\{0, 1, 2, \ldots, 10\}$. The value of the object $v = \max\{x_1, x_2\}$. The object is sold to the highest bidder, who pays the second-highest bid. Bayesian Nash equilibrium of this auction calls for each bidder to bid her signal $b(x_i) = x_i$.[33]

A bidder who neglects that winning the auction conveys negative information about the value of the object acts as if the expected value conditional upon winning equals the expected value conditional upon x_i. Since $v \geq x_i$, such a bidder believes that the average value of the object conditional upon winning exceeds her own signal. When bidders' values are private but unknown, each one has a weakly dominant strategy to bid her expected value.[34] A Bidder 1 who fails to appreciate that winning the auction conveys information about the value of the object won will therefore bid $b(x_1) = E[\max\{X_1, X_2\}|X_1 = x_1] > x_1$, so long as $x_1 \leq 9$.

Subjects in Ivanov, Kagel and Niederle's experiment participate in two treatments. In the first, they play 11 auctions as described, with random and anonymous rematching between each auction. The authors classify subjects into *underbidders*, who bid less than their signals; *signal bidders*, who bid their signals; *overbidders*, who bid more than their signals, but no more than 10; and *above-10 bidders*, who bid more

---

[33] It can readily be checked that this is a BNE. Given that Bidder 1 uses this strategy, if Bidder 2 deviates from the purported BNE to $b > x_2$, then this deviation only makes a difference when $b > x_1 > x_2$, in which case Bidder 2 wins an object worth x_1 at the price x_1, which is not a profitable deviation. If Bidder 2 deviates from the purported BNE to $b < x_2$, then this deviation only makes a difference when $b < x_1 < x_2$, in which case Bidder 2 no longer wins an object worth x_2 at a price below x_2, which is not a profitable deviation. For an argument that the BNE is unique, see Ivanov et al. (2010).

[34] The argument follows the lines of that in the previous footnote.

Table 8 Second-Price Auctions (from Ivanov et al., 2010).

Part I/II	Underbid	Signal bid	Overbid	> 10 bid	Unclassified	Total
Underbidders	2	0	2	1	0	5
Signal bidders	0	5	3	1	0	9
Overbidders	1	5	14	1	4	25
Above-10 bidders	2	1	1	6	0	10
Indeterminate	2	2	3	5	1	13
Total	7	13	23	14	5	

than 10.[35] In order to be classified as one of these types, a subject needed to conform to its prediction in at least 6 of the 11 periods; remaining subjects were unclassified. A subject who fails to appreciate the information content conveyed by winning would be classified by Ivanov, Kagel, and Niederle as an overbidder.

The rightmost column of Table 8 shows that amongst the 49 classified subjects, 51% (25 of 49) overbid—bidding between signal and 10—and 20% (10 of 49) bid more than 10. Whilst the latter is hard to rationalize—bidding more than 10 is weakly dominated—the majority of subjects overbid in a manner consistent with failing to update based on winning the auction.

4.2.3 Social learning

People learn from observing other people's actions in nearly all domains of human decision-making. Consider a simple model in which farmers choose whether to plant their fields with the traditional seed, s, or a new hybrid seed, h. One of these two seeds is superior, but no one farmer knows the identity of the better seed. Each farmer receives a private signal correlated with the state of nature, s or h. Farmers make choices in sequence one at a time, with each one observing the choices of all of her predecessors. Let $\theta \in \left(\frac{1}{2}, 1\right)$ be the probability of receiving an S signal in state s, as well as that of receiving an H signal in state h; assume that S and H are the only two possible signals. Banerjee (1992) and Bikhchandani et al. (1992) show that as soon as the difference in farmer numbers choosing one option over the other reaches two, it becomes optimal for each farmer to ignore her private signal and following the majority of her predecessors.

Beginning with Anderson and Holt (1997), many researchers have tested the striking results of Banerjee (1992) and Bikhchandani et al. (1992). Overall, the experimental literature on observational learning shows that people learn too little from observation of their predecessors' actions (Goeree et al., 2007; Weizsäcker, 2010; Ziegelmeyer et al., 2013). Weizsäcker (2010) crystallizes this insight through a meta-analysis of thirteen lab experiments on social learning. He finds that players only

---

[35] This description of the authors' classification is approximate in the sense that the authors classify those who bid in a narrow band around their signal as signal bidders, etc.

act contrary to the action suggested by their private signal alone when the likelihood that the action suggested their private signal alone is correct falls below one-third, rather than the optimal threshold of one-half. For instance, a player holding an S signal only opts for the hybrid seed when the empirical likelihood that the state is h exceeds two-thirds. This may come about either because people overweight their own private information—often called "overconfidence"—or because they fail to optimally extract their predecessors' private information from observation of their choices. Both theories predict that people overweight their private information relative to the information conveyed by others' choices. Although the two theories differ in the predictions they make about how people weight private information in absolute terms, the standard experimental setting of Anderson and Holt (1997) does not allow one to test for such differences.[36] Outside the lab, Stone and Zafar (2014) present evidence that sports writers ranking American college football teams for the AP Top 25 pay too little attention to the rankings of others.

4.2.4 Voting

A voter who cares only about who wins an election should vote as if she is pivotal, regardless of the likelihood of that event. The event that a voter is pivotal may convey useful information to her when other voters have information that she does not. Feddersen and Pesendorfer (1996) look at settings in which some voters lack private information and show that they strictly prefer to abstain from voting. For a simple illustration of the logic, imagine visiting a friend's home city for the first time. Your friend knows which of two restaurants you would both want to patronize but, rather gallantly, proposes that the two of you vote on whether to dine at Restaurant A or Restaurant B without providing any more information. Specifically, you vote on Restaurant A versus Restaurant B under majority rules; in the event of a tied vote, the winner is chosen by the flip of a fair coin. Notice that your vote only matters in the event of a tie, in which case it will lead to the wrong option with probability one-half. Feddersen and Pesendorfer (1996) label this phenomenon the "swing-voter's curse". By abstaining, you ensure the right choice. Indeed, whenever your information is worse that your friend's (i.e., a Blackwell garbling), you strictly prefer to abstain.

Battaglini et al. (2010) test the model of Feddersen and Pesendorfer (1996) in the lab. In the experiment, the state is either A or B; some subjects receive empty information, whilst others learn the state. In this simplest treatment in which voters have even priors over the two states, subjects receiving no information abstain 91% of the time, which closely matches the BNE prediction of 100%. When voters instead assign A the prior probability of $\frac{5}{9}$, those who receive no information abstain only 73%. Here too BNE predicts 100% abstention. Someone who infers nothing from

---

being pivotal, and regards A as the ex ante better choice, would vote for A, as done by 20% of subjects.[37]

Guarnaschelli et al. (2000) test a related model by Feddersen and Pesendorfer (1998) in which a jury votes whether to convict some defendant of a crime under unanimity: the defendant is convicted if and only if all jurors cast their votes for guilty. (In reality, subjects voted on whether an urn had more red balls or blue balls.) Feddersen and Pesendorfer (1998) describe how in such settings it is not necessarily a BNE for each juror to vote in the direction suggested by her private signal. In a jury of nine using a unanimous-verdict protocol, each voter understands that her vote matters only if all eight others vote guilty. If everyone voted "truthfully", the event that a juror is pivotal would reveal 8 guilty signals, in which the juror might prefer to vote guilty even with an innocent signal. The BNE therefore may involve—depending upon preferences and the signal structure—people with innocent signals sometimes voting guilty; in this way, someone who is pivotal suspects that some signals were in fact innocent, and would not then strictly prefer voting guilty when her own signal suggests innocence.[38] The strategic logic here, like in Feddersen and Pesendorfer (1996) is subtle, and the literature has been criticized on the grounds that real voters do not reason so carefully. Jurors who underinfer their fellow jurors' private information from the event that they are pivotal are more apt to simply vote as directed by their private information.

The data from Guarnaschelli et al. (2000) reveal that people in 3-person juries play roughly consistently with BNE. However, those in 6-person unanimous juries vote guilty too little relative to BNE. (They do so 48% of the time, rather than the 65% in the BNE.)

Esponda and Vespa (2014) conduct a very elegant experiment that tests whether voters correctly extract the information conditional upon being pivotal. In their experiment, the world is Red with probability p and Blue with probability $1 - p$. A subject who knows p votes alongside two computers to predict the state, with the winning prediction decided by the majority vote; the subject's payoffs make her want to predict the state. The computers follow a simple rule: when the state is Red, they vote Red. When the state is Blue, they vote Blue with probability q and Red with probability $1 - q$.

A rational voter should recognize that her vote never matters when the state is Red, since in that case both computers, and thus the majority, vote Red. She should therefore vote Blue. When the subject votes at the same time as the computers, only 22% behave rationally. However, when the subject votes after the computers, 76% behave rationally; actually observing a Blue vote appears to drive most subjects to conclude that the state is Blue.

---

[37] Nevertheless, Battaglini et al. (2010) argue that across all treatments, including those with partisans who always voted one way, aggregated behavior matched the mixed-strategy BNE relatively well.

[38] I ignore BNE in which people play weakly dominated strategies, for instance by all voting innocent.

4.3 Field evidence

In real natural-resource auctions, bidders have private information about the common value of oil, gas, etc. under the tract of land being auctioned. In an important pair of papers, Hendricks et al. (1987) and Hendricks and Porter (1988) provide evidence of systematic overbidding by calculating firms' ex post profits from extraction of the natural resource. Hendricks et al. (1987) check whether firms bid optimally by testing whether any given firm could improve its average profits by shading all of its bids across the many auctions it enters by a fixed amount. They found that nearly 72% of firms, making 77% of bids, would have increased profits by shading all bids by a fixed percentage. Hendricks and Porter (1988) find that bidders for offshore oil rights who did not own neighboring tracts—and therefore found themselves at an informational disadvantage relative to competitors who owned neighboring tracts—lost an average of $0.42 million (with a standard deviation of $1.76 million). Although insignificant, these estimate losses suggest that firms were not bidding optimally: any firm that faced costs of bidding needed to make money on average to cover its costs; any firm with private information should have enjoyed some information rent.

Researchers have uncovered evidence of under inference in other domains. Roll (1986) suggests that companies systematically lose money by overbidding in takeovers because they fail to condition on their bids being accepted.

Several researchers have looked at inference in disclosure games, where one party chooses whether to truthfully reveal some information or remain silent. Brown et al. (2012) and Brown et al. (2013) look at the film industry, where film distributors choose whether to screen the movie to critics in advance. In any reasonable Bayesian Nash equilibrium, distributors should tell all, as rational cinema-goers infer the worst from silence: films that haven't been reviewed are lemons. Less-than-fully-rational cinema-goers may underinfer from silence and overestimate the quality of "cold-opened" films. Brown et al. (2012) report that approximately 10% of films in their sample "open cold" and that opening cold increases box-office revenue by 20–30%.

Many American colleges and universities allow students to choose whether to submit their SAT scores. Admissions offices should recognize the negative selection inherent in such policies: students with low standardized test scores choose not to submit them. Conlin and Dickert-Conlin (2013) look at admissions data from two liberal-arts colleges with optional SAT reporting. By obtaining data from College Board about the SAT scores of those who choose not to submit their scores, they estimate that the colleges' admissions rules implicitly overestimate the SAT scores of non-reporters by approximately 15 to 20 points on an 800-point scale.

Mathios (2000) describes the effect that the Nutrition Labeling and Education Act (NLEA) had on nutrition labeling and market shares. Prior to its implementation in 1994, food manufacturers did not need to use a nutrition label. The NLEA mandated nutrition labeling. Mathios found firstly that prior to the NLEA, not all products used labels, and secondly that previously unlabeled products lost market share in 47 of 50 stores after implementation of the NLEA. Consumers do not seem to be inferring the unhealthiness of unlabeled foods. Other researchers have looked at under-inference from non-disclosure, and mandatory disclosure policies in other contexts (Jin, 2005; Jin et al., 2015; Luca and Smith, 2013).

4.4 Models

Three solution concepts in the literature specifically address people's failure to infer other people's private information from their actions. The first is Eyster and Rabin's (2005) "cursed equilibrium".

4.4.1 Fully cursed equilibrium

Recall that in the Bayesian game $G = (\Omega, A_1, \ldots, A_N; \mathcal{T}_1, \ldots, \mathcal{T}_N; p; u_1, \ldots, u_N)$, the payoff to type $t_k(\omega)$ of Player k from playing action a_k can be written as

$$\sum_{a_{-k} \in A_{-k}} \underbrace{\overline{\sigma}_{-k}(a_{-k}|t_k(\omega))}_{\text{opponents' predicted actions}} \sum_{\omega' \in \Omega} \underbrace{\Pr[\omega'|a_{-k}, t_k(\omega)]}_{\text{inference given actions}} \times \underbrace{u_k(a_k, a_{-k}; \omega')}_{\text{payoff}},$$

In a "fully cursed equilibrium" (Eyster and Rabin, 2005), Player k makes no inference about other players' private information from their actions. Rather than use $\Pr[\omega|a_{-k}, t_k]$ in the formula above, a fully cursed player uses $p(\omega|t_k)$. In a common-values auction, for example, a fully cursed bidder fails to condition her bid upon the information conveyed by event that all other bidders bid lower than she does. Apart from this error of inference, a fully cursed player does everything correctly: she correctly assesses $\overline{\sigma}_{-k}(a_{-k}|t_k(\omega))$, uses the correct priors, and best responds to her beliefs. Fully cursed players use the correct marginal distributions over other players' actions as well over the state space (given their own type); they err simply by neglecting the correlation between the two.

How does fully cursed equilibrium work? Recall that in the Acquire-a-Company Game, the firm has a dominant strategy of accepting if and only if $b \geq v$; a raider who recognizes that the firm is rational therefore chooses b to maximize

$$\frac{b - v_0}{r} \left(\gamma \frac{b + v_0}{2} - b \right);$$

$\frac{b-v_0}{r}$ describes the probability of sale at price b, and $\frac{b+v_0}{2}$ is the expected value of v conditional on sale at price b. A fully cursed raider neglects the relationship between the raider's willingness to sell and b. If all types of raider sell with equal probability, then the expected value of v condition on sale equals the unconditional value of v, $\frac{v_0+(v_0+r)}{2}$. In a fully cursed equilibrium, the raider best responds to beliefs that $\frac{v_0+(v_0+r)}{2}$ is the expected value conditional on sale.

Given the fully cursed raider's misunderstanding of the firm's strategy, how does it perceive the probability of sale as a function of b? Fully cursed equilibrium embeds the closing assumption that the raider correctly perceives the probability of sale for every choice of b. Consequently, the raider perceives the expected payoff from offering b as

$$\frac{b - v_0}{r} \left(\gamma \frac{v_0 + (v_0 + r)}{2} - b \right).$$

As described in Section 4.2.1, the raider bids $b^* = \frac{\gamma+1}{2} v_0 + \frac{\gamma}{4} r$. For Holt and Sherman's parameter choice $\gamma = 1.5$, this yields $b^* = \frac{5}{4} v_0 + \frac{3}{8} r$.

Eyster and Rabin interpret cursedness as people simply not thinking through the logic of others' strategic behavior. Cursedness is an error of omission, not commission. A cursed Player k does not actively believe that other players do not condition their actions upon their information so much as neglect to think through the strategic logic of others' behavior. Indeed, cursed people may appear to be of two minds in the sense that if they were queried about other's strategies, they might report very different beliefs than those to which they appear to best respond.[39] In the Acquire-a-Company Game, a raider queried about the relationship between the firm's value and willingness to trade may correctly articulate the positive relationship. Nevertheless, her bid suggests that she fails to appreciate this relationship. Or, to give another example, a voter may understand that Fox News tilts rightward—she would volunteer that answer if asked to judge Fox News's agenda—without necessarily correcting for that slant at the voting booth. (See DellaVigna and Kaplan, 2007 on the "Fox News effect".)

Indeed, Ivanov et al. (2010) ingenuously illustrate exactly this point. In Part II of their experiment described above, and reported in the columns of Table 7 above, subjects bid against their own past bidding behavior. Naturally, subjects should understand how their own bids increase in their signals. But as Table 7 demonstrates, subjects in Part II of the experiment behaved very much as they did in Part I of the experiment. Ivanov et al. (2010) interpret this as evidence against belief-based solution concepts. But Camerer et al. (2016) view their evidence differently: people do not think through the information revealed by their own past behavior in just the same way that they fail to think through the information revealed by others' behavior.

Eyster and Rabin use the term "cursed" to allude to the winner's curse in common values auctions, the swing-voter's curse of Feddersen and Pesendorfer (1996), and other curses resulting from private information. A number of authors subsequently proposed models of "correlation neglect" in which people neglect correlations between random variables of interest.[40] Fully cursed players neglect the correlation between their opponents' actions and those opponents' private information (conditional on their own private information). Whereas the term "cursed" might be

---

[39] Costa Gomes and Weizsäcker (2008) provide evidence for this that appears in Section 5.

[40] See, *inter alia*, Eyster and Weizsäcker (2011), Levy and Razin (2015), Ellis and Piccione (2017), and Enke and Zimmermann (2017). Spiegler (2016) models agents who imperfectly understand correlation structures, where correlation neglect is a special case, and Spiegler (2017) provides a learning foundation for such models.

obscure, it has the advantage of specificity. In most models of correlation neglect, agents neglect some correlations in the model at the same time as they fully appreciate other correlations, and the model's predictions hinge upon which correlations are ignored versus appreciated. Because the blanket term "correlation neglect" does not identify which correlations are neglected, I prefer "cursedness".[41]

4.4.2 Analogy-based-expectations equilibrium

In a fully cursed equilibrium, each player acts as if she believes that all types of other players choose actions in a way that does not depend upon their types.[42] Consider again the Acquire-a-Company Game, with parameter values $v_0 = 0$, $r = 1$, and $\gamma = 1.5$. A fully cursed raider bids $b = \frac{3}{8}$ with the expectation that acquired firms will have the average value $\frac{1}{2}$.

A more sophisticated raider might categorize firms into two classes, those with values in $\left[0, \frac{1}{2}\right)$ and those with values in $\left[\frac{1}{2}, 1\right]$ and recognize that "low-value firms" act differently than "high-value firms". In particular, the raider may recognize that an offer of $b = \frac{3}{8}$ is only ever accepted by low-value firms and conclude that the expected value of a firm that accepts this offer is $\frac{1}{4}$, which is the unconditional expected value of low-value firms. Of course, we know that only firms with values below $\frac{3}{8}$ accept the offer, and therefore that the expected value conditional upon sale is $\frac{3}{16} < \frac{1}{4}$. This type of raider overestimates the value of firms accepting its offer, yet with less severity than a fully cursed raider. The raider would then choose b to maximize

$$ b\left(\frac{3}{2}\frac{1}{4} - b\right), $$

which is done at $b^* = \frac{3}{16}$.[43]

Using this logic, Jehiel and Koessler (2008) propose another way to embed errors of inference into a solution concept. Following them, I present their formal solution concept in the two-player game $G = (\Omega, A_1, A_2; \mathcal{T}_1, \mathcal{T}_2; p; u_1, u_2)$. Let Player k have a second partition of Ω, denoted by $\mathcal{A}_k$, with typical element α_k. The partition $\mathcal{A}_k$ comprises different "analogy classes" that characterize Player k's coarse understanding of Player j's strategy. In the Acquire-a-Company-Game example, the raider uses the partition $\mathcal{A} = \{[0, \frac{1}{2}), [\frac{1}{2}, 1]\}$.

---

[41] For example, Levy and Razin (2015) assume that players receive two private signals that are correlated conditional on the state of nature, and that players neglect that correlation. Most simply, consider players who receive two copies of the same signal but mistakenly believe that their two signals are iid conditional upon the state. Whereas such players neglect that their signals are correlated conditional on the state, they recognize that each signal is correlated with the state, and therefore that their signals are correlated unconditional on the state. They also recognize that their opponents' actions correlate with the state.

[42] Strictly speaking, this requires that players' types be independent, for each Player k correctly predicts the distribution of actions conditional upon her own type t_k. When t_j, $j \neq k$, is correlated with t_k, then Player k implicitly recognizes that Player j's actions depend upon t_j, but only insofar as they correlate with t_k. This subtlety does not arise in games of one-sided private information.

[43] It falls to the interested reader to verify that the raider does not prefer to offer $b > \frac{1}{2}$.

The perceptions of Player k with analogy class $\mathcal{A}_k$ about Player j's strategy σ_j is given by

$$\hat{\sigma}_j(\omega) := \sum_{\omega' \in \Omega} p(\omega' | \alpha_k(\omega)) \sigma_j(\omega').$$

The perceived strategy $\hat{\sigma}_j(\omega)$ takes Player j's strategy to be constant within each analogy class. Player k categorizes states of nature into different classes, and correctly predicts Player j's behavior within each class, but not necessarily at any greater granularity.[44]

Consider, for example, $\Omega = \{\omega_1, \omega_2, \omega_3\}$. When Player 1 uses the finest possible analogy classes, $\mathcal{A}_1 = \{\{\omega_1\}, \{\omega_2\}, \{\omega_3\}\}$, $\hat{\sigma}_2$ agrees with σ_2. When Player 1 uses the coarsest possible analogy classes, $\mathcal{A}_1 = \{\Omega\}$, $\hat{\sigma}_2(\omega_1) = \hat{\sigma}_2(\omega_2) = \hat{\sigma}_2(\omega_3)$: Player 1 perceives Player 2 as playing the same mixture over actions in each state; moreover, this perceived mixture agrees with Player 2's overall probability of using each action. When $\mathcal{A}_1 = \{\{\omega_1\}, \{\omega_2, \omega_3\}\}$, Player 1 understands how Player 2 behaves in ω_1 but misperceives Player 2 as playing the same mixed action in states ω_2 and ω_3.

In an Analogy-Based-Expectations Equilibrium (ABEE) of a two-player Bayesian game, in each state ω, Player k plays a_k with positive probability only when it solves

$$\max_{a_k \in A_k} \sum_{\omega' \in \Omega} \sum_{a_j \in A_j} p(\omega' | t_k(\omega)) \hat{\sigma}_j(a_j | \omega') u_k(a_j, a_k; \omega').$$

That is, Player k best responds to $\hat{\sigma}_j$ instead of σ_j. When for each k, $\mathcal{A}_k$ is the finest possible partition, $\hat{\sigma}_j = \sigma_j$, and ABEE coincides with BNE. When $\mathcal{A}_k = \mathcal{P}_k$, ABEE coincides with fully cursed equilibrium, for each player correctly predicts the distribution of the other player's action conditional upon her own information but fails to perceive any finer relationship between her opponents' action and information but fails to perceive any finer relationship between her opponent's action and type/information.

ABEE builds upon the idea that people categorize. But how do they categorize? ABEE does not suggest which categories people employ and permits its users great latitude in constructing analogy classes. The many degrees of freedom provide ABEE a great deal of flexibility to accommodate predictions about human behavior. Nevertheless, ABEE rules out certain behavior for all analogy classes—no type of any player can play a dominated action in an ABEE. Moreover, standard game theory also offers users great latitude through the specification of players' information structures $(\Omega, \mathcal{P}_1, \mathcal{P}_2, p)$. In some settings, the players' information might take the form of verifiable information. But in other cases, it merely represents players' beliefs about payoffs, beliefs about others' beliefs about payoffs, etc. In an auction for the oil under some offshore tract, each bidder might possess some estimate of the quantity of oil, and some belief about other bidders' estimates, and some beliefs about other bidders'

---

[44] See Mullainathan et al. (2008) for a related approach.

beliefs about her own estimate, etc. But none of this is hard information. So just as traditional game theorists have learned to make sensible assumptions about unobserved information structures, behavioral game theorists might develop expertise in identifying sensible analogy classes.

4.4.3 Partially cursed equilibrium

Eyster and Rabin also consider the case in which people partially, but not fully, appreciate the information content in others' actions. A "χ-cursed" Player k replaces $\Pr[\omega|a_{-k}, t_k]$ in the formula above with $\chi p(\omega|t_k) + (1 - \chi)\Pr[\omega|a_{-k}, t_k]$. By doing so, a χ-cursed player makes an inference about the state of nature that is a χ-weighted average of her beliefs conditional upon her type alone, $p(\omega|t_k)$, and beliefs that are rationally updated based upon her own type and her opponents' actions, $\Pr[\omega|a_{-k}, t_k]$. When $\chi = 0$, this formula gives rational Bayesian beliefs. When $\chi = 1$, these are the fully-cursed beliefs of someone who fails to appreciate any relationship between her opponents' actions and information. Intermediate values of χ depict situations in which players partially, but not fully, apprehend the connection between what others do and what they know.[45]

Regardless of the value of the parameter χ, cursed players correctly predict the distribution over their opponents' actions conditional upon their private information; they correctly predict $\overline{\sigma}_{-k}(a_{-k}|t_k(\omega))$. In many of the settings of greatest interest to economists, this assumption has no bite. For example, often we are interested in how consumers react to firms' prices, advertisements, product offerings, etc. and attempt to glean hidden information. When the consumer gets to observe the firm's action, it does not make any difference how the consumer would predict the firm to act before seeing it. Even in many settings in which cursed players do not observe their opponents actions, the predictions they make about others actions play no role. In the Wallet Auction above, bidders' predictions about the distribution of others' bids did not matter; the only thing that did matter was bidders' perception of the relationship between others' signals and bids. Likewise, in the speculative-trade example above, traders' estimates of the likelihood of trade did not matter; the only thing that mattered was traders' beliefs about the relationship between others' willingness to trade and their private information.

---

[45] Formally, in a χ-cursed equilibrium of the game G, in each state ω, each player k plays a_k with positive probability only when it solves

$$\max_{a_k \in A_k} \sum_{\omega' \in \Omega} \sum_{a_{-k} \in A_{-k}} p(\omega'|t_k(\omega)) \big((1 - \chi)\sigma_{-k}(a_{-k}|\omega') + \chi\overline{\sigma}_{-k}(a_{-k}|t_k(\omega))\big) u_k(a_k, a_{-k}; \omega').$$

Alternatively, let

$$u_k^{\chi}(a_k, a_{-k}; \omega) = (1 - \chi)u_k(a_k, a_{-k}; \omega) + \chi \sum_{\omega' \in \Omega} p(\omega'|t_k(\omega))u_k(a_k, a_{-k}; \omega').$$

Eyster and Rabin (2005) show that the set of χ-cursed equilibrium of the G coincides with the set of BNE of the game G^{χ}, formed from G by exchanging each player k's payoff u_k for u_k^{χ}. In this way, finding χ-cursed equilibria poses no greater challenge than finding BNE.

In other settings, the assumption that players correctly predict others' actions does matter. In the Samuelson and Bazerman (1985) and Holt and Sherman (1994) examples above, the raider correctly predicts the likelihood with which the firm would accept any offer. In the Samuelson and Bazerman experiment in which $v_0 = 0$ and $r = 1$, the fully cursed equilibrium is to bid $\frac{3}{8}$. Holt and Sherman put forward the natural alternative assumption that the raider believes that the firm would accept any offer at least as large as its average valuation. In this case, a naive bidder would bid $\frac{1}{2}$.[46]

Consider again the adverse selection example of Holt and Sherman (1994), where $v_0 = 0$ and $r = 1$, so that $v \sim U[0, 1]$. A χ-cursed raider chooses b to maximize

$$b\left(\gamma\left((1-\chi)\frac{b}{2} + \chi\frac{1}{2}\right) - b\right).$$

Intuitively, the χ-cursed bidder acts as if the expected value conditional on sale at price b equals its true equilibrium value, $\frac{b}{2}$, with probability $1 - \chi$, and its unconditional expectation, $\frac{1}{2}$ with probability χ. The raider then maximizes by choosing $b^* = \frac{\chi\gamma}{4-2\gamma(1-\chi)}$. When $\chi = 0$, we have the BNE prediction that $b^* = 0$. When $\chi = 1$, we have the fully cursed prediction that $b^* = \frac{\gamma}{4}$. For intermediate values of χ, the raider partially, but not fully, appreciates the adverse-selection problem and bids between the rational and fully cursed levels.

Partially cursed equilibrium modifies BNE through a single parameter χ that measures the players' sophistication. Apart from the choice of one parameter, it requires no more assumptions about the strategic environment than BNE. Fixing the parameter, it has the same degrees of freedom as BNE. Given the wealth of evidence that people fail to fully infer, it seems likely that small values of χ will offer better predictions than BNE in virtually all settings.[47] Eyster and Rabin (2005) note that in the Avery and Kagel (1997) experiment, *every* value of $\chi > 0$ fits the data better than the parameter value $\chi = 0$ that depicts BNE. Table 7 reports prediction for values of the parameter χ that make predictions close to behavior of experienced and inexperienced subjects.

The parameter χ measures players' naivety in a cursed equilibrium. Naturally, different players may have different degrees of naivety. Eyster and Rabin (2005) define an extension to the basic solution concept, "heterogenous cursed equilibrium", that accommodates such heterogeneity. Because χ-cursed players do not directly reason

---

[46] Madarasz (2015) proposes a solution concept for Bayesian games in which players project their own ignorance onto other players. In this setting, a raider ignorant of the firm's value would play as if the firm too did not know its value; a firm that did not know its value would accept any offer above its expected value of $\frac{1}{2}$ in Samuelson and Bazerman's experiment. This assumption better fits the many bidders who bid $b = \frac{1}{2}$ in Samuelson and Bazerman's experiment, although some risk aversion or social preferences would be needed to fit the many bids in excess of one-half.

[47] Of course, an ambitious researcher could certainly construct a setting in which BNE fits better than cursed equilibrium.

about one another's χ, the extension is no more complicated than adding player-specific subscripts to the cursedness parameter χ.

The parameter χ in a partially cursed equilibrium measures the sophistication of the agent by describing the extent to which the agent appreciates the connection between others' private information and action. A natural question is whether a player's expected payoff decreases in her cursedness parameter. This does not generally hold due to strategic effects—someone who knows that he plays against a cursed player will behave differently than he would do if he knew that he was facing a rational opponent; this "strategic effect" can work to the cursed player's benefit or detriment, depending upon the circumstance. Hence, the more pertinent question becomes whether cursedness harms a player *given the behavior of her opponents*. The answer turns out to be yes.[48]

Like the parameter χ measures naivety in cursed equilibrium, the coarseness of players' analogy partitions measures naivety in an ABEE. However, there are some important differences.[49]

---

[48] Letting $EU(a)$ be the expected payoff from playing action a and $\hat{EU}(a)$ be the fully-cursed perception of the expected payoff from playing action a, we want to show that for $\chi' < \chi$,

$$(1 - \chi)EU(a) + \chi\hat{EU}(a) > (1 - \chi)EU(b) + \chi\hat{EU}(b)$$

$$(1 - \chi')EU(b) + \chi'\hat{EU}(b) \geq (1 - \chi')EU(a) + \chi'\hat{EU}(a)$$

implies that $EU(b) \geq EU(a)$. That is, whenever a more cursed player prefers a to b, while a less cursed player prefers b to a, then b yields higher expected utility than a. Rearranging the two inequalities above gives

$$\frac{1 - \chi}{\chi}(EU(a) - EU(b)) > \hat{EU}(b) - \hat{EU}(a)$$

$$\frac{1 - \chi'}{\chi'}(EU(b) - EU(a)) \geq \hat{EU}(a) - \hat{EU}(b)$$

Combining these gives

$$\frac{1 - \chi}{\chi}(EU(a) - EU(b)) > \frac{1 - \chi'}{\chi'}(EU(a) - EU(b)).$$

The condition $\chi' < \chi$ implies that $\frac{1-\chi}{\chi} < \frac{1-\chi'}{\chi'}$, and hence that $EU(a) - EU(b) < 0$, as desired.

[49] Miettinen (2009) unifies partially cursed equilibrium and ABEE by showing that for any partially cursed equilibrium σ in an original game G, one can construct a new game $\hat{G}$ and analogy classes $\mathcal{A}$ such that σ is the ABEE of $\hat{G}$ given $\mathcal{A}$ (projected onto G). Consider a simple example. Player 2 has two ex ante equally likely possible types $T_2 = \{l, h\}$, two possible actions $A_2 = \{L, H\}$ and plays the pure strategy $\sigma_2(l) = L, \sigma_2(h) = H$. There are two kinds of beliefs that Player 1 can hold in an ABEE. When Player 1 uses the finest partition $\{\{l\}, \{h\}\}$, he forms correct beliefs about Player 2's strategy. When Player 1 uses the coarsest partition $\{l, h\}$, he believes that both types of Player 2 mix between L and H independent of type, beliefs that would be shared by a fully cursed Player 1. In this context, all ABEE are equivalent to BNE or fully cursed equilibrium. In particular, no ABEE permits Player 1 to judge the likelihood of h conditional upon H to lie strictly between $\frac{1}{2}$ and 1. Not so for a partially cursed Player 1, who can deem l types more likely to choose L and h types more likely to choose H, whilst assigning positive probability to each type playing each action. How can we get this in an ABEE of an expanded game?

Firstly, partitions cannot be completely ordered by coarseness; whereas χ generates a complete order over sophistication in CE, the coarseness of analogy classes in ABEE do not give a complete order over sophistication. Secondly, fixing her opponent's strategy, a player's payoff does not necessarily decrease in the coarseness of her analogy classes in an ABEE.[50] This can be illustrated in a very simple adverse-selection setting. A venture capitalist (VC) is interested in buying a technology from an entrepreneur. The technology comes in three possible types; the entrepreneur knows the type of technology, but the VC does not and regards all three types as equally likely. Two types of technology are mature and have common value to VC and entrepreneur of either 3 or 6. The third type of technology remains in its infancy, and successful development requires the input of the entrepreneur: the infant technology has value 10 in the hands of the entrepreneur but 0 for the VC. The state space is $\Omega = \{0(10), 3, 6\}$, where $0(10)$ denotes the infant technology worth 0 to VC and 10 to the entrepreneur. Because the technology is worth at least as much to the entrepreneur as to the VC, in no state is it efficient for the two parties to trade.

Consider the trading mechanism under which both parties simultaneously decide whether to trade at the exogenous price of 4. The entrepreneur has a dominant strategy to sell only if the technology is mature and worth 3. If the VC uses the coarsest information partition $\{\{0(10), 3, 6\}\}$, then he believes that the average value to him conditional on sale is $\frac{1}{3}(0 + 3 + 6) = 3 < 4$ and refrains from buying, earning a payoff of 0. What if the VC is more sophisticated and recognizes that an entrepreneur

---

Consider the case in which Player 1 has $\chi = \frac{3}{4}$. He believes that $\Pr[h|H] = \left(1 - \frac{\chi}{2}\right) = \frac{5}{8}$. How can we obtain these beliefs in an ABEE of a related game? We split each type of Player 2 into four identical copies, all equally likely: l becomes (l_1, l_2, l_3, l_4) and h becomes (h_1, h_2, h_3, h_4). Let Player 1 use the analogy classes $\{\{l_1, l_2, l_3, h_4\}, \{h_1, h_2, h_3, l_4\}\}$. Now

$$\Pr[h|H] = \Pr[\{l_1, l_2, l_3, h_4\}|H]\frac{1}{4} + \Pr[\{h_1, h_2, h_3, l_4\}|H]\frac{3}{4}.$$

From Bayes' rule,

$$\Pr[\{l_1, l_2, l_3, h_4\}|H] = \frac{\Pr[H|\{l_1, l_2, l_3, h_4\}]\Pr[\{l_1, l_2, l_3, h_4\}]}{\Pr[H]} = \Pr[H|\{l_1, l_2, l_3, h_4\}] = \frac{1}{4}$$

and, similarly, $\Pr[\{h_1, h_2, h_3, l_4\}|H] = \frac{3}{4}$. Hence,

$$\Pr[h|H] = \frac{1}{4}\frac{1}{4} + \frac{3}{4}\frac{3}{4} = \frac{10}{16} = \frac{5}{8},$$

the same as in the $\chi = \frac{3}{4}$ partially cursed equilibrium.

Based upon this result, it is sometimes claimed that ABEE is more general than CE. Yet we must be careful with what that means. Fixing the game, certain behaviors consistent with CE may not fit any ABEE. Miettinen's result shows that we can construct a new game, with a new information structure and payoff functions whose definition extends over the new, broader type space, in such as way as to allow an ABEE to mimic the behavior in the CE. Yet this is very much an exercise in reverse engineering, and very much depends upon the value of the parameter χ as per above. Unless one knew which feature of CE one wanted to capture, one would not know how to extend the game in the appropriate manner.

[50] Ettinger and Jehiel (2010) make this point in the context of deception: to be deceived, one must be sophisticated enough to comprehend the ruse, but not sophisticated enough to see through it.

with an infant technology behaves differently than one with a mature technology? This more sophisticated VC uses the analogy classes $\{\{0(10)\}, \{3, 6\}\}$. He recognizes that the entrepreneur only sells a mature technology (with probability one-half), but wrongly believes that a mature technology that is sold is equally likely to be worth 3 and 6; since their average of 4.5 exceeds the price of 4, the VC wishes to buy. Whereas the coarsest VC earned a payoff of 0, this more sophisticated VC earns the lower expected payoff $\frac{1}{3}(3 - 4) = -\frac{1}{3}$. In ABEE, sophistication, as measured by the fineness of a player's analogy class, can harm the player, even fixing her opponent's behavior. (Notice that because 3 is the unconditional expected value of the technology to the VC, as well as the value to the VC conditional upon sale, a partially cursed VC perceives the expected value conditional upon sale to be 3 independent of χ; consequently, his payoff is zero for all χ.)

4.4.4 Behavioral equilibrium

In adverse-selection environments such as those of Samuelson and Bazerman (1985) and Holt and Sherman (1994), a cursed buyer can be viewed as making two conceptually distinct forms of error. Firstly, she misperceives the average value of objects that she acquires. Secondly, she misperceives how changing her offer affects the selection of objects that she acquires. In particular, she fails to appreciate that higher offers improve the average quality of those objects that she manages to acquire.

Based on this dichotomy, Esponda (2008) defines "behavioral equilibrium" in adverse-selection environments in a such a way that people correctly perceive the average quality of acquired objects but entirely neglect the effect that raising bids has on selection.

In the environment of Holt and Sherman (1994), the bidder bids b^* with the property that

$$b^* = \arg\max_b \frac{b - v_0}{r} \left(\gamma \frac{v_0 + b^*}{2} - b \right).$$

In both a fully-cursed equilibrium and a behavioral equilibrium, the raider correctly perceives the probability of sale given her offer. In both types of equilibria, the raider treats the average value of the firm conditional upon acquisition as a constant. The only difference lies in the value of the constant. In a fully cursed equilibrium, the raider takes it to be the unconditional mean $\frac{v_0 + v_0 + r}{2}$, whereas in a behavioral equilibrium the raider takes it to equal the equilibrium value of $\frac{v_0 + b^*}{2}$. Esponda's motivation draws on a learning story: a raider who has played this game many times and settled down on bidding b^* should learn that the average value of the firms that she acquires, $\frac{b^* + v_0}{2}$. However, if she receives no feedback about the values of firms that she fails to acquire, then she need not learn their value distribution. Like in a cursed equilibrium, the raider in a behavioral equilibrium neglects that increasing her bid changes the expected value of firms that she acquires. At an interior behavioral equilibrium, $b^* = v_0 \frac{\gamma + 2}{4 - \gamma}$.

When $v_0 = 0$ and $r = 1$—the setting of Samuelson and Bazerman (1985)—$b^* = 0$ as long as $\gamma < 4$. Recall that for $\gamma < 2$, the BNE also has the raider offer zero.

In a behavioral equilibrium in this setting, the raider recognizes that lowering her bid reduces the chance of sale but saves money. But because she misses that lower bids translate into greater adverse selection, she is even more inclined than a rational bidder to lower her bid.

4.5 Social versus private inference

People who fail to infer information from others' actions condition their actions on less information than rational agents. Consequently, solution concepts such as cursed equilibrium and behavioral equilibrium embedding limited inference tend to predict that people rely more on their own private information. Alternatively, people may overweight their own private information because they overestimate its precision. Several authors have put forward this hypothesis across a number of different domains. In the context of trade on financial markets, Daniel et al. (1998) and Daniel et al. (2001) and Odean (1998) show how traders who overestimate the precision of their private information about the value of some asset trade excessively. In the context of social learning, Goeree et al. (2007) posit that people count their own private signal about the state of nature—for instance, whether a new hybrid seed raises crop yields—as $\alpha > 1$ conditionally independent private signals, essentially exaggerating its precision. In the context of voting, Ortoleva and Snowberg (2015) assume that voters overestimate the informativeness of their private signals about whether Candidate A is more qualified than Candidate B. Levy and Razin (2015) assume that voters receive two signals that are correlated conditional upon the state of nature; the voters misperceive these signals as being conditionally uncorrelated. In the extreme case in which the two signals are perfectly correlated conditional upon the state, this assumption is observationally equivalent to Goeree et al.'s (2007) overconfidence with $\alpha = 2$.

People do exhibit overconfidence. Wall Street traders probably regard themselves as better informed than they are. The many small investors who trade actively and systematically underperform the market by going up against "smart money" are also likely to be overconfident. But as Eyster et al. (2019) show, such overconfidence alone does not produce significant trade in large markets with dispersed private information. The reason is that each small trader understands that the price conveys far more information than her own private signal alone, no matter how much she overestimates its precision. In order for overconfidence to generate trade, traders must also be cursed (or otherwise fail to infer much information from price).

A second reason why failures of social inference have more to say about people's excessive trade, naive voting, failure to learn from others' behavior, etc. comes in the form of lab evidence. The typical lab study has two possible states of nature, e.g. one state in which Candidate A is better and the other in which Candidate B is better. Subjects receive private signals about the state of nature. Often this is implemented by telling subjects that one of two urns of balls will be chosen by the flip of a fair coin, and private signals take the form of iid draws from the selected urn. In the A state, an urn with a majority of A balls will be selected. In the B state, an urn with a majority of B balls will be selected. For example, each urn might have 10 balls, 7 that match the state, and 3 that mismatch the state. What does overconfidence mean in this context? An overconfident subject thinks that the probability that her ball matches the state exceeds the true probability of $\frac{7}{10}$. Why would subjects believe that their own ball matches the urn better than anyone else's? Indeed, do they?

The evidence reviewed in Daniel Benjamin's chapter in this handbook suggests that people do not tend to believe that a single draw from an urn imparts more information than it does. Therefore, as argued by Eyster and Rabin (2010), the fact that people behave in ways suggestive of overconfidence or cursedness in lab experiments in which overconfidence feels unlikely should lead a Bayesian researcher to update their beliefs in favor of errors of social inference and against errors in private inference.

4.6 Learning

Jehiel (2005), Jehiel and Koessler (2008), and Esponda (2008) all motivate their solution concepts using stories about learning. In an ABEE, Player k uses a coarse model of the world by thinking about Player j's types in categories. Over time, and very much guided and constrained by the features of her categorical model, she may come to learn the distribution of actions by each category of Player j. Because she does not reason more finely, Player k does not achieve any greater understanding of Player j's strategy. In a behavioral equilibrium, buyers come to learn the average value of objects that they acquire; however, they never learn how increasing their bids affects the distribution of values.

Other researchers have established that people make better inference with experience (Eyster and Rabin, 2005; Fudenberg and Peysakhovich, 2014). Carrillo and Palfrey (2009), Esponda and Vespa (2014), and Ngangoue and Weizsäcker (2016) show that people make better inferences when they observe other people's actions than when they simply condition upon those actions.

We have seen that the χ in χ-cursed equilibrium measures players' sophistication in the sense that fixing a player's opponents' strategies, the lower her χ parameter, the higher her expected payoff. The parameter k in the Level-k model does not have this property: when your opponent plays as a Level 1, you cannot be worse off by being a Level 2 than by being a Level 3. Thus a player's measured k confounds the player's sophistication with her beliefs about others' sophistication. Gill and Prowse (2016) estimate that higher cognitive-ability lab participants have higher levels of k. However, other researchers have estimated whether player's estimated k's are consistent across games. Georganas et al. (2015) find consistency within a class of games, but no correlation in the rank-order of k across subjects across two different classes of games.

4.7 Implications

Eyster et al. (2019) define a market-solution concept, "cursed-expectations equilibrium", which is to rational-expectations equilibrium as cursed equilibrium is to

Bayesian Nash equilibrium. In it, traders underappreciate the information conveyed by market prices. They show that cursedness leads to a much larger volume of trade than REE, even when traders have non-speculative trading motivations arising from liquidity shocks. Kondor and Kőszegi (2015) show how financial firms optimally design securities to exploit small investors' cursedness. Celerier and La Vallee (2017) document how financial firms offer extremely complex derivatives to retail investors at very high margins, contracts that are broadly consistent with the model of Kondor and Kőszegi (2015).

Underinference frequently amplifies the effects of other errors discussed in this volume. Eyster et al. (2019) show how cursedness amplifies overconfidence in financial markets. An informationally small investor whose only mistake is to be overconfident should not trade much because the information conveyed by the market price overwhelms her own private information, aligning her beliefs with those of the market. Cursedness creates a greater role for overconfidence because it limits the trader's inference from market prices.

Underinference also oftentimes serves as an unacknowledged closing assumption in other behavioral models. Many behavioral IO models, surveyed in Heidhues and Kőszegi (2018), implicitly assumed that consumers are cursed in the sense that they do not infer firms' superior information about them from the firms' tariff choices. For example, DellaVigna and Malmendier (2004) describe how firms price for naive β–δ-discounting consumers. Consumers in the model do not attempt to learn about their own time preferences through firms' offerings. Gabaix and Laibson (2006) describe how many consumers do not think about minibar prices when booking hotel rooms unless the hotel mentions them. Rational consumers should of course recognize a hotel that conceals some price is probably concealing a high price. Gabaix and Laibson assume that "myopes" ignore the entire minibar "after-market" when booking their accommodation. Myopes therefore fail to infer anything about minibar prices from hotels' silence. Likewise, Grubb (2009) explains three-part tariffs using a model in which consumers believe that they can predict their demand for mobile telephony more accurately than they actually can. He shows how such "overconfidence" induces firms to essentially bet against their consumers that consumer forecasts are noisier than consumers believe. A consumer whose only mistake is to underestimate the variance in her demand ought to ask herself why the phone company offers such exotic, multi-part tariffs, which are evidently not connected to the marginal costs of provision. Cursed consumers do not ask themselves this questions. Spiegler (2006) proposes a model of "quacks" in which people develop loyalty to a quack based on a single good experience. This creates horizontal differentiation between quacks in the minds of consumers, which allows for supra-competitive pricing. But if consumers rationally interrogated themselves as to why others visit different quacks than their own, then they would see the merits of other quacks, leading to greater price competition.

Eyster et al. (2017) develop a behavioral IO/macro model in which consumers care about fairness as appraised through firms' markups. In the simplest example, consumers observe a monopolist's posted price and infer its hidden (constant) marginal cost. Suppose that the monopolist sets its price as constant proportional markup over marginal cost. Rational consumers recognize that high prices signal high marginal costs, not higher markups. A naive consumer who infers nothing about marginal cost from price concludes that higher prices signal higher markups. Because consumers are assumed to have more elastic demand when they perceive higher markups, a monopolist serving naive consumers would want to set a lower price than one serving rational consumers. Moreover, marginal costs pass through into prices less than one for one. Suppose to the contrary that the monopolist doubled its price when its cost doubled; naive consumers would then perceive a higher markup and show greater price elasticity, in which case the monopolist would optimally lower its price.

4.8 Misinference

Not only may people underinfer others' private information from their actions, but insofar as they do infer, they may infer wrongly. This idea has been applied to social learning more than any other area.

4.8.1 Observational learning

Beginning with Banerjee (1992) and Bikhchandani et al. (1992), a theoretical literature has developed that explores how people rationally learn from observations of their predecessors' choices. Let us return to our simple example in which farmers choose whether to plant their fields with the traditional seed, s, or a new hybrid seed, h. Again one of these two seeds is superior, but no one farmer knows the identity of the better seed. Farmers move in sequence one at a time, with each one observing the choices of all of her predecessors. Each person k receives a private signal t_k correlated with the state of nature, s or h; let F_s be the distribution of signals in state s and F_h be the distribution of signals in state h. Assume that for some $M > 0$, $\frac{1}{M} < \frac{\Pr[s|t_k]}{\Pr[h|t_k]} < M$ for each s_k in the support of F_s and F_h: there exists an upper bound on a private signal's informativeness.

Banerjee (1992), Bikhchandani et al. (1992), and Smith and Sørensen (2000) show that eventually a herd forms with probability one: after some point in time, all farmers choose the same seed. Moreover, when private signals have bounded likelihood ratios, eventually people form a "cascade": each ignores her private signal in favor of following her immediate predecessor. Despite everyone choosing the same action, in the case of bounded likelihood ratios, people recognize that they may be herding on the wrong seed. In the simplest example, people receive one of two kinds of signals. Let $\theta \in \left(\frac{1}{2}, 1\right)$ be the probability of receiving an S signal in state s, as well as that of receiving an H signal in state h. Banerjee (1992) and Bikhchandani et al. (1992) show that as soon as the difference in farmer numbers choosing one option over the other reaches two, it becomes optimal for each farmer to herd by ignoring her private signal and following the majority of her predecessors. This outcome is socially inefficient because farmers fail to learn the truth despite collectively possessing information sufficient to identify the state of nature.

Eyster and Rabin (2010) consider a simple alternative to rational social learning in which people infer naively by neglecting that their predecessors actions depend upon inferences that those predecessors have drawn from their own predecessors. They define a player to engage in best response trailing naive inference (BRTNI) play if she plays a best response to beliefs that each of her predecessors follows his own signal, neglecting that these predecessors in fact make informational inferences from observing their own predecessors' actions. In both BRTNI and rational play, Farmer 1 will base her decision on her private signal; Farmer 2 will base his on the information gleaned from Farmer 1's choice and his own private signal. When rational, Farmer 3 takes account of the fact that Farmer 2's action embodies Farmer 1's signal. However, when BRTNI, Farmer 3 overlooks this dependence, and overcounts Farmer 1's signal by basing her decision on Farmer 1's action, Farmer 2's action (under the assumption that it depends merely on Farmer 2's signal), and her own private signals. A BRTNI Farmer 4 makes the same error, and winds up over counting both Farmer 1 and Farmer 2's signals. In general, people exhibit a social confirmatory bias in the sense that early actions (and hence signals) exert disproportionate effect. Such hysteresis increases inefficiency. Eyster and Rabin (2010) show that even in informationally rich environments in which rational people would learn the truth with probability one, BRTNI players come to believe in the wrong seed with positive probability. In some settings, mislearning may be so bad that BRTNI players earn lower average utility than they would if none of them could observe any past actions. Social learning can be harmful! Gagnon-Bartsch and Rabin (2016) show that with more than two possible states of nature, BRTNI players can unlearn truths that they once learned and find themselves unable to learn certain types of truth, no matter what.

Observational learning has an enormous amount of redundancy, as many people learn from the same set of past observations. Rationality requires that people carefully attend to that redundancy. Eyster and Rabin (2014) show that far milder forms of "redundancy neglect" than BRTNI lead to the same form of mislearning. Guarino and Jehiel (2013) describe ABEE in a social-learning environment in which players play the same game repeatedly, and learn the right action at the end of every game. While behavior in their model appears like BRTNI play early in the game, ABEE players eventually learn the truth because they learn the relationship between complete histories of actions and the state. In simple social-learning games, BRTNI corresponds to level-2 play: when Level 0 acts randomly, Level 1 follows her signal, and Level 2 then best responds to everyone following her signal.[51]

Eyster and Rabin (2014) illustrate how rational social learning becomes far more complex outside the single-file-actor structure used in most of the literature. Sup-

---

[51] However, as illustrated by Eyster and Rabin (2010), when players care about their *successors'* actions, then BRTNI and Level 2 can differ, for they make different predictions about how future players will behave.

pose now that in each period, three farmers simultaneously choose how to plant their fields. Each can choose the traditional seed, the hybrid, or to split their field 50–50 between seeds. Suppose that there are three signal realizations: H favors the hybrid state h; S favors s; and $\emptyset$ provides no information. Farmers begin with beliefs that the traditional and hybrid seeds are equally likely to be good. Let preferences be such that anyone who deems the two states equally likely splits her fields 50–50, whilst anyone who holds beliefs tilted in favor of one of the two seeds dedicates all of her field to that seed. Suppose that in period 1, two farmers choose 50–50, and one chooses the traditional seed. These actions reveal that one farmer must have an S signal and two farmers have $\emptyset$ signals. Now suppose that in period 2, all three farmers plant 50–50. How should a rational farmer plant in period 3? Since period-1 actions reveal one more S than H signal, anyone who receives an S or $\emptyset$ signal in period 2 should plant the traditional seed. Since no farmer in period 2 did so, all must have received H signals. Farmers in period 3 then herd on a hybrid seed that no one has ever planted!

In addition to imitation, rational social learning includes instances of such "anti-imitation" in virtually all observation structures apart from single-file movers.[52] Yet they express skepticism that people truly engage in such complex anti-imitative behavior, and instead predict that people will neglect redundancy in their predecessors' actions. In experiments, Eyster et al. (2018) find scant evidence for anti-imitation in another "multi-file" model in which players move four at a time.[53] Indeed, subjects in their multi-file treatment neglect redundancy to such an extent that they would be better off by not having the opportunity to learn from their predecessors.

People who neglect redundancy wrongly attribute other their predecessors' actions to those predecessors' private information, rather than to the inferences that those predecessors make about their own predecessors. Two recent papers identity redundancy neglect in the field. Murfin and Pratt (2018) look at how banks set interest rates for syndicated loans using prices of "comparables". To identify redundancy neglect, they compare the effect that Loan A has on Loan C in two cases. In the first case, Loan A closes in time to serve as a comparable for Loan B, which in turn is used as a comparable for Loan C. In the second case, Loan A fails to close in time to influence the price of Loan B, yet still serves as a comparable for Loan C. Murfin and Pratt argue that the effect of Loan A on Loan C should be the same in both cases, but they find that it is not. They estimate the size of redundancy neglect to be 40% as large as the effect that comparables have on prices.[54]

---

[52] The reason for the term is that if the traditional planter in period 1 planted hybrid instead, and everything else in the history stayed the same, then the herd in period 3 would have formed on the traditional seed. Fixing the actions in period 2, the more period-1 actions reflect confidence in the traditional seed, the more convinced period-3 players become in the hybrid.

[53] Kübler and Weizsäcker (2004) provide related evidence that social learner's underappreciate how much their predecessors have learned.

[54] They estimate that a 100-basis-point increase in the spread of a comparable leads to a 9–13% increase in the spread of the loan being priced.

Glaeser and Nathanson (2017) study home buyers who forecast future prices based on projections about demand. To estimate future demand, homebuyers estimate current and past demand, using prices. However, they mistakenly interpret past prices as solely reflecting past demand, neglecting that homebuyers in the past also used past prices in their own forecasts. Thus, the structure of error coincides with the naive inference of Eyster and Rabin (2010). Glaeser and Nathanson (2017) show that their model predicts several features of the housing market including short-run momentum, medium-run mean reversion, and excess volatility.

Simonsohn and Ariely (2008) present evidence that buyers on eBay, the online auction platform, herd on auctions with low starting prices. For each item up for sale, eBay displays the current highest bid and the accumulated number of bids, but does not display the starting bid. Conditional on the current price, the lower the starting price, the more bids that took place. Buyers who give the auctions only a cursory inspection do not see the starting price and wrongly interpret more bids as more interest in the object.

People engaged in observational learning may mislearn for reasons other than redundancy neglect. Gagnon-Bartsch (2016) studies people who learn about a payoff-relevant binary state and have preferences that also depend upon their private-information tastes. "Taste projectors" overestimate the popularity of their own tastes, leading them to draw incorrect inferences from others' choices. Madarasz (2015) looks at people who project their own information onto other people, which then bleeds onto their inferences.

4.8.2 Self-confirming equilibrium

Dekel et al. (2004) extend the idea of self-confirming equilibrium (SCE) to Bayesian games. In terms of the taxonomy of errors used in this chapter, they restrict players in Bayesian games to correctly predict other players' actions but permit any inference $\Pr[\omega'|a_{-k}, t_k(\omega)]$ consistent with the prior probability p. Player 1 has a type in $\{l, h\}$, and Player 2 initially regards each type as equally likely. Suppose that the l type of Player 1 plays L, whilst the h type of Player 1 plays H. In a SCE, Player 2 can perceive the mapping between Player 1's type and action exactly backwards by believing that type l plays H and type h plays L. Or he might believe that each type of Player 1 mixes 50–50 over L and H—the fully cursed beliefs.

SCE in Bayesian games is a superset of cursed equilibrium and analogy-based-expectations equilibrium, for in both models, players have correct priors and correct beliefs over the distribution over others' action profiles. This is all that SCE requires, and hence it is more general than the other two concepts. Moreover, SCE surely accommodates real behavior that the other concepts cannot. DellaVigna and Pope (2018) asks expert economists to predict how incentives will motivate Amazon Turk workers. Whereas the experts predict that those on very low piece rates will work less than those on zero piece rates, the opposite turns out to be true. (Setting aside wealth effects, which should be negligible in the experiment, standard economics predicts that higher wages will elicit greater effort. The economists probably cast that familiar logic aside due to Gneezy and Rustichini's (2000) finding that low fines engender more bad behavior than no fines.) Transported into the context of a Bayesian game, DellaVigna and Pope's finding suggests that an expert economist who does not observe a worker's pay scheme—but does observe the worker's effort—will believe that higher effort signals the absence of a piece rate, whereas in fact the opposite is true.

5 Failure to best respond

The final category of error covers people's failure to respond to their beliefs about others' strategies. Costa Gomes and Weizsäcker (2008) provide direct evidence that people fail to best respond to their own beliefs by having people play two-person games as well as state their beliefs about what the other person will do. They find that in more than half their games, players fail to respond to their own stated beliefs. Moreover, their stated beliefs reveal greater confidence in their opponent's rationality than their action. For example, someone who plays as a Level 1 would typically also estimate her opponent's type to be Level 1 (in which case she ought to play as a Level 2).

5.1 Epsilon equilibrium

Radner (1980) proposes that rather than play best responses to others' strategies, people in strategic settings instead play close to best responses. Formally, the strategy profile σ is an ε equilibrium if there exists some $\varepsilon > 0$ such that for each player k, and each $\sigma'_k : T_k \to \Delta A_k$,

$$E[u_k(\sigma_k, \sigma_{-k})] \geq E[u_k(\sigma'_k, \sigma_{-k})] - \varepsilon.$$

When $\varepsilon = 0$, this reduces to Bayesian Nash Equilibrium. In general, an ε equilibrium is a strategy profile wherein each player plays within ε of a best response to the other players' equilibrium strategy profile. It embodies the idea that players play "close to equilibrium" as measured by payoffs.

One justification for ε equilibrium is that players who misperceive the rules of the game, and play a Nash equilibrium in their perceived game, will play an ε equilibrium of the original game. We say that the complete-information game

$$\widetilde{G} = (A_1, \ldots, A_N; \widetilde{u}_1, \ldots, \widetilde{u}_N)$$

lies within a δ-neighborhood of the complete-information game

$$G = (A_1, \ldots, A_N; u_1, \ldots, u_N)$$

if for each Player k, $\max_{a \in A} |u_k(a) - \widetilde{u}_k(a)| < \delta$. Radner (1980) shows that $\widetilde{s}$ is a pure-strategy ε equilibrium of G if and only if it is a Nash Equilibrium of some game $\widetilde{G}$ within an $\varepsilon/2$-neighborhood of G.

Consider again finite repetition of the Prisoner's Dilemma from the table in 3.3.3:

Prisoner's Dilemma

	C	D
C	12, 12	−2, 16
D	16, −2	0, 0

For $\varepsilon \geq 4$, there exist a great many ε equilibria. Consider Grim-Trigger strategies in which both players cooperate until the first defection, at which point they both defect ever after. The most attractive opportunity for unilateral deviation from Grim Trigger in this game comes in the last period, where the gain equals 4. Alternatively, consider a truncated version of the Grim-Trigger strategy in which players play the Grim Trigger through period $K < T$ and defect thereafter. This too meets the definition of ε equilibrium, for $\varepsilon \geq 4$, but gives rise to much less equilibrium cooperation for values of K far below T. Naturally, defect in every period is an ε equilibrium (for any value of ε). Even for fixed ε, the concept of ε equilibrium accommodates SPNE, and many departures from it, whilst providing scant guidance on what behavior to expect.

Friedman and Oprea (2012) look at two continuous-time versions of the Prisoner's Dilemma, where players' payoffs at every instant in time flow according to the table above. In both treatments, the game lasts for one minute. In the "Delay" treatment, players must wait 7.5 seconds before changing their actions; in the "No Delay" treatment, players can react to their opponents as quickly as permitted by their motor neurons. In the No Delay treatment, playing Grim Trigger has little cost, since players can react very quickly to deviations by their opponents. In the Delay treatment, by contrast, cooperating can be costly. Therefore, for any value of ε, one expects more cooperation in the No Delay than in the Delay treatment. This is exactly what Friedman and Oprea find, with cooperation 80–90% in the No Delay treatment.

5.2 Quantal-response equilibrium

The concept of ε equilibrium does not pin down the relationship between a player's expected payoff from playing some action and her likelihood of playing that action. Subsequent researchers have refined ε equilibrium to constrain the form of players' errors. In the realm of decision theory, Luce (1959) formalized the concept of logit to model random choice: people choose all available options with positive probability; their likelihood of choosing a versus b does not depend upon anything else belonging to the choice set (so-called Independence of Irrelevant Alternatives), and increases in the utility of a. McFadden (1976) pioneered the estimation of logit models from empirical choice data.

McKelvey and Palfrey (1995) define a *quantal-response equilibrium (QRE)*, or *logit equilibrium*, to be a completely mixed ε-equilibrium that connects the frequency with which players use each available action to the expected payoff of that action, given other players' behavior. Formally,

Definition 1. The strategy profile $\sigma \in \sum$ is a *quantal-response equilibrium* (QRE) or *logit equilibrium* if for some $\lambda \geq 0$, for each player k, each $a_k \in A_k$, each $\omega \in \Omega$, and each $t_k \in T_k$,

$$\sigma_k(a_k|\omega) = \frac{e^{\lambda\left(\sum_{\omega' \in \Omega} \sum_{a_{-k} \in A_{-k}} p(\omega'|t_k(\omega))\sigma_{-k}(a_{-k}|\omega')u_k(a_k,a_{-k};\omega')\right)}}{\sum_{a_k' \in A_k} e^{\lambda\left(\sum_{\omega' \in \Omega} \sum_{a_{-k} \in A_{-k}} p(\omega'|t_k(\omega))\sigma_{-k}(a_{-k}|\omega')u_k(a_k',a_{-k};\omega')\right)}}$$

$$=: \frac{e^{\lambda E[u_k(a_k,a_{-k},\omega)]}}{\sum_{a_k' \in A_k} e^{\lambda E[u_k(a_k',a_{-k},\omega)]}}$$

When $\lambda = 0$, $\sigma(a_k|\omega) = \frac{1}{|A_k|}$, where $|A_k|$ is the number of actions available to Player k. In this extreme case, QRE coincides with level-0 play. As $\lambda \to \infty$,

$$\lim_{\lambda \to \infty} \sigma_k(a_k|\omega) = \lim_{\lambda \to \infty} \frac{1}{1 + \sum_{a_k' \in A_k \setminus \{a_k\}} e^{\lambda\left(E[u_k(a_k',a_{-k},\omega)] - E[u_k(a_k,a_{-k},\omega)]\right)}}.$$

When k distinct actions maximize expected utility, the probability of playing each one converges to $\frac{1}{k}$ as λ tends to infinity. Let $(\sigma^n)_{n \in \mathbb{N}}$ be a sequence of QRE that correspond to the QRE parameters $(\lambda^n)_{n \in \mathbb{N}} \to \infty$. Whenever $(\sigma^n) \to \sigma$, the strategy profile σ is a Bayesian Nash equilibrium.

The parameter values $\lambda = 0$ and $\lambda = \infty$ correspond to randomly and best-responding to others' behavior, respectively. For interior values of λ, the higher is λ, the closer players come to playing best responses to one another's strategies. Better actions get played with higher probability. In this sense, QRE players play "better", rather than best, responses to their co-players' strategies.[55] QRE ties together two conceptually distinct assumptions: players make errors, and they recognize—and take into account—the fact that others make errors.

Why would people play according to QRE? One reason for this may be rational inattention. People invest more into avoiding costly errors than cheap errors. People do err, and they may make more costly errors less frequently than cheaper errors. Alternatively, QRE can be interpreted as each player best responding to perturbed payoffs $\tilde{u}_k(a_k, a_{-k}; \omega) = u_k(a_k, a_{-k}; \omega) + \varepsilon(a_k, a_{-k}; \omega)$, where $\varepsilon(a_k, a_{-k}; \omega)$ follows the extreme-value distribution.[56] To the extent that people play QRE for the latter reason, the concept does not embed any error and therefore lies outside the purview of this chapter.

Several authors have proposed variants of QRE. Weizsäcker (2003) develops a variant in which players mispredict others' actions in a specific way: they underestimate other players' λ parameter. In the simplest variant of Weizsäcker's (2003)

---

[55] Colin Camerer often says that if Nash had been a statistician, then he would have invented QRE instead of Nash equilibrium.

[56] McKelvey and Palfrey (1995) allow for other distributions, although Haile et al. (2008) point out that QRE lacks predictive power in the absence of specific assumptions about the form of the error term.

model, each player noisily best responds with logit parameter λ to beliefs that her opponent noisily best responds with logit parameter $\lambda' \leq \lambda$. In a sense, each player regards other players as (weakly) less rational than herself. Let $BR_k^\lambda(\sigma_{-k})$ be a Player k's logit best response with parameter λ to the strategy profile (σ_{-k}) by the other players. In a two-player game, $\sigma_1 = BR_1^\lambda(BR_2^{\lambda'}(\sigma_1))$ and $\sigma_2 = BR_2^\lambda(BR_1^{\lambda'}(\sigma_2))$. This nests QRE, where $\lambda' = \lambda$, as well as Level-1 play, where $\lambda = \infty$ and $\lambda' = 0$. Using data from several normal-form games, Weizsäcker (2003) estimates that $\lambda' < \lambda$.

Goeree and Holt (2004) propose a model of "noisy introspection" that combines features of QRE with Level k. They define a concept of noisy rationalizability that resembles QRE as rationalizability resembles Nash equilibrium. In a two-player game, Player 1 plays the action $a_1 = BR_1^{\lambda_1}(BR_2^{\lambda_2}(BR_1^{\lambda_3} \ldots (r))))$, where r is any element in $\Delta(A_1)$, and $(\lambda^n)_{n \in \mathbb{N}}$ is a decreasing sequence that approaches 0. Player 1 noisily best responds to beliefs about Player 2's actions, which itself is an even noisier best response to beliefs about Player 1's action, etc. Goeree and Holt (2004) show that, unlike rationalizability, noisy introspection makes a unique prediction, which depends upon the sequence $(\lambda^n)_{n \in \mathbb{N}}$.

5.3 Applications of QRE

The literature has used QRE in two different ways. First, in many contexts, QRE has been put forward as a stand-alone explanation for experimental anomalies. Second, it has been used as a means of closing other models. Models such as cursed equilibrium or Level k do not have full support in the sense that they predict that some actions will not be chosen with positive probability. Consequently, a researcher who wishes to use these concepts to analyze lab data must add some form of error or noise term. QRE provides a structured way of doing this.

QRE builds upon the premises that people commit errors, that they recognize that others make errors, and that the frequency of error declines with the cost of that error. It helps fit data in the lab to the extent that people make errors and recognize that others do so as well. But does QRE fit data because people make errors and know that others make errors, or simply because they make errors?

Recall Basu's (1994) Traveler's Dilemma of Section 3, where two players choose numbers in $\{80, 81, \ldots, 200\}$, each receives the lower number, and the high player pays the low player R. Whereas the unique rationalizable outcome is for both to choose 80, Capra et al. (1999) find that for $R = 5, 10$, subjects play quite close to 200, whilst for $R = 50, 80$, subjects play very close to 80. This pattern can be well explained by QRE. A subject who expected her partner to bid 195 in the $R = 5$ treatment (which is the average bid in late rounds of that treatment) would lose only 9 by bidding above 195, rather than the optimal 194, and does better by bidding above 195 than by bidding below 185. This game has strategic complementarities: the higher the other player claims, the higher you want to claim. For low values of R, when one player chooses near the top of the range, the other player has incentive to do the same.

When $R = 80$, the game still has strategic complementarities. But the much stronger penalty for overclaiming entices players to make lower claims. Capra et al. (1999) find that in this treatment, subjects play very close to 80. Because being the high bidder accrues such high penalties in this treatment, QRE predicts that subjects should play close to equilibrium, as found in the data.

Thus it appears that subjects in the Traveler's Dilemma both make errors and anticipate others' errors. In other laboratory games, subjects make errors without being so aware of others' errors. For example, in one treatment of Eyster et al.'s (2018) social-learning experiments, players endowed with private integers make entries one at a time, each observing all predecessors' entries, and each attempts to make an entry as close as possible to her own private integer plus the private integers of all of her predecessors. Approximately 10% of subjects neglect that their predecessors incorporate information from their own predecessors' entries into their entries. For example, in a typical sequence Player 1 enters her private integer, and Player 2 adds Player 1's entry to his own private integer. A rational Player 3 would add her own private integer to Player 2's entry—and ignore Player 1, since Player 2's entry already contains the information in Player 1's entry. Yet many Player 3's add Player 1's entry to Player 2's entry to her own private integer.

A Player 4 who understands that his predecessors make errors adjusts his entry accordingly. In the context of this experiment, since the private integers have mean zero, Player 4 would rationally shade his inference towards zero. Eyster et al. (2018) do not find evidence for this. People appear not appreciate other people's proclivity for error.

QRE has also contributed to the literature by closing models lacking error terms. Carrillo and Palfrey (2009) look at an adverse-selection game in which two players with strengths drawn from a uniform distribution on $[0, 1]$ simultaneously choose whether to "fight" or "compromise". If both compromise, then both get $P \in (0, 1)$. If at least one fights, then the stronger player gets $W > P$, and the weaker 0. The unique BNE has both players always fight, for a logic reminiscent of the one that underlies equilibrium in the disclosure game. If no one fought, then the strongest players would want to fight. If only those above some $\bar{t} \in (0, 1)$ fought, then those with strengths just below $\bar{t}$ would rationally anticipate winning any fight that they cause. Subjects in the lab do not fight nearly so much. In treatments where $W = 1$ and $P = \frac{1}{2}$, roughly the strongest half of subjects choose to fight.

In a fully cursed equilibrium, each player would fight if and only if her strength exceeds $\frac{1}{2}$. Carrillo and Palfrey (2009) propose the notion of "α-QRE" in the context of this game to combine α-cursed equilibrium with QRE. In their impressive and comprehensive book on QRE and its applications, Goeree et al. (2016) rename this concept α-cursed QRE, and I will follow this more descriptive nomenclature. Recall from Section 4 that an α-cursed equilibrium can be found as the BNE of a game with transformed payoffs

$$u_k^\alpha(a_k, a_{-k}; \omega) = (1 - \alpha)u_k(a_k, a_{-k}; \omega) + \alpha \sum_{\omega' \in \Omega} p(\omega' | t_k(\omega))u_k(a_k, a_{-k}; \omega').$$

An α-cursed QRE is a QRE of the game formed using these transformed payoffs. Essentially, QRE makes χ- (or α-) cursed equilibrium amenable to data analysis by adding an error term with the QRE feature that dearer errors orthogonal to cursedness get made less frequently than cheaper ones. Since then, other researchers have closed cursed equilibrium with QRE. Indeed, Camerer et al. (2016) close both cursed equilibrium and the Level-k model in this way.[57]

5.4 Failure to understand payoffs

People who fail to appreciate how payoffs depend upon their own actions, or mis-understand the structure of the game, do not necessarily maximize their expected payoffs given their beliefs.

The uniform-price, multi-unit auction generalizes the second-price auction to multiple units. When k units are auctioned, the price is set by the $k + 1$st highest bid. When bidders value more than one unit of the good, they have incentive to shade their bids of less-valued units below their valuations in order to lower the price. Consider for example two bidders who value two units of the good, and a seller with three units for sale. For simplicity, suppose that bidders know each other's values. Bidder A values her first unit at 5 and second at 3. Bidder B values his first unit at 4 and second at 2. Assume that bids must be non-negative. It is a Nash equilibrium for Bidder A to bid her valuations (bidding 5 for the first unit and 3 for the second) and Bidder B to bid 4 for his first unit and 0 for his second unit. The price then is zero. For Bidder B, raising the bid on his second unit above 0 simply increases the price he pays on his first unit until he reaches a bid of 3, at which point he wins a second unit of a good valued at 2 for a price of 3. Evidence that bidders do not optimally shade their bids below valuations in such auctions may be explained by bidders neglecting the impact that their bid has on price.

Grosskopf and Nagel (2008) look at two-player p-beauty pageants. These differ from the many-player games because the approximation $\overline{a}_{-k} \approx \overline{a}$ is no longer valid. When Player 1 chooses a_1, and Player 2 chooses a_2, the average $\overline{a}$ sits halfway between the two; hence, $\frac{1}{2}\overline{a}$ is closer to $\min\{a_1, a_2\}$ than to $\max\{a_1, a_2\}$. In other words, the player who chooses the lower number always wins. In this case, choosing 0 is a weakly dominant strategy: it always wins. This implies that Level 1's, whose beliefs have full support on $[0, 100]$, should choose 0, as should all higher levels. Grosskopf and Nagel find instead that 90% of student subjects chose something different than zero (with the mean and median 35.6 and 33.7, respectively). They also ran their experiment on professionals attending their talks at various game-theory and psychology conferences. Sixty-three percent of professionals also chose something other than zero (with the mean and median 21.7 and 10.0, respectively).

The evidence of Grosskopf and Nagel suggests that people do not literally play as per the Level-k model: they do not maximize payoffs under the belief that their opponents behave as Level $k - 1$. This might happen because people find the required

---

[57] Goeree and Holt (2000) combine QRE with inequity-aversion preferences.

optimization too challenging. Yet people would nearly certainly solve the same problem correctly other contexts. Consider an employee on a defined-benefit pension plan who expects upon retiring to receive a wage equal to half her average career wage; half her career was paid at the low wage w_L and the other half at the high wage w_H. The employee would most likely correctly perceive her retirement income to be closer to w_L than to w_H. In other words, people probably do have access to the right answer, even if they don't provide it without prompting.

Esponda and Pouzo (2016) explore games in which each player misperceives the consequences of players' actions on payoffs. Not only do players not know the true model, but they do not regard it as possible. They propose the solution concept "Berk–Nash equilibrium" in which each player best responds to her misspecified beliefs, and her beliefs minimize a measure of distance to the true model—her beliefs are as close to true as possible, within the class of wrong models she deems possible. They describe learning processes that may lead people to come to play Berk–Nash equilibrium.

When bidders have private values, the sealed-bid, second-price auction is strategically equivalent to the ascending auction. Yet lab participants adhere more closely to equilibrium theory in the ascending auction than in the second-price auction. Li (2017) proposes an explanation due to a failure to understand payoffs. Consider someone who values the object being auctioned at 7. In both auction formats, she has a dominant strategy of bidding 7. However, in the second-price auction, by bidding above 7, she might win the auction at a price below 7 and earn positive payoff. By bidding 7, she might lose the auction and get nothing. Thus, her best payoff from deviating from equilibrium exceeds her worst payoff from playing equilibrium. In Li's terminology, bidding 7 is not obviously dominant. In the ascending auction, by contrast, staying in the auction past 7 can only result in losses. The best payoff from deviating is worse than the worst payoff from playing equilibrium. Li shows that obviously dominant strategies are played more often than mere dominant strategies.

6   From horserace to foxtrot: applying solution concepts

Many settings of interest to economists take the form of simple signaling games. A firm with private information offers choices to consumers, who then make inferences about what the firm knows before acting. In these settings, consumers do not need to predict the firm's action because they observe that action. Through experience with a large number of customers, the firm learns how consumers make choices. In this section, I compare the different solution concepts in this simple but important class of Bayesian games. Despite some differences in predictions amenable to probing in the lab or field, the solution concepts in this chapter all make broadly similar predictions.

Formally, a sender has type t_S in the finite set T_S and chooses action an action a_S from the finite set A_S. For example, a wealth adviser may propose a fund to an investor; the wealth investor gets a kickback from selling the fund, the amount of which is known to the adviser and unknown to the investor. The receiver has no private information, observes the sender's action, and chooses an action a_R in A_R. The sender has no need to infer; the receiver has no need to predict the sender's action. For simplicity, suppose that the sender has an invertible dominant strategy $a_S(t_S)$. In a BNE, a receiver who observes the action $a'_S \in A_S$ would infer that the sender's type is $t'_S = a_S^{-1}(a'_S)$.

A fully cursed receiver observing a'_S infers nothing and keeps priors over t_S. A partially cursed receiver observing a'_S believes that the sender's type is $t'_S = a_S^{-1}(a'_S)$ with probability $1 - \chi + \chi p_R(t'_S)$, where p_R denotes the receiver's priors over T_S. When $\chi = 0$, this formula gives rational inference; when $\chi = 1$, this formula gives the fully cursed inference.

In a heterogenous cursed equilibrium (Eyster and Rabin, 2005), the receiver's χ can be stochastic. For example, the receiver may be rational ($\chi = 0$) with probability π and fully cursed: $\chi = 1$ with probability $1 - \pi$, for some $\pi \in [0, 1]$. Like partially cursed equilibrium, this solution concept has one estimable parameter.

Whether the receiver is partially cursed, or either rational or fully cursed with positive probability, cursed inference leads the receiver to beliefs about the sender that in some sense lie between the truth and the receiver's priors. Partially cursed beliefs are deterministic, and assign to each type a probability between the truth and the receiver's prior probability, whereas heterogenously cursed beliefs are probabilistic and sometimes coincide with rational beliefs and sometimes with fully cursed beliefs.

In an ABEE, the receiver partitions the sender's type space T_S into analogy classes $\mathcal{A}_S := \{\alpha_S^1, \alpha_S^2, \dots\}$. When the receiver observes a'_S, he believes the sender's type is $t'_S = a_S^{-1}(a'_S)$ with probability $\frac{p_R(t'_S)}{\sum_{t_S \in \alpha(t'_S)} p_R(t_S)}$, where $\alpha(t'_S)$ is the element of $\mathcal{A}_S$ that contains t'_S. When $\mathcal{A}_S = \{\{t_S^1\}, \{t_S^2\}, \dots, \}$, namely the receiver uses the finest possible analogy classes, then we get rational inference. When $\mathcal{A}_S = \{T_S\}$, namely the receiver uses the coarsest possible analogy classes, then we get fully cursed inference. For any analogy classes,

$$\underbrace{p_R(t'_S)}_{\text{prior}} \le \underbrace{\frac{p_R(t'_S)}{\sum_{t_S \in \alpha(t'_S)} p_R(t_S)}}_{\text{ABEE inference}} \le \underbrace{1}_{\text{truth}}.$$

Like in cursed equilibrium, the receiver under-infers the sender's type from her action in ABEE.

Now consider the Level-k model, using the random Level 0 who mixes uniformly over all actions independent of type. A Level-1 receiver best responds to a sender who mixes uniformly over A_S independent of t_S, in which case the receiver maintains his priors over t_S after observing a'_S. A Level-2 receiver understands that the sender plays her dominant strategy $a_S(t_S)$ and behaves as per BNE. All higher-level receivers also understand that the seller uses her dominant strategy and behave in the same way.

Thus Level-1 inference coincides with $\chi = 1$ inference, namely neither gives any inference whatsoever. Level-2 inference is $\chi = 0$, namely rational inference. In the cognitive hierarchy model of Camerer et al. (2004), there is a distribution over levels, F; a Level-k player believes that the probability that her opponent has type $j < k$ is $\frac{f(j)}{F(k-1)}$; that is, Level-$k+1$'s beliefs differ from Level-k's only in that she recognizes that some people are Level-k. In this game, Level-2 inference comes from thinking the sender is either Level 0 or Level 1, namely that the sender either mixes uniformly or plays the dominant strategy. Let $F(k|k < 2)$ assign Level 0 probability τ and Level 1 probability $1 - \tau$. Then a Level-2 receiver observing a_S' believes that the sender's type is $t_S' = a_S^{-1}(a_S')$ with probability

$$p_R(t_S') + \frac{p_R(t_S')(1 - p_R(t_S'))(1 - \tau)}{p_R(t_S')(1 - \tau) + \tau/|A_S|} < 1,$$

where $|A_S|$ denotes the cardinality of A_S. The cognitive hierarchy model mixes receivers who make no inference (namely $\chi = 0$), with those who do partial inference.

In ABEE, the Cognitive-Hierarchy Model, cursed equilibrium, and Level-k (for $k \geq 1$), the sender plays her dominant strategy. In all of these concepts, the receiver under-infers about the sender's type from her action. Many of the "horseraces" amongst models in this and related contexts reduce to whether unitary $\chi \in (0, 1)$ or heterogenous χ (namely a mixture of Levels 1 and 2) fit inference better.[58]

Finally, QRE predicts that the sender does not always play her dominant strategy. Like in a χ-cursed equilibrium, when the receiver observes the action optimal for type t_S, he updates his prior beliefs towards t_S more strongly than towards any other type but does not dismiss the possibility of facing any type. That is, the receiver partially uncovers type from action, but this time correctly so. Relative to the other concepts, QRE predicts greater errors on the part of the sender.

ABEE, the Cognitive-Hierarchy Model, cursed equilibrium, and Level-k all predict that the receiver underinfers the sender's type, and QRE predicts something very similar. Researchers who wish to distinguish amongst predictions would more fruitfully work in other environments. Researchers who want to add some element of underinference to standard economics models with this structure can accomplish their goal with any of the models (up to the caveat about QRE).

7 Conclusion

Strategic decision-making requires that people predict others' actions, predict the relationship between what others do and what they know, and optimize according to their beliefs. People err in all three respects. Voters don't think through how others will change their behavior in response to changes in policy. Potential entrants to a market do not think through how incumbents will change their pricing and marketing

---

[58] For example, Crawford and Iriberri's (2007) argument that the Level-k model fits common-values auction data better than partially cursed equilibrium has this flavor.

after entry. Investors do not think through what private interest motivates their advisers to recommend one investment over another. People do not always choose the actions the promise the highest return given their own beliefs.

This chapter has reviewed evidence for each type of failure. It has presented evidence that in strategically simple games, people appear to underappreciate the rationality of other players. For instance, people do not always anticipate that other people will play dominant actions. In settings where people have plenty of opportunity to learn, such as professional sports, people do not always perceive systematic patterns in others' actions such as serial correlation.

In the settings of perhaps greatest interest to economists, people cannot correctly predict others' actions purely based on knowledge of rationality, or knowledge of rationality plus knowledge of knowledge of rationality. They probably also lack any past experience with the exact game at hand. Instead, people probably have some experience with or observation of similar environments and some understanding of the game's actions and incentives. We have little evidence for how people mispredict others' behavior in such environments.[59] In dynamic games, people will likely underappreciate the extent to which other people's actions depend upon the history of the game, like in the model of Jehiel (2005). Apart from this, we currently have few easily articulated notions of how people will mispredict others' actions.

The chapter has described solution concepts that embed the errors listed above. Some models in the literature address just one of these errors: QRE assumes that people correctly predict what others do, and the relationship between what others do and what they know, but fail to optimize against these beliefs; cursed equilibrium and Analogy-Based-Expectations Equilibrium as applied to Bayesian games both assume that people correctly predict what others do, and best respond to their beliefs, but wrongly infer other people's private information from their actions. Other models involve more than one of these errors. The Level-k model has people mispredict others' actions and, as applied to Bayesian games, mispredict the relationship between what others do and what they know.

The models treated in this chapter differ from one another in important ways orthogonal to my taxonomy of errors. Models in the behavioral-economics tradition, such as cursed equilibrium, embed specific errors into equilibrium-style concepts. These models seem most appropriate for games with which players have some familiarity, be it through direct experience or indirect channels such as direct experience with similar environments. The models have the advantage of making plain exactly how people err. They have the disadvantage of only allowing for very a very circumscribed set of errors. Models in the procedural-rationality style, such as the Level-k model, posit some procedure by which people choose their strategies. They seem most appropriate in novel settings where people have little idea how others will

---

[59] Many lab experiments explore how people play matrix games. They can test how experience with Game A influences behavior in Game B. However, since people think about the world through narratives or stories, such tests will likely underestimate learning from related settings.

behave. These models have the advantage of easy applicability, by eschewing fixed-point logic, and offer a wider set of explainable errors. They have the disadvantage of being extremely sensitive to fine modeling details and sometimes obscuring the exact nature of the error committed.

Although most of the models in this chapter inform experimental design and analysis, they have met with limited success in influencing applied theory and empirical work. Partly, this can be attributed to the difficulty in applying them to standard economic settings. Predictions of the Level-k model can crucially depend upon the choice of Level 0, about which the theory gives minimal guidance. Likewise, the predictions of Analogy-Based-Expectations Equilibrium depend upon the choice of analogy classes. This dependence is not necessarily a bad thing. Predictions of standard game theory often crucially depend upon fine details of the game, especially information structures. Just as economists have gained experience over the past few decades in modeling information structures, they may come to learn how to specify Level 0 and analogy classes. Nevertheless, concepts that can be applied mechanistically are likely to be adopted more widely in applications.

Nearly all of the models in this chapter nest Nash equilibrium (or Bayesian Nash equilibrium) as a limiting case. Although this feature may seem somewhat pedestrian and formulaic, it has the potential to sway discourse in the field. A generation ago, researchers interested in the efficiency of financial markets tested the hypothesis that people inferred perfectly from market prices against the alternative hypothesis that people inferred nothing from market prices (Plott and Sunder, 1988). Researchers at the time lacked a language for describing people who partially, but not fully, inferred information from market prices. Yet many of the questions of greatest interest to economists turn on the question of whether people make perfect or imperfect inferences. Do market prices exhibit momentum? Do bidders in large common-values auctions systematically lose money? Do people with common priors and private information agree to speculative trade? Today's researcher has access to more than one language for estimating the sophistication of people's inferences, and these estimates can be used to make predictions about important economic phenomena. Indeed, I hope that in the near future this estimation exercise will spread outside of the laboratory. Finance and industrial-organization economists, for instance, might estimate parameters of the models elaborated in this chapter in conjunction with estimating signal or preference parameters.

Standard game theory has profoundly altered the field of Economics by turning its focus from perfectly competitive markets to strategic interactions. Writers of the next generation of game-theoretic models should aspire to improve our predictions about how people interact strategically in the real world. Lab evidence has played a vital role in identifying ways in which people's behavior departs systematically from equilibrium analysis. But fitting lab data should not be the ultimate goal of model building. Instead, we should strive to write tractable models that can be applied to any economic setting to improve our profession's predictions. Our models should transparently illuminate how people make correct choices, and how they make incorrect choices. Much work remains to be done!

References

Akerlof, G.A., 1970. The market for 'lemons': quality uncertainty and the market mechanism. Quarterly Journal of Economics 84 (3), 488–500.

Akerlof, G.A., 1991. Procrastination and obedience. American Economic Review 81 (2), 1–19.

Anderson, L.R., Holt, C.A., 1997. Information cascades in the laboratory. American Economic Review 87 (5), 847–862.

Andreoni, J., 1990. Donations to public goods: a theory of warm-glow giving. The Economic Journal 100, 464–477.

Aumann, R., Brandenburger, A., 1995. Epistemic conditions for Nash equilibrium. Econometrica 63 (5), 1161–1180.

Avery, C., Kagel, J., 1997. Second-price auctions with asymmetric payoffs: an experimental investigation. Journal of Economics and Management Strategy 6, 573–603.

Bala, V., Goyal, S., 1998. Learning from neighbours. Review of Economic Studies 65 (3), 595–621.

Ball, S.B., Bazerman, M.H., Carroll, J.S., 1991. An evaluation of learning in the bilateral winner's curse. Organizational Behavior and Human Decision Processes 48 (1), 1–22.

Banerjee, A., 1992. A simple model of herd behavior. Quarterly Journal of Economics 107 (3), 797–817.

Basu, K., 1994. The traveler's dilemma: paradoxes of rationality in game theory. American Economic Review 84 (2), 391–395.

Battaglini, M., Morton, R.B., Palfrey, T.R., 2010. The swing voter's curse in the laboratory. The Review of Economic Studies 77 (1), 61–89.

Battigalli, P., 1987. Comportamento razionale ed equilibrio nei giochi e nelle situazioni sociali, unpublished dissertation.

Bazerman, M., Samuelson, W., 1983. I won the auction but don't want the prize. Journal of Conflict Resolution 27, 618–634.

Bernheim, B.D., 1984. Rationalizable strategic behavior. Econometrica, 1007–1028.

Biais, B., Hilton, D., Mazurier, K., Pouget, S., 2005. Judgmental overconfidence, self-monitoring and trading performance in an experimental financial market. Review of Economic Studies 72, 287–312.

Bikhchandani, S., Hirshleifer, D., Welch, I., 1992. A theory of fads, fashion, custom and cultural change as information cascades. Journal of Political Economy 100 (5), 992–1026.

Bosch-Domènech Montalvo, J.G., Nagel, R., Satorra, A., 2002. One, two, (three), infinity, . . . : newspaper and lab beauty-contest experiments. American Economic Review 92, 1687–1701.

Brown, A.L., Camerer, C.F., Lovallo, D., 2012. To review or not to review? Limited strategic thinking at the movie box office. American Economic Journal: Microeconomics 4 (2), 1–26.

Brown, A.L., Camerer, C.F., Lovallo, D., 2013. Estimating structural models of equilibrium and cognitive hierarchy thinking in the field: the case of withheld movie critic reviews. Management Science 59 (3), 733–747.

Camerer, C., 2003. Behavioral Game Theory. Princeton University Press.

Camerer, C.F., Nunnari, S., Palfrey, T.R., 2016. Quantal response and nonequilibrium beliefs explain overbidding in maximum-value auctions. Games and Economic Behavior 98, 243–263.

Camerer, C., Ho, T.-H., 1998. Experience-weighted attraction in normal form games. Econometrica 67, 827–874.

Camerer, C., Ho, T.-H., Chong, J.-K., 2004. A cognitive hierarchy model of games. Quarterly Journal of Economics 119 (3), 861–898.

Capra, C.M., Goeree, J.K., Gomez, R., Holt, C.A., 1999. Anomalous behavior in a traveler's dilemma? American Economic Review 89, 678–690.

Carrillo, J.D., Palfrey, T.R., 2009. The compromise game: two-sided adverse selection in the laboratory. American Economic Journal: Microeconomics 1 (1), 151–181.

Celerier, C., La Vallee, B., 2017. Catering to investors through security design: headline rate and complexity. Quarterly Journal of Economics 132, 1469–1508.

Conlin, M., Dickert-Conlin, S., 2013. Inference by college admission departments. Mimeo.

Corgnet, B., DeSantis, M., Porter, D., 2017. Revisiting information aggregation in asset markets: reflective learning and market efficiency. Mimeo.

Costa Gomes, M., Crawford, V., 2006. Cognition and behavior in two-person guessing games: an experimental study. American Economic Review 96 (5), 1737–1768.

Costa Gomes, M., Crawford, V., Broseta, B., 2001. Cognition and behavior in normal-form games: an experimental study. Econometrica 69 (5), 1193–1235.

Costa Gomes, M., Weizsäcker, G., 2008. Stated beliefs and play in normal-form games. Review of Economic Studies 75 (3), 729–762.

Crawford, V., Iriberri, N., 2007. Level-k auctions: can a non-equilibrium model of strategic thinking explain the winner's curse and overbidding in private-value auctions? Econometrica 75 (6), 1721–1770.

Crawford, V.P., Costa-Gomes, M.A., Iriberri, N., 2013. Structural models of nonequilibrium strategic thinking: theory, evidence, and applications. Journal of Economic Literature 51 (1), 5–62.

Dal Bó, E., Dal Bó, P., Eyster, E., 2018. The demand for bad policy when voters underappreciate equilibrium effects. Review of Economic Studies 85 (2), 964–998.

Daniel, K., Hirshleifer, D., Subrahmanyam, A., 1998. Investor psychology and security market under- and overreactions. Journal of Finance 53 (6), 1839–1885.

Daniel, K., Hirshleifer, D., Subrahmanyam, A., 2001. Overconfidence, arbitrage, and equilibrium asset pricing. Journal of Finance 56 (3), 921–965.

Dekel, E., Fudenberg, D., Levine, D.K., 2004. Learning to play Bayesian games. Games and Economic Behavior 46 (2), 282–303.

DellaVigna, S., Kaplan, E., 2007. The fox news effect: media bias and voting. Quarterly Journal of Economics 122, 1187–1234.

DellaVigna, S., Malmendier, U., 2004. Contract design and self-control: theory and evidence. Quarterly Journal of Economics 119, 353–402.

DellaVigna, S., Pope, D., 2018. Predicting experimental results: who knows what? Journal of Political Economy 126, 2410–2456.

Dhami, S., 2016. The Foundations of Behavioral Economic Analysis. Oxford University Press.

Dranove, D., Jin, G.Z., 2010. Quality disclosure and certification: theory and practice. Journal of Economic Literature 48 (4), 935–963.

Dufwenberg, M., Kirchsteiger, G., 2004. A theory of sequential reciprocity. Games and Economic Behavior 47 (2), 268–298.

Ellis, A., Piccione, M., 2017. Correlation misperception in choice. American Economic Review 107 (4), 1264–1292.

Enke, B., Zimmermann, F., 2017. Correlation neglect in belief formation. Review Economic Studies. https://doi.org/10.1093/restud/rdx081. Forthcoming.

Esponda, I., 2008. Behavioral equilibrium in economies with adverse selection. American Economic Review 98 (4), 1269–1291.

Esponda, I., Pouzo, D., 2016. Berk–Nash equilibrium: a framework for modeling agents with misspecified models. Econometrica 84 (3), 1093–1130.

Esponda, I., Vespa, E., 2014. Hypothetical thinking and information extraction in the laboratory. American Economic Journal: Microeconomics 6 (4), 180–202.

Ettinger, D., Jehiel, P., 2010. A theory of deception. American Economic Journal: Microeconomics 2 (1), 1–20.

Eyster, E., Madarasz, K., Michaillat, P., 2017. Pricing when Customers Care About Fairness but Misinfer Markups. NBER Working Paper 23778.

Eyster, E., Rabin, M., 2005. Cursed equilibrium. Econometrica 73 (5), 1623–1672.

Eyster, E., Rabin, M., 2010. Naive herding in rich-information settings. American Economic Journal: Microeconomics 2 (4), 221–243.

Eyster, E., Rabin, M., 2014. Extensive imitation is irrational and harmful. Quarterly Journal of Economics, 1861–1898.

Eyster, E., Rabin, M., Vayanos, D., 2019. Financial markets where traders neglect the informational content of prices. Journal of Finance. https://doi.org/10.1111/jofi.12729. Forthcoming.

Eyster, E., Rabin, M., Weizsäcker, G., 2018. An Experiment on Social Mislearning. Rationality and Competition, LMU Discussion Paper 73.

Eyster, E., Weizsäcker, G., 2011. Correlation Neglect in Financial Decision-Making. DIW Discussion Paper 1104.

Falk, A., Fischbacher, U., 2006. A theory of reciprocity. Games and Economic Behavior 54 (2), 293–315.

Feddersen, T., Pesendorfer, W., 1996. The swing voter's curse. American Economic Review 86, 408–424.

Feddersen, T., Pesendorfer, W., 1998. Convicting the innocent: the inferiority of unanimous jury verdicts under strategic voting. American Political Science Review 90, 23–35.

Fehr, E., Schmidt, K.M., 1999. A theory of fairness, competition, and cooperation. Quarterly Journal of Economics 114 (3), 817–868.

Forsythe, R., Isaac, R.M., Palfrey, T.R., 1989. Theories and tests of 'blind bidding' in sealed-bid auctions. RAND Journal of Economics 20 (2), 214–238.

Friedman, D., Oprea, R., 2012. A continuous dilemma. The American Economic Review 102 (1), 337–363.

Fudenberg, D., Kreps, D.M., 1998. A Theory of Learning, Experimentation and Equilibrium in Games. Working Paper.

Fudenberg, D., Levine, D.K., 1993. Self-confirming equilibrium. Econometrica 61 (3), 523–545.

Fudenberg, D., Levine, D.K., 1998. The Theory of Learning in Games. MIT Press.

Fudenberg, D., Peysakhovich, A., 2014. Recency, records and recaps: learning and non-equilibrium behavior in a simple decision problem. In: Proceedings of the 15th ACM Conference on Economics and Computation.

Gabaix, X., Laibson, D., 2006. Shrouded attributes, consumer myopia, and information suppression. Quarterly Journal of Economics, 505–540.

Gagnon-Bartsch, T., 2016. Taste projection in models of social learning. Mimeo.

Gagnon-Bartsch, T., Rabin, M., 2016. Naive social learning, mislearning, and unlearning. Mimeo.

Gauriot, R., Page, L., Wooders, J., 2016. Nash at Wimbledon: evidence from half a million serves. Mimeo.

Geanakoplos, J., Pearce, D., Stacchetti, E., 1989. Psychological games and sequential rationality. Games and Economic Behavior 1 (1), 60–79.

Georganas, S., Healy, P., Weber, R., 2015. On the persistence of strategic sophistication. Journal of Economic Theory 159, 369–400.

Gill, D., Prowse, V., 2016. Cognitive ability, character skills, and learning to play equilibrium: a level-k analysis. Journal of Political Economy 124, 1619–1676.

Glaeser, E.L., Nathanson, C.G., 2017. An extrapolative model of house price dynamics. Journal of Financial Economics 126, 147–170.

Gneezy, U., Rustichini, A., 2000. A fine is a price. The Journal of Legal Studies 29 (1), 1–17.

Goeree, J.K., Holt, C.A., 2000. Asymmetric inequality aversion and noisy behavior in alternating-offer bargaining games. European Economic Review 44 (4), 1079–1089.

Goeree, J.K., Holt, C.A., 2004. A model of noisy introspection. Games and Economic Behavior 46 (2), 365–382.

Goeree, J.K., Holt, C.A., Palfrey, T.R., 2016. Quantal Response Equilibrium: A Stochastic Theory of Games. Princeton University Press.

Goeree, J., Palfrey, T., Rogers, B., McKelvey, R., 2007. Self-correcting information cascades. Review of Economic Studies 74 (3), 733–762.

Golub, B., Jackson, M.O., 2010. Naïve learning in social networks and the wisdom of crowds. American Economic Journal: Microeconomics 2 (1), 112–149.

Grosskopf, B., Nagel, R., 2008. The two-person beauty contest. Games and Economic Behavior 62, 93–99.

Grubb, M., 2009. Selling to overconfident consumers. American Economic Review, 1770–1807.

Guarino, A., Jehiel, P., 2013. Social learning with coarse inference. American Economic Journal: Microeconomics 5 (1), 147–174.

Guarnaschelli, S., McKelvey, R., Palfrey, T., 2000. An experimental study of jury decision rules. American Political Science Review 94, 407–423.

Güth, W., Schmittberger, R., Schwarze, B., 2000. An experimental analysis of ultimatum bargaining. Journal of Economic Behavior & Organization 3, 367–388.

Haile, P., Hortacsu, A., Kosenok, G., 2008. On the empirical content of quantal response equilibrium. American Economic Review 98, 180–200.

Harsanyi, J.C., 1967a. Games with incomplete information played by "bayesian" players. Part I: the basic model. Management Science 14 (3), 159–182.

Harsanyi, J.C., 1967b. Games with incomplete information played by "bayesian" players. Part II: Bayesian equilibrium points. Management Science 14 (3), 320–334.

Heidhues, P., Kőszegi, B., 2018. Behavioral industrial organization. In: Bernheim, D.B., DellaVigna, S., Laibson, D. (Eds.), Handbook of Behavioral Economics, vol. 1. Elsevier, pp. 517–612.

Hendricks, K., Porter, R.H., 1988. An empirical study of an auction with asymmetric information. The American Economic Review, 865–883.

Hendricks, K., Porter, R.H., Boudreau, B., 1987. Information, returns, and bidding behavior in ocs auctions: 1954–1969. The Journal of Industrial Economics, 517–542.

Holt, C., Sherman, R., 1994. The loser's curse. The American Economic Review 84, 642–652.

Ispano, A., Schwardmann, P., 2016. Competitive pricing and quality disclosure to cursed consumers.

Ivanov, A., Levin, D., Niederle, M., 2010. Can relaxation of beliefs rationalize the winner's curse?: An experimental study. Econometrica 78 (4), 1435–1452.

Jehiel, P., 2005. Analogy-based expectation equilibrium. Journal of Economic Theory 123 (2), 81–104.

Jehiel, P., Koessler, F., 2008. Revisiting games of incomplete information with analogy-based expectations. Games and Economic Behavior 62 (2), 533–557.

Jin, G., 2005. Competition and disclosure incentives: an empirical study of HMOs. RAND Journal of Economics 36 (1), 93–112.

Jin, G., Luca, M., Martin, D., 2015. Is no news (perceived as) bad news? An experimental investigation of information disclosure. Mimeo.

Johnson, E., Camerer, C., Sen, S., Rymon, T., 2002. Detecting failures of backward induction: monitoring information search in sequential bargaining. Journal of Economic Theory 104 (1), 16–47.

Kagel, J., Levin, D., 1986. The winner's curse and public information in common value auctions. American Economic Review 76 (5), 894–920.

Kagel, J.H., Levin, D., 2002. Common Value Auctions and the Winner's Curse. Princeton University Press, Princeton.

Kneeland, T., 2015. Identifying higher-order rationality. Econometrica 83 (5), 265–279.

Kondor, P., Kőszegi, B., 2015. Cursed financial innovation. Mimeo.

Kübler, D., Weizsäcker, G., 2004. Limited depth of reasoning and failure of cascade formation in the laboratory. Review of Economic Studies 71 (2), 425–441.

Laibson, D., 1997. Golden eggs and hyperbolic discounting. Quarterly Journal of Economics 112 (2), 443–477.

Levitt, S., List, J., Sadoff, S., 2011. Checkmate: exploring backward induction among chess players. American Economic Review 101 (2), 975–990.

Levy, G., Razin, R., 2015. Correlation neglect, voting behavior, and information aggregation. American Economic Review 105 (4), 1634–1645.

Li, S., 2017. Obviously strategy-proof mechanisms. American Economic Review 107 (11), 3257–3287.

Lintner, J., 1969. The aggregation of investor's diverse judgments and preferences in purely competitive security markets. The Journal of Financial and Quantitative Analysis 4 (4), 347–400.

Luca, M., Smith, J., 2013. Salience in quality disclosure: evidence from the US news college rankings. Journal of Economics & Management Strategy 22 (1), 58–77.

Luce, R., 1959. Individual Choice Behavior. Wiley.

Madarasz, K., 2015. Projection Equilibrium: Definition and Applications to Social Investment and Persuasion. CEPR Discussion Paper DP10636.

Magnani, J., Oprea, R., 2014. Why do People Violate No-Trade Theorems? A Diagnostic Test. UCSB Working Paper.

Maskin, E., Tirole, J., 2001. Markov perfect equilibrium. Journal of Economic Theory 100, 191–219.

Mathios, A.D., 2000. The impact of mandatory disclosure laws on product choices: an analysis of the salad dressing market. Journal of Law and Economics 43, 651.

McFadden, D., 1976. Quantal choice analysis: a survey. Annals of Economic and Social Measurement 5, 363–390.

McKelvey, R., Palfrey, T., 1992. An experimental study of the centipede game. Econometrica 60, 803–836.

McKelvey, R., Palfrey, T., 1995. Quantal response equilibria for normal form games. Games and Economic Behavior 10, 6–38.

Miettinen, T., 2009. The partially cursed and the analogy-based expectation equilibrium. Economics Letters 105 (2), 162–164.

Milgrom, P., Roberts, J., 1986. Relying on the information of interested parties. Rand Journal of Economics 17 (1), 18–32.

Milgrom, P., Stokey, N., 1982. Information, trade, and common knowledge. Journal of Economic Theory 26 (1), 17–27.

Mullainathan, S., Schwartzstein, J., Shleifer, A., 2008. Coarse thinking and persuasion. Quarterly Journal of Economics 123 (2), 577–619.

Murfin, J., Pratt, R., 2018. Comparables pricing. Review of Financial Studies. https://doi.org/10.1093/rfs/hhy047. Forthcoming.

Nagel, R., 1995. Unraveling in guessing games: an experimental study. American Economic Review 85 (5), 1313–1326.

Nash, J., 1950. Equilibrium points in n-person games. Proceedings of the National Academy of Sciences 36 (1), 48–49.

Nash, J., 1951. Non-cooperative games. The Annals of Mathematics 54 (2), 286–295.

Ngangoue, K., Weizsäcker, G., 2016. Learning from unrealized versus realized prices.

Odean, T., 1998. Volume, volatility, price, and profit when all traders are above average. Journal of Finance 53 (6), 1887–1934.

O'Donoghue, T., Rabin, M., 1999. Doing it now or later. American Economic Review 89 (1), 103–124.

Ortoleva, P., Snowberg, E., 2015. Overconfidence in political behavior. American Economic Review 105 (2), 504–535.

Palacios-Huerta, I., 2003. Professionals play minmax. Review of Economic Studies, 395–415.

Pearce, D.G., 1984. Rationalizable strategic behavior and the problem of perfection. Econometrica, 1029–1050.

Plott, C., Sunder, S., 1988. Rational expectations and the aggregation of diverse information in laboratory security markets. Econometrica 56, 1085–1118.

Rabin, M., 1993. Incorporating fairness into game theory and economics. American Economic Review, 1281–1302.

Rabin, M., 2002. Inference by believers in the law of small numbers. Quarterly Journal of Economics 117 (3), 775–816.

Rabin, M., 2013. An approach to incorporating psychology into economics. American Economic Review 103 (3), 617–622.

Rabin, M., Vayanos, D., 2010. The gambler's and hot-hand fallacies: theory and applications. Review of Economic Studies 77, 730–778.

Radner, R., 1980. Collusive behavior in epsilon equilibria of oligopolies with long but finite lives. Journal of Economic Theory 22, 136–154.

Roll, R., 1986. The hubris hypothesis of corporate takeovers. The Journal of Business 59 (2), 197–216.

Rosenthal, R., 1981. Games of perfect information, predatory pricing and the chain-store paradox. Journal of Economic Theory, 92–100.

Roth, A., Erev, I., 1995. Learning in extensive form games: experimental data and simple dynamic models in the intermediate term. Games and Economic Behavior 8, 164–212.

Rubinstein, A., 1986. Finite automata play the repeated prisoner's dilemma. Journal of Economic Theory, 83–96.

Rubinstein, A., 2006. Dilemmas of an economic theorist. Econometrica 74, 865–883.

Samuelson, W., Bazerman, M., 1985. The winner's curse in bilateral negotiations. In: Smith, V. (Ed.), Research in Experimental Economics, vol. 3. JAI Press, Greenwich, CT, pp. 105–137.

Schelling, T., 1984. Choice and Consequence. Harvard University Press.

Selten, R., 1965. Spieltheoretische behandlung eines oligopolmodells mit nachfrageträgheit: Teil i: Bestimmung des dynamischen preisgleichgewichts. Journal of Institutional and Theoretical Economics, 301–324.

Simonsohn, U., 2010. eBay's crowded evenings: competition neglect in market entry decisions. Management Science 56 (7), 1060–1073.

Simonsohn, U., Ariely, D., 2008. When rational sellers face non-rational buyers: evidence from herding in online auctions. Management Science 54, 1624–1637.

Smith, L., Sørensen, P., 2000. Pathological outcomes of observational learning. Econometrica 68 (2), 371–398.

Spiegler, R., 2005. Testing threats in repeated games. Games and Economic Behavior 121, 214–235.

Spiegler, R., 2006. The market for quacks. Review of Economic Studies 73 (4), 1113–1131.

Spiegler, R., 2016. Bayesian networks and boundedly rational expectations. Quarterly Journal of Economics 131, 1243–1290.

Spiegler, R., 2017. "Data monkeys": a procedural model of extrapolation from partial statistics. Review of Economic Studies 84, 1818–1841.

Stahl, D.O.I., Wilson, P.W., 1994. Experimental evidence on players' models of other players. Journal of Economic Behaviour & Organization 25 (3), 309–327.

Stone, D.F., Zafar, B., 2014. Do we follow others when we should outside the lab? Evidence from the AP top 25. Journal of Risk and Uncertainty 49 (4), 73–102.

Strotz, R., 1955. Myopia and inconsistency in dynamic utility maximization. Review of Economic Studies 23 (3), 165–180.

Tirole, J., 1988. The Theory of Industrial Organisation. MIT Press.

Walker, M., Wooders, J., 2001. Minimax play at Wimbledon. American Economic Review 91 (5), 1521–1538.

Weizsäcker, G., 2003. Ignoring the rationality of others: evidence from experimental normal-form games. Games and Economic Behavior 44 (1), 145–171.

Weizsäcker, G., 2010. Do we follow others when we should? A simple test of rational expectations. American Economic Review 100 (5), 2340–2360.

Ziegelmeyer, A., March, C., Krügel, S., 2013. Do we follow others when we should? A simple test of rational expectations: comment. American Economic Review 103 (6), 2633–2642.

Behavioral inattention

4

Xavier Gabaix[a]

Harvard University, Cambridge, MA, United States of America
National Bureau of Economic Research, Cambridge, MA, United States of America
e-mail address: xgabaix@fas.harvard.edu

Contents

[a] I thank Vu Chau, Antonio Coppola, and Lingxuan Wu for excellent research assistance. For comments and suggestions, I thank the editors of this *Handbook*, Hunt Allcott, Sandro Ambuehl, Pedro Bordalo, Colin Camerer, Cary Frydman, Nicola Gennaioli, Sam Gershman, David Hirshleifer, Filip Matejka, Antonio Rangel, Gautam Rao, Alex Rees-Jones, Michael Thaler, Laura Veldkamp, Patrick Warren, and Mirko Wiederholt. For sharing their data, I thank Stefano DellaVigna, Josh Pollet, and Devin Pope. I thank the Sloan Foundation for support.

1 Introduction

It is clear that our attention is limited. When choosing, say, a bottle of wine for dinner, we think about just a few considerations (the price and the quality of the wine), but not about the myriad of components (for example, future income, the interest rate, the potential learning value from drinking this wine) that are too minor. Traditional rational economics assumes that we process all the information that is freely available to us.

Modifying this classical assumption is empirically desirable and theoretically doable. Moreover, it is necessary in order to attain greater psychological realism in economic modeling, and ultimately to improve our understanding of markets and to design better policies. This chapter is a user-friendly introduction to this research. The style of this chapter is that of a graduate course, with pedagogical, self-contained derivations.[1] We will proceed as follows.

---

[1] Other surveys exist. DellaVigna (2009) offers a broad and readable introduction to measurement, in particular of inattention, and Caplin (2016) offers a review, from a more information-theoretic point of view.

Section 2 is a high-level overview. I use a simple framework to model the behavior of an inattentive consumer. Attention is parameterized by a value m, such that $m = 0$ corresponds to zero attention (hence, to a very behavioral model in which the agent relies on a very crude "default" perception of the world) and $m = 1$ to full attention (hence, to the traditional rational model). At a formal level, this simple framework captures a large number of behavioral phenomena: inattention to prices and to taxes; base rate neglect; inattention to sample size; over- and underreaction to news (which both stem from inattention to the true autocorrelation of a stochastic time series); local inattention to details of the future (also known as "projection bias"); global inattention to the future (also known as hyperbolic discounting). At the same time, the framework is quite tractable. I also use this framework to discuss the psychology of attention.

Once this framework is in place, Section 3 discusses methods used to measure inattention empirically: from observational ones like eye-tracking to some that more closely approach a theoretical ideal.[2] I then survey concrete findings in the empirics of attention. Measuring attention is still a hard task – we still have only a limited number of papers that measure attention in field settings – but it is often rewarded with very good publications.

Fig. 1 synthesizes this literature measuring attention. On average, the attention parameter estimated in the literature is 0.44, roughly halfway between no attention and full attention. Sensibly, attention is higher when the incentives to pay attention are stronger.

The survey then takes a more theoretical turn, and explores in greater depth the determinants of attention. In Section 4, I start with the most tractable models, those that yield deterministic predictions (that is, for a given situation, there is a deterministic action). Some models rely on the plain notion that more important dimensions should be given more attention – this is plain, but not actually trivial to capture in a tractable model. Some other models put the accent on proportional thinking rather than absolute thinking: in this view, people pay more attention to relatively more important dimensions.

Section 6 then covers models with stochastic decisions – given an objective situation, the prediction is a probability distribution over the agents' actions. These are more complex models. We will cover random choice models, as well as the strand of the literature in which agents pay to acquire more precise signals. We will then move on to the entropy-based penalty that has found particular favor among macroeconomists.

What are the consequences of introducing behavioral inattention into economic models? This chapter reviews many such implications, in industrial organization, taxation, macroeconomics, and other areas. Section 5 presents something elementary that helps unify all of these strands: a behavioral version of the most basic chapter

---

[2] I positioned this section early in the survey because many readers are interested in the measurement of attention. While a small fraction of the empirical discussion uses some notions from the later theoretical analysis, I wished to emphasize that most of it simply relies on the basic framework of Section 2.

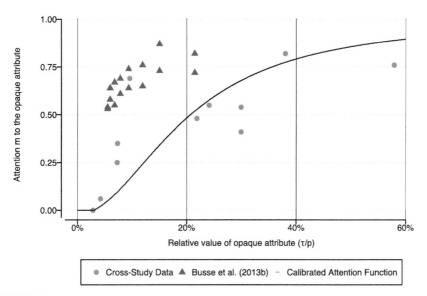

FIGURE 1

Attention point estimates (m) vs. relative value of opaque attribute (τ/p), with overlaid calibrated attention function. Underlying those studies is the following common setup: the full price $q = p + \tau$ of a good is the sum of a base good price p and an opaque price τ. However, an inattentive consumer will perceive $q^s = p + m\tau$, where m captures attention to the opaque attribute. A value $m = 1$ corresponds to full attention, while $m = 0$ implies complete inattention. This figure shows (*circles*) point estimates of the attention parameter m in a cross-section of recent studies (shown in Table 1), against the estimated relative value of the opaque τ add-on attribute relative to the base good or quantity (τ/p). The overlaid curve shows the corresponding calibration of the quadratic-cost attention function in (26), where we impose $\alpha = 1$ and obtain calibrated cost parameters $\bar{\kappa} = 3.0\%$, $q = 22.4$ via nonlinear least squares. Additionally, for comparison, we plot analogous data points (*triangles*) for subsamples from the study of Busse et al. (2013b), who document inattention to left-digit remainders in the mileage of cars sold at auction, broken down along covariate dimensions. Each data point in the latter series corresponds to a subsample including all cars with mileages within a 10,000 mile-wide bin (e.g., between 15,000 and 25,000 miles, between 25,000 miles and 35,000 miles, and so forth). For each mileage bin, we include data points from both retail and wholesale auctions.

of the microeconomics textbook à la Varian (1992), including consumer theory, and Arrow–Debreu. As most of rational economics builds on these pillars, it is useful to have a behavioral alternative.

Section 7 moves on to dynamic models. The key pattern there is that of delayed reaction: people react to novel events, but with some variable lag. Sometimes, they do not attend to a decision altogether – we have then a form of "radical inattention". Useful approaches in this domain include models that introduce costs from changing one's action, or costs from changing one's thinking (these are called "sticky action" and "sticky information" models, respectively). We will also discuss models of "habit formation", and models in which agents optimally choose how to acquire information over time. We will understand the benefits and drawbacks of each of these various models.

Finally, Section 8 proposes a list of open questions. The appendices give mathematical complements and additional proofs.

Notation. I will typically use subscripts for derivatives, e.g. $f_x(x, y) = \frac{\partial}{\partial x} f(x, y)$, except when the subscript is i or t, in which case it is an index for a dimension i or time t.

I differentiate between the true value of a variable x, and its subjectively perceived value, x^s (the s stands for: "subjectively perceived value", or sometimes, the value given by $s$alience or $s$parsity).

2 A simple framework for modeling attention

In this section I discuss a simple framework for thinking about behavioral inattention in economic modeling, and I argue that this simple structure is useful in unifying several themes of behavioral economics, at least in a formal sense. I start from a basic example of prior-anchoring and adjustment toward perceived signals in a model with Gaussian noise, and then move to a more general model structure that captures behavioral inattention in a deterministic fashion.

2.1 An introduction: Anchoring and adjustment via Gaussian signal extraction

Suppose there is a true value x, drawn from a Gaussian distribution $\mathcal{N}(x^d, \sigma_x^2)$, where x^d is the default value (here, the prior mean) and variance σ_x^2. However, the agent does not know this true value, and instead she receives the signal

$$s = x + \varepsilon \tag{1}$$

where ε is drawn from an independent distribution $\mathcal{N}(0, \sigma_\varepsilon^2)$. The agent takes the action a. The agent's objective function is $u(a, x) = -\frac{1}{2}(a - x)^2$, so that if she's rational, the agent wants to take the action that solves: $\max_a \mathbb{E}\left[-\frac{1}{2}(a - x)^2 \mid s\right]$. That is, the agent wants to guess the value of x given the noisy signal s. The first-order condition is

$$0 = \mathbb{E}\left[-(a - x) \mid s\right] = \mathbb{E}\left[x \mid s\right] - a$$

so that the rational thing to do is to take the action $a(s) = \hat{x}(s)$, where $\hat{x}(s)$ is the expected value of x given s,

$$\hat{x}(s) = \mathbb{E}\left[x \mid s\right] = \lambda s + (1 - \lambda) x^d \tag{2}$$

with the dampening factor[3]

$$\lambda = \frac{\sigma_x^2}{\sigma_x^2 + \sigma_\varepsilon^2} \in [0, 1]. \tag{3}$$

Eq. (2) says that the agent should anchor at the prior mean x^d, and partially adjust (with a shrinkage factor m) toward the signal s. The average action $\bar{a}(x) := \mathbb{E}[a(s)|x]$ is then:

$$\bar{a}(x) = mx + (1 - m)x^d \tag{4}$$

with $\lambda = m$. In the rest of this paper, I will analogously use the common notation m to index the limited reaction to a stimulus. In this Bayesian subsection, m is microfounded as a Bayesian ratio of variances λ, but in more general contexts (that we shall see shortly) that need not be the case. In the limit case of an agent who is perfectly well-informed, $\sigma_\varepsilon = 0$, and $m = 1$. In the opposite limit of a very confused agent with infinite noise ($\sigma_\varepsilon \to \infty$), $m = 0$ and the agent relies entirely on her default value.

This is akin to the psychology of "anchoring and adjustment". As Tversky and Kahneman (1974, p. 1129) put it: "People make estimates by starting from an initial value that is adjusted to yield the final answer [...]. Adjustments are typically insufficient". Here, agents start from the default value x^d and on expectation adjusts it toward the truth x. Adjustments are insufficient, as $m \in [0, 1]$, because signals are generally imprecise.

Most models are variants or generalizations of the model in Eq. (4), with different weights m (endogenous or not) on the true value. In this review, I discuss a first class of models that eliminates the noise, as not central, at least for the prediction of the average behavior (see Section 4). I then discuss a second class of frameworks in which noise is central – which often leads to more complicated models (see Section 6).

Before discussing these variants and generalizations, I will present a simple formal framework for modeling inattention.

2.2 Models with deterministic attention and action

Most models of inattention have the following common structure. The agent should maximize

$$\max_a u(a, x) \tag{5}$$

where, as before, a is an action (possibly multidimensional), and x is a vector of "attributes", e.g. price innovations, characteristics of goods, additional taxes, deviations from the steady state, and so on. So a rational agent will choose $a^r(x) = \text{argmax}_a u(a, x)$.

---

[3] The math used here should be familiar, but a refresher is given in Appendix A.

The behavioral agent replaces this by an "attention-augmented decision utility",

$$\max_a u\,(a, x, m) \tag{6}$$

where m is a vector that will characterize the degree of attention – i.e. the agent's subjective *model* of the world. She takes the action

$$a\,(x, m) = \operatorname*{argmax}_a u\,(a, x, m).$$

In inattention models, we will very often take (as in Gabaix and Laibson, 2006; Chetty et al., 2009; DellaVigna, 2009; Gabaix, 2014)[4]

$$u\,(a, x, m) = u\left(a, m_1 x_1 + (1 - m_1)\,x_1^d, \ldots, m_n x_n + (1 - m_n)\,x_n^d\right), \tag{9}$$

where $m_i \in [0, 1]$ is the attention to variable x_i, and where x_i^d is the "default value" for variable i – it is the value that spontaneously comes to mind with no thinking. This is as if x_i is replaced by the *subjectively* perceived x_i^s:

$$x_i^s := m_i x_i + (1 - m_i)\,x_i^d. \tag{10}$$

When $m_i = 0$, the agent "does not think about x_i", i.e. replaces x_i by $x_i^s = x_i^d$.[5] When $m_i = 1$, she perceives the true value ($x_i^s = x_i$). When $0 < m_i < 1$, she perceives partially the true value, though not fully; one microfoundation for that may be the model of Section 2.1, where the agent reacts partially to a noisy signal.[6]

The default x_i^d is typically the prior mean of x_i. However, it can be psychologically richer. For instance, if the mean price of good i is $\mathbb{E}\,[x_i] = \$10.85$, then the normatively simplest default is $x_i^d = \mathbb{E}\,[x_i] = \$10.85$. But the default might be a truncated price, e.g. $x_i^d = \$10$ (see Lacetera et al., 2012).

---

[4] Some other models (e.g. Bordalo et al., 2013, reviewed below in Section 4.2), take the form

$$u\,(a, x, m) = u\,(a, m_{a1} x_1, \ldots, m_{an} x_n) \tag{7}$$

where the attention parameters depend on the goods and the action, so that m has dimensions $A \times n$, where A is the number of goods. We keep a simpler form now, as it allows us to use continuous actions (so $A = \infty$) and take derivatives with respect to action a. Also, the attention parameter m is often deployed multiplicatively "outside the utility", as in

$$u\,(a, x, m) = mu\,(a, x) + (1 - m)\,u\left(a, x^d\right). \tag{8}$$

Still, in most cases with continuous actions placing m inside the utility function makes the model more tractable and more expressive.

[5] Responding to the "default" x_i^d (corresponding to $m_i = 0$) is referred to in the psychology literature alternatively as an automatic, habitual or prepotent response.

[6] The linear form is largely for analytical convenience, and is not essential.

To fix ideas, take the following quadratic example:

$$u\left(a, x\right) = -\frac{1}{2}\left(a - \sum_{i=1}^{n} b_i x_i\right)^2,$$ (11)

with 0 for the default values ($x_i^d = 0$). Then, the traditional optimal action is

$$a^r\left(x\right) = \sum_{i=1}^{n} b_i x_i,$$ (12)

where the r superscript is as in the traditional *rational* actor model. For instance, to choose a, the decision maker should consider not only innovations x_1 in her wealth, and the deviation of GDP from its trend, x_2, but also the impact of interest rate, x_{10}, demographic trends in China, x_{100}, recent discoveries in the supply of copper, x_{200}, etc. There are an innumerable number of factors that should in principle be taken into account. A sensible agent will "not think" about most of these factors, especially the less important ones. We will formalize this notion.

After attention m is chosen, the behavioral agent optimizes under her simpler representation of the world, i.e. chooses

$$a^s\left(x, m\right) = \sum_{i=1}^{n} b_i m_i x_i,$$

so that if $m_i = 0$, she doesn't pay attention to dimension i.

2.3 Unifying behavioral biases: Much of behavioral economics may reflect a form of inattention

Let us see some examples that will show how this form captures – at a formal level at least – many themes of behavioral economics. We shall see that many behavioral biases share a common structure: people anchor on a simple perception of the world, and partially adjusts toward it. Conceptually, there is a "default, simple model" that spontaneously comes to mind,[7] and there is a "true model" that's only imperfectly perceived. Attention m parameterizes the particular convex combination of the default and true models that corresponds to the agent's perception.[8]

This feeling of unity of behavioral economics is tentative – and in part my own speculation, rather than an agreed-upon truth. Still, I find it useful to make a case for it in this chapter. One could imagine doing "attentional interventions" (changing m)

---

[7] Kahneman and Frederick (2002) call something very close to this idea "attribute substitution" – the use of a simplified model, or question, that is cognitively easier than the original problem.

[8] Gabaix (2014, Online Appendix, Section 9.A) contains an early version of this list, with a fuller treatment some of the biases below, including the endogenization of attention m.

to investigate this type of hypothesis experimentally (see e.g. Lombardi and Fehr, 2018 for a step in that direction).

Different cognitive functions underlying limited attention. Attention involves the allocation of scarce cognitive resources. In the examples below, I will not go much into the detailed exploration of what those scarce resources are. They include limited working memory, limited ability to carry out complex algorithms, or lack of readily-accessible knowledge.[9] What drives attention are components of information processing, which are subsumed by the common abstraction m that I use in all these examples.

2.3.1 Inattention to true prices and shrouding of add-on costs

Let us illustrate the misperception of numbers in the context of prices. We start from a default price p^d. The new price is p, while the subjectively price p^s perceived by the agent is

$$p^s = mp + (1 - m) p^d. \tag{13}$$

The perceived price p^s responds only partially (with a strength m) to the true price p, perhaps as in the noisy-signal microfoundation of Section 2.1.

Take the case without income effects, where the rational demand is $c^r(p)$. Then, the demand of a behavioral agent is $c^s(p) = c^r(p^s(p, m))$. So, the sensitivity of demand to price is $c^s(p)' = mc^r(p^s)'$. The demand sensitivity is muted by a factor m.

We can also reason in logarithmic space, so that the perceived price is:

$$p^s = (p)^m \left(p^d\right)^{1-m}. \tag{14}$$

In general, the psychology of numbers (Dehaene, 2011) shows that the latter formulation (in log space) is psychologically more accurate. This Cobb–Douglas formulation is sometimes used in Gabaix (2014) and Khaw et al. (2017) – the latter framework is a stochastic one, and explores how the model's stochasticity is useful to match the empirical evidence.

Similar reasoning applies to the case of goods sold with separate add-ons. Suppose that the price of a base good is p, and the price of an add-on is $\hat{p}$. The consumer might only partially see the add-on, such that she perceives the add-on cost to be $\hat{p}^s = m\hat{p}$. As a result, the myopic consumer perceives total price to be only $p + m\hat{p}$, while the full price is $p + \hat{p}$. Such myopic behavior allows firms to shroud information on add-on costs from consumers in equilibrium (Gabaix and Laibson, 2006).

---

[9] For instance, in the contexts of the examples discussed in this subsection, limited working memory presumably drives the inattention to taxes and the left-digit bias; limited ability to carry out complex algorithms is relevant for the exponential growth bias; and the lack of readily-accessible knowledge is important for the inattention to the future, in that costly simulations may need to be performed.

2.3.2 Inattention to taxes

Suppose that the price of a good is p, and the tax on that good is τ. Then, the full price is $q = p + \tau$. But a consumer may pay only partial attention to the tax, so the perceived tax is $\tau^s = m\tau$, and the perceived price is $q^s = p + m\tau$. Chetty et al. (2009) develop this model, develop the theory of tax incidence, and measure attention to sales taxes in routine consumer purchases. Farhi and Gabaix (2017) provide a systematic theory of optimal taxation (encompassing the Ramsey, Pigou, and Mirrlees problems) with this type of misperceptions and other biases.

2.3.3 Nominal illusion

The notion of nominal illusion is very related. Suppose that the real price change is q, inflation is π, and the nominal price change is p, so that the real price change is:

$$q = p - \pi.$$

People will often anchor to the nominal price, without removing enough inflation. The real price that they will perceive is:

$$q^s = p - m\pi, \tag{15}$$

where $m = 0$ signifies full nominal illusion. Recent research has shown that nominal anchoring has a surprising impact on stock market analysts (Roger et al., 2018), and may be even important for concrete outcomes (Shue and Townsend, 2018).

2.3.4 Hyperbolic discounting: Inattention to the future

In an intertemporal choice setting, suppose that true utility is $U_0 = \sum_{t=0}^{\infty} \delta^t u_t$, and call $U_1 = \sum_{t=1}^{\infty} \delta^{t-1} u_t$ the continuation utility, so that

$$U_0 = u_0 + \delta U_1. \tag{16}$$

A present-biased agent (Laibson, 1997; O'Donoghue and Rabin, 1999) will instead see a perceived utility

$$U_0^s = u_0 + m\delta U_1. \tag{17}$$

The parameter m is equivalent here to the parameter β in the hyperbolic discounting literature.[10]

Still, the normative interpretation is different. If the $m = \beta$ is about misperception, then the favored normative criterion is to maximize over the preferences of the rational agents, i.e. maximize $u_0 + \delta U_1$ (Farhi and Gabaix, 2017). In contrast, with the

---

[10] Gabaix and Laibson (2017) develop an interpretation of discounting via cognitive myopia much along these lines. Abela et al. (2012) present laboratory evidence that damage to the hippocampus (an area of the brain associated with both working memory and long-term memory) increases impulsive decision-making. This may be because, say, the memory of eating peaches in the past is necessary to simulate the future utility from eating a peach.

multiple selves interpretations usually associated with hyperbolic discounting (Thaler and Shefrin, 1981; Fudenberg and Levine, 2012) the welfare criterion is not so clear as one needs to trade off the utility of several "selves". Bernheim and Rangel (2009) similarly advocate for an agnostic welfare criterion for behavioral models that does not privilege the preferences of the rational agent.

2.3.5 When will we see overreaction vs. underreaction?

Suppose that a variable y_{it} follows a process $y_{i,t+1} = \rho_i y_{it} + \varepsilon_{it}$, and ε_{it} is an i.i.d. innovation with mean zero. The decision-maker however has to deal with many such processes, with various autocorrelations, that are ρ^d on average. Hence, for a given process, she may not fully perceive the autocorrelation, and instead use the subjectively perceived autocorrelation ρ_i^s, as in

$$\rho_i^s = m\rho_i + (1 - m)\,\rho^d. \tag{18}$$

That is, instead of seeing precisely the fine nuances of each AR(1) process, the agent anchors on a common autocorrelation ρ^d, and then adjusts partially toward the true autocorrelation of variable y_{it}, which is ρ_i. The agent's prediction is $\mathbb{E}_t^s\left[y_{i,t+k}\right] = \left(\rho_i^s\right)^k y_{i,t}$, so that

$$\mathbb{E}_t^s\left[y_{i,t+k}\right] = \left(\frac{\rho_i^s}{\rho_i}\right)^k \mathbb{E}_t\left[y_{i,t+k}\right]$$

where $\mathbb{E}_t^s$ is the subjective expectation, and $\mathbb{E}_t$ is the rational expectation. Hence, the agent exhibits *overreaction* for processes that are less autocorrelated than ρ^d, as $\rho_i^s/\rho_i > 1$, and *underreaction* for processes that are more autocorrelated than ρ^d, as $\rho_i^s/\rho_i < 1$.[11]

For instance, if the growth rate of a stock price is almost not autocorrelated, and the growth rate of earnings has a very small positive autocorrelation, people will overreact to past returns by extrapolating too much (Greenwood and Shleifer, 2014). On the other hand, processes that are quite persistent (say, inflation) will be perceived as less autocorrelated than they truly are, and agents will underreact by extrapolating too little (as found by Mankiw et al., 2003).[12]

2.3.6 Prospect theory: Inattention to the true probability

There is a literature in psychology (but not widely known by behavioral economists) that finds that probabilities are mentally represented in "log odds space". Indeed, in

---

[11] This sort of model is used in Gabaix (2016, 2018a).

[12] As of now, this hypothesis for the origin of under/overreaction has not been tested, but it seems plausible and has some indirect support (e.g. from Bouchaud et al., 2016). A meta-analysis of papers on under/overreaction, perhaps guided by the simple analytics here, would be useful. There are other ways to generate over/underreaction, e.g. Daniel et al. (1998), which relies on investor overconfidence about the accuracy of their beliefs, and biased self-attribution (see also Hirshleifer et al., 2011).

their survey Zhang and Maloney (2012) assert that this perceptual bias is "ubiquitous" and give a unified account of many phenomena. If $p \in (0, 1)$ is the probability of an event, the log odds are $q := \ln \frac{p}{1-p} \in (-\infty, \infty)$. Then, people may misperceive numbers as in (2) and (4), i.e. their median perception is[13]

$$q^s = mq + (1 - m) q^d. \tag{19}$$

Then, people transform their perceived log odds $q^s = \ln \frac{p^s}{1-p^s}$ into a perceived probability $p^s = \frac{1}{1+e^{-q^s}}$, that is $p^s = \pi(p)$ with:

$$\pi(p) = \frac{1}{1 + \left(\frac{1-p}{p}\right)^m \left(\frac{1-p^d}{p^d}\right)^{1-m}}, \tag{20}$$

which is the median perception of a behavioral agent: we have derived a probability weighting function $\pi(p)$. This yields overweighting of small probabilities (and symmetrically underweighting of probabilities close to 1).[14] Psychologically, the intuition is as follows: a probability of 10^{-6} is just too strange and unusual, so the brain "rectifies it" by dilating it toward a more standard probability such as $p^d \simeq 0.36$, and hence overweighting it.[15] This is exactly as in the simple Gaussian updating model of Section 2.1, done in the log odds space, and gives a probability weighing function much like the one in prospect theory (Kahneman and Tversky, 1979). This theme is pursued (with a different functional form, not based on the psychology of the log odds space surveyed in Zhang and Maloney, 2012) by Steiner and Stewart (2016).[16]

Likewise, for the "diminishing sensitivity" part of prospect theory, one can appeal to the distortions of payoffs as in (14): a payoff is X is perceived as $X^s = X^{m'} \left(X^d\right)^{1-m'}$ (this is done, with experimental evidence, by Khaw et al., 2017). Putting the two themes above (distortions of payoff and distortions of probability) together, we get something much like prospect theory: the perceived value of a gamble offering X with probability p and Y with probability $1 - p$ is:

$$V = \left[\pi(p) X^{m'} - \pi(1-p) Y^{m'}\right] \left(X^d\right)^{1-m'}. \tag{21}$$

In the rational model we have $m' = m = 1$, so that $\pi(p) = p$.

---

[13] I use the median, because perception contains noise around the mean, and the median is more tractable when doing monotonous non-linear transformations.

[14] This behavioral bias is well-documented empirically: DellaVigna and Pope (2018) conduct a meta-analysis of the relevant experimental (and quasi-experimental) literature – averaging across studies, they estimate a mean probability weight of 6% for a true probability of 1%.

[15] Here I take $p^d \simeq 0.36$ as this is the crossover value where $p = p^s$ in Prelec's (1998) survey.

[16] See also Bordalo et al. (2012).

How to obtain loss aversion? To get it, we'd need to assume a "pessimistic prior", saying that the typical gamble in life has negative expected value.[17] For instance the default probability for loss events is higher than the default probability in gains events. This might create loss aversion. A complete treatment of this issue is left to future research.

2.3.7 Projection bias: Inattention to future circumstances by anchoring on present circumstances

Suppose that I need to forecast x_t, a variable at time t. I might use its time-zero value as an anchor, i.e. $x_t^d = x_0$. Then, my perception at time zero of the future variable is

$$x_t^s = m x_t + (1 - m) x_0, \tag{22}$$

hence the agent exhibits projection bias. See also Loewenstein et al. (2003) for the basic analysis, and Chang et al. (2018) as well as Busse et al. (2013a) for empirical evidence in support of this.

2.3.8 Coarse probabilities and partition dependence

Suppose that there are K disjoint potential outcomes $E_1, ..., E_K$ (which form a partition of the event space). It is hard to know their probability, so a sensible default probability for events $E_1, ..., E_K$ is a uniform prior, $P^d(E) = \frac{1}{K}$ for all $E = E_1, ..., E_K$. Then, people may partially adjust toward the truth, and perceive the probability of event E as

$$P^s(E) = m P(E) + (1 - m) P^d(E). \tag{23}$$

A correlated notion is that of "partition dependence". When people are asked "what's the probability of dying of cancer" vs. "what's the probability of dying of lung cancer, or brain cancer, or breast cancer" etc., their assessed probabilities change, in a way that's partition-dependent (Sonnemann et al., 2013). So, as "cancer" is divided into more categories, people perceive that the likelihood of cancer is higher.

2.3.9 Base-rate neglect: Inattention to the base rate

In base-rate neglect (Tversky and Kahneman, 1974) people seem to react a little bit to the base rate, but not enough. A simple way to capture that is to posit that they anchor their perceived based rate on the "uninformative" base rate $P^d(E)$, which is a uniform distribution on the values of E, as in (23). Then, they use Bayes rule with this. This generates base rate neglect.[18]

---

[17] In that hypothesis, people would have "pessimistic prior" about general exchanges in life, and be "overconfident" about their *own* abilities.

[18] Grether (1980) uses a logarithmic variant of this equation. One could imagine a deeper model where people do not used Bayes' rule altogether, but that would take use too far afield.

2.3.10 Correlation neglect

Another way to simplify a situation is to imagine that random variables are uncorrelated, as shown by Enke and Zimmermann (forthcoming). To formalize this, let us say that the true probability of variables $y = (y_1, \ldots, y_n)$ is a joint probability $P(y_1, \ldots, y_n)$, and the (marginal) distribution of y_i is $P_i(y_i)$. Then the "simpler" default probability is the joint density assuming no correlation $P^d(y) = P_1(y_1) \ldots P_n(y_n)$. Correlation neglect is captured by a subjective probability $P^s(y) = m P(y) + (1 - m) P^d(y)$.

2.3.11 Insensitivity to sample size

Tversky and Kahneman (1974) show the phenomenon of "insensitivity to sample size". One way to model this is as follows: the true sample size N is replaced by a perceived sample size $N^s = \left(N^d\right)^{1-m} N^m$, and agents update based on that perceived sample size.

2.3.12 Insensitivity to predictability/misconceptions of regression to the mean/illusion of validity: Inattention to randomness and noise

Tversky and Kahneman (1974) report that, when people see a fighter pilot's performance, they fail to appreciate the role of mean reversion. Hence, if the pilot does less well the next time, they attribute this to lack of motivation, for instance, rather than reversion to the mean.

Call x the pilot's core ability, and $s_t = x + \varepsilon_t$ the performance on day t, where ε_t is an i.i.d. Gaussian noise term and x is drawn from an $N\left(0, \sigma_x^2\right)$ distribution. Given the performance s_t of, say, an airline pilot, an agent predicts next period's performance (Tversky and Kahneman, 1974). Rationally, she predicts $\bar{s}_{t+1} := \mathbb{E}\left[s_{t+1} \mid s_t\right] = \lambda s_t$ with $\lambda = \frac{1}{1+\sigma_\varepsilon^2/\sigma_x^2}$.

However, a behavioral agent may "forget about the noise", i.e. in her perceived model, $\text{Var}^s(\varepsilon) = m\sigma_\varepsilon^2$. If $m = 0$, they don't think about the existence of the noise, and answer $\bar{y}_{t+1}^s = y_t$. Such agent will predict:

$$\bar{s}_{t+1}^s = \frac{1}{1 + \frac{m\sigma_\varepsilon^2}{\sigma_a^2}} s_t.$$

Hence, behavioral agents with $m = 0$, who fully ignore randomness and noise, will just expect the pilot to do next time as he did last time.

2.3.13 Overconfidence: Inattention to my true ability

If x is my true driving ability, with overoptimism my prior x^d may be a high ability value; perhaps the ability of the top 10% of drivers. There are explanations for this kind of overconfidence: people often have to advocate for themselves (on the job, in the dating scene etc.), and one is a better advocate of one's superiority if one actually believes in it (Mercier and Sperber, 2011; see also Bénabou and Tirole, 2002). Rosy perceptions come from this high default ability (for myself), coupled with behavioral neglect to make the adjustment. A related bias is that of "overprecision", in which I think that my beliefs are more accurate than they are: then x is the true precision of my signals, and x^d is a high precision.

2.3.14 Cursedness: Inattention to the conditional probability

In a game theoretic setting, Eyster and Rabin (2005) derive the equilibrium implications of *cursedness*, a behavioral bias whereby players underestimate the correlation between their strategies and those of their opponents. The structure is formally similar, with cursedness χ being $1 - m$: the agent forms a belief that is an average of m times to the true probability, and $1 - m$ times a simplified, naïve probability distribution.[19]

2.3.15 Left-digit bias: Inattention to non-leading digits

Suppose that a number, in decimal representation, is $x = a + \frac{b}{10}$, with $a \geq 1$ and $b \in [0, 1)$. An agent's perception of the number might be

$$x^s = a + m \frac{b}{10} \tag{24}$$

where a low value of $m \in [0, 1]$ indicates left-digit bias. Lacetera et al. (2012) find compelling evidence of left-digit bias in the perception of the mileage of used cars sold at auction.[20]

2.3.16 Exponential growth bias

Many people appear to have a hard time compounding interest rates, something that Stango and Zinman (2009) call the exponential growth bias. Here, if $x = (1 + r)^t$ is the future value of an asset, then the simpler perceived value is $x^d = 1 + rt$, and the perceived growth is just $x^s = mx + (1 - m) x^d$.[21]

2.3.17 Taking stock of these examples

These examples, I submit, illustrate that the simple framework above allows one to think in a unified way about a wide range of behavioral biases, at least in their formal structure. There are four directions in which such baseline examples can be extended. Here I give a brief outline of these four directions, along with a number of examples that are discussed at greater length in later sections of this survey:

---

[19] For empirical evidence linking cursedness to limitations in cognitive skill, see also Carroll et al. (1988), who show that players in two-person negotiation games generally lack knowledge of how to compute conditional expectations from their opponent's point of view.

[20] A variant it to use exponentially-decreasing weights. If the number is $x = \sum_{i=n}^{N} a_i 10^i$ with $N > n$, its perception is $x^s = \sum_{i=n}^{N} a_i 10^i m^{N-n}$.

[21] Kusev et al. (2018) make further progress in modeling anchoring on linear or other non-exponential approximations in the context of subjective time-series forecasting.

1. In the "theoretical economic consequences" direction, economists work out the consequences of partial inattention, e.g. in market equilibrium, or in the indirect effects of all this.
2. In the "empirical economic measurement" direction, researchers estimate attention m.
3. In the "basic psychology" direction, researchers think more deeply about the "default perception of the world", i.e. what an agent perceives spontaneously. Psychology helps determine this default.[22]
4. In the "endogenization of the psychology" part, attention m is endogenized. This can be helpful, or not, in thinking about the two points above. Typically, endogenous attention is useful to make more refined predictions, though most of those remain to be tested. In the meantime, a simple quasi-fixed parameter like m is useful to have, and allows for parsimonious models – a view forcefully argued by Rabin (2013).

2.4 Psychological underpinnings

Here is a digest of some features of attention from the psychology literature. Pashler (1998) and Nobre and Kastner (2014) handbook offer book-length surveys on the psychology of attention, with primary emphasis on perception. Knudsen (2007) offers a neuroscience-oriented perspective.

2.4.1 Conscious versus unconscious attention

Systems 1 and 2. Recall the terminology for mental operations of Stanovich (1999) and Kahneman (2003), where "system 1" is an intuitive, fast, largely unconscious, and parallel system, while "system 2" is a deliberative, slow, relatively conscious, and serial system.

System 2, working memory, and conscious attention. It is likely that we do not consciously contemplate thousands of variables when dealing with a specific problem. For instance, research on working memory documents that people handle roughly "seven plus or minus two" items (Miller, 1956). At the same time, we do know – in our long term memory – about many variables, x. Hence, we can handle consciously relatively few m_i that are different from 0.[23]

System 1/unconscious attention monitoring. At the same time, the mind contemplates unconsciously thousands of variables x_i, and decides which handful it will bring up for conscious examination (that is, whether they should satisfy $m_i > 0$). For instance, my system 1 is currently monitoring if I'm too hot, thirsty, low in blood sugar, but also in the presence of a venomous snake, and so forth. This is not done consciously. But if a variable becomes very alarming (e.g. a snake just appeared), it

---

[22] It would be nice to have a "meta-model" for defaults, unifying the superficial diversity of default models.

[23] In attentional theories, System 1 chooses the attention (e.g. as in Step 1 in Proposition 4.1), while the decision is done by System 2 (as in Step 2 in the same proposition).

will be "brought to consciousness" – that is, to the attention of system 2. Those are the variables with an $m_i > 0$.

To summarize, System 1 chooses the m_i's in an unconscious, parallel fashion, while System 2 takes a decision based on the few elements that have been brought to consciousness (i.e. with $m_i > 0$).

This view has a good degree of support in psychology. In a review paper, Dehaene et al. (2017) say:

> *William James described attention as "the taking possession by the mind, in clear and vivid form, of one out of what seem several simultaneously possible objects or trains of thought". This definition is close to what we mean by [...] the selection of a single piece of information for entry into the global workspace. There is, however, a clear-cut distinction between this final step, which corresponds to conscious access, and the previous stages of attentional selection, which can operate unconsciously. Many experiments have established the existence of dedicated mechanisms of attention orienting and shown that, like any other processors, they can operate nonconsciously.*

2.4.2 Reliance on defaults

What guess does one make when there is no time to think? This is represented by the case $m = 0$: then, variables x are replaced by their default value, which could be some plain average value, or a crude heuristic. This default model ($m = 0$), and the default action a^d (which is the optimal action under the default model) corresponds to "system 1 under extreme time pressure". The importance of default actions has been shown in a growing literature (e.g. Madrian and Shea, 2001; Carroll et al., 2009).[24] Here, the default model is very simple (basically, it is "do not think about anything"), but it could be enriched, following other models (e.g. Gennaioli and Shleifer, 2010).[25]

2.4.3 Neuroscience: The neural correlates of "mental cost" and "limited attention"

It would be great to know the neural correlates of "limited attention" and things like "mental costs" and "mental fatigue" – what exactly is this scarce resource in the brain? Sadly neuroscience research has not found it (Section 4 of Kurzban et al., 2013 is a clear discussion of this). An early proposal was glucose in the brain, but it has been discredited. Hence, the attention literature needs to theorize it without clear guidance from the neuro literature.

---

[24] This literature shows that default actions matter, not literally that default variables matters. One interpretation is that the action was (quasi-)optimal under some typical circumstances (corresponding to $x = 0$). An agent might not wish to think about extra information (i.e., deviate from $x = 0$), and hence deviate from the default action.

[25] There is no systematic theory of the default yet. This default is a close cousin of what Bayesians call the prior (in fact we might imagine that subjective priors would be very crude, for instance a uniform prior). There is no systematic theory of where the prior comes from either.

2.4.4 Other themes

If the choice of attention is largely unconscious, this leads to the curious choice of "attentional blindness". Mack and Rock (1998) studied attentional blindness extensively, and the now canonical experiment for this is the "gorilla" experiment of Simons and Chabris (1999). When asked to perform a task that requires full attentional resources, subjects often didn't see a gorilla in the midst of the experiment.

Another rich field is that of visual attention. Treisman and Gelade (1980) is classic paper in the field, and Carrasco (2011) surveys the literature. One theme – not well integrated by the economics literature, is the "extreme seriality of thought" (see Huang and Pashler, 2007): in the context of visual attention, it means that people can process things only one color at a time. In other contexts, like the textbook rabbit/duck visual experiment, it means that one can see a rabbit or a duck in a figure, but not both at the same time.

From an economic point of view, serial models that represent the agent's action step by step tend to be complicated though instructive (see Rubinstein, 1998; Gabaix et al., 2006; Caplin et al., 2011; Fudenberg et al., 2017, which feature various forms of information search). Because of the limited applicability of process-based models, more "outcome-based models", which directly give the action rather than the intermediary steps, are typically easier to use in economic applications.

3 Measuring attention: Methods and findings

I now turn to the literature on the empirical measurement of attention. I first provide a broad taxonomy of the approaches taken in the literature, and then discuss specific empirical findings. The recent empirical literature on inattention has greatly advanced our ability to understand behavioral biases quantitatively, such that we can now begin to form a synthesis of these results. I present such a synthesis at the end of this section.

3.1 Measuring attention: Methods

There are essentially five ways to measure attention[26]:

1. Deviations from an optimal action (this requires to know the optimal action).
2. Deviations from normative cross-partials, e.g. from Slutsky symmetry (this does not require to know the optimal action).
3. Physical measurement, e.g. time on task and eye-tracking.
4. Surveys: eliciting people's beliefs.
5. Imputations from the impact of attentional interventions: impact of reminders, of advice.

---

[26] This classification builds on DellaVigna's (2009).

As we will see, methods 3–5 can show that attention is not full (hence, help reject the naïve rational and costless-cognition model) and measure correlates of attention (e.g. time spent), and 1 and 2 measure attention as defined in this survey (e.g., measure the parameter m).[27]

3.1.1 Measuring inattention via deviation from an optimal action

Suppose the optimal action function is $a^r(x) := \text{argmax}_a\, u(a, x)$, and the behavioral action is $a^s(x) = a^r(mx)$. Then, the derivative of the action with respect to x is: $a^s_x(x) = m a^r_x(mx)$. Therefore attention can be measured as[28]

$$m = \frac{a^s_x}{a^r_x}.$$

Hence, the attention parameter m is identified by the ratio of the sensitivities to the signal x of the boundedly-rational action function a^{BR} and of the rational action function a^r. This requires knowing the normatively correct slope, a^r_x. How does one do that?

1. This could be done in a "clear and understood" context, e.g. where all prices are very clear, perhaps with just a simple task (so that in this environment, $m = 1$), which allows us to measure a^r_x. This is the methodology used by Chetty et al. (2009), Taubinsky and Rees-Jones (2018), and Allcott and Taubinsky (2015).
2. Sometimes, the "normatively correct answer" is the attention of experts. Should one buy generic drugs (e.g. aspirins) or more expensive "branded drugs" – with the same basic molecule? For instance, to find out the normatively correct behavior, Bronnenberg et al. (2015) look at the behavior of experts – health care professionals – and find that they are less likely to pay extra for premium brands.

We shall review the practical methods later.[29]

3.1.2 Deviations from Slutsky symmetry

We will see below (Section 5.1.2) that deviations from Slutsky symmetry allow one in principle to measure inattention. Aguiar and Riabov (2016) and Abaluck and Adams (2017) use this idea to measure attention. In particular, Abaluck and Adams (2017) show that Slutsky symmetry should also hold in random demand

---

[27] Here, I define measuring attention as measuring a parameter m like in the simple model of this chapter, or its multidimensional generalization $m_1, ..., m_n$. However, one could wish to estimate a whole distribution of actions (i.e., $a(x)$ being a random variable, perhaps parametrized by some m). This is the research program in Caplin and Dean (2015); Caplin et al. (2016). This literature is more conceptual and qualitative at this stage, but hopefully one day it will merge with the more behavioral literature.

[28] To be very precise, $m(x) = \frac{a^s_x(x)}{a^r_x(mx)}$. So, one can get m assuming small deviations x (so that we measure the limit $m(0)$), or the limit of a linearized rational demand $a^r(x)$.

[29] In some cases, the context-appropriate attention parameter m is quite hard to measure. So, people use a "portable already-estimated parameter", e.g. $m = \beta = 0.7$ for hyperbolic discounting.

models. Suppose the utility for good i is $v_i = u_i - \beta p_i$, and the consumer chooses $a = \text{argmax}_i (u_i - \beta p_i + \varepsilon_i)$, where the ε_i are arbitrary noise terms (still, with a non-atomic distribution), which could even be correlated. The probability of choosing i is $c_i (p) = \mathbb{P}(u_i - \beta p_i + \varepsilon_i = \max_j u_j - \beta p_j + \varepsilon_j)$. Define the Slutsky term $S_{ij} = \frac{\partial c_i}{\partial p_j}$. Then, it turns out that we have $S_{ij} = S_{ji}$ again, under the rational model. So, with inattention to prices, and $c^s (p) = c^r (Mp + (1 - M) p^d)$, where $M = diag(m_1, \ldots, m_n)$ is the diagonal matrix of attention, we have

$$S_{ij}^s = S_{ij}^r m_j$$

exactly as in (57). Abaluck and Adams (2017) explore this and similar relations to study the inattention to complex health care plans. They structurally estimate the model described in this section, including in the random choice specification most of the variables that would be available to individuals making Medicare Part D elections, such as premia, deductibles, and so forth. It is nice to see how an a priori abstruse idea (the deviation from Slutsky symmetry in models of limited attention, as in Gabaix, 2014) can lead to concrete real-world measurement of the inattention to health-care plan characteristics.

3.1.3 Process tracking: Time on task, Mouselab, eye tracking, pupil dilatation, etc.

A popular way to measure activity is with a process-tracing experiment commonly known as Mouselab (Camerer et al., 1993; Payne et al., 1993; Johnson et al., 2002; Gabaix et al., 2006), or with eye tracking methods. In Mouselab, subjects need to click on boxes to see which information they contain. In eye tracking (Reutskaja et al., 2011), researchers can follow which part of the screen subjects look at, i.e. track information gathering. There are other physiological methods of measurement as well, such as measuring pupil dilation (which measures effort, Kahneman, 1973). See Schulte-Mecklenbeck et al. (2017) for a recent review.

   Krajbich et al. (2010) and Krajbich and Rangel (2011) introduce a class of algorithmic models that link visual perception and simple choices. These attentional drift-diffusion models (aDDM) posit that – when choosing among multiple responses – the brain accumulates the evidence in favor of one response relative to others until a decision threshold is reached. These relative choice values evolve according to an exogenous visual attention process. The authors find that aDDM models do very well at explaining empirically observed patterns of eye movement and choice in the lab. Arieli et al. (2011) use an eye-tracking experiment to trace the decision process of experiment participants in the context of choice over lotteries, and find that individuals rely on separate evaluations of prizes and probabilities in making their decisions.

   Lahey and Oxley (2016), using eye tracking techniques, examine recruiters, and see what information they look at in resumes, in particular from white vs. African–American applicants. Bartoš et al. (2016) and Ambuehl (2017) study how information acquisition is influenced by incentives.

3.1.4 Surveys

One can also elicit a measurement of attention via surveys. Of course, there is a difficulty. Take an economist. When surveyed, she knows the value of interest rates. But that doesn't mean that she actually takes the interest rate into account when buying a sweater – so as to satisfy her rational Euler equation for consumption. Hence, if people show ignorance in a survey, it is good evidence that they are inattentive. However, when they exhibit knowledge, it does not mean that they actually take into account the variable in their decision. Information, as measured in surveys, is an input of attention, but not the actual attention metric.[30]

For instance, a number of researchers have found that, while people know their average tax rate, they often don't know their marginal one, and often use the average tax rate as a default proxy for the marginal tax rate (De Bartolomé, 1995; Liebman and Zeckhauser, 2004).[31] Relatedly, Handel and Kolstad (2015) survey the employees of a large firm regarding the health insurance plans available to them and find substantial information frictions.

3.1.5 Impact of reminders, advice

If people don't pay attention, perhaps a reminder will help. In terms of modeling, such a reminder could be a "free signal", or an increase in the default attention m_i^d to a dimension.

A reminder could come, for instance, from the newspaper. Huberman and Regev (2001) show how a New York Times article that re-reports stale news creates a big impact for one company's stock price. It is not completely clear how that generalizes. There is also evidence that reminders have an impact on savings (Karlan et al., 2016) and medical adherence (Pop-Eleches et al., 2011). The impact of this type of reminders is typically small, possibly because the reminder (which may be for instance a text message) does not shift attention very much, rather than because attention was almost perfect initially.

In a laboratory context, Johnson et al. (2007) show that the typical endowment effect (Kahneman et al., 1991) can be reversed by simply asking people to first think about what they could do with the proceeds from selling an object (for example, a coffee mug), and only then listing the reasons for which they want to keep that object. This demonstrates that merely altering the order in which people think about the various aspects of a problem has an impact on their eventual decision (presumably via changing their attention to those various aspects): this is an idea that Johnson et al. (2007) call "query theory".

Hanna et al. (2014) provide summary information to seaweed farmers. This allows the farmers to improve their practice, and achieve higher productivity. This is

---

[30] In terms of theory, when asked about the "what is the interest rate", I know the interest rate matters a great deal. When asked "what's the best sweater to buy", the interest rate does not matter much (Gabaix, 2016).

[31] This is, people perceive the marginal tax rate to me $mx^d + (1 - m)x$ with x^d the average tax rate and x the marginal tax rate.

consistent with a model in which farmers were not optimally using all the information available to them. For instance, this could be described by a model such as Schwartzstein's (2014). In this model, if an agent is pessimistic about the fact that some piece of information is useful, she won't pay attention to it, so that she won't be able to realize that it is useful. Knowledge about the informativeness of the piece of information leads to paying more attention, and better learning.

Again, this type of evidence shows that attention is not full, although it doesn't measure it.

3.2 Measuring attention: Findings

Now that we have reviewed the methods, let us move to specific findings on attention.

3.2.1 Inattention to taxes

People don't fully pay attention to taxes, as the literature has established, using the methodology of Section 3.1.1, and this is important for normative taxation (Mullainathan et al., 2012; Farhi and Gabaix, 2017). Chetty et al. (2009) find a mean attention of between 0.06 (by computing the ratio of the semi-elasticities for sales taxes, which are not included in the sticker price, vs. excise taxes, which are included in the sticker price) and 0.35 (computing the ratio of the semi-elasticities for sales taxes vs. more salient sticker prices).[32,33]

Taubinsky and Rees-Jones (2018) design an online experiment and elicit the maximum tag price that agents would be willing to pay when there are no taxes or when there are standard taxes corresponding to their city of residence. The ratio of these two prices is $1 + m\tau$, where τ is the tax. This allows the estimation of tax salience m. Taubinsky and Rees-Jones (2018) find (in their standard tax treatment)[34] that $\mathbb{E}[m] = 0.25$ and $\text{Var}(m) = 0.13$. So, mean attention is quite small, but the variance is high. The variance of attention is important, because when attention variance is high, optimal taxes are generally lower (Farhi and Gabaix, 2017) – roughly, because heterogeneity in attention creates heterogeneity in response, and additional misallocations, which increase the dead-weight cost of the tax. Taubinsky and Rees-Jones (2018) reaffirm this conclusion, and find that accounting for heterogeneity in consumer attention would increase the estimated efficiency losses from realistically-calibrated sales taxes by more than 200%.

---

[32] In an online auction experiment. Greenwood and Hanson (2014) estimate an attention $m = 0.5$ to competitors' reactions and general equilibrium effects.

[33] See also Russo (1977) for earlier field-experimental evidence on the impact of tax salience on consumer purchasing decisions. Relatedly, Finkelstein (2009) studies drivers who pay tolls in cash vs. via electronic toll collection (a more automatic and invisible form of payment). The latter were substantially more likely to respond "I don't know" when asked about how much the toll was, and were also more likely to be incorrect if they offered a guess. Abeler and Jäger (2015) also show that attention to tax incentives is lower when they are more complex.

[34] They actually provide a lower bound on variance, and for simplicity we take it here to be a point estimate.

3.2.2 Shrouded attributes

It is intuitively clear that many people won't pay attention to "shrouded attributes", such as "surprise" bank fees, minibar fees, shipping charges, and the like (Ellison, 2005; Gabaix and Laibson, 2006; Ellison and Ellison, 2009). Gabaix and Laibson (2006) work out the market equilibrium implication of such attributes with naïve consumers – e.g. consumers who are not paying attention to the existence of shrouded attributes when buying the "base good". In particular, if there are enough naïves there is an inefficient equilibrium where shrouded attributes are priced far above marginal costs. In this equilibrium, naïve consumers are "exploited", to put it crudely: they pay higher prices and subsidize the non-naïves.

There is a growing field literature measuring the effects of such fees and consumers' inattention to them. Using both a field experiment and a natural experiment, Brown et al. (2010) find that consumers are inattentive to shrouded shipping costs in eBay online auctions. Grubb (2009) and Grubb and Osborne (2015) show that consumers don't pay attention to sharp marginal charges in three-part tariff pricing schemes,[35] and predict their future demand with excessive ex-ante precision – for example, individuals frequently exhaust their cellular plans' usage allowance, and incur high overage costs. Brown et al. (2012, 2013) show that when film studios withhold movies from critics before their release, moviegoers fail to infer that this may indicate low movie quality – showing that people are indeed behavioral rather than Bayesian (a Bayesian agent should be suspicious of any non-disclosed item, rather than just ignore it like a behavioral agent). Similarly, Jin et al. (2017) use a series of laboratory experiments to show that in general consumers form overly optimistic expectations of product quality when sellers choose not to disclose this information. This literature overlaps with a theoretical literature probing more deeply into firms' incentives to hide these attributes (Heidhues and Kőszegi, 2010, 2017), and a related literature modeling competition with boundedly rational agents (Spiegler, 2011; Tirole, 2009; Piccione and Spiegler, 2012; De Clippel et al., 2014). The companion survey on behavioral industrial organization, by Paul Heidhues and Botond Kőszegi, in this volume, details this.

3.2.3 Inattention in health plan choices

There is mounting evidence for the role of confusion and inattention in the choice of health care plans. McFadden (2006) provides an early discussion of consumers' misinformation in health plan choices, particularly in the context of Medicare Part D elections. Abaluck and Gruber (2011) find that people choose Medicare plans less often if premiums are increased by $100 than if expected out of pocket cost is increased by $100. Handel and Kolstad (2015) study the choice of health care plans at

---

[35] Three-part tariffs are pricing schemes in which a seller offers a good or a service for a fixed fee that comes with a certain usage allowance, as well as a per-unit price that applies to all extra usage in excess of that allowance. One common example is cellphone plans: cellphone carriers commonly offer a certain amount of call minutes and data usage for a fixed price, but charge an extra marginal fee once consumers exceed the allotted quota.

a large firm. They find that poor information about plan characteristics has a large impact on employees' willingness to pay for the different plans available to them, on average leading them to overvalue plans with more generous coverage and lower deductibles (see also Handel, 2013). This study documents a mistake in an important economic context. Ericson (2014) documents consumer inertia in health plan choices, and Abaluck and Adams (2017) show this inertia is largely attributable to inattention.

3.2.4 Inattention to health consequences

It is intuitively clear that we do not always attend to the health consequences of our choices, e.g. when drinking a sugary soda or smoking a cigarette, we underperceive the future health costs (e.g. cancer) from those enjoyments. Several studies have quantified the magnitude of these underperceived costs, and applied them to the normative study of optimal "sin taxation". Allcott et al. (2017) use survey data to measure the price elasticity of demand for sugary beverages, and deliver optimal sin tax formulas in terms of these sufficient statistics. Gruber and Kőszegi (2001) conduct a similar study by postulating hyperbolic discounting, and importing the parameter $m = \beta \simeq 0.7$ into the model.

3.2.5 People use rounded numbers

Lacetera et al. (2012) estimate inattention via buyers' "left-digit bias" in evaluating the mileage of used cars sold at auction. Call x the true mileage of a car (i.e., how many miles it has been driven), and x^d the mileage rounded to the leading digit, and let $r = x - x^d$ be the "mileage remainder." For instance, if $x = 12{,}345$ miles, then $x^d = 10{,}000$ miles and $r = 2{,}345$ miles, and the perceived mileage is $x^s = x^d + m\left(x - x^d\right)$. Lacetera et al. (2012) estimate a structural model for the perceived value of cars of the form $V = -f\left(x^s\left(x, m\right)\right)$. They find a mean attention parameter of $m = 0.69$ (see also Englmaier et al., 2017). Busse et al. (2013b) break down this estimate along covariate dimensions, and find that attention is lower for older and cheaper cars, and lower for lower-income retail buyers.[36]

This is a very nice study, as it offers clean identification and high quality data – hence a more precise estimate of attention than most other papers. It would be nice to see if it matches the quantitative predictions of models discussed in this survey (for example, that in Eq. (35)).

3.2.6 Do people account for the net present value of future costs and benefits?

When you buy a car, you should pay attention to both the sticker price of the car, and the present value of future gasoline payments. But it is very conceivable that some people will pay less than full attention to the future value of gas payments: the

---

[36] In addition to the studies already mentioned, Shlain (2018) estimates a structural model of left-digit bias using retail scanner data; mean estimated attention to the left-digit remainder of prices is $m = 0.74$ in the study's main specification. This work was circulated after the final draft of this survey was completed, so that it could not be integrated in the final tables and figures.

full price of the car $p_{car} + p_{gas}$ will be perceived as $m_{car}p_{car} + m_{gas}p_{gas}$. Two papers explore this, and have somewhat inconsistent findings. Allcott and Wozny (2014) find partial inattention to gas prices: their estimate is $\frac{m_{gas}}{m_{price}} = 0.76$. However, Busse et al. (2013a) find that they cannot reject the null hypothesis of equal attention, $\frac{m_{gas}}{m_{price}} = 1$. One hopes that similar studies, perhaps with data from other countries, will help settle the issue. One can conjecture that people likewise do not fully pay attention to the cost of car parts – this remains to be seen. A related literature, starting with Hausman (1979), has found that people apply high discount rates to future energy costs when purchasing electricity-consuming durables such as refrigerators or air conditioners (see Frederick et al., 2002 for a more recent survey of this literature).

3.2.7 Inattention in finance

There is now a large amount of evidence of partial inattention in finance. This is covered in greater depth in the companion chapter on behavioral finance, by Nick Barberis. Here are some samples from this literature.

When investors have limited attention, the specific format in which accounting statements are presented matters. Hirshleifer and Teoh (2003) is an influential model of that, which relates accounting statements to misvaluations. Relatedly, Hirshleifer et al. (2009) find that when investors are more distracted (as there are more events that day), inefficiencies are stronger: for instance, the post-earnings announcement drift is stronger. Peng and Xiong (2006) study the endogenous attention to aggregate vs. idiosyncratic risk.

DellaVigna and Pollet (2007) find that investors have a limited ability to incorporate some subtle forces (predictable changes in demand because of demographic forces) into their forecasts, especially at long horizons. DellaVigna and Pollet (2009) show that investors are less attentive on Fridays: when companies report their earnings on Fridays, the immediate impact on the price (as a fraction of the total medium run impact) is lower. Hirshleifer et al. (2009) show how investors are less attentive to a given stock when there are lots of other news in the market. In a similar vein, Barber and Odean (2007) show that retail investors overweight attention-grabbing stocks in their portfolios: for example, the stocks of companies that have recently received high media coverage. In a controlled laboratory context, Frydman and Rangel (2014) find that decreasing attention to a stock's purchase price reduces the extent to which people display a disposition effect (i.e., an abnormally high propensity to sell stocks that have realized capital gains).

Cohen and Frazzini (2008) document that investors are quick at pricing the "direct" impacts of an announcement, but slower at pricing the "indirect" impact (e.g. a new plane by Boeing gets reflected in Boeing's stock price, but less quickly in that of Boeing's supplier network). Giglio and Shue (2014) find that investors underreact to the passage of time after merger announcements, even though lack of news is in fact informative of a higher probability that the deal will be successfully completed: in effect, investors pay limited attention to "no news".

Malmendier and Nagel (2011) find that generations who experienced low stock market returns invest less in the stock market. People seem to put too much weight on their own experience when forming their beliefs about the stock market.

Fedyk (2018) shows that positioning of news on the front page of the Bloomberg terminal platform induces abnormally high trading volumes for the affected companies in the first few minutes after new publication: investors appear to pay a disproportionately low amount of attention to news that is not on the front page.

This literature is growing quickly.[37] It would be nice to have more structural models, predicting in a quantitative way the speed of diffusion of information.

3.2.8 Evidence of reaction to macro news with a lag

There is much evidence for delayed reaction in macro data. Friedman (1961) talks about "long and variable lags" in the impacts of monetary stimulus. This is also what motivated models of delayed adjustment, e.g. Taylor (1980). Empirical macro research in the past decades has frequently found that a variable (e.g. price) reacts to shocks in other variables (e.g. nominal interest rate) only after a significant delay (e.g., quarters or years).

Delayed reaction is confirmed by the more modern approaches of Romer and Romer (1989) and Romer and Romer (2004), who identify monetary policy shocks using the narrative account of Federal Open Market Committee (FOMC) Meetings[38] and find that the price level would only start falling 25 months after a contractionary monetary policy shock.

This is confirmed also by more formal econometric evidence with identified VARs. Sims (2003) notes that in nearly all Vector Autoregression (VAR) studies, a variable reacts with delay when responding to shocks in other variables, even though a rational theory would predict that it should instantaneously jump. Such finding is robust in VAR specifications of various sizes, variable sets, and identification methods (Leeper et al., 1996; Christiano et al., 2005). While it is feasible to generate delayed response using adjustment costs, large adjustment costs would imply that a variable's reactions to *all* shocks are smooth, contradicting the VAR evidence that responses to own shocks tend to be large. A model of inattention, however, can account for both phenomena simultaneously.

Finally, micro survey data suggest that macro sluggishness is not just the result of delayed action, but rather the result of infrequent observation as well. Alvarez et al. (2012, 2018) provide evidence of infrequent reviewing of portfolio choice and price

---

[37] A related study – which may also be linked to models of reference dependence – is that of Baker et al. (2012), who find that when thinking about a merger or acquisition price, investors put a lot of weight on recent (trailing 52 weeks) prices. This has real effects: merger waves occur when high returns on the market and likely targets make it easier for bidders to offer a peak price. This shows an intriguing mix of attention to a partially arbitrary price, and its use as an anchor in negotiations and perhaps valuations.

[38] The intended interest rate changes identified in accounts of FOMC Meetings are further orthogonalized by relevant variables in Fed's information set (Greenbook Forecasts), making it plausibly exogenous.

setting, respectively, with clean analytics (see also Abel et al., 2013 for a sophisticated model along those lines). A median investor reviews her portfolio 12 times and makes changes only twice annually, while a median firm in many countries reviews price only 2–4 times a year.

3.2.9 Evidence on level-k thinking in games

An impactful literature on level-k thinking in games has generated a large amount of empirical evidence for the lack of strategic sophistication in games (Nagel, 1995; Ho et al., 1998). Level-k models (Stahl and Wilson, 1995; Camerer et al., 2004) allow players to vary in their levels of strategic sophistication: level-0 players randomize their strategies; level-1 players best-respond under the assumption that all other players are level-0; level-2 players best-respond under the assumption that everyone else is a level-1 thinker, and so forth. Within the framework laid out in this survey, level-k thinking can be understood as lack of attention to higher-order strategical issues, perhaps because of cognitive limitations. Level-0 players corresponds to fully inattentive agents ($m = 0$), while level-∞ players are the traditional rational agents who make full use of all available information ($m = 1$).

Camerer et al. (2004) estimate that an average parameter value $k = 1.5$ fits well empirical data from a wide variety of games, which implies a rather low value of m. A related empirical literature corroborates this finding and contributed to many of the advances in experimental process-tracking methods discussed in Section 3.1.3: see for example Costa-Gomes et al. (2001), Wang et al. (2010), and Brocas et al. (2014).[39]

3.3 Attention across stakes and studies

Attention over many studies. Fig. 1 (in the introduction) and Table 1 contain a synthesis of eleven measurements of attention – I selected all the studies I could find that measured attention (i.e., gave an estimate of the parameter m). They are a tribute to the hard work of many behavioral economists. I am sure that this table will be enriched over time.

Table 1 shows point estimates of the attention parameter m in the literature discussed in this survey. For each distinct study or experimental setting, I report the most aggregated available estimates. In each of these studies, m is measured as the degree to which individuals underperceive the value of an opaque add-on attribute τ to a quantity or price p, such that the subjectively perceived total value of the quantity is $q^s(m) = p + m\tau$.

Correspondingly, for each economic setting I show the estimated ratio of the values p and τ, which is a measure of the relative significance of the add-on attribute τ. Appendix B outlines the details of the methodology used to compile this data. Fig. 1

---

[39] See Avoyan and Schotter (2018) for a related exploration of limited attention in games. Gabaix (2018b) extends the sparsity framework to game-theoretic settings.

Table 1   Attention estimates in a cross-section of studies. This table shows point estimates of the attention parameter m in a cross-section of recent studies, alongside the estimated relative value of the opaque add-on attribute with respect to the relevant good or quantity (τ/p). I report the most aggregated available estimates for each distinct study or experimental setting. The quantity τ is the estimated mean value of the opaque good or quantity against which m is measured; the quantity p is the estimated mean value of the good or quantity itself, exclusive of the opaque attribute. Appendix B describes the construction methodology and details. Studies are arranged by their τ/p value, in descending order.

Study	Good or quantity	Opaque attribute	Attribute importance (τ/p)	Attention estimate (m)
Allcott and Wozny (2014)	Expense associated with car purchase	Present value of future gasoline costs	0.58	0.76
Hossain and Morgan (2006)	Price of CDs sold at auction on eBay	Shipping costs	0.38	0.82
DellaVigna and Pollet (2009)	Public company equity value	Value innovation due to earnings announcements	0.30	0.54
DellaVigna and Pollet (2009)	Public company equity value	Value innovation due to earnings announcements *that occur on Fridays*	0.30	0.41
Hossain and Morgan (2006)	Price of CDs sold at auction on eBay	Shipping costs	0.24	0.55
Taubinsky and Rees-Jones (2018)	Price of products purchased in laboratory experiment	Sales tax, *tripled relative to standard tax*	0.22	0.48
Lacetera et al. (2012)	Mileage of used cars sold at auction	Mileage left-digit remainder	0.10	0.69
Chetty et al. (2009)	Price of grocery store items	Sales tax	0.07	0.35
Taubinsky and Rees-Jones (2018)	Price of products purchased in laboratory experiment	Sales tax	0.07	0.25
Chetty et al. (2009)	Price of retail beer cases	Sales tax	0.04	0.06
Brown et al. (2010)	Price of iPods sold at auction on eBay	Shipping costs	0.03	0.00
Mean	–	–	0.21	0.44
Standard deviation	–	–	0.18	0.28

plots the point estimates of m against the estimated value of τ/p.[40] In addition to this cross-study data, Fig. 1 plots a second set of intra-study data points from Busse et al. (2013b), who offer very precise estimates of attention broken down along covariate dimensions. By looking at subsamples of Busse et al.'s (2013b) dataset of more than 22 million of used car transactions, we are able to effectively highlight the co-movement between m and the relative importance of the add-on attribute. Attention is high for car mileage presumably because the absolute dollar stakes (rather than just the relative stakes $\frac{\tau}{p}$) are particularly high.

As noted above, mean attention is 0.44 – roughly in the middle of the two poles of full rationality and complete inattention. We see that, sensibly, attention does increase with incentives.[41] We can actually propose a model-based calibration of this attention.

Calibrating the attention function. Fig. 1 additionally shows a calibration of an attention model in which estimated attention $\hat{m}$ is a function of the attribute's relative importance τ/p[42]:

$$\hat{m} = \mathcal{A}_\alpha\left(\left[\frac{\tau/p}{\bar{\kappa}}\right]^2\right), \tag{25}$$

where $\mathcal{A}_\alpha$ is an attention function, which will be derived in Section 4.1.1. For now, the reader can think of the attention function $\mathcal{A}_\alpha$ as the solution to a problem in which an agent chooses optimal attention m subject to the tradeoff between the penalty resulting from inattention and the cost of paying attention. For this calibration, I allow the attention cost function to depend quadratically on m, to a degree parameterized by the scalar parameter $q \geq 0$, such that the attention function is given by the following variant of (34),

$$\mathcal{A}_\alpha(\sigma^2) := \arg\min_{m \in [0,1]} \frac{1}{2}(1-m)^2\sigma^2 + \left(m + qm^2\right)^\alpha, \tag{26}$$

---

[40] I use the relative value as a determinant of attention. This arises if, for a given decision, there is a fixed attention budget between different attributes of the problem, and their relative importance determine attention. In the model of Section 4.1.1, this is microfounded by endogenizing the κ and using the "scale-free" κ, as in Gabaix (2014), Section V.C.

[41] It is reassuring to see the attention covarying positively with incentives in Fig. 1. In part, this is because the problems collected in the figure happen to have arguably roughly similar levels of complexity. If problem complexity ("κ" in later notations) varied a lot across studies, a future update of Fig. 1 could potentially show a less clean positive relation between stakes and attention. Likewise, in situations where stakes are very important in dollar terms (e.g. for car purchases), attention is likely to be higher.

[42] Things are expressed in terms of the "scale free cost" $\bar{\kappa}$ (see Gabaix, 2016, Sections 4.2 and 10.2, which conjectures that "a reasonable parameter might be $\bar{\kappa} = 5\%$"), which is unitless, so potentially portable across contexts. It means that agents don't consider attributes τ whose relative importance $\left|\frac{\tau}{p}\right|$ is less than $\bar{\kappa}$. It also justifies the scaling $\frac{\tau}{p}$, where the "natural scale" of the decision is p. This assumes that the attention budget has a fixed amount for the task at hand. Understanding the degree of fungibility of attention across tasks is an interesting research frontier.

where the parameter q captures the curvature of the attention function. In order to retain both continuity and sparsity of the attention function (26), I impose the sparsity-inducing restriction $\alpha = 1$, which results in

$$\mathcal{A}_1(\sigma^2) = \max\left(\frac{\sigma^2 - 1}{\sigma^2 + 2q}, 0\right). \tag{27}$$

I estimate the cost parameters $\bar{\kappa}$ and q on the cross-study data via nonlinear least squares, according to the model in (25). This yields calibrated parameters $\bar{\kappa} = 3.0\%$ and $q = 22.4$.

3.4 Different meanings of "attention"

The concept of "attention" has several meanings. The primary meaning in this survey is that of "the extent to which an agent's cognitive process is able to make use of all available data" (relative to a normative, rational benchmark, so that $m = 1$ means full attention), and is captured by this summary measure m – something we might call "effective attention". Measuring it requires some normative model. In much of psychology, however, attention means "observable sensory inputs devoted to the task" – let us denote this by T, as in time spent on the information, and call T the "observable attention". For instance, a bored student may look at a whole lecture (which lasts for $T = 80$ minutes), but still not really exert effort (let us call M that mental effort) so that the total amount learned (indexed by m) is very low. We have a relation of the type:

$$m = f(T, M),$$

e.g. $m = 1 - e^{-\alpha MT}$. I note that T is directly measurable, m can also be measured, though more indirectly, and M is quite nebulous at this stage. More generally, we can think of attentional inputs as "information gathering" (T in our example) and "information processing" (M).

In this survey I have emphasized m because it's the summary quantity we need to predict behavior, and because in many studies (e.g. on the attention to the tax) we don't have access to the time spent T. Also, even the whole time spent T is not a sufficient statistics for the effective attention m – as active mental effort is hard to measure.

Still, the "observable attention" T is very precious – as it can be directly measured, and much progress of science comes from focusing on directly measurable quantities. Hence, the process tracking studies reviewed in Section 3.1.3 represent great advances. Sometimes, observable attention T yields an excellent prediction of choice (for example, in context of simple choices among two or three alternatives, as in Krajbich and Rangel, 2011).

One can hope that the understanding of observable attention T, and effective attention m will continue to increase, with a healthy interplay between the two.

---

4 Models of endogenous attention: Deterministic action

We have seen that attention can be modeled in a simple way and that it can be measured. In this section, we will study some deterministic models that endogenize attention.

4.1 Paying more attention to more important variables: The sparsity model

The model in Gabaix (2014) aims at a high degree of applicability – to do so, it generalizes the max operator in economics, by assuming that agents can be less than fully attentive. This provides a foundation for a behavioral version of basic textbook microeconomics (Section 5), of the basic theory of taxation (Farhi and Gabaix, 2017), of basic dynamic macroeconomics (Gabaix, 2016), and macroeconomic fiscal and monetary policy (Gabaix, 2018a).[43]

The agent faces a maximization problem which is, in its traditional version, $\max_a u(a, x)$ subject to $b(a, x) \geq 0$, where u is a utility function, and b is a constraint. In this section I present a way to define the "sparse max" operator defined and analyzed in Gabaix (2014)[44]:

$$\underset{a}{\text{smax}}\, u(a, x) \text{ subject to } b(a, x) \geq 0, \tag{28}$$

which is a less than fully attentive version of the "max" operator. Variables a, x and function b have arbitrary dimensions.[45]

The case $x = 0$, will sometimes be called the "default parameter." We define the default action as the optimal action under the default parameter: $a^d :=$ $\arg\max_a u(a, 0)$ subject to $b(a, 0) \geq 0$. We assume that u and b are concave in a (and at least one of them is strictly concave) and twice continuously differentiable around $(a^d, 0)$. We will typically evaluate the derivatives at the default action and parameter, $(a, x) = (a^d, 0)$.

4.1.1 The sparse max without constraints

For clarity, we shall first define the sparse max without constraints, i.e. study $\text{smax}_a\, u(a, x)$.

Motivation for optimization problem. The agent maximizing (6) will take the action

$$a(x, m) := \arg\max_a u(a, x, m) \tag{29}$$

---

[43] This subsection and Section 5 draw extensively from Gabaix (2014).

[44] I draw on fairly recent literature on statistics and image processing to use a notion of "sparsity" that still entails well-behaved, convex maximization problems (Tibshirani, 1996; Candes and Tao, 2006).

[45] We shall see that parameters will be added in the definition of sparse max.

and she will experience utility $v(x, m) = u(a(x, m), x)$. Let us posit that attention creates a psychic cost, parametrized by

$$C(m) = \kappa \sum_i m_i^\alpha$$

with $\alpha \geq 0$. The case $\alpha = 0$ corresponds to a fixed cost κ paid each time m_i is non-zero. The parameter $\kappa \geq 0$ is a penalty for lack of sparsity. If $\kappa = 0$, the agent is the traditional, rational agent model with costless cognition.

It follows that agent would allocate attention m as:

$$\max_m \mathbb{E}[u(a(x, m), x)] - C(m). \tag{30}$$

However, ever since Simon (1955), many researchers have seen that problem (30) is very complicated – more complex than the original problem (we are threatened by "infinite regress" problem). The key step of the sparse max is that the agent will solve a version of this problem.

Definition 4.1 (*Sparse max – abstract definition*). In the sparse max, the agent optimizes in two steps. In Step 1, she selects the optimal attention m^* under a simplified version of the optimal problem (30): (i) she replaces her utility by a linear-quadratic approximation, and (ii) imagines that the vector x is drawn from a mean 0 distribution, with no correlations, but the accurate variances. In Step 2, she picks the best action (29) under the exact utility function, modulated by the attention vector m^* selected in Step 1.

To see this analytically, we introduce some notation. The expected size of x_i is $\sigma_i = \mathbb{E}[x_i^2]^{1/2}$, in the "ex ante" version of attention. In the "ex post allocation of attention" version, we set $\sigma_i := |x_i|$. We define $a_{x_i} := \frac{\partial a}{\partial x_i}$, which indicates how much a change in x_i should change the action, for the traditional agent.[46]

The agent entertaining the simplified problem of Definition 4.1 will want to solve[47]:

$$m^* = \arg\min_{m \in [0,1]^n} \frac{1}{2} \sum_{i=1}^n (1 - m_i)^2 \Lambda_{ii} + \kappa \sum_{i=1}^n m_i^\alpha, \tag{32}$$

---

[46] This implies $a_{x_i} = -u_{aa}^{-1} u_{ax_i}$. Derivatives are evaluated at the default action and parameter, i.e. at $(a, x) = (a^d, 0)$.

[47] The justification is as follows. We call $V(m) = \mathbb{E}[u(a(x, m), x)]$ the expected consumption utility. Then, a Taylor expansion shows that we have, for small x (call $\iota = (1, \ldots, 1)$ the vector corresponding to full attention, like the traditional agent):

$$V(m) - V(\iota) = -\frac{1}{2} \sum_{i,j} (1 - m_i) \Lambda_{ij} (1 - m_j) + o(\sigma^2), \tag{31}$$

defining $\Lambda_{ij} := -\sigma_{ij} a_{x_i} u_{aa} a_{x_j}$, $\sigma_{ij} := \mathbb{E}[x_i x_j]$, and $\sigma^2 = \|(\sigma_i^2)_{i=1\ldots n}\|$. The Taylor expansions is for small noises in x, rather than for m close to 1. The agent drops the non-diagonal terms (this is an optional, but useful, assumption of sparse max).

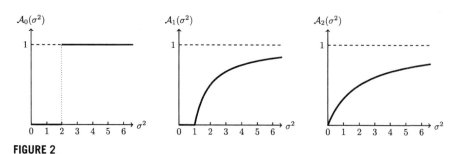

FIGURE 2

Three attention functions $\mathcal{A}_0, \mathcal{A}_1, \mathcal{A}_2$, corresponding to fixed cost, linear cost, and quadratic cost, respectively. We see that $\mathcal{A}_0$ and $\mathcal{A}_1$ induce sparsity – i.e. a range where attention is exactly 0. $\mathcal{A}_1$ and $\mathcal{A}_2$ induce a continuous reaction function. $\mathcal{A}_1$ alone induces sparsity and continuity.

where $\frac{1}{2}\Lambda_{ii} := -\frac{1}{2}\mathbb{E}\left[x_i^2\right]a_{x_i}u_{aa}a_{x_i}$ is the gain that the consumer enjoys when he goes from zero attention to full attention in dimension i (up to third order terms in the Taylor expansion). Hence, (32) shows how the agent trades off the benefits of more attention (captured by $(1-m_i)^2\Lambda_{ii}$) with the costs of attention (captured by κm_i^α).

The attention function. To build at least some intuition, let us start with the case with just one variable, $x_1 = x$ and call $\sigma^2 = \Lambda_{11}$. Then, problem (32) becomes:

$$\min_m \frac{1}{2}(1-m)^2\sigma^2 + \kappa m^\alpha. \tag{33}$$

Optimal attention is $m = \mathcal{A}_\alpha\left(\frac{\sigma^2}{\kappa}\right)$, where the "attention function" $\mathcal{A}_\alpha$ is defined as[48]

$$\mathcal{A}_\alpha\left(\sigma^2\right) := \arg\min_{m\in[0,1]} \frac{1}{2}(1-m)^2\sigma^2 + m^\alpha. \tag{34}$$

Fig. 2 plots how attention varies with the variance σ^2 for fixed, linear, and quadratic cost: $\mathcal{A}_0\left(\sigma^2\right) = 1_{\sigma^2 \geq 2}$, $\mathcal{A}_1\left(\sigma^2\right) = \max\left(1 - \frac{1}{\sigma^2}, 0\right)$, $\mathcal{A}_2\left(\sigma^2\right) = \frac{\sigma^2}{2+\sigma^2}$. In particular, let us examine $\mathcal{A}_1\left(\sigma^2\right)$. When the stakes are small, attention is 0 ($\mathcal{A}_1\left(\sigma^2\right) = 0$ for $\sigma^2 \leq 1$). As stakes increase, attention becomes non-0, and as stakes becomes very large, attention becomes full ($\lim_{\sigma^2 \to \infty} \mathcal{A}_1\left(\sigma^2\right) = 1$).

We now explore the case in which a^s indeed induces no attention to certain variables.[49]

---

[48] If there are multiple minimizers m, we take the highest one.

[49] Lemma 4.1 has direct antecedents in statistics: the pseudonorm $\|m\|_\alpha = \left(\sum_i |m_i|^\alpha\right)^{1/\alpha}$ is convex and sparsity-inducing iff $\alpha = 1$ (Tibshirani, 1996).

Lemma 4.1 (Special status of linear costs). *When $\alpha \leq 1$ (and only then) the attention function $\mathcal{A}_\alpha\left(\sigma^2\right)$ induces sparsity: when the variable is not very important, then the attention weight is 0 ($m = 0$). When $\alpha \geq 1$ (and only then) the attention function is continuous. Hence, only for $\alpha = 1$ do we obtain both sparsity and continuity.*

For this reason $\alpha = 1$ is recommended for most applications. Below I state most results in their general form, making clear when $\alpha = 1$ is required.[50]

The sparse max: Values of attention. The abstract definition of the sparse max, and the functional form assumptions made above, lead to the following concrete procedure that describes that behavioral agent.

Proposition 4.1. *The sparse max of Definition 4.1 is solved in two steps.*
Step 1: Choose the attention vector m^*, which is optimally equal to:

$$m_i^* = \mathcal{A}_\alpha\left(\sigma_i^2 \left| a_{x_i} u_{aa} a_{x_i} \right| / \kappa\right), \tag{35}$$

where $\mathcal{A}_\alpha : \mathbb{R} \to [0, 1]$ is the attention function expressed in (34), σ_i^2 is the perceived variance of x_i^2, $a_{x_i} = -u_{aa}^{-1} u_{ai}$ is the traditional marginal impact of a small change in x_i, evaluated at $x = 0$, and κ is the cost of cognition.
Step 2: Choose the action

$$a^s = \arg\max_a u\left(a, x, m^*\right). \tag{36}$$

Hence more attention is paid to variable x_i if it is more variable (high σ_i^2), if it should matter more for the action (high $\left|a_{x_i}\right|$), if an imperfect action leads to greater losses (high $\left|u_{aa}\right|$), and if the cost parameter κ is low.

The sparse max procedure in (35) entails (for $\alpha \leq 1$): "Eliminate each feature of the world that would change the action by only a small amount".[51] This is how a sparse agent sails through life: for a given problem, out of the thousands of variables that might be relevant, he takes into account only a few that are important enough to significantly change his decision.[52] He also devotes "some" attention to those important variables, not necessarily paying full attention to them.[53]

---

[50] The sparse max is, properly speaking, sparse (in the narrow sense of inducing zero attention) only when $\alpha \leq 1$. When $\alpha > 1$, the abuse of language seems minor, as the smax still offers a way to economize on attention (as it generally shrinks attention toward 0). Perhaps smax should be called a "bmax" or behavioral/boundedly rational max.

[51] For instance, when $\alpha = 1$, eliminate the x_i such that $\left|\sigma_i \cdot \frac{\partial a}{\partial x_i}\right| \leq \sqrt{\frac{\kappa}{|u_{aa}|}}$.

[52] To see this formally (with $\alpha = 1$), note that m has at most $\sum_i b_i^2 \sigma_i^2 / \kappa$ non-zero components (because $m_i \neq 0$ implies $b_i^2 \sigma_i^2 \geq \kappa$). Hence, when κ increases, the number of non-zero components becomes arbitrarily small. When x has infinite dimension, m has a finite number of non-zero components, and is therefore sparse (assuming $\mathbb{E}\left[(a^r)^2\right] < \infty$).

[53] There is anchoring with partial adjustment, i.e. dampening. This dampening is pervasive, and indeed optimal, in "signal plus noise" models (more on this later).

Let us revisit the initial example.[54]

Example 1. In the quadratic loss problem, (11), the traditional action is $a^r = \sum_{i=1}^{n} b_i x_i$, and the behavioral action is:

$$a^s = \sum_{i=1}^{n} m_i^* b_i x_i, \qquad m_i^* = \mathcal{A}_\alpha \left(b_i^2 \sigma_i^2 / \kappa \right). \tag{37}$$

Discrete goods. All this can be extended to discrete actions. For instance, suppose that the agent must choose one good among A goods. Good $a \in \{1...A\}$ has value $u(a, x) = \sum_{i=1}^{n} b_i x_{ia}$. Then, the boundedly rational perception of the utility from good a is $u(a, x, m) = \sum_{i=1}^{n} m_i b_i x_{ia}$, and the optimal attention is again:

$$m_i^* = \mathcal{A}_\alpha \left(b_i^2 \sigma_i^2 / \kappa \right) \tag{38}$$

where σ_i^2 is the variance of x_{ia} across goods. The behavioral action is then $a^s = \arg\max_a u(a, x, m^*)$.

4.1.2 Sparse max allowing for constraints

Let us now extend the sparse max so that it can handle maximization under K (= $\dim b$) constraints, which is problem (28). As a motivation, consider the canonical consumer problem:

$$\max_{c_1, \dots, c_n} u(c_1, \dots, c_n) \text{ subject to } p_1 c_1 + \dots + p_n c_n \leq w. \tag{39}$$

We start from a default price p^d. The new price is $p_i = p_i^d + x_i$, while the price perceived by the agent is $p_i^s(m) = p_i^d + m_i x_i$, i.e.[55]

$$p_i^s(p_i, m) = m_i p_i + (1 - m_i) p_i^d.$$

How to satisfy the budget constraint? An agent who underperceives prices will tend to spend too much – but he's not allowed to do so. Many solutions are possible, but the following makes psychological sense and has good analytical properties. In the traditional model, the ratio of marginal utilities optimally equals the ratio of prices: $\frac{\partial u / \partial c_1}{\partial u / \partial c_2} = \frac{p_1}{p_2}$. We will preserve that idea, but in the space of perceived prices. Hence, the ratio of marginal utilities equals the ratio of *perceived* prices[56]:

$$\frac{\partial u / \partial c_1}{\partial u / \partial c_2} = \frac{p_1^s}{p_2^s}, \tag{40}$$

---

[54] The proof is as follows. We have $a_{x_i} = b_i$, $u_{aa} = -1$, so (35) gives $m_i = \mathcal{A}_\alpha(b_i^2 \sigma_i^2 / \kappa)$.

[55] The constraint is $0 \leq b(c, x) := w - (p^d + x) \cdot c$.

[56] Otherwise, as usual, if we had $\frac{\partial u / \partial c_1}{\partial u / \partial c_2} > \frac{p_1^s}{p_2^s}$, the consumer could consume a bit more of good 1 and less of good 2, and project to be better off.

i.e. $u'(c) = \lambda p^s$, for some scalar λ.[57] The agent will tune λ so that the constraint binds, i.e. the value of $c(\lambda) = u'^{-1}(\lambda p^s)$ satisfies $p \cdot c(\lambda) = w$.[58] Hence, in step 2, the agent "hears clearly" whether the budget constraint binds.[59] This agent is behavioral, but smart enough to exhaust his budget.

Consequences for consumption. Section 5.1.1 develops consumer demand from the above procedure, and contains many examples. For instance, Proposition 5.1 finds that the Marshallian demand of a behavioral agent is

$$c^s(p, w) = c^r(p^s, w'), \tag{41}$$

where the as-if budget w' solves $p \cdot c^r(p^s, w') = w$, i.e. ensures that the budget constraint is satisfied under the true price.

Determination of the attention to prices, m^*. The exact value of attention, m, is not essential for many issues, and this subsection might be skipped in a first reading. Call λ^d the Lagrange multiplier at the default price.[60]

Proposition 4.2 (Attention to prices). *The sparse agent's attention to price i is:*

$$m_i^* = \mathcal{A}_\alpha \left(\left(\frac{\sigma_{p_i}}{p_i^d} \right)^2 \psi_i \lambda^d p_i^d c_i^d / \kappa \right), \text{ where } \psi_i \text{ is the price elasticity of demand for}$$

good i.

Hence attention to prices is greater for goods (i) with more volatile prices (σ_{p_i}/p_i^d), (ii) with higher price elasticity ψ_i (i.e. for goods whose price is more important in the purchase decision), and (iii) with higher expenditure share $(p_i^d c_i^d)$. These predictions seem sensible, though not extremely surprising. What is important is that we have some procedure to pick the m, so that the model is closed. Still, it would be interesting to investigate empirically the prediction of Proposition 4.2.

Generalization to arbitrary problems of maximization under constraints. We next generalize this approach to satisfying the budget constraint to arbitrary problems. The reader may wish to skip to the next section, as this material is more notationally dense. We define the Lagrangian $L(a, x) := u(a, x) + \lambda^d \cdot b(a, x)$, with $\lambda^d \in \mathbb{R}_+^K$ the Lagrange multiplier associated with problem (28) when $x = 0$ (the optimal action in the default model is $a^d = \arg\max_a L(a, 0)$). The marginal action is: $a_x = -L_{aa}^{-1} L_{ax}$.

---

[57] This model, with a general objective function and K constraints, delivers, as a special case, the third adjustment rule discussed in Chetty et al. (2007) in the context of consumption with two goods and one tax.

[58] If there are several λ, the agent takes the smallest value, which is the utility-maximizing one.

[59] See footnote 69 for additional intuitive justification.

[60] This is, $u'(c^d) = \lambda^d p^d$, where p^d is the exogenous default price, and c^d is the (endogenous) optimal consumption as the default.

This is quite natural: to turn a problem with constraints into an unconstrained problem, we add the "price" of the constraints to the utility. Applying the Definition 4.1 to this case this the following characterization.[61]

Proposition 4.3 (Sparse max operator with constraints). *The sparse max,* $\text{smax}_{a|\kappa,\sigma} u(a, x)$ *subject to* $b(a, x) \geq 0$, *is solved in two steps.*

Step 1: Choose the attention m^* as in (32), using $\Lambda_{ij} := -\sigma_{ij} a_{x_i} L_{aa} a_{x_j}$, with $a_{x_i} = -L_{aa}^{-1} L_{ax_i}$. Define $x_i^s = m_i^* x_i$ the associated sparse representation of x.

Step 2: Choose the action. *Form a function* $a(\lambda) := \arg\max_a u(a, x^s) + \lambda b(a, x^s)$. *Then, maximize utility under the true constraint:* $\lambda^* = \arg\max_{\lambda \in \mathbb{R}_+^K} u(a(\lambda), x^s)$ *subject to* $b(a(\lambda), x) \geq 0$. *(With just one binding constraint this is equivalent to choosing* λ^* *such that* $b(a(\lambda^*), x) = 0$; *in case of ties, we take the lowest* λ^*.) *The resulting sparse action is* $a^s := a(\lambda^*)$. *Utility is* $u^s := u(a^s, x)$.

Step 2 of Proposition 4.3 allows generally for the translation of a boundedly rational maximum without constraints into a boundedly rational maximum with constraints. To obtain further intuition on the constrained maximum, we turn to consumer theory.

4.2 Proportional thinking: The salience model of Bordalo, Gennaioli, Shleifer

In a series of papers, Bordalo et al. (2012, 2013, 2016a) introduce a model of context-dependent choice in which attention is drawn toward those attributes of a good that are *salient* – that is, attributes that are particularly unusual with respect to a given reference frame.

4.2.1 The salience framework in the absence of uncertainty

The theory of salience in the context of choice over goods is developed in Bordalo et al. (2013). In a general version of the model, the decision-maker chooses a good from a set $\mathcal{C} = \{\mathbf{x}_a\}_{a=1,...,A}$ of $A > 1$ goods. Each good in the choice set $\mathcal{C}$ is a vector $\mathbf{x}_a = (x_{a1}, \ldots, x_{an})$ of attributes x_{ai} which characterize the utility obtained by the agent along a particular dimension of consumption. In the baseline case without behavioral distortions, the utility of good a is separable across consumption dimensions, with relative weights $(b_i)_{i=1,...,n}$ attached to each dimension, such that $u(a) = \sum_{i=1}^n b_i x_{ai}$. Each weight b_i captures the relative significance of a dimension of consumption, absent any salience distortions. In the boundedly rational case, the agent's valuation of good a instead gets the subjective (or salience-weighted) utility:

$$u^s(a) = \sum_{i=1}^n b_i m_{ai} x_{ai} \tag{42}$$

---

[61] For instance, in a consumption problem (39), λ^d is the "marginal utility of a dollar", at the default prices. This way we can use Lagrangian L to encode the importance of the constraints and maximize it without constraints, so that the basic sparse max can be applied.

where m_{ai} is a weight capturing the extent of the behavioral distortion, which is determined independently for each of the good's attributes. The distortion m_{ai} of the decision weight b_i is taken to be an increasing function of the *salience* of attribute i for good a with respect to a *reference point* $\bar{x}_i$. Bordalo et al. (2013) propose using the average value of the attribute among goods in the choice set as a natural reference point, that is $\bar{x}_i = \frac{1}{A} \sum_{a=1}^{A} x_{ai}$. Valuation is comparative in that what is salient about an option depends on what you compare it to.

Formally, the salience of x_{ai} with respect to $\bar{x}_i$ is given by $\sigma(x_{ai}, \bar{x}_i)$, where the salience function σ satisfies the following conditions:

Definition 4.2. The salience function $\sigma : \mathbb{R} \times \mathbb{R} \to \mathbb{R}$ satisfies the following properties[62]:

1. *Ordering.* If $[x, y] \subset [x', y'] \in \mathbb{R}$, then $\sigma(x, y) < \sigma(x', y')$.
2. *Diminishing sensitivity.* If $x, y \in \mathbb{R}_{>0}$, then for all $\epsilon > 0$, $\sigma(x + \epsilon, y + \epsilon) < \sigma(x, y)$.
3. *Reflection.*[63] If $x, y, x', y' \in \mathbb{R}_{>0}$, then $\sigma(x, y) < \sigma(x', y')$ if and only if $\sigma(-x, -y) < \sigma(-x', -y')$.

According to these axioms, the salience of an attribute increases in its distance to that attribute's reference value, and decreases in the absolute magnitude of the reference point. The agent focuses her attention on those attributes that depart from the usual, but any given difference in an attribute's value is perceived with less intensity when the magnitude of values is uniformly higher. The reflection property guarantees a degree of symmetry between gains and losses. A tractable functional form that satisfies the properties in Definition 4.2 is

$$\sigma(x, y) = \frac{|x - y|}{|x| + |y| + \theta} \tag{43}$$

with $\theta \geq 0$ is an application-dependent parameter. This functional form additionally is symmetric in the two arguments x, y. The model is completed by specifying how the salience values σ translate into the distortion weights m_{ai}. Letting $(r_{ai})_{i=1,\dots,n}$ be the ranking of good a's attributes according to their salience (where rank 1 corresponds to the most salient attribute), Bordalo et al. (2013) propose the functional form

$$m_{ai} = Z_a \delta^{r_{ai}} \tag{44}$$

---

[62] In Bordalo et al. (2013), the additional axiom that σ is symmetric is introduced. Since the assumption of symmetry is relaxed in the case of choice among multiple goods, with multiple attributes, for expository purposes I omit it in Definition 4.2.

[63] This property is only relevant if σ admits both negative and positive arguments. This is discussed in further depth in Bordalo et al. (2012).

where the parameter $\delta \in (0, 1]$ measures the strength of the salience distortion, and Z_a is an application-dependent normalization.[64] In the case $\delta = 1$ we recover the fully rational agent, while in the limit case $\delta \to 0$ the agent only attends to the attribute that is most salient.[65]

To see this model of salience in action, consider the case of a consumer choosing between two bottles of wine, with high (H) and low (L) quality, in a store or at a restaurant. The two relevant attributes for each good $a \in \{H, L\}$ are quality q_a and price p_a. Suppose that utility in the absence of salience distortions is $U_a = q_a - p_a$. The quality of bottle H, $q_H = 30$, is 50 percent higher than the quality of bottle L, $q_L = 20$. At the store, bottle H retails for $20, while bottle L retails for $10. At the restaurant, each bottle is marked up and the prices are $60 and $50, respectively. When is the consumer likely to choose the more expensive bottle?

While in the absence of salience distortions the agent is always indifferent between the two bottles, salience will tilt the choice in one or the other direction depending on the choice context. Taking the reference point for each attribute to be its average in the choice set, at the store we have a "reference good" $(\bar{q}_s, \bar{p}_s) = (25, 15)$, while at the restaurant we have a reference good $(\bar{q}_r, \bar{p}_r) = (25, 55)$. Under the functional form in (43), we can readily verify that in the store price is the more salient attribute for each wine, while at the restaurant quality is. Hence in the store the consumer focuses her attention on price and chooses the cheaper wine, while at the restaurant the markup drives attention away from prices and toward quality, leading her to choose the higher-end wine. Dertwinkel-Kalt et al. (2017) provide evidence for this effect.

Bordalo et al. (2016a) further embed the salience-distorted preference structure over price and quality into a standard model of market competition. This yields a set of predictions that depart from the rational benchmark, as firms strategically make price and quality choices so as to tilt the salience of these attributes in their favor.

4.2.2 Salience and choice over lotteries

Bordalo et al. (2012) develop the salience model in the context of choice over lotteries. The framework is very similar to the one discussed for the case in which we have no uncertainty. The decision-maker must choose among a set $\mathcal{C}$ of $A > 1$ lotteries. We let S be the minimal state space associated with $\mathcal{C}$, defined as the set of distinct payoff combinations that occur with positive probability. The state space S is assumed to be discrete, such that each state of the world $i \in S$ occurs with known probability π_i. The payoff of lottery a in state of the world i is x_{ai}. Absent any salience distortions, the value of lottery a is $u(a) = \sum_{i \in S} \pi_i v(x_{ai})$. Under salient thinking, the agent distorts

---

[64] For the choice over goods, the authors propose $Z_a = \frac{n}{\sum_i \delta^{r_{ai}}}$. For probabilities, Z_a ensures that total probability is 1, $Z_a = 1/\left(\sum_i \pi_i \delta^{r_{ai}}\right)$.

[65] The distortion function (44) can exhibit discontinuous jumps. An alternative specification introduced in Bordalo et al. (2016a) that allows for continuous salience distortions is $m_{ai} = Z_a e^{(1-\delta)\sigma(x_{ai}, \bar{x}_i)}$.

the true state probabilities and correspondingly assigns utility

$$u^s(a) = \sum_{i \in S} \pi_i m_{ai} v(x_{ai}) \qquad (45)$$

to lottery a, where the distortion weights m_{ai} are increasing in the salience of state i. Bordalo et al. (2012) propose evaluating the salience of state i in lottery a by weighing its payoff against the average payoff yielded by the other lotteries in the same state of the world, meaning that the salience is given by $\sigma(x_{ai}, \bar{x}_i)$, where $\bar{x}_i = \frac{1}{A-1} \sum_{\bar{a} \in C: \bar{a} \neq a} x_{\bar{a}i}$.

The salience model of choice under uncertainty presented in this section accounts for several empirical puzzles, including the Allais paradoxes, yielding tight quantitative predictions for the circumstances under which such choice patterns are expected to occur. For a concrete example, we consider the "common-consequence" Allais paradox as presented in Bordalo et al. (2012).[66] In this version of the common-consequence Allais paradox, originally due to Kahneman and Tversky (1979), experimental participants are asked to choose between the two lotteries

$$L_1(z) = (2500, 0.33; \; 0, 0.01; \; z, 0.66)$$
$$L_2(z) = (2400, 0.34; \; z, 0.66)$$

for varying levels of the common consequence z. In a laboratory setting, when the common consequence z is high ($z = 2400$), participants tend to exhibit risk-averse behavior, preferring $L_2(2400)$ to $L_1(2400)$. However, when $z = 0$ most participants shift to risk-seeking behavior, preferring $L_1(0)$ to $L_2(0)$. This empirical pattern is not readily accounted for by the standard theory of choice under uncertainty, as it violates the axiom of independence.

In order to see how the salience model accounts for the Allais paradox, we need only derive the conditions that determine the preference ranking over lotteries in the two cases $z = 2400$ and $z = 0$. For this example, we assume the linear value function $v(x) = x$ and we take σ to be symmetric in its arguments, such that for all states $i \in S$ we have homogeneous salience rankings in the case of choice between two lotteries $a, \tilde{a}$ – that is, $r_{ai} = r_{\tilde{a}i} := r_i$. We further assume the distortion function is defined analogously to (44). These conditions yield the following necessary and sufficient criterion for lottery a to be preferred in a choice between a and $\tilde{a}$:

$$\sum_{i \in S} \delta^{r_i} \pi_i [v(x_{ai}) - v(x_{\tilde{a}i})] > 0. \qquad (46)$$

When $z = 2400$, the minimum state space for the lotteries in the choice set is $S = \{ (2500, 2400), (0, 2400), (2400, 2400)\}$ which from the ordering and diminishing

---

sensitivity properties of σ yields the salience rankings

$$\sigma(0, 2400) > \sigma(2500, 2400) > \sigma(2400, 2400).$$

By criterion (46), in order to account for the preference relation $L_2(2400) \succ L_1(2400)$ it must then hold be that

$$0.01(2400) - 0.33\delta(100) > 0,$$

which is true whenever $\delta < 0.73$. Intuitively, for low enough δ the agent focuses her attention on the salient downside of 0 in $L_1(0)$, which lowers her valuation of it. By an analogous argument, when $z = 0$ a necessary and sufficient condition for $L_1(0) \succ L_2(0)$ is that $\delta \geq 0$. Hence the Allais paradox is resolved for $\delta \in [0, 0.73)$, when the decision-maker exhibits salience bias of great enough significance.

4.3 Other themes

4.3.1 Attention to various time dimensions: "Focusing"

The model of focusing of Kőszegi and Szeidl (2013) expresses a shrinkage assumption similar to that of sparsity (Section 4.1), but with a different emphasis in applications, and an assumption of additivity. The model assumes that the decision-maker gives higher attention on those dimensions of the choice problem that are of primary order – which Kőszegi and Szeidl (2013) take to be the attributes along which her options vary by the largest amount. Given a choice set $\mathcal{C} = \{\mathbf{x}_a\}_{a=1...A}$ of $A > 1$ actions that yield utilities $(x_{ai})_{i=1...n}$ along n dimensions, the decision-maker departs from the rational benchmark $u(a) = \sum_{i=1}^n x_{ai}$ by distorting the importance of each consumption dimension to a degree that is increasing in the latitude of the options available to her in that dimension. Formally, we capture the range σ_i of dimension i as the range (one could imagine another way, e.g. the standard deviation of the x_{ai} across actions a)

$$\sigma_i = \max_a x_{ai} - \min_a x_{ai}. \tag{47}$$

Subjectively perceived utility is:

$$u^s(a) = \sum_{i=1}^n m_i x_{ai}, \tag{48}$$

where the attention weight is

$$m_i = \mathcal{A}(\sigma_i) \tag{49}$$

and the attention function $\mathcal{A}$ is increasing in the range of outcomes σ_i. Intuitively, the decision-maker attends to those dimensions of the problem in which her choice is most consequential. Hence, we obtain a formulation related to sparsity, though it does not use its general apparatus, e.g. the nonlinear framework and microfoundation for attention.

In the context of consumer finance, the focusing model explains why consumers occasionally choose expensive financing options even in the absence of liquidity constraints. Suppose an agent is buying a laptop, and has the option of either paying \$1000 upfront, or enrolling in the vendor's financing plan, which requires 12 future monthly payments of \$100. For simplicity, we assume no time-discounting and linear consumption disutility from monetary payments. We also take consumption in each period of life to be a separate dimension of the choice problem. The agent therefore chooses between two actions a_1, a_2 yielding payoff vectors $x_1 = (-1000, 0, \ldots, 0)$ and $x_2 = (0, -100, \ldots, -100)$ respectively. The vector of utility ranges is therefore $\sigma = (1000, 100, \ldots, 100)$, such that the prospect of a large upfront payment attracts the agent's attention more than the repeated but small subsequent payments. The choice-relevant comparison is between $u^s(a_1) = -\mathcal{A}(1000) \cdot 1000$ and $u^s(a_2) = -\mathcal{A}(100) \cdot 1200$. As long as $\frac{\mathcal{A}(1000)}{\mathcal{A}(100)} > 1.2$, the agent will choose the more expensive monthly payment plan, even though she does not discount the future or face liquidity constraints. Relatedly, Kőszegi and Szeidl (2013) also demonstrate how the model explains present-bias and time-inconsistency in preferences in a generalized intertemporal choice context.

Bushong et al. (2016) develop a related model, where however $\mathcal{A}(\sigma)$ is decreasing in σ, though $\sigma \mathcal{A}(\sigma)$ is increasing in σ. This tends to make the agent relatively insensitive to the absolute importance of a dimension. Interestingly, it tends to make predictions opposite to those of Kőszegi and Szeidl (2013), Bordalo et al. (2013), and Gabaix (2014). The authors propose that this is useful to understand present bias, if "the future" is lumped in one large dimension in the decision-making process.

4.3.2 Motivated attention

The models discussed in this section do not feature motivated attention (a close cousin of motivated reasoning) – e.g. the fact that I might pay more attention to things that favor or are pleasing to me (a self-serving bias), and avoid depressing thoughts. There is empirical evidence for this; for instance Olafsson and Pagel (2017) find that people are more likely to look at their banking account when it is flush than when it is low, an "ostrich effect" (Karlsson et al., 2009; Sicherman et al., 2016). The evidence is complex: in loss aversion, people pay more attention to losses than gains, something prima facie opposite to a self-serving attention bias. Hopefully future research will clarify this.

Let me propose the following simple model of motivated attention. Paying attention m_i to dimension i gives a psychic utility $u_{x_i} x_i \phi(m_i)$, for some increasing function ϕ. Note that x_i is "good news" iff $u_{x_i} x_i \geq 0$ (as a small innovation x_i creates a change in utility $u_{x_i} x_i$). Using a simple variant of Step 1 in the sparsity model yields an optimal attention[67]:

$$m_i^* = \mathcal{A}_\alpha \left(\frac{1}{\kappa} \max \left(\sigma_i^2 \left| a_{x_i} u_{aa} a_{x_i} \right| + \mu u_{x_i} x_i, 0 \right) \right). \tag{51}$$

This is as in (35), but with the extra term for motivated cognition, $\mu u_{x_i} x_i$. It implies that the agent pays more attention to "good news" (i.e. news with $u_{x_i} x_i \geq 0$), with a particular strength μ of motivated cognition that might be empirically evaluated. For instance, in the basic quadratic problem the traditional action is $a^r = \sum_{i=1}^n b_i x_i$, and the behavioral action augmented by motivated reasoning becomes:

$$a^s = \sum_{i=1}^n m_i^* b_i x_i, \qquad m_i^* = \mathcal{A}_\alpha \left(\frac{\max \left(b_i^2 \sigma_i^2 + \mu b_i x_i, 0 \right)}{\kappa} \right). \tag{52}$$

Yet another model is that people might be monitoring information but are mindful of their loss aversion, i.e. avoid "bad news", along the lines of Kőszegi and Rabin (2009), Olafsson and Pagel (2017), and Andries and Haddad (2017).

4.3.3 Other decision-theoretic models of bounded rationality

In the spirit of "model substitution", interesting work of the "bounded rationality" tradition include Jehiel's (2005) analogy-based equilibrium (which has generated a sizable literature), and work of Compte and Postlewaite (2017).

4.4 Limitation of these models

These models are of course limited. They do not feature a refined "cost" of attention: for example, why it's harder to pay attention to tax changes than a funny story remains unmodeled.

Attention can be controlled, but not fully. For instance, consider someone who had a bad breakup, and can't help thinking about it during an exam. That doesn't seem fully optimal, but (in the same way that paying attention to pain is generally useful, but one would like to be able to stop paying attention to pain once under torture) this may be optimal given some constraints on the design of attention.

This notion of "bottom-up attention" may be modeled in a way similar to the "top-down attention" that is the center of this paper. Instead of the attention responding

---

[67] When including psychic utility, the problem (32) becomes

$$m^* = \arg \max_{m \in [0,1]^n} \sum_{i=1}^n \left[\frac{-1}{2} (1 - m_i)^2 \Lambda_{ii} + u_{x_i} x_i \phi (m_i) - \kappa m_i^\alpha \right]. \tag{50}$$

On the right-hand side, the first term is the utility loss from inattention ($\frac{-1}{2} (1 - m_i)^2 \Lambda_{ii}$), the new term is the psychic utility from the news ($u_{x_i} x_i \phi (m_i)$), and the last term is the cost of attention ($-\kappa m_i^\alpha$). If we use, for tractability, $\phi (m) = \frac{\mu}{2} \left(1 - (1 - m)^2 \right)$, where $\mu \geq 0$ parametrizes the importance of motivated cognition, then we obtain (51).

as $m_i^* = \mathcal{A}_\alpha\,(I_i)$ to the "deep" usefulness I_i of a piece of information (as captured by (35) with $I_i = \sigma_i^2\,\left|a_{x_i} u_{aa} a_{x_i}\right|/\kappa$), the agent might rely on the "surface" usefulness of that information, e.g. it's written in red, and in a large font, or with some "emotional" characteristics (that is, she might use a default attention $m_i^* = \mathcal{A}_\alpha\left(I_i^d\right)$, where $I_i^d = \gamma' Y_i$, for some vector Y_i related to the characteristics of information i). Itti and Koch (2000) is an influential empirical model of such visual characteristics.

Rather than seeing those objections as fatal flaws, we shall see them as interesting research challenges.

5 A behavioral update of basic microeconomics: Consumer theory, Arrow–Debreu

Here I present a behavioral version of basic microeconomics, based on limited attention. It is based on Gabaix (2014). Its structure does not, however, depends on the details of the endogenization of attention (i.e. from sparsity or some other procedure). Hence, the analysis applies to a large set of behavioral models, provided they incorporate some inattention to prices.

5.1 Textbook consumer theory

5.1.1 Basic consumer theory: Marshallian demand

We are now ready to see how textbook consumer theory changes for this partially inattentive agent. The rational consumer's Marshallian demand is:

$$c\,(p, w) := \arg\max_{c \in \mathbb{R}^n} u\,(c) \text{ subject to } p \cdot c \le w \tag{53}$$

where c and p are the consumption vector and price vector. We denote by $c^r\,(p, w)$ the demand under the traditional *rational* model, and by $c^s\,(p, w)$ the demand of a behavioral agent (the s stands for: demand given "subjectively perceived prices"). The price of good i is $p_i = p_i^d + x_i$, where p_i^d is the default price (e.g., the average price) and x_i is the deviation between the default price and the true price, as in Section 2.3.1. The price perceived by a behavioral agent is $p_i^s = p_i^d + m_i x_i$, i.e.:

$$p_i^s\,(m) = m_i\,p_i + (1 - m_i)\,p_i^d. \tag{54}$$

When $m_i = 1$, the agent fully perceives price p_i, while when $m_i = 0$, he replaces it by the default price.[68]

---

[68] More general functions $p_i^s\,(m)$ could be devised. For instance, perceptions can be in percentage terms, i.e. in logs, $\ln p_i^s\,(m) = m_i \ln p_i + (1 - m_i) \ln p_i^d$. The main results go through with this log-linear formulation, because in both cases, $\dfrac{\partial p_i^s}{\partial p_i}\bigg|_{p = p^d} = m_i$.

Proposition 5.1 (Marshallian demand). *Given the true price vector p and the perceived price vector p^s, the Marshallian demand of a behavioral agent is*

$$c^s(p, w) = c^r(p^s, w'),\tag{55}$$

where the as-if budget w' solves $p \cdot c^r(p^s, w') = w$, i.e. ensures that the budget constraint is exactly satisfied under the true price (if there are several such w', take the largest one).

To obtain intuition, we start with an example.

Example 2 (*Demand by a behavioral agent with quasi-linear utility*). Take $u(c) = v(c_1, ..., c_{n-1}) + c_n$, with v strictly concave, and assume that the price of good n is correctly perceived. Demand for good $i < n$ is independent of wealth and is: $c_i^s(p) = c_i^r(p^s)$.

In this example, the demand of the behavioral agent is the rational demand given the perceived price (for all goods but the last one). The residual good n is the "shock absorber" that adjusts to the budget constraint. In a dynamic context, this good n could be "savings". Here it is a polar opposite to quasilinear demand.

Example 3 (*Demand proportional to wealth*). When rational demand is proportional to wealth, the demand of a behavioral agent is: $c_i^s(p, w) = \frac{c_i^r(p^s, w)}{p \cdot c^r(p^s, 1)}$.

Example 4 (*Demand by behavioral Cobb–Douglas and CES agents*). When $u(c) = \sum_{i=1}^n \alpha_i \ln c_i$, with $\alpha_i \geq 0$, demand is: $c_i^s(p, w) = \frac{\alpha_i}{p_i^s} \frac{w}{\sum_j \alpha_j \frac{p_j}{p_j^s}}$. When instead $u(c) = \sum_{i=1}^n c_i^{1-1/\eta}/(1 - 1/\eta)$, with $\eta > 0$, demand is: $c_i^s(p, w) = (p_i^s)^{-\eta} \frac{w}{\sum_j p_j (p_j^s)^{-\eta}}$.

More generally, say that the consumer goes to the supermarket, with a budget of $w = \$100$. Because of the lack of full attention to prices, the value of the basket in the cart is actually $\$101$. When demand is linear in wealth, the consumer buys 1% less of all the goods, to hit the budget constraint, and spends exactly $\$100$ (this is the adjustment factor $1/p \cdot c^r(p^s, 1) = \frac{100}{101}$). When demand is not necessarily linear in wealth, the adjustment is (to the leading order) proportional to the income effect, $\frac{\partial c^r}{\partial w}$, rather than to the current basket, c^r. The behavioral agent cuts "luxury goods", not "necessities".[69]

---

[69] For instance, the consumer at the supermarket might come to the cashier, who'd tell him that he is over budget by $\$1$. Then, the consumer removes items from the cart (e.g. lowering the as-if budget w' by $\$1$), and presents the new cart to the cashier, who might now say that he's $\$0.10$ under budget. The consumers now will adjust his consumption a bit (increase w' by $\$0.10$). This demand here is the convergence point of this "tatonnement" process. In computer science language, the agent has access to an "oracle" (like the cashier) telling him if he's over or under budget.

5.1.2 Asymmetric Slutsky matrix, and inferring attention from choice data, and nominal illusion

The Slutsky matrix. The Slutsky matrix is an important object, as it encodes both elasticities of substitution and welfare losses from distorted prices. Its element S_{ij} is the (compensated) change in consumption of c_i as price p_j changes:

$$S_{ij}(p, w) := \frac{\partial c_i(p, w)}{\partial p_j} + \frac{\partial c_i(p, w)}{\partial w} c_j(p, w). \tag{56}$$

With the traditional agent, the most surprising fact about it is that it is symmetric: $S_{ij}^r = S_{ji}^r$. Mas-Colell et al. (1995, p. 70) comment: "Symmetry is not easy to interpret in plain economic terms. As emphasized by Samuelson (1947), it is a property just beyond what one would derive without the help of mathematics."

Now, if a prediction is non-intuitive to Mas-Colell et al., it might require too much sophistication from the average consumer. We now present a less rational, and psychologically more intuitive, prediction.

Proposition 5.2 (Slutsky matrix). *Evaluated at the default price, the Slutsky matrix S^s is, compared to the traditional matrix S^r:*

$$S_{ij}^s = S_{ij}^r m_j, \tag{57}$$

i.e. the behavioral demand sensitivity to price j is the rational one, times m_j, the salience of price j. As a result the behavioral Slutsky matrix is not symmetric in general. Sensitivities corresponding to "non-salient" price changes (low m_j) are dampened.

Proof sketch. For simplicity, here I only show the proof in the quasi-linear case of Example 2, when the price of the last good is correctly perceived at 1. We call $C = (c_1, \ldots, c_{n-1})$, so that $u(C, c_n) = v(C) + c_n$, and set $P = (p_1, \ldots, p_{n-1})$. We restrict our attention to good $i, j < n$. The consumer's first order condition is $v_{c_i} = p_i^s$, i.e. $v'(C) = P^s$, so the demand is $C^s(P^s) = C^r(P^s)$, where $C(P) = v'^{-1}(P)$ is the rational demand. Then, $S_{ij} = \frac{\partial c_i^s(p, w)}{\partial p_j}$, as there is no income effect (by the way, that expression allows to verify that the Slutsky matrix is symmetric in the rational case). So, evaluating the derivatives at $p^s = p^d$,

$$S_{ij}^s = \frac{\partial c_i^s(p)}{\partial p_j} = \frac{dc_i^r\left(m_j p_j + (1 - m_j) p_j^d\right)}{dp_j} = m_j \frac{\partial c_i^r(q_j)}{\partial q_j} = m_j S_{ij}^r.$$

This gives the result.   □

Instead of looking at the full price change, the consumer just reacts to a fraction m_j of it. Hence, he's typically less responsive than the rational agent. For instance, say that $m_i > m_j$, so that the price of i is more salient than price of good j. The model predicts that $\left|S_{ij}^s\right|$ is lower than $\left|S_{ji}^s\right|$: as good j's price isn't very salient, quantities don't react much to it. When $m_j = 0$, the consumer does not react at all to price p_j, hence the substitution effect is zero.

The asymmetry of the Slutsky matrix indicates that, in general, *a behavioral consumer cannot be represented by a rational consumer who simply has different tastes or some adjustment costs.* Such a consumer would have a symmetric Slutsky matrix.

To the best of my knowledge, this is the first derivation of an asymmetric Slutsky matrix in a model of bounded rationality.[70]

Eq. (57) makes tight testable predictions. It allows us to infer attention from choice data, as we shall now see.[71]

Proposition 5.3 (Estimation of limited attention). *Choice data allows one to recover the attention vector m, up to a multiplicative factor $\overline{m}$. Indeed, suppose that an empirical Slutsky matrix S_{ij}^s is available. Then, m can be recovered as*

$$m_j = \overline{m} \prod_{i=1}^{n} \left(\frac{S_{ij}^s}{S_{ji}^s} \right)^{\gamma_i}, \text{ for any } (\gamma_i)_{i=1\ldots n} \text{ such that } \sum_i \gamma_i = 1.$$

Proof. We have $\frac{S_{ij}^s}{S_{ji}^s} = \frac{m_j}{m_i}$, so $\prod_{i=1}^{n} \left(\frac{S_{ij}^s}{S_{ji}^s} \right)^{\gamma_i} = \prod_{i=1}^{n} \left(\frac{m_j}{m_i} \right)^{\gamma_i} = \frac{m_j}{\overline{m}}$, for $\overline{m} := \prod_{i=1}^{n} m_i^{\gamma_i}$.   □

The underlying "rational" matrix can be recovered as $S_{ij}^r := S_{ij}^s / m_j$, and it should be symmetric, a testable implication.[72] There is an old literature estimating Slutsky matrices – but it had not explored the role of non-salient prices (a recent exception is the nascent literature mentioned in Section 3.1.2).

It would be interesting to test Proposition 5.2 directly. The extant evidence is qualitatively encouraging, via the literature on tax salience and shrouded attributes (Sections 3.2.1–3.2.2), and the recent literature exploring this Slutsky asymmetry (Section 3.1.2).

Marginal demand.

Proposition 5.4. *The Marshallian demand $c^s(p, w)$ has the marginals (evaluated at $p = p^d$): $\frac{\partial c^s}{\partial w} = \frac{\partial c^r}{\partial w}$ and*

$$\frac{\partial c_i^s}{\partial p_j} = \frac{\partial c_i^r}{\partial p_j} \times m_j - \frac{\partial c_i^r}{\partial w} c_j^r \times (1 - m_j). \tag{58}$$

This means that, though substitution effects are dampened, income effects ($\frac{\partial c}{\partial w}$) are preserved (as w needs to be spent in this one-shot model).

---

[70] Browning and Chiappori (1998) have in mind a very different phenomenon: intra-household bargaining, with full rationality.

[71] The Slutsky matrix does not allow one to recover $\overline{m}$: for any $\overline{m}$, S^s admits a dilated factorization $S_{ij}^s = (\overline{m}^{-1} S_{ij}^r)(\overline{m} m_j)$. To recover $\overline{m}$, one needs to see how the demand changes as p^d varies. Aguiar and Serrano (2017) explore further the link between Slutsky matrix and bounded rationality.

[72] Here, we find again a less intuitive aspect of the Slutsky matrix.

Nominal illusion. Recall that the consumer "sees" only a part m_j of the price change (Eq. (54)). One consequence is nominal illusion.

Proposition 5.5 (Nominal illusion). *Suppose that the agent pays more attention to some goods than others (i.e. the m_i are not all equal). Then, the agent exhibits nominal illusion, i.e. the Marshallian demand $c(p, w)$ is (generically) not homogeneous of degree 0.*

To gain intuition, suppose that prices and the budget all increase by 10%. For a rational consumer, nothing really changes and he picks the same consumption. However, consider a behavioral consumer who pays more attention to good 1 ($m_1 > m_2$). He perceives that the price of good 1 has increased more than the price of good 2 has (he perceives that they have respectively increased by $m_1 \cdot 10\%$ vs. $m_2 \cdot 10\%$). So, he perceives that the *relative* price of good 1 has increased (p^d is kept constant). Hence, he consumes less of good 1, and more of good 2. His demand has shifted. In abstract terms, $c^s(\chi p, \chi w) \neq c^s(p, w)$ for $\chi = 1.1$, i.e. the Marshallian demand is not homogeneous of degree 0. The agent exhibits nominal illusion.[73]

5.2 Textbook competitive equilibrium theory

We next revisit the textbook chapter on competitive equilibrium, with less than fully rational agents. We will use the following notation. Agent $a \in \{1, ..., A\}$ has endowment $\omega^a \in \mathbb{R}^n$ (i.e. he is endowed with ω_i^a units of good i), with $n > 1$. If the price is p, his wealth is $p \cdot \omega^a$, so his demand is $D^a(p) := c^a(p, p \cdot \omega^a)$. The economy's excess demand function is $Z(p) := \sum_{a=1}^{A} D^a(p) - \omega^a$. The set of equilibrium prices is $\mathcal{P}^* := \{p \in \mathbb{R}_{++}^n : Z(p) = 0\}$. The set of equilibrium allocations for a consumer a is $\mathcal{C}^a := \{D^a(p) : p \in \mathcal{P}^*\}$. The equilibrium exists under weak conditions laid out in Debreu (1970).

5.2.1 First and second welfare theorems: (In)efficiency of equilibrium

We start with the efficiency of Arrow–Debreu competitive equilibrium, i.e. the first fundamental theorem of welfare economics.[74] We assume that competitive equilibria are interior, and consumers are locally non-satiated.

Proposition 5.6 (First fundamental theorem of welfare economics revisited: (In)efficiency of competitive equilibrium). *An equilibrium is Pareto efficient if and only if the perception of relative prices is identical across agents. In that sense, the first welfare theorem generally fails.*

Hence, typically the equilibrium is not Pareto efficient when we are not at the default price. The intuitive argument is very simple (the appendix has a rigorous

---

[73] See Eyster et al. (2017) for progress on the impact of nominal illusion from inattention.
[74] This chapter does not provide the producer's problem, which is quite similar and is left for a companion paper (and is available upon request). Still, the two negative results in Propositions 5.6 and 5.7 apply to exchange economies, hence apply a fortiori to production economies.

proof): recall that given two goods i and j, each agent equalizes relative marginal utilities and relative perceived prices (see Eq. (40)):

$$\frac{u^a_{c_i}}{u^a_{c_j}} = \left(\frac{p^s_i}{p^s_j}\right)^a, \qquad \frac{u^b_{c_i}}{u^b_{c_j}} = \left(\frac{p^s_i}{p^s_j}\right)^b, \tag{59}$$

where $\left(\frac{p^s_i}{p^s_j}\right)^a$ is the relative price perceived by consumer a. Furthermore, the equilibrium is efficient if and only if the ratio of marginal utilities is equalized across agents, i.e. there are no extra gains from trade, i.e.

$$\frac{u^a_{c_i}}{u^a_{c_j}} = \frac{u^b_{c_i}}{u^b_{c_j}}. \tag{60}$$

Hence, the equilibrium is efficient if and only if any consumers a and b have the same perceptions of relative prices ($\left(\frac{p^s_i}{p^s_j}\right)^a = \left(\frac{p^s_i}{p^s_j}\right)^b$).

The second welfare theorem asserts that any desired Pareto efficient allocation $(c^a)_{a=1...A}$ can be reached, after appropriate budget transfers (for a formal statement, see e.g., Mas-Colell et al., 1995, Section 16.D). The next Proposition asserts that it generally fails in this behavioral economy. The intuition is as follows: typically, if the first welfare theorem fails, then a fortiori the second welfare theorem fails, as an equilibrium is typically not efficient.

Proposition 5.7 (Second theorem of welfare economics revisited). *The second welfare theorem generically fails, when there are strictly more than two consumers or two goods.*

5.2.2 Excess volatility of prices in a behavioral economy

To tractably analyze prices, we follow the macro tradition, and assume in this section that there is just one representative agent. A core effect is the following.

Bounded rationality leads to excess volatility of equilibrium prices. Suppose that there are two dates, and that there is a supply shock: the endowment $\omega(t)$ changes between $t = 0$ and $t = 1$. Let $dp = p(1) - p(0)$ be the price change caused by the supply shock, and consider the case of infinitesimally small changes (to deal with the arbitrariness of the price level, assume that $p_1 = p^d_1$ at $t = 1$). We assume $m_i > 0$ (and will derive it soon).

Proposition 5.8 (Bounded rationality leads to excess volatility of prices). *Let $dp^{[r]}$ and $dp^{[s]}$ be the change in equilibrium price in the rational and behavioral economies, respectively. Then:*

$$dp^{[s]}_i = \frac{dp^{[r]}_i}{m_i}, \tag{61}$$

i.e., after a supply shock, the movements of price i in the behavioral economy are like the movements in the rational economy, but amplified by a factor $\frac{1}{m_i} \geq 1$. Hence, ceteris paribus, the prices of non-salient goods are more volatile. Denoting by σ_i^k the price volatility in the rational ($k = r$) or behavioral ($k = s$) economy, we have $\sigma_i^s = \frac{\sigma_i^r}{m_i}$.

Hence, non-salient prices need to be more volatile to clear the market. This might explain the high price volatility of many goods, such as commodities. Consumers are quite price inelastic, because they are inattentive. *In a behavioral world, demand underreacts to shocks; but the market needs to clear, so prices have to overreact to supply shocks.*[75]

5.3 What is robust in basic microeconomics?

I distinguish what appears to be robust and not robust in the basic microeconomic theory of consumer behavior and competitive equilibrium – when the specific deviation is a sparsity-seeking agent. I use the sparsity benchmark not as "the truth", of course, but as a plausible extension of the traditional model, when agents are less than fully rational. I contrast the traditional (or "classical") model to a behavioral model with inattention.

Propositions that are not robust.

Tradition: There is no money illusion. *Behavioral* model: There is money illusion: when the budget and prices are both increased by 5%, the agent consumes less of goods with a salient price (which he perceives to be relatively more expensive); Marshallian demand $c(p, w)$ is not homogeneous of degree 0.

Tradition: The Slutsky matrix is symmetric. *Behavioral* model: It is asymmetric, as elasticities to non-salient prices are attenuated by inattention.

Tradition: The competitive equilibrium allocation is independent of the price level. *Behavioral* model: Different aggregate price levels lead to materially different equilibrium allocations, as implied by a Phillips curve.

Greater robustness: Objects are very close around the default price, up to second order terms.

Tradition: People maximize their "objective" welfare. *Behavioral* model: people maximize in default situations, but there are losses away from it.

Tradition: Competitive equilibrium is efficient, and the two Arrow–Debreu welfare theorems hold. *Behavioral* model: Competitive equilibrium is efficient if it happens at the default price. Away from the default price, competitive equilibrium has inefficiencies, unless all agents have the same misperceptions. As a result, the two welfare theorems do not hold in general.

---

[75] Gul et al. (2017) offer a very different model leading to volatile prices, with a different mechanism linked to endogenous heterogeneity between agents.

Traditional economics gets the signs right – or, more prudently put, the signs predicted by the rational model (e.g. Becker-style price theory) are robust under a sparsity variant. Those predictions are of the type "if the price of good 1 goes down, demand for it goes up", or more generally "if there's a good incentive to do X, people will indeed tend to do X."[76,77] Those sign predictions make intuitive sense, and, not coincidentally, they hold in the behavioral model[78]: those sign predictions (unlike quantitative predictions) remain unchanged even when the agent has a limited, qualitative understanding of his situation. Indeed, when economists think about the world, or in much applied microeconomic work, it is often the sign predictions that are used and trusted, rather than the detailed quantitative predictions.

6 Models with stochastic attention and choice of precision

We now move on to models with noisy signals. They are more complex to handle, as they provide a stochastic prediction, not a deterministic one. There are pros and cons to that. One pro is that economists can stick to optimal information processing. In addition, the amount of noise may actually be a guide to the thought process, hence might be a help rather than a hindrance: see Glimcher (2011) and Caplin (2016). The drawback is basically the complexity of this approach – these models become quickly intractable.

Interestingly, much of the neuroeconomics (Glimcher and Fehr, 2013) and cognitive psychology (Gershman et al., 2015; Griffiths et al., 2015) literatures sees the brain as an optimal information processor. Indeed, for low-level processes (e.g. vision), the brain may well be optimal, though for high-level processes (e.g. dealing with the stock market) it is not directly optimal.

6.1 Bayesian models with choice of information

There are many Bayesian models in which agents pay to get more precise signals. An early example is Verrecchia (1982): agents pay to receive more precise signals in a financial market. In Geanakoplos and Milgrom (1991), managers pay for more information. They all essentially work with linear-quadratic settings – otherwise the

---

[76] Those predictions need not be boring. For instance, when divorce laws are relaxed, spouses kill each other less (Stevenson and Wolfers, 2006).

[77] This is true for "direct" effects, though not necessarily once indirect effects are taken into account. For instance, this is true for compensated demand (see the part on the Slutsky matrix), and in partial equilibrium. This is not necessarily true for uncompensated demand (where income effects arise) or in general equilibrium – though in many situations those "second round" effects are small.

[78] The closely related notion of strategic complements and substitutes (Bulow et al., 1985) is also robust to a sparsity deviation.

task is intractable. In the basic problem of Section 2.1, the expected loss is

$$\mathbb{E}\left[\max_a \mathbb{E}\left[-\frac{1}{2}(a-x)^2 \,|s\right]\right] = -\frac{1}{2}(1-m)\sigma_x^2$$

so that the agent's problem is:

$$\max_\tau -\frac{1}{2}(1-m)\sigma_x^2 - \kappa G(\tau) \text{ subject to } m = \frac{\tau}{1+\tau}$$

where $\tau = \frac{\sigma_x^2}{\sigma_\varepsilon^2}$ is the relative precision of the signal, and G is the cost of precision, which is increasing. This can be equivalently reformulated as:

$$\max_m -\frac{1}{2}(1-m)\sigma_x^2 - \kappa g(m)$$

by defining $g(m)$ appropriately ($g(m) := G(\frac{m}{1-m})$). So, we have a problem very much like (33).

This allows us to think about the optimal choice of information. When actions are strategic complements, you can get multiple equilibria in information gathering (Hellwig and Veldkamp, 2009). When actions are strategic substitutes, you often obtain specialization in information (Van Nieuwerburgh and Veldkamp, 2010). More generally, rational information acquisition models do seem to predict qualitatively relevant features of real markets (Kacperczyk et al., 2016).

6.2 Entropy-based inattention: "Rational inattention"

Sims (1998, 2003) extends the ideas to allow for larger choice sets in which agents freely choose the properties of their signals. He uses the entropy penalty to handle non-Gaussian variables.

6.2.1 Information theory: A crash course

Here is a brief introduction to information theory, as developed by Shannon (1948). The basic textbook for this is Cover and Thomas (2006).

Discrete variables. Take a random variable X with probability p_i of a value x_i. Throughout, we will use the notation f to refer to the probability mass function of a given random variable (when discrete), or to its probability density function (when continuous). Then the entropy of X for the discrete case is defined as

$$H(X) = -\mathbb{E}\left[\log f(X)\right] = -\sum_i p_i \log p_i$$

so that $H \geq 0$ (for a discrete variable; it won't be true for a continuous variable). In the case where uncertainty between outcomes is greatest, X can take n equally probable values, $p_i = \frac{1}{n}$. This distribution gives the maximum entropy,

$$H(X) = \log n$$

which illustrates that higher uncertainty yields higher entropy.

This measure of "complexity" is really a measure of the complexity of communication, not of finding or processing information. For instance, the entropy of a coin flip is $\log 2$ – one bit if we use the base 2 logarithm. But also, suppose that you have to communicate the value of the 1000th figure in the binary expansion of $\sqrt{17}$. Then, the entropy of that is again simply $\log 2$. This is not the cost of actually processing information (which is a harder thing to model), just the cost of transmitting the information.

Suppose we have two independent random variables, with $X = (Y, Z)$. Then, $f^X(y, z) = f^Y(y) f^Z(z)$ so

$$H(X) = -\mathbb{E}\left[\log f^X(X)\right] = -\mathbb{E}\left[\log\left(f^Y(Y) f^Z(Z)\right)\right]$$

$$= -\mathbb{E}\left[\log f^Y(Y) + \log f^Z(Z)\right]$$

$$H(X) = H(Y) + H(Z). \tag{62}$$

This shows that the information of independent outcomes is additive. The next concept is that of mutual information, for which we drop the assumption that the two variables of interest are independent. It is defined by the reduction of entropy of X when you know Y:

$$I(X, Y) = H(X) - H(X|Y)$$

$$= -\mathbb{E}\left[\log f^X(X)\right] + \mathbb{E}\left[\log f^{X|Y}(X|Y)\right]$$

$$= -\mathbb{E}\left[\log f^X(X)\right] + \mathbb{E}\left[\log \frac{f(X, Y)}{f^Y(Y)}\right]$$

$$= -\mathbb{E}\left[\log f^X(X) + \log f^Y(Y)\right] + \mathbb{E}\left[\log f(X, Y)\right]$$

$$= H(X) + H(Y) - H(X, Y) = I(Y, X),$$

and so it follows that mutual information is symmetric. The next concept is the Kullback–Leibler divergence between two distributions p, q,

$$D(p\|q) = \mathbb{E}^P\left[\log \frac{p(X)}{q(X)}\right] = \sum_i p_i \log \frac{p_i}{q_i}. \tag{63}$$

Note that the Kullback–Leibler divergence is not actually a proper distance, since $D(p\|q) \neq D(q\|p)$, but it is similar to a distance – it is nonnegative, and equal to 0 when $p = q$.

Hence, we have:

$$I(X, Y) = D\left(f(x, y) \| f^X(x) f^Y(y)\right) = \sum_{x,y} f(x, y) \log \frac{f(x, y)}{f^X(x) f^Y(y)}, \tag{64}$$

or, in other words, mutual information $I(X, Y)$ is the Kullback–Leibler divergence between the full joint probability $f(x, y)$ and its "decoupled" approximation $f^X(x) f^Y(y)$.

Continuous variables. With continuous variables with density $f(x)$, entropy is defined to be:

$$H(X) = -\mathbb{E}\big[\log f(X)\big] = -\int f(x) \log f \, dx$$

with the convention that $f(x) \log f(x) = 0$ if $f(x) = 0$. For instance, if X is a uniform $[a, b]$, then $f(x) = \frac{1}{b-a} 1_{x \in [a,b]}$ and

$$H(X) = \log(b - a) \tag{65}$$

which shows that we can have a negative entropy, $(H(X) < 0)$ with continuous variables.

If $Y = a + \sigma X$, then because $f^Y(y) \, dy = f^X(x) \, dx$, i.e. $f^Y(y) = \frac{1}{\sigma} f^X(x)$, we have

$$H(Y) = -E\left[\log f^Y(Y)\right] = -E\left[\log f^X(X)\right] + \log \sigma$$

$$H(Y) = H(X) + \log \sigma \tag{66}$$

so with continuous variables, multiplying a variable by σ increases its entropy by $\log \sigma$.

The entropy of a Gaussian $N(\mu, \sigma^2)$ variable is, as shown in Appendix A,

$$H(X) = \frac{1}{2} \log \sigma^2 + \frac{1}{2} \log(2\pi e) \tag{67}$$

and for a multi-dimensional Gaussian with variance–covariance matrix V, the entropy is

$$H(X) = \frac{1}{2} \log(\det V) + \frac{n}{2} \log(2\pi e) \tag{68}$$

which is analogous to the one-dimensional formula, but σ^2 is replaced by $\det V$.

Mutual information in a Gaussian case. Suppose X, Y are jointly Gaussian with correlation ρ. Then, their mutual information is

$$I(X, Y) = \frac{1}{2} \log \frac{1}{1 - \rho^2} \tag{69}$$

so that the mutual information is increasing in the correlation.

6.2.2 Using Shannon entropy as a measure of cost

Sims (2003) proposed the following problem, which had two innovations: the use of entropy, and a reformulation of the choice of the signal structure (both of which can be generalized). Consider an agent that has no information or attention costs and makes choices by maximizing $u(a, x)$. In the Sims version, the agent will pick a stochastic action A drawn from an endogenously chosen density $q(a|x)$ – i.e., the probability density of a given the true state is x – where q is chosen by the optimization problem

$$\max_{q(a|x)} \int u(a, x) q(a|x) f(x) \, da \, dx \text{ s.t. } I(A, X) \leq K, \tag{70}$$

that is, the agent instructs some black box to give him a stochastic action: the box sees the true x, and then returns a noisy prescription $q(a|x)$ for his action.[79] Of course, the nature of this black box is a bit unclear, but may be treated as some thought process.[80]

A simple example. To get a feel for this problem, revisit the "targeting problem" seen above, where $x \sim N(0, \sigma^2)$, and $u(a, x) = -\frac{1}{2}(a - x)^2$. The solution is close to that in Section 2.1: the agent receives a noisy signal $s = x + \varepsilon$, and takes the optimal action $a(s) = \mathbb{E}[x|s] = mx + m\varepsilon$ with $m = \frac{\sigma^2}{\sigma^2 + \sigma_\varepsilon^2}$. The loss utility achieved is:

$$U = \mathbb{E}[u(a(s), x)] = -\frac{1}{2}(mx + m\varepsilon - x)^2 = -\frac{1}{2}(1 - m)\sigma^2. \tag{71}$$

The analytics in (92) shows that $\rho^2 = \operatorname{corr}(a(s), x)^2 = m$, and using equation (69), the mutual information is $I(a(s), x) = \frac{1}{2}\log\frac{1}{1-\rho^2} = \frac{1}{2}\log\frac{1}{1-m}$. Hence, the decision problem (70) boils down to:

$$\max_m -\frac{1}{2}(1 - m)\sigma^2 \text{ s.t. } \frac{1}{2}\log\frac{1}{1 - m} \leq K.$$

This gives:

$$m = 1 - e^{-2K} \tag{72}$$

and the action has the form:

$$a^{\text{Sims}} = mx + \eta$$

with $\eta = m\varepsilon$. So, we get a solution as in the basic problem of Section 4.1, with a cost function $C(m) = \frac{1}{2}\log\frac{1}{1-m}$.

---

[79] The density chosen is non-parametric, and does not involve explicitly sending intermediary signals as in the prior literature – which is an innovation by Sims (2003).

[80] In the Shannon theory, this nature is clear. Originally, the Shannon theory is a theory of communication. Someone has information x at one end of the line, and needs to communicate information a at the other end of the line. Under the setup of the Shannon theory, the cost is captured by the mutual information $I(A, X)$.

If we wish to calibrate an attention $m \leq 0.9$, Eq. (72) implies that we need $K \leq \frac{-\log(1-m)}{2}$, which gives $K \leq 1.15$ "natural units" or a capacity of at most 1.7 bits. This is a very small capacity.

Extensions to multiple dimensions. Now, let us see the multidimensional version, with the basic quadratic problem (11): $u(a, x) = -\frac{1}{2}(a - \sum_{i=1}^{n} b_i x_i)^2$. We assume that the x_i are uncorrelated, jointly Gaussian, that $\text{Var}(x_i) = \sigma_i^2$. Then, one can show that the solution takes the form

$$a^{\text{Sims}} = m \sum_i b_i x_i + \eta \tag{73}$$

with an η orthogonal to the x.

This may be a good place to contrast the Sims approach and sparsity. For the same quadratic problem, Eq. (37) yields

$$a^s = \sum_{i=1}^{n} m_i b_i x_i \tag{74}$$

so that the agent can pay more attention to source 1 than to source 10 (if $m_1 > m_{10}$). Hence, with the global entropy constraint of Sims we obtain uniform dampening across all variables (i.e. $m_i = m$ for all i in Eq. (73)) – not source-specific dampening as in (37)–(74).[81]

Now, a drawback of sparsity (and related models like Bordalo et al., 2013) is that framing (in the sense of partitioning of attributes into dimensions) matters in this model, whereas it does not in the Sims approach. This is important to its ability to generate non-uniform dampening across dimensions. On the other hand, this seems realistic: in the base example of the price with a tax (Section 2.3.2), it does matter empirically whether the price is presented as two items (price, tax), or as one composite information price plus tax.

Discussion. One advantage of the entropy-based approach is that we have a universally applicable measure of the cost of information. In simple linear-quadratic-Gaussian cases, the models are similar (except for the important fact that Sims generates uniform, rather than source-dependent, dampening). When going away from this linear-quadratic-Gaussian case, the modeling complexity of sparsity remains roughly constant (and attention still obtains in closed form). In Sims, this is not the case, and quickly problems become extremely hard to solve. For instance, in Jung et al. (2015), the solution has atoms – it is non-smooth. One needs a computer to solve it.[82] All in all, it is healthy for economics that different approaches are explored in parallel.

---

[81] There is a "water-filling" result in information theory that generates source-dependent attention, but it requires different channels, not the Sims unitary attention channel.

[82] This is can be seen as a drawback, but Matějka (2016) proposes that this can be used to model pricing with a discrete set of prices.

Sims called this modeling approach "rational inattention". This name may be overly broad, as Sims really proposed a particular modeling approach, not at all the general notion that attention allocation responds to incentives. That notion comes from the 1960s and information economics – dating back at least to Stigler (1961), where agents maximize utility subject to the cost of acquiring information, so that information and attention responds to costs and benefits. There are many papers under that vein, e.g. Verrecchia (1982), Geanakoplos and Milgrom (1991). Hence, a term such as "entropy-based inattention" seems like a proper name for the specific literature initiated by Sims.[83]

Still, a great virtue of the entropy-based approach is that it has attracted the energy of many economists, especially in macro (Maćkowiak and Wiederholt, 2009, 2015; Veldkamp, 2011; Khaw et al., 2016), e.g. to study the inattention to the fine determinants of pricing by firms. Many depart from the "global entropy penalty", which allows one to have source-specific inattention. But then, there is no real reason to stick to the entropy penalty in the first place – other cost functions will work similarly. Hence researchers keep generalizing the Shannon entropy, for instance Caplin et al. (2017), Ellis (2018).

6.3 Random choice via limited attention

6.3.1 Limited attention as noise in perception: Classic perspective

A basic model is the random choice model. The consumer must pick one of n goods. Utility is v_i, drawn from a distribution $f(v)$. In the basic random utility model à la Luce–McFadden (Manski and McFadden, 1981), the probability of choosing v_i is

$$p_i = \frac{e^{v_i/\sigma}}{\sum_j e^{v_j/\sigma}}, \tag{75}$$

with the following classic microfoundation: agents receive a signal

$$s_i = v_i + \sigma \varepsilon_i \tag{76}$$

where the ε_i are i.i.d. with a Gumbel distribution, $\mathbb{P}(\varepsilon_i \leq x) = e^{-e^{-x}}$. The idea is that ε_i is noise in perception, and perhaps it could be decreased actively by agents, or increased by firms.

Agents have diffuse priors on v_i. Hence, they choose the good j with the highest signal s_t, $p_i = \mathbb{P}(i \in \text{argmax}_j s_j)$. With Gumbel noise, this leads (after some calculations as in e.g. Anderson et al., 1992) to (75). When the noise scaling parameter σ is higher, there is more uncertainty; when $\sigma \to \infty$, then $p_i \to \frac{1}{n}$. The choice is completely random.

This is a useful model, because it captures in a simple way "noisy perceptions". It has proven very useful in industrial organization (e.g. Anderson et al., 1992) – where

---

[83] Maćkowiak et al. (2016) is a recent survey.

the typical interpretation is "rational differences in tastes", rather than "noise in the perception". It can be generalized in a number of ways, including with correlated noises, and non-Gumbel noise (Gabaix et al., 2016). This framework can be used to analyze equilibrium prices when consumers are confused and/or when firms create noise to confuse consumers. Then, the equilibrium price markup (defined as price minus cost) is generally proportional to σ, the amount of noise. For a related model with two types of agents, see Carlin (2009).

6.3.2 Random choice via entropy penalty

Matějka and McKay (2015) derive an entropy-based foundation for the logit model. In its simplest form, the idea is as follows. The consumer must pick one of n goods. Utility is v_i, drawn from a distribution $f(v)$. The endogenous probability of choosing i is p_i. The problem is to maximize utility subject to a penalty for having an inaccurate probability:

$$\max_{(p_i(v))_{i=1...n}} \mathbb{E}\left[\sum_i p_i(v)\, v_i\right] - \kappa D\left(P \| P^d\right)$$

where the expectation is taken over the value of v, and $D\left(P \| P^d\right)$ is the Kullback–Leibler distance between the probability and a default probability, P^d. Hence, we have a penalty for a "sophisticated" probability distribution that differs from the default probability.[84] So, the Lagrangian is

$$L = \int \sum_i p_i(v)\, v_i\, f(v)\, dv - \kappa \int \left[\sum_i p_i(v) \log \frac{p_i(v)}{p_i^d}\right] f(v)\, dv$$
$$- \int \mu(v)\left(\sum p_i(v) - 1\right) f(v)\, dv.$$

Differentiation with respect to $p_i(v)$ gives $0 = v_i - \kappa(1 + \log \frac{p_i(v)}{p_i^d}) - \mu(v)$, i.e. $p_i(v) = p_i^d e^{v_i/\kappa} K(v)$ for a value $K(v)$. Ensuring that $\sum_i p_i(v) = 1$ gives

$$p_i(v) = \frac{p_i^d e^{v_i/\kappa}}{\sum_j p_j^d e^{v_j/\kappa}}, \tag{77}$$

so this is like (75), with σ replaced by κ, and with default probabilities being uniform. When the cost κ is 0, then the agent is the classical rational agent.

---

[84] The math is analogous to the basic derivation of the "Boltzmann distribution" familiar to statistical mechanics. Maximizing the entropy $H(P)$ subject to a given energy constraint $\sum_i p_i v_i = V$ yields a distribution $p_i = \frac{e^{-\beta v_i}}{\sum_j e^{-\beta v_j}}$ for some β.

Matějka and McKay's setup (2015) actually gives the default:

$$\max_{(p_i^d)} \mathbb{E}\left[\log\left(\sum_i p_i^d e^{v_i/\kappa}\right)\right] \text{ s.t. } \sum_i p_i^d = 1.$$

So, when the v_i are drawn from the same distribution, $p_i^d = 1/n$.

In some cases, some options will not even be looked at, so $p_i^d = 0$. This gives a theory of consideration sets. For related work, see Masatlioglu et al. (2012), Manzini and Mariotti (2014), Caplin et al. (2016). This in turn helps explore dynamic problems, as in Steiner et al. (2017).

7 Allocation of attention over time

The models discussed so far were static. We now move on to models that incorporate the allocation of attention over time. One important theme is that people are initially inattentive to a new piece of information, but over time they adjust to the news – a form of "sluggishness". I cover different ways to generate sluggishness, particularly over time. They are largely substitutes for inattention from a modeling standpoint, but they generate sometimes different predictions, as we shall see.

7.1 Generating sluggishness: Sticky action, sticky information, and habits

7.1.1 Sticky action and sticky information

The most common models are those of sticky action and sticky information. In the sticky action model, agents need to pay a cost to change their action. In the sticky information model, agents need to pay a cost to change their information. Sticky action has been advocated in macroeconomics by Calvo (1983) and Caballero (1995), and in a finance context by Duffie and Sun (1990) and Lynch (1996). Sticky information has been advocated in macro by Gabaix and Laibson (2002), Carroll (2003), and then by Mankiw and Reis (2002), Reis (2006a), Bacchetta and Van Wincoop (2010) and numerous authors since. Coibion and Gorodnichenko (2015) finds evidence for slow adjustment to information. Intuitively, this generates sluggishness in the aggregate action. To see this, consider the following tracking problem. The agent should maximize

$$V = \sum_{t=0}^{\infty} \beta^t u(a_t, x_t) \tag{78}$$

$$u(a, x) = -\frac{1}{2}(a - x)^2 \tag{79}$$

where a_t is a decision variable, and x_t an exogenous variable satisfying:

$$x_{t+1} = \rho x_t + \varepsilon_{t+1} \tag{80}$$

with $|\rho| \leq 1$. In the frictionless version, the optimal action at date t is:

$$a_t^r = x_t.$$

Simple case: Random walk. To keep the math simple, take $\rho = 1$ at first. Consider first the "sticky action" case. We will consider two benchmarks. In the "Calvo" model (as in the pricing model due to Calvo, 1983) the agent changes her action only with a Poisson probability $1 - \theta$ at each period. In the "fixed delay D" model (as in Gabaix and Laibson, 2002; Reis, 2006a), the agent changes her action every D periods. Both models imply that the action is changed with a lag.

Call $a_{t,s}^A$ (respectively $a_{t,s}^I$) the action of an agent at time t, who re-optimized her action (respectively, who refreshed her information) s periods ago, in the sticky Action model (respectively, Information). Then

$$a_{t,s}^A = a_{t-s}^r = x_{t-s}$$

and

$$a_{t,s}^I = \mathbb{E}_{t-s}\left[a_t^r\right] = x_{t-s}.$$

Hence, in the random walk case, sticky action and sticky information make the same prediction. However, when we go beyond the random walk, predictions are different (see Section A.2).

So, consider the impact of a change in ε_t in x_t, on the aggregate action

$$\bar{a}_t = \sum_{s=0}^{\infty} f(s) a_{t,s}.$$

In the Calvo model, $f(s) = (1 - \theta)\theta^s$. In the "fixed delay D" model, $f(s) = \frac{1}{D} 1_{0 \leq s < D}$. Look at $\bar{a}_t(\varepsilon_t, \varepsilon_{t-1}, ...)$, and $\mathbb{E}_t \frac{d\bar{a}_{t+T}}{d\varepsilon_t}$. Then:

$$\mathbb{E}_t\left[\frac{d\bar{a}_{t+T}}{d\varepsilon_t}\right] = \sum_{s=0}^{T} f(s) =: F(T)$$

with

$$F(T) = 1 - \theta^{T+1} \tag{81}$$

in the Calvo model; and

$$F(T) = \min\left(\frac{T+1}{D}, 1\right)$$

in the updating-every-D periods model. Hence, we have a delayed reaction. This is the first lesson. Models with sticky action, and sticky reaction, generate a sluggish, delayed response in the aggregate action.

Put another way, in the Calvo model, aggregate dynamics are:

$$\bar{a}_t^A = \theta \bar{a}_{t-1}^A + (1 - \theta) x_t \tag{82}$$

and they are the same (in the random walk case that we are presently considering) in the sticky information case.

7.1.2 Habit formation generates inertia

Macroeconomists who want to generate inertia often use habits. That is, instead of a utility function $u(a_t, x_t)$, one uses a utility function

$$v(a_t, a_{t-1}, x_t) := u \left(\frac{a_t - ha_{t-1}}{1 - h}, x_t \right) \tag{83}$$

where $h \in [0, 1)$ is a habit parameter. This is done in order to generate stickiness. To see how, consider again the targeting problem (78), but with no frictions except for habit:

$$\max_{a_t} - \sum_{t=0}^{\infty} \beta^t \left(\frac{a_t - ha_{t-1}}{1 - h} - x_t \right)^2.$$

The first best can be achieved simply by setting the square term to 0 at each date, e.g. $\frac{a_t - ha_{t-1}}{1-h} - x_t = 0$. That is,

$$a_t = ha_{t-1} + (1 - h) x_t \tag{84}$$

which is exactly an AR(1) process, like (82), replacing θ by h. This is a sense in which a habit model can generate the same behavior as a sticky action/information model. In more general setups, the correspondence is not perfect, but it qualitatively carries over.

Macroeconomists have used this habit model to generate inertia in consumption, and even in investment – see Christiano et al. (2005). Havranek et al.'s (2017) meta-analysis finds a median estimate of $h = 0.5$ for macro studies, and $h = 0.1$ for micro studies. The discrepancy is probably due to the fact that at the micro level there is so much volatility of consumption, that this is only consistent with a small degree of habit formation. In macro studies, aggregate consumption is much smoother, so aggregate sluggishness of the reaction to information results in a higher measured h.

Of course, for normative purposes the analysis is completely different. In the habit model above, the agent achieves the first best utility. However, in the sticky information model, if the agent could remove her friction (e.g. lower the stickiness θ to 0), she would do it. In a more complex macro model, the same holds. Likewise for optimal retirement savings policy, the specific reason for people's sensitivity to the default matters a great deal (Bernheim et al., 2015).

Which is true? Most macroeconomists acknowledge that habits are basically just a device to generate stickiness. Carroll et al. (2017) argue that stickiness is indeed about inattention, rather than habits.

7.1.3 Adjustment costs generate inertia

Adjustment costs also generate inertia. Suppose that the problem is

$$\max_{a_t} - \sum_{t=0}^{\infty} \beta^t \left[(a_t - x_t)^2 + \kappa (a_t - a_{t-1})^2 \right]$$

such that the first order condition with respect to a_t is

$$a_t - x_t + \kappa (a_t - a_{t-1}) - \beta\kappa (\mathbb{E}_t a_{t+1} - a_t) = 0 \tag{85}$$

so we obtain a second order difference equation. When x_t is a random walk, we have

$$a_t = \theta a_{t-1} + (1 - \theta) x_t \tag{86}$$

where θ solves $\theta = \frac{\kappa}{\kappa+1+\beta\kappa(1-\theta)}$.[85] So, θ is 0 when $\kappa = 0$, and $\theta = 1$ as $\kappa \to \infty$.

Hence again, adjustment costs yield an isomorphic behavior, but with a more complex mathematical result, as θ has to be solved for.

7.1.4 Observable difference between inattention vs. habits/adjustment costs: Source-specific inattention

Both inattention and habits/adjustment costs create delayed reaction. Let us see this in a one-period model.

In an adjustment cost model, the agent solves $\max_a - (a - \sum_i b_i x_i)^2 - \kappa (a - a_{-1})^2$, which yields an action:

$$a = m a^r + (1 - m) a_{-1} \tag{87}$$

with $m = \frac{1}{1+\kappa}$. Likewise, a habit

$$\max_a u \left(\frac{a - h a_{-1}}{1 - h}, x \right) \tag{88}$$

creates the same expression (87) for the action, this time with $m = 1 - h$.

---

[85] *Proof.* We use (86) at $t + 1$, which gives

$$\mathbb{E} a_{t+1} - a_t = (\theta - 1) a_t + (1 - \theta) \mathbb{E}_t x_{t+1} = (1 - \theta) (x_t - a_t).$$

Then, we plug it into (85),

$$0 = a_t - x_t + \kappa (a_t - a_{t-1}) - \beta\kappa (\mathbb{E} a_{t+1} - a_t)$$
$$= (1 + \beta\kappa (1 - \theta)) (a_t - x_t) + \kappa (a_t - a_{t-1}).$$

Solving for a_t, this implies (86) at time t, provided that $\theta = \frac{\kappa}{\kappa+1+\beta\kappa(1-\theta)}$.

In contrast, inattention creates an action:

$$a = \sum_i m_i b_i x_i.$$

Hence we can differentiate between them as follows. The presence of adjustment costs (or the sticky action model) creates *uniform* under-reaction ($m_i = m$ for all i's), while inattention (of the sticky information kind) creates *source-specific* under-reaction (the m_i in general differ across i's).

7.1.5 Dynamic default value

Within behavioral models, a simple way to model dynamic attention is via the default value. For instance, the default value could jump to the optimal default value, with some Poisson probability, much as in the sticky information model. In a Bayesian context, the "prior" could be updated with some Poisson probability.

7.2 Optimal dynamic inattention

How to optimize the allocation of attention? The agent minimizes the following objective function over the information acquisition policy, in which a denotes a state-contingent policy:

$$V(a, \beta) = -\mathbb{E}\left[\sum_{t \geq 0}(1 - \beta)\beta^t \left(\frac{1}{2}(a_t - x_t)^2 + \kappa C_t\right)\right]$$

where $C_t = 1$ if a cost is paid, 0 otherwise. Here, to simplify calculations and concentrate on the economics, we take the "timeless perspective", and take the limit $\beta \to 1$. That is, the agent maximizes, over the adjustment policy, $V(a) = \lim_{\beta \to 1} V(a, \beta)$, that is

$$V(a) = -\mathbb{E}\left[\frac{1}{2}(a_t - x_t)^2 + \kappa C_t\right]$$

which is the average consumption loss plus a penalty for the average cost of looking up information.[86]

If the information is s periods old, then $a_{t,s} - x_t = \sum_{u=1}^{s} \varepsilon_{t-u}$, so

$$\mathbb{E}\left[(a_{t,s} - x_t)^2\right] = s\sigma^2$$

hence, the losses from misoptimization are:

$$\mathbb{E}\left[(a_t - x_t)^2\right] = \sigma^2 \mathbb{E}[T] = \sigma^2 \frac{D - 1}{2} \quad \text{for the } D\text{-period model,}$$

---

[86] Indeed, as $\sum_{t \geq 0}(1 - \beta)\beta^t X_t \to \mathbb{E}[X_t]$ as $\beta \to 1$ if X is an "ergodic" process.

$$\mathbb{E}\left[(a_t - x_t)^2\right] = \sigma^2 \frac{\theta}{1-\theta} \text{ for the Calvo model.}$$

Now, we calculate[87]

$$\mathbb{E}[C_t] = \frac{1}{D} \text{ for the } D\text{-period model,}$$
$$\mathbb{E}[C_t] = 1 - \theta \text{ for the Calvo model,}$$

so that the optimal reset time solves, in the D period model:

$$\min_D \frac{1}{2}\sigma^2 \frac{D-1}{2} + \kappa \frac{1}{D}$$

i.e. a frequency of price adjustments

$$\frac{1}{D} = \frac{\sigma}{2\sqrt{\kappa}} \tag{89}$$

as in Gabaix and Laibson (2002), Reis (2006a, 2006b), Alvarez et al. (2011). Likewise, in the Calvo model, the optimal frequency θ is

$$\min_\theta \frac{1}{2}\sigma^2 \frac{\theta}{1-\theta} + \kappa(1-\theta)$$

i.e. the frequency of price adjustments is

$$1 - \theta = \min\left(\frac{\sigma}{\sqrt{2\kappa}}, 1\right). \tag{90}$$

The same generalizes to the case where the signal has n components. Suppose that

$$x_t = \sum_i x_{it}$$
$$x_{it} = x_{i,t-1} + \varepsilon_{it}$$

and reset costs are κ_i. Then the average per-period loss is

$$\sum_i \left[\frac{1}{2}\sigma_i^2 \frac{D_i - 1}{2} + \kappa_i \frac{1}{D_i}\right]$$

so that the frequency at which agents look up source i is

$$\frac{1}{D_i} = \frac{\sigma_i}{2\sqrt{\kappa_i}}. \tag{91}$$

---

[87] In the D model, the information is looked up every D periods. In the Calvo model, the probability of looking up the information next period is $1 - \theta$.

I do know not of systematic evidence on this, although the research on this topic is progressing vigorously (e.g. Alvarez et al., 2011, 2018).

7.3 Other ways to generate dynamic adjustment

7.3.1 Procrastination

Another way to generate sluggishness is to use procrastination, as in Carroll et al. (2009). In this view, agents hope to act, but procrastinate for a long time – because they are optimistic about their future behavior (O'Donoghue and Rabin, 1999). Related issues are forgetting and lapsed attention. For instance, Ericson (2017) finds that an important factor is that people overestimate the likelihood that they will remember that they have to make a decision, which amplifies sluggishness (see also Ericson, 2011).

7.3.2 Unintentional inattention

Most models are about fairly "intentional" attention – agents choose to pay attention (though, given attention is dictated more so by System 1 than by System 2, in the language of Kahneman (2003), the distinction isn't completely clear cut). If unintentional inattention is the first-order issue, how do we model that? A simple way would be to say that the agent has the wrong "priors" over the importance of variable x_i. That is, in truth σ_i is high, but the agent thinks that σ_i is low – for instance, at the allocation of attention stage the agent thinks that an employer's retirement savings match rate is small. Concretely, at Step 1 in Proposition 4.1, the agent might have too low a perception of σ_i. One could imagine an iterated allocation problem, where the agent also optimizes over his perception of the costs and benefits.

7.3.3 Slow accumulation of information with entropy-based cost

Sims (1998) was motivated by evidence for sluggish adjustment. Maćkowiak and Wiederholt (2009, 2015) pursue that idea in macroeconomics – while breaking the unitary entropy of Sims, such that agents are allowed to have heterogeneous attention to different news sources. The dynamics are much more complex to derive, but are not unrealistic.

7.4 Behavioral macroeconomics

There has been a recent interest in behavioral macroeconomics. It is too early to present a comprehensive survey of this literature. Themes includes rules of thumb (Campbell and Mankiw, 1989), limited information updating (Caballero, 1995; Gabaix and Laibson, 2002; Mankiw and Reis, 2002; Reis, 2006a; Alvarez et al., 2011), and noisy signals (Sims, 2003; Maćkowiak and Wiederholt, 2015). A small but growing literature in theoretical macroeconomics draws consequences for general equilibrium and policy from features like inattention and imperfect information (Woodford, 2013; García-Schmidt and Woodford, 2015; Angeletos and Lian, 2017, 2016; Farhi and Werning, 2017; Bordalo et al., 2016b). For instance, Gabaix (2018a) presents a behavioral version of the textbook New Keynesian model, which gives a way to model monetary and fiscal policy with behavioral agents. There is also a budding literature on limited attention by firms beyond the issues of price stickiness (Goldfarb and Xiao, 2016). We can expect this literature to grow in the future.

8 Open questions and conclusion

The field of inattention has become extremely active. Here are some important open issues.

We need more measures of inattention, and go beyond rejecting the "full attention" null hypothesis. Currently, to produce one good measure of attention m, we need a full paper. It would be nice to scale up production – in particular, to always attempt to provide a quantitative measure of attention, rather than a demonstration that it is not full.

Investigating Varian in the lab. Consider the difference between a physics textbook and a microeconomics textbook. In a physics textbook, assertions and results (e.g. force = mass × acceleration) have been verified exquisitely in the lab. Not so in economics. When one opens a textbook such as Mas-Colell et al. (1995) or Varian (1992), one is confronted with a few chapters that have been extensively investigated: for example, expected utility (with prospect theory as a behavioral benchmark), or basic game theory, with some behavioral models as an alternative (Camerer, 2003). But other chapters, such as basic microeconomics of the consumer-theory and Arrow–Debreu styles, have been investigated very little.[88] One sees many assertions and predictions, with very few experimental counterparts – and indeed, one suspects that the assertions will actually be wrong if they are to be tested.

This is a result – I believe – of the lack of a systematic behavioral alternative. The material in Section 5 fills this gap by proposing a behavioral counterpart of the major parts of basic microeconomics, including directions in which inattention will modify the rational predictions. It would be a great advance to implement procedures to investigate its predictions empirically. Such a study would be very useful for economics.

The challenges are: (i) to implement a notion of "clearly perceived" and "more opaque" prices, (ii) measure attention m, and (iii) implement in a roughly natural way the basic problem (53). The outcome of this would be very valuable, as we would then have a worked-out and tested counterpart of basic microeconomics.

---

[88] There is a literature estimating GARP and Afriat's theorem, but it is generally not guided by a specific behavioral alternative, so that "rejection of rationality" usually gives little guidance to a behavioral alternative. See Aguiar and Serrano (2017) for progress on this, and the references therein to this strand of literature.

We need more experimental evidence on the determinants of attention. There are now several theories of attention, but measurement is somewhat lagging in refinement (the reason is that it is already hard to measure attention in the first place, so that the study of the determinants of attention is even harder). What's the cost of inattention? Could we get some sense of the shape of the cost, and of the attention function (e.g. that in Fig. 1)? At a more basic level, the global-entropy constraint à la Sims predicts a unitary shadow value of attention, as in Eq. (73), without source-dependent inattention. Other models, e.g. behavioral models and older models where people pay for precision (Verrecchia, 1982; Veldkamp, 2011), predict source-dependent inattention, as in (37). Other theories emphasize the fact that attention is commodity- and action-dependent (Bordalo et al., 2013). Empirical guidance would be useful.

More structural estimation. The early papers found evidence for imperfect attention, with large economic effects. A more recent wave of papers has estimated inattention – its mean, variance, and how it varies with income, education, and the like. A third generation of papers might estimate more structural models of inattention, to see if the predictions do fit, and perhaps suggest newer models.

Using this to do better policy: Generating attention. All this work may lead to progress in how to generate attention, e.g. for policy. Making consumers more rational is difficult even when the right incentives are in place – for example, consumers overwhelmingly fail to minimize fees in allocating their portfolios (Choi et al., 2009). The work on nudges (Thaler and Sunstein, 2008) is based on psychological intuition rather than quantified principles. Also, knowing better "best practices" for disclosure would be helpful. Firms are good at screening for consumer biases (Ru and Schoar, 2016), but public institutions less so, and debiasing is quite hard.

Appendix A Further derivations and mathematical complements

A.1 Further derivations

Basic signal-extraction problem (Section 2.1). We have $s = x + \varepsilon$. So $\mathbb{E}[x|s] = ms$, with $m = \frac{\text{Cov}(x,s)}{\text{Var}(s)} = \frac{v_x}{v_s}$, with $v_x = \sigma_x^2$ and $v_s = \sigma_x^2 + \sigma_\varepsilon^2$. Hence, the optimal $a = \mathbb{E}[x|s]$ is $a = ms = mx + m\varepsilon$. A little bit of algebra gives $v_\varepsilon = v_s - v_x = v_x \left(\frac{1}{m} - 1\right)$ and

$$\text{Var}(m\varepsilon) = m^2 v_\varepsilon = m(1 - m) v_x$$

so a is distributed as:

$$a = mx + \sqrt{m(1-m)}\eta_x \tag{92}$$

where η_x is another draw from the distribution of x. This implies $\text{Var}(a) = m\text{Var}(x)$, and $\mathbb{E}\left[(a - x)^2\right] = (1 - m)\sigma_x^2$.

Derivation of the losses from inattention (Eq. (31)). Let us start with a 1-dimensional action, with a utility function $u\,(a)$. Call a^* the optimum. But the agent does $a = a^* + \hat{a}$, where $\hat{a}$ is a deviation (perhaps coming from inattention). Then utility losses are

$$L\left(\hat{a}\right) := u\left(a^* + \hat{a}\right) - u\left(a^*\right).$$

Let's do a Taylor expansion,

$$L_a\left(\hat{a}\right) = u'\left(a^* + \hat{a}\right), \quad L_{aa}\left(\hat{a}\right) = u''\left(a^* + \hat{a}\right)$$

$$L\left(\hat{a}\right) = L\left(0\right) + L_a\left(0\right)\hat{a} + \frac{1}{2}L_{aa}\left(0\right)\hat{a}^2 + o\left(\hat{a}^2\right)$$

which implies $L\left(0\right) = L_a\left(0\right) = 0$. Hence:

$$L\left(\hat{a}\right) = \frac{1}{2}u_{aa}\left(0\right)\hat{a}^2 + o\left(\hat{a}^2\right).$$

Next, for a small x, the deviation is

$$\hat{a} = a^*\left(x^s\right) - a^*\left(x\right) = a_x\left(x^s - x\right) + o\left(x\right) = a_x\left(m - 1\right)x + o\left(x\right)$$

hence, for a one-dimensional x, the loss is:

$$2L\left(x\right) = u_{aa}\left(a^*\left(x\right)\right)\hat{a}^2 + o\left(\hat{a}^2\right) = u_{aa}\left(a^*\left(0\right)\right)\hat{a}^2 + o\left(\hat{a}^2\right)$$

$$= u_{aa}a_x^2 x^2\left(1 - m\right)^2 + o\left(|x|^2\right).$$

With an n-dimensional x, the math is similar, with matrices:

$$\hat{a} = a^*\left(x^s\right) - a^*\left(x\right) = a_x\left(x^s - x\right) = a_x\left(M - I\right)x + o\left(x\right)$$

with $M = diag\,(m_1, ..., m_n)$, I the identity matrix of dimension n. So, neglecting $o\left(\|\hat{a}\|^2\right)$ terms,

$$2L = \hat{a}'u_{aa}\left(0\right)\hat{a} + o\left(\|\hat{a}\|^2\right) = x'\left(I - M\right)'a_x'u_{aa}\left(0\right)a_x\left(I - M\right)x$$

$$= \sum_{i,j}\left(1 - m_i\right)x_i a_{x_i}'u_{aa}\left(0\right)a_{x_j}x_j\left(1 - m_j\right)$$

$$= -\sum_{i,j}\left(1 - m_i\right)\tilde{\Lambda}_{ij}\left(1 - m_j\right) = -\left(\iota - m\right)\tilde{\Lambda}\left(\iota - m\right)'$$

$$\tilde{\Lambda}_{ij} = -x_i a_{x_i}'u_{aa}\left(0\right)a_{x_j}x_j, \quad \iota := \left(1, ..., 1\right).$$

We then obtain (31) by taking expectations.

Derivation of the entropy of Gaussian variables (Section 6.2.1). The entropy doesn't depend on the mean, so we normalized it to 0.

One dimension. The density is $f(x) = \frac{e^{-\frac{x^2}{2\sigma^2}}}{\sqrt{2\pi\sigma^2}}$, so

$$H(X) = -\mathbb{E}\left[\log f(X)\right] = -\mathbb{E}\left[-\frac{x^2}{2\sigma^2} - \frac{1}{2}\log\left(2\pi\sigma^2\right)\right]$$
$$= \frac{1}{2} + \frac{1}{2}\log\left(2\pi\sigma^2\right) = \frac{1}{2}\log\sigma^2 + \frac{1}{2}\log(2\pi e).$$

Higher dimensions. The density is $f(x) = \frac{e^{-\frac{1}{2}x'V^{-1}x}}{(2\pi)^{n/2}(\det V)^{1/2}}$, where $V = \mathbb{E}\left[XX'\right]$ is the variance covariance matrix. Using the notation $|V| = \det V$, and Tr for the trace, we first note

$$\mathbb{E}\left[x'V^{-1}x\right] = \mathbb{E}\left[\text{Tr}\left(x'V^{-1}x\right)\right] = \mathbb{E}\left[\text{Tr}\left(xx'V^{-1}\right)\right]$$
$$= \text{Tr}\,\mathbb{E}\left[xx'V^{-1}\right] = \text{Tr}\,\mathbb{E}\left[VV^{-1}\right] = \text{Tr}\,I_n = n.$$

Then, the entropy is

$$H(X) = -\mathbb{E}\left[\log f(X)\right] = -\mathbb{E}\left[-\frac{n}{2}\log(2\pi) - \frac{1}{2}\log|V| - \frac{1}{2}x'V^{-1}x\right]$$
$$= \frac{1}{2}\log\left((2\pi)^n |V|\right) + \frac{n}{2} = \frac{1}{2}\log\left((2\pi e)^n |V|\right).$$

Mutual information of two Gaussian variables (Section 6.2.1). Suppose X, Y are jointly Gaussian, with variance–covariance matrix

$$V = \begin{pmatrix} \sigma_X^2 & \rho\sigma_X\sigma_Y \\ \rho\sigma_X\sigma_Y & \sigma_Y^2 \end{pmatrix},$$

where $\rho = \text{corr}(X, Y)$. Then, $\det V = \sigma_X^2\sigma_Y^2(1 - \rho^2)$, so

$$H(X, Y) = \frac{1}{2}\log(\det V) + \log(2\pi e)$$

and using (67) gives

$$I(X, Y) = H(X) + H(Y) - H(X, Y) = -\frac{1}{2}\log\left(1 - \rho^2\right).$$

Proof of Proposition 5.1. From Definition 4.3, the optimum satisfies: $u'(c) = \lambda p^s$ for some λ. Hence, this consumption is the consumption of a rational agent facing prices p^s, and wealth $w' = p^s \cdot c$. $\qquad\square$

Proof of Proposition 5.2. Here I show only the proof in the most transparent case – see the original paper for the general case. Utility is $u(c) = U(C) + c_n$, where $C = (c_1, \ldots, c_{n-1})$, and the price of good n is 1 and correctly perceived. Then, demand satisfies $u'(c) = \lambda p^s$. Applying this to the last good gives $1 = \lambda$. So, demand for the other goods satisfies $U'(C) = P^s$, where $P = (p_1, \ldots, p_n)$. Differentiating w.r.t. P, $U''(C) C_P^s = M$, where $M = diag(m_1, \ldots, m_{n-1})$ is the vector of attention to prices. Now, the Slutsky matrix (for the goods $1, \ldots, n-1$) is $S^s = C_P^s = U''^{-1}(C) M$, as all the income effects are absorbed by the last good ($\frac{\partial c_i}{\partial w} = 0$ for $i < n$). As a particular case where $M = I$, the rational Slutsky matrix is $S^r = U''^{-1}(C)$. So, we have $S^s = S^r M$. □

Proof of Proposition 5.4. The part $\frac{\partial c^s}{\partial w} = \frac{\partial c^r}{\partial w}$ follows from Proposition 5.1: at the default prices $p = p^s$, so $c^s(p^d, w) = c^r(p^d, w)$, which implies $\frac{\partial c^s}{\partial w} = \frac{\partial c^r}{\partial w}$. Then, the definition of the Slutsky matrix and Proposition 5.2 imply (58). □

Proof of Proposition 5.8. In an endowment economy, equilibrium consumption is equal to the endowment, $c(t) = \omega(t)$. We have $\frac{u_i(c(t))}{u_1(c(t))} = \frac{p_i^s(t)}{p_1^s(t)}$ for $t = 0, 1$: the ratio of marginal utilities is equal to the ratio of perceived prices – both in the rational economy (where perceived prices are true prices) and in the behavioral economy (where they're not). Using $p_1^s(t) = p_1^r(t) = p_1(0)$, that implies that the perceived price needs to be the same in the behavioral and rational economy: $\left(p_i^{[s]}(t)\right)^{\text{perceived}} = p_i^{[r]}(t)$. Thus, we have $m_i dp_i^{[s]} = d\left[\left(p_i^{[s]}\right)^{\text{perceived}}\right] = dp_i^{[r]}$, i.e. $dp_i^{[s]} = \frac{1}{m_i} dp_i^{[r]}$. □

A.2 Mathematical complements

Here I provide some mathematical complements.

Dynamic attention: Beyond the random walk case. Here I expand on Section 7.1, beyond the random cases which made the analytics very transparent. I consider the case (80) with ρ not necessarily equal to 1. The sticky action is a bit more delicate to compute. Consider an agent who can change her action at time t. At period $t + s$, she will still have to perform action $a_{t,s}^A = a_{t,0}^A$ with probability θ^s (we use the Calvo formulation here). Hence, the optimal action at t satisfies

$$\max_a - \mathbb{E}_t \sum_{s=0}^{\infty} \beta^s \theta^s (a - x_{t+s})^2.$$

The first order condition is

$$\mathbb{E}_t \sum_{s=0}^{\infty} \beta^s \theta^s (a - x_{t+s}) = 0$$

i.e. $\frac{1}{1-\beta\theta} a - \sum_{s=0}^{\infty} \beta^s \theta^s \mathbb{E}_t [x_{t+s}] = 0$, i.e. $a = a_{t,0}^A$ with

$$a_{t,0}^A = (1 - \beta\theta) \mathbb{E}_t \sum_{s=0}^{\infty} \beta^s \theta^s \mathbb{E}_t [x_{t+s}]. \tag{93}$$

In the AR(1) case, $\mathbb{E}_t [x_{t+s}] = \rho^s x_t$, and

$$a_{t,0}^A = \frac{1 - \beta\theta}{1 - \beta\theta\rho} x_t. \tag{94}$$

In the sticky information model, the problem is, for each period t,

$$\max_{a_{t,s}^I} - \mathbb{E}_{t-s} \left(a_{t,s}^I - x_t \right)^2$$

which yields

$$a_{t,s}^I = \mathbb{E}_{t-s} [x_t]. \tag{95}$$

Hence, we see that the two models are generally different – even though they generate the same predictions in the random walk case.

Appendix B Data methodology

This appendix outlines the details of the methodology used to compile the data in Table 1 and Fig. 1, which present point estimates of the attention parameter m in a cross-section of recent studies, alongside the estimated relative value of the opaque add-on attribute with respect to the relevant good or quantity (τ/p).

- In the study of Allcott and Wozny (2014), we take τ to be the standard deviation of the present discounted value of future gasoline costs in the authors' sample; p is correspondingly the standard deviation of vehicle price, such that $\tau = \$4,147$ and $p = \$9,845$. The point estimate for m is as reported by the authors.
- Hossain and Morgan (2006) and Brown et al. (2010) both conduct a series of paired experiments by selling various goods on eBay and varying the shrouded shipping costs. This setup allows us to deduce the implied degree of inattention, following the same methodology as in DellaVigna (2009). We consider auction pairs in which the auction setup and the sum of reserve price are held constant, while the shipping cost is altered. As in DellaVigna (2009), we assume buyers are bidding their true willingness to pay in eBay's second price auctions, such that their bid is $b = p + m\tau$, where p is the buyer's valuation of the object and τ is the shipping cost. Seller's revenue is $p + (1 - m)c$. Under this model, the ratio of the difference in revenues to the difference in shipping costs across the two auction conditions corresponds to the quantity $1 - m$.

The estimates for the attention parameter m in the experiments of Hossain and Morgan (2006) are as reported in DellaVigna (2009). We use the same methodology to derive the analogous estimate for the eBay Taiwan field experiment of Brown et al. (2010). The raw implied estimate for the latter experimental setting is negative ($m = -0.43$), as the mean revenue difference between the two auction conditions is greater than the difference in shipping costs. For consistency with the definition of m and in order to account for measurement error, we constrain the final implied estimate of m to the interval [0, 1].

Given that each estimate of m is inferred from a set of two paired auctions, the value p of the good under auction is defined as average revenue minus shipping costs across the two auction conditions. The value τ of the opaque attribute is analogously defined as the average shipping cost across the two auction conditions.

- For the study of DellaVigna and Pollet (2009) we take τ/p to be the ratio of the standard deviation of abnormal returns at earnings announcement to abnormal returns for the quarter, pooled across all weekdays and computed following the methodology in DellaVigna and Pollet (2009). The quarterly cadence is chosen to match the frequency of earnings announcements in the authors' sample. The return at earnings announcement is for two trading days from the close of the market on the trading day before the earnings announcement to the close of the trading day after the earnings announcement. The standard deviation of the abnormal returns at earnings announcement is 0.0794. The standard deviation of the abnormal returns for the quarter, starting from the close of the market on the trading day before the earnings announcement and continuing to the close of the market on trading day 60 after the announcement, is 0.2651. The estimates for the attention parameter m are as in DellaVigna (2009).

- In the case of Lacetera et al. (2012), τ is taken to be the average mileage remainder in the sample, which is approximately 5,000, per correspondence with the authors. The quantity p is obtained by subtracting $\tau = 5{,}000$ from the mileage of the median car in the sample, which is 56,997. Hence $p = 51{,}997$. The estimate for m is as reported by the authors in the full-sample specification that includes all car transactions, pooled across fleet/lease and dealer categories.

- For the field experiment of Chetty et al. (2009), we take τ/p to be the relevant sales tax rate of 7.38%. Correspondingly, for the natural experiment of Chetty et al. (2009) we take τ/p to be 4.30%, which is the mean sales tax rate for alcoholic products across U.S. states as reported by the authors. The estimates for the attention parameter m are as reported by the authors.

- For the study of Taubinsky and Rees-Jones (2018), we analogously let τ/p be the sales tax rate applied in the laboratory experiment, which is 7.31% in the standard-tax treatment arm, and triple that value in the triple-tax treatment arm. The estimate for the attention parameter m are as reported by the authors for the two treatment arms.

- Fig. 1 additionally shows data points from Busse et al. (2013b), who measure inattention to left-digit remainders in the mileage of used cars in auctions along several covariate dimensions. Each data point corresponds to a subsample of cars with mileages within a 10,000 mile-wide bin (e.g., between 15,000 and 25,000 miles, between 25,000 and 35,000 miles, and so forth). Data is available for two data sets, one including retail auctions and one including wholesale auctions. For each mileage bin, we include data points from both of these data sets. The estimates of m are as reported by the authors. The metric τ/p is the average ratio of mileage remainder to true mileage net of mileage remainder in the subsamples. As this ratio is most readily available for the data set of wholesale car auctions, we compute the τ/p estimates on subsamples of the wholesale data set only, under the assumption that the mileage distribution is not systematically different across the two data sets. We do not expect substantive impact on our results from this assumption.

References

Abaluck, Jason, Adams, Abi, 2017. What Do Consumers Consider Before They Choose? Identification from Asymmetric Demand Responses. NBER Working Paper No. 23566.

Abaluck, Jason, Gruber, Jonathan, 2011. Heterogeneity in choice inconsistencies among the elderly: evidence from prescription drug plan choice. The American Economic Review: Papers and Proceedings 101 (3), 377–381.

Abel, Andrew B., Eberly, Janice C., Panageas, Stavros, 2013. Optimal inattention to the stock market with information costs and transactions costs. Econometrica 81 (4), 1455–1481.

Abela, Andrew R., Dougherty, Stephen D., Fagen, Erin D., Hill, Carolyn J.R., Chudasama, Y., 2012. Inhibitory control deficits in rats with ventral hippocampal lesions. Cerebral Cortex 23 (6), 1396–1409.

Abeler, Johannes, Jäger, Simon, 2015. Complex tax incentives. American Economic Journal: Economic Policy 7 (3), 1–28.

Aguiar, Victor H., Riabov, Nickolai, 2016. Estimating High Dimensional Demand Under Bounded Rationality: The ESMAX Demand System. Working Paper.

Aguiar, Victor H., Serrano, Roberto, 2017. Slutsky matrix norms: the size, classification, and comparative statics of bounded rationality. Journal of Economic Theory 172, 163–201.

Allcott, Hunt, Lockwood, Benjamin B., Taubinsky, Dmitry, 2017. A Theory of Regressive Sin Taxes, with an Application to the Optimal Soda Tax. Working Paper.

Allcott, Hunt, Taubinsky, Dmitry, 2015. Evaluating behaviorally motivated policy: experimental evidence from the lightbulb market. The American Economic Review 105 (8), 2501–2538.

Allcott, Hunt, Wozny, Nathan, 2014. Gasoline prices, fuel economy, and the energy paradox. Review of Economics and Statistics 96 (5), 779–795.

Alvarez, Fernando, Gonzalez-Rozada, Martin, Neumeyer, Andy, Beraja, Martin, 2018. From hyperinflation to stable prices: Argentina's evidence on menu cost models. The Quarterly Journal of Economics. https://doi.org/10.1093/qje/qjy022. Forthcoming.

Alvarez, Fernando, Guiso, Luigi, Lippi, Francesco, 2012. Durable consumption and asset management with transaction and observation costs. The American Economic Review 102 (5), 2272–2300.

Alvarez, Fernando, Lippi, Francesco, Paciello, Luigi, 2018. Monetary shocks in models with observation and menu costs. Journal of the European Economic Association 16 (2), 353–382.

Alvarez, Fernando E., Lippi, Francesco, Paciello, Luigi, 2011. Optimal price setting with observation and menu costs. The Quarterly Journal of Economics 126 (4), 1909–1960.

Ambuehl, Sandro, 2017. An Offer You Can't Refuse. Working Paper.

Anderson, Simon P., De Palma, Andre, Thisse, Jacques François, 1992. Discrete Choice Theory of Product Differentiation. MIT Press.

Andries, Marianne, Haddad, Valentin, 2017. Information Aversion. NBER Working Paper No. 23958.

Angeletos, George-Marios, Lian, Chen, 2016. Forward Guidance Without Common Knowledge. NBER Working Paper No. 23379.

Angeletos, George-Marios, Lian, Chen, 2017. Dampening General Equilibrium: From Micro to Macro. NBER Working Paper No. 22785.

Arieli, Amos, Ben-Ami, Yaniv, Rubinstein, Ariel, 2011. Tracking decision makers under uncertainty. American Economic Journal: Microeconomics 3 (4), 68–76.

Avoyan, Ala, Schotter, Andrew, 2018. Attention in Games: An Experimental Study. Working Paper.

Bacchetta, Philippe, Van Wincoop, Eric, 2010. Infrequent portfolio decisions: a solution to the forward discount puzzle. The American Economic Review 100 (3), 870–904.

Baker, Malcolm, Pan, Xin, Wurgler, Jeffrey, 2012. The effect of reference point prices on mergers and acquisitions. Journal of Financial Economics 106 (1), 49–71.

Barber, Brad M., Odean, Terrance, 2007. All that glitters: the effect of attention and news on the buying behavior of individual and institutional investors. The Review of Financial Studies 21 (2), 785–818.

Bartoš, Vojtěch, Bauer, Michal, Chytilová, Julie, Matějka, Filip, 2016. Attention discrimination: theory and field experiments with monitoring information acquisition. The American Economic Review 106 (6), 1437–1475.

Bénabou, Roland, Tirole, Jean, 2002. Self-confidence and personal motivation. The Quarterly Journal of Economics 117 (3), 871–915.

Bernheim, B. Douglas, Fradkin, Andrey, Popov, Igor, 2015. The welfare economics of default options in 401(k) plans. The American Economic Review 105 (9), 2798–2837.

Bernheim, B. Douglas, Rangel, Antonio, 2009. Beyond revealed preference: choice theoretic foundations for behavioral welfare economics. The Quarterly Journal of Economics 124 (1), 51–104.

Bordalo, Pedro, Gennaioli, Nicola, Shleifer, Andrei, 2012. Salience theory of choice under risk. The Quarterly Journal of Economics 127 (3), 1243–1285.

Bordalo, Pedro, Gennaioli, Nicola, Shleifer, Andrei, 2013. Salience and consumer choice. Journal of Political Economy 121 (5), 803–843.

Bordalo, Pedro, Gennaioli, Nicola, Shleifer, Andrei, 2016a. Competition for attention. The Review of Economic Studies 83 (2), 481–513.

Bordalo, Pedro, Gennaioli, Nicola, Shleifer, Andrei, 2016b. Diagnostic Expectations and Credit Cycles. NBER Working Paper No. 22266.

Bouchaud, Jean-Philippe, Krueger, Philipp, Landier, Augustin, Thesmar, David, 2016. Sticky Expectations and the Profitability Anomaly. HEC Paris Research Paper No. FIN-2016-1136.

Brocas, Isabelle, Carrillo, Juan D., Wang, Stephanie W., Camerer, Colin F., 2014. Imperfect choice or imperfect attention? understanding strategic thinking in private information games. The Review of Economic Studies 81 (3), 944–970.

Bronnenberg, Bart J., Dubé, Jean-Pierre, Gentzkow, Matthew, Shapiro, Jesse M., 2015. Do pharmacists buy Bayer? Informed shoppers and the brand premium. The Quarterly Journal of Economics 130 (4), 1669–1726.

Brown, Alexander L., Camerer Colin, F., Lovallo, Dan, 2012. To review or not to review? Limited strategic thinking at the movie box office. American Economic Journal: Microeconomics 4 (2), 1–26.

Brown, Alexander L., Camerer, Colin F., Lovallo, Dan, 2013. Estimating structural models of equilibrium and cognitive hierarchy thinking in the field: the case of withheld movie critic reviews. Management Science 59 (3), 733–747.

Brown, Jennifer, Hossain, Tanjim, Morgan, John, 2010. Shrouded attributes and information suppression: evidence from the field. The Quarterly Journal of Economics 125 (2), 859–876.

Browning, Martin, Chiappori, Pierre-Andre, 1998. Efficient intra-household allocations: a general characterization and empirical tests. Econometrica 66 (6), 1241–1278.

Bulow, Jeremy I., Geanakoplos, John D., Klemperer, Paul D., 1985. Multimarket oligopoly: strategic substitutes and complements. Journal of Political Economy 93 (3), 488–511.

Bushong, Benjamin, Rabin, Matthew, Schwartzstein, Joshua, 2016. A Model of Relative Thinking. Working Paper.

Busse, Meghan R., Knittel, Christopher R., Zettelmeyer, Florian, 2013a. Are consumers myopic? Evidence from new and used car purchases. The American Economic Review 103 (1), 220–256.

Busse, Meghan R., Lacetera, Nicola, Pope Devin, G., Silva-Risso, Jorge, Sydnor, Justin R., 2013b. Estimating the effect of salience in wholesale and retail car markets. The American Economic Review: Papers and Proceedings 103 (3), 575–579.

Caballero, Ricardo J., 1995. Near-rationality, heterogeneity, and aggregate consumption. Journal of Money, Credit, and Banking 27 (1), 29–48.

Calvo, Guillermo A., 1983. Staggered prices in a utility-maximizing framework. Journal of Monetary Economics 12 (3), 383–398.

Camerer, Colin, 2003. Behavioral Game Theory: Experiments in Strategic Interaction. Princeton University Press.

Camerer, Colin F., Ho, Teck-Hua, Chong, Juin-Kuan, 2004. A cognitive hierarchy model of games. The Quarterly Journal of Economics 119 (3), 861–898.

Camerer, Colin F., Johnson, Eric, Rymon, Talia, Sen, Sankar, 1993. Cognition and framing in sequential bargaining for gains and losses. Frontiers of Game Theory 104, 27–47.

Campbell, John Y., Mankiw, N. Gregory, 1989. Consumption, income, and interest rates: reinterpreting the time series evidence. NBER Macroeconomics Annual 4, 185–216.

Candes, Emmanuel J., Tao, Terence, 2006. Near-optimal signal recovery from random projections: universal encoding strategies? IEEE Transactions on Information Theory 52 (12), 5406–5425.

Caplin, Andrew, 2016. Measuring and modeling attention. Annual Review of Economics 8, 379–403.

Caplin, Andrew, Dean, Mark, 2015. Revealed preference, rational inattention, and costly information acquisition. The American Economic Review 105 (7), 2183–2203.

Caplin, Andrew, Dean, Mark, Leahy, John, 2016. Rational Inattention, Optimal Consideration Sets and Stochastic Choice. Working Paper.

Caplin, Andrew, Dean, Mark, Leahy, John, 2017. Rationally Inattentive Behavior: Characterizing and Generalizing Shannon Entropy. NBER Working Paper No. 23652.

Caplin, Andrew, Dean, Mark, Martin, Daniel, 2011. Search and satisficing. The American Economic Review 101 (7), 2899–2922.

Carlin, Bruce I., 2009. Strategic price complexity in retail financial markets. Journal of Financial Economics 91 (3), 278–287.

Carrasco, Marisa, 2011. Visual attention: the past 25 years. Vision Research 51 (13), 1484–1525.

Carroll, Christopher D., 2003. Macroeconomic expectations of households and professional forecasters. The Quarterly Journal of Economics 118 (1), 269–298.

Carroll, Christopher D., Crawley, Edmund, Slacalek, Jiri, Tokuoka, Kiichi, White, Matthew N., 2017. Sticky Expectations and Consumption Dynamics. Working Paper.

Carroll, Gabriel D., Choi, James J., Laibson, David, Madrian, Brigitte C., Metrick, Andrew, 2009. Optimal defaults and active decisions. The Quarterly Journal of Economics 124 (4), 1639–1674.

Carroll, John S., Bazerman, Max H., Maury, Robin, 1988. Negotiator cognitions: a descriptive approach to negotiators' understanding of their opponents. Organizational Behavior and Human Decision Processes 41 (3), 352–370.

Chang, Tom Y., Huang, Wei, Wang, Yongxiang, 2018. Something in the air: pollution and the demand for health insurance. The Review of Economic Studies 85 (3), 1609–1634.

Chetty, Raj, Looney, Adam, Kroft, Kory, 2007. Salience and Taxation: Theory and Evidence. NBER Working Paper No. 13330.

Chetty, Raj, Looney, Adam, Kroft, Kory, 2009. Salience and taxation: theory and evidence. The American Economic Review 99 (4), 1145–1177.

Choi, James J., Laibson, David, Madrian, Brigitte C., 2009. Why does the law of one price fail? An experiment on index mutual funds. The Review of Financial Studies 23 (4), 1405–1432.

Christiano, Lawrence J., Eichenbaum, Martin, Evans, Charles L., 2005. Nominal rigidities and the dynamic effects of a shock to monetary policy. Journal of Political Economy 113 (1), 1–45.

Cohen, Lauren, Frazzini, Andrea, 2008. Economic links and predictable returns. The Journal of Finance 63 (4), 1977–2011.

Coibion, Olivier, Gorodnichenko, Yuriy, 2015. Information rigidity and the expectations formation process: a simple framework and new facts. The American Economic Review 105 (8), 2644–2678.

Compte, Olivier, Postlewaite, Andrew, 2017. Ignorance and uncertainty. Unpublished manuscript.

Costa-Gomes, Miguel, Crawford, Vincent P., Broseta, Bruno, 2001. Cognition and behavior in normal-form games: an experimental study. Econometrica 69 (5), 1193–1235.

Cover, Thomas M., Thomas, Joy A., 2006. Elements of Information Theory. John Wiley & Sons.

Daniel, Kent, Hirshleifer, David, Subrahmanyam, Avanidhar, 1998. Investor psychology and security market under- and overreactions. The Journal of Finance 53 (6), 1839–1885.

De Bartolomé, Charles A.M., 1995. Which tax rate do people use: average or marginal? Journal of Public Economics 56 (1), 79–96.

De Clippel, Geoffroy, Eliaz, Kfir, Rozen, Kareen, 2014. Competing for consumer inattention. Journal of Political Economy 122 (6), 1203–1234.

Debreu, Gerard, 1970. Economies with a finite set of equilibria. Econometrica 38 (3), 387–392.

Dehaene, Stanislas, 2011. The Number Sense: How the Mind Creates Mathematics. Oxford University Press.

Dehaene, Stanislas, Lau, Hakwan, Kouider, Sid, 2017. What is consciousness, and could machines have it? Science 358 (6362), 486–492.

DellaVigna, Stefano, 2009. Psychology and economics: evidence from the field. Journal of Economic Literature 47 (2), 315–372.

DellaVigna, Stefano, Pollet, Joshua M., 2007. Demographics and industry returns. The American Economic Review 97 (5), 1667–1702.

DellaVigna, Stefano, Pollet, Joshua M., 2009. Investor inattention and Friday earnings announcements. The Journal of Finance 64 (2), 709–749.

DellaVigna, Stefano, Pope, Devin, 2018. What motivates effort? Evidence and expert forecasts. The Review of Economic Studies 85 (2), 1029–1069.

Dertwinkel-Kalt, Markus, Köhler, Katrin, Lange, Mirjam R.J., Wenzel, Tobias, 2017. Demand shifts due to salience effects: experimental evidence. Journal of the European Economic Association 15 (3), 626–653.

Duffie, Darrell, Sun, Tong-sheng, 1990. Transactions costs and portfolio choice in a discrete-continuous-time setting. Journal of Economic Dynamics and Control 14 (1), 35–51.

Ellis, Andrew, 2018. Foundations for optimal inattention. Journal of Economic Theory 173, 56–94.

Ellison, Glenn, 2005. A model of add-on pricing. The Quarterly Journal of Economics 120 (2), 585–637.

Ellison, Glenn, Ellison, Sara Fisher, 2009. Search, obfuscation, and price elasticities on the internet. Econometrica 77 (2), 427–452.

Englmaier, Florian, Schmöller, Arno, Stowasser, Till, 2017. Price discontinuities in an online market for used cars. Management Science 64 (6), 2754–2766.

Enke, Benjamin, Zimmermann, Florian, forthcoming. Correlation neglect in belief formation. The Review of Economic Studies. https://doi.org/10.1093/restud/rdx081.

Ericson, Keith M., 2014. Consumer inertia and firm pricing in the Medicare Part D prescription drug insurance exchange. American Economic Journal: Economic Policy 6 (1), 38–64.

Ericson, Keith M. Marzilli, 2011. Forgetting we forget: overconfidence and memory. Journal of the European Economic Association 9 (1), 43–60.

Ericson, Keith M. Marzilli, 2017. On the interaction of memory and procrastination: implications for reminders, deadlines, and empirical estimation. Journal of the European Economic Association 15 (3), 692–719.

Eyster, Erik, Madarasz, Kristof, Michaillat, Pascal, 2017. Pricing when Customers Care About Fairness but Misinfer Markups. NBER Working Paper No. 23778.

Eyster, Erik, Rabin, Matthew, 2005. Cursed equilibrium. Econometrica 73 (5), 1623–1672.

Farhi, Emmanuel, Gabaix, Xavier, 2017. Optimal Taxation with Behavioral Agents. NBER Working Paper No. 21524.

Farhi, Emmanuel, Werning, Iván, 2017. Monetary Policy, Bounded Rationality, and Incomplete Markets. NBER Working Paper No. 23281.

Fedyk, Anastassia, 2018. Front Page News: The Effect of News Positioning on Financial Markets. Working Paper.

Finkelstein, Amy, 2009. E-ztax: tax salience and tax rates. The Quarterly Journal of Economics 124 (3), 969–1010.

Frederick, Shane, Loewenstein, George, O'Donoghue, Ted, 2002. Time discounting and time preference: a critical review. Journal of Economic Literature 40 (2), 351–401.

Friedman, Milton, 1961. The lag in effect of monetary policy. Journal of Political Economy 69 (5), 447–466.

Frydman, Cary, Rangel, Antonio, 2014. Debiasing the disposition effect by reducing the saliency of information about a stock's purchase price. Journal of Economic Behavior & Organization 107, 541–552.

Fudenberg, Drew, Levine, David K., 2012. Timing and self-control. Econometrica 80 (1), 1–42.

Fudenberg, Drew, Strack, Philipp, Strzalecki, Tomasz, 2017. Speed, Accuracy, and the Optimal Timing of Choices. Working Paper.

Gabaix, Xavier, 2014. A sparsity-based model of bounded rationality. The Quarterly Journal of Economics 129 (4), 1661–1710.

Gabaix, Xavier, 2016. Behavioral Macroeconomics via Sparse Dynamic Programming. NBER Working Paper No. 21848.

Gabaix, Xavier, 2018a. A Behavioral New Keynesian Model. NBER Working Paper No. 22954.

Gabaix, Xavier, 2018b. Some game theory with sparsity-based bounded rationality. In progress.

Gabaix, Xavier, Laibson, David, 2002. The 6D bias and the equity-premium puzzle. NBER Macroeconomics Annual 16, 257–312.

Gabaix, Xavier, Laibson, David, 2006. Shrouded attributes, consumer myopia, and information suppression in competitive markets. The Quarterly Journal of Economics 121 (2), 505–540.

Gabaix, Xavier, Laibson, David, 2017. Myopia and Discounting. NBER Working Paper No. 23254.

Gabaix, Xavier, Laibson, David, Li, Deyuan, Li, Hongyi, Resnick, Sidney, Vries, Casper Gde, 2016. The impact of competition on prices with numerous firms. Journal of Economic Theory 165, 1–24.

Gabaix, Xavier, Laibson, David, Moloche, Guillermo, Weinberg, Stephen, 2006. Costly information acquisition: experimental analysis of a boundedly rational model. The American Economic Review 96 (4), 1043–1068.

García-Schmidt, Mariana, Woodford, Michael, 2015. Are Low Interest Rates Deflationary? A Paradox of Perfect-Foresight Analysis. NBER Working Paper 21614.

Geanakoplos, John, Milgrom, Paul, 1991. A theory of hierarchies based on limited managerial attention. Journal of the Japanese and International Economies 5 (3), 205–225.

Gennaioli, Nicola, Shleifer, Andrei, 2010. What comes to mind. The Quarterly Journal of Economics 125 (4), 1399–1433.

Gershman, Samuel J., Horvitz, Eric J., Tenenbaum, Joshua B., 2015. Computational rationality: a converging paradigm for intelligence in brains, minds, and machines. Science 349 (6245), 273–278.

Giglio, Stefano, Shue, Kelly, 2014. No news is news: do markets underreact to nothing? The Review of Financial Studies 27 (12), 3389–3440.

Glimcher, Paul W., 2011. Foundations of Neuroeconomic Analysis. Oxford University Press.

Glimcher, Paul W., Fehr, Ernst, 2013. Neuroeconomics: Decision Making and the Brain. Academic Press.

Goldfarb, Avi, Xiao, Mo, 2016. Transitory Shocks, Limited Attention, and a Firm's Decision to Exit. Working Paper.

Greenwood, Robin, Hanson, Samuel G., 2014. Waves in ship prices and investment. The Quarterly Journal of Economics 130 (1), 55–109.

Greenwood, Robin, Shleifer, Andrei, 2014. Expectations of returns and expected returns. The Review of Financial Studies 27 (3), 714–746.

Grether, David M., 1980. Bayes rule as a descriptive model: the representativeness heuristic. The Quarterly Journal of Economics 95 (3), 537–557.

Griffiths, Thomas L., Lieder, Falk, Goodman, Noah D., 2015. Rational use of cognitive resources: levels of analysis between the computational and the algorithmic. Topics in Cognitive Science 7 (2), 217–229.

Grubb, Michael D., 2009. Selling to overconfident consumers. The American Economic Review 99 (5), 1770–1807.

Grubb, Michael D., Osborne, Matthew, 2015. Cellular service demand: biased beliefs, learning, and bill shock. The American Economic Review 105 (1), 234–271.

Gruber, Jonathan, Kőszegi, Botond, 2001. Is addiction "rational"? Theory and evidence. The Quarterly Journal of Economics 116 (4), 1261–1303.

Gul, Faruk, Pesendorfer, Wolfgang, Strzalecki, Tomasz, 2017. Coarse competitive equilibrium and extreme prices. The American Economic Review 107 (1), 109–137.

Handel, Benjamin R., 2013. Adverse selection and inertia in health insurance markets: when nudging hurts. The American Economic Review 103 (7), 2643–2682.

Handel, Benjamin R., Kolstad, Jonathan T., 2015. Health insurance for "humans": information frictions, plan choice, and consumer welfare. The American Economic Review 105 (8), 2449–2500.

Hanna, Rema, Mullainathan, Sendhil, Schwartzstein, Joshua, 2014. Learning through noticing: theory and evidence from a field experiment. The Quarterly Journal of Economics 129 (3), 1311–1353.

Hausman, Jerry A., 1979. Individual discount rates and the purchase and utilization of energy-using durables. Bell Journal of Economics, 33–54.

Havranek, Tomas, Rusnak, Marek, Sokolova, Anna, 2017. Habit formation in consumption: a meta-analysis. European Economic Review 95, 142–167.

Heidhues, Paul, Kőszegi, Boton, 2010. Exploiting naivete about self-control in the credit market. The American Economic Review 100 (5), 2279–2303.

Heidhues, Paul, Kőszegi, Botond, 2017. Naivete-based discrimination. The Quarterly Journal of Economics 132 (2), 1019–1054.

Hellwig, Christian, Veldkamp, Laura, 2009. Knowing what others know: coordination motives in information acquisition. The Review of Economic Studies 76 (1), 223–251.

Hirshleifer, David, Lim, Sonya Seongyeon, Teoh, Siew Hong, 2009. Driven to distraction: extraneous events and underreaction to earnings news. The Journal of Finance 64 (5), 2289–2325.

Hirshleifer, David, Lim, Sonya S., Teoh, Siew Hong, 2011. Limited investor attention and stock market misreactions to accounting information. The Review of Asset Pricing Studies 1 (1), 35–73.

Hirshleifer, David, Teoh, Siew Hong, 2003. Limited attention, information disclosure, and financial reporting. Journal of Accounting & Economics 36 (1), 337–386.

Ho, Teck-Hua, Camerer, Colin, Weigelt, Keith, 1998. Iterated dominance and iterated best response in experimental "p-beauty contests". The American Economic Review 88 (4), 947–969.

Hossain, Tanjim, Morgan, John, 2006. . . . Plus shipping and handling: revenue (non) equivalence in field experiments on eBay. Advances in Economic Analysis & Policy 5 (2).

Huang, Liqiang, Pashler, Harold, 2007. A boolean map theory of visual attention. Psychological Review 114 (3), 599.

Huberman, Gur, Regev, Tomer, 2001. Contagious speculation and a cure for cancer: a nonevent that made stock prices soar. The Journal of Finance 56 (1), 387–396.

Itti, Laurent, Koch, Christof, 2000. A saliency-based search mechanism for overt and covert shifts of visual attention. Vision Research 40 (10–12), 1489–1506.

Jehiel, Philippe, 2005. Analogy-based expectation equilibrium. Journal of Economic Theory 123 (2), 81–104.

Jin, Ginger Zhe, Luca, Michael, Martin, Daniel, 2017. Is No News (Perceived as) Bad News? An Experimental Investigation of Information Disclosure. NBER Working Paper No. 21099.

Johnson, Eric J., Camerer, Colin, Sen, Sankar, Rymon, Talia, 2002. Detecting failures of backward induction: monitoring information search in sequential bargaining. Journal of Economic Theory 104 (1), 16–47.

Johnson, Eric J., Häubl, Gerald, Keinan, Anat, 2007. Aspects of endowment: a query theory of value construction. Journal of Experimental Psychology: Learning, Memory, and Cognition 33 (3), 461.

Jung, Junehyuk, Kim, Jeong-Ho, Matějka, Filip, Sims, Christopher A., 2015. Discrete Actions in Information-Constrained Tracking Problems. Working Paper.

Kacperczyk, Marcin, Van Nieuwerburgh, Stijn, Veldkamp, Laura, 2016. A rational theory of mutual funds' attention allocation. Econometrica 84 (2), 571–626.

Kahneman, Daniel, 1973. Attention and Effort, vol. 1063. Prentice-Hall.

Kahneman, Daniel, 2003. Maps of bounded rationality: psychology for behavioral economics. The American Economic Review 93 (5), 1449–1475.

Kahneman, Daniel, Frederick, Shane, 2002. Representativeness revisited: attribute substitution in intuitive judgment. In: Heuristics and Biases: The Psychology of Intuitive Judgment. pp. 49, 81.

Kahneman, Daniel, Knetsch, Jack L., Thaler, Richard H., 1991. Anomalies: the endowment effect, loss aversion, and status quo bias. The Journal of Economic Perspectives 5 (1), 193–206.

Kahneman, Daniel, Tversky, Amos, 1979. Prospect theory: an analysis of decision under risk. Econometrica, 263–291.

Karlan, Dean, McConnell, Margaret, Mullainathan, Sendhil, Zinman, Jonathan, 2016. Getting to the top of mind: how reminders increase saving. Management Science 62 (12), 3393–3411.

Karlsson, Niklas, Loewenstein, George, Seppi, Duane, 2009. The ostrich effect: selective attention to information. Journal of Risk and Uncertainty 38 (2), 95–115.

Khaw, Mel Win, Li, Ziang, Woodford, Michael, 2017. Risk Aversion as a Perceptual Bias. NBER Working Paper No. 23294.

Khaw, Mel Win, Stevens, Luminita, Woodford, Michael, 2016. Discrete Adjustment to a Changing Environment: Experimental Evidence. NBER Working Paper No. 22978.

Knudsen, Eric I., 2007. Fundamental components of attention. Annual Review of Neuroscience 30, 57–78.

Kőszegi, Botond, Rabin, Matthew, 2009. Reference-dependent consumption plans. The American Economic Review 99 (3), 909–936.

Kőszegi, Botond, Szeidl, Adam, 2013. A model of focusing in economic choice. The Quarterly Journal of Economics 128 (1), 53–104.

Krajbich, Ian, Armel, Carrie, Rangel, Antonio, 2010. Visual fixations and the computation and comparison of value in simple choice. Nature Neuroscience 13 (10), 1292.

Krajbich, Ian, Rangel, Antonio, 2011. Multialternative drift-diffusion model predicts the relationship between visual fixations and choice in value-based decisions. Proceedings of the National Academy of Sciences 108 (33), 13852–13857.

Kurzban, Robert, Duckworth, Angela, Kable, Joseph W., Myers, Justus, 2013. An opportunity cost model of subjective effort and task performance. Behavioral and Brain Sciences 36 (6), 661–679.

Kusev, Petko, Schaik, Paulvan, Tsaneva-Atanasova, Krasimira, Juliusson, Asgeir, Chater, Nick, 2018. Adaptive anchoring model: how static and dynamic presentations of time series influence judgments and predictions. Cognitive Science 42 (1), 77–102.

Lacetera, Nicola, Pope, Devin G., Sydnor, Justin R., 2012. Heuristic thinking and limited attention in the car market. The American Economic Review 102 (5), 2206–2236.

Lahey, Joanna N., Oxley, Douglas, 2016. The power of eye tracking in economics experiments. The American Economic Review: Papers and Proceedings 106 (5), 309–313.

Laibson, David, 1997. Golden eggs and hyperbolic discounting. The Quarterly Journal of Economics 112 (2), 443–478.

Leeper, Eric M., Sims, Christopher A., Zha, Tao, 1996. What does monetary policy do? Brookings Papers on Economic Activity 27 (2), 1–78.

Liebman, Jeffrey B., Zeckhauser, Richard J., 2004. Schmeduling. Working Paper.

Loewenstein, George, O'Donoghue, Ted, Rabin, Matthew, 2003. Projection bias in predicting future utility. The Quarterly Journal of Economics 118 (4), 1209–1248.

Lombardi, Gaia, Fehr, Ernst, 2018. The Attentional Foundations of Framing Effects. Working Paper.

Lynch, Anthony W., 1996. Decision frequency and synchronization across agents: implications for aggregate consumption and equity return. The Journal of Finance 51 (4), 1479–1497.

Mack, Arien, Rock, Irvine, 1998. Inattentional Blindness. MIT Press.

Maćkowiak, Bartosz, Matějka, Filip, Wiederholt, Mirko, 2016. Rational Inattention: A Disciplined Behavioral Model. Working Paper.

Maćkowiak, Bartosz, Wiederholt, Mirko, 2009. Optimal sticky prices under rational inattention. The American Economic Review 99 (3), 769–803.

Maćkowiak, Bartosz, Wiederholt, Mirko, 2015. Business cycle dynamics under rational inattention. The Review of Economic Studies 82 (4), 1502–1532.

Madrian, Brigitte C., Shea, Dennis F., 2001. The power of suggestion: inertia in 401(k) participation and savings behavior. The Quarterly Journal of Economics 116 (4), 1149–1187.

Malmendier, Ulrike, Nagel, Stefan, 2011. Depression babies: do macroeconomic experiences affect risk taking? The Quarterly Journal of Economics 126 (1), 373–416.

Mankiw, N. Gregory, Reis, Ricardo, 2002. Sticky information versus sticky prices: a proposal to replace the New Keynesian Phillips curve. The Quarterly Journal of Economics 117 (4), 1295–1328.

Mankiw, N. Gregory, Reis, Ricardo, Wolfers, Justin, 2003. Disagreement about inflation expectations. NBER Macroeconomics Annual 18, 209–248.

Manski, Charles F., McFadden, Daniel (Eds.), 1981. Structural Analysis of Discrete Data with Econometric Applications. MIT Press.

Manzini, Paola, Mariotti, Marco, 2014. Stochastic choice and consideration sets. Econometrica 82 (3), 1153–1176.

Mas-Colell, Andreu, Whinston, Michael Dennis, Green, Jerry R., 1995. Microeconomic Theory. Oxford University Press, New York.

Masatlioglu, Yusufcan, Nakajima, Daisuke, Ozbay, Erkut Y., 2012. Revealed attention. The American Economic Review 102 (5), 2183–2205.

Matějka, Filip, 2016. Rationally inattentive seller: sales and discrete pricing. The Review of Economic Studies 83 (3), 1125–1155.

Matějka, Filip, McKay, Alisdair, 2015. Rational inattention to discrete choices: a new foundation for the multinomial logit model. The American Economic Review 105 (1), 272–298.

McFadden, Daniel, 2006. Free markets and fettered consumers. The American Economic Review 96 (1), 3–29.

Mercier, Hugo, Sperber, Dan, 2011. Why do humans reason? Arguments for an argumentative theory. Behavioral and Brain Sciences 34 (2), 57–74.

Miller, George A., 1956. The magical number seven, plus or minus two: some limits on our capacity for processing information. Psychological Review 63 (2), 81.

Mormann, Milica Milosavljevic, Frydman, Cary, 2016. The Role of Salience and Attention in Choice Under Risk: An Experimental Investigation. Working Paper.

Mullainathan, Sendhil, Schwartzstein, Joshua, Congdon, William J., 2012. A reduced-form approach to behavioral public finance. Annual Review of Economics 4 (1), 511–540.

Nagel, Rosemarie, 1995. Unraveling in guessing games: an experimental study. The American Economic Review 85 (5), 1313–1326.

Nobre, Anna C. (Kia), Kastner, Sabine, 2014. The Oxford Handbook of Attention, 1st edition. Oxford University Press.

O'Donoghue, Ted, Rabin, Matthew, 1999. Doing it now or later. The American Economic Review 89 (1), 103–124.

Olafsson, Arna, Pagel, Michaela, 2017. The Ostrich in Us: Selective Attention to Financial Accounts, Income, Spending, and Liquidity. NBER Working Paper No. 23945.

Pashler, Harold E., 1998. The Psychology of Attention. MIT Press.

Payne, John W., Bettman, James R., Johnson, Eric J., 1993. The Adaptive Decision Maker. Cambridge University Press.

Peng, Lin, Xiong, Wei, 2006. Investor attention, overconfidence and category learning. Journal of Financial Economics 80 (3), 563–602.

Piccione, Michele, Spiegler, Ran, 2012. Price competition under limited comparability. The Quarterly Journal of Economics 127 (1), 97–135.

Pop-Eleches, Cristian, Thirumurthy, Harsha, Habyarimana, James P., Zivin, Joshua G., Goldstein, Markus P., De Walque, Damien, Mackeen, Leslie, Haberer, Jessica, Kimaiyo, Sylvester, Sidle, John, et al., 2011. Mobile phone technologies improve adherence to antiretroviral treatment in a resource-limited setting: a randomized controlled trial of text message reminders. AIDS 25 (6), 825.

Prelec, Drazen, 1998. The probability weighting function. Econometrica 66 (3), 497–527.

Rabin, Matthew, 2013. Incorporating limited rationality into economics. Journal of Economic Literature 51 (2), 528–543.

Reis, Ricardo, 2006a. Inattentive consumers. Journal of Monetary Economics 53 (8), 1761–1800.

Reis, Ricardo, 2006b. Inattentive producers. The Review of Economic Studies 73 (3), 793–821.

Reutskaja, Elena, Nagel, Rosemarie, Camerer, Colin F., Rangel, Antonio, 2011. Search dynamics in consumer choice under time pressure: an eye-tracking study. The American Economic Review 101 (2), 900–926.

Roger, Tristan, Roger, Patrick, Schatt, Alain, 2018. Behavioral bias in number processing: evidence from analysts' expectations. Journal of Economic Behavior & Organization 149, 315–331.

Romer, Christina D., Romer, David H., 1989. Does monetary policy matter? A new test in the spirit of Friedman and Schwartz. NBER Macroeconomics Annual 4, 121–170.

Romer, Christina D., Romer, David H., 2004. A new measure of monetary shocks: derivation and implications. The American Economic Review 94 (4), 1055–1084.

Ru, Hong, Schoar, Antoinette, 2016. Do Credit Card Companies Screen for Behavioral Biases? NBER Working Paper No. 22360.

Rubinstein, Ariel, 1998. Modeling Bounded Rationality. MIT Press.

Russo, J. Edward, 1977. The value of unit price information. Journal of Marketing Research, 193–201.

Samuelson, Paul A., 1947. Foundations of Economic Analysis. Harvard University Press.

Schulte-Mecklenbeck, Michael, Johnson, Joseph G., Böckenholt, Ulf, Goldstein, Daniel G., Russo, J. Edward, Sullivan, Nicolette J., Willemsen, Martijn C., 2017. Process-tracing methods in decision making: on growing up in the 70s. Current Directions in Psychological Science 26 (5), 442–450.

Schwartzstein, Joshua, 2014. Selective attention and learning. Journal of the European Economic Association 12 (6), 1423–1452.

Shannon, Claude E., 1948. A mathematical theory of communication. The Bell System Technical Journal 27 (4), 623–656.

Shlain, Avner S., 2018. More than a Penny's Worth: Left-Digit Bias and Firm Pricing. Working Paper.

Shue, Kelly, Townsend, Richard, 2018. Can the Market Multiply and Divide? Non-Proportional Thinking in Financial Markets. Working Paper.

Sicherman, Nachum, Loewenstein, George, Seppi, Duane J., Utkus, Stephen P., 2016. Financial attention. The Review of Financial Studies 29 (4), 863–897.

Simon, Herbert A., 1955. A behavioral model of rational choice. The Quarterly Journal of Economics 69 (1), 99–118.

Simons, Daniel J., Chabris, Christopher F., 1999. Gorillas in our midst: sustained inattentional blindness for dynamic events. Perception 28 (9), 1059–1074.

Sims, Christopher A., 1998. Stickiness. Carnegie–Rochester Conference Series on Public Policy 49 (1), 317–356.

Sims, Christopher A., 2003. Implications of rational inattention. Journal of Monetary Economics 50 (3), 665–690.

Sonnemann, Ulrich, Camerer, Colin F., Fox, Craig R., Langer, Thomas, 2013. How psychological framing affects economic market prices in the lab and field. Proceedings of the National Academy of Sciences 110 (29), 11779–11784.

Spiegler, Ran, 2011. Bounded Rationality and Industrial Organization. Oxford University Press.

Stahl, Dale O., Wilson, Paul W., 1995. On players' models of other players: theory and experimental evidence. Games and Economic Behavior 10 (1), 218–254.

Stango, Victor, Zinman, Jonathan, 2009. Exponential growth bias and household finance. The Journal of Finance 64 (6), 2807–2849.

Stanovich, Keith E., 1999. Who Is Rational?: Studies of Individual Differences in Reasoning. Psychology Press.

Steiner, Jakub, Stewart, Colin, 2016. Perceiving prospects properly. The American Economic Review 106 (7), 1601–1631.

Steiner, Jakub, Stewart, Colin, Matějka, Filip, 2017. Rational inattention dynamics: inertia and delay in decision-making. Econometrica 85 (2), 521–553.

Stevenson, Betsey, Wolfers, Justin, 2006. Bargaining in the shadow of the law: divorce laws and family distress. The Quarterly Journal of Economics 121 (1), 267–288.

Stigler, George J., 1961. The economics of information. Journal of Political Economy 69 (3), 213–225.

Taubinsky, Dmitry, Rees-Jones, Alex, 2018. Attention variation and welfare: theory and evidence from a tax salience experiment. The Review of Economic Studies 85 (4).

Taylor, John B., 1980. Aggregate dynamics and staggered contracts. Journal of Political Economy 88 (1), 1–23.

Thaler, Richard H., Shefrin, Hersh M., 1981. An economic theory of self-control. Journal of Political Economy 89 (2), 392–406.

Thaler, Richard H., Sunstein, Cass R., 2008. Nudge. Yale University Press.

Tibshirani, Robert, 1996. Regression shrinkage and selection via the lasso. Journal of the Royal Statistical Society, Series B, Methodological, 267–288.

Tirole, Jean, 2009. Cognition and incomplete contracts. The American Economic Review 99 (1), 265–294.

Treisman, Anne M., Gelade, Garry, 1980. A feature-integration theory of attention. Cognitive Psychology 12 (1), 97–136.

Tversky, Amos, Kahneman, Daniel, 1974. Judgment under uncertainty: heuristics and biases. Science 185, 1124–1130.

Van Nieuwerburgh, Stijn, Veldkamp, Laura, 2010. Information acquisition and under-diversification. The Review of Economic Studies 77 (2), 779–805.

Varian, Hal R., 1992. Microeconomic Analysis. W.W. Norton.

Veldkamp, Laura L., 2011. Information Choice in Macroeconomics and Finance. Princeton University Press.

Verrecchia, Robert E., 1982. Information acquisition in a noisy rational expectations economy. Econometrica 50 (6), 1415–1430.

Wang, Joseph T., Spezio, Michael, Camerer, Colin F., 2010. Pinocchio's pupil: using eyetracking and pupil dilation to understand truth telling and deception in sender–receiver games. The American Economic Review 100 (3), 984–1007.

Woodford, Michael, 2013. Macroeconomic analysis without the rational expectations hypothesis. Annual Reviews of Economics 5, 303–346.

Zhang, Hang, Maloney, Laurence T., 2012. Ubiquitous log odds: a common representation of probability and frequency distortion in perception, action, and cognition. Frontiers in Neuroscience 6.

Behavioral development economics[*]

5

Michael Kremer[a,c,*], Gautam Rao[a,c], Frank Schilbach[b,c]

[a]*Harvard University, Cambridge, MA, United States of America*
[b]*MIT, Cambridge, MA, United States of America*
[c]*National Bureau of Economic Research, Cambridge, MA, United States of America*
Corresponding author: e-mail address: mkremer@fas.harvard.edu

Contents

[*] We thank the editors—Douglas Bernheim, David Laibson, and especially Stefano DellaVigna—for their detailed comments and helpful suggestions, and their patience and sophistication in the face of our naïve present focus. We are grateful to Pedro Bessone, Kevin Carney, Joshua Dean, Emily Gallagher, Rachel Glennerster, Tomoko Harigaya, Karla Hoff, Matt Lowe, Maddie McKelway, David McKenzie, Matthew Ridley, Mattie Toma, Pierre-Luc Vautrey, and Jack Willis for thoughtful feedback and comments on a draft version. Audiences at the NBER Development Economics workshop, SITE and ESA conference provided helpful comments on early versions of this chapter. We thank Fanelesibonge Mashwama, Stephen Nyarko, and especially Xinyue Lin for excellent research assistance. Michael Kremer discloses that he is a board member of Precision Agriculture for Development (PAD). PAD is a non-profit organization and Kremer receives no financial compensation from PAD.

Handbook of Behavioral Economics, Volume 2
ISSN 2352-2399, https://doi.org/10.1016/bs.hesbe.2018.12.002

1 Introduction

Modern development economics was born in part as a reaction against a widespread view among scholars that peasants in poor societies were bound by tradition and could not be subject to the same type of economic analysis as people in modern industrialized societies. From the work of Schultz (1964) through the early 1990s, most development economists instead took it as axiomatic that people in developing countries were "poor but efficient".

The field of development economics has been transformed since the 1990s in part by the growth in experiments. Most of these have focused either on issues of importance to development economics, such as the rate of return to capital for small enterprises, or policy issues, such as finding ways to increase use of fertilizer to increase agricultural production in Africa. Until recently, only a few were designed to test behavioral theories or to identify the parameters of behavioral models. Yet, in the past decade, development economics has increasingly come to incorporate theories and ideas from behavioral economics into the study of questions in development, giving birth to the subfield of *behavioral development economics.*

Our definition of "behavioral" economics hews closely to those in other chapters in this handbook. We view behavioral economics as consisting of systematic deviations from the standard economic model in terms of preferences, beliefs, and decision-making. These deviations are motivated by insights from psychology but are typically captured using economic models (Rabin, 1998; DellaVigna, 2009). In parts of this chapter, we extend this definition to include systematic deviations by firms from profit-maximization, even if the underlying psychology is not yet well understood.

We discuss several areas in which concepts from behavioral economics have proved useful in shedding light on issues in development economics. We focus on three types of non-standard preferences—present bias, reference-dependent preferences (loss aversion), and social preferences—and three key areas of non-standard beliefs—naïveté about present bias, projection bias and deviations from Bayesian learning. We touch upon other behavioral concepts related to non-standard decision-making, including limited attention and memory, mental accounting, and default effects. We also discuss the literature on the psychology of poverty, which argues that the conditions of living in poverty themselves have a causal effect on cognitive function and economic behavior.

We begin by examining a key puzzle in development economics. The Euler equation derived from intertemporal choice models directly relates consumption growth to rates of return on available investment opportunities. Calibrated versions of this equation using standard preference parameter values, rational expectations, and the high rates of return to investments identified in recent studies in developing countries predict high consumption growth of over forty percent annually. Observed consumption growth is much lower. We argue that the puzzle cannot be explained by credit constraints, non-concave production functions, or stochastic production.

Present bias can play an important role in resolving this puzzle, because it can explain impatient short-run behavior while maintaining realistic predictions about longer-run choices. The modified Euler equation implied by present-biased preferences can generate a significantly lower effective discount factor and thus substantially reduce the implied rate of consumption growth.

Under-investment in preventive health is a particularly striking and widely documented example of individuals' failure to take advantage of high-return investment opportunities. We argue that this underinvestment in preventive, as opposed to curative, health care is difficult to explain in a purely rational model. For instance, positing large disutility costs from preventive health activities would not be enough to explain the low levels of health investments, as this explanation is at odds with the high sensitivity of demand for preventive health to small differences in price or convenience.

We use the case of health to explore a more general issue: the role of **misprediction of future preferences** in shaping current mis-optimization and choices. A general insight from behavioral economics is that the distortions arising from non-standard preferences (such as present bias or loss aversion) can be greatly magnified by biased beliefs about these preferences. In the case of present bias, realistic parameter values of present bias alone can explain some failures to invest in high-return investments. However, explaining failures to invest in very high return investments (in preventive health or elsewhere) typically requires another ingredient: at least partial **naïveté regarding future present bias**.

A (partially) naïve individual underestimates the degree of their future present bias. Such naïveté can magnify the welfare losses associated with present bias since individuals may delay very high return investments with small short-run utility costs because they incorrectly anticipate making these investments later. Fully naïve individuals will not take advantage of commitment devices to overcome their self-control problems, while partially naïve individuals will mis-predict whether a given commitment device is likely to work for them. Naïveté and uncertainty in the environment (which increases the value of flexibility) are likely to drive down demand for commitment and may explain why commitment devices are not more widespread.

People in developing countries are often highly exposed to risk, enjoy little social insurance from governments, and live close to subsistence, giving them little margin of adjustment. Many also have limited scope for borrowing. Whereas standard theory suggests that risk-averse households without access to borrowing should build up buffer stocks to insulate themselves from risk, present-biased consumers will have difficulty saving and maintaining liquid assets and hence will wind up liquidity constrained. This will leave them exposed to shocks and unable to self-insure.

A standard finding in development economics is that demand for even actuarially-fair weather insurance or health insurance is surprisingly low. Present bias, by generating liquidity constraints, may also reduce demand for standard insurance contracts which require up-front payment of premia.

Another implication of these endogenous liquidity constraints is that it will be difficult for present-biased agents to respond to surprise opportunities for investment without accompanying provisions for credit. This issue makes it difficult to interpret some standard tests for willingness to pay that are common in the health and environmental literatures.

Loss aversion may help explain why many apparently high expected return investments in developing countries remain unexploited. Just as present bias yields much larger distortions when combined with naïveté, loss aversion can have much more negative effects on investment when combined with narrow bracketing, the tendency to consider decisions in isolation from each other. Loss aversion may generate stickiness of assets, which arguably better matches some of the dynamics of assets than many poverty-trap models based on increasing returns. In contrast, loss aversion has ambiguous theoretical effects on the demand for insurance.

Individuals may mis-predict their future preferences in various ways. As discussed above, naïveté may greatly exacerbate the consequences of present bias. **Projection bias**, the tendency to overestimate the degree to which one's future tastes will resemble one's current tastes, may reduce investment in preventive health and insurance, to the extent that people find it difficult to imagine that they may become sick in the future and the extent to which they will need resources if they or their family might be hit by a health shock.

Beyond mis-predicting future preferences, individuals may hold **non-standard beliefs**, which might interfere with many important decisions, including technology adoption, health investments, or insurance and savings decisions.

Individuals may exhibit a **failure to correctly interpret information** for various reasons, among them redundancy neglect, belief in the law or small numbers, and selection neglect. For instance, under redundancy neglect, people may overweight information from others because they do not consider the possibility that multiple apparently independent signals may all ultimately stem from a common source. Theory suggests the possibility of potentially dramatic equilibrium effects on social learning, in which people become confident in false beliefs about the efficacy of technologies or health investments, and society becomes locked in to an incorrect choice.

Failures to seek or share valuable information can also cause biased beliefs to persist in large shares of the population. On the supply side of information, envy or pride may hinder people from sharing valuable information with others. On the demand side, fear of shame or stigma could inhibit learning by preventing individuals from asking questions that might make them look ignorant or stupid. **Limited attention and memory** may also distort learning and thus interfere with technology adoption. Beyond interfering with learning, these factors could also cause underinvestment in preventive health or savings choices.

Finally, beliefs might also be biased due to **motivated reasoning**. Individuals may derive utility from thinking of themselves highly (ego utility) or from foreseeing a bright future for themselves (anticipatory utility), which may distort decisions to acquire valuable information as well as the processing of received information. Such biased beliefs could be particularly important for choices involving protection of health or other disaster risks.

In addition to non-standard preferences and beliefs, we consider **non-standard decision-making**, i.e. failures to optimize, given preferences and beliefs. We consider non-standard decision-making in the context of savings choices, including mental accounting, susceptibility to default effects, and limited attention and memory. While these topics have received less attention in recent development economics research, they provide opportunities for relatively minor policy and product design choices to have major impacts on individuals. For instance, labeling savings accounts as "health savings", setting default choices to desired options, or providing reminders to adhere to medication can powerfully impact behavior at minimal costs.

Most of this review, like much of the behavioral development economics literature, treats **behavioral distortions as universal features of human behavior**, and examines the ways in which behavioral biases interact with features of developing societies or play out differently given the differing circumstances and institutions of the developing world. The same psychological forces often seem to be at play in developed and developing countries. For instance, present bias has been shown to explain how individuals allocate work over time in both the United States and in India (e.g. Augenblick et al., 2015 and Kaur et al., 2015); the endowment effect exists both in labs in college students in Canada and in the field in dairy-farmers in Kenya (e.g. Knetsch, 1989 and Carney et al., 2018).

Similarly, default effects powerfully affect savings choices in the US and Afghanistan (Madrian and Shea, 2001; Blumenstock et al., 2018), while DellaVigna and Pope (2018) show that the treatment effects on worker effort of ten different behavioral treatments, leveraging social preferences, time preferences, probability-weighting, crowd-out and other ideas from psychology, are very similar in Indian and US samples of online workers.

However, differences in institutions and markets imply that the same behavioral factors that are at play in developing and developed countries have different implications for behaviors. For example, present bias may impact preventive health investments less severely in a society in which most people receive clean water through a municipally managed system than in a society in which people need to make active choices to boil water or treat it with purchased supplies of dilute chlorine solution. Similarly, in the section on "behavioral labor", we argue that behavioral factors such as present bias and reference dependence may matter more for labor supply and work-effort decisions in developing countries, where labor markets are characterized by high levels of self-employment and informality. Self-employment and informality mean that workers in developing countries often do not face the commitment and monitoring provided by the formal firms common in rich countries.

To take another example of how the features of institutions and markets interact with behavioral factors, note that developing countries typically have much smaller firms than rich countries, arguably because large firms are open to predation, and that those large firms which do exist often enjoy considerable market power. This implies that selection pressures that might drive out managers or firms that systematically fail to maximize profits might be weaker in poor countries. Hence, one should expect more "**behavioral firms**" in poor countries. While in rich societies the consequence of wide-spread present bias and naiveté may be some workers failing to take advantage of employer match programs for retirement savings, in poor countries, this may lead to unexploited high-return investment opportunities for a wide range of firms.

In the final sections of the chapter, we go beyond considering such "universal" psychology to discuss two more speculative literatures which raise the possibility that behavioral factors themselves may operate differently across societies or levels of income. Many forms of **social preferences** may be fairly universal. Thus, for example, work on fairness norms in developing countries suggests that wages may be constrained by fairness norms even independent of some of the institutions, such as unions, that are thought to play a major role in developed societies, suggesting more similarity across societies than one might have expected. However, even if social preferences are based on universal psychological building blocks, the very fact that they are social creates more scope for them to be shaped by the cultural environment. To take a trivial example, humans may be susceptible to creating in groups and out groups, but who is in what group will be defined by culture.

In fact, there might be systematic differences between developed and developing societies in social preferences and attitudes such as trust, reciprocity, and the ability to cooperate. Indeed, some go so far as to argue that the cultural ability to cooperate outside of small kin-based groups is rare and key to development. In this view, the scarcity of large firms in developing societies, and hence the potential role for behavioral factors in firm behavior, is not driven simply by policy mistakes such as state predation on large firms, but rather reflects fundamental cultural features of societies that make cooperation difficult outside of the extended family. Similar factors may interfere with state capacity. We discuss the evidence for differences in social preferences across societies, and the extent to which these differences may be thought of as causes or consequences of development, and how they may be shaped by policy.

Finally, we discuss the nascent literature on the **psychology of poverty**, which investigates whether poverty itself affects cognitive function and economic decision-making in meaningful ways. The main argument of this literature is that the conditions associated with poverty, such as the constant worries about money, greater exposure to factors such as pain, sleep deprivation, noise and malnourishment, and less access to mental health care, may influence cognitive function (largely negatively). Worse cognitive function may in turn affect decision-making and productivity in ways that generate a psychological poverty trap. While the literature provides some evidence of effects on cognitive function, studies evaluating effects on economic outcomes and behaviors remain scarce.

This chapter complements several **existing review articles** on behavioral development economics. An accessible and thorough review of empirical research in behavioral development economics is provided in World Bank (2015). While that report is aimed at policy makers, this chapter is written for researchers and graduate students, and is thus somewhat more technical. Schilbach et al. (2016) and Dean et al. (2018) cover in detail the relationship between poverty and cognitive function, which we touch on in Section 10. Datta and Mullainathan (2014) describe principles of behaviorally-informed design of development policy. Finally, Demeritt and Hoff (2018) provide a history of the rise of behavioral development economics. While our chapter concentrates on "universal" behavioral models such as present bias, reference-dependence and limited attention, Demeritt and Hoff point to a different strand of behavioral development economics, which emphasizes the importance of the "cultural mental models" – categories, concepts, identities and worldviews – that individuals use to interpret situations and make decisions.

Before proceeding, we discuss a few **caveats and critiques of behavioral development economics.** First, just as behavioral economics seeks to build on and improve upon existing neoclassical models, behavioral development economics seeks to augment existing theories of development economics by capturing systematic and relevant aspects of human behavior, often using parsimonious extensions of existing models (Rabin, 1998).

Second, behavioral development economics does not deny the importance of institutions or economic policy in economic development. Instead, it takes local economic environments seriously, and studies how universal behavioral factors play out in the context of the choices, markets and institutions common in developing countries. Rather than diverting attention from the study of important structural issues, behavioral development may sometimes help better identify and understand these issues and potential reforms.

Third, a critique of behavioral development is that such work is too quick to abandon the possibility that apparently irrational actions by people may reflect real economic incentives and constraints. For example, Rosenzweig and Udry (2014) argue that it is difficult to generalize about the effectiveness of agricultural inputs even from several seasons, because agricultural production is highly stochastic and returns to inputs may vary across seasons. This view implies that one should not too quickly jump to the conclusion that certain behaviors (such as not using more fertilizer) are irrational. We see merit in this view. One way that behavioral economists can address this critique is by designing experiments to more precisely identify specific behavioral mechanisms and to test for those, rather than to simply reject a single rational model and label any residual as "behavioral". We believe that the best work in behavioral development economics takes precisely such an approach. The solution to the problem of bad behavioral-development research is more careful and rigorous behavioral-development research.

Fourth, some see behavioral development economics as blaming the poor for their poverty. In fact, behavioral development is largely concerned with universal psychological factors and does not generally attribute poverty to having greater behavioral biases. Moreover, we do not view having behavioral biases as in any way deserving blame, since there is no reason whatsoever to believe that they are freely chosen.

Fifth, behavioral economics is often seen as opening the door to paternalistic policies and restrictions on individual choice. While we believe that understanding the role of behavioral factors in a scientific way does not automatically translate into any policy or political implications, we also argue that misunderstanding human behavior can also lead to bad policy outcomes.

Policymakers are sometimes enthusiastic about behavioral economics due to the perception that it promises inexpensive but effective interventions, and want to apply it to policy right away. However, behavioral economics should arguably make policy makers more cautious for two reasons. One is the subtlety of thinking about **welfare** in a behavioral world, a topic which we do not cover, and for which we refer readers to the chapter by Bernheim and Taubinsky (2018) in this handbook. In addition to philosophical issues involved in conducting welfare analysis with behavioral agents, in the case of behavioral development, behavioral biases will often interact with multiple market failures, potentially leading to second-best issues and making welfare analysis more challenging. Another reason for humility in policymaking is precisely because behavioral economics demonstrates that small details can matter for people's choices. Consequently, unintended consequences may be more likely in a world with behavioral agents.

Finally, while we have argued that many behavioral phenomena are relevant for development economics, it is worth noting that other ideas, which have been found to be important in laboratory experiments, and in some cases in some real-world developed-country contexts, have not turned out to play an important role in popular applications in development. Research provides little support for some views widely espoused by development practitioners and NGOs regarding the alleged coun-terproductive behavioral effects of more favorable financial treatment of poor people. Rather, the growth of scientific behavioral development economics research has led to the formal testing and rejection of several of these hypotheses, and in some cases, this has arguably influenced policy debates.

For example, some have conjectured that reducing the cost of preventive health products such as mosquito nets or distributing them for free would lead people to value them less and use them less. Rigorous testing by Cohen and Dupas (2010) and Ashraf et al. (2010) yields no support for this conjecture. Broadly speaking, this evidence has moved the policy debate towards free distribution of preventive health goods such as mosquito nets. Similarly, while many practitioners have voiced concern that financial compensation for community health workers could crowd out intrinsic motivation or lead to selection of less motivated staff, and indeed in some labora-tory experiments there is evidence of a tradeoff, most real-world experiments provide little evidence that extrinsic financial incentives crowd out intrinsic incentives mean-ingfully, and indeed provide evidence that recruiting community health workers in ways that emphasize career benefits leads to better selection. To take a final example, many development practitioners were concerned that unconditional cash transfers to the poor would be largely dissipated on alcohol and cigarettes, but evidence from Haushofer and Shapiro (2016) does not support this view.

Roadmap. The remainder of this chapter is organized according to topics in devel-opment economics, rather than by behavioral biases. Section 2 examines the puzzle of high rates of return without rapid growth. Section 3 examines behavioral factors that may contribute to low investment in preventive health. Sections 4 and 5 discuss how non-standard preferences, beliefs and decision-making can affect savings be-havior and demand for insurance. Section 6 investigates how technology adoption decisions may be affected by limited attention and present bias, as well as by failures in learning.

Section 7 discusses behavioral labor economics in developing economies. We first consider how some characteristics of labor markets in developing countries may potentially exacerbate behavioral biases. We then discuss the labor supply and worker productivity, as well as the role of fairness norms in wage-setting, the selection of workers, and female labor-force participation. Section 8 discusses behavioral firms, arguing that firms in developing countries may be more subject to behavioral biases, since limits on the span of control in developing societies weaken the opportunities for market forces to eliminate behavioral firms, and imply that a greater proportion of the population in developing countries acts as managers or owners of firms.

Sections 9 and 10 discuss culture, social preferences, and the psychology of poverty. We first briefly review the intellectual history of this field and then cover questions regarding the existence of differences in social preferences across soci-eties, whether these preferences matter for development, and the potential to change these attitudes through social contact across groups, or other deliberate policies. We then review the recent literature on the psychology of poverty, including the effects of scarcity on cognitive function and economic behaviors, the potential role of other deprivations beyond lack of money, and mental health. Finally, we explore question around aspirations, hope, and religiosity.

---

2 High rates of return without rapid growth

A recent body of research in development economics finds that, although there is considerable heterogeneity, many potential investments in developing countries yield very high returns (Banerjee and Duflo, 2005).

Among the direct estimates, Banerjee and Duflo (2014) exploit exogenous policy-variation over time and estimate that the returns to capital in certain Indian firms must be at least 105%. De Mel et al. (2008) use randomized grants to generate shocks to capital stock for a set of Sri Lankan microenterprises and find the average real return to capital in these enterprises is 55% to 63% per year. Kremer et al. (2013) use administrative data on whether firms purchased enough to take advantage of quantity discounts from wholesalers and estimate a lower bound on rates of return for the median shop of well over 100 percent per year. Duflo et al. (2008) estimate an annual rate of return of about 70 percent for the most profitable quantity of fertilizer in their study.

High rates of return are also evidenced by high interest rates people are willing to pay to borrow (Aleem, 1990; Fafchamps, 2000). Individuals in developing countries often borrow at annual interest rates upwards of 70%. For example, many small-scale fruit vendors in Chennai borrow at a daily interest rate of 5% (Karlan et al., 2018). The authors payed off high-interest moneylender debt for a randomly selected subset of vendors. Most borrowers returned to debt as soon as six weeks after the payoff of their original debt obligations. Moreover, treatment individuals were again borrowing at the same rate as control households one to two years after intervention.

In this section, we demonstrate that such high rates of return are difficult to reconcile with the standard neoclassical model under reasonable parameter assumptions, even when considering that income and returns may be stochastic, people are risk averse, that individuals may face "taxes" either from the state or from family/social pressure, and that production functions are sometimes non-concave. We will then consider whether various behavioral factors can help solve this puzzle, focusing on present bias and loss aversion as potential explanations.

2.1 The Euler equation puzzle

In a standard dynamic optimization model, the Euler equation implies that high returns to capital predict rapid rates of consumption growth, even in the absence of any capital market. To see the underlying logic, consider first a simple deterministic discrete-time intertemporal consumption model, in which infinitely-lived households maximize their lifetime utility. Assume households solve the following optimization problem: $\max_{\{C_t\}} \sum_{t=0}^{\infty} \delta^t u(C_t)$, where $0 < \delta < 1$ is the annual exponential discount factor; C_t is the household's consumption in period t; $u(C_t)$ measures the utility derived from consuming C_t in period t. $u(C)$ is increasing and concave and satisfies the usual Inada conditions: $u'(C) > 0$ and $u''(C) < 0$, $\lim_{c \to 0} u'(C) = \infty$ and $\lim_{c \to \infty} u'(C) = 0$.

The budget constraint of the household is $x_{t+1} = f'(K_t)(x_t - C_t)$, where x_t is household assets ("cash on hand") in period t, with x_0 given; $f(K)$ is the production function denoting the value of the output in the next period including any remaining value of the capital; $f'(K)$ is the gross rate of return to capital; $f(K)$ satisfies $f'(K) > 0$ and $f''(K) < 0$, $\lim_{K \to 0} f'(K) = \infty$, $\lim_{K \to \infty} f'(K) = 1$.

Solving for the optimal consumption path gives the discrete-time Euler equation:

$$u'(C_t) = f'(K_t)\delta u'(C_{t+1}) \tag{1}$$

Assume a constant-elasticity-of-substitution (CES) utility, $u(C) = \frac{C^{1-\sigma}}{1-\sigma}$ if $\sigma \neq 1$; $u(C) = \log(C)$ if $\sigma = 1$.[1] Then, the Euler equation implies that the growth rate of consumption is $(\delta f'(K_t))^{\frac{1}{\sigma}} - 1$. With standard values for discount rates and the intertemporal elasticity of substitution, it follows from that high returns to capital imply high consumption growth.

For example, suppose that the gross rate of return on capital, $f'(K) = 150\%$ (well within the range of estimated returns to capital in developing-country settings) and $\delta = 0.96$. Then, with log utility ($\sigma = 1$ and elasticity of intertemporal substitution equal to one), the implied growth rate of consumption is $\frac{\dot{C}}{C} = 44\%$. No country grows at anything like this rate. One does not observe sustained consumption growth rates of this magnitude even for the subset of the population that appears to have access to returns of this magnitude.

Alternatively, using a ballpark estimate from the macro literature for the elasticity of intertemporal substitution of 0.5 (and therefore $\sigma = 2$), the implied consumption growth is $\frac{\dot{C}}{C} = 20\%$ per year.[2] This number implies a 38-fold increase in consumption in 20 years, far higher than actual growth rates of consumption.[3] Working in reverse, a consumption growth rate of 5% implies that $f'(K) = 115\%$, i.e. net rates of return of 15%, which is much lower than the rates observed in many contexts.

The finding that many people in developing countries face high rates of return yet do not have dramatic growth in consumption thus poses a puzzle in the framework of the neoclassical model. Some would try to resolve this puzzle by arguing that

---

[1] Under CES utility, the elasticity of intertemporal substitution is equal to $\frac{1}{\sigma}$.

[2] A value of 0.5 is used in standard calibrations in macro studies (e.g., Hall, 2009, 2016). See Havránek (2015) for a review.

[3] Suppose individuals instead had a Stone-Geary utility function incorporating subsistence levels of consumption. Then, they would become unwilling to intertemporally substitute at very low levels of income. However, being close to such subsistence constraints does not seem consistent with the observed high-frequency variation in consumption even among the poor (Collins et al., 2009) and the high share of income spent on goods which are not necessities, such as low-calorie foods, alcohol, and cigarettes (Banerjee and Duflo, 2007). Moreover, high rates of return are observed not just for the ultra-poor, but also for some people who are not near that absolute consumption floor, for example, shopkeepers in Sri Lanka or Kenya.

households face a high implicit tax on the return on capital, for example, due to predation by corrupt government officials, or due to redistributive pressures from extended family members.

Allowing for realistic levels of such distortions, it is difficult to reconcile the data with standard calibrated values for an exponential discount rate. For instance, Jakiela and Ozier (2015) show with a lab-in-the-field experiment that women (but not men) face a "kin tax" of 4% when making an observable investment, which would not dramatically change the above calibration. Moreover, their experiment also includes men for whom the authors do not find such kin taxes. Further, marginally increasing inventories for a shopkeeper or marginally increasing fertilizer use by a farmer would not easily be observable either by the state or by kin outside the nuclear family, and as such would not be subject to such a tax. Finally, "taxes" by kin or other social groups are not pure taxes but would likely generate either some reciprocal obligations from those receiving the transfers or some utility benefits to the household making the transfers. It thus seems difficult to believe that such taxes would fully resolve the puzzle.[4]

It is worth noting that the same households who hold high-interest debt often hold low-return assets. For instance, Collins et al. (2009) report that every household they survey has both low-interest savings and high-interest debt at the same time. Anagol et al. (2017) estimate that cows and buffaloes earn large negative returns in India, and yet are owned by 45% of rural households. Similarly, the shopkeepers in Kremer et al. (2013) who leave unexploited inventory-investment returns of over 100% per year simultaneously deposit money in savings accounts returning a few percentage points. As discussed below, one interpretation might be that people hold these low return assets to diversify risk, while another is that they are seeking to manage liquidity.

Poverty traps. Could a non-concave production function help square such high rates of return with the lack of dramatic growth in consumption? Under the usual concave production function, poor households will have higher returns to investment, will accumulate wealth, and thus converge to richer households. With an S-shaped production function that is convex for low levels of capital and then concave at higher levels, there may instead be multiple steady states. Which of these steady states a household converges to may depend on its initial capital stock, and the long-run distribution of wealth may depend on the initial distribution. Such a model can feature poverty traps: households that fall below a certain threshold may be stuck at low levels of returns and be unable to accumulate wealth. In general, there is limited ev-

---

[4] A given percentage informal "tax" leveled by extended family could potentially be more distortionary if it was levied on capital itself rather than simply on capital income, especially if they were particularly high for certain types of investment, for example, on more observable capital goods, but in general there is no reason to assume that informal taxation systems would be more distortionary than formal taxation systems used in developed countries, and in any case, even a 4% tax on capital would not be a big deterrent if gross returns were on the order of 150%.

idence that such poverty traps are widespread, but they are likely to be present in at least some situations (Kraay and McKenzie, 2014; Bandiera et al., 2017).[5]

Yet even in models with poverty traps and non-concave production functions, the observed initial conditions still need to be consistent with the model. An S-shaped production function allows for a steady state with a low rate of return (at either low or high wealth), but it nevertheless also implies that individuals who face a high marginal rate of return to investment should exhibit fast consumption growth. Thus, even under a model with a non-concave production function, one would not observe households with high marginal returns and low growth. Even the presence of assets with increasing returns would not explain high returns to divisible fertilizer investments for farmers or inventory for shopkeepers or fruit sellers.

Lumpy investments with high rates of return can remain unexploited in the presence of credit constraints. Thus, households might not be able to purchase an asset, like a cow, even if it generated a high return. However, even lumpy investments with credit constraints are not a sufficient condition for unexploited high returns. For example, consider a household that has a discount factor of 0.96, a non-lumpy liquid investment opportunity offering a 10% return and a lumpy investment opportunity yielding a 50% rate of return on a discrete investment. The households would initially save in the liquid non-lumpy investment and then reallocate assets to the lumpy investment once a sufficient amount was accumulated. Even with a zero rate of return on the non-lumpy investment, the household would save up for the lumpy investment unless it required a very large investment.

Moreover, even if certain physical assets are lumpy, the financial returns to investment could potentially be smoothed with appropriate financial products, informal institutions, or government programs. Lumpy investments could be exploited using mechanisms such as ROSCAs, borrowing and lending contracts, or government programs that would either simply transfer resources to individuals stuck in poverty traps or would lend them resources and then use the power of the state to collect repayments. Lotteries and ROSCAs are indeed very popular, suggesting that there are ways to address potential non-concavities in the production function, but they do not seem to enable the rates of consumption growth one would expect with a gross rate of return to capital of 150% or more.

In any case, one should not observe high returns to non-lumpy investments without rapid consumption growth. Yet, research has documented high returns to fertilizer (Duflo et al., 2008) and to small increases in working capital for small firms (Beaman et al., 2014; Kremer et al., 2013). Moreover, extending credit to poor households does not result in transformative effects (Banerjee et al., 2015a; Meager, 2019). Credit constraints cannot in themselves explain high rates of return.

---

[5] One rarely observes multi-modal distributions of income; there is little evidence that temporary positive shocks lead to sustained increases in income over time; and unconditional transfers such as Give Directly and the Georgia land lottery did not provide evidence of poverty traps (Haushofer and Shapiro, 2016; Bleakley and Ferrie, 2016).

Stochastic returns and risk aversion. If returns are stochastic, risk aversion might deter individuals from making investments, even if expected returns exceed the discount rate. Can we explain the Euler equation puzzle with stochastic income and risk aversion? Suppose, for example, income in period t is:

$$Y_{it} = Y_0 + \varepsilon_t + \sum_{i=1}^{n} \mu_{it} f_i(K_{it}) \tag{2}$$

where there are n assets or capital goods and capital goods i has stochastic return μ_{it} in period t with an arbitrary pattern of correlation. In this setting, the stochastic Euler equation is:

$$u'(C_t) = \delta E_t \left[\mu_{it} f_i'(K_{it}) u'(C_{t+1}) \right], \quad i = 1, 2, \ldots, n \tag{3}$$

Given an initial capital stock, risk aversion will decrease investment in assets that co-vary positively with consumption and increase investment in assets that co-vary negatively with consumption. In this framework, it will be optimal for risk-averse households to build a buffer stock of low-risk savings that they can draw upon when they experience negative shocks (Deaton, 1991; Carroll, 1997). In the ergodic distribution, few people will have a low buffer stock. Keeping a high buffer stock will allow most people to smooth consumption, so that consumption will be largely insensitive to high-frequency income shocks or predictable changes in income. It follows, for example, that most market traders in the ergodic distribution should be willing to invest in working capital and most farmers should be willing to invest in fertilizer.

All but those who recently experienced a string of negative shocks would have a sufficient buffer stock of relatively safe assets to allow them to invest in assets like fertilizer. Even if the returns to fertilizer investment in a season are highly correlated with harvest during that season, for example, because they depend on rainfall during the season, they should only be modestly correlated with lifetime income and thus consumption. Therefore, risk aversion should only modestly reduce investment, and cannot fully explain the Euler equation puzzle.

In fact, however, liquid buffer stocks are typically modest (Deaton, 1989). While consumption is smoother than income, it does still co-vary substantially with income shocks (Townsend, 1995; Collins et al., 2009). For instance, Jalan and Ravallion (1999) estimate that the pass-through of income shocks to consumption is 40% among the poorest decile of households in rural China. Kazianga and Udry (2006), studying a period of severe drought in Burkina Faso, find little evidence of consumption smoothing.

Moreover, consumption varies not just with shocks to income, but also with predictable variation in income, contrary to models with patient consumers. Both food and non-food consumption have been documented to vary seasonally with the harvest cycle: consumption is lower before harvest in the lean season, and higher after harvest, when farmers are cash rich (Mani et al., 2013; Kaminski et al., 2014; Basu and Wong, 2015). While some of this variation can be explained by seasonal price fluctuations and lack of storage opportunities, consumption varies across the pay cycle also among the poor in rich countries, where markets are thick and food prices do not show similar fluctuations. For instance, Shapiro (2005) shows that caloric intake declines by 10–15% over the course of a month after delivery of food stamps. Stephens (2003) similarly shows that social security recipients in the United States fail to smooth consumption between checks.

A related finding is that investment decisions of farmers are affected by the timing of predictable variation in prices and expenditures. For instance, Burke et al. (2018) show that farmers fail to exploit arbitrage opportunities created by seasonal price variation in local grain markets. That is, they sell when prices are low, and buy for personal consumption when prices are high in the lean season. Providing access to credit reduces this failure to arbitrage and generates returns on investment of 29%. The question, however, is why farmers are not able to build up liquid buffer stocks to exploit this investment opportunity themselves, even in the absence of credit markets.

One could further enrich the model, for example, by allowing for illiquid investments. Households might indeed be more reluctant to invest in fertilizer or inventories if they might be subject to income shocks and thus require liquidity before the payoff on those investments was realized. However, the same basic approach of building up a buffer stock, for example, of cash or grain or other relatively liquid assets such as jewelry or livestock that could be sold in bad times could help address this problem.

In summary, we have argued that the high rates of return without rapid consumption growth, evident in many parts of the developing world, pose a puzzle that cannot be explained by the standard neoclassical model, non-concave production functions or risk aversion. We now discuss theories from behavioral economics that may shed light on this puzzle.

2.2 Present bias

Modest rates of consumption growth can be reconciled with high rates of return to capital if discount rates are high. For example, if the discount rate is approximately the same magnitude as the net return to capital, then one would not expect much consumption growth. High constant discount rates on the order of 50% per year, however, would generate implausible predictions for individuals' willingness to make long-run investments: people would not give up one dollar today for one billion dollars in 30 years. With such a high discount rate that was constant over different time horizons, no one would hold on to land or get an education.

A discounting model involving a high, constant discount rate makes unrealistic predictions because the model only has one parameter to fit two different empirical regularities: a high degree of impatience in the short run (to match high short-run rates of return and borrowing rates) and a relatively high degree of patience in the long run (to match relatively low longer-run returns to investments in land or education). Since the constant discounting model assumes that the short-run and long-run discounting parameters are the same, it cannot match both moments at the same time (Frederick et al., 2002).

Laibson's (1997) model of quasi-hyperbolic discounting posits that individuals discount all future periods by a present bias parameter β relative to the immediate present.[6] Discounting between all future periods follows the standard exponential model. Having a present-bias parameter β in addition to the exponential parameter δ allows this model to resolve some of the puzzles described above. The recent literature in behavioral economics provides structural estimates of β ranging from about 0.7 to 0.9 on average across studies, although with substantial individual heterogeneity.[7]

How can present bias be incorporated into the Euler equation we discussed above, and can plausible values of present bias help resolve the Euler equation puzzle? Harris and Laibson (2001) derive a hyperbolic Euler equation incorporating present bias:

$$u'(C_t) = f'(K_t)\big[\beta\delta C'(x_{t+1}) + \delta\big(1 - C'(x_{t+1})\big)\big]u'(C_{t+1}), \qquad (4)$$

where $C'(x_{t+1}) = \frac{dC_{t+1}}{dx_{t+1}}$ is the marginal propensity to consume out of liquid assets.

Comparing the standard Euler equation in Eq. (1) to this hyperbolic Euler equation reveals that the standard exponential discount factor δ is replaced by an effective discount factor $[\beta\delta C'(x_{t+1}) + \delta(1 - C'(x_{t+1}))]$. This effective discount factor is a weighted average of the short-run discount factor $\beta\delta$ and the long-run exponential discount factor δ. Crucially, the weights are given by the (anticipated) marginal propensity to consume (MPC) out of cash on hand in period $t + 1$. If an individual expects high MPC in the next period (for example, if she expects low cash-on-hand), then her effective discount factor will be closer to $\beta\delta$, and she will appear impatient. In contrast, if an individual expects a low MPC in the next period (if she expects high cash-on-hand), then her effective discount factor will be closer to δ and she will appear patient.

Given that households in developing countries typically have low cash-on-hand and a high MPC, present bias might make them appear particularly impatient, even if they have the same time preferences as richer individuals (Dean and Sautmann, 2018; Cassidy, 2018). If the household expects to be liquidity-constrained in the next period, with an MPC out of liquid assets approaching 1, their effective discount factor, with $\beta = 0.8$ and $\delta = 0.95$, will be 0.76, compared to 0.95 for an exponential agent. Thus, incorporating present bias goes some way towards resolving the Euler equation puzzle posed above, although it does not eliminate it altogether. (As discussed below, naïveté can greatly increase the welfare cost of present bias.)

While heterogeneity in cash-on-hand and MPC themselves generate variation in patience in a present-bias model, there is reason to believe that there also exists sub-

---

[6] In this chapter, we discuss time preferences and self-control problems through the lens of the present-bias model, which has emerged as a workhorse model in this literature. However, numerous other models of limited self-control and intertemporal choice exist, some of which make similar (or even identical) predictions in the problems we consider. We refer readers to Ericson and Laibson (2018) in this handbook for a broader perspective on this literature.

[7] On estimation of time preferences, see Ericson and Laibson (2018) in this volume and Cohen et al. (2016) for details as well as a brief discussion further below in this section.

stantial heterogeneity in present bias itself. Augenblick and Rabin (2018) estimate that 78% of individuals are present biased, with the rest either acting as exponential discounters or even exhibiting future bias.[8] The mean estimate of β in their sample is 0.79, with a standard deviation across individuals of 0.29. The extent to which observed heterogeneity in the returns to capital or unexploited investment opportunities can be explained by heterogeneity in discount factors is an open question for future research.

The quasi-hyperbolic model can explain another important set of facts about the poor: low levels of precautionary savings in liquid form, and high covariance of income and consumption. Under standard lifecycle models, individuals will save up substantial buffer stocks of liquid savings. They will thus be able to self-insure against shocks, and income and consumption will not co-vary much. In contrast, present-biased agents will have low levels of liquid savings (e.g. Angeletos et al., 2001). When such agents are hit with shocks, their lack of buffer-stock savings implies that they will be unable to self-insure, and consumption will thus co-vary substantially with transitory income shocks.[9] In fact, consumption will also vary with perfectly predictable changes in income, as is the case with farmers over the harvest cycle. Standard lifecycle models typically cannot explain the sensitivity of consumption to predictable falls in income, even in the absence of credit markets (Jappelli and Pistaferri, 2010). Note also that these endogenous liquidity constraints generate the high MPC discussed above, which causes present-biased agents to appear impatient.

In contrast to their failure to build up liquid savings, sophisticated present-biased agents may build up substantial *illiquid* assets since they correctly forecast their future self-control problems (Angeletos et al., 2001). Such individuals may invest in education or hold on to land, rather than selling it, since land and human capital are both illiquid assets that provide valued protection against over-consuming. Thus, these agents will be willing to save up even in low-return illiquid assets (such as land or, to a lesser extent, jewelry and cattle), which may partly explain why households do not appear to equate marginal returns across assets.

In the case of completely naïve present-biased agents, who think they will be exponential discounters without self-control problems beginning tomorrow, illiquid assets will only be accumulated if they are perceived to be attractive, high-return investments. Apart from this feature, the level of naïveté or sophistication has been found to matter relatively little for quantitative predictions about savings and consumption paths in lifecycle consumption models (Beshears et al., 2015).[10,11]

---

[8] Some of this estimated variation might be estimation noise.

[9] Karlan et al. (2014a) find that providing rainfall insurance increases agricultural investment and leads to riskier investment choices in Ghana. Present bias can explain why farmers did not self-insure by saving, despite substantial demand for insurance.

[10] In the case of the naïve hyperbolic Euler equation, the MPC term will be replaced by the agents (incorrectly) perceived MPC in the next period.

[11] As shown by O'Donoghue and Rabin (1999, 2001), the level of sophistication theoretically matters a great deal for procrastination and the demand for commitment. We will discuss this in detail in Section 3,

Given that present-biased agents are (endogenously) effectively liquidity constrained, how does providing access to credit affect their behaviors and welfare? Angeletos et al. (2001) show that present-biased agents will frequently use revolving credit. They will do so not just in response to shocks, but also to fund instant gratification, and for entirely predictable expenditure events. While the use of credit to smooth shocks enhances welfare, present-biased agents may be harmed by access to credit to fuel consumption binges.

Self-control and poverty traps. Banerjee and Mullainathan (2010) investigate the possibility that self-control (or, alternatively, time preferences) may depend on people's income. Specifically, their model introduces the possibility that specific goods such as sugar, fat, and alcohol are temptation goods. Such goods that are valued in the moment, but one does not want the future self to consume. The authors focus on the implications of assuming "declining temptations", i.e. that the fraction of the marginal dollar spent on temptation goods decreases with overall consumption. For instance, one can only eat so many donuts or so much ice cream, or drink so much alcohol or cups of chai on any given day. This model creates several novel and important predictions, including the possibility of temptation-based poverty traps. However, little existing empirical work provides rigorous tests of this model's assumptions and predictions. Experiments testing them—especially the ones that deviate from other models of discounting—would be valuable.

Measuring time preferences. Development economists are often interested in measuring time preferences, including present bias, using surveys or lab experiments in the field. Such measures have been used for parameter identification (Mahajan and Tarozzi, 2011), to test mechanisms by estimating heterogeneous treatment effects (Ashraf et al., 2006), or as outcome measures responding to some treatment themselves (Alan and Ertac, 2018). In principle, time preferences should be measured by identifying indifference points between units of utility in different time periods. For instance, a present-biased individual may be indifferent between 1 util today and 1.3 utils tomorrow and indifferent between 1 util in 300 days and 1.001 utils in 301 days. In practice, time preferences are difficult to measure, and the literature has not converged on a broadly accepted and easily implementable approach. Cohen et al. (2016) as well as Ericson and Laibson (2018) in this volume provide for thoughtful discussions.

The most common approach in the literature is to provide choices between monetary payments earlier or later in time. This approach has many benefits, including that it is relatively easy to implement using off-the-shelf experimental protocols (e.g. Andersen et al., 2008; Andreoni and Sprenger, 2012), and that choices elicited in this way have been shown to correlate, albeit weakly, with real-world behaviors such as exercise and smoking (Chabris et al., 2008), credit scores (Meier and Sprenger, 2011), income (Tanaka et al., 2010), and procrastination (Reuben et al., 2015).

---

in the context of preventive health behavior, another example of apparently under-exploited high-return investments.

This widely popular approach rests on shaky theoretical foundations. Cubitt and Read (2007), for instance, show that choices over money payments at different time horizons need not reveal anything about time preferences since individuals' marginal propensity to consume from such payments will likely deviate from one. Optimizing individuals should smooth consumption over their lifecycle. Thus, receiving $100 today (say, in experimental payouts) may only increase consumption today by pennies. Even with reasonable liquidity constraints, one would expect consumption to be smoothed over weeks or more, whereas present bias is thought to operate over a shorter time horizon of hours or days (e.g. McClure et al., 2007; Augenblick, 2018). Indeed, choices over money earlier or later may reveal more about effective interest rates faced by individuals, or about their time-varying liquidity and financial shocks, even among the poor in developing countries (Dean and Sautmann, 2018; Cassidy, 2018).

A promising recent alternative approach to measuring time preferences is to offer participants choices between actual consumption events or effort. For example, McClure et al. (2007) offer sips of juice to thirsty individuals, while Augenblick et al. (2015) ask participants to choose between different amounts of tedious work on different dates. This approach offers some distinct advantages, since the participant cannot as easily smooth away the (dis)utility associated with these tasks. Perhaps for this reason, present bias is more evident in tasks using such real rewards. Augenblick et al. (2015) estimate a mean β of 0.9 when using an effort task, compared to $\beta = 0.974$, much closer to exponential discounting, when using monetary payments with a parallel design. However, such approaches come with their own challenges, particularly the logistical difficulty of implementation, the practical problems of subject comprehension, and the remaining possibility that consumption or effort outside the experiment adjusts in response to consumption in the experiment.

Where does this leave development economists who would like to measure time preferences or present bias using surveys or experiments in the field? Unfortunately, there are no easy answers. If measuring time preferences is central to the research, implementing a real-effort task as in Augenblick et al. (2015) or Augenblick (2018) may be the best option. If not, utilizing a money-earlier-or-later task may still provide some signal of patience over monetary payments, even if it does not cleanly isolate time preferences.

Recent evidence suggests that hypothetical and incentivized choices over money provide fairly similar results (Ubfal, 2016; Madden et al., 2004; Falk et al., 2016), making hypothetical choices over money an even lower-cost approach. However, hypothetical choices over money may still fail to pin down present bias precisely for the reasons described above in the discussion of the incentivized cases. These questions may be supplemented with qualitative survey questions on self-assessed willingness to wait for larger rewards, as in Falk et al. (2018).[12]

---

[12] The Global Preference Survey of Falk et al. (2018) is worth highlighting here. The authors provide an accessible dataset of unincentivized survey measures of risk, time and social preferences from 80,000

2.3 Reference-dependent preferences

A large body of evidence in psychology and economics suggests that individuals evaluate and experience outcomes—such as consumption, wages, investment returns, or hours worked—not in terms of absolute levels, but relative to reference points (Markowitz, 1952; Kahneman and Tversky, 1979). Moreover, losses relative to that reference point loom larger than gains, a phenomenon termed loss aversion. Lab and field estimates provide estimates of loss aversion in the range of $\lambda = 2 - 2.5$, meaning that a loss of $1 is weighted on average as much as a gain of $2 to $2.5.[13] We will now consider whether reference-dependence and particularly loss aversion can explain aspects of the Euler equation puzzle described above.

The first empirical fact motivating the Euler equation puzzle is the high estimated rate of return on a variety of investments among many small firms. A different way to frame this fact is that numerous high-return investments appear to be left unexploited at equilibrium. Loss aversion may help explain this fact, at least in part. The intuition is that high-return investments invariably involve some possibility of losses relative to forgoing the investment; loss aversion will make such investments less attractive. More generally, loss aversion can explain substantial risk aversion over small to moderate stakes, contrary to standard expected utility models.

Why turn to loss aversion to understand risk aversion over modest stakes, when the textbook already provides diminishing marginal utility of wealth as an explanation? The reason is that expected utility cannot explain small-to-moderate stakes risk aversion without implying nonsensically high levels of risk aversion over large stakes, a point eloquently made by Rabin (2000). Experiments show that many individuals will reject a gamble with equal chances of gaining $2 or losing $1, or of gaining $200 or losing $100. Rabin shows that being indifferent to such a gamble (at any wealth level) due to diminishing marginal utility of wealth would require such rapidly diminishing marginal utility of wealth that such an individual would reject a gamble with a 50% chance of a $4 loss and a 50% chance of *any* level of gain (O'Donoghue and Sprenger, 2018). In contrast, a person with a loss aversion parameter $\lambda = 2$ would be indifferent to a gamble with a 50–50 chance of losing $1 and winning $2 but, much more reasonably, would accept a bet with a 50–50 chance of losing $4 and winning $10. Loss aversion can thus explain the rejection of positive expected-value gambles at small or moderate stakes. Expected-utility maximizers, in contrast, should be approximately risk-neutral over small stakes.

Consider the example of low take-up of fertilizer in Kenya, which was estimated by Duflo et al. (2008) to have an average return of just over 50%. Suppose a unit of fertilizer costs $2, and its use increases output by $6 with 50% probability and has no

---

individuals in 76 countries. Their measure of patience is a function of both answers to quantitative money earlier or later questions, as well as a qualitative self-assessment of patience. In a paper exploiting these data, Dohmen et al. (2018) document a positive correlation between patience and income, both within and across countries.

[13] O'Donoghue and Sprenger (2018) in the first volume of this handbook provide a detailed discussion of reference dependence.

effect with 50% probability. Then, the expected return of fertilizer is 50%. Given the relatively small stakes, an expected-utility agent would be approximately risk neutral, and would make the investment, since the expected value is $0.5 \cdot (\$6 - \$2) + 0.5 \cdot (-\$2) = +\$1$. In contrast, a loss-averse agent with $\lambda = 2.5$ who narrowly brackets returns for this investment would not invest, since $0.5 \cdot (\$6 - \$2) + \lambda \cdot 0.5 \cdot (-\$2) = -\$0.5$.

Despite the clear intuition for how loss aversion could cause individuals to forgo high-return investments, we have relatively limited field evidence of the importance of loss aversion in developing countries. Kremer et al. (2013) provide correlational evidence: shopkeepers in Kenya who exhibit greater small-stakes risk aversion in experimental tasks (presumably due to loss aversion) also maintain lower inventories, thus forgoing bulk-purchase discounts and increasing the probability of creating stock-outs.

Carney et al. (2018) provide field-experimental evidence on loss aversion, credit and technology adoption among dairy farmers in Kenya. The authors study the demand for collateralized loans to fund the purchase of durable assets (both domestic and productive assets). They show that the endowment effect—a canonical implication of loss aversion—causes borrowers to dislike taking loans in which the collateral is an asset they already own, since already-owned assets (such as land, jewelry, or cattle) are already in the borrower's reference point. The prospect of losing such assets in case of loan default (say, due to a negative income shock) makes such loans unattractive. In contrast, the authors show that loans collateralized using the new asset being financed by the loan itself, as in mortgages or car loans, are more attractive to borrowers, since the new asset is not yet in the reference point at the time of loan take-up, and borrowers do not anticipate experiencing as great a sense of loss in case of default.

To isolate this effect, the experimenters endow potential borrowers with a randomly-selected durable asset. A week later, individuals are offered a loan to finance the purchase of a second randomly-selected asset, varying whether the collateral required is the endowed asset, or the new asset itself. The authors find that borrowers are willing to pay approximately 9 percentage points per month higher interest rates to collateralize using the new asset. Interestingly, the same-asset collateralized loans do not result in higher default rates, despite the higher take-up. This suggests that, after taking possession of the new asset, borrowers' reference points update such that they come to develop a comparable endowment effect over their new asset, even before it is paid off. Crucially, individuals systematically under-estimate their future endowment effect before possessing an asset, an example of naïveté or projection bias.

Carney et al. illustrate a general theme of this chapter, the interaction between universal behavioral phenomena and institutions that differ across societies. To the extent that people are reluctant to use goods they already own as collateral, creditors operating in markets with institutions that make it easy to repossess collateral will simply ask them to collateralize loans with the new items they are buying with the loan. On the other hand, where the institutional environment is weak enough that it's hard to collect certain types of collateral, lenders may accept only the easiest to collect forms of collateral.

For example, in the environment studied by Carney et al., the financial institution making the loans, like most of its type, normally required that one-third of each loan be collateralized with the borrower's own deposits held in the financial institution, and the remaining two-thirds be guaranteed by deposits by co-signers. Work by Jack et al. (2016), suggests that substituting the ability to collateralize loans with newly purchased assets, rather than with deposits in the financial institution, increased take-up of loans for rainwater harvesting tanks used by dairy farmers from 2.4% to 44%. This is thus an example of how in the context of developing country institutions, loss aversion may prevent individuals from undertaking potentially high return investments, since financing these investments requires putting existing assets at risk.

The above discussion is all based on either static decisions, or on models with limited dynamics. Unlike the literature on present bias, we only have a limited understanding of the implications of reference-dependence in life-cycle models. One exception is Pagel (2017) who studies life-cycle consumption with expectations-based reference dependence. We conjecture that dynamic models with reference dependence may yield more reasonable dynamic predictions, with a fair amount of stickiness in asset levels, but without the dramatically different dynamic behavior around a threshold asset level than poverty trap models.

Loss aversion is less directly helpful in understanding the second empirical fact underlying the Euler equation puzzle: borrowing at high interest rates without a corresponding increase in consumption over time. One way in which loss aversion may increase demand for credit is if credit is used to insure against consumption losses or losses of assets in case of negative income shocks. Of course, the question remains why individuals are not able to self-insure by building up liquid buffer stocks, which could be due to present bias as described in the previous subsection.

Narrow bracketing. The effects of loss aversion on choices involving risk are particularly likely to be important when individuals engage in narrow bracketing. Narrow bracketing refers to an individual considering each choice or source of uncertainty they face in isolation, failing to integrate it with other choices and risk from other sources (Tversky and Kahneman, 1981). Narrow bracketing is implicitly assumed in a range of economic models and analyses. It has bite in the case of loss aversion, due to the importance of the sharp kink in the utility function at the reference point, which would effectively be smoothed out if individuals were considering many sources of uncertainty simultaneously.

Narrow bracketing can also reduce dynamic problems to repeated static problems if individuals bracket, for instance, daily income or annual stock-performance. Bracketing also helps explain the so-called Samuelson bet problem: an individual may turn down a single 50–50 gamble of losing $100 or gaining $120 but would be willing to accept a hundred such gambles if offered together (Haigh and List, 2005; Bellemare et al., 2005). Such choices are not compatible with expected utility but are easily explained by the decision-maker bracketing the bets more broadly when a hundred bets are presented together.

Lab evidence suggests narrow bracketing is in fact common and leads individuals to make first-order stochastically dominated choices (Tversky and Kahneman, 1981; Rabin and Weizsäcker, 2009). Field evidence on reference-dependence also presents cases of narrow bracketing, from taxi drivers bracketing daily labor supply and earnings (Camerer et al., 1997; Crawford and Meng, 2011; Thakral and Tô, 2018) to investors bracketing realized financial gains or losses from each asset (Barberis and Xiong, 2012). Many open research questions remain in this area, including determining in which cases individuals narrowly bracket, how these brackets are formed, whether individuals can be taught to bracket more broadly, and whether such interventions translate into reduced risk aversion in investment decisions in the field.

Narrow bracketing may be particularly relevant in developing countries. Many households run small firms and face a host of potentially risky decisions. For example, a shopkeeper might have to make decisions of how much inventory to buy on each of many different products and in each case if they are loss averse, they might be concerned about the potential that some of the types of goods might go unsold, creating a loss. A farmer makes decisions every growing season about whether to use each of several different agricultural inputs, as well as whether to invest in livestock, farm equipment such as irrigation pumps, etc. If the manager of a shop or a farm treats each of these decisions in isolation, they may wind up turning down gambles that are very attractive. Loss aversion combined with narrow bracketing could help explain the high unrealized rate of return on additional inventory investment in Kremer et al. (2013).

Reference-point formation. Models of reference-dependence come with an important degree of freedom: the assumption about what constitutes the reference point. The literature has taken different approaches to selecting the relevant reference point: the status-quo level of wealth or assets (e.g. Kahneman and Tversky, 1979) and rational expectations of consumption (Kőszegi and Rabin, 2006, 2009) are the most common. Other papers have chosen different reference points, such as the average of lagged outcomes (DellaVigna et al., 2017) or salient targets such as round-number finishing times among marathon runners (Allen et al., 2016).

Different assumptions about reference-point formation can generate important differences in predicted behavior. Assuming a status quo reference point can predict staying in place, and sticky asset allocations, as well as a high degree of local risk aversion. With expectations-based reference points, multiple equilibria are possible (Kőszegi and Rabin, 2006, 2009). If people have a stochastic reference point (and are already anticipating uncertainty in outcomes), they will often be somewhat more willing to take risks. We conjecture that both types of reference points are relevant and important in different contexts. When people face decisions that they have much experience with (e.g. planting usual crops), expectations will likely determine their reference points. In contrast, if they face new choices (e.g. trying new technologies), the status quo may be more likely to determine their reference point. Investigating this question and the formation of reference points more generally remain important areas for future research.

2.4 Other behavioral factors

There is no reason to think that present bias and loss aversion are the only behavioral factors affecting individuals' consumption and investment choices over time. As we discussed above, quantitative estimates of present bias can explain why high-return investments are not exploited, but not failure to exploit very high return investments. Biased beliefs, in particular, naïveté about present bias, can dramatically distort behavior, as discussed in Section 3. Similarly, narrow bracketing can dramatically increase the consequences of loss aversion.

Other behavioral concepts might also help explain some of the facts described above. We will not discuss these in detail here but refer to the remaining sections of this chapter. For instance, pessimistic beliefs about the returns to various investments may provide an explanation for why high-return investments remain unexploited. Beliefs may be biased due to inattention, as argued for the case of the seaweed farmers by Hanna et al. (2014), as discussed in Section 6.

Moreover, beliefs may be biased due to failures of social learning, as discussed in Section 6.3 (Eyster and Rabin, 2014). Entrepreneurs and CEOs in rich countries are thought to display overconfidence (e.g. Malmendier and Tate, 2005), but we have little evidence on whether owners of small businesses in poor countries do the same. Indeed, it is possible that the poor display under-confidence and low self-efficacy (McKelway, 2018). Individuals may also feel shame or stigma from asking others for information (e.g. Chandrasekhar et al., 2018), or may dislike standing out from others and risking public failure by attempting to adopt a new technology or acquire new skills.

All the above factors might interact in important ways. Present-biased individuals might also have biased beliefs, possibly precisely because present bias prevents them from engaging in costly information-acquisition and correcting their beliefs.

3 Health

Low investment in preventative health is one specific case of apparently underinvestment in high-return opportunities.[14] The neoclassical model has difficulties explaining such behavior, especially when paired with the high sensitivity of this investment to price and convenience. We argue that present bias combined with at least partial naïveté can help explain some cases of low investment in preventive health due to procrastination and liquidity constraints. However, other cases remain unexplained by present bias alone. We argue that biased beliefs could play an important role in explaining other cases of low investment.

---

[14] Behavioral economists have also studied other aspects of health economics, such as health insurance. We do not cover those topics here, in part due to less evidence on those topics from poor countries, and refer readers instead to the chapter by Chandra et al. (2018) in this handbook.

3.1 **Underinvestment in preventive health**

The recent literature has established several stylized facts regarding health behavior in developing countries. These have been extensively discussed in recent reviews by Dupas (2011a), Kremer and Glennerster (2011), Dupas and Miguel (2017). After briefly summarizing some of these facts, we explore the extent to which potential behavioral explanations can help explain them.

Health is both a consumption and an investment good. It influences people's utility directly, but also impacts their productivity and ability to generate income in the near and distant future. Medical advances made over the past century have greatly expanded the ability to treat infectious disease and have dramatically decreased the costs of doing so. Today, many highly effective life-saving technologies that prevent and treat disease, such as insecticide-treated bed nets, deworming pills, and chlorine treatment for water are available for a few dollars or less.[15] While adoption of these technologies has driven massive health improvements in the developing world, and generated life expectancies much higher than those historically achieved by currently developed countries when they were at similar levels of income, there is still apparent under-adoption of preventive health and treatment for chronic conditions. Take-up rates of many health investments are surprisingly low considering their low costs and immense long-term benefits.

One way to see this is as a special case of the more general problem of under-exploitation of apparently high-return investments highlighted in the section on the Euler equation puzzle. An alternative interpretation could be that people have a low value of health, but demand for treatment (rather than prevention) of health conditions seems much higher (e.g. Cohen et al., 2015) and this is inconsistent with that alternative interpretation. Indeed, there is considerable evidence of relatively ineffective health expenditure (e.g. Das and Hammer, 2007). In fact, Banerjee et al. (2015a) and Dupas and Robinson (2013b) find that out-of-pocket health expenditure among Indian slum dwellers and rural Kenyan households comprises about 10% and 8% of total household expenditure, respectively. While the data are not broken down into acute and preventive spending in their studies, it is unlikely that these households are spending these sums on cheap prevention products.

Low willingness-to-pay for preventive health. Fig. 1, taken from Dupas and Miguel's review chapter on field experiments in health, illustrates this point. In different demand experiments offering individuals in developing countries health-investment goods, a significant fraction of individuals decided not to purchase the goods, even at low prices well within the budget constraint of most poor households. Such choices are remarkable given that the large expected future benefits of these health goods exceeded the investment costs, sometimes by orders of magnitude.

---

[15] Taking deworming pills is not prevention but treatment. However, from a behavioral perspective, treatment for chronic conditions is more similar to prevention than acute care: (1) acute conditions are salient, but the worm load builds up over time and people don't see a sudden worsening of health; (2) there is a short-run disutility of taking deworming medicine as the worms are expelled. Any nutritional or other gains take place over time.

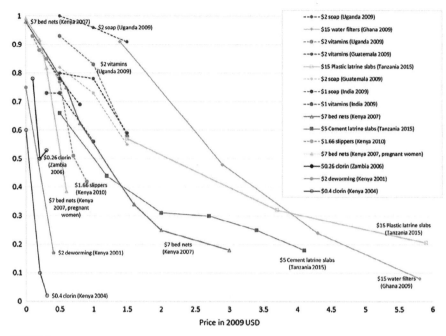

FIGURE 1

Demand for preventative health products. The y-axis plots the share of individuals or households taking up the product.

From Dupas and Miguel (2017).

For example, deworming has a large impact on a variety of outcomes, including future school attendance, work hours, and education, with an estimated private NPV financial benefit of deworming of $142 (Baird et al., 2016). However, only 18% of parents purchased medication when they had to pay a small fee of about $1 (Kremer and Miguel, 2007). Similarly, Berry et al. (2018) find that individuals' willingness to pay for clean water technology is less than 15% of production costs. Kremer et al. (2011) show that households in Kenya have low willingness-to-pay for cleaner water, implied through the additional distance they are willing to walk to use an exogenously cleaner water source. Their calculations imply a WTP to avert one disability-adjusted life year of $23, while policy-makers typically apply much higher values.

(Un)healthy behaviors. In addition to investing in their future health via purchasing bed nets, getting immunizations, or deworming, individuals can choose to lead a healthier lifestyle by limiting or avoiding certain behaviors. Such behaviors include eating unhealthy food options (e.g. high intake of fat and sugar), consuming addictive substances such as alcohol and cigarettes, or not sleeping or exercising sufficiently. In both developed and developing countries, significant fractions of the population express a desire to engage in a healthier lifestyle in the future, while having difficulties to do so in the present. The health consequences of such behaviors can be severe, and their importance has been strongly on the rise in developing countries (Bloom et al., 2011). Non-communicable diseases such as hypertension, cancer, and, diabetes are the leading cause of death worldwide (Islam et al., 2014; WHO, 2015), yet, until recently, have received less attention by researchers and policymakers compared to acute conditions with similar burdens of disease.

High sensitivity of health investments to price and convenience. In addition to illustrating low levels of demand, Fig. 1 also displays high demand elasticity for preventative health investments. Even small price increases seem to lead to precipitous declines in demand for products such as water treatment (Ashraf et al., 2010), deworming (Kremer and Miguel, 2007), insecticide-treated bed nets (Cohen and Dupas, 2010), and vitamins (Meredith et al., 2013). Take-up of health investments is also sensitive to convenience in some cases. Thornton (2008) finds that whether people pick up HIV test results is very sensitive to relatively small differences in walking distance to obtain results.

A mirror image of these large effects of small price increases is the finding that providing small incentives for healthy choices can have large effects on healthy behaviors and investments among the poor. For instance, providing small, time-limited non-financial incentives for child immunization leads to large increases in immunization (Banerjee et al., 2010), and small, time-limited financial incentives greatly increase the proportion of people who pick up their HIV test results in Malawi (Thornton, 2008).

Lower price-sensitivity for acute care. In contrast to high price-sensitivity for preventive-health products, households appear to have a relatively low price-elasticity for acute care. Cohen et al. (2015) look at price sensitivity for antimalarial treatment. In this study consumers are offered vouchers for subsidized anti-malarials to be redeemed at the closest drug shop. Increasing the price of an antimalarial treatment course for young children by 250 percent, from $0.30 to $1.5, does not reduce the share of households buying the treatment (about a third). However, as expected, demand does fall at much higher prices. Only 4 percent of households buy the treatment at $3.

Knife-edge interpretation. One story might be that people who do not take up preventive health goods perceive large benefits from preventive health investments, but they perceive even higher costs, and hence make a rational decision not to take up the preventive health measures. Thus, for example, they might worry that vaccines carry side effects or have religious objections to vaccination; they might be worried about the unpleasantness associated with expelling worms in response to taking deworming medication; they might find mosquito nets inconvenient and uncomfortable, and they might prefer not to know if they are HIV positive.

It would be difficult to reconcile this type of story with the high sensitivity to price and convenience observed across several different preventive-health items and services, however. In a standard optimizing model, with individuals comparing the (discounted) costs and benefits of the action, observing a large mass of consumers change their decision in response to a small change in prices has a clear interpretation: a large share of consumers must be very close to indifferent between taking up the health investment or not. Therefore, the small incentive could easily tip the balance between costs and benefits and change their decision. That is, the costs and benefits associated with investing in their health must have been nearly equal, such that they were making decisions balanced on a knife's edge. While possible for a single product, it appears extremely unlikely that this situation would occur for so many different households (at the same price), and across a range of different technologies and settings.

This reasoning suggests that households which do not adopt these preventive behaviors either do not perceive large benefits, or that decisions are not being made in the way conventionally modeled by economists. Of course, some health investments (e.g. vaccination against rare diseases) likely indeed have small private benefits. However, there are also cases of low take-up of health investments with large private benefits. In at least some of these cases, individuals report believing in the effectiveness of health investments (Kremer et al., 2011). A careful investigation of such beliefs, including rigorous ways to address social desirability bias, and potential other explanations for low demand would be a highly valuable contribution to this literature.

3.2 Present bias

Present bias might explain some of the findings described above through two channels.

First, many health behaviors feature tradeoffs either between immediate costs and delayed benefits, or alternatively, immediate gratification and delayed costs. Such behaviors include getting vaccinated, seeing the doctor for a check-up, taking medication, purchasing a bed net, and avoiding potato chips, risky sexual activities, or smoking. Immediate costs often include hassle and psychological costs, for instance, of going to the doctor, walking to a water source farther away than the nearest one, taking medication, or other health-promoting behaviors. Present bias can cause individuals to procrastinate indefinitely on taking such healthy actions, as we explain in detail below. Time-limited incentives and discounts may help reduce procrastination, as can reducing hassle costs and providing individuals with commitment devices.

Second, as discussed in Section 2 above, present bias can generate endogenous liquidity constraints for households. These liquidity constraints may, in turn, cause households to leave high-return investments unexploited, including preventive-health purchases. They may also generate high price-sensitivity in the take-up of such investments.

3.2.1 Procrastination and health behaviors

Many preventive-health behaviors involve a utility cost in the present, paid in return for health benefits in the future. For instance, treating one's water, walking to a farther-but-cleaner water source, getting a vaccination, getting more exercise, improving one's diet, drinking less alcohol all involve utility or hassle costs (as distinguished from purely financial costs) in the present, with benefits potentially years in the future.

The degree to which present bias hinders the take-up of such behaviors depends crucially on two factors: (a) how sophisticated an individual is about their present bias (O'Donoghue and Rabin, 1999, 2001), and (b) whether the task involves clear deadlines.

Naïveté and sophistication. A naïve, present-biased individual prefers and expects to do a painful but worth-doing task tomorrow but fails to account for the fact that they will also be present-biased then. The naïveté required for present bias is usually thought of as overconfidence about future self-control.[16] Sophistication, on the other hand, makes the individual realize that if they do procrastinate today, they will also likely do so tomorrow, increasing the cost of putting off the difficult task today. In this way, naïveté can greatly amplify the impact of present bias on behavior and lead to large distortions and welfare consequences (O'Donoghue and Rabin, 2001).

To better understand the extent to which present bias can explain low take-up of preventive-health behaviors and the extent to which the explanation depends on naïveté, we distinguish between the following categories of health behaviors:

Case I: Health investments without deadlines

Consider first a health investment good or action without a deadline for take-up. Theory tells us that a sophisticated present-biased individual might delay taking up such an investment good for a few time periods (say, days or weeks) due to present bias. However, she will take up the good eventually, since she will foresee her future present bias and thus avoid lengthy and costly delays. More generally, sophisticates have rational expectations, so they anticipate correctly what they will do it if they wait. For them, delaying from period t to period τ is a single decision to procrastinate. Therefore, small self-control problems cannot cause severe welfare losses in such investment decisions for sophisticates (O'Donoghue and Rabin, 2001).

In contrast, (partially) naïve individuals do not (fully) understand their future self-control problems. Such individuals may think every day that they will incur the cost investing on the following day, and never actually follow through with their plans. Naïveté can compound the impact of self-control problems by inducing individuals to make repeated decisions to procrastinate, each time believing they will do it next period.[17] The welfare costs arising from procrastination can become arbitrarily large since a naïve individual never compares the immediate costs to future benefits. Instead the individual keeps comparing the costs of taking up the good today to the costs of doing so tomorrow, wrongly anticipating that she will take up the good regardless of the choice of doing it immediately (O'Donoghue and Rabin, 2001).

---

[16] Sometimes, however, this is observationally equivalent to overconfidence about future availability of time, or even overconfidence about not forgetting in the future.

[17] This also holds for partial naïveté. Any degree of naïveté is sufficient to generate procrastination and can cause much more severe welfare losses than complete sophistication.

Many of the lifestyle choices with important health consequences involve habits that could at least in principle be changed every day. On any given day, a smoker or drinker may decide to quit. An individual may start improving their food intake, sleep, or exercising behavior on any day. In such situations, the structure of costs and benefits is the same as for take-up decisions without deadlines. A change in habit often causes short-run costs for a limited time and yields significant benefits in the often-distant future. While the short-run costs of such behavioral change can be substantial (e.g. quitting smoking), they are arguably far outweighed by the long-run benefits in many cases (e.g. avoiding lung cancer). There is typically no enforced deadline that determines when to start changing a habit. As discussed above, while a sophisticated person may delay changing their habits for a few days, present bias cannot lead to large costs caused by the delay for this person. In contrast, a (partially) naïve person may procrastinate for a long time, possibly forever telling themselves that they will start developing virtuous habits soon but never actually following through.

The above discussion highlights the importance of considering naïveté in models of present bias. For instance, if an individual is observed to never get a flu shot despite being well-informed about the benefits and perhaps even displaying some stated intention to do so, they may be procrastinating. If a researcher were to attempt to fit a model of sophisticated present bias to the data, they would conclude that the individual has such pathological levels of present bias, that they simply don't care about the future. If instead they allowed the individual to be naïve about their present bias, plausible values of present bias may be able to fit the data quite well. While evidence of demand for commitment suggest at least some sophistication (Schilbach, 2019; Casaburi and Macchiavello, 2018), the best direct estimates of individuals' sophistication suggest that individuals are largely naïve on average (e.g. Augenblick and Rabin, 2018).

Similarly, it is important to make sensible assumptions about the length of a time period when modeling choices under present bias. A naïve present-biased individual deciding whether to get a flu vaccination today or tomorrow may be tempted to wait until tomorrow, since the expected cost of delay (i.e. the chance that he may get the flu this evening) will be small compared to the lower discounted cost of getting the vaccination tomorrow (which is down-weighted by the present bias factor). The cost of delay might instead appear quite large if the choice is between going now and going next month. The empirical literature suggests that the "present" in present bias is a matter of hours or, at most, a day (Augenblick, 2018). Thus, it will often be appropriate to model daily decision-making, unless the opportunity to take the costly action truly only occurs once a month.

Impact of small incentives. In the absence of other issues, present bias will not lead to large distortions for fully sophisticated present-biased individuals (O'Donoghue and Rabin, 2001). As a result, there is only limited potential for small incentives to alter take-up behavior of sophisticated agents, nor is there much need for them to do so. Small incentives might accelerate take-up by sophisticated present-biased individuals, but they are unlikely to cause large shifts in the extensive margin of demand. In contrast, small but time-limited discounts can have large effects for naïve present-biased individuals facing costly actions without deadlines. The time limit on these incentives is crucial: on the last day of the incentives (or at some sooner date, in case of uncertainty), the choice is between making the investment today at a lower price or in the future at a higher price. The time limit makes acting immediately more attractive and can thus inhibit procrastination. In contrast, this reasoning does not apply for permanent incentives. Essentially, time-limited discounts provide a deadline, which can help overcome procrastination problems, as we discuss below.

Case II: Health investments involving deadlines (but no or small monetary costs)

Consider next a one-shot decision of an investment good that is otherwise not available. An example could be a one-time visit by an NGO that offers to provide you with deworming pills free-of-cost, or a vaccination camp at a local health clinic where age-sensitive vaccines are provided for free. For realistic parameter values and in the absence of other behavioral biases, present bias cannot explain the lack of take-up of such high-return, time-limited investment goods. Present bias induces individuals to put less weight on future benefits relative to current costs. However, realistic estimates of present bias find values of $\beta \approx 0.7$, which implies a 30% reduction in weight on future periods relative to the present. Even a present-biased individual with $\beta = 0.5$ or $\beta = 0.3$ (on the low end of empirical estimates) would take up the deworming or vaccination for their child (assuming they care about them sufficiently) since the associated benefits outweigh costs by orders of magnitude. This insight does not depend on the level of sophistication about present bias, since individuals do not need to make predictions about their future behavior to make this one-shot decision.

The present bias model similarly has difficulty explaining individuals' lack of take-up of investment behaviors that are available for a longer but still finite time with a clear deadline. Essentially, on the day of the deadline, the individual's choice problem reduces to the one-shot decision as described in the previous paragraph, and the present-biased individual will take up on that day if he has not done so already, regardless of naïveté or sophistication.

The above conclusion is not greatly affected by the presence of shocks to the cost of taking the action on any given day (subject to the deadline), provided the individual has accurate beliefs about the distribution of shocks. For example, on any given day, individuals may find it particularly costly to go to the clinic to get an immunization since they may be busy or unwell. If they are forward-looking and think through the optimal stopping problem, they will have in mind a reservation cost below which they will take the action on each day, with the reservation cost rising over time. Naïve and sophisticated agents may have different reservation costs on any given day, since the naïve agent expects to be more patient in the future. But, again, both will do the task on the last day if not done already, barring an extreme or unlucky shock. The welfare losses from present bias in this case are thus bounded by the cost of delaying until the deadline. Naïve individuals are, however, more likely than sophisticates to delay the task up to the deadline before finally completing it.

If individuals have biased beliefs about the probability of future shocks, even deadlines may not ensure take-up. For instance, suppose individuals have imperfect memory, with a probability of simply forgetting about the task on any given day. If they are sophisticated about this imperfect memory, they will act similarly to a sophisticated present-biased individual and will not delay for long, since they realize they might forget to do the task in the future. If they instead underestimate their chances of forgetting in the future, they might put off the task until tomorrow, and then forget to complete it despite the deadline.

3.2.2 Low willingness to pay and high price sensitivity

Above, we considered cases in which costly health behavior did not involve substantial monetary costs. We discussed that present bias with naïveté can generate low adoption of healthy behaviors due to procrastination problems, at least in the absence of strict deadlines. However, many health investments involve some monetary cost up front (in addition to any hassle costs), for example, purchasing bed nets, paying for deworming pills, and buying water filters or chlorine tablets. We discuss how present bias can drive down demand for such goods, and cause high price-sensitivity, through the mechanism of liquidity constraints.

However, many health investments involve some monetary cost up front (in addition to any hassle costs). For example, purchasing bed nets when they are offered for sale rather than given away for free, paying for deworming pills, buying water filters or chlorine tablets, etc. Next, we discuss how present bias can drive down demand for such goods, and cause high price-sensitivity, through the mechanism of liquidity constraints.

Case III: Health investments involving significant financial costs (with or without deadlines)

Present bias has been invoked as an explanation for the overall low willingness-to-pay and high demand-elasticity for preventative health goods (Dupas, 2011a; Kremer and Glennerster, 2011). The empirical facts of low WTP and high price-sensitivity are not directly related to the mechanism of procrastination described above. That is, even when a researcher unexpectedly shows up at a household's door and offers a preventive-health good for purchase with a one-time-only offer, demand is low, and price-sensitivity is high, despite no possibility of procrastinating over the purchase. However, present bias may still curb demand by generating liquidity constraints.

Liquidity constraints. Although the related empirical evidence is mixed, liquidity constraints are an often-cited reason for individuals' low demand for health investments (Dupas and Miguel, 2017). Some studies have found that offering preventive health products with a line of credit greatly increases take-up (e.g. Devoto et al., 2012 on piped water connections and Tarozzi et al., 2014 on bed nets). Offering savings technologies such as safe-boxes labeled as being specifically for health savings increased health investments (Dupas and Robinson, 2013b). On the other hand, unconditional cash transfers (Haushofer and Shapiro, 2016) and the ultra-poor graduation program, which may each ease liquidity constraints, did not have detectable effects on health or health expenditures.

While at any given point in time, lack of liquidity may explain why individuals do not invest in their future health, liquidity itself is endogenous. As described in Section 2, risk-averse non-present biased people living in an environment where they are subject to shocks, should build up buffer stocks over time, even if they are initially very poor. However, present-biased individuals will find it difficult to build up substantial buffer stocks and hence will be much more liquidity constrained (Angeletos et al., 2001). As such, evidence of liquidity constraints preventing individuals from making investments in their health can be interpreted as evidence *in favor* of the importance of present bias rather than evidence against it.

Moreover, once an individual is effectively liquidity-constrained, present bias can further reduce their demand for an investment good, since the monetary cost of the investment will reduce immediate consumption more severely in the presence of liquidity constraints (since consumption smoothing is hampered by liquidity constraints). Such a reduction in immediate consumption to finance the health investment will be particularly unattractive to a present-biased agent.

Demand estimation. An important frontier in this area is how to estimate demand for health investments or other goods in the presence of liquidity constraints.[18] Unannounced visits to study participants, offering to sell a good, will not measure long-run demand under liquidity constraints. Several approaches have been pursued. One is to endow people with money first. However, it is unclear how much money is needed in a buffer stock world. In a model in which people are subject to shocks and hold buffer stocks, WTP is likely to rise smoothly with the amount of money that people are given in the experiment. Demand will only level off with a high buffer stock. Separately from this issue, endowing individuals with cash and then offering them items for sale is likely to result in experimenter demand effects. A second approach is to allow individuals time to purchase the good or to allow them to pay with their time (Dupas, 2009). Offering coupons to purchase the good at a local shop may reduce demand effects (Duflo et al., 2018). A third approach is to allow individuals to pay using credit (Devoto et al., 2012).

Present bias and liquidity constraints complicate welfare calculations using willingness-to-pay estimates. Welfare may be underestimated for at least two reasons. First, present-biased individuals are likely to face liquidity constraints, which will lower demand estimates. Second, even in the absence of liquidity constraints, present bias may lower demand estimates for durables and long-run investments if costs are upfront and not smoothed over the lifetime. Of course, behavioral models including more generally some challenges to using revealed preference to infer welfare (Kőszegi and Rabin, 2007; Bernheim and Taubinsky, 2018 in this handbook).

3.2.3 Commitment devices

Demand for commitment devices can provide decisive evidence revealing present bias, or more generally, self-control problems, contributing to certain behaviors.

---

[18] We refer the reader to Dupas and Miguel (2017) for a detailed discussion of this topic.

Commitment devices are arrangements entered into by an individual with the aim of helping fulfill a plan for future behavior that would otherwise be difficult owing to intrapersonal conflict stemming from, for example, a lack of self-control (Bryan et al., 2010). Demand for such devices is often interpreted as "smoking-gun" evidence of time-inconsistency and self-control problems. It is difficult to rationalize why someone would elect to constrain their future choice set in the absence of time-consistent preferences. Laibson's (1997) model of quasi-hyperbolic preferences features time-inconsistent preferences (induced by present bias) and can thus generate demand for commitment. Alternative models of self-control are equally consistent with demand for commitment (Thaler and Shefrin, 1981; Gul and Pesendorfer, 2001, 2004; Fudenberg and Levine, 2006).

Ashraf et al. (2006) provide a proof of concept that offering commitment devices can cause important changes in behaviors, as discussed in Section 4.1. More recently, development economists have documented demand for commitment to achieve health-related goals. Giné et al. (2010) offered smokers a voluntary commitment product to support their attempts to quit smoking. Eleven percent of individuals who were offered the commitment device took it up, with modest but significant impacts on smoking six months later, which persisted in surprise tests at 12 months.

Schilbach (2019) explores the relationship between alcohol consumption and self-control among rickshaw drivers in Chennai. As part of the experiment, participants were offered a choice between receiving an unconditional payment of a fixed amount or a conditional payment that had a high payoff for sobriety (measured using a breathalyzer) and a lower payoff otherwise. The amount of the unconditional payment varied, such that one of the unconditional options weakly dominated the conditional option and another strictly dominated the conditional option. Schilbach (2019) finds substantial demand for costly commitment to sobriety: more than half of those offered the choices chose the weakly dominated option that incentivized sobriety over the unconditional payment, and more than a third chose the strictly dominated conditional incentives over the larger unconditional payment.

Despite this promising evidence, commitment devices have not taken off as a policy tool or in real-world markets. Two weaknesses are at the heart of this issue. First, while Schilbach (2019) and Casaburi and Macchiavello (2018) find high take-up for costly commitment, demand for commitment devices is relatively low in many other settings (Laibson, 2015).[19] Second, many of the individuals who demand commitment fail to follow through with their plans despite the commitment device, such that they ex post appear to be made worse off by being offered commitment (John, 2018; Bai et al., 2017).

Does the mixed (at best) success of commitment contracts imply that self-control problems are not an important driver of preventive health behavior? To answer this question, it is important to keep in mind determinants of commitment demand. A key requirement for generating demand for commitment is a sufficient level of sophistication about self-control problems. A completely naïve present-biased individual

---

[19] See Table 1 in Schilbach (2019) and Table 1 in John (2018) for overviews of the existing evidence.

would never demand commitment, since they believe they have no self-control problems beginning in the next period. Thus, demand for commitment is a one-sided test for self-control problems: finding demand for commitment indicates self-control problems (in the absence of confusion or social pressure to sign up), but absence of demand does not necessarily mean self-control problems do not exist or are not important in that domain or in other domains. It could instead be that (a) individuals are not sufficiently sophisticated to demand commitment, (b) that the commitment device is perceived as being ineffective, or (c) that uncertainty in the environment makes commitment unattractive despite self-control problems (Laibson, 2015).

The variation in take-up across settings could partly be explained by variation in the extent of individuals' present bias, as well their awareness of such problems. While standard models of present bias assume that both the level of present bias β and the level of sophistication about it ($\hat{\beta}$) are the same across all dimensions, it could be that individuals are more aware of their self-control problems in some dimensions than in others. Of course, it is surely the case that much of the variation is simply explained by difference in beliefs or long-run preferences: many people may simply not think the task is worth doing and would not want their future selves to do it either. People may also have varying beliefs about the likely effectiveness of the contract, which in turn might be related to individuals' experience with the device. Better understanding the role of individuals' beliefs in commitment decisions remains an important area for future research.

Individuals' failure to follow through is a second reason why commitment has not become a more successful policy tool (John, 2018). If people are only partially aware of their present bias, there may be systematic failures of commitment, with plausibly negative effects on welfare. Those who are partially naïve may accept a commitment contract without realizing the true extent of their present bias, resulting in them incurring the cost of the commitment device without its intended benefit.

Bai et al. (2017) show how people may be willing to take out commitment contracts that are ultimately welfare harming. They study attendance at "Hypertension Day" health camps organized by a healthcare provider in rural India. In partnership with the provider, they offer contracts in which individuals make a large up-front payment, which reduces future attendance fees or, in the case where the payment exceeds the visit fee, provides a conditional payment for each future visit to the camp. The authors find low demand for the commitment contracts, but among those who do take up a commitment contract, a large proportion do not follow through with their future visits to the camp. These people lose the paid up-front fee and do not gain the health benefits that the contracts were intended to facilitate. This behavior is consistent with partial naïveté, where individuals demand some commitment, but not enough to overcome their present bias, which they do not fully anticipate.[20]

---

[20] The authors also design a contract intended to appeal to naïve individuals: they bundle together price discounts and commitment. The idea is that naïve individuals who expect to attend the health camp in any case might sign up to take advantage of the discount, but then be helped ex-post by the commitment aspect of the contract. Yet, even for this contract, follow-through rates are disappointing.

Future research on commitment devices might fruitfully focus on how to improve their success rates and increase their demand. One approach might be to attempt to de-bias individuals about the extent of their self-control problems, say by drawing their attention to the gap between their intentions and actions, or similar gaps among others. Another would be to facilitate learning by providing individuals with guided experience with selecting commitment devices.

Finally, even if agents are fully sophisticated regarding their present bias and have accurate beliefs regarding costs and benefits, commitment may not be optimal if there is uncertainty about the future (Amador et al., 2006; Laibson, 2015). In environments with uncertainty that will be resolved in future periods, commitment becomes less valuable insofar as it limits the agent's ability to act upon any new information. Therefore, with uncertainty or (partial) naïveté, a more promising approach may be to reduce hassle costs, provide direct time-limited incentives, or ease liquidity constraints. Another approach in the face of uncertainty is to utilize "soft" commitments, as discussed in Section 4.1.

In summary, present bias appears to have explanatory power for some of the low demand for health investments described above, through two channels: procrastination (in the case of health behaviors without deadlines, and naïve agents), and liquidity constraints (in case of naïve or sophisticated present-biased agents who endogenously create liquidity constraints). The classic tool in the literature to deal with self-control problems—commitment devices—have shown some promise but have yet to overcome important shortcomings to become an important policy tool.

Present bias on its own is by no means sufficient to explain all the patterns observed in the data. However, it is important to keep in mind that the different behavioral explanations we discuss in this chapter are by no means mutually exclusive. For instance, present bias and biased beliefs may well jointly explain some of the behaviors that cannot be explained by each of these factors on their own. However, some of the above patterns in behavior cannot be explained by liquidity constraints, for instance, individuals' high sensitivity to convenience as documented by Thornton (2008). Explanations involving biased beliefs appear more plausible in such cases.

3.3 Biased beliefs

To make good decisions regarding their health, individuals must form accurate beliefs about several variables. What is the likelihood of falling sick with different conditions in the future? How severe would the consequences of falling sick be? What is the causal effect of different interventions on the likelihood of falling sick, or of being cured? How good are various providers and should one trust their recommendations?

Learning the right answer to these questions is difficult even for a fully rational (Bayesian) agent who has perfect memory and the ability to process complex information. There are many reasons why it is difficult for an individual to form accurate beliefs, including fundamental uncertainty and heterogeneity across individuals in risks and responses to treatment, the self-limiting nature of many diseases, externalities, long time-horizons, and the complicated nature of many medical conditions.

Indeed, this point was made by Arrow (1963) in a paper sometimes considered the founding work of modern health economics.

In addition to the general difficulty of learning about health, individuals often face additional challenges to learning, especially in developing countries. For instance, sometimes they may simply not have access to relevant information, and there may be few trained experts around to learn from. Once we additionally account for the fact that human beings systematically depart from the Bayesian learning benchmark (see Benjamin, 2018 in this volume), the likelihood that individuals have inaccurate beliefs—and perhaps systematically biased beliefs—becomes even greater.

Below, we discuss how inaccurate beliefs may explain some patterns in health behavior in developing countries. We describe reasons for inaccurate beliefs including simple lack of access to information, as well as specific biases in learning and beliefs which may be important, including information avoidance and motivated reasoning, incorrect mental models, and non-Bayesian social learning.

Inaccurate beliefs. Misperceived returns to health investments could help explain the stylized facts described in Section 3.1. Underestimating returns will drive down the demand for preventive health investments. Perceived returns close to zero could also help explain the high demand elasticity for such investments. Surprisingly little work directly elicits individuals' beliefs regarding the returns to different health investments. While quantitative belief elicitation is challenging, methods have been developed to elicit even probabilistic beliefs meaningfully in low-literacy populations in the developing world (see Delavande et al., 2011 and Delavande, 2014 for reviews).

One example is Delavande and Kohler (2009), who elicit subjective probabilities of HIV infection in Malawi. Compared to the actual HIV prevalence of 6.9% in Sub-Saharan Africa at the time, 67% of respondents report that their likelihood of being currently infected with HIV is 0, while only 1% think the likelihood is 100 percent. Godlonton et al. (2016) elicit men's beliefs about male circumcision and HIV transmission risk and find that only 36% correctly believe circumcision is related to lower HIV transmission risk.

It remains to be seen whether inaccurate beliefs, by themselves, can help explain under-investment in preventive health. It could even be that eliciting beliefs heightens the puzzle in some contexts, if many individuals over-estimate the returns to healthy behaviors or the risks involved in unhealthy behaviors such as for the risks associated with smoking in the US (Viscusi, 1990) and the risks of HIV transmission in Malawi (Anglewicz and Kohler, 2009). However, our lack of understanding of these beliefs constitutes a glaring gap in the literature at present. More systematic elicitation of beliefs—including quantitative beliefs—in the health domain will be a valuable agenda for future research.

Information interventions. A substantial body of work has studied the effects of information interventions on health behaviors (although often without measuring beliefs themselves). These have been treated as tests for whether information is a binding constraint on preventive health behaviors. Put differently, providing information and measuring changes in health behaviors is an indirect way of testing for errors in beliefs in the baseline. However, this approach depends on numerous assumptions which are rarely tested: that the information treatment was effective in changing beliefs in the intended direction, and that the information intervention did not impact behavior in other ways such as through increased salience or demand effects.

Dupas and Miguel (2017) provide a thorough review of this literature and point to the mixed overall findings. While some information interventions such as informing students about how to avoid worm infections (Kremer and Miguel, 2007) and providing information about HIV/AIDS to students (Dupas, 2011b) had no effects on behaviors, other cases show more promising results, especially when providing personalized information. Madajewicz et al. (2007) show that informing households about well safety regarding arsenic levels causes large switches from unsafe to safe water sources. Dupas (2011b) finds that teenage girls in Kenya falsely believed older men would expose them to lower HIV risk than younger partners, an informing them about the higher risk of infection of older men led to changes in behavior.

Several other well-known examples of effective information campaigns exist, for instance, Egypt's campaign on oral rehydration for diarrhea treatment (Levine and Kinder, 2004). However, similar information campaigns implemented over a long period of time have not had a transformative effect on infant death rates from diarrhea (Rao et al., 1998). Other examples show more mixed results of information campaigns. For instance, while health warnings on packaging have been shown to decrease tobacco use in some settings (Borland et al., 2009), similar warnings have been less effective at decreasing alcohol consumption (Anderson et al., 2009).

We only have a limited understanding why information interventions can have large impacts in some contexts, but small to null impacts in others. Dupas (2011a) points to several determinants that could be important of the success of information campaigns. One possible explanation is that it matters who receives the information, due to individual-level differences in returns to health investments. An alternative hypothesis is that multiple behavioral biases are jointly affecting individuals' decisions and only addressing one of them is insufficient. For example, in the case of alcohol consumption, information interventions could play a role, but only if individuals also receive help in overcoming potential self-control problems. A different hypothesis is that in cases of motivated beliefs, information interventions will not be successful since individuals are actively trying to avoid updating their beliefs, as discussed below.

Motivated reasoning. Information avoidance and motivated reasoning may arise when beliefs enter directly into an individual's utility function, in addition to their instrumental value. A variety of theoretical concepts can capture this phenomenon, including anticipatory utility (utility from anticipating the future; Kőszegi (2003), Mayraz (2011), Caplin and Leahy (2001, 2004), Brunnermeier and Parker (2005)) or news/realization utility (utility from learning good or bad news; Kőszegi and Rabin, 2009). In these models, acquiring more information does not necessarily make individuals better off, such that they will sometimes eschew seemingly useful information.

One compelling example from the developed world is Oster et al. (2013) who study genetic testing among individuals at risk for Huntington's Disease (HD). While Huntington's is a degenerative neurological disorder without cure, it may still be very useful to learns one's HD status as it can inform important life decisions regarding childbearing, retirement plans, savings, or education. However, despite the relatively low economic cost, pre-symptomatic testing is rare. Moreover, actions among untested individuals are strongly skewed toward the optimal action of those who do not carry the HD mutation. Finally, individuals often get tested when their symptoms paired with their genetic disposition predicts a positive result with near certainty.

The standard neoclassical framework has difficulties explaining this set of results. Oster et al. (2013) explain the patterns in the data using a model of anticipatory utility. Untested individuals have the option to choose their beliefs about the future, at the cost of increasing the probability of choosing the wrong action. Avoiding information may be optimal if the increase in anticipatory utility outweighs the costs associated with making choices based on wrong beliefs. Oster et al. (2013) explain the patterns in the data using a model of anticipatory utility. Untested individuals have the option to choose their beliefs about the future, at the cost of increasing the probability of choosing the wrong action. Avoiding information may be optimal if the increase in anticipatory utility outweighs the costs associated with making choices based on wrong beliefs.

Work on this topic in developing countries is scarce, but there is little reason to think that a similar psychology might not apply also in poor countries, and with respect to important health conditions ranging from HIV to hypertension and diabetes. Indeed, Li et al. (2018) provide suggestive evidence on information aversion in the case of diabetes blood-testing at a rural hospital near Beijing.

Although Oster et al. (2013) and Li et al. (2018) both use the same model of anticipatory utility to rationalize their results, anticipatory utility alone cannot fully explain people's preferences over medical testing. In line with the evidence for other health products, Li et al. (2018) and Thornton (2008) show that demand for medical test results can be highly sensitive to small changes in prices, even among relatively high-risk populations. It is hard for anticipatory utility by itself to drive this result: it would require individuals to be close to indifferent, once accounting for both the total expected benefits and costs of getting tested, and the change in anticipatory utility from being tested. It seems unlikely that this would occur by chance for many individuals.

Incorporating present bias into models of information preferences might help explain this behavior. If people are averse to learning medical test results, say due to news utility or simply because they dislike focusing their attention on their health status, then a present-biased person could forgo testing because they put disproportionate weight on the immediate welfare costs of learning the test's result.[21]

---

[21] News-utility is different than anticipatory utility. In the case of news utility, the utility cost of receiving news is at the moment that the news is received. By the next period, once the information has been incor-

Especially in the case of naïve present bias, small psychological costs of learning new information may cause individuals to procrastinate indefinitely on obtaining their test result, as in Thornton (2008).

Redundancy neglect. Individuals may learn about health choices—such as which provider to go to—by observing their peers' decisions and experiences. To interpret peer behavior, they must employ some theory as to how and why others made their own decisions. For example, an individual who observes her two neighbors go to a local witch doctor needs to think through what information their choice reveals. One possibility is that both those neighbors chose to visit the witch doctor due to independent private information. Another is that one of those neighbors simply observed and imitated the other. In the latter case, the signal in support of visiting the witch doctor is weaker—despite observing two neighbors, there is effectively just one information source.

Eyster and Rabin (2010) provide a model of naïve social learning in which people fail to appreciate the redundancy in their predecessors' actions by naively interpreting their actions as independent. The authors show that societies which behave in this way can converge to confident and wrong beliefs, an outcome that is impossible in standard rational-actor economics. Eyster et al. (2018) run a lab experiment in which student subjects act in precisely this way: by failing to account for the redundancy in one another's actions, subjects do worse than they would do without the possibility for social learning. While we do not have tests of this from the health domain, social learning about health behaviors and providers might be a promising domain in which to study these biases. We discuss applications related to technology adoption in Section 6.

Sampling and statistical biases. People often generalize from small amounts of information—they tend to exaggerate the extent to which a small sample of outcomes represents the distribution of outcomes they will face in the future (Tversky and Kahneman, 1971; Griffin and Tversky, 1992; Rabin, 2002). For example, an individual who recovered from an illness after visiting a health provider and following their instructions may be excessively confident that the provider is highly able.

Furthermore, summary statistics about a health behavior or product might not be sufficient to correct beliefs: people also display a tendency to under-infer from large samples (Griffin and Tversky, 1992; Benjamin et al., 2016). Information campaigns that provide scientific evidence supporting a new treatment may thus have limited effect, since individuals might continue to overweight individual negative experiences or anecdotes relative to seemingly conclusive statistical evidence that runs counter. Countering these statistical biases is potentially critical for more accurate beliefs and better health behaviors.

---

porated into the reference point, the past news no longer "hurts". In contrast, in the case of anticipatory utility, news once learned will continue to affect one's anticipatory utility in future time periods.

3.4 Incorrect mental models

Individuals may interpret what they see through the wrong causal model or theory, as investigated by Schwartzstein (2014). Gagnon-Bartsch et al. (2018) show theoretically that, if individuals have in mind the wrong theory, and they use that theory to direct their attention to information, they may fail to correct their beliefs despite repeatedly observing outcomes which are inconsistent with their beliefs.

One potential source of mistakes in causal inference in health behaviors is that many health conditions are self-correcting. That is, most individuals will naturally recover, given time, from most illnesses. Individuals may misattribute their recovery to any health care choices they made while sick.

Relatedly, an incorrect mental model which seems important in health behaviors in poor countries is a belief in magical theories of sickness such as curses, witchcraft, the evil eye, and superstitions. If individuals see the world through such beliefs, then they may mis-infer from observing episodes of sickness, recovery or even death by updating about irrelevant variables while not attending to causally relevant factors.

Ashraf et al. (2017) provide another example in the context of traditional beliefs about maternal risk in Zambia. The authors describe a wide-spread traditional belief that marital infidelity is a primary cause of health complications during childbirth. This superstition discourages women from sharing their experience with others, and even from seeing medical help when complications arise during delivery, since revealing difficulties would cause stigma for the pregnant woman. In addition, the authors argue, the traditional mental model causes the community to misattribute maternal deaths to infidelity, making it harder for social learning about the true risk factors to occur.

Beliefs regarding diarrhea can cause dehydration and is fatal for more than half a million infants annually. Oral Rehydration Solution (ORS) made of sugar and salts is highly effective at preventing dehydration and decreasing fatalities from diarrhea. Yet in many areas it is not widely used, despite its low cost. While one could come up with behavioral explanations that could arguably limit ORS take-up, evidence suggests that a key constraint is simply access to information about its effectiveness, which is in part not demanded or valued since many parents have the wrong mental model of diarrhea.

Parents observe their infant's watery stools and infer that they should *decrease* their child's fluid intake (which is exactly the wrong thing to do, but is an intuitive conclusion). In India, when poor women were asked how to treat an infant's diarrhea, 30 to 50 percent recommended decreasing fluids to keep the infant "dry" (Datta and Mullainathan, 2014). In fact, reducing fluid intake is a common response to infant diarrhea in many regions of the world (Carter et al., 2015). In this case people are not merely unsure of the right course of action, but instead confidently hold utterly false beliefs.

3.5 Other behavioral factors

Emotions and decision-making. Making rational economic decisions is difficult even in the best of times. Decisions regarding health care must often be made in very difficult times. When an individual or a family-member is sick, emotions of sadness, fear, and anger are likely to be prominent. While behavioral economics has not studied the role of emotions in as much detail as phenomena like present bias or loss aversion, evidence exists in psychology that emotions systematically affect decision-making (Loewenstein and Lerner, 2003; Lerner et al., 2015). Health behaviors may be a valuable application of those ideas to studying economic behaviors.

Salience. Incentives for health behavior might operate not only due to the incentive-effect itself, but because the incentives make the importance of the behavior salient to individuals. Such salience effects could increase individuals' perceived benefits from investing in their health or they could serve as reminders in situations that necessitate repeated actions, for instance, vaccinations or medical adherence. The role of salience in the context of health investments remains to be investigated in future work.

Social image. In an innovative study in Sierra Leone, Karing (2018) studies how social image concerns can be leveraged to increase vaccination rates. She provides mothers with colored bracelets that allow them to signal to others whether their child is vaccinated. The author cleverly designed her study to enable her to disentangle social-image motives from memory and salience (for instance, by providing placebo bracelets that do not communicate information about the number of vaccinations completed, but which plausibly still remind the mother about vaccinations). Karing finds that the intervention increases timely and complete vaccination at a cost of 1 USD per child.

Zero-pricing and the absence of sunk-cost effects. Policy-makers often want to encourage take-up of preventive health, sometimes due to behavioral internalities, but also due to straightforward epidemiological externalities or social concerns for children or fiscal externalities from increased labor supply and taxation (Baird et al., 2016). From a policy perspective, the above discussion suggests that charging a low price is not likely to be a good solution, since it deters many people from purchasing, while not raising much revenue. Demand is sensitive enough to price that it will typically make sense to go all the way down to a zero price. This argument does not depend upon arguing for any special psychology around zero pricing.[22] Logistical costs of dealing with any payment provide another argument for a zero price instead of a small positive price.

In tension with the desire to increase take-up, development organizations, including international financial institutions such as the World Bank, have at times

---

[22] One might argue even for negative prices, but these create obvious incentives for people to take the good, accept the subsidy, and then not use it.

advocated charging users for preventive health products and services. The main motivation for this is the pursuit of financial sustainability. However, another reason that is often cited in support of positive prices is that higher prices may stimulate higher usage through a sunk-cost effect. The sunk cost effect describes a direct effect that price has on use: it predicts that paying a price for a good makes an individual more likely to use it (Thaler, 1980; Eyster, 2002). These effects have been demonstrated in evidence from the field and the lab in rich countries. For instance, Arkes and Blumer (1985) experimentally offered discounts to season ticket holders at a theater and show a positive relationship between the effective price paid for a ticket and performance attendance.

In the context of preventive health products in the developing world, there is good evidence that higher prices (or even positive relative to zero prices) do *not* cause greater product use. Ashraf et al. (2010) use a field experiment to estimate the impact of the price of a drinking water disinfectant on its use. Their experimental design uses a two-stage randomization procedure as in Karlan and Zinman (2009) to distinguish between a screening effect, through which prices limit take-up to buyers who are more likely to use the product, and a sunk-cost effect. Conditional on a household's willingness to pay, they randomize surprise price-discounts to obtain variation in the actual price paid by a household. The authors find a strong screening effect, but no evidence of a sunk-cost effect on ultimate usage of the product. While willingness to pay sensibly predicts usage, the actual transaction amount paid does not. Those who paid a positive price were no more likely to use the product at endline than those who received it for free.

Cohen and Dupas (2010) use a similar two-stage price randomization design to study the influence of prices on use of insecticide-treated bed nets. Conditional on purchase of a net at a posted price, they surprise buyers with a randomly determined discount and estimate the relationship between the discount size and net use. Consistent with the results of Ashraf et al. (2010), they find no significant effect of effective price on usage, suggesting that the sunk cost effect is not an important determinant of usage of health products.

Overall, therefore, the evidence suggests that a policy-maker looking to increase usage of preventive-health products should avoid small positive prices, as they lead to large reductions in take-up without increasing utilization.

4 Savings

In recent years, an active field-experimental literature has studied savings in developing countries.[23] At the individual level, as described in Section 2, savings are

---

[23] See Karlan et al. (2014b) for an excellent recent review of neoclassical and behavioral constraints on saving in developing countries.

necessary to self-insure against risks and to finance lumpy investments. Barriers to savings might thus reduce welfare and opportunities for growth.

One part of the recent literature on savings has studied "standard" barriers to saving, such as a lack of access to formal savings products, for instance, due to prohibitive costs of opening a bank account. Several papers randomize subsidies for opening various types of bank accounts or other savings products, with mixed results. Dupas et al. (2018a) conduct experiments in three countries and find only small effects of providing bank accounts to poor individuals. Many participants in these experiments do not actively use their newly-opened bank accounts. The authors conclude that merely expanding access to bank accounts is unlikely to lead to noticeable welfare improvements among the poor. In contrast, other papers find increases in productive investment (Dupas and Robinson, 2013a), savings (Prina, 2015), and even income (Schaner, 2018). One interpretation is that a subset of individuals has high returns to access to formal savings products, while for most poor individuals, access is not the only constraint on saving.[24]

What other constraints may be important in reducing savings among the poor? In this section, we discuss various behavioral factors which may play a role in reducing savings, as well as behavioral tools which have been used by policy-makers to increase savings.

4.1 Commitment savings devices

Commitment savings. Present bias can greatly influence savings decisions. A key prediction of the present-bias is that households accumulate few liquid savings over time, while building up substantial illiquid wealth. This prediction seems broadly consistent with savings patterns in both rich and poor countries (Angeletos et al., 2001; Banerjee and Duflo, 2007; Collins et al., 2009). For more detail, we refer the reader to Section 2 of this chapter and the discussion of time preferences in Ericson and Laibson (2018).

Present bias paired with at least some level of sophistication implies demand for commitment, as discussed in detail in Section 3.2 in the context of health behavior. If present bias reduces savings, individuals might have demand for commitment devices to increase their savings. There is evidence of such demand for commitment in the domain of savings. In a founding paper in this literature, Ashraf et al. (2006) offered a commitment savings account to a random subset of study participants through a bank in the Philippines. About a quarter of respondents took up this offer, electing to restrict their future access to their savings until a savings goal was met, or until a target date. A year later, those offered commitment savings had substantially higher average bank account savings than those in the control group.

A subsequent literature has investigated how different types of commitments impact savings. An important contribution by Dupas and Robinson (2013b) compared

---

[24] This evidence raises the question of why the individuals with high returns to savings accounts do not borrow or save enough to pay the fees (typically a few dollars) associated with opening these accounts.

different types of commitment devices of varying strength. They compare the effects, relative to a control group, of providing participants with either a safe box in which to store money at home (to which the participants have the key) or instead a lock box (whose key is held by the research staff). The idea is that the former provides a softer commitment than the latter treatment. Both treatments were motivated as targeting saving to cover health expenses. A year later, the authors find high sustained use of both products, but only the more flexible, softer commitment of the safe box led to increased spending on preventive care.

The findings of Dupas and Robinson (2013b) connect to a key open question surrounding the usefulness of commitment devices: the optimal tradeoff between commitment and flexibility (Beshears et al., 2017). A commitment that is too weak will not overcome self-control problems, while one which is too restrictive will drive down take-up due to the real costs of commitment in uncertain environments (Amador et al., 2006; Laibson, 2015).

The tradeoff between weak and strong commitment is complicated by the existence of partial naïveté. John (2018) studies savings commitment accounts in the Philippines (in the same context as Ashraf et al., 2006) and shows that many of the individuals who demand commitment savings fail to follow through with their commitment and incur financial penalties. As a result, these individuals are (ex post) made worse off by being offered the commitment device. Partial naïveté about present bias can explain this result: partially naïve individuals realize that they have a self-control problem, so they will have demand for commitment. However, they might under-estimate the needed strength of the commitment, so they might sign up for commitment contracts that do not provide sufficient incentives to follow through.

It is worth noting that savings commitments are not restricted to formal savings accounts. Instead, social networks and savings groups such as ROSCAs may effectively provide commitment. Kast et al. (2018) show large impacts of public goal-setting and group monitoring on savings, emphasizing the potential for social ties to pay a role in motivating individuals to save. Breza and Chandrasekhar (2015) randomly assign "monitors" to savers within the same village and show that monitors cause an increase in savings of over 40% a year later, with some evidence of a social image or reputation channel driving the effects.

We speculate that such socially-provided commitment might also be able to more flexibly deal with uncertainty and shocks. While it is difficult for a formal provider to contract on and verify shocks which may affect savings, others in the same social or economic network may be better placed to do so.

Another potential weakness of commitment savings accounts is that they merely prevent individuals from withdrawing money that they have already deposited. However, present-biased individuals might have difficulties depositing money into their savings account in the first place. Alternative designs that include automatic payments into savings accounts (e.g. using M-Pesa in Kenya) could prove to be highly effective.

4.2 Designing financial products for behavioral agents

Numerous behavioral factors beyond present bias can impact individuals' savings decisions, including mental accounting, default effects, limited attention, and memory issues. Some of the existing evidence in support of the importance of these factors for savings decisions is limited, especially in developing countries. Better understanding these factors could uncover cheap and highly effective ways to impact savings behavior (Chetty, 2015). Further evidence would greatly improve policymakers' ability to design savings accounts and financial products to better serve the poor.

Mental accounting. Money from different sources and in different accounts should be fungible and is treated as such in standard economic models. However, in practice people may have "mental accounts" for different types of expenditures, which makes money effectively non-fungible across accounts (Thaler, 1985; Shefrin and Thaler, 2004; Hastings and Shapiro, 2013). Such mental accounts may in part be used to avoid overspending and thus deal with self-control problems. The existence of mental accounting implies that small details in the specific design of financial products can powerfully impact behavior. For instance, an individual might use unconditional transfers labeled as "health resources" primarily on health expenditures, simply because the label causes these resources to become part of the individual's "health" mental account.

Dupas and Robinson (2013b), discussed above, find evidence of the importance of mental accounting. For instance, earmarking expenses for health emergencies increased individuals' ability to cope with health shocks. Similarly, in a horse race between a hard and soft commitment savings account, Karlan and Linden (2018) find that the weaker commitment account causes stronger increases in savings for educational supplies, which in turn increased test scores, in contrast to the stronger commitment account. The authors argue that the labeling of the resources for educational purposes was a strong enough commitment while also allowing some flexibility for individuals.

Default effects. Setting default choices is a cheap but often highly powerful option in the behavioral-economics toolbox, as shown in the context of retirement savings (Madrian and Shea, 2001) and organ donations (Johnson and Goldstein, 2004) in rich countries. For instance, setting the default to automatic enrollment (wherein individuals are enrolled unless they explicitly opt out) as opposed to a non-enrollment default option can have enormous impacts on individuals' retirement choices, with impacts lasting over a decade (Chetty et al., 2014; Choi et al., 2002).

In a starkly different developing-country context, Blumenstock et al. (2018) find similar results. They take advantage of rising financial inclusion and show large impacts of setting opt-in defaults on savings behavior among workers in Afghanistan who receive their salaries using mobile money. Moreover, the authors provide evidence of the underlying mechanisms driving default effects and argue that present bias and the hassle costs of thinking through different options play an important role, while other factors such as limited memory are less important.

These findings highlight the importance of the economic environment and institutions in shaping savings behaviors. In contrast to developed countries, most individuals in developing countries do not have the option to automatically save for retirement (such as using 401k savings vehicles) or to have their salary paid into their bank account monthly. Instead, many workers are paid daily or even hourly, which may increase individuals' susceptibility to temptation. For instance, Casaburi and Macchiavello (2018) argue that farmers may prefer to sell milk to the dairy where they get paid monthly, rather than to sell it on the spot market for a higher price because this creates a form of savings since they get paid at the end of the month.

Memory and attention. Limited memory and attention might distort individuals' decision-making in various ways, ranging from medical adherence to savings behavior. Memory constraints might be particularly important for the poor since low literacy levels make it difficult to effectively use of written reminders or similar technologies. Karlan et al. (2016) study the impact of reminders in a field experiment with three different banks in Bolivia, Peru, and the Philippines. Their idea is that, when making consumption decisions in the moment, individuals may forget or not attend to their future consumption of investment goals. They find that reminder messages which increase the salience of the savings goal help individuals follow through on their weak-commitment savings plan, suggesting important interactions between memory and self-control (as in Ericson, 2017).

Exponential growth bias. Financial literacy can greatly impact individuals' savings choices (Lusardi, 2009). For instance, individuals may also underestimate the returns to savings due to a systematic under-estimation of the power of compound interest (Stango and Zinman, 2009). Song (2015) provides evidence consistent with exponential growth bias using a field experiment in China. A treatment group which is taught the principles of compound interest contributes substantially more to a government pension plan.

New technologies. The development of new technologies such as mobile money creates great opportunities for the financial inclusion and empowerment of the poor (Jack and Suri, 2014, 2016; Suri, 2017). Such technologies can greatly help individuals with behavioral biases, for instance, through automatic payment schemes or reminders (Cadena and Schoar, 2011). A thorough understanding of the above behavioral biases can greatly improve the design of adequate financial products. However, new technologies also create potential for behavioral agents to be targeted and exploited, raising important questions of consumer protection (Ru and Schoar, 2016). For instance, recent increases in sports-betting using mobile phones in East Africa, and the growth of an industry making small loans at very high interest rates are important topics for future research.

5 Risk and insurance

Risk plays a central role in the lives of the poor (Collins et al., 2009). Poor households are simultaneously exposed to numerous risks, including market risks (e.g. prices), production risks (weather shocks, pests), health risks, asset risks (e.g. theft), and even political risk (e.g. civil conflict) (Hazell, 1992; Dercon, 2005). Under most plausible utility functions, the sharply diminishing marginal utility of income at very low consumption levels implies a particularly strong need for insurance. Yet, little social insurance (whether health or income insurance) is provided by governments in poor countries. Poor countries also have less well-developed markets for dealing with risk through private insurance.

Instead, societies have developed non-market institutions for coping with risk (Besley, 1995; Townsend, 1994). A large literature studies informal risk-sharing in developing countries, and how risk considerations affect crop choice, migration choice, and marriage, and other decisions. Evidence on the extent of risk sharing within villages (or other networks, such as sub-caste networks in India) is mixed. In some cases, one cannot reject the hypothesis that consumption moves only with village-wide income shocks, not idiosyncratic shocks, but in other cases consumption and even mortality and long-run health outcomes move with idiosyncratic shocks (Paxson, 1992; Townsend, 1995; Yang and Choi, 2007; Rose, 1999; Maccini and Yang, 2009). There is also evidence that consumption moves with health shocks, sometimes dramatically (Gertler and Gruber, 2002; Collins et al., 2009).

Since people in poor countries are often exposed to weather risk, and since such risk is not generally subject to asymmetric information, it is a puzzle that rainfall insurance is not more common. Weather risk is different from other risks (e.g. illness or death in the family) because it is not idiosyncratic, but correlated within regions, and therefore cannot be easily insured away within villages or even across villages. These reasons make rainfall insurance a particularly interesting context to study behavioral biases, since other reasons for market failures or low take-up may be less relevant here.

Weather insurance remains uncommon despite subsidies from governments and NGOs. In India, rainfall-indexed insurance was introduced in 2003, but despite monsoons being notoriously unpredictable, and a large share of the population being dependent on rainfall, take-up has been disappointing (Stein, 2016). Several field experiments have found low levels of take-up, despite heavy subsidies and significant marketing efforts (Giné et al., 2008; Cole et al., 2013). Some of this low take-up may be explained by standard reasons, e.g. basis risk (Clarke, 2016) or fear of contractual non-performance (Doherty and Schlesinger, 1991).[25]

Below, we focus on potential behavioral reasons that might contribute to inefficiently low take-up levels of insurance. We first consider existing evidence of non-standard preferences affecting the demand for insurance. We then investigate the role of non-standard beliefs.

---

[25] Lack of trust is more generally correlated with low levels of participation in financial markets (Guiso et al., 2006). Low social trust may have deep historical roots and be culturally-determined, as discussed in Section 9.

5.1 **Non-standard preferences affecting insurance demand**

Present bias. In textbook models of insurance, resources are transferred only across states of the world. In practice, however, insurance almost always additionally entails shifting resources over time. That is, in period t, individuals need to decide whether they would like to purchase insurance that pays out in a pre-specified bad state in period $t + 1$. This time structure of decisions and payments allows for the possibility of time preferences affecting lowering individuals' demand for insurance.

Casaburi and Willis (2018) test this idea by offering Kenyan farmers crop-insurance in which the premium is charged only when uncertainty is resolved, that is, at the time of harvest. Their unusual insurance product thus purely distributes resources between future states. They find that demand for such insurance is dramatically higher than for standard contracts with upfront payments of insurance premia, even at highly subsidized levels. The authors argue that this result is driven by present bias. They also find that offering farmers a commitment to purchase insurance a month later increases take-up by 21 percentage points, suggesting present bias and liquidity constraints as important inhibitors of demand for standard insurance contracts.

The authors could enforce post-harvest premium payments due to the contract-farming setting they study. Their insight suggests a comparative advantage in insurance provision for entities which have the power to enforce contemporaneous transfers from those experiencing good states to those receiving bad shocks. In rich countries, governments have a major role in providing social insurance. In poor countries, social groups such as kinship networks, villages, or sub-caste groups may play a key role, and formal sector jobs may be desirable in part because of the capacity of large firms to provide such insurance.

Reference-dependent utility. Loss aversion can have ambiguous impacts on demand for insurance (Eckles and Wise, 2011). On the one hand, reference-dependence increases risk aversion over small and moderate stakes, as argued by Sydnor's (2010) study of home-owner insurance in the US. On the other hand, if up-front insurance premia are bracketed separately from insurance payouts and considered as losses, loss aversion could curb demand for insurance by making the premium payment particularly unattractive. In fact, loss aversion could play some role in explaining the results by Casaburi and Willis (2018) described above. This highlights the importance of understanding what reference-point individuals use when evaluating their insurance choices, as well as how they bracket their decisions.

Finally, Kahneman and Tversky's (1979) Prospect Theory argues that individuals overweight small probability events in their evaluation of risky gambles. Such overweighting would tend to increase demand for insurance against low-probability but high-risk events, potentially heightening the puzzle of low insurance demand in developing countries.

5.2 Non-standard beliefs affecting insurance demand

Projection bias and recency effects. Individuals may exhibit projection bias when evaluating insurance products. In good states of the world, they may have difficulty appropriately valuing bad states of the world, i.e. they may underestimate their marginal utility in potential bad states if the present state is good (Loewenstein et al., 2003). Relatedly, individuals might place disproportionate weight on observations from the recent past or extrapolate recent trends, and thus overestimate the probability of their current state occurring in the future (Hogarth and Einhorn, 1992; Fuster et al., 2010).

Such individuals value future insurance less than when they are currently in a good state (holding everything else equal), thus curbing insurance demand for individuals who are currently in good states. In contrast, individuals in bad states may overvalue insurances, but bad states are more likely to generate liquidity constraints, which could reduce take-up despite a high valuation.[26] Moreover, if bad states are rare, projection bias will systematically depress demand for insurance (since demand will typically be elicited during a good state). This is ironic because insurance offers its largest benefit for low-probability high-loss events.

Recent work in developing countries provides evidence that the current idiosyncratic state of the world does affect individuals' demand for insurance.[27] Chang et al. (2018) find that fluctuations in daily air pollution levels predict individuals' decision to purchase or cancel health insurance in China. Since these fluctuations are hardly predictive of future pollution levels and thus the value of insurance, such effects are difficult to reconcile with the neoclassical model. Instead, these demand patterns are consistent with individuals over- and under-weighting future pollution-related health risk depending on the state of pollution on the day of their purchase or cancellation decision.

Karlan et al. (2014a) find evidence consistent with recency bias in their study of agricultural decision-making among small-scale farmers in Ghana. They find that demand for insurance is higher for farmers following a payout to themselves or someone their network. In contrast, demand is lower for previously insured farmers who did not receive payouts due to good rain. Such demand patterns are consistent with projection and recency bias, and salience, though they might also be explained by limited trust in the insurance agency, with observed payouts increasing trust.

Motivated reasoning and over-optimism. As discussed in Section 3.3, motivated reasoning could explain individuals' lack of health investments. If individuals directly derive utility from beliefs about their future wellbeing, they may seek to maintain biased beliefs about their current health status or the future. Such biased beliefs might

---

[26] Bad states may also fail to come to mind or be salient when times are good, and vice versa (Bordalo et al., 2012).

[27] Further evidence on recency effects in insurance choices includes a body of work by Slovic et al., 1974; Kunreuther et al., 1978; and Gallagher, 2014.

lower demand for insurance. To the best of our knowledge, no existing evidence considers this hypothesis.

Beliefs in higher powers. Individuals' beliefs might deviate in more dramatic ways from standard probability assessments, including beliefs in higher powers, witchcraft, and magic. In a clever lab-in-the-field study in Ghana, Auriol et al. (2018) find that enrolling individuals in a commercial funeral-insurance policy lowers individuals' investment behavior in religious goods, as measured by choices between payments for themselves and contributions to church. The authors interpret their results as evidence of individuals perceiving the church as a source of insurance, derived from beliefs in an interventionist god. Such beliefs could be relevant barriers to demand for formal insurance in other settings as well.

6 Technology adoption

The development literature has identified various instances of seemingly sub-optimal technology choices. In Pakistan, Atkin et al. (2017) showed that take-up of a new technology that reduced waste in the production of soccer balls was surprisingly low, despite its potential to increase profits.[28] Other examples of apparently non-optimal technology choice in the development literature include fertilizer use in Kenya (Duflo et al., 2008) and textile factories in India (Bloom et al., 2013).

Below, we discuss two behavioral factors that could potentially either interfere with technology adoption: present bias, and limited attention. We then argue that behavioral social learning could produce badly distorted social outcomes.

6.1 Limited attention

Hanna et al. (2014) provide an explanation why individuals might not take advantage of apparently useful and readily available information. Given that attention is limited, individuals can only focus on and process a small subset of all the potentially available information. Rational attention theories predict that individuals focus on what they think is most important, and their beliefs about what is important are assumed to be accurate (Sims, 2003, 2010). Therefore, such theories predict only limited inefficiencies and welfare losses due to limited attention.

In contrast, Schwartzstein's (2014) model of attention argues that current beliefs about what is important in the world guide individuals' attention and learning, which in turn shape individuals' beliefs in the future. If individuals have incorrect beliefs about the importance of different aspects of the world, they might pay less than optimal attention to them, and thus might never learn that their beliefs were wrong. Therefore, wrong beliefs can persist indefinitely even in the presence of data which

---

[28] The authors point to the role of agency problems within the firm.

would otherwise lead to revision of beliefs. In such models, inattention can create significant inefficiencies and lead to large welfare losses.

Hanna et al. (2014) apply this insight to technology adoption among seaweed farmers in Indonesia. Given the complex production function with many possibly important dimensions, the authors argue that farmers will only pay attention to the dimensions of production they think are important. Hanna et al. (2014) track the relationship between the size of planted seaweed pods and farmers' output, arguing that larger pods lead to greater output. Farmers, when asked, did not suggest that pod size is an important determinant of output. 86% of farmers did not even know the pod sizes they themselves planted, even though 83% of them were literate and the average farming experience amongst the sample was 18 years.

Moreover, natural variation in pod size created numerous quasi-experiments that farmers could have learned from. Hanna et al. (2014) argue that despite large amounts of data being available for free on their own farms, inattention appears to have prevented farmers from noticing this relationship. Hanna et al.'s (2014) data is based on only a single season and there is significant cross-sectional variation in optimal pod size. Since the authors did not collect impacts of their intervention on subsequent profits, some questions remain whether optimal pod sizes for given farms vary over time and whether the intervention indeed increased profits. Additional data to shed light on this issue would be valuable.

If attention is limited, providing simple information with tips about optimizing production may be more effective than providing full information. In an RCT to test the above theory of inattention, Hanna et al. (2014) find that presenting farmers with summaries that draw their attention to the importance of pod sizes changed their farming techniques and increased output, but simply providing them with data on initial pod size and eventual yield from each of their pods did not induce learning and did not change farming behavior.

Similarly, Bennear et al. (2013) find in Bangladesh that a simpler message (providing red versus green labels) about whether a well has dangerous levels of arsenic is more effective than providing more continuous information. In the Dominican Republic, Drexler et al. (2014) find that a simple "rule-of-thumb" training significantly improved the financial practices of participating firm relative to a fuller training about accounting. This evidence suggests that there are cases when limited attention may lead to sub-optimal decisions and providing well-chosen limited information may be more effective than providing the full set of available information.

There are also potential downsides of presenting simplified information. First, there may be heterogeneity in the population and some individuals may benefit from fuller information. Second, external analysts may not understand the decision problem as well as the people to whom they are trying to transmit information, or they may pursue different objectives. They may therefore offer inappropriate advice. For example, in an agricultural context, agricultural scientists or government departments may seek to maximize agricultural production rather than profits and thus may not appropriately value farmer time.

6.2 **Present bias**

Duflo et al. (2011) study the extent to which present bias influences agricultural technology adoption and how policy can mitigate its effect. In previous work with small-scale maize farmers in Western Kenya, Duflo et al. (2008) find high returns to top-dressing fertilizer in Western Kenya if used at the right quantity. However, despite these potentially high returns at the time of the study, only about 20 percent of farmers used fertilizer in any given season, which suggests mis-optimization.

Farmers have money around the time of harvest and report plans to purchase fertilizer before planting begins. However, few farmers then follow through on their plans. Duflo et al. (2011) posit a model of stochastic present bias and partial naïveté. A partially naïve, present-biased farmer may put off purchasing fertilizer until the last minute, expecting to purchase the fertilizer later. Then, having underestimated how likely she is to be impatient in the last period, the farmer may also be impatient in the last period that buying is possible, and thus end up not purchasing the fertilizer.

This sort of model of decision-making has important implications for debates over fertilizer subsidies. Agriculture experts sometimes feel that farmers are using too little of particular inputs and they sometimes advocate heavy subsidies to encourage adoption. Economists have historically been more sceptical, arguing that this may distort input use away from the optimal level, potentially with negative environmental consequences. The model suggests that while heavy subsidies could help present-biased farmers overcome any immediate utility costs of purchasing fertilizer, they could induce overuse of fertilizer by farmers who are not present biased.

Duflo et al. (2011) argue that the tradeoff could be improved through better policy design: smaller, time-limited subsidies offered just after harvest could mitigate present bias while causing only second-order distortions among farmers without time inconsistent preferences. If farmers have more cash on hand in the period immediately following the harvest, then offering small, time-limited subsidies could lead to an increase in fertilizer use among present-biased farmers while limiting other distortions. These early discounts would only need to be large enough to overcome the utility costs of purchasing fertilizer if offered after the harvest, whereas discounts offered later, when the farmer is poorer would also need to cover part of the out-of-pocket fertilizer costs.

Based on these predictions, Duflo et al. (2011) designed a program to offer time-limited discounts for fertilizer that allowed farmers to purchase a voucher for fertilizer immediately after the harvest at the regular price, with free delivery around planting time. Time-limited discounts around the time of harvest substantially increased take-up of fertilizer. Moreover, this program was more effective than offering a 50 percent discount on fertilizer later in the season.

This evidence suggests that time-limited discounts around times when individuals have money available could be an efficient policy tool to increase fertilizer use or other desirable behaviors. However, as always, scaling any given policy presents challenges. In the case of time-limited discounts for fertilizer use, a specific scaled-up version of the program led to positive yet significantly smaller impacts on fertilizer adoption than the original study (Schilbach, 2015).

We hypothesize that present bias may also induce procrastination in learning about new technologies. If adoption requires costly experimentation and costly attention, present-biased individuals might procrastinate over conducting such experimentation. Such individuals would benefit, again, from decreasing the costs of learning through the provision of simplified information. Moreover, commitment devices for future experimentation could help overcome such procrastination problems. Agricultural extension services that incorporate self-help groups and encourage public commitments to attempt experimentation with new technologies may, in addition to solving failures of social learning, help solve such self-control problems.

Finally, present bias may induce non-adoption through the usual mechanism of generating liquidity constraints, as described in previous section. Lee et al. (2016) experimentally estimate the demand curve for an electricity connection in rural Kenya and conclude that consumer surplus—as revealed by willingness to pay—is considerably lower than the cost of provision. However, liquidity constraints may contribute to their estimates of low demand. The authors present evidence that credit constraints are indeed binding, which may influence welfare calculations and induce low adoption of even desired technologies.

6.3 Behavioral learning

For individual farmers, identifying the best technologies to adopt and how to use them is challenging, given that experimentation is costly, and outcomes are noisy. Thus, learning from the experiences and knowledge of others—social learning—may promote adoption of useful technologies (e.g., Munshi, 2004; Bandiera and Rasul, 2006; Conley and Udry, 2010).

Behavioral economics suggests several ways in which individuals may misinterpret information. For example, individuals may neglect the extent to which the pieces of information they hear from multiple sources are "redundant", in that they themselves derive from a common source (Eyster and Rabin, 2010). They may also over-generalize from small amounts of information, such as the recommendations of a handful of neighbors (Tversky and Kahneman, 1971), and underestimate how much can be learned from a large sample, such as the aggregated recommendations of hundreds of farmers (Benjamin et al., 2016).

Below, we discuss these behavioral factors in more detail, discuss the existing evidence, and argue that theory suggests they may interact to seriously distort.

6.3.1 Barriers to sharing or seeking information

On the demand side, social learning in agriculture requires farmers to actively seek, or at least be receptive to, information and recommendations from others. On the supply side, social learning similarly requires farmers who have some information or experience to be willing to share it with others. Certain behavioral which might make farmers hesitant to seek or share information with others.

Distributional preferences. Whether and whom farmers are willing to share information with may depend on social preferences such as altruism and envy, and how these apply to others within the farmers' social networks. For example, if farmers' have envious or competitive preferences towards their peers, they may avoid sharing information to remain or become relatively more successful. Farmers might even choose to share false information to maintain an advantage. In contrast, individuals are likely to be altruistic towards others from their own extended families, kin or ethnic groups, and might therefore be willing to provide advice to such individuals.

Existing research from Uganda provides some evidence for such differential effects: agricultural extension workers target information towards farmers from their own social group, while withholding information from others (Bandiera et al., 2018). This evidence suggests that accounting for the structure of social networks and distributional preferences across those networks may help explain patterns of social learning and allow for the design of more efficient methods to seed and transmit information.

Social-image concerns. Social-image concerns may keep farmers from asking others for information or advice, since doing so may signal ignorance or low ability on the part of the asker. An experiment conducted by Chandrasekhar et al. (2018) in rural India provides some evidence for such an effect. They design a field experiment in which "seekers" must acquire information from a paired "advisor". In one arm of the experiment, the seeker's need for the information is (artificially) correlated with their ability from a baseline test, such that choosing to ask for advice may signal low ability. In the other arm, ability is revealed to the advisor regardless of the seeker's choice to ask for information, such that the signaling channel is shut down, although low-ability seekers may still feel some shame from interacting with an advisor who has learned of his low ability. The authors find that signaling is the dominant force overall and that low ability individuals do face large stigma inhibitions: there is a 55% decline in the probability of seeking when the need for information is correlated with cognitive ability.

If such mechanisms are more broadly relevant—that is, if asking for information about technology signals low ability even without artificially creating a correlation between low ability and need for information—then interventions to reduce the stigma of asking for information, for instance by using technology to make accessing such information private, could increase the demand for social learning.

Social image concerns might also affect the supply of social information. On the one hand, if acquiring the image of being a helpful community member is valued, then social-image incentives such as publicly acknowledging those who share information might increase the supply of information. On the other hand, social-image motives might instead reduce the supply or quality of information. For instance, farmers may want to selectively share positive experiences that create an image of success, while suppressing their failures, thus providing biased information. Similarly, farmers may fear unfairly acquiring an image of being either incompetent or malicious, if accurate information they share leads a peer to make a decision that ends poorly due to chance.

6.3.2 Barriers to correctly interpreting information

A literature in psychology and economics documents several biases in learning and errors in probabilistic reasoning (see Benjamin, 2018 in this volume for a thorough review). Little research on these biases, however, has occurred in field settings or in developing countries. Biases in learning could be important to technology adoption, causing people to put too much or too little stock in available information. This could influence their willingness to experiment and take risks, potentially slowing learning and adoption of productive technologies.

Redundancy neglect. Section 3.3 discussed redundancy bias extensively in the context of health choices. Recall that redundancy neglect describes a failure of Bayesian learning wherein an individual trying to learn by observing others' actions does not account for the fact that other individuals are also engaged in social learning. For instance, an individual may observe multiple neighbors behaving in the same fashion. He may take those separate actions as independent signals of private information whereas, in fact, those neighbors might have in turn have been basing their choice on a single signal from a common source.

This concept is relevant in the context of technology adoption as well. Take, for instance, the context of input adoption amongst smallholder farmers. To correctly interpret the observed behavior of their neighbors, and thereby enhance social learning, farmers must correctly account for these potential "information redundancies" in the network structure of information in their village, for example. Failure to do so could have an outsized effect on how followers value technology. If initial farmers choose suboptimal practice by happenstance, then this inefficient practice may grow entrenched amongst those that follow, creating a situation in which a population is locked into confidentially held false beliefs.

Eyster et al. (2018) and Enke and Zimmermann (2019) conduct lab experiments in which subjects act in precisely this way: by failing to account for the redundancy in signals, subjects do worse than they would do without the possibility for social learning. Murfin and Pratt (2019) provide field evidence that finance professionals exhibit redundancy neglect when pricing loans, as well.

Sampling and statistical biases. In Section 3.3, we discussed sampling and statistical biases and that generalizing from small samples is a widespread phenomenon in a variety of contexts.[29] This evidence is relevant to behavioral development economics since farmers, for instance, might form excessively strong negative opinions about the value of a new technology based on a few unlucky experiences of his own. Agricultural outcomes have high variance, and the inference drawn from a small sample of observations is likely to be misleading. Furthermore, over-inference from small samples might be particularly relevant in rural contexts where farmers' information is often limited to their own experience and that of their neighbors

Moreover, even summary statistics about a technology's profitability based on ample data might not be sufficient to remedy statistical biases: people also dis-

---

[29] This has been termed "Belief in the Law of Small Numbers" by Tversky and Kahneman (1971).

play a tendency to under–infer from large samples (Griffin and Tversky, 1992; Benjamin et al., 2016). Information campaigns that provide scientific evidence supporting a new technology may thus have limited effect, since farmers might continue to overweight individual negative experiences or anecdotes relative to seemingly conclusive statistical evidence that runs counter. This bias prevents farmers from growing confident when they should, meaning that their beliefs are too easily swayed by new data. Such a bias, along with other statistical errors that give undue weight to recent outcomes (e.g., base-rate neglect; see Kahneman and Tversky, 1973 and Benjamin et al., 2018), may therefore underlie why some farmers seem to switch in and out of using a new technology over time (e.g. Suri, 2011). Countering these statistical biases is potentially critical for sustained adoption.

Selection neglect. Above, we highlighted several ways that farmers may selectively transmit information (e.g. due to distributional concerns or for social image motives). For those who receive this information to properly interpret its content, they must properly account for the selection process underlying when and why farmers share information in the first place. Farmers might, for instance, be excited to tell their neighbors and friends when a newly adopted technology works well but say nothing when it works poorly. Alternatively, competitive farmers may decide to keep information about profitable technologies to themselves.

In each of these scenarios, rational inference requires special attention to the selection rule: in the first case, taking recommendations at face value would lead farmers to become overly optimistic about the technology; in the latter, it would lead them to be overly pessimistic. Enke (2017) provides laboratory evidence that many individuals completely neglect the fact that the signals they receive are selected, especially when the environment itself is somewhat complex. However, nudging participants by drawing their attention to the bias leads to much better inference.

7 Labor

This section discusses behavioral issues in labor markets in developing countries. First, we highlight how work patterns in poor countries differ from those in rich countries. Instead of 9-to-5 work in the formal sector as in rich countries, labor markets in developing countries are instead characterized by three features that might potentially increase the importance of behavioral biases: high levels of informality, casual labor, and self-employment.

We discuss evidence on worker productivity and labor supply in developing countries, including female labor-force participation; wage-setting and incentives with behavioral workers; and the selection of workers.

7.1 Labor markets in developing countries

Many economists assume that the natural default type of labor-force participation is full-time employment on a regular schedule (e.g. 9 to 5, Monday to Friday), with time during those hours being devoted to work, and other time being devoted to domestic responsibilities. We typically assume impersonal employment norms and laws governing interactions between workers and their managers during the work period. Such work patterns are far from the historical norm or the current situation in developing countries, where many individuals work in family firms without a sharp delineation of work and domestic time; and others are subject to sometimes coercive, multi-stranded relationships, for example, working as domestic servants or for feudalistic landowners with de facto political authority.

Some historians of the Industrial Revolution argue that it is not at all natural for people to work regular hours in factories under factory discipline, and that peasants had to be turned into workers through pressures like enclosures and through devices like factory bells and provisions to lock out workers who showed up late. Many historians and some economists (e.g., Thompson, 1967; Marglin, 1974) have argued that the introduction of the new management technology of factory discipline was as important to the Industrial Revolution as any purely technological innovation. Such scholars tend to see factory discipline as imposed on workers by capitalists, and perhaps as made possible only by the dispossession of farmers by enclosure of the commons.

Clark (1994) turns this interpretation on its head, with a much more benign view of the role of factory discipline. He argues that workers themselves preferred the introduction of factory discipline as a commitment device. He notes that under the older putting-out system, workers "frequently kept irregular hours, often taking off Monday ('St. Monday') and even Tuesday and working long hours on Thursday and Friday" (Clark, 1994). Clark posits that workers valued the constraints imposed on their behavior by factory discipline because this helped mitigate their self-control problems.

Informality and self-employment. Labor markets in developing countries are characterized by high levels of informality and self-employment. Most people in developing countries are self-employed. The majority of the rural population operates a farm in most developing countries, while many additionally operate a non-agricultural business. The poor are highly likely to be self-employed entrepreneurs, potentially running multiple microenterprises or juggling casual labor and business (Banerjee and Duflo, 2007). In contrast, only 12% of employment in OECD countries is self-employment.

Some standard explanations for the lack of large firms, and the prevalence of self-employment in developing countries, are agency problems, credit constraints and predation. A potential additional explanation is that regular employment may simply be costlier for workers in poor countries. First, it may be harder to hold a formal job simply because of the likelihood of unpredictable demands on one's time. For example, you may have to go to the hospital with family members when they get sick to ensure they receive quality care, or you may yourself be more likely to get sick. Second, preferences for work schedules may feature strategic complementarities, which make fixed scheduled unattractive when others do not also have them.

In the United States, Mas and Pallais (2017) show that workers place little value on work-hours flexibility, and instead have a strong preference for Monday–Friday 9-to-5 jobs. In contrast, in developing countries, where most others are self-employed or engaged in casual day-labor, having a fixed schedule may be unattractive. Social expectations for participation in events like weddings and funerals may be shaped by the fact that most adults have flexible schedules. This fact may partly explain why formal-sector jobs in poor countries often come with a wage premium. Such a premium may in part be a compensating differential and not simply reflect a higher marginal product of labor in the formal sector. It is also consistent with the documented high absence rates of employees even in the private sector in developing countries (Kremer et al., 2005).

In standard models of development such as the Harris and Todaro (1970) model, factory jobs are highly desirable and provide large rents. Many economists assume that distortionary unions, or state-owned firms, or labor legislation provide these rents. An alternative perspective is that these jobs are not particularly desirable. Blattman and Dercon (2018) randomly assign industrial jobs in Ethiopia and find that workers quickly quit and move to different sectors.

One implication of self-employment and informal employment is that workers often set their own work hours and effort, without the structure, commitment and norms provided by formal employers. This feature makes behavioral phenomena such as limited self-control and income-targeting potentially more important in labor markets in developing countries. Consistent with this hypothesis, Fafchamps (1993) and Baird et al. (2016) find very low hours worked in agriculture in some parts of Africa: just 9.8 hours per week among young Kenyan adults employed in agriculture. In contrast, Bick et al. (2018) harmonize survey evidence from 49 countries (although missing India, China and large parts of Sub-Saharan Africa) and conclude that people in poor countries work *more* hours on average than those in rich countries. While we do not yet have a full understanding of labor supply differences across rich and poor countries, we discuss direct evidence on self-control problems at work in Section 7.2 below.

Casual labor in agricultural labor markets. The share of the population employed in agriculture is much higher in poor countries than in rich countries. While most agricultural production in poor countries occurs on smallholder farms, with family labor as an input, there is also a highly active agricultural labor market. Most farms employ outside workers for short spells using informal contracts; providing labor in such markets is an important source of earnings, especially for the poorest amongst the poor (Kaur, 2019).

How efficient are these labor markets? At first glance, agricultural labor markets in poor countries would appear to satisfy many of the conditions for competitive markets: many small buyers and sellers of labor, without formal unions or enforced minimum wages. Yet, surprisingly, such markets exhibit several features such as wage rigidity and limited wage dispersion. We discuss these in Section 7.3 below.

Role of the public sector. Formal employment in developing countries is often dominated by the state. The public sector in poor countries is an attractive employer.

It provides a large wage premium over the private sector (much more so than in rich countries), provides job security with few chances of being fired, and rarely utilizes incentives or performance pay (Finan et al., 2017). This public sector typically does quite poorly at providing public services such as education, health, sanitation and law-and-order, relative to rich countries. A recent literature in development economics has used field experiments to study the personnel economics of the state, including topics related to behavioral labor: the selection of prosocial workers, and the response to monetary and non-monetary incentives. We discuss some of these issues in Section 7.4 below.

While many have seen the high absence rates among government social service employees like teachers and health workers as evidence of weak incentives and poor accountability in the public sector, it is worth noting that absence rates of teachers in private schools are also very high (e.g., 22.8% in Indian private schools, Kremer et al., 2005). One interpretation of this fact is that high absence rates are in fact part of an efficient contract because employees find a regular 9-to-5 schedule to be very costly.

Social norms and networks. Social norms and networks play an important role in labor markets in developing countries, just as in rich countries. However, the nature of the norms and social pressures may differ. For instance, many developing countries have strong norms against female labor force-participation. In India, the caste system prescribes norms regarding appropriate occupations for individuals based on their inherited caste (although surprisingly little recent work in economics studies how this distorts occupational choice). Given the importance of kin or caste networks in poor countries, job search and referrals often flow along these networks, leading to potentially inefficient matching of workers with jobs (Beaman and Magruder, 2012). The barriers to the efficient allocation of workers to jobs—such as due to norms against women or other disadvantaged groups working—may have large aggregate effects on growth, as has been studied in the case of the United States (Hsieh et al., 2018).

In addition, life for workers and even employers in poor countries features many deprivations: the scarcity of money, the prevalence of environmental factors such as noise and heat, and health issues such as chronic sleep deprivation among the urban poor. While we discuss these factors in detail in Section 10 on the psychology of poverty, they may also have implications for worker productivity.

7.2 Labor supply and worker productivity

Self-control problems. One implication of informal work is that productivity may be more influenced by behavioral biases. Given the lack of direct or indirect supervision by workers in informal labor markets, the consequences of workers' self-control problems could be particularly pronounced. Someone who is self-employed will likely not face the same consequences of arriving late at work or of not showing up at all, for example, as someone with a fixed schedule and a supervisor to report to. The Indian rickshaw drivers and other low-income workers studied in Schilbach

(2019), who often work while inebriated, are only able to do so because they are self-employed.

Kaur et al. (2010) study whether workers prefer contracts that help them commit to working more to overcome self-control problems. Such self-control problems at work may be different than in other domains because, in addition to reducing the worker's welfare, they can hurt profits. The existence of self-control problems fundamentally changes the nature of the contracting problem, in that both parties have interests in incentivizing the worker to exert more effort in the future. Furthermore, whereas in other contexts commitment mechanisms will only arise if agents are sophisticated and demand them, employers may elect to design contracts that mitigate self-control problems even if the employee is naïve or does not demand them explicitly. The authors speculate that this may be the reason why employers often impose contracts with production minimums, such as the forty-hour work week, where employees have little authority over how much they work, and instead must elect to either work the designated amount or risk being fired.

Using evidence from a 13-month field experiment in India, Kaur et al. (2015) investigate whether commitment contracts can help workers tackle their self-control problems and increase their productivity. Study participants were hired as full-time data-entry workers and paid a piece rate for output, without restrictions on their hours, so that they could largely determine themselves how much they would produce and be paid. Then, on randomly selected days, the experimenters gave workers the option to set a target output level for the day. If their realized output fell below the chosen target, workers received a piece rate that was half of the usual rate; if their output exceeded the target, they receive the usual piece rate. Choosing a positive target creates a dominated contract, in that the contract punishes low output but does not reward high output relative to a contract with no target. Crucially, apart from potential boosts in productivity and labor supply, there is no reason for workers to choose a positive target since doing so can only reduce workers' pay for any given worker effort.

Workers set a positive target 36% of the time when offered the option to choose a target level, thus selecting a dominated contract that incentivized reaching the target. Workers also exerted more effort as the randomly assigned payday approached, suggesting high levels of worker impatience and the existence of self-control problems.[30] The authors argue that workers chose these dominated contracts to overcome self-control problems and commit themselves to working a certain amount. Indeed, choosing such a contract increased worker output, with an effect of the same size as an 18% increase in the piece rate. Those who had greater payday effects were more likely to choose positive targets when offered and had larger increases in output under these contracts relative to the standard contract. As some workers may be naïve about their level of self-control, and thus may not choose commitment despite having self-control problems, these estimates may be a lower bound on the extent of time inconsistency and the potential of these kinds of contracts to increase productivity.

---

[30] Although note that a standard model of present bias would not imply higher effort closer to the payday, unless workers are severely liquidity-constrained.

This result is consistent with the explanation that the workers with the greatest self-control problems benefited the most from the dominated contracts. However, if there is heterogeneity among workers in the extent of self-control problems, workers who do not have strong self-control problems may be made worse off by the fact that other workers have self-control problems. This insight stands in sharp contrast to other equilibrium settings in which, for example, the gym membership setting in which agents with more standard preferences effectively benefit from the firm's efforts to exploit the preferences of behavioral agents since firms are subject to a zero-profit condition in equilibrium. In this context, there is an adverse selection problem in which firms may be forced to offer contracts with draconian work rules to avoid selecting undesirable workers, even if those draconian work rules are not appropriate for most workers.

Reference-dependence and income targeting. Another implication of self-employment with flexible schedules is that workers may engage in various forms of income or effort targeting. In his book, *The Protestant Ethic and the Spirit of Capitalism*, Weber argued that peasants in traditional societies have what modern economists would label a backward-bending labor supply curve and contrasted this to what he saw as the predictions of models of rational economic actors.

In a static labor-supply model, there are opposing income and substitution effects, so the response to a wage increase is theoretically ambiguous. However, in a dynamic model in which there are high-frequency wage shocks, and individuals have a constant exponential discount factor, for any plausible parameter values, labor supply would increase in response to temporary wage increases (e.g., Lucas and Rapping, 1969). Backward bending labor supply could be generated under at least two behavioral stories: reference-dependent preferences and present bias. First, we discuss reference-dependent labor supply, which has received a great deal of attention in the behavioral literature.

An active literature has studied whether workers such as taxi-drivers, who can set their own hours, respond to wage shocks as neoclassical models would predict (by increase labor supply when wages are high), or if they instead exhibit income-targeting due to reference-dependence (such that fewer hours of work are supplied when the wage is high, since the reference point/income target is attained sooner on high-wage days).[31] While there remains a debate in this literature, most evidence points towards some role for income targets and reference dependence, with negative daily wage elasticities (e.g. Thakral and Tô, 2018).

The literature on reference-dependent labor supply has largely been used to provide sharp tests of reference-dependence in the field, rather than because of the inherent economic importance of daily labor supply in rich countries (O'Donoghue and Sprenger, 2018 in Volume 1 of this handbook). In poor countries, given the high share of self-employment, this phenomenon could be rather more important.

---

[31] See, for instance, Camerer et al. (1997), Farber (2005, 2015), Crawford and Meng (2011), and Thakral and Tô (2018).

Economists studying developing countries have begun to apply this idea to studying labor supply (Giné et al., 2017; Andersen et al., 2014; Dupas et al., 2018b). Below, we discuss one such paper in detail.

Dupas et al. (2018b) study the labor supply of Kenya bicycle-taxi drivers. They depart from the existing literature in two ways. First, instead of estimating the reference point, or using the typical earnings as the reference point, they collect daily data on the worker's "cash needs" for the day—unexpected (until recently) expenses such as repairs or entirely anticipated needs such as a savings-club payment coming due. Second, instead of relying on instruments for the wage, they use experimental cash drops on workers to generate variation in how quickly the cash needs for the day may be reached.

The authors find evidence of income targeting, in that labor supply responds positively to cash needs, even entirely anticipated needs. However, a cash drop at the beginning of the day does not decrease labor supply, implying that the reference point is over earned income, rather than over total daily income.[32] Finally, Dupas et al. (2018b) develop a model in which being below the reference point reduces effort costs (rather than the usual assumption that being below the reference point induces a sense of loss). The authors calibrate this model to conclude that in the absence of such income targeting, workers would earn 19% *less*, even in the absence of factors like present bias. Since their model does not feature the exogenous wage shocks (as opposed to cash drops) considered by the previous papers, they do not capture a potential opposite effect of income targeting: that income-targeters will earn less for the same total number of hours supplied, since they will work too long on low-wage days, and too little on high-wage days.

Dupas et al. (2018b) thus implicitly connect the literature on reference-dependent labor supply with a potential alternative or complementary explanation: liquidity constraints caused by present bias. In a standard model, individuals should not react sharply to predictable daily expenditure needs, since they would be building up savings over time. If people are severely present-biased, as discussed in Section 2, then they may hold no liquid assets and may also be incapable of saving funds from the period with high wages and using them in periods with lower wages. In this case, the dynamic labor supply problem approximately reduces to the static problem with opposing income and substitution effects and the theoretical impact of a temporary positive wage shock on labor supply is again ambiguous.

Environmental factors. Heat and noise are ubiquitous features of developing countries, especially in large cities. Dean (2018) conducts an ingenious set of experiments in Kenya with factory workers who are accustomed to working in a noisy environment, recruiting them to work in an environment where the experimenter can control noise levels. The author shows using a randomized intervention that a 10 dB increase in ambient noise (akin to the increase in noise from running a vacuum cleaner compared to a dishwasher) leads to a 5% decline in output of textile workers. Using lab

---

[32] The literature studying cab-drivers has implicitly made the same assumption, since those papers only consider a single source of income.

measures, he shows that the increase in noise also causes a worsening of cognitive function. Specifically, executive function (also known as cognitive control), a set of higher-order cognitive functions which direct one's attention and manipulate working memory (Diamond, 2013), declines by 0.07 standard deviations. While the decline in cognitive function cannot be directly linked to the decline in the textile-production output, some alternative channels such as direct effects on health can be ruled out. Moreover, noise has no effects on a cognitively unchallenging effort task (the a–b task of DellaVigna and Pope, 2017).

Importantly, Dean (2018) finds that workers seem unaware of the effect of noise on their productivity, despite having frequently experienced exposure to such noise. Stated beliefs about the productive effect of noise were generally inaccurate, and workers were not willing to pay more for a quiet work environment when pay depended on productivity compared to when pay was fixed (although the latter comparison is somewhat under-powered). This evidence suggests that while the amenity value of quiet was valued to some extent, its productive value was not appreciated. Workers are thus unlikely to take steps by themselves to sufficiently insulate themselves from noise.

Adhvaryu et al. (2018a) show similar effects for the consequences of heat in the workplace. They work with 26 textile factories in India and show that replacing incandescent bulbs with LED lighting reduced temperature on the factory floor, boosting output substantially, and particularly on hot days. Daily variation in temperature similarly affects output. While the authors do not formally elicit workers' or managers' beliefs about the effect of heat, they note that the managers were unaware of the productivity benefits of lowering temperature, and that the change in lighting was implemented to reduce lighting costs. We return to this point when we discuss behavioral firms in Section 8.

7.3 Wages and behavioral workers

We now turn to understanding aspects of wage and incentive-setting in labor markets in developing countries. We discuss wage rigidity in markets for casual agricultural labor, the absence of pay dispersion across workers, and evidence on gift exchange at work.

Wage rigidity. Many analysts of labor markets in developed countries assume that features like downward nominal wage rigidity and wage compression are driven by labor market institutions such as unions, labor market regulation and the threat of union or regulatory action. Looking at sectors of the labor market of developing countries where both unions and effectively enforced government regulations are close to absent, such as agricultural labor markets, suggests that behavioral factors play an important role.

Kaur (2019) revisits nominal wage rigidity in the context of Indian agricultural labor markets. First, she documents that nominal wages appear sticky from year-to-year. Next, she finds that positive rainfall shocks, which increase the marginal product of labor temporarily, increase nominal wages. In contrast, negative shocks do not reduce wages. Moreover, transitory positive shocks lead to *persistently* higher nominal wages, even when the marginal product of labor has returned to a lower level. The asymmetry in response to positive and negative shocks is precisely what is predicted with nominal rigidity. Such rigidities distort employment: agricultural employment is 9% lower in the year following a positive shock. Consistent with the importance of fairness motives, Kaur shows survey evidence that nominal wage cuts are widely perceived as being unfair, as in the classic findings of Kahneman et al. (1986) and Bewley (1998).

Breza et al. (2018a) provide field-experimental evidence on how such nominal wage rigidities persist in the absence of enforced minimum wages or formal institutions such as unions. The authors partner with small employers to offer jobs to workers in spot labor markets in India during the lean season, when unemployment is high. They vary both the wage offered to the worker—either the prevailing market wage, or 10% below the wage—as well as the observability of the wage offer (either inside the worker's home, or on a public street). Offers below the market wage are often accepted when made in private (18%, compared to 26% acceptance at the full market wage). However, acceptance of low offers drops to only 2% when the low-wage offers are made publicly. In contrast, offers made at the market wage are equally likely to be accepted in the private and public conditions. Workers thus appear to be subject to social pressure to prevent them from accepting job offers below the prevailing market wage. Nearly a quarter of workers are willing to forego a day's work to avoid being seen as a "scab".

The authors provide indirect evidence that the wage floor is enforced through social sanctions: when playing a costly punishment game in the lab, players impose large penalties on their partners when they are informed that the partner previously accepted a job at below-market wages. Interestingly, players impose these punishments even on scabs in other villages, whose labor supply does not affect their own outcomes, implying that punishing scabs is an internalized social norm. The paper leaves one puzzle unanswered: why are employers not able to make such offers in private themselves, especially given the repeated nature of the employment relationships, and the potentially substantial efficiency losses?

Pay equality. An existing literature in behavioral labor studies the consequences of pay inequality in the workplace. Card et al. (2012) show using a field experiment at a large employer that disclosing information on peers' salaries reduces job satisfaction among workers with below-median salaries in their work unit and makes them more likely to look for a new job. Breza et al. (2018b) build on this literature by studying how social preferences over pay inequality affect not just satisfaction and job-search, but also workers' labor supply and productivity. The authors set up a manufacturing workshop, in which 378 workers are randomized into small units of three workers each, for one month of full-time employment. Workers are paid a flat daily wage for attendance but select their own effort levels.

Breza et al. (2018b) randomly assigned work units to one of four different pay structures. In the "pay disparity" treatment condition, each worker in the unit is assigned to a different wage (w_{low}, w_{medium}, w_{high}), based on their own baseline productivity levels, with the most productive worker receiving the highest wage. The pay differences between the three levels are modest (less than 5%). In three control conditions, all workers in a unit were paid the same—either w_{low}, w_{medium}, w_{high}, depending on the group. This design allows the authors to compare two individuals earning the same daily wage, with one being in a group with pay inequality (the treatment group), and the other in a group with homogeneous pay (the control conditions). Importantly, the design allows the authors to identify the effects of pay inequality separately on high earners and on low earners.

The key finding is that when coworker productivity is hard to observe, introducing pay inequality reduces output by 0.45 standard deviations, driven largely by an 18-percentage point reduction in attendance. Somewhat surprisingly, while the reduction is largest for the workers who are paid the least in their group, even those receiving the high or medium pay reduce their attendance, suggesting that pay inequality makes the workplace a less attractive environment. Overall, workers appear to give up 9% of their earnings to avoid a workplace where they are paid differently than their peers. Interestingly, these negative effects on worker morale vanish if the wage inequality is more clearly justified: when output is more observable, or when coworkers' baseline productivity levels are further apart, pay disparity does not reduce output.

Kaur (2019) and Breza et al. (2018a, 2018b) help explain why even decentralized informal markets in developing countries have high levels of nominal wage rigidity and little dispersion in wages across workers.

Incentives in the public and non-profit sectors. Developing countries often have poor provision of public services such as education and health. An active area of research in development is thus on how to improve the productivity of workers in the public and allied non-profit sectors. Recent work has evaluated financial incentives for performance, with mixed results. Some papers find positive effects: for instance, financial incentives for teachers can reduce teacher absence (Duflo et al., 2012) and improve student test scores (Muralidharan and Sundararaman, 2011). However, providing incentives to multi-tasking agents is well known to be difficult (Holmstrom and Milgrom, 1991). Indeed, some papers show that incentives are gamed when employed, and argue they are of limited utility (Glewwe et al., 2010). Perhaps the bottom line is that such financial incentive programs, whether effective or not, are often politically unpopular and are rarely adopted and scaled up by governments (Finan et al., 2017).

One alternative, lower-cost strategy is to provide non-monetary incentives such as social recognition and awards. The idea is to increase and harness prosocial motivation, to provide social-image or competitive motives to exert effort, and to align the worker's identity with the employer's goals. Despite a great deal of interest in such interventions, and evidence that social incentives broadly matter in organizations (Ashraf and Bandiera, 2018), there is relatively little evidence on their effectiveness in the field in poor countries, especially with the public sector or over an extended period.

An exception is Ashraf et al. (2014), who compare financial and social incentives for the sale of condoms by agents of a non-profit organization in Zambia. The authors find that a simple non-monetary incentive—providing agents with a publicly-displayed "thermometer" display and awarding stars based on sales—outperforms even providing them with a 90% margin on selling condoms. However, in this case, even the largest financial incentives were modest, given the low cost and demand for the condoms. It is unclear what role the prosocial nature of the task played in making the thermometer display effective. More research remains to be done on whether such non-monetary incentives are more broadly effective, on which types of such incentives are most promising, and what the underlying mechanisms are. The same challenges with providing incentives to multi-tasking agents that apply to financial incentives will also likely apply to non-monetary incentives.

Crowd-out of intrinsic motivation. One question that has garnered much interest in both development policymaking and in behavioral research is whether extrinsic incentives crowd out intrinsic motivations. Influential lab evidence from social psychology has shown that extrinsic rewards *can* reduce individuals' intrinsic motivation to do a task. A famous paper by Deci (1971) shows that after a temporary incentive for solving puzzles in the lab is withdrawn, effort in a subsequent unincentivized round is lower than in a group where incentives were never offered to begin with. Several lab experiments provide similar evidence of crowd-out of intrinsic motivation, and theoretical work in economics provides potential explanations for this phenomenon: e.g. incentives can signal information such as task difficulty and extrinsic rewards can muddy the self- or social-signaling value of a prosocial task (Bénabou and Tirole, 2003, 2006).

Yet, there is little field evidence that extrinsic incentives crowd out intrinsic motivation substantially.[33] Lacetera et al. (2013) review field studies on incentives for blood donation—an example of a prosocial task in which policy makers are concerned about potential crowd-out—and conclude that in 18 out of 19 cases, providing incentives increase donation, without evidence of long-run reductions in donations if incentives are removed. Some papers also find that more pro-socially motivated workers respond more to financial incentives, perhaps due to the correlations of prosociality and other omitted variables in the underlying population (e.g. Ashraf et al., 2014).

Overall, there seems little reason to think that extrinsic incentives systematically crowd out intrinsic motivation in practice in real-world situations. This result is relevant, for instance, for the ongoing policy debate about whether community health workers should be paid more. In the following section, we describe evidence that paying higher wages does not generally lead to increased select of less prosocial workers.

---

[33] An exception is Gneezy and Rustichini (2000), who find that introducing a small fine for late pickup of children from day-care centers in Israel increased the incidence of late pick-ups.

Gift exchange. Incentives are often limited in real-world workplaces, particularly when output is multi-dimensional or hard to measure (Holmstrom and Milgrom, 1991). Theories in labor and behavioral economics suggest that workers' identities, alignment with the employers' missions, and their social preferences towards their employers may all play an important motivating role (Akerlof and Kranton, 2005; Besley and Ghatak, 2005). The theory of gift exchange argues that employers can benefit by paying workers above market wages, since workers may respond by working harder, even absent repeated-game motives (Akerlof, 1982). A recent field-experimental literature in behavioral economics uses one-shot employment opportunities to evaluate whether workers reciprocate by working harder (or less hard) when employers surprise them with higher (or lower) pay. The findings are mixed, with recent studies mostly finding small, if any, gift-exchange effects, particularly in response to pay increases (Gneezy and List, 2006; DellaVigna et al., 2016; Esteves-Sorenson, 2017).

Two recent field studies from developing countries study gift-exchange in entirely natural settings in real organizations, although with repeated-game incentives in play, since they consider long-term employment relationships. Both studies find little evidence of gift exchange. de Ree et al. (2018) conduct a large-scale randomized experiment with a representative sample of schools in Indonesia and find that a *doubling* of base pay for teachers led to no improvement in measures of teacher effort or student learning.

Jayaraman et al. (2016) study a government-induced contract change for tea pickers in an Indian plantation. For most workers, the contract changes led to increased base pay with constant or reduced piece-rate incentives. The authors find that, in the first month after the more generous contract is introduced, output increases by 20 to 80%. Yet, this effect dissipates over subsequent months, and eventually output is reduced below the original level. The results are consistent with an initial "behavioral" response, but a longer-run adjustment to the neoclassical prediction. This result highlights one benefit of studying incentives and wages in the field with longer-run studies, even at the risk of failing to isolate precise mechanisms.

7.4 Selection of workers

Given the lack of incentives, and often even accountability, in the public sector in developing countries, there has been a great deal of policy interest in selecting prosocial and intrinsically motivated workers into the public sector. The optimal selection of workers for the public sector, or for other pro-socially oriented professions, has been a subject of a recent field-experimental literature in development economics.

One question has been whether offering higher wages, which might attract more talented workers, will negatively select on the prosocial motivation of workers. Dal Bó et al. (2013) work with the Mexican federal government to randomize wage offers across 167 municipalities to fill 350 positions. Applicants complete a battery of tests of ability, personality traits and prosocial motivations. The authors find that higher wage offers attract a higher-ability applicant pool in terms of fluid intelligence, better personality traits, and experience. Yet this increase in applicants did not come with a cost in terms of lower public-service motivation (measured using survey questions). Ashraf et al. (2018) find similar results with a field experiment in Zambia, where they vary across locations whether job postings to recruit health workers emphasized either career prospects or instead the possibility of helping one's community. Emphasizing career prospects led to recruiting applicants with higher high-school grades, but no lower prosocial motivation. Moreover, those recruited under the career concerns condition have much better job performance.

In contrast, Deserranno (2018) finds that posting job notices with a higher implied pay attracts candidates who donate less money in dictator games, and who perceive lower social benefits to the job at the time of applying. Such candidates subsequently have higher turnover on the job. However, one important way this experiment differs from the others is that Deserranno studies applicants to an entirely new position, such that the advertised wages may communicate a great deal more information about the position that will typically be the case. This feature makes it perhaps more likely that the theoretical mechanism of Bénabou and Tirole (2006) applies, but it is not clear that such an effect would persist once information about the jobs is more widely diffused.

While paying less and yet recruiting more motivated workers is no doubt an attractive proposition for governments and non-profits, the bulk of the evidence suggests that this is unlikely to be the case. This evidence is consistent with the underlying correlation of cognitive ability and pro-sociality in the population: Falk et al. (2018) find in their Global Preference Survey that altruism and reciprocity are both strongly positively correlated with cognitive ability within countries. In addition, the previous section argued that crowd-out of intrinsic motivation is similarly not typically found in the field. Clearly, one should not generally expect to find that higher wages will select out prosocial motives.

7.5 Female labor-force participation

Another striking aspect of labor markets in some low-to-middle income countries is the low rate of female labor force participation (FLFP). Only 52% of women in poor countries participate in the labor force, compared to 78% of men (Duflo, 2012b). However, there are large differences across cultures and regions. Labor force participation seems more equal by gender in sub-Saharan Africa where, in 2017, World Bank data suggest that the labor force participation rate of women was 63%, compared to 74% of men (ILO, 2018).

In contrast, female labor market participation is particularly low in South Asia, the Middle East and North Africa. For instance, FLFP in India has hovered below 30% in recent years, with some evidence of a decline since 2005, despite economic female education growth (Fletcher et al., 2017). Low FLFP is worrying to policy makers, both because of the aggregate effects of likely misallocation of talented women (Hsieh et al., 2018) and because working outside the home increases female empowerment (Heath and Jayachandran, 2016).

Why is female labor-force participation so low in some countries? A standard economic answer would involve gender specialization in home and wage work, possibly due to biological reasons such as women's role in childbearing and nursing. However, standard economic answers do not explain much of the variation in FLFP, even conditional on GDP per capita. A literature in cultural economics, described also in Section 9 below, provides evidence on the historical roots of FLFP. And two recent papers in behavioral economics provide evidence of specific behavioral mechanisms which depress FLFP.

Self-efficacy. McKelway (2018) studies internal psychological constraints on women's employment in India. She implements a field experiment with women and their families in partnership with a large firm which offers employment opportunities to women. The key treatment is an intervention to increase women's self-efficacy—beliefs in one's own ability to attain one's desired outcomes. The author finds large and sustained increases in women's employment due to the treatment. In a second experiment, the author randomizes job offers to women, and finds that receiving a job offer increases self-efficacy months later. Thus, living in a setting with low female labor-force participation may reduce women's self-efficacy, which in turn depressed women's employment.

Social norms. Bursztyn et al. (2018) provide evidence for the importance of social norms in suppressing female labor force participation in Saudi Arabia. The authors show that most young married men in Saudi Arabia privately support women working outside the home. However, these men underestimate the level of such support among similar men in their neighborhoods. Correcting these beliefs—that is, informing men about the true rates of private support—causes men to become substantially more likely to sign their wives up for a job-search service.

Four months after this intervention, the wives of treated men are more likely to have applied and interviewed for jobs outside the home. The paper thus provides evidence that social norms may suppress female labor force participation, and how those norms may remain sticky, since individuals who support the taboo behavior may be hesitant to reveal their views to others for fear of social sanction. However, it is not clear if there are many such situations in which second-order beliefs are biased. For instance, men in conservative communities in India might well be accurate in thinking that their neighbors will judge them harshly if their wives work outside the home. Measuring such second-order beliefs systematically in areas where norms may be important could be a promising avenue for future research.

While the above two studies provide careful evidence on specific mechanisms constraining FLFP, they do not in themselves explain variation in FLFP across societies. Preferences and cultural transmission might play an important role. Fernandez and Fogli (2009) show that the labor supply decisions of second-generation American women depend on the FLFP rates in the country of familial origin, despite presently facing the same economic environment. This result suggests a role for cultural transmission of attitudes or values regarding FLFP. Alesina et al. (2011) show that regions with a history of the use of the plough in agriculture—in which men had a comparative advantage—are associated with more gender inequality in present-day attitudes, and with less female participation in the labor force. Thus, at least to some extent, FLFP appears to be driven by sticky cultural and preference factors.

8 Firms

Behavioral economics investigates how *individual* decision-making, preferences, and beliefs systematically depart from standard economic models. It is thus not surprising that even behavioral industrial organization (Heidhues and Koszegi, 2018) has mostly assumed sophisticated, profit-maximizing firms responding to behavioral consumers.

Is it reasonable to assume that firms successfully maximize profits? There are numerous justifications for this assumption. First, one longstanding argument for treating firms as neoclassical actors is that market forces should weed out firms that systematically deviate from profit-maximizing behavior. Therefore, at equilibrium, surviving firms will be profit-maximizers.

Second, applying the same argument to competition within firms and building on Lucas's (1978) span of control model, even if a significant share of individuals exhibits behavioral biases, individuals without such biases may rise to become the key managers and decision-makers in firms. In contrast, workers with particularly severe behavioral biases might get fired. Of course, forms of principal-agent problems within firms can attenuate this advantageous selection.

Third, many important decisions in large firms are made jointly by several actors and often under intense scrutiny by stakeholders and the company's board, potentially limiting the scope for persistent mistakes, to the extent that groups are more rational than individuals (Cooper and Kagel, 2005; Charness and Sutter, 2012; Kugler et al., 2012). Moreover, workers typically receive considerable training and operate within structures that are designed to limit the impact of behavioral factors.

8.1 Are firms in developing countries more "behavioral"?

Given these arguments, there are several reasons to think that firms in developing countries are more likely to deviate from the neoclassical benchmark than firms in rich countries. First, competitive pressures may be lower in poor countries. Imports are often restricted by high tariffs and the entry of new firms as well as the expansion of existing firms may be restricted for various reasons including financing constraints, agency problems, and regulations. High travel costs, especially in rural areas, mean that buyers may have only a limited number of firms available to choose from, providing firms with some amount of local monopoly power. Prices are sometimes fixed by manufacturers, preventing price competition. State ownership of large enterprises in countries such as India and China, weak anti-trust regulations and a higher importance of political connections, cronyism, and corruption may also contribute to lower levels of competitiveness in developing countries.

Second, firms in developing economies are small. Hsieh and Olken (2014) find that about 90 percent of firms in Mexico employ less than 10 workers. In India and

Indonesia, the corresponding number is close to 100 percent. This firm distribution is in sharp contrast to rich countries (Tybout, 2000). Thus, firms in poor countries involve a limited span of control: decisions are often made by one person only, the owner-operator. There is little scope for within-firm competition that might cause non-behavioral agents to rise to the top of the firm via an efficient selection process. Nor are firm owners necessarily highly selected. As described in the previous section, self-employment rates are much higher in poor than in rich countries: a large share of individuals operate some sort of firm.

A classic theme in development economics is the lack of separation between household economics and firm economics for smallholder farmers. Under the conditions for the separation theorem, family labor supply or risk preferences of household members would not affect the type of agricultural production chosen. In reality, they seem to have an impact (e.g., Lopez, 1984; Grimard, 2000; Le, 2010). Given this finding in development economics, it is only natural to expect that behavioral factors, like other household factors, would have important impacts on production in family-run firms.

Behavioral issues might also be particularly powerful due to limited training and education, and limited potential to learn from co-workers or to receive on-the-job training. While new workers in a large firm are thoroughly instructed and trained, such training does not exist in small firms in developing countries. Few owner-operators have much business-training or adequate schooling, such that making optimal decisions might be more challenging.

Some factors instead point in the opposite direction. One might argue that behavioral issues are less likely to have bite since the stakes are a lot higher for self-employed individuals and owners of small firms—their consumption is directly tied to profits. Moreover, within any given marketplace in Kenya or India, one can often observe many seemingly identical retail shops that offer nearly identical products, suggesting high levels of local competition. Yet, none of these shops appear to grow rapidly and few go out of business. Nor do behavioral issues only matter for small decisions: even high-stakes decisions such as retirement savings choices or decisions to take one's potentially life-saving medications seem to involve behavioral biases, as described in other chapters in this handbook. Moreover, some behavioral factors such as present bias and loss aversion could have more bite precisely because firm profits and individual consumption are so intimately linked.

The topic of behavioral firms departs from an emphasis on the classic behavioral biases such as present bias, loss aversion, etc. By "behavioral firms", we simply mean firms that depart from profit-maximization in systematic ways. We do not yet have enough research on this to be sure if these cases are due to the same psychological factors studied in consumer behavior or if other biases and behavioral phenomena are more relevant in the case of firm decision-making. Almost surely, limited attention, salience, failures of Bayesian learning, and self-control issues can matter for firms too.

8.2 Behavioral firms: evidence and applications

Once we start considering firm decision-making, many unexplored and potentially important areas of research arise.

Trust, firm structure, and missing firm growth. Behavioral economics may provide some insights into why firms in developing countries are small and typically run as a family business with little decentralization in decision-making. Standard explanations for small firms include taxation, regulation (e.g. labor regulation), and predation. While these factors may well play some role, many firms are even smaller than these thresholds (e.g. Hsieh and Olken, 2014), suggesting there may be additional reasons for firms to fail to grow. Credit constraints again likely play some role, but even with incomplete credit markets, profitable firms should grow over time and increase their market share.

Low levels of trust may play an important role in keeping firms small is. As described in detail in Section 9, developing countries have systematically lower levels of social trust than rich countries (Falk et al., 2018). Lower levels of trust have been shown to be associated with smaller firm sizes and less decentralization of decisions made within firms, both between and within countries (Cingano and Pinotti, 2012; Algan and Cahuc, 2014). Non-Western countries are also more likely to have moral values emphasizing the importance loyalty to one's group and respect for authority (Haidt, 2012). This in turn might make firm owners less likely to hire or cooperate with out-group members, and less likely to decentralize decision-making, potentially inhibiting firm growth. Moreover, these differences are driven at least in part by deep historical factors (Enke, 2018; Schulz et al., 2018), and might thus causally explain variation in firm size across countries.

This argument echoes an existing literature on agency issues in firms in developing countries. Ilias (2006) argues that some managers decide to hire only family members as an organizational way of dealing with agency costs. Consistent with this hypothesis, Ilias shows that there is a positive relationship between family size and firm size in the surgical-instrument industry in Pakistan. Firm founders with more brothers (and therefore a larger pool of potential managers) end up with larger firms. Similarly, Bertrand et al. (2008) study 93 large business families in Thailand and find a positive relationship between family size and family involvement in the company. When the founder dies, sons play a larger role in the company, and their increased involvement following the founder's death is associated with lower firm-level performance. The authors' interpretation of these results is that the sons engage in a "race to the bottom" to tunnel out company resources.

Bloom et al. (2013), discussed below, argue that the mid-sized firms they study were constrained from taking up high-return management practices due to a lack of management time. They implicate a low level of trust: firm owners do not trust non-family members to make important decisions or occupy important managerial slots. Managerial human capital even in these relatively large firms in India is thus constrained by the number of male children in the owner's family.[34]

Objective function. Standard producer theory assumes that a firm's goal is to maximize expected profits. When firms are instead run as a small (family) business, the objective function of the firm might be quite different. For instance, the owner's risk preferences likely matter, making risk-neutrality and thus expected-profit maximization not a safe assumption. Firm owner-operators might not even desire growth, given the increased effort and lifestyle changes firm growth might entail. Their objectives may include providing employment to their family or descendants. They may operate microenterprises as a coping strategy to diversify risk, given the potential for shocks to other sources of household income such as agricultural output (e.g., Adhvaryu et al., 2016). Yet, at present, we have a limited understanding of what the actual objectives of firm-owners in developing countries are and the extent to which the preferences and skills of household members affect firm decisions.

Pricing. Firms might make suboptimal pricing or product choices. They may have trouble estimating consumer demand accurately, leading to suboptimal pricing or product choices. Even if firms perfectly understand demand, they might deviate from optimal pricing decisions. Recent work has begun to document substantial failures of profit-maximization among even large and highly sophisticated firms in rich countries. For instance, DellaVigna and Gentzkow (2017) show that a large grocery-store chain in the US prices its products uniformly within large geographical zones, despite substantial variation in the incomes of shoppers across stores. The authors calculate that the firm gives up 7% of profit by failing to price optimally. Given that such large firms US chains leave plenty of money on the table by making suboptimal pricing choices, it seems worth scrutinizing firms' pricing choices in developing countries. To the best of our knowledge, no such studies exist.

Inventory management. A recent literature has begun to point to examples of small-business owners in developing countries leaving profitable investments unexploited. Kremer et al. (2013) show that many shopkeepers in rural Kenya fail to make small inventory investments with high expected returns. First, shopkeepers often fail to take advantage of bulk-purchase discounts from distributors. A considerable mass of inventory purchase orders is for quantities which fall just below thresholds at which additional discounts kick in. In addition, shops frequently experience stock-outs due to not maintaining enough inventory, even for relatively low-price goods which can be purchased in small increments, such as phone cards. The correlation of returns to inventory across goods is also low, suggesting that shopkeepers may not be equalizing marginal returns to inventory across goods. Inventory levels are predicted by small-stakes risk aversion displayed by the owners in a lab game, as well as by their math skills, but not by their self-reported credit constraints.

---

[34] This example provides another illustration of the inefficiencies caused by the norms against female labor-force participation.

Beaman et al. (2014) provide another example of small firms failing to maximize profits. They show that a representative sample of micro-enterprises in two Kenyan cities lose 5–8% of total profits for a surprisingly simple reason: they fail to keep enough change on hand to break larger bills, and thus lose potential sales to customers. The authors study 508 typically small firms, with 60% having just one worker, the owner. The firms include a variety of businesses, from vegetable vendors to furniture shops, and service providers such as small restaurants, repair shops, and barbers.

Simply drawing firms' attention to the frequency of "change-outs" and lost sales—through a randomized information intervention, or simply by asking them questions about it—led to a reduction in change-outs and an increase in sales and profits. This result parallels Hanna et al.'s (2014) results on inattention and technology adoption: firms may not think that change-outs are important, and they thus fail to attend to them. But once their attention is drawn to the neglected factor, or if they are directly provided with the summary information, they make the high-return investment. If the change-outs were instead due to other (rational) factors such as an aversion to keeping cash on hand due to the risk of theft, providing information on the frequency and cost of change-outs would not be expected to change behavior.

Labor and capital choices. Firms might also deviate from profit-maximization in their labor and capital-investment decisions, although we have few direct tests of this. Adhvaryu et al. (2018b) show that even large firms may under-invest in worker skills: an experimentally introduced low-cost soft-skills training for workers in a large textile firm increased worker productivity by 20% without raising turnover, resulting in a large internal rate of return (over 250% over eight months). How could such large returns remain unexploited by a large firm? One possibility is that the owners and managers simply under-estimate the returns to soft skills among workers.

Firms might also manage their staff inadequately, e.g. by providing suboptimal incentives to workers, by making inefficient hiring choices, or by discriminating certain types of workers or by hiring their friends and family members. One suggestive example is from Abebe et al. (2017), who document that firms in Ethiopia do not understand how skills among workers are correlated with barriers to applying to jobs. Specifically, they show that a firm that provides a small monetary subsidy for people to apply to its open jobs attracts a more talented applicant pool than it can achieve by even doubling the offered wage. The crucial finding from the behavioral perspective is that firms systematically under-estimate the effect of providing such a subsidy. In fact, managers on average expect applicant quality to *decrease* due to the subsidy.

Finally, firms may fail to adopt the highest-return technologies, as discussed with numerous examples in Section 6, although these focus on agricultural technology adoption by small-scale farmers. Even larger firms may not adopt appropriate technologies. For instance, Adhvaryu et al. (2018a) describe how managers of the 28 textile factories in their study largely neglected the effect of heat on worker productivity, and thus undervalued LED-lighting technology. When LED lighting was adopted to satisfy environmentally-motivated international buyers, the side-effect of reducing temperatures led to substantial unanticipated increases in productivity. Similarly,

Atkin et al. (2017) document organizational barriers to the adoption of a profitable technology among soccer-ball manufacturers in Pakistan. They argue that employees resist adoption of a new, more efficient technique due to fears that adoption will reduce their effective wages.

Management practices.   Bloom et al. (2013) investigate firms' management practices by running a management field experiment with large, multi-plant textile firms in India. Firms in this study receive free consulting on management practices to a treatment group of firms and find that this intervention increases productivity by 17% in the first year. Annual profitability increased by over $300,000, and treatment firms grew faster and opened more production plants within three years.

Given these large positive impacts, why had firms not already adopted these practices? While in some cases firms were simply not aware of practices such as daily factory meetings, owners appeared to systematically underestimate the profitability of simple and known practices such measuring quality defects, machine downtime, and inventory. Importantly, despite these failures to adopt high-return management practices, control-group firms were not weeded out of the market. Competitive pressures, the authors argue, were restricted by high tariffs, credit constraints, and particularly by limited managerial time. As in DellaVigna and Gentzkow (2017), this paper provides evidence that failures of profit-maximization are not restricted to small firms.

A related paper by Bruhn et al. (2018) examines the impact of access to one year of management consulting services on the outcomes of small and medium enterprises in Mexico. The authors randomly assigned enterprises that applied to receive subsidized consulting services to either receive the subsidized services or not. The authors find that the consulting intervention increased owners' "entrepreneurial spirit" (an index that measures entrepreneurial confidence and goal setting) and had positive short-run impacts on productivity and profits.

While many of the studies described above mostly do not take a behavioral perspective, the evidence they provide for failures of profit-maximization is compelling. Given this evidence, and given the arguments we presented for why behavioral firms are more likely to exist in developing countries, we believe that studying firm decisions in developing countries could be a promising new agenda for behavioral economics. In addition to studying standard behavioral-economic topics such as loss aversion, biased beliefs, and inattention in a new high-stakes economic setting, such an agenda might uncover new and previously understudied biases in human decision-making.

Indeed, one could argue that development economics has led the way in pointing out the importance of behavioral firms, an area that may find an increasing number of applications also to firms in rich countries.

9   Social preferences, culture, and development

So far in this chapter, we have considered the implications of behavioral models while treating the models and even parameter values as universal. In the remaining two sections, however, we describe arguments and recent evidence for systematic differences in psychology across rich and poor countries, and across rich and poor individuals. Section 9 describes a literature studying differences in social preferences (such as trust and reciprocity) and culture across societies and then discusses its possible implications for development. Section 10 describes the new literature on the psychology of poverty.

These sections are more speculative, in part because the modern economics literature on these topics is newer. However, some of the ideas in Section 9 echo an older tradition of thought on economic development, which viewed development as a process involving important changes in social structure and in ways of thinking. We begin by briefly sketching a history of the views of human behavior implicit in thinking about development and growth.

9.1 History of views of human behavior in economic development

Historically, many social scientists, including classical economists, did not see humans as rational and purely self-interested actors. As behavioral economists enjoy pointing out, Adam Smith anticipated much of behavioral economics (Ashraf et al., 2005).[35]

Prior to the emergence of modern economics, a long history of thought argued that what we now see as the process of economic development involves fundamental changes in economic psychology. Modern economists assume that firms maximize profits and individuals maximize utility across history and across societies, but for many Marxist writers, the "icy water of egotistical calculation" is a feature of capitalism, not of pre-capitalist societies or of the human condition more broadly (Marx and Engels, 1848). Famously, Weber (1905) argued that modern capitalism and the pervasive role of rationality emerged historically in response to changes in ways of thinking induced by Protestantism.

Modernization theory, prominent in the 1950s, influenced by Weber and Durkheim, drew a distinction between "traditional" and "modern" societies, including differences between societies based on achievement versus societies based on birth; orientation towards the nuclear family versus extended kinship ties; individualism versus communal orientation; relations based on tradition and loyalty versus those based on rational exchange. Proponents of modernization theory thought that people in traditional societies are not necessarily motivated by the rational calculation of self-interest of their modern counterparts. The process of modernization was thought of as a process of dramatic change in social structures, but also in ways of thinking. For instance, McClelland (1961) emphasized the "need for achievement"

---

[35] In his *Theory of Moral Sentiments*, Smith argued that behavior was determined by the struggle between what Smith termed the "passions" and the "impartial spectator." The passions included drives, emotions, and motivational feeling. Smith viewed behavior as under the direct control of the passions but believed that people could override passion-driven behavior by viewing their own behavior from the perspective of an outsider—the impartial spectator (Ashraf et al., 2005).

as a psychological characteristic that was key to entrepreneurial activity and modernization, and Inkeles and Smith (1974) defined uniquely "modern" personality traits.

After the 1950s and 1960s, modernization theory fell out of favor. In economics, Schultz (1964) argued that those in developing countries are "poor but efficient".[36] In this view, *homo economicus* did not need to be created; he or she was there all along. Whereas development experts influenced by modernization theory may have seen farmers as irrationally clinging to outdated farming techniques because of an attachment to tradition and may have favored coercion or heavy subsidies to encourage adoption of new techniques, modern development economists began with the assumption that farmers knew what they were doing.

Economists studying growth and development also reacted against cultural explanations for differences in economic development across societies that seemed unfalsifiable and therefore unscientific in the cross section, and that later turned out to be false once a longer panel data emerged: India was thought to be stuck with a low "Hindu rate of growth" while China's development was said to be held back by Confucian traditions (as described in Acemoglu and Robinson, 2013).

In part as a reaction to this sort of claim, development economists perhaps went to the opposite extreme of presuming that people in developing countries (and elsewhere) are fully rational *homo economicus*. If Weber argued that farmers in traditional societies were irrational and stuck with traditional techniques even when this was not profitable, modern development economists responded by demonstrating that farmers changed their behavior in response to prices. Yet, such evidence is far from showing that farmers are fully rational or are quantitatively (and sometimes even qualitatively) well-described by standard neoclassical theory.

In the past two decades, with the rise of behavioral economics, the pendulum has begun to swing back towards a more psychologically-realistic view of human behavior in development economics. Development economists have increasingly incorporated systematic departures from pure rationality and self-interest while approaching substantive questions in development. Crucially, this approach has involved rigorous empirical tests of the underlying behavioral ideas. Perhaps the clearest sign of the new openness of development economics to ideas from behavioral economics was the publication in 2015 of the World Bank's flagship annual World Development Report, "*Mind, Society, and Behavior*", with the theme of behavioral development economics.

A key difference between behavioral development economics and the older modernization-theory literature, however, is that the behavioral economics literature has mostly focused on universal features of human behavior, rather than on variation across individuals or societies. Recent work in cultural economics and behavioral economics, however, has begun to explore variation across societies. The rest of this section describes this new literature.

---

[36] Modernization theory also fell out of favor in sociology, but for somewhat different reasons: it was criticized as conflating features of Western society with necessary requirements for development, and was subject to criticism with the rise of dependency theory.

9.2 Differences in social preferences across societies

Behavioral economists and psychologists have argued that in addition to being motivated by private consumption, people have numerous social and moral motives. For instance, they often care about others' outcomes, by being altruistic (placing a positive weight on others' utility) or envious (placing a negative weight on others' utility). Individuals care about the fairness of outcomes and processes, such as by preferring to split unearned money in a dictator game equally with a recipient. They care what others think of them, for both instrumental and hedonic reasons, and thus have social image motives. They care that others act fairly and mean well, and may incur a cost to punish others who misbehave or hurt them, an example of negative reciprocity. People also care about conforming to social norms regarding appropriate behavior and may internalize these norms such that they are influenced by them even in private.

The above broad set of frequently powerful motives have been termed *social preferences* in the behavioral economics literature. While these preferences may have evolved for functional reasons—for example, negative reciprocity may have evolved because it helps sustain cooperation in repeated interactions—the experimental economics literature suggests that these motives are now "hard-wired" and partly unconscious rather than being simply deliberate strategic behavior. For example, individuals share money with anonymous recipients in a dictator game, even in the absence of repeated interactions or any role for reputation effects.

We next discuss certain aspects of social preferences which may differ systematically across societies, and which have been argued to matter for economic development.

Trust and reciprocity. Trust can be broadly defined as willingness to cooperate with others. Conceptually, trust is a somewhat complex concept, involving both beliefs (particularly beliefs about whether the other party is trustworthy) as well as preferences (such as "warm glow" from the act of cooperating, and altruism towards the other party), and potentially norms towards appropriate behavior. Reciprocity is the tendency to reward someone who cooperated or was generous (positive reciprocity), and to punish someone who defected or behaved poorly (negative reciprocity). Both trust and reciprocity are considered key ingredients for generating cooperative behavior, especially in situations requiring cooperation with those outside one's immediate family or kin group (Henrich et al., 2010a).

Multiple pieces of evidence suggest that developing countries have lower levels of trust and reciprocity than rich countries.

First, cross-country survey evidence from sources such as the World Values Survey shows substantial variation across countries in levels of self-reported generalized trust in others. Generalized trust is trust towards other members of society (rather than trust towards close family or friends), including trust towards one's neighbors, co-ethnics, fellow citizens, and even trust in strangers and foreigners.[37] An influential

---

[37] In surveys, generalized trust is measured with questions such as "Generally speaking, would you say that most people can be trusted or that you can't be too careful in dealing with people?"

body of work shows that such measures of trust (and trustworthiness) are correlated with per-capita income and institutional features of countries: poorer countries and regions have lower levels of trust (e.g. LaPorta et al., 1997; Knack and Keefer, 1997; Tabellini, 2010).

Some economists view survey measures as unreliable and prefer incentivized or revealed-preference outcomes. An innovative early paper by a team of anthropologists and behavioral economists ran incentivized social-preference lab experiments in 15 small-scale societies across the world (Henrich et al., 2001). The authors report considerable variation across these societies in play in dictator games, ultimatum games, and public-goods games, although in each case outcomes deviate from self-interested choices without social preferences or fairness concerns. The author point to a correlation in their results between the degree of market integration (at the society level) and greater cooperation in experimental games.

More recently, using the Global Preference Survey (GPS), a dataset covering 80,000 respondents who constitute nationally-representative samples from 76 countries, Falk et al. (2018) find systematic differences across countries in measures of social preferences. Specifically, the authors find that developing countries have lower levels of both trust and reciprocity. However, variation within countries substantially exceeds variation between countries. Moreover, the measure of patience is more predictive of per-capita GDP than measures of trust and social preferences, and controlling for patience makes the coefficient on trust non-significant in a regression on per-capita GDP.[38]

It is worth noting that there need be nothing irrational about low levels of trust. To establish some failure of rationality, one would need to show, for example, systematically biased beliefs about how trustworthy others are, and separate this from differences in preferences. Differences in societies across trust could, for example, be driven by differences in history or institutions or could simply reflect multiple equilibria (e.g. Aghion et al., 2010, 2011; Alesina and Giuliano, 2015). We are not aware of systematic evidence on this question.

Moral attitudes. In addition to the standard notions of social preferences in behavioral economics such as altruism, fairness, reciprocity, and social image concerns, psychologists have in recent years expanded our understanding of *moral* preferences. Such authors point out that psychology has focused excessively on WEIRD—Western, Educated, Industrialized, Rich, Democratic—populations (Henrich et al., 2010b). In such populations, morality is conceptualized as being primarily about harm and fairness. Outside of these populations, for example, in developing countries, and in less-educated and lower-income populations in rich countries, moral attitudes are broader than these two principles (Haidt, 2012). These conceptions of morality include not only harm and fairness, but also deeply-held beliefs in moral ideals of loyalty to one's group, respect for authority, and purity or sanctity. Haidt

---

[38] As discussed in Section 2, some of the correlation between GDP and measured patience could be due to liquidity constraints affecting the measures of patience, even for hypothetical choices.

(2012) argues that these beliefs are extremely important to people and correlate with important political and social behaviors. The implications of these different moral frameworks for economic and political behavior are ripe for exploration.

Culture. A recent literature in economics takes an even broader view of cross-society variation in values, beliefs and social preferences. Guiso et al. (2006) define culture as "those customary beliefs and values that ethnic, religious, and social groups transmit fairly unchanged from generation to generation". Nunn (2012) instead defines culture as heuristics and rules of thumb that aid in decision making, with a role not just for values and beliefs, but also for emotions and "gut feelings".

Nunn (2012) summarizes the evidence on differences in culture across societies. One empirical strategy has been to compare individuals from different cultures brought into the same environment. For instance, Fernandez and Fogli (2009) show that the fertility and labor-force participation of second-generation US women is positively correlated with historical fertility and labor-force participation in their parents' country-of-origin. Fisman and Miguel (2007) study national variation in a culture of corruption by documenting differences in rates of unpaid parking tickets accumulated by diplomats from different countries who are all stationed in New York City.

Another strategy has been to conduct similar economic lab experiments across different societies, such as the work of Henrich et al. (2001) or Gneezy et al. (2009). More commonly, survey evidence has been used to document differences across countries in the stated importance to the respondent of family, the importance of children showing obedience and respect, the role of hard work versus luck in success, or the degree to which people prefer to be self-reliant versus integrating closely with a group (Alesina and Giuliano, 2015).

9.3 Do social preferences and culture matter for development?

Since at least the work of Banfield (1958), Coleman (1990), and Putnam (2000), social scientists have argued that trust plays a crucial role in generating desirable economic outcomes. More generally, achieving cooperation—including with strangers and in one-shot interactions—is often argued to be central to the process of development (Algan and Cahuc, 2014). In economics, an understanding of incomplete contracts and imperfect enforcement has led some scholars to agree. For instance, Arrow (1972) emphasized the importance of trust as follows: "virtually every commercial transaction has within itself an element of trust, certainly any transaction conducted over a period of time. It can be plausibly argued that much of the economic backwardness in the world can be explained by the lack of mutual confidence."

This idea is consistent with the cross-country correlations described above: trust and reciprocity are positively correlated with economic outcomes. However, one might worry that trust is simply a consequence of development. Poor countries tend to have worse contract enforcement and legal institutions, and thus it may simply be rational to distrust others more in poor countries. The process of development and growth might in turn strengthen state capacity and improve contract enforcement, thus increasing trust.

In recent years, some scholars of long-run growth and of cultural economics have argued that trust and related social attitudes are not only an outcome of development, but are instead (at least in part) deeper drivers of development themselves.[39]

One body of work provides evidence that modern-day trust and related concepts such as trustworthiness have deep historical roots. Nunn and Wantchekon (2011) show that current differences in trust levels within Africa can be traced back to the transatlantic and Indian Ocean slave trades, and that individuals who have ancestors from areas that were heavily raided through the slave trade show lower levels of trust in survey data. This evidence provides a potential mechanism to explain the large differences in modern-day development across the same regions of Africa (Nunn, 2008).

Other scholars have pointed to the importance of historical kindship structure in generating variation in modern-day culture. Enke (2018) shows that historical tightness of kinship structure predicts modern-day moral attitudes and social behaviors. Enke classifies societies by whether they historically had tighter kinship structures, in which people were deeply embedded in extended family networks, or conversely looser kinship structures, in which such extended family networks were less important. Groups which historically had tighter kinship have lower levels of trust, more in-group favoritism, higher willingness to cheat on and distrust outsiders, and more local rather than broader institutions today.

Schulz et al. (2018) argue that this psychological variation arose as a response to different institutions governing kinship, descent and marriage. They propose that the Catholic Church's policies led to the dissolution of traditional kinship institutions in Europe, creating the specific modern-day psychology specific to Western countries, including the increased importance of impartiality, universal moral principles, generalized trust, cooperation, and fairness.

The above evidence suggests that present-day levels of trust, social preferences and culture more broadly are not entirely determined by present-day outcomes, making a causal role for trust on development more plausible. Other work more directly attempts to link trust causally to economic outcomes. Algan and Cahuc (2010) use an ingenious approach to determine historical levels of trust in various countries. They examine trust levels in present-day individuals in the United States and, using variation in when the ancestors of those individuals first immigrated to the US, infer the levels of trust in the sending country at the time of immigration.

Algan and Cahuc (2010) make a key assumption, well-accepted in cultural economics, that present-day trust among individuals is correlated with the trust levels of their ancestors. Moreover, they assume that the nature of selection into migration by trust does not change substantially over time. The authors then relate the inferred level of trust in each sender country in a given year to income-per-capita in that country in that year and estimate substantial causal effects of trust on per-capita income.

---

[39] Recent reviews of this literature include Algan and Cahuc (2014), Spolaore and Wacziarg (2013) and Nunn (2012).

In subsequent work, Algan and Cahuc (2014) calculate that Africa would have a 5.5 times higher per-capita income if it had the same trust levels as Sweden (Algan and Cahuc, 2014).

Discussing the determinants and impact of ethnic diversity on economic, political and social outcomes is beyond the scope of this chapter, but it is worth noting that some studies using micro data suggest that, at least in some circumstances, there may be costs to diversity. Moreover, these costs may be context dependent and subject to policy influence.

Hjort (2014) examines how inter-group preferences can affect output. He collects data from a large flower farm in Kenya and shows that workers have strong social preferences featuring an in-group bias: they act to increase the payoffs of their co-ethnics relative to members of a rival ethnic group. Workers work in small teams of three, with one upstream worker and two downstream workers in each team. Hjort (2014) shows that upstream workers distort their effort and direct more of the intermediate goods they produce towards their co-ethnics downstream, resulting in both productivity losses of 4 to 8 percent and lower earnings even for themselves. These distortions worsen when ethnic divisions become more salient after electoral violence, until the firm finally reacts by adoption a team-pay scheme which eliminates incentives to discriminate. The paper thus also provides an illustration of how institutions (in this case, within-firm rules and incentives) can be adapted to reduce the distortions arising from ethnic preferences.

Ethnic diversity is also associated with worse local public goods. For instance, higher ethnic diversity is correlated with lower primary school funding and worse school facilities in Kenya (Miguel and Gugerty, 2005). The authors argue that diversity makes it more difficult to impose social sanctions, creating collective action failures. However, as discussed in Section 9.4 below, such effects are not found in Tanzania, a country with a history of policies designed to reduce ethnic conflict.

Not all the evidence suggests substantial individual-level ethnic prejudice. For instance, Berge et al. (2015) run lab experiments in a large sample of participants in Nairobi, Kenya, and find no evidence of ethnic favoritism in dictator games, public-goods games, and choose-your-dictator games, in which the participant can choose which other individual must decide how to share some money with them. Intriguingly, Berge et al. do find evidence of bias among recent movers to Nairobi, suggesting that living in a more cosmopolitan urban setting, with frequent interaction across ethnic groups, may have played some role in reducing ethnic preferences. In contrast to the overall null effects on behaviors, the authors detect a small amount of ethnic "bias" in Implicit Association Tests.[40] The incongruence in the findings on behaviors and implicit associations echoes with an ongoing debate in social psychology over whether IATs meaningfully predict real-world behaviors (Greenwald et al., 2009; Oswald et al., 2013).

---

[40] The Implicit Associate Test (IAT) is a test developed by social psychologists to measure the extent to which certain categories (such as race or gender) are associated with stereotypes, or with generally positive or negative valence (Greenwald et al., 1998).

Low levels of trust and the structure of in-group versus out-group preferences may also be related to several other important economic and political outcomes. For instance, some evidence suggests that levels of trust predict the structure of firms: higher trust in Italian regions predicts larger firm size and more decentralized decision-making (Cingano and Pinotti, 2012). Firms in Asia are substantially more centralized in terms of decision-making than firms in the United States or Europe and the extent of centralization is correlated with regional trust. (Bloom et al., 2012). Similarly, a sense of duty towards family and kin, and a lack of trust towards strangers may contribute to a culture of corruption and patronage in politics.

9.4 The impact of contact and policies on social preferences and norms

The previous discussion suggested that differences in social preferences and culture are driven at least in part by long-run historical factors. Should cultural differences and social trust or conversely social divisions therefore be thought of as fixed and immune to policy? Recent research suggests that at least some of these factors are malleable. Policy-relevant factors such as social contact, media exposure, and education can all affect social preferences.

Inter-group contact. A recent body of work in economics and psychology has provided rigorous tests of Allport's (1954) prediction that inter-group contact will (at least under certain favorable conditions) reduce social prejudice and improve social behavior.

Rao (2018) shows that the integration of rich and poor children in schools reduces social discrimination and increases willingness to socialize. Additionally, contact with poor children increases rich children's generosity towards others in both the lab (measuring using dictator games) and the field (volunteering for charities in school). Finally, it increases the strength of fairness preferences: rich students integrated with poor classmates become more inequity-averse in lab games. Corno et al. (2018) find similar reductions in racial prejudice using randomized roommate assignments of university students in South Africa, as do Boisjoly et al. (2006) in a university in the United States.

Lowe (2018) pushes this literature forward by investigating how the precise conditions under which contact occurs improve or instead worsen prejudice and mutually-beneficial economic transactions. He runs a field experiment involving a cricket league in villages in India and shows that cooperative contact (playing on the same team with members of a different caste) reduces caste prejudice in young men, while competitive contact (playing against others of a different caste) somewhat worsens attitudes. Cooperative contact also makes individuals more likely to engage in trade across caste lines and thus earn greater surplus in an innovative field task created by the author.

Okunogbe (2018) studies the consequences of mandatory national service in Nigeria, where college graduates are required to temporarily serve in other provinces in the country. She finds that inter-ethnic exposure causes individuals to have greater national pride and more positive attitudes towards Nigeria, but simultaneously increases the salience of one's own ethnic identity, resulting in more positive attitudes towards one's own group (but not others). These results point to the need for a nuanced understanding of national identity and ethnic diversity: it is possible to build national identity without weakening ethnic identity, even in a diverse developing country.

Media. Exposure to media has been shown to be a powerful driver of change in social preferences and attitudes in developing countries. For instance, exposure to Rwandan government radio propaganda, which focused on post-genocide nation-building, decreased the salience of ethnicity and increased inter-ethnic trust (Blouin and Mukand, 2017). Most intriguingly, the authors show that individuals from treated locations become less likely to use ethnicity (Hutu versus Tutsi) to categorize individuals, suggesting that even the salience of ethnic categories is malleable and could be influenced by governments or private media. Of course, such effects cut both ways: the same media tools can effectively be used to worsen social attitudes, stoke distrust, and even incite violence (Yanagizawa-Drott, 2014).

Exposure to television has also been shown to change attitudes and behaviors. La Ferrara et al. (2012) find that telenovelas in Brazil reduce fertility for the exposed cohorts in regions with access to telenovelas. Similarly, Jensen and Oster (2009) show evidence that the arrival of cable television in villages in India changed stated gender attitudes and some measures of behavior.

In contrast to the evidence on the effects of radio and television, little rigorous evidence exists on the effect of the print media on social and economic attitudes. Similarly, the rapid adoption of social media using internet-enabled cellphones in developing countries offer another important topic for future research.

Education. Education is generally shown to be positively correlated with trust and measures of prosocial preferences (e.g. Falk et al., 2018). However, we have relatively little causal evidence on this topic. Miguel (2004) argues that Tanzanian "nation-building" policies, partly implemented through school curriculum, allowed ethnically diverse communities in rural Tanzania to achieve considerably better local public goods outcomes than diverse communities in the nearby Kenyan region without similar policies.

School curriculum changes in China have been shown to have substantially affected students' political attitudes, making them more skeptical of free markets and more supportive of Chinese governance (Cantoni et al., 2017). Algan et al. (2013) argued that horizontal teaching practices in school—wherein students work together in groups—builds social capital. Rao (2018) similarly showed that direct personal interactions between students, caused by quasi-random assignment of students to study groups, reduced discriminatory behavior towards outgroup-members even outside the classroom. Further evidence on how education affects in-group preference and moral and social preferences is a promising area for future research.

This section has described the evidence on cross-society differences in social preferences and other aspect of culture. It has pointed to both evidence that variation in culture has deep historical roots, but also that social preferences, beliefs and values are at least somewhat malleable at the individual level and respond to a variety of interventions.

---

10 The psychology of poverty

A recent body of work suggests that living in poverty may *directly* affect cognitive function and economic behaviors, thus potentially exacerbating behavioral biases and deepening poverty (Haushofer and Fehr, 2014; Schilbach et al., 2016). In this section, we discuss the emerging literature on the psychology of poverty and point to both its promises and its present shortcomings.

10.1 Scarcity

In an influential book, Mullainathan and Shafir (2013) argue that poverty impedes cognitive function by capturing people's minds with thoughts of scarcity. At any point in time, a poor person may worry about paying their rent, their children's school fees, cellphone bills, or an adverse health shock with the potential to cause financial ruin. Everyday events such as seeing the doctor or buying groceries are also more likely to trigger thoughts about money or cost among the poor (Shah et al., 2018).

One might expect this increased focus to result in better decision-making. Models of rational inattention would predict that when the stakes are higher, which they often are for the poor, individuals will pay more attention and thus make better choices. There is some evidence in support of this theory. The poor have higher awareness of certain prices (Mullainathan and Shafir, 2013), and they pay more attention than the rich to sales taxes (Goldin and Homonoff, 2013). They also display more consistent valuations of goods across contexts, making them less likely to display biases such as proportional thinking in money (Shah et al., 2015).[41]

However, according to Mullainathan and Shafir (2013), while some of this attention is intentional and productive, much of it is not. Since cognitive capacity is limited and money-related thoughts take up some of this valuable capacity, mental "bandwidth" available for other tasks is reduced. As a result, they argue, poverty itself impedes cognitive function among the poor, degrading also the quality of decision-making and lowering productivity.

---

[41] Shah et al. (2015) provide examples in which lower-income individuals hew more closely to a rational model than the rich do. For instance, the poor appear to engage less in proportional thinking (Tversky and Kahneman, 1981): they report being equally willing to travel 30 minutes to save $50 off a purchase, regardless of whether the item they are purchasing costs $300, $500, or $1000. In contrast, high-income consumers are more willing to spend 30 minutes to save $50 on a $300 purchase than on a $1000 purchase, a classic finding in behavioral economics (Thaler, 1985). The poor also express the same willingness to pay for an item across contexts, unlike the rich. Specifically, their WTP for a beer to be consumed on a beach is the same whether the beer was purchased from a hotel or a store, while higher-income consumers report being willing to pay more for the same beer from a hotel.

Mani et al. (2013) provide empirical evidence in support of this hypothesis. Their study features two complementary designs: a "lab study" in a mall in Trenton, NJ, and a field study with farmers in India. The lab study induces thoughts about finances by making individuals consider a financial scenario and then measures cognitive function using tasks developed by psychologists to measure fluid intelligence (IQ) and cognitive control. Results from four different trials show a subtle but highly intriguing picture. Performance by rich individuals, defined as those higher than median income in the sample, is unaffected by whether the financial scenario concerns involve large or small amounts of money. In contrast, when asked about the high-amount scenario, the poor perform significantly worse compared to being asked about the low-amount scenario, suggesting that induced thoughts about money lowered their cognitive function.

The complementary field study in Mani et al. (2013) cleverly exploits within-person variation in financial status before and after harvest among sugarcane farmers rural India. The harvest cycle for sugarcane, a cash crop, is about 18 months and farmers have trouble evenly spreading the resources received at harvest over the entire cycle, possibly due to present bias. Consequently, farmers are significantly poorer in the months before harvest compared to the months after harvest, as reflected in belongings pawned, outstanding loans, and reported ability to cope with ordinary bills. Farmers' cognitive performance right before harvest is significantly worse compared to their performance right after harvest. The authors provide evidence against competing channels such as nutrition or uncertainty and conclude that poverty itself impedes cognitive function.

The results in Mani et al. are striking and important for several reasons. First, the estimated effects are enormous. While the effect sizes in the lab study are difficult to interpret, the authors argue that the differences in the field study correspond to differences of about 10 IQ points, comparable to the impacts of losing a night of sleep or being moderately inebriated. Lower cognitive performance is known to be correlated with lower levels of patience and willingness to accept risk (Dohmen et al., 2010), worse job performance (Kuncel and Hezlett, 2010) and even higher mortality (Batty et al., 2009). If these effects translate causally into worse real-world decisions and behaviors, they could help explain puzzling behaviors among the poor, such as evidence of lower parenting effort, lower medication adherence, and food-consumption patterns. If such effects indeed exist, they may make an additional case for the effectiveness of unconditional cash transfers, reducing hassles among the poor, or subsidizing insurance to facilitate peace of mind.

There is also some, albeit disputed, inconsistently measured and hard-to-interpret evidence of differences in cognitive ability across the rich and poor, and even across rich and poor countries (Ervik, 2003; Palairet, 2004). Previous explanations of such differences include differences in childhood nutrition (such as iodine supplements in diet), education, and other omitted variables.

In contrast, Mullainathan and Shafir (2013) offer a new perspective: poverty itself may lower cognitive function. In fact, in the mall study of Mani et al. (2013), described above, the cognitive performance of the rich and the poor was indistinguishable from each other in the absence of the financially-stressful question. The argument is thus not one of fixed differences across individuals, but of the importance of the situation of poverty. This echoes the long-running debate in psychology between social psychology, which argues that variation in human behavior is overwhelmingly driven by variation in the situation or context (Ross and Nisbett, 1991; Bertrand et al., 2004), and personality psychology, which argues that stable individual differences in personality traits explain a great deal of variation in behavior (e.g. Borghans et al., 2008).

However, important gaps and shortcomings in this promising research agenda remain. First, the existing studies have understandable methodological limitations. For instance, the field study of Mani et al. is a simple pre-post comparison without a control group, which raises the question of potential learning effects or time trends explaining the results. Second, to the best of our knowledge, neither of the two studies appears to have been replicated. In a related setting, Carvalho et al. (2016) find no differences in cognitive function and decision-making around paydays in the US, though this finding may be in explained by the smaller differences in financial hardship before and after payday in their sample relative to those among farmers in India.

Third, to date, little evidence exists of impacts on economic outcomes such as productivity, preferences, or decision-making. Ong et al. (2018) analyze the impacts of a debt-relief program among low-income individuals in Singapore. While the authors find intriguing impacts on a range of cognitive and economic outcomes, the study does not feature a control group, causing identification concerns similar to the ones regarding Mani et al.'s (2013) field evidence. Bartos et al. (2018) measure the impact of poverty on time preferences. Experimentally-induced thoughts about poverty increased Ugandan farmers' impatience, as measured by their preference to consume entertainment early and instead to delay work effort.

Kaur et al. (2018) consider the impact of poverty on productivity in a field experiment with low-income piece rate workers in rural India. The authors randomly vary the timing of wage payments to workers—generating variation in the timing of cash receipt while holding overall income fixed—with the payment amount corresponding to about 2 to 3 weeks' worth of baseline earnings. Since workers are severely cash-constrained at baseline, receiving early payments significantly alters workers' expenditure patterns following the days of the payment. Workers reduce debt overhang and increase food purchases.

The authors interpret the early-pay intervention as changing the experienced financial constraints among study participants. Upon receiving their early pay, workers significantly increase their hourly output compared to the control group, with effects concentrated among poorer workers. Kaur et al. (2018) find evidence of decreased attentional errors in production, suggesting improved cognition as a contributing channel for the productivity effects. The authors argue that the impacts are not driven by gift exchange, trust in the employer, affect, or nutrition. The results provide evidence that the alleviation of experienced financial constraints may have a direct link with productivity and offer suggestive support for cognition as a channel.

The effects of scarcity are most likely to translate into important real-world out-comes if people are not self-aware of such effects. Individuals in both of Mani et al.'s (2013) studies were not given a choice as to when to perform the cognitive tasks. Individuals who understand the impacts of scarcity on their decision-making might choose to make important decisions at times when they are cash-rich and thus to mitigate the impacts of scarcity. To date, there is no evidence of people's (lack of) awareness of the impacts of scarcity on their cognitive function. In an experimental study on the impact of noise on cognitive function and productivity, Dean (2018) finds near-complete naïveté regarding impairments of cognitive function and worker productivity due to noise.

10.2 Deprivations beyond lack of money

Poverty entails many other deprivations and potentially detrimental situations beyond lack of money (Schilbach et al., 2016). Perhaps most well-known among these and well-studied in the development literature, the poor are often affected by malnutrition (FAO, 2018). Another recent literature has documented that poverty and negative income shocks are associated with higher levels of stress (Haushofer and Fehr, 2014), although evidence on the effects of stress on economic decision-making is mixed at best (Haushofer et al., 2018).

However, the urban poor are also disproportionately exposed to poor sleeping conditions (Grandner et al., 2010; Patel et al., 2010) as well as environmental and noise pollution and heat (Harlan et al., 2006; Dean et al., 2018). Physical labor, lack of education and limited access to medical care also lead to higher prevalence of physical pain among the poor (Krueger and Stone, 2008; Poleshuck and Green, 2008; Case and Deaton, 2015). While rigorous evidence on the underlying causal re-lationships is scarce, poverty has also been associated with hazardous alcohol consumption patterns and other forms of substance abuse (Neufeld et al., 2005; Subramanian et al., 2005; Patel, 2007). Moreover, poverty often entails stigma, shame, and social exclusion, which could all affect cognition and decision-making (Hall et al., 2014; Ghosal et al., 2017; Chandrasekhar et al., 2018).

For each of these factors, a rich literature in psychology, medicine, and other fields has studied and often established impacts on cognitive function, decision-making, and health, mostly via experimental lab studies and observational data, as summa-rized in Dean et al. (2018). A key open question is whether the known impacts on cognition and health translate into economically meaningful effects on productivity, labor supply, and decision-making. A second line of research is whether these factors can *cause* behavioral biases. Behavioral economics to date has primarily shown the existence and relevance of behavioral biases, mostly focusing on average parame-ter estimates, for instance, the fraction of present-biased individuals and the average degree of present bias among those individuals. Uncovering some of the underlying sources of behavioral biases could help to identify some of the determinants of varia-tion across individuals and over time. Since the poor are disproportionately exposed by these factors, they could lead to more pronounced behavioral biases among the poor.

Recently completed and ongoing work has attempted to make inroads into each of these two lines of research. Studies have found significant impacts of noise, environmental pollution, nutrition on worker learning, productivity, and earnings (Schofield, 2014; Chang et al., 2018; Dean, 2018; Jagnani, 2018). Many of the poor are exposed to several of these factors, such that impacts on productivity and earning might well add up to economically large magnitudes. There could also be important interaction effects between these factors that are yet to be explored.

There is less evidence on the impacts of factors surrounding poverty on preferences and decision-making. Schofield (2014) finds evidence of increased nutrition on effort discounting among low-income workers in India. Sleep deprivation appears to make individuals less altruistic, trusting and trustworthy (Dickinson and McElroy, 2017). Similarly, Koppel et al. (2017) find that acute pain makes individuals less patient and more risk-seeking. Finally, Schilbach (2019) finds that incentives for sobriety significantly increased savings among low-income drivers in India, particularly among individuals without access to commitment savings. Additional evidence linking the above factors to preferences and decision-making would be valuable.

In an ongoing study, Bessone et al. (2018) study the impacts of improving sleeping conditions among the urban poor in Chennai, India. They find that study participants sleep on average under 5.5 hours per night, implying severe chronic sleep deprivation, in part due to environmental irritants such as heat, noise, mosquitoes, and physical discomfort. The authors evaluate different randomized interventions (such as improving individuals' home sleep environment and offering them a place to nap at the workplace) to investigate the impacts of improved sleep on labor market outcomes as well as behavioral biases and preferences (time, risk, and social preferences, susceptibility to defaults, and inattention).

10.3 Mental health

There is mixed evidence on the relationship between poverty and mental ill-health. On the one hand, income and consumption measures do not appear to strongly correlate with mental health, even when mental health is itself measured in representative surveys, such that differential rates of diagnosis are not a factor (Das et al., 2007). However, other measures and aspects of poverty, such as food insecurity, lack of education, poor housing, and self-reported financial stress are associated with mental ill-health in numerous epidemiological studies (Patel and Kleinman, 2003; Lund et al., 2010).

Regardless of the income gradients of mental health, the prevalence of mental health conditions in developing countries is high and is paired with extremely low levels of diagnosis and treatment options, especially for the poor. For instance, India has only about 0.3 psychiatrists per 100,000 individuals (3,600 psychiatrists to serve a population of 1.2 billion), compared to 12.4 per 100,000 individuals in the United States. In addition to inadequate care, mental ill-health is often associated with stigma, exclusion, and shame, further reducing the propensity to seek mental health care in times of need.

Major Depressive Disorder ("depression") is the single leading cause of disability worldwide (Friedrich, 2017). At a global level, over 300 million people are estimated to suffer from depression, equivalent to 4.4% of the world's population. Scholars in global mental health have shown that simple psychotherapy interventions can be effective in treating depression in low-income contexts (Bolton et al., 2003). These methods usually involve trained laypeople delivering psychotherapy as volunteers. Patel et al. (2017) use a community health approach to psychotherapy in Goa, India. A short-run evaluation of a behavioral-activation treatment delivered by lay counselors showed high effectiveness in reducing depression incidence and symptom severity three months after the end of the intervention.

Baranov et al. (2017) show impacts of a similar intervention, delivered by community health workers, on depression and female empowerment seven years after the end of the treatment. While these results are encouraging, it is too early to tell whether low-cost psychotherapy is a scalable and effective way to improve mental health in developing countries. Numerous other trials are in the field, including evaluations of therapy provided over cellphones and using text-messaging (Fairburn and Patel, 2017).

Psychotherapies have been employed to support individuals in other ways than alleviating depression. Two trials have recently been completed in developing countries. Blattman et al. (2017) evaluate the impact of a cognitive-behavioral therapy (CBT) intervention and the distribution of unconditional cash transfers on the behavior of high-risk young men in Liberia. The authors find reduced criminal behavior and improved self-control and self-image among participants. McKelway (2018) evaluates a four-week psycho-social intervention to improve generalized self-efficacy and found large impacts on female labor supply (as discussed in more detail in Section 7.5).

Suicide is a particularly severe consequence of mental ill-health and one of the leading causes of death for individuals suffering from severe mental ill-health (Hawton et al., 2013). Suicides cause 800,000 deaths annually, with about three-quarters of these deaths occurring in developing countries. Stress, mental illness, and depression have been identified as major causes of suicides (Mann et al., 1999; Boldrini and Mann, 2015). While economic conditions have been linked to each of these factors, few studies have been able to provide a direct link between economic wellbeing and suicides. Using a difference-in-differences approach in Indonesia, Christian et al. (2018) find that cash transfers reduced yearly suicides by 0.36 per 100,000 people, corresponding to an 18 percent decrease.

While we have learned much about mental health and the impact of psychotherapies, many open questions remain. A high priority for future research is to better understand the underlying mechanisms. How does depression affect preferences, beliefs, and decision-making? More generally, how should economists model depression?[42] As a first step toward better understanding these questions, a follow-up evaluation of Patel et al. (2017) is underway, which will investigate the medium-run effects of this intervention on depression, earnings and consumption (de Quidt et al., 2018). Specifically, the study seeks to shed light on the underlying channels of potential treatment effects, by measuring individuals' risk, social, and time preferences as well as beliefs in one's own ability and information processing.

Numerous questions remain for future investigation. How does the effectiveness of mental health treatments interact with cash payments or available economic opportunities (e.g. job offers)? Existing evidence shows cash transfers can improve wellbeing and mental health (Haushofer and Shapiro, 2016). But do such effects persist over a longer time horizon? Can we better understand determinants of entry into and exit from depression? Do cash transfers and/or mental health interventions have intergenerational effects on children's mental health? What is the relationship between physical pain, mental health and substance abuse? These and many questions remain to be explored in future research on this topic.

10.4 Aspirations, hope, and religiosity

We now turn to positive psychological factors, particularly hope and aspirations, which may be helpful in generating better economic outcomes and psychological well-being among the poor. We also discuss suggestive evidence on how religious beliefs and practices may, at least in some cases, provide similar benefits.

Aspirations and hope. Development economists have investigated the role of aspirations and hope in the lives of the poor at least since Sen (1985, 1999). Appadurai (2004) proposed that 'aspirations to the good life' are not evenly distributed in society, with lower capacity to aspire among the poor—not because of any fundamental cognitive differences, but simply due to a lack of opportunity to practice the 'exploration, conjecture and refutation' of possible futures. Low levels of aspirations and hope in turn can limit social mobility and even create a poverty trap (Ray, 2006; Dalton et al., 2015; Genicot and Ray, 2017).

An important challenge in this literature is the definition and modeling of aspirations. Aspirations are broadly a hope or ambition of achieving something.[43] While such broad definitions are useful and intuitive, it has proven difficult to map aspirations into existing economic frameworks. Aspirations are conceptually distinct from both beliefs about the future and preferences for outcomes. Endogenous reference points might come closest to existing theories in behavioral economics. In recent years, models of aspirations and hope as reference points have made progress in this direction (Dalton et al., 2015; Genicot and Ray, 2017; Lybbert and Wydick, 2018). They are also closely related to existing models of goals

---

[42] One approach is provided by de Quidt and Haushofer (2016), who model depression essentially as having low beliefs about returns to effort. They show how this simple assumption can rationalize several behaviors associated with depression.

[43] For excellent discussions of the recent literature, see La Ferrara (2018) and Duflo (2012a).

as endogenously set references point, useful to motivate one's effort when facing self-control problems (Hsiaw, 2013).

Dalton et al. (2015) propose a model of aspirations as reference points, wherein aspirations influence effort choices, and effort produces future wealth. Future wealth in turn causes aspirations to adjust, potentially producing a virtuous cycle. A key assumption is that individuals do not realize how their future aspirations will be affected by their current effort levels. That is, they do not internalize the future motivating or demotivating effects of their present effort choice. Since the authors additionally (reasonably) assume that poor individuals need to exert greater effort to reach the same final wealth level, the model can generate poverty traps: even if they start with the same aspirations, poor individuals will exert less effort, which will cause their future aspirations to become lower, further reducing effort, and so on.

Genicot and Ray (2017) provide another model of aspirations as reference points. In their model, parents have aspirations for children's future wealth levels. Parents receive a utility boost proportional to the extent to which their children exceed their parents' aspirations, creating a kink in the utility function akin to models of reference dependence. Aspirations in their model are not (necessarily) rational expectations or status-quo levels, but instead may depend upon the distribution of outcomes in society. Aspirations moderately above the individual's present level provide incentives to invest, while avoiding frustration.

A key empirical question in this literature is whether aspirations are malleable and how different policies might be able to affect them. Bernard et al. (2014) consider the impact of exposing individuals to documentaries showing similar individuals from their community who managed to escape poverty through their own efforts in agriculture or business. The authors find remarkably large five-year impacts on aspirations as well as investments in education, livestock, and agricultural inputs. More research in this area is underway, with the goal to confirm and expand upon these striking and surprising impacts from such a light-touch intervention.

Aspirations for one's children could be particularly important for economic development and poverty alleviation. Beaman et al. (2012) show that role models are an important aspect in shaping individuals' aspirations. The authors find that Indian parents are less ambitious for the education and careers of their daughters than their sons. However, random exposure to female politicians at the local level (due to a reservation policy in India) sharply reduced this gender gap in aspirations as well as actual educational achievement among teenage girls.

An open question is whether improving economic outcomes via cash transfers or broader programs such as the ultra-poor program fosters higher aspirations. While Banerjee et al. (2015b) do not report findings regarding aspirations in their six-country evaluation of the multi-faceted "graduation program", Sulaiman and Barua (2013) report that changing aspirations is often cited by the implementers as the most important challenge in the ultra-poor graduation program in the context of Afghanistan. [44]

Religiosity. The poor often spend considerable time and money on festivals, funeral, pilgrimages, and other religious activities (Banerjee and Duflo, 2007). Such activities may foster social cohesion and trust in societies (Clingingsmith et al., 2009). Moreover, work going back to Adam Smith and Max Weber argues that religiosity (specifically, the Protestant faith) causes economic wellbeing by fostering diligence, thriftiness, and norms prescribing virtuous behavior (Iannaccone, 1998; Iyer, 2016). Religiosity has been linked to many aspects of lives that are favorable for individuals' economic wellbeing including human capital formation, income, savings, and health (Freeman, 1986; Gruber, 2005; Ellison, 1991; Gruber and Hungerman, 2008).[45]

Despite these prominent arguments for the importance of religion and specific religious traditions for economic activity, rigorously establishing causal relationships between contemporaneous religious practices and beliefs, income, and wealth has been difficult due to obvious identification challenges, particularly at the individual level. Moreover, research on the economic and psychological consequences of religiosity we described above mostly focuses on various denominations of Christianity. Given the diversity of religious traditions in the developing world, a potentially important research agenda in behavioral development economics is to consider a wider range of religions and contexts and their implications for the lives of the poor.

Bryan et al. (2018) make progress toward improving our understanding of the causal impacts of religiosity by randomizing exposure to religion in the Philippines. They randomly assign over 6,000 poor households in 160 communities in the Philippines to receive invitations to attend an evangelical Protestant Christian values-and-theology education program consisting of 15 weekly half-hour sessions. This treatment significantly increases both religiosity and income. Puzzlingly, the authors detect no effect on either total labor supply, assets, or consumption, begging the question of where the increase in income comes from and how they are spent. A partial answer could be a shift from agricultural to non-agricultural self-employment, which may involve a higher implicit wage.

Beyond impacts on human capital, earnings, and wealth, religion could influence individuals' hope and aspirations, as well as their expectations about the future. As discussed in Section 5 on insurance, beliefs in higher, interventionist powers could crowd out demand for formal or informal insurance (Auriol et al., 2018). Such beliefs

---

[44] Related evidence is provided by Laajaj (2017), who shows that an intervention providing input subsidies and a savings match to farmers in Mozambique increases their self-reported planning horizons. The author provides a model in which the agent's planning horizon is endogenously determined by how bright their future prospects appear. The idea is that a gloomy future causes distress due to anticipatory utility, and the agent responds by avoiding thinking about the future, worsening planning and reducing long-term investments.

[45] Bryan et al. (2018) provide a more thorough review of this literature.

could also foster individuals' hopes and aspirations, and even boost mental health, as argued in a contentious literature going back as far as Freud (Levin, 2010).

Cooley Fruehwirth et al. (2019) consider the possibility that religiosity directly impacts depression. To address endogeneity concerns, the authors exploit across-cohort variation in the religiosity of students' peers at school. They report that increased exposure to religious peers among US adolescents increased own religiosity and lowered depression. The authors provide evidence that the mechanism through which religiosity protects against depression is not by strengthening friendships or increasing social activities. Instead, they argue, religiosity increases psychological resilience and ability to deal with stressors. While this evidence is intriguing and important, identification concerns remain, and more work along these lines would be valuable.

11 Conclusion

In this chapter, we discussed canonical topics in development economics through the lens of behavioral economics. We argued that models and ideas from behavioral economics can help explain important puzzles in development, and have applications to understanding preventive health behavior, savings, demand for insurance, technology adoption, labor markets and firms. We also discussed evidence of variation in social preferences and culture across societies, and of the relationship between poverty and psychology.

We have not discussed several important topics in development, due to limited existing work on these topics in behavioral development. One such topic is education. As an investment good, education may be particularly subject to behavioral biases if children and youth themselves have substantial agency over educational investments (Bursztyn and Coffman, 2012). Existing evidence suggests that the time preferences of students may be malleable and important (Alan and Ertac, 2018; Alan et al., 2018) and that students may have systematically biased beliefs about the returns to education (Jensen, 2010). Another under-explored topic for behavioral development could be the economics of the family. Social preferences and norms within the household could matter for consumption and investment decisions, as could biased beliefs. For instance, Dizon-Ross (2018) shows that parents do not fully understand their children's (relative) ability and returns to education. Another topic we have only touched on in passing is the political economy of development, where social preferences, biased beliefs and norms may all be important (e.g. Finan and Schechter, 2012; Chen and Yang, 2018). We believe that these are equally important areas for future work in behavioral development economics as those we have covered in this chapter.

While policy design is not the focus of our paper, we have discussed some cases of success of behaviorally-informed solutions, for instance, the use of small incentives to encourage desirable health behaviors, and the use of mental accounts to direct savings. In other cases, the solutions proposed by behavioral economics are yet to show reliable impacts on outcomes, for instance, in the case of commitment devices to address self-control problems. Yet other interventions show promising initial evidence, but with much more investigation warranted, as in the case of psychotherapies to improve mental health and economic outcomes.

We close by encouraging researchers in behavioral development economics to take behavioral theory seriously and ideally quantitatively, providing calibrations or estimations where possible (DellaVigna, 2018). This approach entails designing experiments to more precisely identify specific behavioral mechanisms and to test for them (Ludwig et al., 2011).

References

Abebe, G., Caria, S., Ortiz-Ospina, E., 2017. The Selection of Talent: Experimental and Structural Evidence from Ethiopia. Technical report. Mimeo.

Acemoglu, Daron, Robinson, James A., 2013. Why Nations Fail: The Origins of Power, Prosperity, and Poverty. Broadway Business, New York.

Adhvaryu, Achyuta, Kala, Namrata, Nyshadham, Anant, 2016. Management and Shocks to Worker Productivity. Mimeograph. University of Michigan Working Paper.

Adhvaryu, Achyuta, Kala, Namrata, Nyshadham, Anant, 2018a. The Light and the Heat: Productivity Co-Benefits of Energy-Saving Technology. NBER Working Paper No. 24314.

Adhvaryu, Achyuta, Kala, Namrata, Nyshadham, Anant, 2018b. The Skills to Pay the Bills: Returns to On-the-Job Soft Skills Training. Technical report. National Bureau of Economic Research.

Aghion, Philippe, Algan, Yann, Cahuc, Pierre, et al., 2011. Can policy affect culture? Minimum wage and the quality of labor relations. Journal of the European Economic Association 9 (1), 3–42.

Aghion, Philippe, Algan, Yann, Cahuc, Pierre, Shleifer, Andrei, 2010. Regulation and distrust. The Quarterly Journal of Economics 125 (3), 1015–1049.

Akerlof, George A., 1982. Labor contracts as partial gift exchange. The Quarterly Journal of Economics 97 (4), 543–569.

Akerlof, George A., Kranton, Rachel E., 2005. Identity and the economics of organizations. The Journal of Economic Perspectives 19 (1), 9–32.

Alan, Sule, Boneva, Teodora, Ertac, Seda, 2018. Ever failed, try again, succeed better: results from a randomized educational intervention on grit. Mimeograph.

Alan, Sule, Ertac, Seda, 2018. Fostering patience in the classroom: results from a randomized educational intervention. Journal of Political Economy 126 (5), 1865–1911.

Aleem, Irfan, 1990. Imperfect information, screening, and the costs of informal lending: a study of a rural credit market in Pakistan. World Bank Economic Review 4 (3), 329–349.

Alesina, Alberto, Giuliano, Paola, 2015. Culture and institutions. Journal of Economic Literature 53 (4), 898–944.

Alesina, Alberto, Giuliano, Paola, Nunn, Nathan, 2011. Fertility and the plough. The American Economic Review 101 (3), 499–503.

Algan, Yann, Cahuc, Pierre, 2010. Inherited trust and growth. The American Economic Review 100 (5), 2060–2092.

Algan, Yann, Cahuc, Pierre, 2014. Trust, growth, and well-being: new evidence and policy implications. In: Handbook of Economic Growth, vol. 2. Elsevier, pp. 49–120.

Algan, Yann, Cahuc, Pierre, Shleifer, Andrei, 2013. Teaching practices and social capital. American Economic Journal: Applied Economics 5 (3), 189–210.

Allen, Eric J., Dechow, Patricia M., Pope, Devin G., Wu, George, 2016. Reference-dependent preferences: evidence from marathon runners. Management Science 63 (6), 1657–1672.

Allport, Gordon Willard, 1954. The Nature of Prejudice. Doubleday.

Amador, Manuel, Werning, Iván, Angeletos, George-Marios, 2006. Commitment vs. flexibility. Econometrica 74 (2), 365–396.

Anagol, Santosh, Etang, Alvin, Karlan, Dean, 2017. Continued existence of cows disproves central tenets of capitalism? Economic Development and Cultural Change 65 (4), 583–618.

Andersen, Steffen, Brandon, Alec, Gneezy, Uri, List, John A., 2014. Toward an Understanding of Reference-Dependent Labor Supply: Theory and Evidence from a Field Experiment. NBER Working Paper No. 20695.

Andersen, Steffen, Harrison, Glenn W., Lau, Morten I., Rutström, E. Elisabet, 2008. Eliciting risk and time preferences. Econometrica 76 (3), 583–618.

Anderson, Peter, Chisholm, Dan, Fuhr, Daniela C., 2009. Effectiveness and cost-effectiveness of policies and programmes to reduce the harm caused by alcohol. The Lancet 373 (9682), 2234–2246.

Andreoni, James, Sprenger, Charles, 2012. Estimating time preferences from convex budgets. The American Economic Review 102 (7), 3333–3356.

Angeletos, George-Marios, Laibson, David, Repetto, Andrea, Tobacman, Jeremy, Weinberg, Stephen, 2001. The hyperbolic consumption model: calibration, simulation, and empirical evaluation. The Journal of Economic Perspectives 15 (3), 47–68.

Anglewicz, Philip, Kohler, Hans-Peter, 2009. Overestimating HIV infection: the construction and accuracy of subjective probabilities of HIV infection in rural Malawi. Demographic Research 20 (6), 65.

Appadurai, Arjun, 2004. The capacity to aspire: culture and the terms of recognition. In: Rao, Vijayendra, Walton, Michael (Eds.), Culture and Public Action. Stanford University Press, Stanford.

Arkes, Hal R., Blumer, Catherine, 1985. The psychology of sunk cost. Organizational Behavior and Human Decision Processes 35 (1), 124–140.

Arrow, Kenneth J., 1963. Uncertainty and the welfare economics of medical care. The American Economic Review 53 (5), 941–973.

Arrow, Kenneth J., 1972. Gifts and exchanges. Philosophy & Public Affairs, 343–362.

Ashraf, Nava, Bandiera, Oriana, 2018. Social incentives in organizations. Annual Review of Economics 10, 439–463.

Ashraf, Nava, Bandiera, Oriana, Jack, B. Kelsey, 2014. No margin, no mission? A field experiment on incentives for public service delivery. Journal of Public Economics 120, 1–17.

Ashraf, Nava, Bandiera, Oriana, Lee, Scott, 2018. Losing Prosociality in the Quest for Talent? Sorting, Selection, and Productivity in the Delivery of Public Services. London School of Economics and Political Science Working Paper.

Ashraf, Nava, Berry, James, Shapiro, Jesse M., 2010. Can higher prices stimulate product use? Evidence from a field experiment in Zambia. The American Economic Review 100 (5), 2383–2413.

Ashraf, Nava, Camerer, Colin F., Loewenstein, George, 2005. Adam Smith, behavioral economist. The Journal of Economic Perspectives 19 (3), 131–145.

Ashraf, Nava, Field, Erica, Rusconi, Giuditta, Voena, Alessandra, Ziparo, Roberta, 2017. Traditional beliefs and learning about maternal risk in Zambia. The American Economic Review 107 (5), 511–515.

Ashraf, Nava, Karlan, Dean, Yin, Wesley, 2006. Tying Odysseus to the mast: evidence from a commitment savings product in the Philippines. The Quarterly Journal of Economics 121 (2), 635–672.

Atkin, David, Chaudhry, Azam, Chaudry, Shamyla, Khandelwal, Amit K., Verhoogen, Eric, 2017. Organizational barriers to technology adoption: evidence from soccer-ball producers in Pakistan. The Quarterly Journal of Economics 132 (3), 1101–1164.

Augenblick, Ned, 2018. Short-term time discounting in unpleasant tasks. Mimeograph.

Augenblick, Ned, Niederle, Muriel, Sprenger, Charles, 2015. Working over time: dynamic inconsistency in real effort tasks. The Quarterly Journal of Economics 130 (3), 1067–1115.

Augenblick, Ned, Rabin, Matthew, 2018. An experiment on time preference and misprediction in unpleasant tasks. The Review of Economic Studies, rdy019.

Auriol, Emmanuelle, Lassebie, Julie, Panin, Amma, Raiber, Eva, Seabright, Paul, 2018. God Insures Those Who Pay? Formal Insurance and Religious Offerings in Ghana. Toulouse School of Economics Working Paper.

Bai, Liang, Handel, Benjamin, Miguel, Edward, Rao, Gautam, 2017. Self-Control and Demand for Preventive Health: Evidence from Hypertension in India. NBER Working Paper No. 23727.

Baird, Sarah, Hamory Hicks, Joan, Kremer, Michael, Miguel, Edward, 2016. Worms at work: long-run impacts of a child health investment. The Quarterly Journal of Economics 131 (4), 1637–1680.

Bandiera, Oriana, Burgess, Robin, Das, Narayan, Gulesci, Selim, Rasul, Imran, Sulaiman, Munshi, 2017. Labor markets and poverty in village economies. The Quarterly Journal of Economics 132 (2), 811–870.

Bandiera, Oriana, Burgess, Robin, Deserranno, Erika, Rasulk, Imran, Sulaiman, Munshi. 2018. Social ties and the delivery of development programs. Mimeograph.

Bandiera, Oriana, Rasul, Imran, 2006. Social networks and technology adoption in Northern Mozambique. The Economic Journal 116 (514), 869–902.

Banerjee, Abhijit, Duflo, Esther, Glennerster, Rachel, Kinnan, Cynthia, 2015a. The miracle of microfinance? Evidence from a randomized evaluation. American Economic Journal: Applied Economics 7 (1), 22–53.

Banerjee, Abhijit, Duflo, Esther, Goldberg, Nathanael, Karlan, Dean, Osei, Robert, Parienté, William, Shapiro, Jeremy, Thuysbaert, Bram, Udry, Christopher, 2015b. A multifaceted program causes lasting progress for the very poor: evidence from six countries. Science 348 (6236), 1260799.

Banerjee, Abhijit, Mullainathan, Sendhil, 2010. The Shape of Temptation: Implications for the Economic Lives of the Poor. NBER Working Paper No. 15973.

Banerjee, Abhijit V., Duflo, Esther, 2005. Growth theory through the lens of development economics. In: Handbook of Economic Growth, vol. 1. Elsevier, Amsterdam, pp. 473–552.

Banerjee, Abhijit V., Duflo, Esther, 2007. The economic lives of the poor. The Journal of Economic Perspectives 21 (1), 141–168.

Banerjee, Abhijit V., Duflo, Esther, 2014. Do firms want to borrow more? Testing credit constraints using a directed lending program. The Review of Economic Studies 81 (2), 572–607.

Banerjee, Abhijit V., Duflo, Esther, Glennerster, Rachel, Kothari, Dhruva, 2010. Improving immunisation coverage in rural India: clustered randomised controlled evaluation of immunisation campaigns with and without incentives. BMJ British Medical Journal 340, c2220.

Banfield, Edward C., 1958. The Moral Basis of a Backward Society. Free Press, Glencoe, IL.

Baranov, Victoria, Bhalotra, Sonia R., Biroli, Pietro, Maselko, Joanna, 2017. Maternal Depression, Women's Empowerment, and Parental Investment: Evidence from a Large Randomized Control Trial. IZA Discussion Papers.

Barberis, Nicholas, Xiong, Wei, 2012. Realization utility. Journal of Financial Economics 104 (2), 251–271.

Bartos, Vojtech, Bauer, Michal, Chytilová, Julie, Lively, Ian, 2018. Effects of poverty on impatience: preferences or inattention? Mimeograph

Basu, Karna, Wong, Maisy, 2015. Evaluating seasonal food storage and credit programs in East Indonesia. Journal of Development Economics 115, 200–216.

Batty, G. David, Wennerstad, Karin Modig, Smith, George Davey, Gunnell, David, Deary, Ian J., Tynelius, Per, Rasmussen, Finn, 2009. IQ in early adulthood and mortality by middle age: cohort study of 1 million Swedish men. Epidemiology 20 (1), 100–109.

Beaman, Lori, Duflo, Esther, Pande, Rohini, Topalova, Petia, 2012. Female leadership raises aspirations and educational attainment for girls: a policy experiment in India. Science 335 (6068), 582–586.

Beaman, Lori, Magruder, Jeremy, 2012. Who gets the job referral? Evidence from a social networks experiment. The American Economic Review 102 (7), 3574–3593.

Beaman, Lori, Magruder, Jeremy, Robinson, Jonathan, 2014. Minding small change among small firms in Kenya. Journal of Development Economics 108, 69–86.

Bellemare, Charles, Krause, Michaela, Kröger, Sabine, Zhang, Chendi, 2005. Myopic loss aversion: information feedback vs. investment flexibility. Economics Letters 87 (3), 319–324.

Bénabou, Roland, Tirole, Jean, 2003. Intrinsic and extrinsic motivation. The Review of Economic Studies 70 (3), 489–520.

Bénabou, Roland, Tirole, Jean, 2006. Incentives and prosocial behavior. The American Economic Review 96 (5), 1652–1678.

Benjamin, Dan, Bodoh-Creed, Aaron, Rabin, Matthew, 2018. Base-rate neglect: foundations and implications. Mimeograph.

Benjamin, Daniel J., 2018. Errors in Probabilistic Reasoning and Judgment Biases. NBER Working Paper No. 25200.

Benjamin, Daniel J., Rabin, Matthew, Raymond, Collin, 2016. A model of nonbelief in the law of large numbers. Journal of the European Economic Association 14 (2), 515–544.

Bennear, Lori, Tarozzi, Alessandro, Pfaff, Alexander, Balasubramanya, Soumya, Ahmed, Kazi Matin, Van Geen, Alexander, 2013. Impact of a randomized controlled trial in arsenic risk communication on household water-source choices in Bangladesh. Journal of Environmental Economics and Management 65 (2), 225–240.

Berge, Lars Ivar Oppedal, Bjorvatn, Kjetil, Galle, Simon, Miguel, Edward, Posner, Daniel N., Tungodden, Bertil, Zhang, Kelly, 2015. How Strong are Ethnic Preferences? NBER Working Paper No. w21715.

Bernard, Tanguy, Dercon, Stefan, Orkin, Kate, Taffesse, Alemayehu, 2014. The future in mind: aspirations and forward-looking behaviour in rural Ethiopia. Mimeograph.

Bernheim, B. Douglas, Taubinsky, Dmitry, 2018. Behavioral public economics. In: Handbook of Behavioral Economics, vol. 1.

Berry, James, Fischer, Greg, Guiteras, Raymond P., 2018. Eliciting and utilizing willingness to pay: evidence from field trials in Northern Ghana.

Bertrand, Marianne, Johnson, Simon, Samphantharak, Krislert, Schoar, Antoinette, 2008. Mixing family with business: a study of Thai business groups and the families behind them. Journal of Financial Economics 88 (3), 466–498.

Bertrand, Marianne, Mullainathan, Sendhil, Shafir, Eldar, 2004. A behavioral-economics view of poverty. The American Economic Review 94 (2), 419–423.

Beshears, John, Choi, James J., Harris, Christopher, Laibson, David, Madrian, Brigitte C., Sakong, Jung, 2015. Self Control and Commitment: Can Decreasing the Liquidity of a Savings Account Increase Deposits? NBER Working Paper No. 21474.

Beshears, John, Choi, James J., Harris, Christopher, Laibson, David, Madrian, Brigitte C., Sakong, Jung, 2017. Which early withdrawal penalty attracts the most deposits to a commitment savings account? Mimeograph

Besley, Timothy, 1995. Savings, credit and insurance. In: Behrman, Jere, Srinivasan, T.N. (Eds.), Handbook of Development Economics, vol. 3 (Part A). Elsevier, Amsterdam, pp. 2123–2207.

Besley, Timothy, Ghatak, Maitreesh, 2005. Competition and incentives with motivated agents. The American Economic Review 95 (3), 616–636.

Bessone, Pedro, Rao, Gautam, Schilbach, Frank, Schofield, Heather, Toma, Mattie, 2018. Sleepless in Chennai: The Economic Effects of Sleep Deprivation Among the Poor. Working paper. MIT.

Bewley, Truman F., 1998. Why not cut pay? European Economic Review 42 (3–5), 459–490.

Bick, Alexander, Fuchs-Schündeln, Nicola, Lagakos, David, 2018. How do hours worked vary with income? Cross-country evidence and implications. The American Economic Review 108 (1), 170–199.

Blattman, Christopher, Dercon, Stefan, 2018. The impacts of industrial and entrepreneurial work on income and health: experimental evidence from Ethiopia. American Economic Journal: Applied Economics 10 (3), 1–38.

Blattman, Christopher, Jamison, Julian C., Sheridan, Margaret, 2017. Reducing crime and violence: experimental evidence from cognitive behavioral therapy in Liberia. The American Economic Review 107 (4), 1165–1206.

Bleakley, Hoyt, Ferrie, Joseph, 2016. Shocking behavior: random wealth in Antebellum Georgia and human capital across generations. The Quarterly Journal of Economics 131 (3), 1455–1495.

Bloom, David E., Cafiero, Elizabeth, Jané-Llopis, Eva, Abrahams-Gessel, Shafika, Reddy Bloom, Lakshmi, Fathima, Sana, Feigl, Andrea B., Gaziano, Tom, Hamandi, Ali, Mowafi, Mona, O'Farrell, Danny, Ozaltin, Emre, Pandya, Ankur, Prettner, Klaus, Rosenberg, Larry, Seligman, Benjamin, Stein, Adam Z., Weinstein, Cara, Weiss, Jonathan, 2011. The Global Economic Burden of Noncommunicable Diseases. World Economic Forum.

Bloom, Nicholas, Eifert, Benn, Mahajan, Aprajit, McKenzie, David, Roberts, John, 2013. Does management matter? Evidence from India. The Quarterly Journal of Economics 128 (1), 1–51.

Bloom, Nicholas, Sadun, Raffaella, Van Reenen, John, 2012. The organization of firms across countries. The Quarterly Journal of Economics 127 (4), 1663–1705.

Blouin, Arthur Thomas, Mukand, Sharun W., 2017. Erasing ethnicity? Propaganda, nation building and identity in Rwanda. Mimeograph.

Blumenstock, Joshua, Callen, Michael, Ghani, Tarek, 2018. Why do defaults affect behavior? Experimental evidence from Afghanistan. The American Economic Review 108 (10), 2868–2901.

Boisjoly, Johanne, Duncan, Greg J., Kremer, Michael, Levy, Dan M., Eccles, Jacque, 2006. Empathy or antipathy? The impact of diversity. The American Economic Review 96 (5), 1890–1905.

Boldrini, Maura, Mann, J. John, 2015. Depression and suicide. In: Zigmond, Michael J., Rowland, Lewis P., Coyle, Joseph T. (Eds.), Neurobiology of Brain Disorders. Academic Press, London, pp. 709–729.

Bolton, Paul, Bass, Judith, Neugebauer, Richard, Verdeli, Helen, Clougherty, Kathleen F., Wickramaratne, Priya, Speelman, Liesbeth, Ndogoni, Lincoln, Weissman, Myrna, 2003. Group interpersonal psychotherapy for depression in rural Uganda: a randomized controlled trial. Journal of the American Medical Association 289 (23), 3117–3124.

Bordalo, Pedro, Gennaioli, Nicola, Shleifer, Andrei, 2012. Salience theory of choice under risk. The Quarterly Journal of Economics 127 (3), 1243–1285.

Borghans, Lex, Lee Duckworth, Angela, Heckman, James J., Ter Weel, Bas, 2008. The economics and psychology of personality traits. The Journal of Human Resources 43 (4), 972–1059.

Borland, Ron, Wilson, Nick, Fong, Geoffrey T., Hammond, David, Cummings, K. Michael, Yong, Hua H., Hosking, Warwick, Hastings, Gerard B., Thrasher, James, McNeill, Ann, 2009. Impact of graphic and text warnings on cigarette packs: findings from four countries over five years. Tobacco Control, 358–364.

Breza, Emily, Chandrasekhar, Arun G., 2015. Social Networks, Reputation and Commitment: Evidence from a Savings Monitors Experiment. NBER Working Paper No. 21169.

Breza, Emily, Kaur, Supreet, Krishnaswamy, Nandita, 2018a. Scabs: the social suppression of labor supply. Mimeograph.

Breza, Emily, Kaur, Supreet, Shamdasani, Yogita, 2018b. The morale effects of pay inequality. The Quarterly Journal of Economics 133 (2), 611–663.

Bruhn, Miriam, Karlan, Dean, Schoar, Antoinette, 2018. The impact of consulting services on small and medium enterprises: evidence from a randomized trial in Mexico. Journal of Political Economy 126 (2), 635–687.

Brunnermeier, Markus K., Parker, Jonathan A., 2005. Optimal expectations. The American Economic Review 95 (4), 1092–1118.

Bryan, Gharad, Karlan, Dean, Nelson, Scott, 2010. Commitment devices. Annual Review of Economics 2, 671–698.

Bryan, Gharad T., Choi, James J., Karlan, Dean, 2018. Randomizing Religion: The Impact of Protestant Evangelism on Economic Outcomes. London School of Economics and Political Science Working Paper.

Burke, Marshall, Falcao Bergquist, Lauren, Miguel, Edward, 2018. Sell Low and Buy High: Arbitrage and Local Price Effects in Kenyan Markets. NBER Working Paper No. 24476.

Bursztyn, Leonardo, Coffman, Lucas C., 2012. The schooling decision: family preferences, intergenerational conflict, and moral hazard in the Brazilian favelas. Journal of Political Economy 120 (3), 359–397.

Bursztyn, Leonardo, González, Alessandra L., Yanagizawa-Drott, David, 2018. Misperceived Social Norms: Female Labor Force Participation in Saudi Arabia. NBER Working Paper No. 24736.

Cadena, Ximena, Schoar, Antoinette, 2011. Remembering to pay? Reminders vs. Financial Incentives for Loan Payments. NBER Working Paper No. 17020.

Camerer, Colin, Babcock, Linda, Loewenstein, George, Thaler, Richard, 1997. Labor supply of New York City cabdrivers: one day at a time. The Quarterly Journal of Economics 112 (2), 407–441.

Cantoni, Davide, Chen, Yuyu, Yang, David Y., Yuchtman, Noam, Zhang, Y. Jane, 2017. Curriculum and ideology. Journal of Political Economy 125 (2), 338–392.

Caplin, Andrew, Leahy, John, 2001. Psychological expected utility theory and anticipatory feelings. The Quarterly Journal of Economics 116 (1), 55–79.

Caplin, Andrew, Leahy, John, 2004. The supply of information by a concerned expert. The Economic Journal 114 (497), 487–505.

Card, David, Mas, Alexandre, Moretti, Enrico, Saez, Emmanuel, 2012. Inequality at work: the effect of peer salaries on job satisfaction. The American Economic Review 102 (6), 2981–3003.

Carney, Kevin, Kremer, Michael, Lin, Xinyue, Rao, Gautam, 2018. The endowment effect and collateralized loans.

Carroll, Christopher D., 1997. Buffer-stock saving and the life cycle/permanent income hypothesis. The Quarterly Journal of Economics 112 (1), 1–55.

Carter, Emily, Bryce, Jennifer, Perin, Jamie, Newby, Holly, 2015. Harmful practices in the management of childhood diarrhea in low- and middle-income countries: a systematic review. BMC Public Health 15 (1), 788.

Carvalho, Leandro S., Meier, Stephan, Wang, Stephanie W., 2016. Poverty and economic decisionmaking: evidence from changes in financial resources at payday. The American Economic Review 106 (2), 260–284.

Casaburi, Lorenzo, Macchiavello, Rocco, 2018. Demand and supply of infrequent payments as a commitment device: evidence from Kenya. The American Economic Review. Forthcoming.

Casaburi, Lorenzo, Willis, Jack, 2018. Time vs. state in insurance: experimental evidence from contract farming in Kenya.

Case, Anne, Deaton, Angus, 2015. Suicide, Age, and Wellbeing: An Empirical Investigation. NBER Working Paper No. 21279.

Cassidy, Rachel, 2018. Are the Poor so Present-Biased? Institute for Fiscal Studies Working Paper No. 18/24.

Chabris, Christopher F., Laibson, David, Morris, Carrie L., Schuldt, Jonathon P., Taubinsky, Dmitry, 2008. Individual laboratory-measured discount rates predict field behavior. Journal of Risk and Uncertainty 37 (2–3), 237–269.

Chandra, Amitabh, Handel, Benjamin, Schwartzstein, Joshua, 2018. Behavioral economics and health-care markets.

Chandrasekhar, Arun G., Golub, Benjamin, Yang, He, 2018. Signaling, Shame, and Silence in Social Learning. NBER Working Paper No. 25169.

Chang, Tom Y., Huang, Wei, Wang, Yongxiang, 2018. Something in the air: projection bias and the demand for health insurance. The Review of Economic Studies 85 (3), 1609–1634.

Charness, Gary, Sutter, Matthias, 2012. Groups make better self-interested decisions. The Journal of Economic Perspectives 26 (3), 157–176.

Chen, Yuyu, Yang, David Y., 2018. The impact of media censorship: 1984 or brave new world? Mimeograph

Chetty, Raj, 2015. Behavioral economics and public policy: a pragmatic perspective. The American Economic Review 105 (5), 1–33.

Chetty, Raj, Friedman, John N., Leth-Petersen, Søren, Heien Nielsen, Torben, Olsen, Tore, 2014. Active vs. passive decisions and crowd-out in retirement savings accounts: evidence from Denmark. The Quarterly Journal of Economics 129 (3), 1141–1219.

Choi, J., Laibson, D., Madrian, B., Metrick, A., 2002. Defined contribution pensions: plan rules, participant decisions, and the path of least resistance. Tax Policy and the Economy 16, 67–114.

Christian, Cornelius, Hensel, Lukas, Roth, Christopher, 2018. Income shocks and suicides: causal evidence from Indonesia. Available at SSRN 2716684.

Cingano, Federico, Pinotti, Paolo, 2012. Trust, firm organization and the structure of production. Carlo F. Dondena Centre for Research on Social Dynamics Working Paper No. 053.

Clark, Gregory, 1994. Factory discipline. The Journal of Economic History 54 (1), 128–163.

Clarke, Daniel J., 2016. A theory of rational demand for index insurance. American Economic Journal: Microeconomics 8 (1), 283–306.

Clingingsmith, David, Khwaja, Asim Ijaz, Kremer, Michael, 2009. Estimating the impact of the hajj: religion and tolerance in Islam's global gathering. The Quarterly Journal of Economics 124 (3), 1133–1170.

Cohen, Jessica, Dupas, Pascaline, 2010. Free distribution or cost-sharing? Evidence from a randomized malaria prevention experiment. The Quarterly Journal of Economics 125 (1), 1–45.

Cohen, Jessica, Dupas, Pascaline, Schaner, Simone, 2015. Price subsidies, diagnostic tests, and targeting of malaria treatment: evidence from a randomized controlled trial. The American Economic Review 105 (2), 609–645.

Cohen, Jonathan D., Ericson, Keith Marzilli, Laibson, David, Myles White, John, 2016. Measuring Time Preferences. NBER Working Paper No. 22455.

Cole, Shawn, Giné, Xavier, Tobacman, Jeremy, Topalova, Petia, Townsend, Robert, Vickery, James, 2013. Barriers to household risk management: evidence from India. American Economic Journal: Applied Economics 5 (1), 104–135.

Coleman, James, 1990. Foundations of Social Theory. Harvard University Press, Cambridge, MA.

Collins, D., Morduch, J., Rutherford, S., Ruthven, O., 2009. Portfolios of the Poor: How the World's Poor Live on $2 a Day. Princeton University Press.

Conley, Timothy G., Udry, Christopher R., 2010. Learning about a new technology: pineapple in Ghana. The American Economic Review 100 (1), 35–69.

Cooley Fruehwirth, Jane, Iyer, Sriya, Zhang, Anwen, 2019. Religion and depression in adolescence. Journal of Political Economy. Forthcoming.

Cooper, David J., Kagel, John H., 2005. Are two heads better than one? Team versus individual play in signaling games. The American Economic Review 95 (3), 477–509.

Corno, Lucia, La Ferrara, Eliana, Burns, Justine, 2018. Interaction, Prejudice and Performance. Evidence from South Africa. Mimeo.

Crawford, Vincent P., Meng, Juanjuan, 2011. New York City cab drivers' labor supply revisited: reference-dependent preferences with rational-expectations targets for hours and income. The American Economic Review 101 (5), 1912–1932.

Cubitt, Robin P., Read, Daniel, 2007. Can intertemporal choice experiments elicit time preferences for consumption? Experimental Economics 10 (4), 369–389.

Dal Bó, Ernesto, Finan, Frederico, Rossi, Martín A., 2013. Strengthening state capabilities: the role of financial incentives in the call to public service. The Quarterly Journal of Economics 128 (3), 1169–1218.

Dalton, Patricio S., Ghosal, Sayantan, Mani, Anandi, 2015. Poverty and aspirations failure. The Economic Journal 126 (590), 165–188.

Das, Jishnu, Do, Quy-Toan, Friedman, Jed, McKenzie, David, Scott, Kinnon, 2007. Mental health and poverty in developing countries: revisiting the relationship. Social Science & Medicine 65 (3), 467–480.

Das, Jishnu, Hammer, Jeffrey, 2007. Money for nothing: the dire straits of medical practice in Delhi, India. Journal of Development Economics 83 (1), 1–36.

Datta, Saugato, Mullainathan, Sendhil, 2014. Behavioral design: a new approach to development policy. The Review of Income and Wealth 60 (1), 7–35.

Dean, Emma Boswell, Schilbach, Frank, Schofield, Heather, 2018. Poverty and cognitive function. In: Barrett, Christopher B., Carter, Michael R., Chavas, Jean-Paul (Eds.), The Economics of Poverty Traps. University of Chicago Press, Chicago.

Dean, Joshua T., 2018. Noise, cognitive function, and worker productivity. Mimeo.

Dean, Mark, Sautmann, Anja, 2018. Credit constraints and the measurement of time preferences. Mimeo.

Deaton, Angus, 1989. Saving and Liquidity Constraints. Technical Report w3196. National Bureau of Economic Research.

Deaton, Angus S., 1991. Saving and liquidity constraints. Econometrica 59 (5), 221–248.

Deci, Edward L., 1971. Effects of externally mediated rewards on intrinsic motivation. Journal of Personality and Social Psychology 18 (1), 105.

Delavande, Adeline, 2014. Probabilistic expectations in developing countries. Annual Review in Economics 6 (1), 1–20.

Delavande, Adeline, Giné, Xavier, McKenzie, David, 2011. Measuring subjective expectations in developing countries: a critical review and new evidence. Journal of Development Economics 94 (2), 151–163.

Delavande, Adeline, Kohler, Hans-Peter, 2009. Subjective expectations in the context of HIV/aids in Malawi. Demographic Research 20, 817–874.

DellaVigna, Stefano, 2009. Psychology and economics: evidence from the field. Journal of Economic Literature 47 (2), 315–372.

DellaVigna, Stefano, 2018. Structural Behavioral Economics. NBER Working Paper No. 24797.

DellaVigna, Stefano, Gentzkow, Matthew, 2017. Uniform Pricing in US Retail Chains. NBER Working Paper No. 23996.

DellaVigna, Stefano, Lindner, Attila, Reizer, Balázs, Schmieder, Johannes F., 2017. Reference-dependent job search: evidence from Hungary. The Quarterly Journal of Economics 132 (4), 1969–2018.

DellaVigna, Stefano, List, John A., Malmendier, Ulrike, Rao, Gautam, 2016. Voting to tell others. The Review of Economic Studies 84 (1), 143–181.

DellaVigna, Stefano, Pope, Devin, 2017. What motivates effort? Evidence and expert forecasts. The Review of Economic Studies 85 (2), 1029–1069.

DellaVigna, Stefano, Pope, Devin, 2018. Stability of experimental results: forecasts and evidence. Mimeo.

De Mel, Suresh, McKenzie, David, Woodruff, Christopher, 2008. Returns to capital in micro enterprises: evidence from a field experiment. The Quarterly Journal of Economics 123 (4), 1329–1372.

Demeritt, Allison Davis, Hoff, Karla, 2018. The making of behavioral development economics. History of Political Economy 50, 303–322.

de Quidt, Jonathan, Haushofer, Johannes, 2016. Depression for Economists. NBER Working Paper No. 22973.

de Quidt, Jonathan, Haushofer, Johannes, Rao, Gautam, Schilbach, Frank, Vautrey, Pierre-Luc, 2018. The economics consequences of depression. Mimeograph.

Dercon, Stefan, 2005. Insurance Against Poverty. Oxford University Press.

de Ree, Joppe, Muralidharan, Karthik, Pradhan, Menno, Rogers, Halsey, 2018. Double for nothing? The effects of unconditional teacher salary increases in Indonesia. Quarterly Journal of Economics 133 (2), 923–1039.

Deserranno, Erika, 2018. Financial incentives as signals: experimental evidence from the recruitment of village promoters in Uganda. American Economic Journal: Applied Economics. Forthcoming.

Devoto, Florencia, Duflo, Esther, Dupas, Pascaline, Parienté, William, Pons, Vincent, 2012. Happiness on tap: piped water adoption in urban Morocco. American Economic Journal: Economic Policy 4 (4), 68–99.

Diamond, Adele, 2013. Executive functions. Annual Review of Psychology 64, 135–168.

Dickinson, David L., McElroy, Todd, 2017. Sleep restriction and circadian effects on social decisions. European Economic Review 97, 57–71.

Dizon-Ross, Rebecca, 2018. Parents' Beliefs About Their Children's Academic Ability: Implications for Educational Investments. NBER Working Paper No. 24610.

Doherty, Neil A., Schlesinger, Harris, 1991. Rational insurance purchasing: consideration of contract non-performance. In: Cummins, J. David, Derrig, Richard A. (Eds.), Managing the Insolvency Risk of Insurance Companies. Springer, Dordrecht, pp. 283–294.

Dohmen, Thomas, Enke, Benjamin, Falk, Armin, Huffman, David, Sunde, Uwe, 2018. Patience and comparative development. Mimeograph.

Dohmen, Thomas, Falk, Armin, Huffman, David, Sunde, Uwe, 2010. Are risk aversion and impatience related to cognitive ability? The American Economic Review 100 (3), 1238–1260.

Drexler, Alejandro, Fischer, Greg, Schoar, Antoinette, 2014. Keeping it simple: financial literacy and rules of thumb. American Economic Journal: Applied Economics 6 (2), 1–31.

Duflo, Esther, 2012a. Human values and the design of the fight against poverty. Tanner Lectures, 1–55.

Duflo, Esther, 2012b. Women empowerment and economic development. Journal of Economic Literature 50 (4), 1051–1079.

Duflo, Esther, Hanna, Rema, Ryan, Stephen P., 2012. Incentives work: getting teachers to come to school. The American Economic Review 102 (4), 1241–1278.

Duflo, Esther, Kremer, Michael, Robinson, Jonathan, 2008. How high are rates of return to fertilizer? Evidence from field experiments in Kenya. The American Economic Review 98 (2), 482–488.

Duflo, Esther, Kremer, Michael, Robinson, Jonathan, 2011. Nudging farmers to use fertilizer: theory and experimental evidence from Kenya. The American Economic Review 101 (6), 2350–2390.

Duflo, Esther, Kremer, Michael, Robinson, Jonathan, Schilbach, Frank, 2018. Technology diffusion and appropriate use: evidence from western Kenya. Mimeograph.

Dupas, Pascaline, 2009. What matters (and what does not) in households' decision to invest in malaria prevention? The American Economic Review 99 (2), 224–230.

Dupas, Pascaline, 2011a. Health behavior in developing countries. Annual Review of Economics 3 (1), 425–449.

Dupas, Pascaline, 2011b. Do teenagers respond to HIV risk information? Evidence from a field experiment in Kenya. American Economic Journal: Applied Economics 3 (1), 1–34.

Dupas, Pascaline, Karlan, Dean, Robinson, Jonathan, Ubfal, Diego, 2018a. Banking the unbanked? Evidence from three countries. American Economic Journal: Applied Economics 10 (2), 257–297.

Dupas, Pascaline, Miguel, Edward, 2017. Impacts and determinants of health levels in low-income countries. In: Banerjee, Abhijit V., Duflo, Esther (Eds.), Handbook of Economic Field Experiments, vol. 2. Elsevier, Amsterdam, pp. 3–93.

Dupas, Pascaline, Robinson, Jonathan, 2013a. Savings constraints and microenterprise development: evidence from a field experiment in Kenya. American Economic Journal: Applied Economics 5 (1), 163–192.

Dupas, Pascaline, Robinson, Jonathan, 2013b. Why don't the poor save more? Evidence from health savings experiments. The American Economic Review 103 (4), 1138–1171.

Dupas, Pascaline, Robinson, Jonathan, Saavedra, Santiago, 2018b. The daily grind: cash needs and labor supply.

Eckles, David L., Wise, J. Volkman, 2011. Prospect Theory and the Demand for Insurance. The Risk Theory Society, American Risk and Insurance Association (ARIA), Philadelphia, PA, USA. Available at: http://www.aria.org/rts/proceedings/2012/default.htm. (Accessed 18 September 2013).

Ellison, Christopher G., 1991. Religious involvement and subjective well-being. Journal of Health and Social Behavior, 80–99.

Enke, Benjamin, 2017. Complexity, mental frames, and neglect.

Enke, Benjamin, 2018. Kinship, Cooperation, and the Evolution of Moral Systems. NBER Working Paper No. 23499.

Enke, Benjamin, Zimmermann, Florian, 2019. Correlation neglect in belief formation. Review of Economic Studies. Forthcoming.

Ericson, Keith Marzilli, 2017. On the interaction of memory and procrastination: implications for reminders, deadlines, and empirical estimation. Journal of the European Economic Association 15 (3), 692–719.

Ericson, Keith Marzilli, Laibson, David, 2018. Intertemporal choice. NBER Working Paper No. 25358.

Ervik, Astrid Oline, 2003. IQ and the wealth of nations. The Economic Journal 113 (488), F406–F408.

Esteves-Sorenson, Constanca, 2017. Gift exchange in the workplace: addressing the conflicting evidence with a careful test. Management Science 64 (9), 4365–4388.

Eyster, Erik, 2002. Rationalizing the past: a taste for consistency. Mimeograph.

Eyster, Erik, Rabin, Matthew, 2010. Naive herding in rich-information settings. American Economic Journal: Microeconomics 2 (4), 221–243.

Eyster, Erik, Rabin, Matthew, 2014. Extensive imitation is irrational and harmful. The Quarterly Journal of Economics 129 (4), 1861–1898.

Eyster, Erik, Rabin, Matthew, Weizsäcker, Georg, 2018. An experiment on social mislearning. Mimeograph.

Fafchamps, Marcel, 1993. Sequential labor decisions under uncertainty: an estimable household model of West-African farmers. Econometrica 61 (5), 1173–1197.

Fafchamps, Marcel, 2000. Ethnicity and credit in African manufacturing. Journal of Development Economics 61 (1), 205–235.

Fairburn, Christopher G., Patel, Vikram, 2017. The impact of digital technology on psychological treatments and their dissemination. Behaviour Research and Therapy 88, 19–25.

Falk, Armin, Becker, Anke, Dohmen, Thomas, Enke, Benjamin, Huffman, David, Sunde, Uwe, 2018. Global evidence on economic preferences. The Quarterly Journal of Economics 133 (4), 1645–1692.

Falk, Armin, Becker, Anke, Dohmen, Thomas, Huffman, David B., Uwe, Sunde, 2016. The Preference Survey Module: A Validated Instrument for Measuring Risk, Time, and Social Preferences. IZA Institute of Labor Economics Discussion Paper 9674.

Farber, Henry S., 2005. Is tomorrow another day? The labor supply of New York City cabdrivers. Journal of Political Economy 113 (1), 46–82.

Farber, Henry S., 2015. Why you can't find a taxi in the rain and other labor supply lessons from cab drivers. The Quarterly Journal of Economics 130 (4), 1975–2026.

Fernandez, Raquel, Fogli, Alessandra, 2009. Culture: an empirical investigation of beliefs, work, and fertility. American Economic Journal: Macroeconomics 1 (1), 146–177.

Finan, Frederico, Olken, Benjamin A., Pande, Rohini, 2017. The personnel economics of the developing state. In: Banerjee, Abhijit V., Duflo, Esther (Eds.), Handbook of Economic Field Experiments, vol. 2. Elsevier/North-Holland, Amsterdam, pp. 467–514.

Finan, Frederico, Schechter, Laura, 2012. Vote-buying and reciprocity. Econometrica 80 (2), 863–881.

Fisman, Raymond, Miguel, Edward, 2007. Corruption, norms, and legal enforcement: evidence from diplomatic parking tickets. Journal of Political economy 115 (6), 1020–1048.

Fletcher, Erin, Pande, Rohini, Troyer Moore, Charity Maria, 2017. Women and work in India: descriptive evidence and a review of potential policies.

Food and Agriculture Organization of the United Nations (FAO), 2018. The State of Food Security and Nutrition in the World 2018: Building Climate Resilience for Food Security and Nutrition.

Frederick, Shane, Loewenstein, George, O'Donoghue, Ted, 2002. Time discounting and time preference: a critical review. Journal of Economic Literature 40 (2), 351–401.

Freeman, Richard B., 1986. Who escapes? The relationship of churchgoing and other background factors to the socioeconomic performance of black male youths from inner-city tracts. In: Freeman, Richard B., Holzer, Harry J. (Eds.), The Black Youth Employment Crisis. University of Chicago Press, Chicago.

Friedrich, M.J., 2017. Depression is the leading cause of disability around the world. Jama 317 (15), 1517.

Fudenberg, Drew, Levine, David K., 2006. A dual-self model of impulse control. The American Economic Review 96 (5), 1449–1476.

Fuster, Andreas, Laibson, David, Mendel, Brock, 2010. Natural expectations and macroeconomic fluctuations. The Journal of Economic Perspectives 24 (4), 67–84.

Gagnon-Bartsch, Tristan, Rabin, Matthew, Schwartzstein, Joshua, 2018. Channeled attention and stable errors. Mimeo.

Gallagher, Justin, 2014. Learning about an infrequent event: evidence from flood insurance take-up in the United States. American Economic Journal: Applied Economics, 206–233.

Genicot, Garance, Ray, Debraj, 2017. Aspirations and inequality. Econometrica 85 (2), 489–519.

Gertler, Paul, Gruber, Jonathan, 2002. Insuring consumption against illness. The American Economic Review 92 (1), 51–70.

Ghosal, Sayantan, Jana, Smarajit, Mani, Anandi, Mitra, Sandip, Roy, Sanchari, 2017. Stigma, discrimination and self-image: evidence from Kolkata brothels. Mimeograph.

Giné, Xavier, Karlan, Dean, Zinman, Jonathan, 2010. Put your money where your butt is: a commitment contract for smoking cessation. American Economic Journal: Applied Economics 2 (4), 213–235.

Giné, Xavier, Martinez-Bravo, Monica, Vidal-Fernández, Marian, 2017. Are labor supply decisions consistent with neoclassical preferences? Evidence from Indian boat owners. Journal of Economic Behavior & Organization 142, 331–347.

Giné, Xavier, Townsend, Robert, Vickery, James, 2008. Patterns of rainfall insurance participation in rural India. World Bank Economic Review 22 (3), 539–566.

Glewwe, Paul, Ilias, Nauman, Kremer, Michael, 2010. Teacher incentives. American Economic Journal: Applied Economics 2 (3), 205–227.

Gneezy, Uri, Leonard, Kenneth L., List, John A., 2009. Gender differences in competition: evidence from a matrilineal and a patriarchal society. Econometrica 77 (5), 1637–1664.

Gneezy, Uri, List, John A., 2006. Putting behavioral economics to work: testing for gift exchange in labor markets using field experiments. Econometrica 74 (5), 1365–1384.

Gneezy, Uri, Rustichini, Aldo, 2000. A fine is a price. The Journal of Legal Studies 29 (1), 1–17.

Godlonton, Susan, Munthali, Alister, Thornton, Rebecca, 2016. Responding to risk: circumcision, information, and HIV prevention. Review of Economics and Statistics 98 (2), 333–349.

Goldin, Jacob, Homonoff, Tatiana, 2013. Smoke gets in your eyes: cigarette tax salience and regressivity. American Economic Journal: Economic Policy 5 (1), 302–336.

Grandner, Michael A., Patel, Nirav P., Gehrman, Philip R., Xie, Dawei, Sha, Daohang, Weaver, Terri, Gooneratne, Nalaka, 2010. Who gets the best sleep? Ethnic and socioeconomic factors related to sleep complaints. Sleep Medicine 11 (5), 470–478.

Greenwald, Anthony G., McGhee, Debbie E., Schwartz, Jordan L.K., 1998. Measuring individual differences in implicit cognition: the implicit association test. Journal of Personality and Social Psychology 74 (6), 1464.

Greenwald, Anthony G., Poehlman, T. Andrew, Uhlmann, Eric Luis, Banaji, Mahzarin R., 2009. Understanding and using the implicit association test: III. Meta-analysis of predictive validity. Journal of Personality and Social Psychology 97 (1), 17.

Griffin, Dale, Tversky, Amos, 1992. The weighing of evidence and the determinants of confidence. Cognitive Psychology 24 (3), 411–435.

Grimard, Franque, 2000. Rural labor markets, household composition, and rainfall in Côte d'Ivoire. Review of Development Economics 4 (1), 70–86.

Gruber, Jonathan, Hungerman, Daniel M., 2008. The church versus the mall: what happens when religion faces increased secular competition? The Quarterly Journal of Economics 123 (2), 831–862.

Gruber, Jonathan H., 2005. Religious market structure, religious participation, and outcomes: is religion good for you? The BE Journal in Economic Analysis & Policy 5 (1).

Guiso, Luigi, Sapienza, Paola, Zingales, Luigi, 2006. Does culture affect economic outcomes? The Journal of Economic Perspectives 20 (2), 23–48.

Gul, Faruk, Pesendorfer, Wolfgang, 2001. Temptation and self-control. Econometrica 69 (6), 1403–1435.

Gul, Faruk, Pesendorfer, Wolfgang, 2004. Self-control and the theory of consumption. Econometrica 72 (1), 119–158.

Haidt, Jonathan, 2012. The Righteous Mind: Why Good People Are Divided by Politics and Religion. Vintage Books, New York.

Haigh, Michael S., List, John A., 2005. Do professional traders exhibit myopic loss aversion? An experimental analysis. Journal of Finance 60 (1), 523–534.

Hall, Crystal C., Zhao, Jiaying, Shafir, Eldar, 2014. Self-affirmation among the poor: cognitive and behavioral implications. Psychological Science 25 (2), 619–625.

Hall, Robert E., 2009. Reconciling cyclical movements in the marginal value of time and the marginal product of labor. Journal of Political Economy 117 (2), 281–323.

Hall, Robert E., 2016. Macroeconomics of persistent slumps. In: Taylor, John B., Uhlig, Harald (Eds.), Handbook of Macroeconomics, vol. 2. Elsevier, Amsterdam, pp. 2131–2181.

Hanna, Rema, Mullainathan, Sendhil, Schwartzstein, Joshua, 2014. Learning through noticing: theory and evidence from a field experiment. The Quarterly Journal of Economics 129 (3), 1311–1353.

Harlan, Sharon L., Brazel, Anthony J., Prashad, Lela, Stefanov, William L., Larsen, Larissa, 2006. Neighborhood microclimates and vulnerability to heat stress. Social Science & Medicine 63 (11), 2847–2863.

Harris, Christopher, Laibson, David, 2001. Dynamic choices of hyperbolic consumers. Econometrica 69 (4), 935–957.

Harris, John R., Todaro, Michael P., 1970. Migration, unemployment and development: a two-sector analysis. The American Economic Review 60 (1), 126–142.

Hastings, Justine S., Shapiro, Jesse M., 2013. Fungibility and consumer choice: evidence from commodity price shocks. The Quarterly Journal of Economics 128 (4), 1449–1498.

Haushofer, Johannes, Fehr, Ernst, 2014. On the psychology of poverty. Science 344 (6186), 862–867.

Haushofer, Johannes, Jang, Chaning, Lynham, John, Abraham, Justin, 2018. Stress and temporal discounting: Do domains matter? Mimeo.

Haushofer, Johannes, Shapiro, Jeremy, 2016. The short-term impact of unconditional cash transfers to the poor: experimental evidence from Kenya. Quarterly Journal of Economics 131 (4), 1973–2042.

Havránek, Tomáš, 2015. Measuring intertemporal substitution: the importance of method choices and selective reporting. Journal of the European Economic Association 13 (6), 1180–1204.

Hawton, Keith, Casañas i Comabella, Carolina, Haw, Camilla, Saunders, Kate, 2013. Risk factors for suicide in individuals with depression: a systematic review. Journal of Affective Disorders 147 (1–3), 17–28.

Hazell, Peter B.R., 1992. The appropriate role of agricultural insurance in developing countries. Journal of International Development 4 (6), 567–581.

Heath, Rachel, Jayachandran, Seema, 2016. The Causes and Consequences of Increased Female Education and Labor Force Participation in Developing Countries. NBER Working Paper No. 22766.

Heidhues, Paul, Köszegi, Botond, 2018. Behavioral industrial organization. In: Bernheim, B. Douglas, DellaVigna, Stefano, Laibson, David (Eds.), Handbook of Behavioral Economics: Foundations and Applications 1, vol. 1. Elsevier/North-Holland, Amsterdam.

Henrich, Joseph, Boyd, Robert, Bowles, Samuel, Camerer, Colin, Fehr, Ernst, Gintis, Herbert, McElreath, Richard, 2001. In search of homo economicus: behavioral experiments in 15 small-scale societies. The American Economic Review 91 (2), 73–78.

Henrich, Joseph, Ensminger, Jean, McElreath, Richard, Barr, Abigail, Barrett, Clark, Bolyanatz, Alexander, Cardenas, Camilo Juan, Gurven, Michael, Gwako, Edwins, Henrich, Natalie, Lesorogol, Carolyn, Marlowe, Frank, Tracer, David, Ziker, John, 2010a. Markets, religion, community size, and the evolution of fairness and punishment. Science 327 (5972), 1480–1484.

Henrich, Joseph, Heine, Steven J., Norenzayan, Ara, 2010b. The weirdest people in the world? Behavioral and Brain Sciences 33 (2–3), 61–83.

Hjort, Jonas, 2014. Ethnic divisions and production in firms. The Quarterly Journal of Economics 129 (4), 1899–1946.

Hogarth, Robin M., Einhorn, Hillel J., 1992. Order effects in belief updating: the belief-adjustment model. Cognitive Psychology 24 (1), 1–55.

Holmstrom, Bengt, Milgrom, Paul, 1991. Multitask principal-agent analyses: incentive contracts, asset ownership, and job design. Journal of Law, Economics, & Organization 7 (24).

Hsiaw, Alice, 2013. Goal-setting and self-control. Journal of Economic Theory 148 (2), 601–626.

Hsieh, Chang-Tai, Hurst, Erik, Jones, Charles I., Klenow, Peter J., 2018. The Allocation of Talent and US Economic Growth. NBER Working Paper No. 18693.

Hsieh, Chang-Tai, Olken, Benjamin A., 2014. The missing "missing middle". The Journal of Economic Perspectives 28 (3), 89–108.

Iannaccone, Laurence R., 1998. Introduction to the economics of religion. Journal of Economic Literature 36 (3), 1465–1495.

Ilias, Nauman, 2006. Families and firms: agency costs and labor market imperfections in Sialkot's surgical industry. Journal of Development Economics 80 (2), 329–349.

Inkeles, Alex, Smith, David H., 1974. Becoming modem. In: Seligson, Mitchell A., Passe-Smith, John T. (Eds.), Development and Underdevelopment: The Political Economy of Global Inequality (Lynne Rienner Publishers, 1998, Boulder).

International Labour Office (ILO). 2018. Ilostat database.

Islam, Sheikh Mohammed Shariful, Dannemann Purnat, Tina, Phuong, Nguyen Thi Anh, Mwingira, Upendo, Schacht, Karsten, Fröschl, Günter, 2014. Non-communicable diseases (NCDS) in developing countries: a symposium report. Globalization and Health 10 (1), 81.

Iyer, Sriya, 2016. The new economics of religion. Journal of Economic Literature 54 (2), 395–441.

Jack, William, Kremer, Michael, De Laat, Joost, Suri, Tavneet, 2016. Borrowing Requirements, Credit Access, and Adverse Selection: Evidence from Kenya. NBER Working Paper No. 22686.

Jack, William, Suri, Tavneet, 2014. Risk sharing and transactions costs: evidence from Kenya's mobile money revolution. The American Economic Review 104 (1), 183–223.

Jack, William, Suri, Tavneet, 2016. The long-run poverty and gender impacts of mobile money. Science 354 (6317), 1288–1292.

Jagnani, Maulik, 2018. Poor sleep: sunset time and human capital production. Mimeograph.

Jakiela, Pamela, Ozier, Owen, 2015. Does Africa need a rotten kin theorem? Experimental evidence from village economies. The Review of Economic Studies 83 (1), 231–268.

Jalan, Jyotsna, Ravallion, Martin, 1999. Are the poor less well insured? Evidence on vulnerability to income risk in rural China. Journal of Development Economics 58 (1), 61–81.

Jappelli, Tullio, Pistaferri, Luigi, 2010. The consumption response to income changes. Annual Review of Economics 2, 479–506.

Jayaraman, Rajshri, Ray, Debraj, de Véricourt, Francis, 2016. Anatomy of a contract change. The American Economic Review 106 (2), 316–358.

Jensen, Robert, 2010. The (perceived) returns to education and the demand for schooling. The Quarterly Journal of Economics 125 (2), 515–548.

Jensen, Robert, Oster, Emily, 2009. The power of TV: cable television and women's status in India. The Quarterly Journal of Economics 124 (3), 1057–1094.

John, Anett, 2018. When commitment fails—evidence from a field experiment. Management Science. Forthcoming.

Johnson, Eric J., Goldstein, Daniel G., 2004. Defaults and donation decisions. Transplantation 78 (12), 1713–1716.

Kahneman, Daniel, Knetsch, Jack L., Thaler, Richard, 1986. Fairness as a constraint on profit seeking: entitlements in the market. The American Economic Review 76 (4), 728–741.

Kahneman, Daniel, Tversky, Amos, 1973. On the psychology of prediction. Psychological Review 80, 237–251.

Kahneman, Daniel, Tversky, Amos, 1979. Prospect theory: an analysis of decision under risk. Econometrica 47 (2), 263–292.

Kaminski, Jonathan, Christiaensen, Luc, Gilbert, Christopher L., 2014. The End of Seasonality? New Insights from Sub-Saharan Africa. World Bank Policy Research Working Paper No. 6907.

Karing, Anne, 2018. Social Signaling and Childhood Immunization: A Field Experiment in Sierra Leone. Innovations for Poverty Action (IPA) Working Paper.

Karlan, Dean, McConnell, Margaret, Mullainathan, Sendhil, Zinman, Jonathan, 2016. Getting to the top of mind: how reminders increase saving. Management Science 62 (12), 3393–3411.

Karlan, Dean, Mullainathan, Sendhil, Roth, Benjamin N., 2018. Debt Traps? Market Vendors and Moneylender Debt in India and the Philippines. NBER Working Paper No. 24272.

Karlan, Dean, Osei, Robert, Osei-Akoto, Isaac, Udry, Christopher, 2014a. Agricultural decisions after relaxing credit and risk constraints. The Quarterly Journal of Economics 129 (2), 597–652.

Karlan, Dean, Lakshmi Ratan, Aishwarya, Zinman, Jonathan, 2014b. Savings by and for the poor: a research review and agenda. The Review of Income and Wealth 60 (1), 36–78.

Karlan, Dean, Zinman, Jonathan, 2009. Observing unobservables: identifying information asymmetries with a consumer credit field experiment. Econometrica 77 (6), 1993–2008.

Karlan, Dean S., Linden, Leigh, 2018. Loose knots: strong versus weak commitments to save for education in Uganda.

Kast, Felipe, Meier, Stephan, Pomeranz, Dina, 2018. Saving more in groups: field experimental evidence from Chile. Journal of Development Economics 133, 275–294.

Kaur, Supreet, 2019. Nominal wage rigidity in village labor markets. American Economic Review. Forthcoming.

Kaur, Supreet, Kremer, Michael, Mullainathan, Sendhil, 2010. Self-control and the development of work arrangements. The American Economic Review 100 (2), 624–628.

Kaur, Supreet, Kremer, Michael, Mullainathan, Sendhil, 2015. Self-control at work. Journal of Political Economy 123 (6), 1227–1277.

Kaur, Supreet, Mullainathan, Sendhil, Oh, Suanna, Schilbach, Frank, 2018. Does poverty lower productivity?

Kazianga, Harounan, Udry, Christopher, 2006. Consumption smoothing? Livestock, insurance and drought in rural Burkina Faso. Journal of Development Economics 79 (2), 413–446.

Knack, Stephen, Keefer, Philip, 1997. Does social capital have an economic payoff? A cross-country investigation. The Quarterly Journal of Economics 112 (4), 1251–1288.

Knetsch, Jack, 1989. The endowment effect and evidence of nonreversible indifference curves. The American Economic Review 79 (5), 1277–1284.

Koppel, Lina, Andersson, David, Posadzy, Kinga, Västfjäll, Daniel, Tinghög, Gustav, 2017. The effect of acute pain on risky and intertemporal choice. Experimental Economics 20 (4), 878–893.

Kőszegi, Botond, 2003. Health anxiety and patient behavior. Journal of Health Economics 22 (6), 1073–1084.

Kőszegi, Botond, Rabin, Matthew, 2006. A model of reference-dependent preferences. The Quarterly Journal of Economics 121 (4), 1133–1165.

Kőszegi, Botond, Rabin, Matthew, 2007. Reference-dependent risk attitudes. The American Economic Review 97 (4), 1047–1073.

Kőszegi, Botond, Rabin, Matthew, 2009. Reference-dependent consumption plans. The American Economic Review 99 (3), 909–936.

Kraay, Aart, McKenzie, David, 2014. Do poverty traps exist? Assessing the evidence. Journal of Economic Perspectives 28 (3), 127–148.

Kremer, Michael, Chaudhury, Nazmul, Halsey Rogers, F., Muralidharan, Karthik, Hammer, Jeffrey, 2005. Teacher absence in India: a snapshot. Journal of the European Economic Association 3 (2–3), 658–667.

Kremer, Michael, Glennerster, Rachel, 2011. Improving health in developing countries: evidence from randomized evaluations. In: Pauly, Mark V., Mcguire, Thomas G., Barros, Pedro P. (Eds.), Handbook of Health Economics, vol. 2. Elsevier, Amsterdam, pp. 201–315.

Kremer, Michael, Lee, Jean, Robinson, Jonathan, Rostapshova, Olga, 2013. Behavioral biases and firm behavior: evidence from Kenyan retail shops. The American Economic Review 103 (3), 362–368.

Kremer, Michael, Leino, Jessica, Miguel, Edward, Peterson Zwane, Alix, 2011. Spring cleaning: rural water impacts, valuation, and property rights institutions. The Quarterly Journal of Economics 126 (1), 145–205.

Kremer, Michael, Miguel, Edward, 2007. The illusion of sustainability. The Quarterly Journal of Economics 122 (3), 1007–1065.

Krueger, Alan B., Stone, Arthur A., 2008. Assessment of pain: a community-based diary survey in the USA. The Lancet 371 (9623), 1519–1525.

Kugler, Tamar, Kausel, Edgar E., Kocher, Martin G., 2012. Are groups more rational than individuals? A review of interactive decision making in groups. Wiley Interdisciplinary Reviews: Cognitive Science 3 (4), 471–482.

Kuncel, Nathan R., Hezlett, Sarah A., 2010. Fact and fiction in cognitive ability testing for admissions and hiring decisions. Current Directions in Psychological Science 19 (6), 339–345.

Kunreuther, Howard, Ginsberg, Ralph, Miller, Louis, Sagi, Philip, Slovic, Paul, Borkan, Bradley, Katz, Norman, 1978. Disaster Insurance Protection: Public Policy Lessons. Wiley, New York.

Laajaj, Rachid, 2017. Endogenous time horizon and behavioral poverty trap: theory and evidence from Mozambique. Journal of Development Economics 127, 187–208.

Lacetera, Nicola, Macis, Mario, Slonim, Robert, 2013. Economic rewards to motivate blood donations. Science 340 (6135), 927–928.

La Ferrara, Eliana, 2018. Aspirations, Social Norms and Development. European Economic Association Presidential Address – Cologne.

La Ferrara, Eliana, Chong, Alberto, Duryea, Suzanne, 2012. Soap operas and fertility: evidence from Brazil. American Economic Journal: Applied Economics 4 (4), 1–31.

Laibson, David, 1997. Golden eggs and hyperbolic discounting. The Quarterly Journal of Economics 112 (2), 443–478.

Laibson, David, 2015. Why don't present-biased agents make commitments? The American Economic Review 105 (5), 267–272.

LaPorta, Rafael, Lopez-De-Silanes, Florencio, Shleifer, Andrei, Vishny, Robert W., 1997. Trust in large organizations. American Economic Review: Papers and Proceedings 87 (2), 333–338.

Le, Kien T., 2010. Separation hypothesis tests in the agricultural household model. American Journal of Agricultural Economics 92 (5), 1420–1431.

Lee, Kenneth, Miguel, Edward, Wolfram, Catherine, 2016. Experimental Evidence on the Demand for and Costs of Rural Electrification. NBER Working Paper No. 22292.

Lerner, Jennifer S., Li, Ye, Valdesolo, Piercarlo, Kassam, Karim S., 2015. Emotion and decision making. Annual Review of Psychology 66.

Levin, Jeff, 2010. Religion and mental health: theory and research. International Journal of Applied Psychoanalytic Studies 7 (2), 102–115.

Levine, Ruth, Kinder, Molly, 2004. Millions Saved: Proven Successes in Global Health, vol. 3. Center for Global Development, Washington, DC.

Li, Yufei, Meng, Juanjuan, Song, Changcheng, Zheng, Kai, 2018. Information avoidance and medical screening: a field experiment in China.

Loewenstein, George, Lerner, Jennifer S., 2003. The role of affect in decision making. In: Davidson, Richard J., Scherer, Klaus R., Goldsmith, H. Hill (Eds.), Handbook of Affective Science. Oxford University Press, Oxford and New York.

Loewenstein, George, O'Donoghue, Ted, Rabin, Matthew, 2003. Projection bias in predicting future utility. The Quarterly Journal of Economics 118 (4), 1209–1248.

Lopez, Ramon E., 1984. Estimating labor supply and production decisions of self-employed farm producers. European Economic Review 24 (1), 61–82.

Lowe, Matt, 2018. Types of contact: a field experiment on collaborative and adversarial caste integration. Mimeo.

Lucas Jr., Robert E., 1978. On the size distribution of business firms. Bell Journal of Economics, 508–523.

Lucas Jr., Robert E., Rapping, Leonard A., 1969. Real wages, employment, and inflation. Journal of Political Economy 77 (5), 721–754.

Ludwig, Jens, Kling, Jeffrey R., Mullainathan, Sendhil, 2011. Mechanism experiments and policy evaluations. The Journal of Economic Perspectives 25 (3), 17–38.

Lund, Crick, Breen, Alison, Flisher, Alan J., Kakuma, Ritsuko, Corrigall, Joanne, Joska, John A., Swartz, Leslie, Patel, Vikram, 2010. Poverty and common mental disorders in low and middle income countries: a systematic review. Social Science & Medicine 71 (3), 517–528.

Lusardi, Annamaria, 2009. Overcoming the Saving Slump: How to Increase the Effectiveness of Financial Education and Saving Programs. University of Chicago Press.

Lybbert, Travis J., Wydick, Bruce, 2018. Poverty, aspirations, and the economics of hope. Economic Development and Cultural Change 66 (4), 709–753.

Maccini, Sharon, Yang, Dean, 2009. Under the weather: health, schooling, and economic consequences of early-life rainfall. The American Economic Review 99 (3), 1006–1026.

Madajewicz, Malgosia, Pfaff, Alexander, Van Geen, Alexander, Graziano, Joseph, Hussein, Iftikhar, Momotaj, Hasina, Sylvi, Roksana, Ahsan, Habibul, 2007. Can information alone change behavior? Response to arsenic contamination of groundwater in Bangladesh. Journal of Development Economics 84 (2), 731–754.

Madden, Gregory J., Raiff, Bethany R., Lagorio, Carla H., Begotka, Andrea M., Mueller, Angela M., Hehli, Daniel J., Wegener, Ashley A., 2004. Delay discounting of potentially real and hypothetical rewards: II. Between- and within-subject comparisons. Experimental and Clinical Psychopharmacology 12 (4), 251.

Madrian, Brigitte C., Shea, Dennis F., 2001. The power of suggestion: inertia in 401(k) participation and savings behavior. The Quarterly Journal of Economics 116 (4), 1149–1187.

Mahajan, Aprajit, Tarozzi, Alessandro, 2011. Time inconsistency, expectations and technology adoption: the case of insecticide treated nets.

Malmendier, Ulrike, Tate, Geoffrey, 2005. CEO overconfidence and corporate investment. Journal of Finance 60 (6), 2661–2700.

Mani, Anandi, Mullainathan, Sendhil, Shafir, Eldar, Zhao, Jiaying, 2013. Poverty impedes cognitive function. Science 341 (6149), 976–980.

Mann, J. John, Waternaux, Christine, Haas, Gretchen L., Malone, Kevin M., 1999. Toward a clinical model of suicidal behavior in psychiatric patients. The American Journal of Psychiatry 156 (2), 181–189.

Marglin, Stephen A., 1974. What do bosses do? The origins and functions of hierarchy in capitalist production. Review of Radical Political Economics 6 (2), 60–112.

Markowitz, Harry, 1952. The utility of wealth. Journal of Political Economy 60 (2), 151–158.

Marx, Karl, Engels, Friedrich, 1848. The Communist Manifesto.

Mas, Alexandre, Pallais, Amanda, 2017. Valuing alternative work arrangements. The American Economic Review 107 (12), 3722–3759.

Mayraz, Guy, 2011. Wishful thinking.

McClelland, David C., 1961. The Achievement Society. Von Nostrand, Princeton, NJ.

McClure, Samuel M., Ericson, Keith M., Laibson, David I., Loewenstein, George, Cohen, Jonathan D., 2007. Time discounting for primary rewards. The Journal of Neuroscience 27 (21), 5796–5804.

McKelway, Madeline, 2018. Women's self-efficacy and women's employment: experimental evidence from India.

Meager, Rachael, 2019. Understanding the average impact of microcredit expansions: a bayesian hierarchical analysis of seven randomized experiments. American Economic Journal: Applied Economics. Forthcoming.

Meier, Stephan, Sprenger, Charles D., 2011. Time discounting predicts creditworthiness. Psychological Science 23 (1), 56–58.

Meredith, Jennifer, Robinson, Jonathan, Walker, Sarah, Wydick, Bruce, 2013. Keeping the doctor away: experimental evidence on investment in preventative health products. Journal of Development Economics 105, 196–210.

Miguel, Edward, 2004. Tribe or nation? Nation building and public goods in Kenya versus Tanzania. World Politics 56 (3), 327–362.

Miguel, Edward, Gugerty, Mary Kay, 2005. Ethnic diversity, social sanctions, and public goods in Kenya. Journal of Public Economics 89 (11–12), 2325–2368.

Mullainathan, Sendhil, Shafir, Eldar, 2013. Scarcity: Why Having Too Little Means So Much. Macmillan.

Munshi, Kaivan, 2004. Social learning in a heterogeneous population: technology diffusion in the Indian green revolution. Journal of Development Economics 73 (1), 185–213.

Muralidharan, Karthik, Sundararaman, Venkatesh, 2011. Teacher performance pay: experimental evidence from India. Journal of Political Economy 119 (1), 39–77.

Murfin, Justin, Pratt, Ryan, 2019. Comparables pricing. The Review of Financial Studies 32 (2), 688–737.

Neufeld, K.J., Peters, D.H., Rani, M., Bonu, S., Brooner, R.K., 2005. Regular use of alcohol and tobacco in India and its association with age, gender, and poverty. Drug and Alcohol Dependence 77 (3), 283–291.

Nunn, Nathan, 2008. The long-term effects of Africa's slave trades. The Quarterly Journal of Economics 123 (1), 139–176.

Nunn, Nathan, 2012. Culture and the historical process. Economic History of Developing Regions 27 (1), S108–S126.

Nunn, Nathan, Wantchekon, Leonard, 2011. The slave trade and the origins of mistrust in Africa. The American Economic Review 101 (7), 3221–3252.

O'Donoghue, Ted, Rabin, Matthew, 1999. Doing it now or later. The American Economic Review 89 (1), 103–124.

O'Donoghue, Ted, Rabin, Matthew, 2001. Choice and procrastination. The Quarterly Journal of Economics 116 (1), 121–160.

O'Donoghue, Ted, Sprenger, Charles, 2018. Reference-dependent preferences. In: Bernheim, B. Douglas, DellaVigna, Stefano, Laibson, David (Eds.), Handbook of Behavioral Economics: Foundations and Applications 1. Elsevier, Amsterdam.

Okunogbe, Oyebola, 2018. Does exposure to other ethnic regions promote national integration? Evidence from Nigeria.

Ong, Qiyan, Theseira, Walter, Ng, Irene Y.H., 2018. Reducing debt improves psychological functioning and changes decision making in the poor.

Oster, Emily, Shoulson, Ira, Dorsey, E., 2013. Optimal expectations and limited medical testing: evidence from Huntington disease. The American Economic Review 103 (2), 804–830.

Oswald, Frederick L., Mitchell, Gregory, Blanton, Hart, Jaccard, James, Tetlock, Philip E., 2013. Predicting ethnic and racial discrimination: a meta-analysis of IAT criterion studies. Journal of Personality and Social Psychology 105 (2), 171.

Pagel, Michaela, 2017. Expectations-based reference-dependent life-cycle consumption. The Review of Economic Studies 84 (2), 885–934.

Palairet, M.R., 2004. IQ and the wealth of nations.

Patel, Nirav P., Grandner, Michael A., Xie, Dawei, Branas, Charles C., Gooneratne, Nalaka, 2010. "Sleep disparity" in the population: poor sleep quality is strongly associated with poverty and ethnicity. BMC Public Health 10 (1), 475.

Patel, Vikram, 2007. Alcohol use and mental health in developing countries. Annals of Epidemiology 17 (5), S87–S92.

Patel, Vikram, Kleinman, Arthur, 2003. Poverty and common mental disorders in developing countries. Bulletin of the World Health Organization 81, 609–615.

Patel, Vikram, Weobong, Benedict, Weiss, Helen A., Anand, Arpita, Bhat, Bhargav, Katti, Basavraj, Dimidjian, Sona, Araya, Ricardo, Hollon, Steve D., King, Michael, Vijayakumar, Lakshmi, Park, A-La, McDaid, David, Wilson, Terry, Velleman, Richard, Kirkwood, Betty R., Fairburn, Christopher G., 2017. The healthy activity program (HAP), a lay counsellor-delivered brief psychological treatment for severe depression, in primary care in India: a randomised controlled trial. The Lancet 389 (10065), 176–185.

Paxson, Christina H., 1992. Using weather variability to estimate the response of savings to transitory income in Thailand. The American Economic Review, 15–33.

Poleshuck, Ellen L., Green, Carmen R., 2008. Socioeconomic disadvantage and pain. Pain 136 (3), 235.

Prina, Silvia, 2015. Banking the poor via savings accounts: evidence from a field experiment. Journal of Development Economics 115, 16–31.

Putnam, Robert D., 2000. Bowling Alone: The Collapse and Revival of American Community. Simon and Schuster, New York.

Rabin, Matthew, 1998. Psychology and economics. Journal of Economic Literature 36 (1), 11–46.

Rabin, Matthew, 2000. Risk aversion and expected-utility theory: a calibration theorem. Econometrica 68 (5), 1281–1292.

Rabin, Matthew, 2002. Inference by believers in the law of small numbers. The Quarterly Journal of Economics 117 (3), 775–816.

Rabin, Matthew, Weizsäcker, Georg, 2009. Narrow bracketing and dominated choices. The American Economic Review 99 (4), 1508–1543.

Rao, Gautam, 2018. Familiarity does not breed contempt: diversity, discrimination and generosity in Delhi schools. The American Economic Review. Forthcoming.

Rao, K.V., Mishra, Vinod K., Retherford, Robert D., 1998. Effects of Exposure to Mass Media on Knowledge and Use of Oral Rehydration Therapy for Childhood Diarrhea in India. National Family Health Survey Subject Report (10).

Ray, Debraj, 2006. Aspirations, Poverty, and Economic Change. In: Banerjee, Abhijit V., Benabou, Roland, Mookherjee, Dilip (Eds.), Understanding Poverty. Oxford University Press, New York.

Reuben, Ernesto, Sapienza, Paola, Zingales, Luigi, 2015. Procrastination and impatience. Journal of Behavioral and Experimental Economics 58, 63–76.

Rose, Elaina, 1999. Consumption smoothing and excess female mortality in rural India. Review of Economics and Statistics 81 (1), 41–49.

Rosenzweig, Mark R., Udry, Christopher, 2014. Rainfall forecasts, weather, and wages over the agricultural production cycle. The American Economic Review 104 (5), 278–283.

Ross, Lee, Nisbett, Richard E., 1991. The Person and the Situation: Perspectives of Social Psychology. Pinter & Martin Publishers.

Ru, Hong, Schoar, Antoinette, 2016. Do Credit Card Companies Screen for Behavioral Biases? NBER Working Paper No. 22360.

Schaner, Simone, 2018. The persistent power of behavioral change: long-run impacts of temporary savings subsidies for the poor. American Economic Journal: Applied Economics 10 (3), 67–100.

Schilbach, Frank, 2019. Alcohol and self-control: a field experiment in India. The American Economic Review. Forthcoming.

Schilbach, Frank, Schofield, Heather, Mullainathan, Sendhil, 2016. The psychological lives of the poor. The American Economic Review 106 (5), 435–440.

Schilbach, Frank N., 2015. Essays in Development and Behavioral Economics. PhD thesis.

Schofield, Heather, 2014. The economic costs of low caloric intake: evidence from India. Unpublished Manuscript.

Schultz, Theodore W., 1964. Transforming Traditional Agriculture. Studies in Comparative Economics. Economics 37 (1), 47–61.

Schulz, Jonathan, Bahrami-Rad, Duman, Beauchamp, Jonathan, Henrich, Joseph, 2018. The origins of WEIRD psychology.

Schwartzstein, Joshua, 2014. Selective attention and learning. Journal of the European Economic Association 12 (6), 1423–1452.

Sen, Amartya, 1985. Commodities and capabilities.

Sen, Amartya, 1999. Freedom as development.

Shah, Anuj K., Shafir, Eldar, Mullainathan, Sendhil, 2015. Scarcity frames value. Psychological Science 26 (4), 402–412.

Shah, Anuj K., Zhao, Jiaying, Mullainathan, Sendhil, Shafir, Eldar, 2018. Money in the mental lives of the poor. Social Cognition 36 (1), 4–19.

Shapiro, Jesse M., 2005. Is there a daily discount rate? Evidence from the food stamp nutrition cycle. Journal of Public Economics 89 (2–3), 303–325.

Shefrin, Hersh M., Thaler, Richard H., 2004. Mental accounting, saving, and self-control. In: Camerer, Colin F., Loewenstein, George, Rabin, Matthew (Eds.), Advances in Behavioral Economics. Russell Sage Foundation/Princeton University Press, Princeton and Oxford, pp. 395–428.

Sims, Christopher A., 2003. Implications of rational inattention. Journal of Monetary Economics 50 (3), 665–690.

Sims, Christopher A., 2010. Rational inattention and monetary economics. In: Friedman, Benjamin M., Woodford, Michael (Eds.), Handbook of Monetary Economics, vol. 3. Elsevier, Amsterdam, pp. 155–181.

Slovic, Paul, Kunreuther, Howard, White, Gilbert F., 1974. Decision processes, rationality and adjustment to natural hazards. In: White, Gilbert F. (Ed.), Natural Hazards: Local, National, Global. Oxford University Press, New York, pp. 187–205.

Song, Changcheng, 2015. Financial illiteracy and pension contributions: a field experiment on compound interest in China.

Spolaore, Enrico, Wacziarg, Romain, 2013. How deep are the roots of economic development? Journal of Economic Literature 51 (2), 325–369.

Stango, Victor, Zinman, Jonathan, 2009. Exponential growth bias and household finance. The Journal of Finance 64 (6), 2807–2849.

Stein, Daniel, 2016. Dynamics of demand for rainfall index insurance: evidence from a commercial product in India. World Bank Economic Review 32 (3), 692–708.

Stephens, Melvin Jr., 2003. "3rd of tha month": do social security recipients smooth consumption between checks? The American Economic Review 93 (1), 406–422.

Subramanian, S.V., Nandy, Shailen, Irving, Michelle, Gordon, David, Smith, George Davey, 2005. Role of socioeconomic markers and state prohibition policy in predicting alcohol consumption among men and women in India: a multilevel statistical analysis. Bulletin of the World Health Organization 83, 829–836.

Sulaiman, Munshi, Barua, Proloy. 2013 Improving livelihood using livestock: impact evaluation of 'targeting ultra-poor' programme in Afghanistan.

Suri, Tavneet, 2011. Selection and comparative advantage in technology adoption. Econometrica 79 (1), 159–209.

Suri, Tavneet, 2017. Mobile money. Annual Review of Economics 9 (1), 497–520.

Sydnor, Justin, 2010. (Over) insuring modest risks. American Economic Journal: Applied Economics 2 (4), 177–199.

Tabellini, Guido, 2010. Culture and institutions: economic development in the regions of Europe. Journal of the European Economic Association 8 (4), 677–716.

Tanaka, Tomomi, Camerer, Colin F., Nguyen, Quang, 2010. Risk and time preferences: linking experimental and household survey data from Vietnam. The American Economic Review 100 (1), 557–571.

Tarozzi, Alessandro, Mahajan, Aprajit, Blackburn, Brian, Kopf, Dan, Krishnan, Lakshmi, Yoong, Joanne, 2014. Micro-loans, insecticide-treated bednets, and malaria: evidence from a randomized controlled trial in Orissa, India. The American Economic Review 104 (7), 1909–1941.

Thakral, Neil Tô, Linh T., 2018. Daily labor supply and adaptive reference points. Mimeo.

Thaler, Richard, 1980. Toward a positive theory of consumer choice. Journal of Economic Behavior & Organization 1 (1), 39–60.

Thaler, Richard, 1985. Mental accounting and consumer choice. Marketing Science 4 (3), 199–214.

Thaler, Richard H., Shefrin, Hersh M., 1981. An economic theory of self-control. Journal of Political Economy 89 (2), 392–406.

Thompson, Edward P., 1967. Time, work-discipline, and industrial capitalism. Past & Present 38, 56–97.

Thornton, Rebecca L., 2008. The demand for, and impact of, learning HIV status. The American Economic Review 98 (5), 1829–1863.

Townsend, Robert M., 1994. Risk and insurance in village India. Econometrica: Journal of the Econometric Society, 539–591.

Townsend, Robert M., 1995. Consumption insurance: an evaluation of risk-bearing systems in low-income economies. The Journal of Economic Perspectives 9 (3), 83–102.

Tversky, Amos, Kahneman, Daniel, 1971. Belief in the law of small numbers. Psychological Bulletin 76 (2), 105.

Tversky, Amos, Kahneman, Daniel, 1981. The framing of decisions and the psychology of choice. Science 211 (4481), 453–458.

Tybout, James R., 2000. Manufacturing firms in developing countries: how well do they do, and why? Journal of Economic Literature 38 (1), 11–44.

Ubfal, Diego, 2016. How general are time preferences? Eliciting good-specific discount rates. Journal of Development Economics 118, 150–170.

Viscusi, W. Kip, 1990. Do smokers underestimate risks? Journal of Political Economy 98 (6), 1253–1269.

Weber, Max, 1905. The protestant ethic and the spirit of capitalism.

World Bank, 2015. World Development Report 2015: Mind, Society, and Behavior. World Bank Group.

World Health Organization, 2015. Noncommunicable Diseases Progress Monitor 2015. Technical report. World Health Organization.

Yanagizawa-Drott, David, 2014. Propaganda and conflict: evidence from the Rwandan genocide. The Quarterly Journal of Economics 129 (4), 1947–1994.

Yang, Dean, Choi, HwaJung, 2007. Are remittances insurance? Evidence from rainfall shocks in the Philippines. World Bank Economic Review 21 (2), 219–248.

Behavioral economics and health-care markets[*]

Amitabh Chandra[a,c,d], Benjamin Handel[b], Joshua Schwartzstein[c,*]

[a]*Harvard Kennedy School, Cambridge, MA, United States of America*
[b]*UC Berkeley, Berkeley, CA, United States of America*
[c]*Harvard Business School, Boston, MA, United States of America*
[d]*National Bureau of Economic Research, Cambridge, MA, United States of America*
*Corresponding author: e-mail address: jschwartzstein@hbs.edu

Contents

[*] We thank Douglas Bernheim, Stefano DellaVigna, and Matthew Rabin for helpful comments.

Handbook of Behavioral Economics, Volume 2
ISSN 2352-2399, https://doi.org/10.1016/bs.hesbe.2018.11.004

1 Introduction

Writing in 1963, Kenneth Arrow—the father of health-economics—explained the many ways in which markets for health-insurance and health-care services were different than other markets. Arrow's emphasis was on how uncertainty of various types is pervasive in medical-care markets. It showed up in the form of unpredictable illness that required costly interventions, which in turn created demand for health-insurance. It showed up as uncertainty about the effect of illness on health, earnings, and recovery. And it showed up as uncertainty in the value of medical treatments themselves, not knowing product quality or the therapeutic benefit of treatment. Arrow argued that such characteristics of the medical-care market established a special place for it in economic analysis.

In this chapter, we return to themes from Arrow's seminal work and update them with insights from behavioral economics, a field that wasn't born at the time of his writing. Like him, we focus on insurance markets and product markets in health care. And, like Arrow, we focus on special characteristics of medical-care markets. But while his emphasis was on the importance of uncertainty in these markets, ours is on the importance of choice difficulties and biases leading to mistakes. Our approach overlaps with Arrow's because the presence of uncertainty increases the difficulty of choosing insurance and care wisely, and the likelihood that a health-care consumer succumbs to various forms of behavioral biases.

Indeed, health economics markets abound in difficult choices and other enablers for biases. It is not easy to choose between health insurance plans; to forecast the need for care; to assess the benefits and costs of treatment. The presence of uncertainty creates space for many biases, such as errors in statistical-reasoning, projection bias, and mis-weighting of probabilities. But special features of medical-care markets are great enablers of potential mistakes more broadly. For example, the benefits of care are often in the distant future while the costs appear now, so present bias is likely important. While, as we discuss below, the behavioral health-economics literature has done a better job of documenting choice mistakes than explaining *why* those mistakes occur, it is clear that we should not ignore these mistakes in our analyses.

Health-care economics is a broad field containing many possible specific applications of behavioral economics. To focus our chapter, we primarily analyze health-care markets rather than health more broadly. Table 1 presents a range of applications, separating ones that we cover in this handbook chapter from ones that we do not. We focus this chapter on the topics of (i) consumer insurance choices and corresponding market implications and (ii) health-care utilization choices, with corresponding normative and positive implications for the design of insurance contracts. The topics that we focus on are close in spirit to the topics discussed in Arrow (1963).

Table 1 This table presents a range of behavioral health-economics applications, together with sample references.

Behavioral health economics applications	
Topics covered	**Sample references**
Consumer insurance choices	Handel (2013)
	Bhargava et al. (2017)
Impact of insurance on consumer health-care utilization	Baicker et al. (2015), Brot-Goldberg et al. (2017)
Provider-consumer joint treatment choices	
Consumer adherence to medications/treatments	Sokol et al. (2005)
Topics not covered	
Diet	Volpp et al. (2008)
	Oster (2018)
Exercise	DellaVigna and Malmendier (2006)
	Carrera et al. (2018)
Addiction	Gruber and Kőszegi (2013)
	Bernheim and Rangel (2004)
End-of-life care	Halpern et al. (2013), Sudore et al. (2017)
Medical-testing decisions	Kőszegi (2003)
	Oster et al. (2013)
Provider treatment choices	Chandra et al. (2012)
Provider responses to incentives/quality programs	
Provider use of information/information technology	Kolstad (2013)
Residency match mechanism design	Rees-Jones (2018)

Topics that we do not cover in detail, but are fertile ground for behavioral economics research, include (i) diet; (ii) exercise; (iii) addiction; (iv) end-of-life care; (v) provider responses to financial incentives and quality programs; (vi) provider integration of information; and (vii) mechanism design in the context of the medical residency match. Many of these topics involve decisions that are either physician-directed, primarily influenced by factors other than market prices, and/or influenced by non-standard preferences. Table 1 presents examples of research on these topics.

Since health-insurance plan choice is a point of entry into decision making in the health-care sector, we start by considering this choice. Research shows that consumers leave lots of money on the table in their plan choices, sometimes thousands of dollars. This research takes several approaches to identifying poor consumer choices and to characterizing the underlying mechanisms behind those choices. It focuses on active choice issues, arising when consumers are engaged in the choice process.

It also focuses on passive choice issues, arising from inertia when consumers have a default option. We discuss the implications of this body of work for questions in industrial organization such as the design and regulation of insurance markets, including the interaction between consumer choice difficulties or biases and adverse selection.

We then consider how consumers respond to changes in prices such as copayments and deductibles in their medical-treatment choices, conditional on their choice of health plan. A large and influential literature in economics notes that increases in patient cost-sharing through copayments and deductibles reduce the demand for health care. This effect is often referred to as the "price elasticity of demand for medical care" and is conventionally used by economists as a measure of moral hazard under the assumption that, by letting a low price discourage treatment, a patient reveals that the treatment has little value to them. Put differently, in the conventional model, moral hazard would point to some marginal-value care being reduced when prices increase—so there would be an adverse, but small, health cost. However, choice difficulties and biases may lead the patient to cut back on treatment that in fact is of great value, muddying the argument that the price elasticity of demand meaningfully captures the degree of moral hazard.

Additional issues on consumer treatment choices that we cover include patterns of patient adherence to treatment recommendations, as well as how patients respond to the highly non-linear structure of high-deductible health plans (which have low first-dollar coverage but generous last dollar coverage). We discuss the many potential biases and frictions that contribute to mis-behavior in these areas, as well as the empirical literature suggesting the prevalence of such mis-behavior. Following typical assumptions made in this literature, we also describe welfare implications.[1]

As with most work in the area of empirical behavioral economics, the positive and normative implications of key results depend on the maintained assumptions. In his book on identification, Manski (1999) discusses a tradeoff between the credibility of an empirical analysis and the assumptions required for sharp predictions. In empirical research in behavioral economics, this tradeoff is particularly relevant for welfare calculations where the researcher needs to know structural parameters whose estimation necessitates modeling assumptions about consumer decision-making. While we strive to present a healthy skepticism of the assumptions maintained in the empirical work we analyze, we also believe that relevance necessitates some use of plain and accessible language.

---

[1] While we include only a very brief discussion of pre-system health behaviors like diet and exercise, see, e.g., Cawley and Ruhm (2011) for a survey covering individual behaviors in these areas. Also, since patient choices are often made jointly with physicians, we briefly discuss physician decision-making. There has been relatively little research studying behavioral economics in the context of physician treatment decisions, likely because of the empirical difficulty of identifying physician biases and/or mistakes separately from their (and their patients') private information. See, e.g., Chandra et al. (2012) for a survey of the literature on physician decision-making, as well as Chandra and Staiger (2017) and Chandra and Staiger (2010) for examples of physician bias in treatment decisions.

For example, we will refer to some decisions that consumers make as mistakes when the preponderance of evidence suggests that consumers would have been better off making another choice. However, we acknowledge the concern that consumers may respond to idiosyncratic preferences that economists and physicians observing them do not observe—we will point out the kinds of assumptions that a neoclassical observer would have to make in order to refute our preferred interpretation.

We also follow the empirical literature and assume that the correct welfare frame is that of a consumer without choice frictions or behavioral biases making a choice at the same time that he/she does in practice (e.g., during open enrollment in health-insurance markets). While we discuss this assumption in more depth throughout the chapter, we defer to the discussion of welfare and behavioral economics in Bernheim and Taubinsky (2018) for a more detailed treatment of the underlying issues.

Finally, we want to highlight the nascent nature of our topic area. Other chapters in this Handbook concern areas like retirement savings and financial markets, where the cumulative amount of knowledge on the role of mistakes (and which mistakes are important) is higher. But this makes behavioral health economics an especially exciting area in which to work going forward. We lay out some directions for future research in the concluding section.

2 Consumer choice of insurance

Consumer purchase and use of health insurance are central components of their experiences in health-care markets. Insurance protects consumers from potentially crippling financial risk, and serves as a crucial intermediary between consumers and medical providers. In many settings, consumers are presented with a range of insurance options to choose from, with the goal of facilitating the best matches between consumers and plans. For instance, the health-insurance exchanges set up under the Affordable Care Act of 2010 and drug-plan markets set up under Medicare Part D in 2003 encourage private insurers to enter and compete for consumers' business. In these managed competition environments, consumers typically have many choices, in some cases up to 40 or 50. Similarly, large employers offering coverage often present employees with several choices to encourage both competition between insurers and efficient employee-plan experiences. The rationale in favor of market environments with a meaningful number of choices is clear: if consumers are well informed and make unbiased choices, having a greater number of options facilitates efficient matching, drives premiums down through increased competition, and forces insurers to improve non-pecuniary aspects of their products such as provider networks. Even in markets with single-payer systems such as the UK, many patients still choose supplemental coverage plans that have these features and require consumers to choose between alternative plans.

Yet it may be difficult for consumers to assess the many complex features of insurance plans, and to synthesize those assessments into plan choices. There is ample empirical evidence that consumers have difficulty making active choices in insurance markets, as well as passive choices where inertia plays a role and consumers are placed into a default option if they take no new action. As detailed in subsequent sections, consumers often leave hundreds, and sometimes thousands, of dollars on the table in their plan choices. They frequently lack or fail to process key pieces of information about financial and non-financial plan characteristics. In certain cases, they even choose options that are financially dominated by another plan in their choice set, losing a significant amount of money with certainty. Broadly, the implications of these issues are two-fold: (i) conditional on the market environment, consumers are worse off due to poorer plan matches and (ii) insurance prices and products do not improve to the extent they would in competitive markets with frictionless and bias-free consumers.

The literature on consumer choice in insurance markets has exploded over the past decade and continues to be very active. In addition to being an important market with a lot at stake, researchers have been attracted to health insurance due to the paradigm-shifting ACA (and related) reform efforts. Finally, researchers have been able to obtain individual-level datasets with detailed information on health-risk heterogeneity and insurance purchases. This latter feature allows researchers to infer what consumers *should* choose much more easily than they can in standard product markets, making health-insurance markets an excellent context to study behavioral economics.

Overall, this literature shows several clear patterns. First, consumers often leave meaningful sums of money on the table when making active insurance choices. Though there are many potential explanations, primary ones include (see, e.g., Handel and Schwartzstein, 2018) (i) information frictions, including costs of processing information, and (ii) mental gaps, including biases in integrating information and limited insurance competence. Consumer choices become even worse when a previously chosen option is the default: inertia causes consumers to lose substantial sums of money, above and beyond what they lose in active choice settings. Consumer choice mistakes also have important implications for the industrial organization of health-insurance markets and, more broadly, the regulation of health-insurance markets. We now discuss each of these areas in turn.

2.1 Demand for insurance
2.1.1 Simple model

Most prior research studying the potential for consumer mistakes in health insurance markets focuses on broadly documenting these mistakes and, when possible, linking them to specific micro-foundations. We begin with a simple model (borrowed from Handel et al., 2015) that nests most of these micro-foundations: this model is especially useful when thinking about the market implications of behavioral consumers, which we discuss later in this chapter.

Consider a consumer choosing between two insurance options. Define w_i as a consumer's willingness-to-pay for plan 1 relative to plan 2. Denote a consumer's true value for plan 1 relative to plan 2 as v_i. Here, we define true value as the ex ante willingness-to-pay for a consumer with no information frictions or behavioral biases. Given this, a consumer's relative surplus will be the difference between a consumer's true valuation and the expected cost to the insurer c_i; that is, surplus equals $v_i - c_i$. Positive surplus from one insurance plan relative to another could reflect, e.g., increased risk protection for a risk averse consumer, or a broader provider network granting access to preferable providers.

Sources of consumer mistakes in this setup are reflected in the difference between willingness-to-pay, which impacts consumer demand, and true consumer ex ante value, which impacts consumer welfare:

$$\varepsilon_i = w_i - v_i. \tag{1}$$

A positive value of ε_i implies that the entire set of frictions and biases a consumer faces causes her to overvalue plan 1 relative to plan 2 by ε_i. This impacts purchases and market outcomes: a consumer purchases plan 1 if w_i exceeds the relative price of plan 1, ΔP, but, in a frictionless and bias-free market, a consumer should only purchase that plan if $v_i > \Delta P$.[2] This simple model is useful to have in mind during our discussion of more complex micro-founded models, which propose specific underpinnings of ε_i and v_i. Additionally, it is useful for thinking about the sufficient statistics necessary to evaluate different policy interventions, something we discuss at the end of this section. Also, this framework relates closely to the behavioral hazard framework discussed for consumer medical-treatment choices in the next section of this chapter.

This framework, by definition, assumes that the "correct" welfare criterion, both for the consumer and policymaker, is derived from consumers' decision utility at the time of choice assuming they were to make that choice without behavioral biases and without information frictions. Throughout this chapter, we abide by this criterion because (i) it is parsimonious in modeling the distinction between revealed preference with and without both frictions and biases and (ii) it is the approach followed (at least implicitly) by much of the empirical literatures in behavioral health economics, behavioral industrial organization, and behavioral public finance. See, e.g., Kőszegi and Rabin (2008) and Bernheim and Taubinsky (2018) for an extended discussion of welfare economics for behavioral consumers.

When empirical behavioral papers model specific mechanisms underlying poor consumer-plan choices, the typical starting point is a model of a rational frictionless expected utility maximizing consumer. Behavioral models typically modify the baseline expected-utility setup to reflect distinct choice biases and/or frictions. There are many ways such modifications can be made, some sticking closely to the classical expected-utility framework and others moving further away.

---

[2] This presumes that a consumer chooses one plan or the other. This could be, e.g., because of a fully-enforced individual mandate, as specified by the Affordable Care Act.

2.1.2 Modified expected utility to study active choices: Handel and Kolstad (2015b)

The first model we discuss, from Handel and Kolstad (2015b), closely follows a classical expected utility setup. This allows the authors to show how bringing additional data to bear on consumers' lack of knowledge (interpreted as the result of information frictions) impacts the conclusions that are drawn, relative to assuming biases and frictions away in a classical expected-utility framework.

The consumer's problem is to choose a plan j from set $\mathcal{J}$. To analyze this problem, we will first consider consumer utility in a given insurance plan conditional on a specific health risk outcome (ex post utility). Then, we will discuss *ex ante* consumer utility from an insurance plan, i.e., in advance of knowing the health-risk outcome.

Consumer i's ex post utility in health plan j is:

$$u(W_i - P_{ij} + \pi_j(\psi_j, \mu_i) - s, \gamma_i). \tag{2}$$

u is assumed to be a concave utility function, implying that consumers have diminishing marginal utility for wealth and are risk averse. A typical functional form assumption is constant absolute risk aversion (CARA), meaning that the curvature of the utility function doesn't depend on baseline wealth. This is a one-parameter functional form where γ describes the degree of curvature: γ close to 0 means low curvature (risk-neutral) while high γ means high curvature (quite risk averse). This ex-post utility includes several components, some of which are the same regardless of health during the year. W_i is consumer wealth and P_{ij} is the premium contribution an individual i pays in plan j. π_j reflects the consumer's value for non-financial plan characteristics, such as provider networks or tax-advantaged health-savings accounts: this depends on plan characteristics ψ_j and a consumer's health type μ_i. In this formulation, each of these components is assumed to be independent of the health-risk realization.[3]

Finally, the payment s is the consumer's out-of-pocket payment for health care, given an ex post realization of their health risk. This is the element consumers have uncertainty about, which is why, given risk aversion, insurance is valuable for them ex ante.

We now turn to *ex ante* consumer utility, which captures their expected utility from an insurance plan. Assume that a consumer faces uncertainty about their out-of-pocket spending in a given plan j, following the probability distribution $f_{ij}(s|\psi_j, \mu_i)$. The distribution of payments depends on the plan design and the consumer's health-risk type. Given this uncertainty, a consumer's expected utility for plan j is:

$$U_{ij} = \int_0^\infty f_{ij}(s|\psi_j, \mu_i) u(W_i - P_{ij} + \pi_j(\psi_j, \mu_i) - s, \gamma_i) ds. \tag{3}$$

---

[3] In certain settings, one may want to model π as a function of the ex post risk realization as well, since provider networks and health risk interact. We don't do so here for simplicity.

The expected utility function averages the utility the consumer gets across her possible health-risk realizations. For example, if consumers are very risk-averse, then high s outcomes in a plan will strongly discourage the consumer from choosing that plan. Within this setup, the consumer will choose the plan j that maximizes her expected utility U_{ij}. If we map this frictionless and bias-free expected utility framework to our earlier simple model of plan choice ($\varepsilon_i = 0$), both the consumer's relative willingness-to-pay for one plan vs. another (w_i) as well as her true welfare (v_i) line up with the difference in certainty equivalents implied by U_{ij} and $U_{ij'}$.

Handel and Kolstad (2015b) depart from this baseline expected utility model by allowing for the consumer's beliefs (notated with "hats") to deviate from what they would be under full information and rational expectations:

$$\widehat{U_{ij}} = \int_0^\infty f_{ij}(s|\widehat{\psi_{i,j}}, \widehat{\mu_i}) u(W_i - P_{ij} + \widehat{\pi_{i,j}}(\widehat{\psi_{i,j}}, \widehat{\mu_i}) - s, \gamma_i) ds. \tag{4}$$

Here, beliefs about plan characteristics, health risk, and health benefits are modeled allowing for both population-level and individual-level departures from the rational-model values.

Empirically, this framework allows for departures from baseline beliefs and information due to information frictions or biases more broadly. These frictions and biases may result from (i) consumers not having easy access to key information; (ii) consumers not attending to readily available information; or (iii) consumers having difficulty integrating certain types of information into decisions. Handel and Kolstad consider data from a large firm with over 50,000 employees where employees choose between two plans: a broad network PPO plan with no premium and no (in network) cost sharing, and a high-deductible plan with the same network and a linked health savings account subsidy (essentially a reverse premium). The paper presents descriptive evidence showing that consumers seem to substantially under-purchase the high-deductible plan (HDHP) based on its financial value relative to the simpler PPO option. The standard non-behavioral explanation is that these purchasing patterns reflect consumer risk aversion—but the degree of risk aversion necessary to rationalize these choices is very high.

Given this backdrop, the authors implemented a comprehensive survey to measure consumer information sets shortly after they make plan choices during open enrollment. The survey asks multiple choice questions to consumers about all aspects of plan choice, including perceptions about the health savings account subsidy, provider networks, and financial characteristics such as deductibles or coinsurance. In addition, the survey asks about perceived hassle costs of enrolling in a high-deductible plan where medical bills and health savings accounts may involve time and hassle costs relative to the hassle-free PPO option. The survey is linked to enrollment and detailed claims data at the individual-level, allowing the authors to study how individual choices relate to limited information. The authors show that consumers who lack knowledge about the high-deductible plan relative to the PPO plan are more likely to leave substantial sums of money on the table in their plan choices. The key point is that this money left on the table is not due to risk aversion, but to frictions or biases that result in limited knowledge.

The primary structural model the authors estimate is a baseline expected utility model with shifters that reflect changes in willingness-to-pay for the high-deductible plan as a function of limited information about that plan (as measured in the survey). This is very similar to the theoretical model in Eq. (4) but incorporates measures of limited information in a specific way. The main specification is:

$$U_{ij} = \int_0^\infty f_{ij}(s) u_i(x_{ij}) ds \tag{5}$$

$$u_i(x) = -\frac{1}{\gamma_i(\mathbf{D}_i)} e^{-\gamma_i(\mathbf{D}_i)x} \tag{6}$$

$$x_{ij} = W_i - P_{ij} - s + \eta(\mathbf{D}_i)\mathbf{1}_{j_t = j_{t-1}} + \mathbf{Z}'_i \beta \mathbf{I}_{HDHP} + \epsilon_{ij}. \tag{7}$$

Here, U_{ij} is an expected utility function for a risk averse consumer, following the model just discussed. Eq. (6) describes the functional form used to implement the constant absolute risk aversion model. x_{ij} measures the outcome (translated into monetary units) for each consumer during the year, given a realization of their health uncertainty. η is a term that addresses consumer inertia, modeled as an implied switching cost. Risk aversion γ and inertia η both vary with observable demographics D_i.

The authors include indicator variables related to consumers' information sets in the vector $\mathbf{Z}$. For each question, they construct indicator variables for 'informed', 'uninformed' or 'not sure' answers as well as variables derived from answers to questions about hassle costs and knowledge of own health expenditures. $Z = 0$ indicates that a consumer is perfectly informed, while $Z = 1$ indicates that a consumer lacks information on a certain dimension. The coefficient β then measures the impact of that lack of information on willingness-to-pay for the high-deductible plan relative to the less complex PPO option.

This empirical approach to studying the impact of consumer frictions and biases has several advantages and disadvantages. One advantage is that measuring effective consumer information sets with surveys is often feasible. Another advantage is that the approach is simple, in the sense that the estimates tell us about the impact of survey-measured limited information on willingness-to-pay for different options. One disadvantage is that it doesn't posit a specific structural mechanism for how limited information impacts choices: a more structured version would allow for answers to survey questions to imply something specific about the precise nature of beliefs. But it is also difficult to link the responses directly to belief objects. This disadvantage makes it difficult to assess whether specific policy interventions to improve consumers' choices would be successful. Another potential disadvantage is that the baseline model used is a specific expected utility model that does not capture behavioral notions of how consumers respond to risk and uncertainty, which is an important topic.[4]

Handel and Kolstad (2015b) offer several results on the knowledge consumers lack and the resulting amount of money they leave on the table. The most influential gaps in knowledge are about available providers and treatments, and the perceived time and hassle costs for the high-deductible plan. For example, a consumer who incorrectly believes that the PPO option grants greater medical access than the high-deductible plan (they grant the same access in reality) is willing to pay $2267 more on average for the PPO over the one-year period of the insurance contract than a correctly informed consumer. Aggregating across all included measures for incomplete knowledge, the average consumer is willing to pay $1694 more for the PPO relative to a fully informed consumer with zero perceived hassle costs. Consumer perceptions of relative hassle costs, which likely overstate true hassle costs, have a major impact, equaling approximately $100 per perceived extra hour of time spent on plan hassle.[5]

Next, they find that including measures of consumer information into the model together with risk aversion significantly changes estimates of risk aversion. Framed in terms of a simple hypothetical gamble, a consumer with baseline model risk aversion (where information frictions are not taken into account) would be indifferent between taking on a gamble in which he gains $1000 with a 50 percent chance and loses $367 with a 50 percent chance. In other words, he would have to be paid a risk premium of roughly $633 in expectation to take this risky bet. In the primary model with survey variables included, the consumer is instead found to be indifferent between taking on a gamble with a $1000 gain and $913 loss (with 50% chance of each). This has meaningful implications for policy, for example altering conclusions of the benefits of forcing consumers into high-deductible plans.

2.1.3 Dominated choices and mechanisms behind mistakes in active choices: Bhargava et al. (2017)

Bhargava et al. (2017) also study mistakes in health insurance plan choice, but focus more on empirically identifying the mechanisms underlying those mistakes. They use data from a large firm with approximately 24,000 employees, where employees chose from a flexible menu with up to 48 different possible plans. For almost all employees, choosing the low deductible (most generous plan) is strictly financially dominated by another plan, meaning that for *any possible* level of total health expenditures (insurer

---

[4] While we are unaware of empirical papers studying non-standard consumer responses to risk and uncertainty in health insurance, Barseghyan et al. (2013) study non-linear probability weighting for consumers choosing car and property insurance policies and Grubb and Osborne (2015) study overconfidence and myopia in cellular phone markets. These projects structurally identify alternative choice models, but typically assume full consumer information to do so. It should be possible to combine the Handel and Kolstad (2015b) approach with these others.

[5] The authors consider different possible welfare interpretations of perceived time and hassle costs. Perceived costs are higher than stated costs, suggesting that some component of perceived time and hassle costs are not actually experienced by people once they enroll in the high-deductible plan.

+ insuree) during the year, the consumer is better off financially in that other plan.[6] Since the low deductible option is financially dominated, no consumer in a standard expected utility model should choose that option. The authors document that the majority of employees do in fact choose a financially dominated plan, losing on average $400 relative to choosing otherwise equivalent high-deductible options.

The authors conduct a series of lab experiments to study why the employees might be choosing dominated plans. They consider the following possibilities:

1. **Menu complexity:** The authors define menu complexity based on the number of plans in the choice set N and the number of attributes K that define each plan. As either N or K increases, the authors say that the menu becomes more complex.
2. **Alternative preferences:** The authors consider preferences that depart from the baseline expected utility model. Consumers may, for example, gain some extra value from not making an out-of-pocket payment. This could occur if consumers have (perceived) liquidity constraints, a desire for budget predictability, or just a distaste for making payments related to medical care.
3. **Insurance literacy:** If consumers have low insurance literacy, then they may have incorrect beliefs about plan costs. For example, if a consumer does not appropriately understand what an out-of-pocket maximum is, he may project that a plan has substantial tail-spending risk when it in fact does not. A good illustration of this possibility comes from evidence in Loewenstein et al. (2013), which presents results from surveys where consumers are (i) asked whether they think they understand key insurance concepts (e.g., deductibles, coinsurance, and the out-of-pocket maximum) and (ii) tested to see if they correctly work with these concepts in practice. The paper finds, e.g., that 93% of consumers claim to understand the out-of-pocket maximum while only 55% of those consumers actually pass a simple comprehension test for this feature (it shows analogous results for the deductible, coinsurance, and copays). In the Handel and Kolstad (2015b) notation, this kind of limited insurance literacy could, e.g., enter into mis-specified beliefs about out-of-pocket spending $f_{ij}(s|\widehat{\psi}_{ij}, \widehat{\mu}_i)$ resulting from a poor understanding of how insurance plan characteristics map to final payments.

In their first lab experiment, Bhargava et al. (2017) randomly give their online subjects menus with different levels of complexity that always include some dominated options. The authors find that even when they reduce plan menus from 12 plans and 2 attributes to 4 plans and 1 attribute, consumers continue to choose dominated plans at a similar rate, suggesting that menu complexity/size is not a primary reason for dominated-plan choices in this particular context.

Their second experiment exposed consumers to high and low clarity presentations. The low clarity presentation was similar to that faced by employees at the firm, while the high clarity presentation included additional information about the plan

---

[6] Typically, researchers discuss one plan as dominated by another only when networks of providers are also identical between the options, so that there is no standard rationale to choose the dominated option.

options that highlighted the financial consequences of those options. The fraction of consumers choosing dominated plans is substantially reduced but not eliminated under the high-clarity presentation—the fraction choosing dominated plans goes from 48% in the low-clarity presentation to 18% in the high-clarity presentation. This suggests that non-standard preferences play a relatively minor (though still potentially meaningful) role in consumers choosing dominated plans. Instead, explanation three, low insurance literacy, seems to be the primary driver of dominated-plan choices in their setting: when consumers receive substantial help translating plan menus into simple value propositions, they are much less likely to choose dominated plan options. The authors also elicit measures of insurance competence from study participants, and find that low insurance competence is correlated with choosing dominated plans.

2.1.4 Additional empirical evidence on mistakes in active choices

Both the Handel and Kolstad (2015b) and Bhargava et al. (2017) papers document mistakes in active insurance purchases. There are a number of complementary studies that provide evidence of similar mistakes. Abaluck and Gruber (2011) show that consumers forego substantial savings in Medicare Part D choices, controlling for spending risk, risk preferences, and average brand preferences. Medicare Part D is an especially interesting market to study from a behavioral economics standpoint because consumers have many options (typically around 40) and may not have the time, information, or knowledge to understand the subtleties of what differentiates these options from one another. In addition, Medicare Part D, which was introduced in 2006, was set up with an underlying premise that rational and well-informed consumers would choose effectively from these many options, delivering value to themselves and disciplining the market. If consumers do not choose effectively from the options in the market, the motivation for this style of insurance reform is called into question.

Abaluck and Gruber (2011) find that a key reason consumers lose money on their plan choices is that they overweight premiums by a factor of 5 to 1 relative to expected out-of-pocket spending. (This finding is consistent with results from more recent work, both in Medicare Part D and other health insurance markets.) Abaluck and Gruber (2011) model this bias with a modified expected utility model, similar in spirit to that described above from Handel and Kolstad (2015b), where the key modification is allowing the weight consumers place on premiums to differ from the weight they place on expected out-of-pocket spending. Further work is necessary to better understand the sources of this bias. Potential explanations include, but are not limited to, consumers having better information on premiums than other characteristics (premiums are known with certainty and are prominently posted); consumers having greater relative comprehension of what premiums mean; and consumers being overconfident that out-of-pocket spending will be low.

Heiss et al. (2010) also study consumer choice quality in Medicare Part D and find results that are consistent with those from Abaluck and Gruber (2011). They find that fewer than 10% of consumers enroll in a plan that is ex post optimal and that consumers on average lose roughly $300 per year in their plan choices. Ketcham et al. (2012) show similar patterns in Part D plan choices and also study whether consumers learn to make better choices over time. They find evidence of poor consumer choices but, leveraging panel data, find that consumers may make better choices over time as they gain experience in the market. Specifically, they find that consumer overspending is reduced, on average, by $298 in their second year in the Part D market relative to their first. Some of this may be due to plan switching and some to plans delivering better value over time.

2.1.5 Interventions to improve active choices

While there are several papers documenting how health-insurance consumers make mistakes in their active choices, there are fewer papers that study interventions to help consumers make better enrollment decisions. Ericson and Starc (2016) study consumer choice on the Massachusetts Health Insurance Exchange. The authors study a natural experiment where the exchange implemented meaningful product standardization reforms. Specifically, moving from one year to the next, the exchange significantly reduced the scope for plans to differ along many financial attributes (e.g., deductibles and coinsurance rates). The exchange complemented this change with a web design that helped consumers compare plans with the same financial attributes, though the plans could still differ on premiums and provider networks.

The authors model two channels by which product standardization impacts allocations: (i) the availability channel, whereby the products in the market change and (ii) the valuation channel, whereby consumers' decision weights attached to different plan attributes change. When standardization impacts the valuation channel, consumers' decision-utilities change, e.g., because consumers attend more to certain attributes. To complement their empirical analyses, the authors run an experiment to differentiate between impacts of product standardization itself and the improved presentation of the choice set via a new web design. The experiment finds that product standardization matters, but that the better presentation of the standardized options also improves choices conditional on the choice set.

Several other papers study interventions to help improve consumers' insurance choices, though there is still much to be done in this literature. Kling et al. (2012) studies a targeted intervention to seniors choosing in the Medicare Part D market. The authors run a randomized control trial where members of the treatment group get individually-tailored letters with key information about how they could switch Part D plans and save money in the process. This intervention increased plan switching, with those in the treatment group switching 28% of the time and those in the control group 17% of the time. Those in the treatment group had an average decline in spending of approximately $100.

Abaluck and Gruber (2016b) study the plan choices of Oregon school district employees and begin by showing that consumers leave substantial sums of money on the table in their plan choices, consistent with their findings on choices in Medicare Part D. The authors then study several interventions to help improve these choices. First, they study whether forcing some employees to make active choices substantially reduces their foregone savings. They identify the effect of active choice by comparing the choices of consumers whose prior plans were canceled to those of consumers whose plans were not canceled. They find little effect, presumably because consumers' active choices were privately suboptimal. Next, they study an information intervention that gave employees access to an individually-tailored online tool giving them help shopping for insurance plans. They also find that this intervention has essentially no impact on plan-choice quality, though they note some key issues with the implementation of the online tool that they study. Their third intervention, choice-set regulation by the school district, is effective in improving consumer welfare. This regulation removed the lower quality options from the choice set without removing too much match-specific value between insurers and consumers. We discuss this analysis in greater detail later in this chapter.

An important caveat to studies that investigate interventions to improve consumer choices in health-insurance markets (e.g. online tools or mailed letters) is that their results depend on the specific qualities and features of those interventions and are fairly context dependent. Without a robust literature that studies a range of carefully documented interventions it is difficult to derive general lessons on the potential for such interventions to improve consumer choices.

2.1.6 Mistakes in passive choices: inertia

While the papers we have discussed so far show that consumers have difficulty making active choices in insurance markets, there has been as much if not more empirical research on consumer inertia and the significant value consumers leave on the table in *passive choice settings*—where the default is that they will continue to be enrolled in their prior option if they make no new choice. Consumer inertia reduces the quality of consumer choices in such settings, as products evolve over time and consumers do not adjust accordingly.

Handel (2013) studies inertia using data from a large employer that spans six years (2004–2009). The employer changed the menu of options employees could choose from during the middle of this time frame and forced all employees to make active (non-default) choices from this new menu of options. Following that forced active choice, consumers had a default option of their previously chosen plan, despite the fact that the plan premiums and features changed significantly over time. The paper presents several pieces of descriptive evidence suggesting that inertia causes consumers to leave meaningful sums of money on the table. First, one product changed over time such that it became dominated by other options (similar to Bhargava et al., 2017) and, despite losing over a thousand dollars for sure, consumers continued to enroll in the newly dominated plan when it was their default option. Second, the active choices that new enrollees made were significantly better (in terms of money left on the table) than the choices of similar incumbent employees who had a default option. While active choices are far from perfect, choices become worse in an environment with a suboptimal default option.

The paper estimates a structural model of consumer inertia, modeled as a switching or adjustment cost that could result from consumers having research/paperwork costs of switching or learning costs of using a new plan. The expected utility framework is similar to that in Handel and Kolstad (2015b) as described in Eqs. (5)–(7). A simplified version of the Handel (2013) analog to Eq. (7), representing the money at stake for consumers for each health state, is:

$$x_{ij} = W_i - P_{ij} - s + \eta(\mathbf{X}_i)\mathbf{1}_{j_t=j_{t-1}} + \epsilon_{ij}. \tag{8}$$

Inertia is quantified by the amount of money consumers are willing to leave on the table to stick with their incumbent plan. In effect, the premium for the incumbent plan is lowered by η for consumers in this model. η is allowed to depend on observable characteristics, X, including other benefits choices consumers make (such as flexible spending account choices that must be actively made every year). Inertia in this environment (and most health insurance environments) could result from any of the following micro-foundations:

1. **Switching costs:** Consumers could incur paperwork or hassle costs of switching plans. Consumers may also incur adjustment costs of learning how to use their new plan, or costs associated with needing to switch care providers. While this last cost (of switching providers) is not an issue in the Handel (2013) analysis, such costs will be relevant in many settings.
2. **Search costs:** Consumers could incur costs of searching through the different available plan options to determine if they want to switch. Typically, this would be modeled as a two stage model (as in Ho et al., 2017 described below) where consumers first decide whether to search and then decide whether to switch after searching.
3. **Inattention:** Consumers could be inattentive. They could rationally decide not to engage in the search process because search is too costly relative to expected benefits. Or they could less rationally neglect potential benefits of carefully considering plans and plan options.
4. **Naive present bias:** Consumers could believe that they will conduct research and make a new choice right before the choice deadline, but then when the time arrives not be willing or able to invest the time and effort to do so.

Handel (2013) does not distinguish between these micro-foundations, but shows how welfare conclusions are sensitive to the micro-foundation. In particular, his welfare analysis allows for a range of results that depend on whether or not inertia primarily results from a rational response to costs (e.g., of search) or a less rational response to perceived benefits and/or perceived costs.[7]

The paper finds that consumers exhibit significant inertia: on average, consumers with a default option are estimated to leave $2032 on the table annually to stay with

---

[7] The welfare analysis presumes the same normative standard for a consumer's "true" plan valuation discussed earlier in this chapter, i.e., the valuation of a rational and frictionless consumer with no biases at the time of choice. The welfare costs of inertia are added on top of this framework: the author investigates a range of assumptions spanning from the case where estimated costs are all welfare-relevant when incurred to the case where estimated switching costs are not at all welfare relevant.

their default. Consumers who also make active flexible spending account elections leave an average of \$551 less on the table.[8] Families, who have more money at stake, leave \$751 more on the table than single employees. There is no evidence that recent health shocks lead to active choices. The paper studies counterfactual policies where the extent of inertia is reduced by some proportion and consumers re-choose plans in the market. In the partial equilibrium analysis where plan prices do not adjust from re-sorting, a 75% reduction in the magnitude of inertia improves consumer welfare by 5.2% of paid premiums. Later in this section, when we discuss the market implications of poor choices, we will discuss the case where prices are allowed to re-adjust as consumers make better choices due to reduced inertia.

A range of other papers study inertia in health insurance markets and show that it causes meaningful financial losses for consumers. Ho et al. (2017) study inertia in Medicare Part D with a model of inattention. They model consumers with a default option making choices in two stages. First, they decide whether or not to engage with the market. This decision is influenced by a series of shocks (e.g., changes to the premium of their current plan) related to the market and their default option. Second, consumers who decide to engage in the market choose a plan following a standard active discrete choice model, where consumer i's utility for option j is denoted by $u_{i,j}$.

As the market evolves over time, consumers costlessly learn about how their current plan changes but have to pay a cost ψ to learn about how the characteristics of other plans change. Consumers choose to pay this cost if the expected benefit of doing so outweighs the cost:

$$\mathbb{E}\left[\max_{j=1,\dots,J} u_{i,j,t+1} | \bar{X}_{i,k,t+1}\right] - u_{i,k,t+1} > \psi_{i,t}.$$

Here, plan k is the one a consumer is currently enrolled in and $\bar{X}_{i,k,t+1}$ includes the known characteristics for that plan. The expectation is taken over the characteristics of other plans that the consumer discovers if she pays the cost to search through the set of available plans. If the consumer pays the cost to search then she learns the characteristics of all plans in the market. The consumer is more likely to search if (i) she has a health shock that changes the value she receives from different plans; (ii) the characteristics of her current plan change; and/or (iii) she receives a signal that the market significantly evolved to make search valuable.

Empirically, the authors estimate this model without fully specifying consumers' beliefs about other options in the market prior to search. They model consumer attention as being a function of whether consumers experience shocks (v) that cause them to pay attention:

$$v_{i,t} = v_{i,p,t}\beta_1 + v_{i,c,t}\beta_2 + v_{i,h,t}\beta_3 + v_{i,e,t}.$$

---

[8] Consumers who elect to make a flexible spending account (FSA) contribution must do so actively each year—they cannot default into their previous year's contribution. As a result, when a consumer elects to contribute to an FSA, she is making an active-benefits decision.

Here, v_p equals 1 if there is a premium increase for a consumer's own plan that exceeds the median weighted increase in the market; v_c equals 1 if there is a meaningful change to the out-of-pocket coverage characteristics for a consumer's own plan; v_h equals 1 if the consumer experienced an acute health shock in the past year, e.g., a significant increase in drug spending; and v_e is a random shock that spurs consumer search. With this framework, a consumer searches if her composite shock v is greater than some threshold value (related to $\psi_{i,t}$ above). Then, if the consumer searches, she picks the plan that maximizes her expected utility, with full updated knowledge of all plan characteristics. If the consumer does not search then she remains in the plan that she is already enrolled in.

Ho et al. (2017) find substantial inertia in the Medicare Part D context: only approximately 10% of consumers switch plans each year and leave a lot of money on the table by not switching. Consistent with the model of inattention, consumers are more likely to switch when their own plan features (e.g., premium or cost-sharing) change but are less likely to search when alternative plan features change by similar amounts. The paper then studies how insurers price given the degree of inertia in the market, which we discuss later in this section. It is interesting to note that Handel (2013) and Ho et al. (2017) use similar data and identification strategies to study inertia, but assume different micro-foundations. Future work that empirically distinguishes between mechanisms for inertia will be valuable in this literature (Handel and Schwartzstein, 2018).

A range of other papers also document inertia in Medicare Part D. These papers include Ericson (2014), Polyakova (2016), Heiss et al. (2016), and Abaluck and Gruber (2016a), with each approaching the inertia question from a distinct angle. In addition, Abaluck and Gruber (2016a) find limited evidence that consumers learn to shop effectively for plans over time, contrary to the findings in Ketcham et al. (2012). Finally, in the large employer and Medicaid managed care contexts, respectively, Strombom et al. (2002) and Marton et al. (2015) both show significant value left on the table due to consumer inertia.

Research on inertia in health-insurance choices is also consistent with powerful default effects in other domains. See, e.g., Beshears et al. (2018) for examples in household finance.

2.2 Implications for insurance markets and their regulation

The literature on consumer choice in insurance markets shows several patterns. First, consumers often leave meaningful sums of money on the table when making active insurance choices. While some of this may reflect search or other welfare-relevant costs, the magnitudes involved make it likely that many consumers are making mistakes. Second, inertia causes consumers to leave even more on the table when their previously chosen option is the default. These patterns have important implications for the industrial organization of health insurance markets and, more broadly, the regulation of health-insurance markets.

2.2.1 Welfare revisited

One key theme in the Handel et al. (2015) paper, and others in both the behavioral health and broader empirical behavioral economics literature, is the subtlety involved in measuring welfare in markets where consumers make mistakes (see, e.g., Bernheim and Rangel, 2009 for an extended treatment). The Handel et al. (2015) framework models true consumer welfare as the *ex ante* value that a consumer without behavioral biases and choice frictions would derive from a given insurance plan, while demand reflects *ex ante* willingness-to-pay. Drawing a distinction between demand and welfare is crucial in policy analyses in markets with behavioral consumers: Handel and Kolstad (2015b), Abaluck and Gruber (2016b), Abaluck and Gruber (2016a), and Handel (2013) all differentiate between demand and welfare; Baicker et al. (2015) (which we discuss in the next section) uses a similar framework to analyze consumer demand for health care. Crucially, if researchers don't distinguish between demand and welfare, they are implicitly assuming that consumers choose the options that make them best off, contradicting much of the empirical evidence in this literature.[9]

Fig. 1 illustrates a simple and common case where the distinction between demand and welfare is crucial. The figure considers a population of consumers choosing between a comprehensive and basic insurance option. The demand curve reflects the incremental willingness-to-pay between the comprehensive and basic options, and the welfare curve reflects the incremental consumer value. Quantity reflects the proportion of consumers in the market purchasing comprehensive coverage. All other consumers are assumed to choose the basic option, e.g., because of a fully-enforced individual mandate that rules out being uninsured. The welfare curve is drawn conditional on demand, in the sense that it presents the welfare for consumers at that quantity point of the demand curve. To keep things simple, we assume that marginal cost is constant across all consumers. This could reflect the case of perfect risk adjustment, for example, where insurers receive transfers for enrolling sick consumers and pay transfers for enrolling healthy consumers. In this framework, which follows that in Einav et al. (2010) and Handel et al. (2015), the welfare curve reflects the benefit consumers gain from incremental insurance, and the marginal cost curve reflects the social cost of that incremental insurance.

Competitive equilibrium occurs in the market where demand crosses the average cost curve (which here is the same as the marginal cost curve because it is flat). In the Einav et al. (2010) approach, also applied empirically, e.g., by Hackmann et al. (2015), the competitive equilibrium point in this picture is the welfare-maximizing point. This is because demand is assumed to be the same as welfare. However, if consumers have frictions or biases that drive a wedge between demand and welfare, the competitive equilibrium is no longer the welfare-maximizing point. Instead, the

---

[9] See Bernheim and Taubinsky (2018) for an extended discussion of related empirical work in public finance and see that chapter, along with an article by Handel and Schwartzstein (2018), for more in-depth discussions of the theoretical and empirical assumptions typically made within such frameworks.

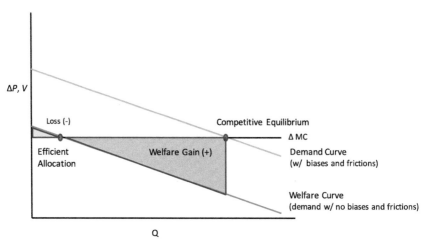

FIGURE 1

This figure portrays outcomes in an insurance market with two types of plans: comprehensive and basic. Demand, true welfare, and marginal cost are portrayed for comprehensive relative to basic coverage. The figure shows the welfare impact of a policy that eliminates the possibility of choosing comprehensive coverage. The policy would be welfare reducing if demand was taken to reflect welfare.

welfare-maximizing point is the point labeled as the efficient allocation, where the welfare curve crosses the marginal cost curve. The graph illustrates a case where consumers in the population over-demand comprehensive insurance, so they have a willingness-to-pay higher than true welfare for such coverage. This is similar to the empirical case described earlier in Handel and Kolstad (2015b).

With this framework in mind, think about a policymaker who is deciding whether or not to implement a policy that removes comprehensive coverage from the market entirely. This is similar, e.g., to a firm requiring employees to enroll in high-deductible insurance, or a regulator removing the most comprehensive options from a market such as an ACA exchange or the Medicare Part D drug insurance market. Without modeling the wedge between welfare and demand, this policy will be seen as strictly welfare reducing. However, with the separate modeling of demand and welfare, this policy now has the welfare effect shown in the picture, which depicts the case where the welfare gains for consumers are bigger than the welfare losses. Consumers who had erroneously been over-purchasing comprehensive coverage are now enrolled in the more preferable option, while only a small portion of consumers who would have been better off in comprehensive coverage experience welfare losses.

This simple example illustrates potential policy implications of modeling welfare separately from demand in environments with behavioral consumers. This is true in more realistic and complex settings where other issues, such as adverse selection, are a concern.

2.2.2 Consumer mistakes and adverse selection

Consumers' mistakes are bad for them given a specific market structure. However, empirical research has shown that in insurance markets where adverse selection is a prime concern, improving choices may ultimately make consumers worse off. This presents a challenge for policymakers considering avenues to improve consumers' decisions.

Adverse selection is an important potential inefficiency that arises in insurance markets where the costs to the insurer depend on who is insured. When sicker consumers choose more comprehensive insurance coverage, the premiums for those plans increase to reflect greater costs to the insurer. As a result, healthier consumers, who could prefer plans with greater network coverage or risk protection, may be priced out of the market.

Handel (2013) studies the interaction between inertia and adverse selection using a counterfactual analysis where, as consumer inertia is reduced, consumers pick different insurance plans and the prices of those plans adjust as a result. When inertia is reduced by 75% of its baseline estimate, the premiums for comprehensive coverage increase sharply as healthy people who had been choosing that coverage and losing value shift to less generous coverage. This leads to a death spiral, where the comprehensive plan essentially disappears from the market with an extremely high premium, and consumers who want higher coverage are forced into lower-coverage options. Quantitatively, reduced inertia leads to a 7.7% unintended welfare *reduction* in this environment: helping consumers make better choices is bad for the sample overall.

Polyakova (2016) studies a similar question in Medicare Part D, but emphasizes that whether reduced inertia will be good or bad for consumers depends on how initial prices in the market are set. This paper shows that in Part D, where initial prices for comprehensive coverage are relatively far away from those for less generous coverage, reduced inertia actually helps the prices of more comprehensive coverage adjust downward over time (under the assumption that insurers use lagged average cost pricing). This is because initial prices were set further apart than steady-state equilibrium prices, so reduced inertia, which helps prices move more quickly towards the steady-state equilibrium, reduces the price gap. Thus, in the Part D environment, reduced inertia may both help consumers conditional on the market environment and, by lowering the price of comprehensive coverage in the market, reduce adverse selection.

Handel et al. (2015) provide a general framework for studying when improved choices exacerbate adverse selection. They use the simple model given at the beginning of this insurance section to analyze a population of consumers that are heterogeneous across many dimensions: costs, willingness-to-pay, true value, and choice frictions driving a wedge between willingness-to-pay and true value. The authors derive several theoretical results for competitive insurance markets where consumers make active choices. They show that, as both the mean and variance of consumer surplus rise relative to the mean and variance of costs, improving consumer choices is more likely to be beneficial. This is because the feedback loop between costs and premiums generating adverse selection becomes dominated by improved matching of consumers to the plans they value the most. For example, if heterogeneous consumer values for insurance as a tool for risk protection are relatively large and varied, then improved decision-making facilitates large improvements to welfare through better matching. If these values are not strongly correlated with costs, then there will be limited incremental selection but substantial gains from better choices. The converse is also true: as the mean and variance of costs become more important contributors to insurance value relative to surplus from risk protection, helping consumers make better decisions is worse for the market: these improved decisions cause additional adverse selection which dominates the benefit from better matching. The authors illustrate the interactions between these key objects with simulations as well as an empirical application based on Handel and Kolstad (2015b).

In addition to studying the pricing impacts of improved choices in competitive markets with adverse selection, several papers study how firms price in markets with inertial consumers. Ericson (2014) documents the invest-then-harvest pricing patterns in Medicare Part D, finding that firms initially set prices low in order to attract consumers and then raise prices to take advantage of consumers' inertia. Ho et al. (2017) also study dynamic firm pricing to inertial consumers in Medicare Part D, with a model of imperfect competition. The authors find that premiums would be meaningfully reduced if inertia were removed entirely, and that the government could save approximately 550 million dollars each year in the process since they provide substantial subsidies for plan purchases. But, overall, there has been quite limited work studying how firms price to behavioral consumers in health-insurance and health-care markets. See Heidhaus and Kőszegi (2018) for a broader discussion of behavioral industrial organization and some of the approaches that could be applied to studying related questions in health-care markets.

2.2.3 Paternalistic interventions

There are also important regulatory questions that directly relate to consumer-choice mistakes. Abaluck and Gruber (2016a) study whether including more options in the consumers' choice sets is good or bad. This is similar in spirit to the work of Bhargava et al. (2017) mentioned earlier, but studies a specific empirical environment to model and identify a tradeoff between improved consumer-plan matches from greater choice and increased consumer-choice errors from having more options. The authors leverage a unique data set from Oregon school district employees where each district had the opportunity to offer any combination of 13 approved plans to consumers. Thus, the overall set of plans each district could offer was fixed, but each district could curate its own set of options. As a result, both cross-sectionally and over time, the authors observe similar consumers with a number of choices ranging from 1 to 13, drawn from the same overall set of plans.

Abaluck and Gruber (2016a) find in their environment that a greater number of plans is associated with worse outcomes for consumers. Using the average consumer's empirical decision function, choosing from sets with 7–8 plans leads to about $400–$500 more in total costs than choosing from sets with 2–3 plans. A meaningful proportion of the higher foregone savings in the larger choice sets is due to the incremental options being worse on average than those included in the choice sets with 2–3 plans. Inertia raises consumers' foregone savings by approximately $85 on average. Moreover, consumers are estimated to be quite insensitive to reducing their out-of-pocket costs. This leads to estimates of minimal consumer plan matching benefits (on average $30) from offering 7–8 plans relative to 2–3 plans.

This result calls into question the managed competition paradigm underlying many health insurance markets. As we mention above, such markets allow many plans to enter and compete with one another, with the idea being that more plans mean greater value for consumers in terms of matching and premium competition. If instead more options confuse consumers, and allow firms to prey on them, regulators may want to curate these markets closely and serve as intermediaries between plans and consumers.[10]

A related topic that researchers should investigate is the extent to which targeted (or "smart") default options can help or hurt consumers. Handel and Kolstad (2015a) propose a targeted default policy and analyze the tradeoffs involved in some simulations. Targeted defaults give consumers a default option that is best matched for them, determined by an algorithm implemented by a regulator or market designer. These defaults can be tailored based on a consumer's health risk, risk preference, and preference for providers. The ability to target defaults precisely depends on the extent of data available to the regulator and her ability to use those data in forming defaults. Defaults can be implemented with different levels of aggressiveness: a very aggressive default policy would default consumers into a new plan if it improved their expected value by a little bit, without exposing them to more risk or changing their key providers. A less aggressive policy would require a large gain in expected value to change their plan. As defaults become more aggressive, the expected gain for the population overall is likely to increase, but the number of consumers who lose because of the policy also increases. There is currently no empirical work that we are aware of that investigates smart default policies in health-insurance markets. One interesting issue that arises is how an effective smart default policy interacts with a competitive market paradigm. On the one hand, effective smart defaults allow the market to function as advocates of managed competition intend, with many consumers choosing the best plans for them and competition creating value. On the other hand, if a regulator's algorithm is driving this competition, it calls into question whether or not insurers can game this algorithm, and whether a heavily regulated market with few options chosen by the regulator is preferable.

In Section 4 we discuss promising avenues for future behavioral research on health-insurance markets.

---

[10] Certain ACA state exchanges, such as, e.g., Massachusetts and California, use this kind of model to offer more curated options.

3 Treatment choices

Behavioral insights change how we think about health treatment choices by patients. As noted earlier, while there is an active role for physicians in what gets prescribed and why, our focus will be on consumer-driven decisions like whether to fill a prescription given the cost of doing so. In the standard model, the concern is that people will seek too much care relative to the cost of treatment because treatment is subsidized by insurance. According to this model, the inefficiency generated by insurance—the moral hazard cost of insurance—is analogous to the deadweight loss generated by below marginal cost pricing. We know from deadweight loss calculus that this inefficiency is greater when the elasticity of demand for treatment is higher: moral hazard requires that patients have heterogeneous responses to treatment and that they know these responses better than the insurer. The higher the price elasticity, the greater this heterogeneity and the more low (utility) value care is encouraged when prices are reduced.

But evidence and behavioral principles suggest that systematic biases influence treatment choices. Misutilization is not just driven by insurance, but also by mistakes. Underutilization is a concern in addition to overutilization. The inefficiency generated by the combination of biases and insurance cannot be determined only by examining the demand curve. In fact, as we will spell out below, a greater elasticity of demand for treatment may signal a greater *benefit* of expanding insurance coverage, for example if underuse is the big concern and the large price sensitivity suggests that reducing prices will in fact mitigate underuse. To really tell, we need to examine health impacts of treatments — we cannot assume the demand curve tells us everything we need to know about these impacts. Likewise, taking a step back, people may not be sophisticated enough about their own biases to demand insurance contracts that successfully counteract those biases. This means that there is room for behaviorally-minded policy interventions that improve the efficiency of insurees' treatment choices beyond what we see under equilibrium insurance contracts.

3.1 Consumer demand for treatment

In the standard neo-classical model, a person decides whether to treat—fill a prescription, take a pill, get a procedure, etc.—by trading off the benefit b of treatment against the price p. In insurance contexts, this price reflects copays, coinsurance rates, or deductibles. In other contexts, this may reflect a market price. Treatment benefits are net of non-pecuniary costs, such as side effects, and as such are not restricted to be positive. In this model, a person treats whenever $b > p$ and does not treat whenever $b < p$. This model says that if a person chooses not to treat at a given price he must value treatment at less than the price.

Evidence on actual treatment choices challenges this perspective. While we will note caveats in describing some of the evidence below, in many situations people seem not to treat when benefits likely exceed the price; in others people seek treatments that are very unlikely to help. Treatment choices are also sensitive to nudges and respond in inconsistent ways to different price levers. In short, rather than choosing to treat according to whether $b > p$, people seem to treat according to whether

$$b + \varepsilon > p, \tag{9}$$

where, as described below, ε is viewed as varying systematically as a function of disease, treatment, prices, and nudges. In Eq. (9), ε captures misbehavior due to mistakes or "behavioral hazard" (Baicker et al., 2015). When $\varepsilon > 0$ behavioral hazard increases people's tendency to treat (e.g., in seeking ineffective treatment for back pain) and when $\varepsilon < 0$ behavioral hazard reduces people's tendency to treat (e.g., in not adhering to effective diabetes treatment). Behavioral hazard can reflect misunderstandings of price levers, such as non-linear schedules. It may also differ across individuals.

This framework—which builds on Mullainathan et al. (2012)—nests behavioral models where people misbehave because of mistakes, capturing a divide between preference as revealed by choice and utility as it is experienced, or between "decision utility" and "experienced utility" (Kahneman et al., 1997).[11] While $b - p$ affects the experienced utility of taking the pill or treatment, individuals instead choose as if $b + \varepsilon - p$ affects this utility. For example, Baicker et al. (2015) show how it nests models of present-bias, inattention, and false beliefs. Viewing ε, e.g., as a function of p, it also nests models where people misreact to price levers.[12]

3.1.1 Over and underutilization

Behavioral first principles suggest many reasons why people are likely to misbehave in health treatment decisions. The benefits of care are often in the distant future while the costs appear now, so present bias (Laibson, 1997; O'Donoghue and Rabin, 1999) is likely important (Newhouse, 2006). Symptoms of many conditions like elevated glucose levels for diabetics are not salient, so inattention—modeled in economics by, e.g., DellaVigna (2009), Bordalo et al. (2012, 2013), Kőszegi and Szeidl (2013), Schwartzstein (2014), Gabaix (2014)—often matters (Osterberg and Blaschke, 2005). Given the complicated nature of many decisions and the scope for bad theories in this context to persist (Eyster and Rabin, 2014; Gagnon-Bartsch et al., 2017), false beliefs likely play an important role (Pauly and Blavin, 2008).

A variety of evidence also points to such misbehavior—systematically non-zero wedges, ε, between willingness to pay and true consumer value/welfare—but the interpretation of that evidence is non-trivial. To see the potential difficulty, index patients by $i \in \mathcal{I}$ and de-compose the benefit of treatment for patient i as $b_i = v_i(h_i)$. Here, h_i is the net (of side effects) clinical benefit of treatment for patient i and v_i represents how much patient i cares about that benefit. The marginal clinical benefit

---

[11] Gabaix and Farhi (2017) develop a more general framework that nests previous contributions.

[12] Note that non-standard preferences, for example where anticipation and anxiety are important contributors to utility (Kőszegi, 2003), influence choices through their impact on how people view benefits b—they do not necessarily lead to mistakes.

of treatment at price p is then $\mathbb{E}[h_i|b_i + \varepsilon_i = p]$, while the marginal private benefit (true value/consumer welfare) is $\mathbb{E}[v_i(h_i)|b_i + \varepsilon_i = p]$.[13] To identify the marginal amount of behavioral hazard (which determines whether mistakes are driving over- or underuse at the margin), we need to know the marginal private benefit since $\mathbb{E}[\varepsilon_i|b_i + \varepsilon_i = p]$ equals the difference between willingness-to-pay, p, and the marginal private benefit of treatment. As discussed above, this wedge may be non-zero as the result of any number of biases. But, at best, we typically only have a good sense of the demand curve and the marginal clinical benefit of treatment.

As an illustration of how this could create problems in identifying over- or underuse due to behavioral hazard, consider panel A of Fig. 2. In this figure, the demand curve and marginal clinical benefit are sloped in opposite directions. This could occur, for example, if the salience of symptoms (e.g., pain) drives treatment decisions, but clinical treatment benefits tend to be higher when patients are asymptomatic (perhaps because patients are asymptomatic earlier in a disease progression when clinical treatment benefits are the highest). We'd be tempted to say that the marginal patient when prices are high is making a mistake by seeking treatment and the marginal patient when prices are low is making a mistake by not seeking treatment. But perhaps $v_i(h_i)$ is such that, while the patient does mis-react to symptoms, she in fact experiences the greatest utility benefit from treatment when symptoms are salient and the lowest when symptoms are not salient.

Despite such difficulties, there is highly suggestive evidence of under- and overuse due to behavioral hazard, even if there is no empirical proof. Panels B and C in Fig. 2 depict the sorts of situations we have in mind. These panels show situations where the demand and marginal clinical benefit curves are known with confidence, while the marginal private benefit curves are unknown (hence the dotted curves in the panels) but believed not to deviate much from the marginal clinical benefit curves. For example, the private benefits of pills treating chronic conditions with few side effects likely line up closely with monetized clinical benefits. In these cases, despite not knowing the precise marginal private benefit curve, we're fairly confident that conclusions derived from equating this curve with the marginal clinical benefit aren't too misleading.

Much of the evidence on underutilization ($\varepsilon < 0$) comes from (lack of) adherence to prescribed drugs, where the marginal clinical benefit seems to lie above the prices patients face. Panel B of Fig. 2 pictures the situation we have in mind. In the case of diabetes, for example, adherence to glucose-controlling drugs is only between 60 and 80% (Rubin, 2005), despite severe health consequences of unmanaged diabetes. One study showed that almost half of diabetic patients did not have their prescriptions

---

[13] In empirical work, h_i could reflect clinical benefits either gross or net of side effects. For practical purposes, if h_i is gross of side effects (i.e. does not include them) then the dis-utility from those side effects is included in the wedge between the measured marginal clinical benefit and the marginal private benefit. Other factors that could be a part of the wedge between marginal clinical benefit and marginal private benefit include patients' intrinsic values for health versus money and patient satisfaction (or lack thereof) from receiving medical care.

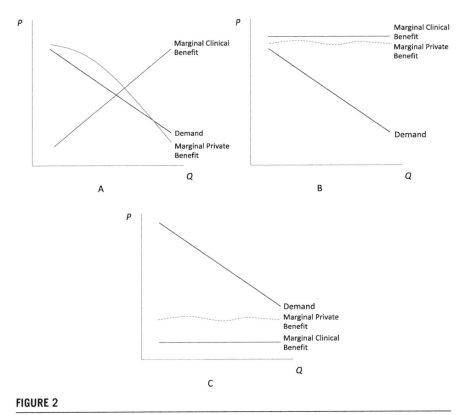

FIGURE 2

The relationship between the demand for treatment and the marginal private/clinical benefit of treatment.

filled consistently, despite consistent filling cutting the risk of hospitalization in half (Sokol et al., 2005).[14]

   There are also examples of overuse that are hard to reconcile with the standard model, suggesting positive behavioral hazard ($\varepsilon > 0$). Panel C of Fig. 2 pictures a situation where we'd be confident of overuse driven by mistakes. While we know of no perfect empirical examples, consider (over)treatment of back pain. Back pain is widespread and expensive: it is a leading symptomatic cause of physician visits and cost more than $25 billion in 1998 (Deyo et al., 1992, 2006; Strine and Hootman, 2007; Luo et al., 2004). Doctors prescribe screenings (e.g., fMRIs) and treatments despite evidence suggesting they are ineffective (Di Iorio et al., 2000; Jarvik et al., 2003; Lehnert and Bree, 2010; Chou et al., 2009; Sheehan, 2010). The treatment of prostate

---

[14] Beyond prescription drug non-adherence, patients do not receive recommended care across a wide range of categories, including recommended preventive care (e.g., colonoscopies) and follow-up care (e.g., for asthma management) (McGlynn et al., 2003; Denberg et al., 2005; Ness et al., 2000).

cancer is another potential example. The disease is rarely fatal and the cancers grow slowly, so the five-year survival rate for those diagnosed is 99.4% (Howlader et al., 2012). Perlroth et al. (2010) show that while "watchful waiting" is as effective as more expensive clinical treatments, a large portion of prostate cancer patients pursue these more aggressive options that expose them to risk and don't improve their prognosis.

These documented behaviors (particularly of underuse) likely reflect misutilization due to behavioral hazard. First, the magnitudes involved often make the case for unobservable factors less plausible. As an example, reducing copayments from fairly low levels even after an event as salient as a heart attack still produce improvements in adherence: providing medications to prevent future heart attacks for free (instead of at roughly a $10–$25 copayment) increased adherence by about 5 percentage points (relative to a base of 35–50 percent), and this increase was associated with a reduced rate of subsequent major vascular events (Choudhry et al., 2011).

Second, while there is plenty of evidence of heterogeneous treatment benefits, there is less evidence that people self sort in the manner we'd expect under a model where willingness to pay is increasing in treatment benefits. For example, Goldman et al. (2006) look at the impact of a small ($10) increase in copayments for cholesterol-lowering medications. They find that it drives similar reductions in use of those medications among those with high risk (and thus high health benefits) as those with much lower risk. One possibility is that willingness-to-pay does not increase with treatment benefits because some unobserved factor (let's call it "sick tolerance") tends to correlate with willingness-to-pay and treatment benefits, making the marginal private benefit curve look quite different from the marginal clinical benefit curve. But it strikes us that a more natural hypothesis is that some people are making mistakes.

How consumers respond to the structure of health incentives further builds the case that the demand for treatment is richer than predicted by the standard model.

3.1.2 Inconsistent responses to price levers

The degree of behavioral hazard is not only a function of the disease and treatment. Evidence suggests that insurees respond in inconsistent ways (from the perspective of a neo-classical model) to different price levers: ε is influenced by levers that make up the price p.

Insurees appear to overreact to "spot prices" (out-of-pocket expenses tied to care) relative to expected end-of-year prices (how care influences out-of-pocket expenses over the course of the insurance cycle). Suppose the deductible is $X and there is no cost sharing beyond the deductible. Also, suppose (for sake of example) that the insuree will for sure exhaust the deductible by the end of the year. Then, no matter what, the insuree will pay $X on care over the course of the year. The evidence says, however, that the insuree is more reluctant to seek care towards the beginning of the year when he has not yet exhausted the deductible than towards the end when he has (Einav et al., 2015; Dalton et al., 2015; Abaluck et al., 2015; Aron-Dine et al., 2015;

Brot-Goldberg et al., 2017). It is as if he does not recognize that $X is in expectation a sunk cost.[15]

Such differential reactions imply that the shape of a non-linear insurance schedule influences how much care insurees consume, fixing how much care a fully rational insuree would consume under different plans. For example, in high-deductible health plans spot prices decrease over the course of an insurance cycle, so such plans reduce spending by more when insurees overreact to spot prices. This spending reduction may have adverse and undesirable consequences for health, as discussed below.

Reactions to price levers may interact with levers that influence insurees' understanding of health insurance, as insurees seem to lack a basic understanding of many plan features (e.g., Loewenstein et al., 2013).

3.1.3 Nudge responses

Evidence also suggests that insurees respond to nudges (Thaler and Sunstein, 2009). Following Mullainathan et al. (2012), we conceptualize nudges as levers that would not influence consumer demand in the neo-classical model: nudges n influence decisions through impacting ε but not b or p. There is ample evidence that interventions targeting patient communication (not just by influencing what information is conveyed but also how it is conveyed) can produce substantial changes in adherence (e.g., Cutrona et al., 2010), as can text message reminders or simplifications of dosage schedules (Schedlbauer et al., 2010; Schroeder et al., 2004; Strandbygaard et al., 2010; Long et al., 2012; Lafeber et al., 2017; Patel et al., 2015).[16]

But which combination of nudges work to improve treatment outcomes (and when) is a complex and open question. The REMIND trial—a large-scale randomized trial evaluating the adherence effects of low-cost medication reminder devices, including a digital timer cap and a pill-bottle strip with toggles—did not find improvements in adherence (Choudhry et al., 2017). The HeartStrong intervention, which involved a mix of nudge and non-nudge interventions such as providing electronic pill bottles, lottery financial incentives, and social support for survivors of acute myocardial infarction, also did not boost adherence (Volpp et al., 2017). Right now, it seems that the most reliable lever that influences outcomes is a traditional one: prices. We next take up the question of how behavioral economics influences how we think about basic health-insurance tradeoffs involving prices.

---

[15] Explanations for the overreaction to spot prices include myopia (Dalton et al., 2015), "schmeduling" (Liebman and Zeckhauser, 2004), limited information (Handel and Kolstad, 2015b), and liquidity constraints. There are contexts where the last explanation is unlikely to be at play because consumers overreact to spot prices even when they are relatively well off and have easy access to credit (Brot-Goldberg et al., 2017). Interestingly, insurees appear even more responsive to copays than out-of-pocket-equivalent deductibles (Stockley, 2016).

[16] There are also nudges that effectively increase preventive care like vaccinations. Milkman et al. (2011), for example, find that a "planning prompt" that encouraged adults to plan a date and time to get a flu shot boosted the number of adults who obtained a flu shot by 4.2 percentage points. The nudge perhaps operated by reducing forgetfulness. Chapman et al. (2010) find that automatically scheduling individuals for vaccination appointments (which they could opt out of) likewise increased vaccination rates.

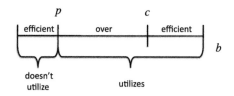

FIGURE 3

Model with only moral hazard. This figure previously appeared in Baicker, Katherine, Mullainathan, Sendhil, Schwartzstein, Joshua, 2015. Behavioral hazard in health insurance. The Quarterly Journal of Economics 130 (4), 1623–1667. It is reprinted here by permission of Oxford University Press and the authors.

Source: Baicker et al. (2015).

3.2 Re-thinking basic health insurance tradeoffs

The neo-classical model identifies a fundamental moral hazard tradeoff: lowering the price of care increases insurance value but leads to overutilization (Arrow, 1963; Pauly, 1968; Zeckhauser, 1970; Cutler and Zeckhauser, 2000). To illustrate, suppose a person may get a headache of severity s, where s is drawn from some distribution and is private information. Treatment provides benefit $b(s)$ ($b'(\cdot) > 0$) and costs society c. It is socially efficient for the person to get treated only if the headache is sufficiently severe that $b(s)$ exceeds c. But providing insurance means that the price for treatment, which for simplicity we will equate with a copay in this section, is below cost, $p < c$. So if a person is rationally deciding whether to get treated then he seeks treatment whenever $b(s) > p$, generating situations where the person chooses to treat headaches (e.g., by going to the doctor) in situations where it is socially inefficient for him to do so.

More generally, suppose as in Fig. 3 that treatment benefits b are distributed on a line, where sometimes benefits exceed and other times fall below the social cost of treatment c. Then whenever the treatment is insured ($p < c$) there is overuse in the region where benefits exceed copays but fall below costs ($b \in (p, c)$). According to the moral hazard model, overutilization is the big concern—and overutilization is created by insurance.

3.2.1 Re-interpreting the benefits of health insurance

Behavioral hazard modifies this analysis. Misutilization is not only driven by insurance, but also by mistakes. As discussed above, underutilization—not just overutilization—is a concern. When behavioral hazard is negative ($\varepsilon < 0$), for example, a person inefficiently fails to get treated when $b > c$ but $b + \varepsilon < p$.

In natural cases, then, behavioral hazard reverses the risk-protection/moral hazard tradeoff. Fig. 4 compares the welfare impact of reducing the copay (price) from $p = c$ to 0 when there is no behavioral hazard to when there is significantly negative behavioral hazard, under the assumption of local risk neutrality to isolate the moral/behavioral hazard impact. The dark gray area represents the standard deadweight loss triangle—the moral hazard cost of insurance. This area is positive because

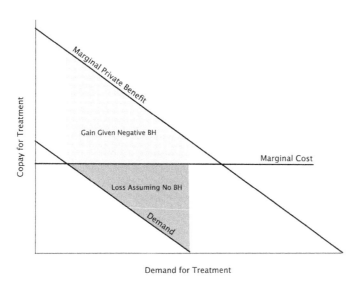

FIGURE 4

Welfare impact of a treatment price change: behavioral hazard vs. moral hazard alone. *Notes*: This figure considers the welfare impact of reducing the price of treatment to zero when there is only moral hazard to when there is also negative behavioral hazard. It is drawn for the case where all people share the same $\varepsilon < 0$. This figure previously appeared in Baicker, Katherine, Mullainathan, Sendhil, Schwartzstein, Joshua, 2015. Behavioral hazard in health insurance. The Quarterly Journal of Economics 130 (4), 1623–1667. It is reprinted here by permission of Oxford University Press and the authors.

Source: Baicker et al. (2015).

getting treated only when the price is below marginal cost signals that a person's willingness to pay must be below this cost.

The standard approach makes an often implicit assumption: analogous to identifying welfare curves in insurance choices (described above), we can equate willingness to pay for treatment with the true marginal benefit of treatment. That is, being marginal at a copay signals that $b = p$. Behavioral hazard drives a wedge between these objects. Being marginal at a copay signals that $b = p - \varepsilon$. The figure illustrates the case where all people have a propensity to underuse because of negative behavioral hazard and share the same $\varepsilon < 0$. In this case, the marginal benefit curve lies above the demand curve and the vertical difference equals $|\varepsilon|$. When the magnitude of negative behavioral hazard ($|\varepsilon|$) is sufficiently large, the marginal benefit of treatment outweighs the marginal cost even when the copay equals 0. In this case, reducing the copay to 0 no longer generates a welfare cost of increased utilization but a welfare benefit equal to the light gray area in the figure.

3.2.2 Re-interpreting the price elasticity of demand for medical care

Behavioral hazard also changes how we empirically measure the benefits and costs of insurance. Define $m(p)$ to be an individual's forecasted demand for care at a given copay: it equals 1 if and only if $b + \varepsilon > p$. Aggregate demand then equals $M(p) = \mathbb{E}[m(p)]$. The extent of moral hazard is typically calibrated by the price sensitivity of demand for medical care (either $M'(p)$ or the elasticity of demand). As can be seen in the figure, absent behavioral hazard the welfare cost of insurance (the dark gray area) is greater the flatter the demand curve: more elastic demand means a greater moral hazard cost of insurance.

There is much work measuring the elasticity of demand for medical care for the purpose of calibrating the degree of moral hazard (e.g., Feldstein, 1973; Manning et al., 1987; Feldman and Dowd, 1991; Newhouse, 1993). Perhaps the most famous example is work on the RAND Health Insurance Experiment, which randomly assigned insurees to different degrees of cost sharing and found a demand elasticity of roughly −0.2. Recent work (e.g., Aron-Dine et al., 2013; Finkelstein, 2014) has made a lot of progress developing ways to more accurately measure how changes in cost sharing impact medical-care spending, especially taking into account the non-linear nature of insurance coverage. But for the most part it maintains the assumption that the price-sensitivity of demand for medical care meaningfully captures the degree of moral hazard.

The presence of behavioral hazard complicates this analysis. This is because the care that is encouraged when co-pays are reduced may in fact be high value. Indeed, the light gray area of the figure is greater the flatter is demand: with sufficiently negative behavioral hazard, up to a point more elastic demand now means a greater *benefit* of insurance.

As an empirical matter, changes in cost-sharing (from small levels) impact the demand for both high *and* low-value care (Lohr et al., 1986; Goldman et al., 2006; Chandra et al., 2010; Brot-Goldberg et al., 2017). For a recent example, Brot-Goldberg et al. (2017) examine data from a large self-insured firm that switched from a plan with free health care to a high deductible plan and find that insurees responded by not only reducing the quantity of potentially wasteful care (identified following Schwartz et al., 2014), but also by meaningfully reducing the quantity of high value care (e.g., drugs for diabetes, cholesterol, depression etc.). Moreover, spending reductions were almost entirely due to quantity reductions and not to price shopping or substitution across procedures by insurees. Equating the price-sensitivity of demand for medical care with the degree of moral hazard is potentially quite misleading.

3.2.3 Re-interpreting health impacts of price changes

To examine the welfare impact of cost-sharing changes, it is beneficial to "get under the hood" and examine health impacts of discouraging care by increasing prices. One approach is to directly measure health markers like blood pressure, adverse health events (e.g., heart attacks), mortality, etc. This is an approach taken by, e.g., Choudhry et al. (2011).[17] Another approach, which is less direct but sometimes more empirically feasible, is to measure how a decrease in medical care (e.g., prescription drug

---

[17] Sommers et al. (2017) provide a summary of the evidence on how health insurance coverage impacts health.

use) in response to higher cost sharing (e.g., higher drug copays) results in "offsetting" increases in other forms of medical care (e.g., hospital utilization). Using a quasi-experimental design of the effects of increases in copayments for prescription drugs and physician visits among retirees in California, Chandra et al. (2010) show that there are significant offsetting increases in hospital utilization. It's possible that the retirees are rationally trading off the risk of hospitalization against copays and side effects, but in interpreting the findings it's useful to keep in mind that much of the cost of hospitalization is large and uninsurable (e.g., many procedures in the hospital are painful and come with a significant time cost).

Incorporating behavioral hazard provides a foundation for value-based insurance design (Chernew et al., 2007), specifying lower cost-sharing for higher value care. To take a very simple example, suppose the demand curve for a given (disease, treatment) combination slopes down only because of behavioral hazard ($\text{Var}(b) = 0$, $\text{Var}(\varepsilon) > 0$) and insurees are approximately risk neutral. Then the welfare impact of a co-pay change can be identified by examining the average value of the treatment b. In this case, it is optimal to set the copay below cost (perhaps even subsidizing treatment) if and only if $b > c$.[18]

3.3 Implications for insurance markets and policy

The analysis above suggests that socially efficient health insurance contracts should be designed to help counteract biases.[19] Will equilibrium health insurance contracts be designed with this in mind? Is there room for behaviorally-minded welfare-improving government intervention?[20]

We derive the equilibrium insurance contract in a competitive market. This contract may differ from the optimal contract because people may not fully understand how they are biased and misforecast their demand for treatment. Formally, define $\hat{m}(p)$ to be an individual's forecasted demand for care at a given copay: it equals 1 if and only if $b + \hat{\varepsilon} > p$, where $\hat{\varepsilon}$ represents the forecasted degree of behavioral hazard. At the time of contracting, the insuree may not appreciate that she will undervalue the need to take a chronic disease medication or that she will seek out any treatment for back pain. Define forecasted aggregate demand to equal $\hat{M}(p) = \mathbb{E}[\hat{m}(p)]$. In common with much of the behavioral literature, we will highlight two extreme cases: the case where the insuree perfectly understands her biases and the case where she thinks

---

[18] Value-based insurance designs are attracting increasing attention in policy circles. For example, the Centers for Medicare and Medicaid Services are testing such designs, as is the Department of Defense (Frakt, 2017).

[19] Much of this section's content and language previously appeared in Baicker et al. (2012)—a working paper version of Baicker et al. (2015).

[20] This analysis follows much of the existing theoretical literature (e.g., as implicit in Blomqvist, 1997) and formally models a situation where insurers compete directly to attract potential insurees. By closely following this work, the analysis isolates the market failure resulting from behavioral hazard, holding other institutional features constant.

she is unbiased at the time of contracting. Formally, the agent is said to be *sophisticated* when $\hat{\varepsilon} = \varepsilon$ (e.g., correctly forecasting that she will act as if she undervalues the need to take a chronic disease medication) and to be *naive* when $\hat{\varepsilon} = 0$ (e.g., incorrectly thinking she will act as if she properly values the need to take a chronic disease medication).[21]

In equilibrium, the market will supply an insurance plan to maximize the agent's *perceived* expected utility subject to zero profit constraint.[22] The agent's perceived expected utility can differ from her actual utility because she may misforecast her demand for treatment.

Since the optimal contract maximizes perceived expected utility subject to a zero profit constraint, it is immediate that the optimal and equilibrium contract coincide when the agent is sophisticated. In the more general case, the agent may misforecast demand and consequently view the tradeoff between a higher co-pay and a lower premium as being more or less favorable than it actually is. Overforecasting the degree to which the premium should go down reduces the apparent desirability of raising the co-pay; underforecasting raises the apparent desirability.

3.3.1 Market failures arising from consumers' naivete

The equilibrium co-pay differs from the optimal co-pay because the agent misforecasts demand: there is a market failure resulting from lack of sophistication. To gain more intuition for how this works, consider the simple case of a risk-neutral naive agent. In this case, the optimal co-pay formula reduces to

$$p^B = c + \varepsilon(p^B), \tag{10}$$

where $\varepsilon(p^B)$ is the degree of behavioral hazard of the marginal insuree given co-pay p^B. At the optimal co-pay, the marginal agent fully internalizes her "internality" (the difference between p and c acts as a Pigouvian tax set at the level of the marginal internality $\varepsilon(p)$).[23]

---

[21] There is another potential form of naivete, namely that insurees misperceive treatment benefits at the time of contracting, not just at the time of making a treatment decision (i.e., at the time of contracting, they misforecast the benefit of getting treated as $b + \varepsilon$). It would be natural to assume this form of naivete if decision errors are the result of incorrect beliefs about treatment benefits, for example, but not if these errors are the result of biases such as procrastination. We abstract from this form of naivete to limit the number of cases considered. However, we note that it is particularly easy to characterize the equilibrium outcome given this form of naivete: it is just the solution to the planner's problem if the planner mistakenly perceives treatment benefits as equaling $\hat{b} = b + \varepsilon$.

[22] As is well known, the solution to this problem will coincide with the outcome when insurers maximize profits subject to an "individual rationality" constraint for the representative agent, where the consumer's outside option is such that the solution to this problem yields zero profits. In fact, the logic of the equilibrium co-pay holds for *any* outside option, so the degree of market power does not change the logic of how co-pays will be set in equilibrium.

[23] Since the optimal co-pay in this case acts as a Pigouvian tax to get the agent to internalize his internality, it is tempting to think that the analysis would be the same if we were to think of ε as an externality rather than an internality. However, there are important differences. If ε were an externality then market forces

On the other hand, Baicker et al. (2012) show that the equilibrium co-pay in this case, p^E, is instead set to take advantage of the difference between actual and predicted demand: the larger this difference, the greater the co-pay.[24] To illustrate how the equilibrium copay differs from the optimal copay, suppose insurees are inattentive and forget to get treated with some probability that is independent of decision benefits and costs. The optimal copay does not depend on the forgetting probability because this probability does not influence decisions at the margin. Yet, at the same time, forgetfulness leads agents to overforecast their usage and, in equilibrium, profit maximizing firms will have an incentive to lower the copay (and create "fictitious surplus") in response to this bias.

3.3.2 Insurers' failure to provide nudges that benefit consumers may flow from consumers' naivete about the impact of such nudges

Now suppose insurers are also able to use nudges. Define $\hat{m}_n(p)$ as the individual's forecasted demand for care at a given price conditional on nudge n: $\hat{m}_n(p)$ equals 1 if and only if $b + \hat{\varepsilon}_n > p$. Let $\hat{M}_n(p) \equiv \mathbb{E}[\hat{m}_n(p)]$ equal forecasted aggregate demand given a nudge. For a sophisticated consumer, $\hat{\varepsilon}_n = \varepsilon_n$ for all n: sophisticates completely understand how nudges will affect their decisions. For a naive consumer, $\hat{\varepsilon}_n = 0$ for all n: naifs think their decisions will be independent of nudges. Naifs do not appreciate that reminders and educational programs will improve adherence, or that small hassle factors will greatly influence whether they seek treatment.

We assume that nudges can be contracted over. If the representative agent is sophisticated it is again immediate that the equilibrium insurance contract will be efficient. In particular, nudges will be supplied optimally. Matters are different if the agent is naive. In this case, $\hat{m}_n$ is independent of n, so nudges will only affect perceived expected utility insofar as they influence the size of the premium through the zero profit constraint. Fixing the co-pay, the nudge that maximizes perceived expected utility subject to the zero profit constraint will be the one that minimizes insurer costs. When the equilibrium co-pay is lower than cost c, this means the equilibrium nudge will (weakly) discourage care relative to the default nudge. This is

---

alone would not correct the problem (Coasian bargaining seems unlikely in this setting)—government intervention would be necessary. However, when people are sophisticated, market forces may correct an internality. Likewise, even when people are naive, market forces can lead to an equilibrium in which agents partially internalize their internality, as we will soon see.

[24] Under regularity conditions, Baicker et al. (2012) show that p^E satisfies

$$p^E = c + \frac{M(p^E) - \hat{M}(p^E)}{|M'(p^E)|}. \tag{11}$$

p^E deviates from c for reasons analogous to why profit-maximizing firms may charge high up-front fees and below-cost usage prices for "investment goods" when consumers are partially naive about their self-control problems (DellaVigna and Malmendier, 2004). In this way, our model may help explain why the insurance plans we see in the world appear "too generous" (too low co-pays and deductibles) relative to simulated optimal plans (Cutler and Zeckhauser, 2000).

independent of the initial bias: when nudges are available, equilibrium insurance contracts may exacerbate rather than help counteract biases.

Matters are different when insurers' bottom line depends indirectly on whether agents are treated, perhaps because a failure to get treated will lead to greater expenses within the horizon of the insurer. For example, it may be costly to the insurer if an insuree does not get a flu shot. The equilibrium nudge may encourage care in this situation even when agents are naive, as such a nudge may improve the insurer's bottom line.

These results suggest that competitive forces do not lead to efficient equilibrium insurance contracts when insurees are naive about their biases, but that the insurer will have an incentive to counteract biases when this saves *the insurer* money. For example, Starc and Town (2016) find that Medicare prescription drug coverage plans spend more on drugs when they cover all medical expenses than when they are only responsible for prescription drug spending, and this spending is concentrated on drugs that produce offsets. This is consistent with such plans having more of an incentive to counteract behavioral hazard.

4 Future directions for behavioral health economics

There are many interesting topics for future research in behavioral health economics. To conclude, we highlight some of these topics. We follow the structure of this chapter and divide our discussion into topics related to insurance choices and those related to treatment choices.

4.1 Future work on health-insurance choices

While there has been much research showing that consumers have a difficult time choosing insurance options in both active and passive settings, there is much to be done to better understand why and to investigate policies to improve these choices. Policies that should be studied further include:

- Providing information to consumers. What forms of information are effective and what is the upper bound for effectiveness in this domain?
- Impact of consumer education/literacy. How do we educate consumers to make better choices?
- Active choice. When consumers have a default option, is forced active choice a welfare-enhancing policy?
- Targeted/smart defaults. What is the impact of targeted/smart defaults on choices? What are the impacts of setting such defaults on competitive markets? How can targeted defaults be best designed to fulfill social objectives?
- Curated choice sets. What are welfare-maximizing curated choice sets in competitive markets?

To think about such policy questions, it is important to more broadly understand how insurers respond to consumer biases. While we mentioned some findings on this topic above, there is room for much more empirical and theoretical work speaking to whether, how, and when insurers set prices or design products to take advantage of consumer mistakes.

An additional area for future research is to investigate the role of non-standard risk preferences and systematic biases in health-insurance choices. As discussed in Section 2, empirical analyses typically focus on classical expected utility models, with minor modifications, or reduced-form frameworks that nest a slew of models. Future work in this area could estimate models that incorporate reference-dependent preferences (e.g., Kőszegi and Rabin, 2007) or context-dependent choices arising from salience, focusing, and relative thinking (e.g., Bordalo et al., 2012; Kőszegi and Szeidl, 2013, and Bushong et al., 2018).

A related topic concerns the degree to which consumers make consistent choices across domains (from the perspective of given models of risk preferences). Einav et al. (2012) studies whether consumers make consistent choices, in terms of ordering of riskiness, across multiple benefit choices at Alcoa. Within one private firm, Barseghyan et al. (2016) perform a similar study of consumers making multiple non-health insurance choices across the domains of property and auto insurance. Investigating consistency across health-insurance choices (and across other related choices) could provide insights that are useful for positive and normative analyses.

4.2 Future work on health-treatment choices

In our earlier discussion of health-treatment choices, we abstracted from several important issues by analyzing a single "choice to treat". Unpacking what we mean by a treatment choice reveals many more areas to apply insights from behavioral economics.

First, before people are treated, they often must be tested. If people rationally respond to information and hold classical expected utility preferences, then testing must be valuable because it provides potentially useful information. While we've mostly focused this chapter on mistakes rather than non-standard preferences, anxiety or a desire to remain optimistic (e.g., Kőszegi, 2003 and Oster et al., 2013) may lead people to avoid testing—and perhaps be made better off as a result. More relevant to discussions in this chapter, mistakes at the treatment stage may create small or even negative returns at the testing stage, resulting in larger benefits to counteracting behavioral hazard (Baicker et al., 2015). For example, recent large scale clinical trials indicate that Prostate Specific Antigen (PSA) screening for prostate cancer has, at best, a small effect in reducing mortality, and that the risks likely outweigh the benefits (Andriole et al., 2009; Djulbegovic et al., 2010). A natural question is whether such a conclusion would be reversed if more patients diagnosed with prostate cancer were nudged or incentivized to pursue "watchful waiting".

Second, treatment choices are often made in consultation with a doctor who may also be subject to behavioral biases. Chandra et al. (2012) review behavioral influences in clinical decisions. One example is the availability heuristic (Tversky and Kahneman, 1973)—the idea that people predict the frequency of an event by the ease with which it comes to mind. This suggests that a physician who has just seen a patient with influenza may be more likely to make the diagnosis of influenza for the next patient. Choudhry et al. (2006) found evidence for availability influencing clinical decisions. They showed that physicians who treated a patient with Warfarin (a blood-thinning drug with the risk of bleeding) and saw that patient experience an adverse bleeding event were 21 percent less likely to prescribe Warfarin to other patients for which Warfarin is indicated, even 90 days after the adverse event. Physicians are humans too and are subject to the same influences (e.g., of framing, status-quo bias, and messaging) that systematically influence other humans. A topic for future work is to better understand the interaction between physician and patient biases.

Third, if the treatment is medication, people have to not only fill their prescriptions but also take their pills. There is a large literature on patient adherence, reviewed by Osterberg and Blaschke (2005), that we briefly discussed. While the evidence suggests that making high-value drugs free will promote people filling prescriptions and taking their pills, many people will not be adherent even if they have their pills on hand. For example, they may forget to take them. Much research is exploring ways to boost adherence, such as the REMIND trial discussed above. Improving adherence should increase the benefits of counteracting behavioral hazard in decisions to fill prescriptions.

Fourth, the benefits of treatment will interact with "lifestyle behaviors", for example involving diet, exercise, and smoking. Loewenstein et al. (2012) provide a nice review of behaviorally-informed attempts to help people help themselves. Many of these attempts to date take the form of financial incentives, but framed or structured in a way to have a reasonable bang-for-buck given the errors people make. As a recent illustration, Halpern et al. (2015) conduct a randomized trial of financial-incentive programs for smoking cessation among CVS Caremark employees and find that individual rewards of $800 come close to tripling the rate of cessation. Paying careful attention to the structure of incentives (e.g., paying separate and salient rewards rather than incorporating them into insurance-premium adjustments) seems particularly important in these cases because the people we want to target have revealed that they do not respond to big (but perhaps not salient) incentives to change their behaviors (Volpp et al., 2011).

Future research could use a behavioral lens to further unpack the dimensions of treatment decisions and explore interactions between them.

Finally, a theme throughout this chapter is that we're often more confident that people are making *some* mistake in their health-insurance or health-treatment choices than *why* they are making a mistake in these choices. We believe the explosion of research described above convincingly points to pitfalls in analyzing demand curves for insurance or medical care while maintaining the assumption that choices perfectly reveal preferences. And we believe it shows that researchers are able to make progress in studying these decisions (and difficulties in making them) without understanding the precise mechanisms behind consumer mistakes. That said, parallel work described in other chapters of this Handbook suggest large future gains to understanding the "whys" behind poor insurance and treatment choices.

References

Abaluck, Jason, Gruber, Jonathan, 2011. Choice inconsistencies among the elderly: evidence from plan choice in the Medicare Part D program. The American Economic Review 101 (4), 1180–1210.

Abaluck, Jason, Gruber, Jonathan, 2016a. Evolving choice inconsistencies in choice of prescription drug insurance. The American Economic Review 106 (8), 2145–2184.

Abaluck, Jason, Gruber, Jonathan, 2016b. Improving the Quality of Choices in Health Insurance Markets. NBER Working Paper No. 22917.

Abaluck, Jason, Gruber, Jonathan, Swanson, Ashley, 2015. Prescription Drug Use Under Medicare Part D: A Linear Model of Nonlinear Budget Sets. National Bureau of Economic Research.

Andriole, Gerald L., David Crawford, E., Grubb III, Robert L., Buys, Saundra S., Chia, David, Church, Timothy R., Fouad, Mona N., Gelmann, Edward P., Kvale, Paul A., Reding, Douglas J., et al., 2009. Mortality results from a randomized prostate-cancer screening trial. The New England Journal of Medicine 360 (13), 1310–1319.

Aron-Dine, Aviva, Einav, Liran, Finkelstein, Amy, 2013. The RAND health insurance experiment, three decades later. The Journal of Economic Perspectives 27 (1), 197–222.

Aron-Dine, Aviva, Einav, Liran, Finkelstein, Amy, Cullen, Mark, 2015. Moral hazard in health insurance: do dynamic incentives matter? Review of Economics and Statistics 97 (4), 725–741.

Arrow, Kenneth, 1963. Uncertainty and the welfare economics of medical care. The American Economic Review 53 (5), 141–149.

Baicker, Katherine, Mullainathan, Sendhil, Schwartzstein, Joshua, 2012. Behavioral Hazard in Health Insurance. Working Paper.

Baicker, Katherine, Mullainathan, Sendhil, Schwartzstein, Joshua, 2015. Behavioral hazard in health insurance. The Quarterly Journal of Economics 130 (4), 1623–1667.

Barseghyan, Levon, Molinari, Francesca, O'Donoghue, Ted, Teitelbaum, Joshua, 2013. The nature of risk preferences: evidence from insurance choices. The American Economic Review 103 (6), 2499–2529.

Barseghyan, Levon, Molinari, Francesca, Teitelbaum, Jeff, 2016. Inference under stability of risk preferences. Quantitative Economics 7 (2), 367–409.

Bernheim, B. Douglas, Rangel, Antonio, 2004. Addiction and cue-triggered decision processes. The American Economic Review 94 (5), 1558–1590.

Bernheim, B. Douglas, Rangel, Antonio, 2009. Beyond revealed preference: choice-theoretic foundations for behavioral welfare economics. The Quarterly Journal of Economics 124 (1), 51–104.

Bernheim, Douglas, Taubinsky, Dmitry, 2018. Behavioral Public Economics. University of California at Berkeley working paper.

Beshears, John, Choi, James J., Laibson, David, Madrian, Brigitte, 2018. Behavioral household finance. In: Handbook of Behavioral Economics, vol. 1. Elsevier, pp. 177–276.

Bhargava, Saurabh, Loewenstein, George, Sydnor, Justin, 2017. Choose to lose: health plan choices from a menu with dominated option. The Quarterly Journal of Economics 132 (3), 1319–1372.

Blomqvist, Åke, 1997. Optimal non-linear health insurance. Journal of Health Economics 16 (3), 303–321.

Bordalo, Pedro, Gennaioli, Nicola, Shleifer, Andrei, 2012. Salience theory of choice under risk. The Quarterly Journal of Economics 127 (3), 1243–1285.

Bordalo, Pedro, Gennaioli, Nicola, Shleifer, Andrei, 2013. Salience and consumer choice. Journal of Political Economy 121 (5), 803–843.

Brot-Goldberg, Zarek C., Chandra, Amitabh, Handel, Benjamin R., Kolstad, Jonathan T., 2017. What does a deductible do? The impact of cost-sharing on health care prices, quantities, and spending dynamics. The Quarterly Journal of Economics 132 (3), 1261–1318.

Bushong, Benjamin, Rabin, Matthew, Schwartzstein, Joshua, 2018. A Model of Relative Thinking. Working Paper. Harvard University, Cambridge, MA.

Carrera, Mariana, Royer, Heather, Stehr, Mark, Sydnor, Justin, 2018. Can financial incentives help people trying to establish new habits? Experimental evidence with new gym members. Journal of Health Economics 58, 202–214.

Cawley, John, Ruhm, Christopher J., 2011. The economics of risky health behaviors. In: Handbook of Health Economics, vol. 2, pp. 95–199 (Chapter 3).

Chandra, Amitabh, Staiger, Douglas O., 2010. Identifying provider prejudice in healthcare.

Chandra, Amitabh, Staiger, Douglas O., 2017. Identifying sources of inefficiency in health care.

Chandra, Amitabh, Cutler, David, Song, Zirui, et al., 2012. Who ordered that? The economics of treatment choices in medical care. In: Handbook of Health Economics, vol. 2, pp. 397–432.

Chandra, Amitabh, Gruber, Jonathan, McKnight, Robin, 2010. Patient cost sharing in low income populations. The American Economic Review 100 (2), 303–308.

Chapman, Gretchen B., Li, Meng, Colby, Helen, Yoon, Haewon, 2010. Opting in vs opting out of influenza vaccination. JAMA 304 (1), 43–44.

Chernew, Michael E., Rosen, Allison B., Mark Fendrick, A., 2007. Value-based insurance design. Health Affairs 26 (2), w195–w203.

Chou, Roger, Fu, Rongwei, Carrino, John A., Deyo, Richard A., 2009. Imaging strategies for low-back pain: systematic review and meta-analysis. The Lancet 373 (9662), 463–472.

Choudhry, Niteesh K., Anderson, Geoffrey M., Laupacis, Andreas, Ross-Degnan, Dennis, Normand, Sharon-Lise T., Soumerai, Stephen B., 2006. Impact of adverse events on prescribing warfarin in patients with atrial fibrillation: matched pair analysis. BMJ 332 (7534), 141–145.

Choudhry, Niteesh K., Avorn, Jerry, Glynn, Robert J., Antman, Elliott M., Schneeweiss, Sebastian, Toscano, Michele, Reisman, Lonny, Fernandes, Joaquim, Spettell, Claire, Lee, Joy L., et al., 2011. Full coverage for preventive medications after myocardial infarction. The New England Journal of Medicine 365 (22), 2088–2097.

Choudhry, Niteesh K., Krumme, Alexis A., Ercole, Patrick M., Girdish, Charmaine, Tong, Angela Y., Khan, Nazleen F., Brennan, Troyen A., Matlin, Olga S., Shrank, William H., Franklin, Jessica M., 2017. Effect of reminder devices on medication adherence: the REMIND randomized clinical trial. JAMA Internal Medicine 177 (5), 624–631.

Cutler, David M., Zeckhauser, Richard J., 2000. The anatomy of health insurance. In: Handbook of Health Economics, vol. 1, pp. 563–643.

Cutrona, Sarah L., Choudhry, Niteesh K., Fischer, Michael A., Servi, Amber, Liberman, Joshua N., Brennan, Troyen, Shrank, William H., 2010. Modes of delivery for interventions to improve cardiovascular medication adherence. The American Journal of Managed Care 16 (12), 929.

Dalton, Christina M., Gowrisankaran, Gautam, Town, Robert, 2015. Myopia and Complex Dynamic Incentives: Evidence from Medicare Part D. National Bureau of Economic Research.

DellaVigna, Stefano, 2009. Psychology and economics: evidence from the field. Journal of Economic Literature 47 (2), 315–372.

DellaVigna, Stefano, Malmendier, Ulrike, 2004. Contract design and self-control: theory and evidence. The Quarterly Journal of Economics 119 (2), 353–402.

DellaVigna, Stefano, Malmendier, Ulrike, 2006. Paying not to go to the gym. The American Economic Review 96 (3), 694–719.

Denberg, Thomas D., Melhado, Trisha V., Coombes, John M., Beaty, Brenda L., Berman, Kenneth, Byers, Tim E., Marcus, Alfred C., Steiner, John F., Ahnen, Dennis J., 2005. Predictors of nonadherence to screening colonoscopy. Journal of General Internal Medicine 20 (11), 989–995.

Deyo, Richard A., Mirza, Sohail K., Martin, Brook I., 2006. Back pain prevalence and visit rates: estimates from US national surveys, 2002. Spine 31 (23), 2724–2727.

Deyo, Richard A., Rainville, James, Kent, Daniel L., 1992. What can the history and physical examination tell us about low back pain? JAMA 268 (6), 760–765.

Di Iorio, Daniel, Henley, Eric, Doughty, Andrea, 2000. A survey of primary care physician practice patterns and adherence to acute low back problem guidelines. Archives of Family Medicine 9 (10), 1015.

Djulbegovic, Mia, Beyth, Rebecca J., Neuberger, Molly M., Stoffs, Taryn L., Vieweg, Johannes, Djulbegovic, Benjamin, Dahm, Philipp, 2010. Screening for prostate cancer: systematic review and meta-analysis of randomised controlled trials. BMJ 341, c4543.

Einav, Liran, Finkelstein, Amy, Cullen, Mark, 2010. Estimating welfare in insurance markets using variation in prices. The Quarterly Journal of Economics 125 (3), 877–921.

Einav, Liran, Finkelstein, Amy, Pascu, Iuliana, Cullen, Mark, 2012. How general are risk preferences? Choices under uncertainty in different domains. The American Economic Review 102 (6), 2606–2638.

Einav, Liran, Finkelstein, Amy, Schrimpf, Paul, 2015. The response of drug expenditure to nonlinear contract design: evidence from Medicare Part D. The Quarterly Journal of Economics 130 (2), 841–899.

Ericson, Keith, 2014. Market design when firms interact with inertial consumers: evidence from Medicare Part D. American Economic Journal: Economic Policy 6 (1), 38–64.

Ericson, Keith, Starc, Amanda, 2016. How product standardization affects choice: evidence from the Massachusetts health insurance exchange. Journal of Health Economics 50, 71–85.

Eyster, Erik, Rabin, Matthew, 2014. Extensive imitation is irrational and harmful. The Quarterly Journal of Economics 129 (4), 1861–1898.

Feldman, Roger, Dowd, Bryan, 1991. A new estimate of the welfare loss of excess health insurance. The American Economic Review 81 (1), 297–301.

Feldstein, Martin S., 1973. The welfare loss of excess health insurance. Journal of Political Economy 81 (2, Part 1), 251–280.

Finkelstein, Amy, 2014. Moral Hazard in Health Insurance. Columbia University Press.

Frakt, Austin. 2017. Health plans that nudge patients to do the right thing. The New York Times.

Gabaix, Xavier, 2014. A sparsity-based model of bounded rationality. The Quarterly Journal of Economics 129 (4), 1661–1710.

Gabaix, Xavier, Farhi, Emmanuel, 2017. Optimal Taxation with Behavioral Agents. Working Paper. Harvard.

Gagnon-Bartsch, Tristan, Rabin, Matthew, Schwartzstein, Joshua, 2017. Channeled Attention and Stable Errors. Working Paper. Harvard.

Goldman, Dana P., Joyce, Geoffrey F., Karaca-Mandic, Pinar, 2006. Varying pharmacy benefits with clinical status: the case of cholesterol-lowering therapy. The American Journal of Managed Care 12 (1), 21–29.

Grubb, Michael, Osborne, Matthew, 2015. Cellular service demand: biased beliefs, learning, and bill shock. The American Economic Review 105 (1), 234–271.

Gruber, Jon, Kőszegi, Botond, 2013. Is addiction rational? Theory and evidence. The Quarterly Journal of Economics 103 (6), 2499–2529.

Hackmann, Martin, Kolstad, Jonathan, Kowalski, Amanda, 2015. Adverse selection and the individual mandate: when theory meets practice. The American Economic Review 105 (3), 1030–1066.

Halpern, Scott D., French, Benjamin, Small, Dylan S., Saulsgiver, Kathryn, Harhay, Michael O., Audrain-McGovern, Janet, Loewenstein, George, Brennan, Troyen A., Asch, David A., Volpp, Kevin G., 2015. Randomized trial of four financial-incentive programs for smoking cessation. The New England Journal of Medicine 372 (22), 2108–2117.

Halpern, Scott, Loewenstein, George, Volpp, Kevin, Cooney, Elizabeth, Vranas, Kelly, Quill, Caroline, McKenzie, Mary, Harhay, Michael, Gabler, Nicole, Silva, Tatiana, Arnold, Robert, Angus, Derek, Bryce, Cindy, 2013. Default options in advance directives influence how patients set goals for end-of-life care. Health Affairs 32 (2), 408–417.

Handel, Benjamin, 2013. Adverse selection and inertia in health insurance markets: when nudging hurts. The American Economic Review 103 (7), 2643–2682.

Handel, Benjamin, Kolstad, Jonathan, 2015a. Getting the Most From Marketplaces: Smart Policies on Health Insurance Choice. Brookings Hamilton Project Discussion Paper 2015-08.

Handel, Benjamin, Kolstad, Jonathan, 2015b. Health insurance for humans: information frictions, plan choice, and consumer welfare. The American Economic Review 105 (8), 2449–2500.

Handel, Benjamin, Kolstad, Jonathan, Spinnewijn, Johannes, 2015. Information Frictions and Adverse Selection: Policy Interventions in Health Insurance Markets. NBER Working Paper No. 21759.

Handel, Benjamin, Schwartzstein, Joshua, 2018. Frictions or mental gaps: what's behind the information we (don't) use and when do we care? The Journal of Economic Perspectives 32 (1), 155–178.

Heidhaus, Paul, Kőszegi, Botond, 2018. Behavioral industrial organization. In: Bernheim, Douglas B., Dellavigna, Stefano, Laibson, David (Eds.), Handbook of Behavioral Economics, vol. 1, pp. 517–612.

Heiss, Florian, McFadden, Daniel, Winter, Joachim, 2016. Inattention and Switching Costs as Sources of Inertia in Medicare Part D. NBER Working Paper No. 22765.

Heiss, Florian, McFadden, Daniel, Winter, Joachim, Wupperman, Amelie, Zhou, Bo, 2010. Mind the gap! Consumer perceptions and choices of Medicare Part D prescription drug plans. Research Findings in the Economics of Aging, 413–481.

Ho, Kate, Hogan, Joseph, Morton, Fiona Scott, 2017. The impact of consumer inattention on insurer pricing in the Medicare Part D program. The RAND Journal of Economics 48 (4), 877–905.

Howlader, N., Noone, A.M., Krapcho, M., Neyman, N., Aminou, R., Waldron, W., Altekruse, S.F., Kosary, C.L., Ruhl, J., Tatalovich, Z., Cho, H., Mariotto, A., Eisner, M.P., Lewis, D.R., Chen, H.S., Feuer, E.J., Cronin, K.A., 2012. SEER Cancer Statistics Review, 1975–2009.

Jarvik, Jeffrey G., Hollingworth, William, Martin, Brook, Emerson, Scott S., Gray, Darryl T., Overman, Steven, Robinson, David, Staiger, Thomas, Wessbecher, Frank, Sullivan, Sean D., et al., 2003. Rapid magnetic resonance imaging vs radiographs for patients with low back pain: a randomized controlled trial. JAMA 289 (21), 2810–2818.

Kahneman, Daniel, Wakker, Peter P., Sarin, Rakesh, 1997. Back to Bentham? Explorations of experienced utility. The Quarterly Journal of Economics 112 (2), 375–406.

Ketcham, Jonathan, Lucarelli, Claudio, Miravete, Eugenio, Roebuck, Christopher, 2012. Sinking, swimming, or learning to swim in Medicare Part D? The American Economic Review 102 (6), 2639–2673.

Kling, Jeffrey, Mullainathan, Sendhil, Shafir, Eldar, Vermeulen, Lee, Wrobel, Marian, 2012. Comparison friction: experimental evidence from Medicare drug plans. The Quarterly Journal of Economics 127 (1), 199–235.

Kolstad, Jonathan, 2013. Information and quality when motivation is intrinsic: evidence from surgeon report cards. The American Economic Review 103 (7), 2875–2910.

Kőszegi, Botond, 2003. Health anxiety and patient behavior. Journal of Health Economics 22 (6), 1073–1084.

Kőszegi, Botond, Rabin, Matthew, 2007. Reference-dependent risk attitudes. The American Economic Review 97 (4), 1047–1073.

Kőszegi, Botond, Rabin, Matthew, 2008. Revealed mistakes and revealed preferences. In: The Foundations of Positive and Normative Economics: A Handbook, pp. 193–209.

Kőszegi, Botond, Szeidl, Adam, 2013. A model of focusing in economic choice. The Quarterly Journal of Economics 128 (1), 53–104.

Lafeber, Melvin, Spiering, Wilko, Visseren, Frank L.J., Grobbee, Diederick E., Bots, Michiel L., Stanton, Alice, Patel, Anushka, Prabhakaran, Dorairaj, Webster, Ruth, Thom, Simon, et al., 2017. Impact of switching from different treatment regimens to a fixed-dose combination pill (polypill) in patients with cardiovascular disease or similarly high risk: the influence of baseline medication on LDL-cholesterol, blood pressure and calculated risk reduction when switching to a cardiovascular polypill. European Journal of Preventive Cardiology 24 (9), 951–961.

Laibson, David, 1997. Golden eggs and hyperbolic discounting. The Quarterly Journal of Economics 112 (2), 443–478.

Lehnert, Bruce E., Bree, Robert L., 2010. Analysis of appropriateness of outpatient CT and MRI referred from primary care clinics at an academic medical center: how critical is the need for improved decision support? Journal of the American College of Radiology 7 (3), 192–197.

Liebman, Jeffrey B., Zeckhauser, Richard J., 2004. Schmeduling.

Loewenstein, George, Friedmen, Joelle, McGill, Barbara, Ahmad, Sarah, Linck, Suzanne, Sinkula, Stacy, Beshears, John, Choi, James, Kolstad, Jonathan, Laibson, David, Madrian, Brigitte, List, John, Volpp, Kevin, 2013. Consumers' misunderstanding of health insurance. Journal of Health Economics 32, 850–862.

Loewenstein, George, John, Leslie K., Volpp, Kevin, 2012. Using decision errors to help people help themselves.

Lohr, Kathleen N., Brook, Robert H., Kamberg, Caren J., Goldberg, George A., Leibowitz, Arleen, Keesey, Joan, Reboussin, David, Newhouse, Joseph P., 1986. Use of medical care in the RAND health insurance experiment: diagnosis-and service-specific analyses in a randomized controlled trial. Medical Care 24 (9), S1–S87.

Long, Judith A., Jahnle, Erica C., Richardson, Diane M., Loewenstein, George, Volpp, Kevin G., 2012. Peer mentoring and financial incentives to improve glucose control in African American veterans: a randomized trial. Annals of Internal Medicine 156 (6), 416–424.

Luo, Xuemei, Pietrobon, Ricardo, Sun, Shawn X., Liu, Gordon G., Hey, Lloyd, 2004. Estimates and patterns of direct health care expenditures among individuals with back pain in the United States. Spine 29 (1), 79–86.

Manning, Willard G., Newhouse, Joseph P., Duan, Naihua, Keeler, Emmett B., Leibowitz, Arleen, 1987. Health insurance and the demand for medical care: evidence from a randomized experiment. The American Economic Review, 251–277.

Manski, Charles, 1999. Identification Problems in the Social Sciences. Harvard University Press.

Marton, James, Yelowitz, Aaron, Talbert, Jeffrey, 2015. Medicaid Program Choice and Participant Inertia. University of Kentucky Working Paper.

McGlynn, Elizabeth A., Asch, Steven M., Adams, John, Keesey, Joan, Hicks, Jennifer, DeCristofaro, Alison, Kerr, Eve A., 2003. The quality of health care delivered to adults in the United States. The New England Journal of Medicine 348 (26), 2635–2645.

Milkman, Katherine L., Beshears, John, Choi, James J., Laibson, David, Madrian, Brigitte C., 2011. Using implementation intentions prompts to enhance influenza vaccination rates. Proceedings of the National Academy of Sciences 108 (26), 10415–10420.

Mullainathan, Sendhil, Schwartzstein, Joshua, Congdon, William J., 2012. A reduced-form approach to behavioral public finance. Annual Review of Economics 4, 511–540.

Ness, Reid M., Holmes, Ann M., Klein, Robert, Dittus, Robert, 2000. Cost-utility of one-time colonoscopic screening for colorectal cancer at various ages. The American Journal of Gastroenterology 95 (7), 1800–1811.

Newhouse, Joseph P., 1993. Free for All? Lessons From the RAND Health Insurance Experiment. Harvard University Press.

Newhouse, Joseph P., 2006. Reconsidering the moral hazard-risk avoidance tradeoff. Journal of Health Economics 25 (5), 1005–1014.

O'Donoghue, Ted, Rabin, Matthew, 1999. Doing it now or later. The American Economic Review, 103–124.

Oster, Emily, 2018. Diabetes and diet: purchasing behavior change in response to health information. American Economic Journal: Applied Economics 10 (4), 308–348.

Oster, Emily, Shoulson, Ira, Dorsey, E. Ray, 2013. Optimal expectations and limited medical testing: evidence from Huntington disease. The American Economic Review 103 (2), 804–830.

Osterberg, Lars, Blaschke, Terrence, 2005. Adherence to Medication. The New England Journal of Medicine 353 (5), 487–497.

Patel, Anushka, Cass, Alan, Peiris, David, Usherwood, Tim, Brown, Alex, Jan, Stephen, Neal, Bruce, Hillis, Graham S., Rafter, Natasha, Tonkin, Andrew, et al., 2015. A pragmatic randomized trial of a polypill-based strategy to improve use of indicated preventive treatments in people at high cardiovascular disease risk. European Journal of Preventive Cardiology 22 (7), 920–930.

Pauly, Mark V., 1968. The economics of moral hazard: comment. The American Economic Review, 531–537.

Pauly, Mark V., Blavin, Fredric E., 2008. Moral hazard in insurance, value-based cost sharing, and the benefits of blissful ignorance. Journal of Health Economics 27 (6), 1407–1417.

Perlroth, Daniella J., Goldman, Dana P., Garber, Alan M., 2010. The potential impact of comparative effectiveness research on U.S. health care expenditures. Demography 47 (Suppl. 1), S173–S190.

Polyakova, Maria, 2016. Regulation of insurance with adverse selection and switching costs: evidence from Medicare Part D. American Economic Journal: Applied Economics 8 (3), 165–195.

Rees-Jones, Alex, 2018. Suboptimal behavior in strategy-proof mechanisms: evidence from the residency match. Games and Economic Behavior 108, 317–330.

Rubin, Richard R., 2005. Adherence to pharmacologic therapy in patients with type 2 diabetes mellitus. The American Journal of Medicine 118 (5), 27–34.

Schedlbauer, Angela, Davies, Philippa, Fahey, Tom, 2010. Interventions to improve adherence to lipid lowering medication. Cochrane Database of Systematic Reviews 3 (3).

Schroeder, Knut, Fahey, Tom, Ebrahim, Shah, 2004. How can we improve adherence to blood pressure–lowering medication in ambulatory care?: Systematic review of randomized controlled trials. Archives of Internal Medicine 164 (7), 722–732.

Schwartz, Aaron L., Landon, Bruce E., Elshaug, Adam G., Chernew, Michael E., McWilliams, J. Michael, 2014. Measuring low-value care in Medicare. JAMA Internal Medicine 174 (7), 1067–1076.

Schwartzstein, Joshua, 2014. Selective attention and learning. Journal of the European Economic Association 12 (6), 1423–1452.

Sheehan, N.J., 2010. Magnetic resonance imaging for low back pain: indications and limitations. Postgraduate Medical Journal 86 (1016), 374–378.

Sokol, Michael C., McGuigan, Kimberly A., Verbrugge, Robert R., Epstein, Robert S., 2005. Impact of medication adherence on hospitalization risk and healthcare cost. Medical Care 43 (6), 521–530.

Sommers, Benjamin D., Gawande, Atul A., Baicker, Katherine, 2017. Health insurance coverage and health—what the recent evidence tells us.

Starc, Amanda, Town, Robert J., 2016. Externalities and benefit design in health insurance.

Stockley, Karen, 2016. Evaluating rationality in responses to health insurance cost-sharing: comparing deductibles and copayments. Mimeo. http://scholar.harvard.edu/kstockley/JMP.

Strandbygaard, Ulla, Thomsen, Simon Francis, Backer, Vibeke, 2010. A daily SMS reminder increases adherence to asthma treatment: a three-month follow-up study. Respiratory Medicine 104 (2), 166–171.

Strine, Tara W., Hootman, Jennifer M., 2007. US national prevalence and correlates of low back and neck pain among adults. Arthritis Care and Research 57 (4), 656–665.

Strombom, B., Buchmueller, C., Feldstein, J., 2002. Switching costs, price sensitivity, and health plan choice. Journal of Health Economics 21, 89–116.

Sudore, Rebecca, Boscardin, John, Feuz, Mariko, McMahan, Ryan, Katen, Mary, Barnes, Deborah, 2017. Effect of the PREPARE website vs an easy-to-read advance directive on advance care planning documentation and engagement among veterans: a randomized clinical trial. JAMA Internal Medicine 177 (8), 1102–1109.

Thaler, Richard H., Sunstein, Cass R., 2009. Nudge: Improving Decisions About Health, Wealth, and Happiness. Penguin (Non-Classics).

Tversky, Amos, Kahneman, Daniel, 1973. Availability: a heuristic for judging frequency and probability. Cognitive Psychology 5 (2), 207–232.

Volpp, Kevin G., Asch, David A., Galvin, Robert, Loewenstein, George, 2011. Redesigning employee health incentives—lessons from behavioral economics. The New England Journal of Medicine 365 (5), 388–390.

Volpp, Kevin G., John, Leslie K., Troxel, Andrea B., Norton, Laurie, Fassbender, Jennifer, Loewenstein, George, 2008. Financial incentive-based approaches for weight loss: a randomized trial. JAMA 300 (22), 2631–2637.

Volpp, Kevin G., Troxel, Andrea B., Mehta, Shivan J., Norton, Laurie, Zhu, Jingsan, Lim, Raymond, Wang, Wenli, Marcus, Noora, Terwiesch, Christian, Caldarella, Kristen, et al., 2017. Effect of electronic reminders, financial incentives, and social support on outcomes after myocardial infarction: the heartstrong randomized clinical trial. JAMA Internal Medicine.

Zeckhauser, Richard, 1970. Medical insurance: a case study of the tradeoff between risk spreading and appropriate incentives. Journal of Economic Theory 2 (1), 10–26.

Index

CPI Antony Rowe
Eastbourne, UK
March 14, 2019